Library of Congress Cataloging in Publication Data

Groth, Alexander J
  Contemporary politics.

  Includes bibliographical references and index.
  1. Europe — Politics and government — 1945–
  2. Europe — Economic conditions — 1945–
  I. Lieber, Robert J., joint author.
  II. Lieber, Nancy I., joint author.
  D1058.G74   320.9'4'055   76-173
  ISBN 0-87626-156-X

Cover design and interior design by Designworks, Inc.

contemporary
politics: europe

Alexander J. Groth
Robert J. Lieber
Nancy I. Lieber

University of California, Davis

Winthrop Publishers, Inc.
Cambridge, Massachusetts

CONTENTS

PREFACE

In writing a book that treats the live stuff of politics and policy, while deemphasizing institutional preoccupations, we have had to come to grips with differences of political and methodological viewpoint among ourselves. Perhaps it is a mark of successful collegiality that these disagreements have stimulated genuinely creative tension among the authors. Divergences of viewpoint have also had the utility of keeping each of us sensitive to the need for mustering the necessary evidence in support of our arguments.

All the authors contributed critically and editorially to each and every chapter and have cooperated conceptually in developing the framework for the book as well as the ideas set forth in Chapters One and Eight. For the record, the principal contributions to substantive chapters by Alexander Groth have been to Chapter Four (the Two Germanies), Chapter Five (The Soviet Union), and Chapter Seven (Alternative European Politics). Robert Lieber has borne the primary responsibility for Chapter Two (Britain) and Chapter Five (The European Community). Nancy Lieber has been chiefly responsible for the execution of Chapter Three (France).

to M. G.
B. Y. L.
K. A. L.

1

introduction

1 INTRODUCTION

We have written this book about politics in Europe from a new and different perspective. It is designed for the student interested in the major problems and policy issues faced by contemporary Europeans, in the different policy-making processes of Europe, and also in the quality of life which results from political activity.

But why study Europe, one might ask, particularly in view of the enhanced importance of states in other parts of the world today? We think that there are vital political, intellectual, and practical reasons for the study of European politics. The origins of most of the political institutions and ideologies of the modern world are to be found in Europe. The problems faced by the largely industrialized and urbanized peoples of the European continent are much more analogous to those of the United States than to the developing world. Above all, the facts of contemporary world interdependence are such that the fate of Europe is, and for a long time will undoubtedly be, closely linked to that of the United States itself.

In the 1970's, about 40 percent of U.S. trade volume has been with Europe, far exceeding American trade with Latin America, or with Asia, Africa, Canada, or Australia. Some of the most pressing challenges to American security—and in the age of thermonuclear weapons, even survival—are linked to the historic confrontation between the United States and the Soviet Union and between NATO in Western Europe and the Warsaw Pact in Eastern Europe. The territories between the Ural Mountains and the Straits of Gibraltar contain the greatest reservoir of

3

technology and productive capacity outside the United States itself, with enormous economic and strategic consequences for the fate of the entire world.

Europe has been the originator and the scene of most of the central political dramas of recent history and of our time. Whether we consider the Protestant ethic and early capitalism, the intellectual foundations of Western liberal democracy, democratic socialism, Marxism, fascism, or the welfare state and the managed economy, the relevance of the European experience is manifest. Moreover, no convincing historical or political evidence exists to indicate that the continued evolution and development of industrial or postindustrial society in Europe (and elsewhere) has come to a halt. The point is applicable whether one considers the Western democracies (despite a series of arguments which have heralded the development of prosperity, Keynesian economics, and the welfare state as contributing to an "end of ideology") or the Marxist notion that human social–political–economic evolution will suddenly stop with the attainment of communism.

Problems which Europe now faces—such as those involving popular participation in politics as well as in the work-place, representation, income distribution, economic growth, education, leisure, the balance between full employment and inflation, between regionalism and centralization, between social and individual needs, between pollution and production—typify matters which do or will confront advanced industrial societies throughout the world. The range of choices and solutions which Europe faces may therefore offer us something tangible, because they widen our sense of what is possible.

An understanding of the European perspective on these questions is particularly important at a time when many of the issues and problems spill beyond national borders and strain the capabilities of individual nation-states to provide adequate solutions. World crises of energy, food, and inflation all indicate the increasing interdependence of political systems; such crises also highlight some of our common vulnerabilities with the Europeans.

innovations of analysis

Our treatment of European politics breaks with the institutional and technical preoccupations of most standard texts. Instead, we seek to provide the reader with a real grasp of the "live stuff of politics"—the dominant issues and struggles in recent times of each area. Thus, our book is oriented to a series of specific objectives.

First, we focus upon *salient political issues* and controversies since World War II. We explain the technical, institutional, and historical aspects of the political process mainly as they relate to these issues. Our principal task is to enable the reader to understand what the themes and conflicts of recent European political life have been and why; how these conflicts have been carried on; who has participated in them and why; and what has resulted from them. In each chapter, we follow the analysis of major issues with an overview of the policy process and note the principal similarities and differences among systems.

Second, our treatment is *transnational* throughout. That is, we de-emphasize what we consider to be the increasingly artificial distinction between domestic and international or "foreign" politics and policies. Any perceptive observer of the contemporary politics of Europe recognizes that many of the supposedly domestic issues of individual countries have foreign antecedents and connections; equally, the problems and crises of the international and regional communities of the world often originate in largely domestic sources. As a result of advances in technology, transportation, and communications, as well as growing economic and even political interdependence, national governments possess far less ability to achieve their domestic objectives than is commonly assumed. Illustratively, the pattern of Europe's politics cannot be adequately understood without reference to the Common Market; yet, the evolution of the Common Market cannot be adequately explained without reference to France's late President, Charles de Gaulle, and to Gaullism. For many of the political systems we study, matters such as inflation, unemployment, economic growth, pollution, energy supply, and even national security are substantially shaped by factors only partly within national control. In addition, actors other than centralized governments frequently play crucial roles across and within national boundaries. Thus multinational corporations, pressure groups, international organizations, foundations, political movements, terrorist groups, and even decentralized agencies of government may exercise significant influence. The effect of this is noted by two political scientists:

> As the decision domains of corporations, banks, and (to a lesser extent) trade unions transcend national boundaries, a wide range of domestic politics come to impinge upon each other. These effects are further reinforced by transnational communications, which occur even in the absence of organizations. This growing policy sensitivity means that foreign economic policies touch a wider range of domestic economic activity than has been true in the past quarter century, thus blurring the lines

between domestic and foreign policy and increasing the numbers of issues relevant to foreign policy.[1]

As a case in point, the impact of the energy crisis on the principal countries of Western Europe has been substantially determined by a war in the Middle East, relations with the United States and the oil producing countries, actions of the European Community, the international oil companies, the Organization of Oil Exporting Countries (OPEC), the International Energy Agency (IEA), The International Monetary Fund (IMF), and other bodies. Yet the effect on European politics and economics has been considerable, involving increased energy costs, inflation and unemployment, concern about energy shortages, limits on governmental abilities to carry out political programs because of decreased tax revenues, and greater governmental instability.

Third, our treatment is more *comprehensive in its "Europeanness,"* based on an in-depth analysis of the European Community (Common Market) as well as on the political systems of Britain, France, the two Germanies, the Soviet Union, and a brief comparative examination of two alternative political models—Yugoslavia and the Mediterranean dictatorships. In our discussion of the individual European states we examine the background of the major issues, the characteristic forms and processes of political activity, and the contending political forces. We also treat the similarities and differences among European systems and assess how well each system works in terms of policy ("output") gratifications. We thus aim to provide the reader with an appreciation of the different solutions applied to analogous problems such as representation, participation, welfare, security, equality, and justice under a variety of systems. We also give thorough treatment to the European Community (EC). In our discussion we describe the needs (usually associated with the idea of interdependence) shaping its evolution and we treat the economic, political, and cultural factors that have led to its creation and development. We briefly survey the processes and mechanisms involved in Common Market operation and the fluctuating struggle among various social, economic, and political forces throughout the continent which are alternately seeking to construct or to subvert a larger European order. Finally, we analyze the practical impact of the EC on the lives of people—and then compare its performance to that of Comecon (the Soviet–East European common market).

Fourth, in each chapter our analyses—functional, institutional, histori-

---

[1] Robert O. Keohane and Joseph S. Nye, "World Politics and the International Economic System," in C. Fred Bergsten, ed., *The Future of the International Economic Order: An Agenda for Research* (Lexington, Mass.: Lexington Books, D.C. Heath, 1973), pp. 129–130.

cal, sociological, ideological, and political—are related to *the American experience.* This will be of value to those readers who have had some exposure to the American political system, yet rarely have the opportunity to compare the U.S. experience with that of other Western systems. It will also overcome any temptation to treat each of the European political systems in splendid isolation without considering relevant comparisons or attempting to assess overall system performance.

Fifth, we employ a *policy-making or problem-solving framework,*[2] applicable to each European (and indeed any other) political system. This approach is sensitive to more open and closed political systems. Simultaneously, it brings out the operation of the political process and alerts the student to the complexity of political contrasts. In effect, we hope that this framework will facilitate better understanding of how policy problems are handled in particular political systems, how political systems differ with respect to policy-making processes, and what the results, or outcomes, of political activity are likely to be.

organization

Each of the chapters dealing with specific political systems is divided into four sections: Background; Policy Agenda: Problems, Cleavages, and Conflicts; Policy Process; and Conclusion: Performance and Prospects. Let us examine what each section will cover.

BACKGROUND

We begin by presenting information useful to the appreciation of the specific contemporary issues and problems in a particular political system. In a sense, all polities share certain kinds of problems or face comparable demands—for example, security, distribution or redistribution of resources, political participation and representation, and the role of government in economy and society. Yet the importance of these issues, and the context in which they are faced, differs sharply from one political system to another. What constitutes a dramatic political problem in one country may be of minor significance in another. Thus it is essential to consider background factors such as political history, political culture,

[2] Recent books which explore problem-solving in politics include Yehezkel Dror, *Public Policy-Making Re-examined* (San Francisco: Chandler, 1968); Charles O. Jones, *An Introduction to the Study of Public Policy* (Belmont: Wadsworth, 1970); Daniel Lerner and Harold Lasswell, eds., *The Policy Sciences* (Stanford: Stanford University Press, 1960); Austin Ranney, ed., *Political Science and Public Policy* (Chicago: Markham, 1968); Ira Sharkansky, ed., *Policy Analysis in Political Science* (Chicago: Markham, 1970); more specific applications of problem-solving approaches are illustrated by Aaron Wildavsky, *The Politics of the Budgetary Process* (Boston: Little, Brown, 1964).

.ideology, and even geography, which enable us to understand why people and governments react in certain ways to new problems. A great deal depends on the political heritage or "political memories" of a people, and our appreciation of the legacy of ancient Russian despotism, the French Revolution of 1789, or the extraordinary continuity of British constitutional tradition can provide clues to present European politics and even to the future.

POLICY AGENDA: PROBLEMS, CLEAVAGES, AND CONFLICTS

Within the context of background and political history, the second section of each chapter presents the fundamental problems, cleavages, and conflicts which constitute the policy agenda within a given political system and which give rise to the live stuff of politics. First, this section examines the basic *problems*, which almost always have their origins on a longer term basis. These include such matters as governmental representativeness, responsiveness, democracy and stability, international relations and foreign policy; quality of life and the provision of social services; problems of the welfare state and the managed economy; class, religious, and ethnic differences; and questions of "who gets what," as in the choice between variants of capitalist, socialist, or "mixed" economic-political systems.*

These problems give rise to political and social *cleavages,* as people and groups respond in different ways and with different preferences and proposed solutions. Here we get an idea of what separates the "right" from the "left" and of the assumptions, strategies, and strengths of contending political forces, interest groups, or parties. In some societies these cleavages may be so profound as to make the solution of common problems virtually impossible on any basis on which the major contending groups can approve or acquiesce. In other systems, differences may be resolved with considerable success. Thus within the British system, we find a remarkable blend of continuity and change, while in France these cleavages have given rise to periodic upheavals in the political system itself, and in the Soviet Union the real or potential cleavages are dealt with by preventing the articulation of grievances or by suppressing those who would express demands or policies differing from the prevailing orthodoxy. In turn, these problems and cleavages lead to specific *conflicts.* Here we examine the major issues and struggles as they are played out in the contemporary political arena.

* Our list of problems or conflicts in each chapter is *not* meant to be exhaustive, of course. As students and teachers we could all find both additional issues and further ramifications in each of the systems discussed in the book.

The third section of each chapter deals with the resolution of these political issues through formal and informal means. In any society, institutions and individuals often take part in several phases of their policy process. We have divided the process into seven related stages, each of which we consider in turn.

Initiation   The first stage of the policy process (following the identification of an issue or problem) involves the formulation of proposals for action—for example, through legislation or perhaps some form of nongovernmental societal action. In pluralistic political systems, policy proposals may emanate quite openly from a great variety of sources, within and without the structure of government. As in the United States, interest groups, parties, newspapers, private individuals, legislators, academicians, bureaucrats, churchmen (and under some circumstances, transnational actors) all originate action and policy proposals from time to time. This right of public initiative may be more or less widely circumscribed in any society. In some of the more closed political systems, certain agencies and individuals may substantially preempt the right of initiative. In the German and Russian regimes of Hitler and Stalin, for example, people were very careful *not* to suggest publicly anything which could be interpreted as a rejection of, or drastic departure from, the policies pursued by the leaders. This was a hazardous and rarely indulged pastime for any citizen. Even privately, within a close circle of a leader's presumably most trusted and privileged advisors, people took great care to appear conformist. However, most of the political systems which we will analyze are relatively open insofar as this stage of policy initiation is concerned, and even the Soviet Union is somewhat less closed than it once was.

Deliberation   This stage of the policy process also takes both official and unofficial forms. In political systems with representative governments, this is the point at which the legislature typically enters the scene as a forum for debate. However, much official policy-making takes place outside the legislature—for example, within the executive (decrees or decisions of prime ministers), the administrative agencies of government (the bureaucracy and civil service), and the judiciary. Here, a whole panoply of public debate and efforts to exert influence come into play. The media (press, television, radio), pressure groups, public meetings or demonstrations, lobbying, private arm twisting, letter writing, and numerous other activities provide a means of broader involvement in policy deliberation or of influencing those charged with the official responsibility for deliberation. Even in highly authoritarian regimes, a certain amount of deliberation occurs, though usually behind the scenes.

Approval In most political systems, decisions and policies require the approval or concurrence of one or more public bodies before becoming binding rules upon members of the society as a whole. In the United States, for example, taxing and spending measures as well as most other legislation, require approval by both houses of Congress and of the president (a presidential veto, however, can be overridden by a two-thirds vote of both houses). Other U.S. laws require various federal and regulatory agencies to hold hearings and even conduct referenda (as in the administration of farm price supports) before putting into effect a rule or action.[3]

In most of the European political systems, comparable institutional arrangements exist. Thus Britain, France, the German Federal Republic —and even the USSR—require approval by their legislatures and by the head of state. What is of interest, however, is to determine in what circumstances this approval is only a mechanical or ceremonial formality rather than a matter of real political power or political controversy. Thus in Britain, although the upper legislative body, the House of Lords, must process and approve a bill in a manner comparable to the legislation's passage through the elected House of Commons, the Lords, an ancient hereditary and appointive body, have little real power to oppose the will of the House of Commons. Instead they serve mainly as a debating chamber and arena for occasional technical amendments to legislation. Even more striking is the role of the British monarch: Queen Elizabeth II must give royal assent before a bill becomes law, yet she is "constitutionally" obligated to approve whatever Parliament proposes. In the Soviet Union, however, it is the legislature which is a rubber stamp. There real power rests with the ruling Communist Party of the Soviet Union (CPSU), and parliamentary approval is only *pro forma*.

To the extent that the process of approval is a public one, there is an opportunity for the involvement of a much larger, more inclusive, national audience through the media, political parties, specialized interest groups, and so forth. Even a government which has the votes or the political muscle to get its way on a particular policy may find it necessary or prudent to defend publicly the wisdom of its policies. In part it may do so in anticipation of forthcoming elections and the need to maintain

[3] See Zbigniew Brzezinski and Samuel Huntington for a discussion of this in a comparison of Soviet and American agricultural policy in *Political Power USA/USSR* (New York: Viking Press, 1964), pp. 301–330; and Roy D. Laird, *The Soviet Paradigm* (New York: Macmillan, 1970), Chapter 9, pp. 133–143.

popular or legislative support. Approval is also required for reasons of due process, for if a government's activities are irregular there may be —in a democratic system at least—legal as well as political consequences.

Popular elections also play a significant role in the process by which policy is approved. Usually this approval is indirect and only periodic; thus, every few years voters elect a particular government and thereby indirectly approve the programs and policies which its political élites present during the election campaign. However, the process is remote, since it does not give voters a chance to indicate which of a party's policies it favors and which it opposes. Thus some states, such as Switzerland, sanction regular popular referenda on public issues. France has utilized the popular referendum six times in the Fifth Republic, and Britain resorted to a hitherto unprecedented referendum in order to settle the divisive question of whether to remain within the Common Market. At times, public approval is also expressed and made relevant by opinion polls. On the occasions when the polls—and sometimes the media—do convey a clear and unambiguous sense of public attitudes on a major policy question, governments are usually reluctant to act against this consensus.

There is, however, a major alternative channel by which policy approval is sought or obtained. In most of the democratic countries of Europe, governments have become deeply involved in managing their national economies to avoid extreme economic cycles of depression, unemployment, and inflation, and to maintain a measure of prosperity and economic growth to meet the needs and desires of their citizens. In addition, governments are frequently involved in regulating the economy or individual industries to prevent or lessen specific abuses (child labor, pollution, sanitation problems) or to promote desired public values (decentralization of industry, regulation or subsidy of public transport). Yet in complex and advanced economies, government is deeply dependent on the expertise, information, advice, and cooperation of the groups and enterprises it seeks to regulate. In an authoritarian or totalitarian society a government may compel compliance through repression or even force (though often at real costs in efficiency). However, in a free society it has little choice but to secure voluntary compliance. In a country such as Britain, where the process of policy approval is most advanced, this has given rise to a kind of functional representation, whereby pressure groups provide a direct link between society and government and their approval or acquiescence must be obtained in order for government policies to succeed.[4]

[4] See Robert J. Lieber on the politicization process in which, by focusing national attention on an issue, democratic leaders can frequently lessen if not eliminate the

Application In the words of the old adage, "there's many a slip 'twixt the cup and the lip". . . . The application of policy, in any system, may well determine its content, in some cases completely modifying or distorting the objectives of a bill or a directive. In all systems, the implementation or application of policy often involves the use of many different resources, organizations, and communication channels, all with considerable discretionary authority for people in the field to make decisions in carrying out the policy. Thus in virtually every political system a certain amount of slippage, between the mandate from the top and the execution of it at the grass roots, is all but inevitable.

In Britain, for example, an electoral change brings to power a mere hundred or so members of Parliament from the winning party. These members occupy positions at cabinet and sub-cabinet level, while the chief civil service officials in each government department (Foreign Office, Defense, Treasury, and so on) remain unchanged. These permanent administrators are the ones who carry out government policy, but they will have developed their own views based on individual experience, education, and personal background. In effect, they often influence the detailed application of policy in directions not fully anticipated or desired by political officials. They also influence policy-making, because cabinet officials rely heavily upon their technical advice. According to R. H. S. Crossman, a late and prominent Labour party cabinet member and intellectual, cabinet ministers often become captives of the very departments they are supposed to direct. In general, bureaucrats tend to prefer established procedures and are often at least passively resistant to change, whether the new policies involve innovations or the abandonment of established programs.

In making distinctions among different kinds of regimes, however, we are particularly concerned with the relative autonomy of implementing agencies. In some systems, the process of policy application is more fragmented than in others, not just in the number of agencies involved, but in terms of the legal–political autonomy of the participants. In the United States the constitutional obligation of federal employees is to enforce the laws, not to provide political service to any particular president or political leader. When civil service officials (bureaucrats) do not see eye to eye with the president on issues of mutual concern, he is not free to fire, demote, or otherwise directly punish these officials as a dictatorial leader such as Brezhnev or Franco might do. The corporate

veto power of otherwise potent interest groups, *British Politics and European Unity* (Berkeley: University of California Press, 1970); and also "Interest Groups and Political Integration: British Entry Into Europe," *American Poiltical Science Review* 57, no. 2 (March 1972): 53–67.

existence and autonomy of the different components of the bureaucracy are generally safeguarded by statutes (in addition, state and local governments and their employees are substantially independent of the federal government). Attempts to bypass them sometimes result in a stormy public reaction against political interference with the bureaucracy and illegal conduct by the government. The angry response of the American public to revelations that former President Nixon and his aides misused the Internal Revenue Service, the Federal Bureau of Investigation, and the Central Intelligence Agency is a case in point.

The case of the United States, a federal system, has certain parallels among other pluralistic political systems, both federal (West Germany) and unitary (Britain and France). Ordinarily a British, French, or West German prime minister or chancellor cannot issue direct commands to lower ranking civil servants, officers, or soldiers without "going through channels"; this is so concerning judges, courts, and media as well. In these systems, effective implementation or application of policy (that is, application that is compliant with the directives and objectives of leaders) depends very little on coercion and direct intervention by political leaders; it depends much more on such factors as the existence (or nonexistence) of a value consensus between the bureaucrats and their masters; the degree of professional dedication on the part of the bureaucracy; the technical resources and abilities of the bureaucracy; and the skillful manipulation of opinion throughout the political system by the leaders.

Adjudication and Enforcement   The attempt to apply rules and policies inevitably involves disputes, conflicts, and ambiguities. Often these have to do with questions of jurisdiction: Who is responsible for what? What agency or official? Sometimes conflicts or ambiguities arise with respect to special, marginal, or deviant cases. Given particular situations, and several possible applicable rules, how should they be handled? On occasion, people may believe that a conflict of laws or rights exists, or that governmental actions are not grounded in lawful authority. Issues of this sort require adjudication through one or more agencies, which can sort things out and relate the facts of each particular case to the general rules of the system.

It makes a great deal of difference as to how the participants can pursue their claims or "rights"; what sanctions may be invoked against individuals and public agencies; how these are enforced (or unenforced, as the case may be); to what extent the procedural and substantive rights of all participants are protected; and very importantly, too, how open and autonomous the whole adjudication process is.

Can citizens sue the government, for example, or any of its officials or agencies? Are trials held in public? Are the rights of accused persons protected in the courts? Is there access by mass media to the judicial process? To what extent is the judicial process a prerogative one—that is, subject to private, unstructured, and capricious decisions? To what extent are all the components of the adjudication process—all the way from a hearing to determine if sufficient cause exists for an adjudicative proceeding to the execution of a verdict—under the control of one agency, person, or group of people? Or, to what extent is it an interactive process with some independent or at least loosely interdependent actors?

In certain political systems, jurisdictional or agency conflicts may be resolvable not by relatively independent courts, publicly, but generally by easily manipulable political organs. Those who give the directions and issue the decrees may also be the same persons who resolve conflicts among the implementors of policy. In other systems, there may be appeal to a judiciary substantially independent of the rule-makers and rule implementors.

Such is the case in the United States and in France, for example, where the Supreme Court and the Council of State, respectively, serve as agencies for the resolution of such conflicts—with public proceedings, published verdicts and records of the case, and wide media access. In these systems, as well as the other constitutional–pluralistic regimes discussed in this book, citizens may sue the government as well as specific government officials for damages in wrongful actions, for malperformance or failure to perform their legal duties. Chances of recovery or reversal may be considerable. In other political systems, such suits may not be launched at all. Thus, we find that even after the very substantial, open disclosure of the criminal excesses of the secret police in Stalin's Russia (by his successor Khrushchev in 1956) not a single suit for damages has even been brought against any KGB police official.

The rule of law exists in many societies, thus providing a means for the resolution of disputes among individuals, and between individuals or groups and governments without the aggrieved party feeling it has no recourse but violence to obtain justice. Processes vary enormously, however. Compared to the United States, where the Supreme Court exists as an independent branch of government and can declare laws unconstitutional, the British Parliament is supreme and—at least in theory—can pass whatever legislation it desires. In France, no right of habeas corpus exists; police officials can arrest, imprison, and interrogate people for considerable lengths of time without lodging formal charges. In the USSR, Communist legality dictates that judicial decisions be based on criteria of ideology and the strengthening of communism within the

Soviet Union rather than on notions of "bourgeois" justice or objectivity.

In all political systems there also exists a basic problem of bringing about citizen compliance with policies or rules. Policy enforcement is not always automatic; it may involve the threat or use of punitive sanctions. Even so, some laws may be unenforceable if there is wide scale public resistance or a sense that the policy in question violates tradition or lacks legitimacy. The examples of the prohibition of alcoholic beverages in the U.S. during the 1920's, and of widespread evasion of French income tax laws throughout the twentieth century are cases in point. Authoritarian regimes, such as those of Stalin and his successors in Russia, and of Franco in Spain, were often able to enforce unpopular policies through coercion, terror, and murder. However, the collapse of the military dictatorship in Greece (1974), and the quasi-fascist Salazar-Caetano dictatorship in Portugal (1974), as well as upheavals against Communist dictatorships in East Germany (1953), Hungary (1956), Poland (1956, 1970), and Czechoslovakia (1968), indicate that even coercion has its limits. In the open and pluralistic societies of Western Europe, compliance must be largely voluntary and enforcement will mainly serve to maintain government credibility, provided some legitimacy already exists.

Auditing and Monitoring of Policy Politics and the policy process do not cease with the implementation of a policy. The actual operation of a policy as well as its consequences, both intended and unintended, may become the subject of intense controversy. Indeed, in order for a government, or any organization, group, or individual, to achieve its goals it must obtain information on the actual performance of a policy as compared to what was previously anticipated. The *feedback* of this information is essential, and—if there is to be effective system performance—it must be used to modify on-going policy performance.[5] This is not only a matter of efficiency, but often of governmental responsiveness, legitimacy, and stability.

In practice, auditing and monitoring of policy are carried out in numerous ways. In Western Europe and the United States, the media are particularly important in this phase of problem-solving. Americans are familiar with the role of the press in exposing the Watergate scandals and of television in bringing the issue of the Indochina war into their livingrooms. Comparable events, which served to mobilize public opinion with considerable impact on the decision-making process, have taken

[5] This is a fundamental tenet of cybernetics (the study of communication and control in organizations). See R. Lieber, *Theory and World Politics* (Cambridge, Mass.: Winthrop Publishers, 1972), pp. 68–87.

place in Western Europe. For example, British newspapers helped to expose the Profumo affair (a lurid sex and spy scandal), and undermined the Conservative government of Prime Minister Macmillan. In Germany, the *Spiegel* news magazine controversy (involving abuses of police power by the ambitious Franz Joseph Strauss) caused Strauss's ouster from government and a revision of police procedures.

The media are by no means the only source for auditing and monitoring of policy. Governments try to institutionalize such procedures, sometimes by contracting with independent analysts (or "think tanks") and more often by conducting their own inquiries. These may take place within administrative departments or sometimes may be undertaken by the legislature, as in the case of Senator Sam Ervin's Senate investigation of Watergate, or may be carried out by the executive, as in the case of British select committees or Royal Commissions. Individuals and private groups also exercise their rights to speak out, organize, assemble, and disseminate information in an effort to modify policies which are harmful to them or with which they disagree.

In authoritarian political systems, monitoring is mostly a private and highly privileged affair. The very attempt to elicit information about a particular policy, let alone disseminate information and criticism, may be considered treasonable—except for a handful of ruling élites, who may dominate a military dictatorship (for example, Greece from 1967 to 1974) or a bureaucratic collectivist dictatorship (contemporary Russia). There may thus be no legitimate public forum for the open review of policy, and the media and legislature (if it exists) will often be used to rubber stamp or to applaud policy but not to scrutinize it. Similarly, political parties, independent organizations, interest groups, and the like, may be suppressed or often manipulated to endorse or to rally support for existing policies.

There is no certainty that democratic societies will always speedily and effectively modify policies which prove unsuccessful or unpopular —as the French experience in Indochina (1946–1954) and Algeria (1954–1962) or the American involvement in Vietnam illustrate—nor can all the ongoing activities of huge and complex governments be scrutinized on a daily basis. Yet the auditing and monitoring capabilities of open and pluralistic political systems do create a greater likelihood that unsuccessful policies and past failures will sooner or later be investigated and criticized and that salutary lessons will be learned from these experiences. Autocratic power holders, however, often fear that exposure of the misdeeds of their own or of their predecessors may undermine their power, and so they tend to discourage or limit investigative processes.

Thus military defeats or other damaging involvements suffered by the United States (Pearl Harbor, 1941) or Britain (Narvik, 1940 and Suez, 1956) have been matters of public attention leading to modification in policy and sometimes to changes in government. By contrast, the calamitous defeat suffered by Nazi Germany at Stalingrad (1943), brought on largely by Hitler's personal policy, could not be the subject of public or even private inquiry. Germany continued the war until the bitter end, when its cities were nearly obliterated, millions of its civilians killed or made refugees, and huge portions of its territory annexed by Russia and Poland. Similarly, the devastating Nazi attack on Russia in June 1941 found the Soviets unable to defend themselves properly because vigorous defense preparations would have implied criticism of Stalin's policy of alliance with Hitler. As a result the Soviet Union lost some 20 million lives during World War II. Only the route of conspiracy and assassination lay open to those profoundly disenchanted by their leaders in these events.[6] More mundane examples also exist. According to one account, during the 1960's, most Soviet refrigerators manufactured were approximately six inches too wide to fit into the appropriate kitchen space designed for them in most Soviet apartments constructed during that period, but there was no resultant public uproar in the media.

Termination and Amendment In all political systems policies are terminated or changed from time to time. In all systems, change of policy is liable to occur in the application phase—often unintentionally—and without any formal sanction. But how can policy be changed or terminated formally and intentionally? In pluralistic systems, this may involve an extended public process with different, mutually independent actors participating. A practical consequence of this process is that one agency can legitimately pull the rug from under others. Legislative or parliamentary agencies, and in some cases courts, may openly amend or even reject policies. We should also remember that the modification or termi-

---

[6] Insightful biographies of some of these authoritarian leaders include Alan Bullock, *Hitler, a Study in Tyranny* (Oxford: Oxford University Press, 1952); H. M. Hyde, *Stalin* (New York: Farrar, Straus and Giroux, 1972); and Brian Crozier, *Franco: A Biographical History* (London: Eyre and Spottiswoode, 1967). See also Harison Salisbury, *900 Days: The Siege of Leningrad* (New York: Harper & Row, 1969) and Seweryn Bialer, *Stalin's Generals* (New York: Columbia University Press, 1971). In the case of Nazi Germany, the option of conspiracy was involved in the abortive assassination attempt by Colonel Graf von Stauffenberg and others against Hitler on July 20, 1944. In the case of Stalin, no internal conspiracy can be documented, although some defections among high-ranking Russian officers captured by Germans (Vlasov) did occur. Even now, long after Stalin's death, the responsibilities of the political leaders in the events of 1941–1945 have received only guarded, partial, and fragmentary airing, with bits and pieces of evidence subsequently collected not in the USSR but in the West.

nation of policy may be secured through elections, through referenda, and in parliamentary regimes through votes of censure or of no confidence against particular ministries.

However, some regimes are organized on such authoritarian principles that only the initiators of a policy can legitimately amend or terminate it. Except for the kind of universal bureaucratic slippage, noted with respect to policy application earlier, there may be no legitimate organs of interposition in the political system—that is, any that could openly and freely say "no," or "enough," to a Hitler, Stalin, Brezhnev, or Franco.

CONCLUSION: PERFORMANCE AND PROSPECTS

The final section of each chapter poses the crucial questions of performance and output. That is, given the history, issues, actors, conflicts, and processes of politics, what has this added up to for the citizens of each country, and what are the future prospects of the political system likely to be in terms of both stability and change?

We can assess performance by asking how successful each system has been in meeting common needs. At a minimum, European citizens expect a degree of physical safety and security from foreign invasion, civil war, and domestic violence. In much of Europe they may expect not only a stable and effective government but an open political system as well, one which respects individual liberties and responds to the needs and desires of the majority of its population. While assessing these political systems we can also compare their performance against three classical tenets of democratic theory:

1. The common man ought to participate in the making of those decisions that most directly affect him;
2. There ought to be ways in which those who rule can be called to account by those who are ruled;
3. The government ought to ensure that available resources are distributed in a reasonably equitable manner, particularly those goods and services necessary to basic human welfare.[7]

In short, we may evaluate system performance in terms which encompass not only human welfare but also personal rights and collective choices.

Not only political criteria but also economic and social ones are thus highly significant. Europeans may judge their political systems and specific governments according to the standard of living, the likelihood of full employment, the management of inflation, overall production and

[7] Richard B. Fagen and William S. Tuohy, *Politics and Privilege in a Mexican City* (Stanford: Stanford University Press, 1972), p. 161. See David Baybroke, *Three Tests for Democracy: Personal Rights, Human Welfare, Collective Preference* (New York: Random House, 1968).

growth as well as the security of property, social status, and cultural–national identifications. In social terms, people are likely to ask whether their system has provided relief from the problems of illness, disability, old age, and unemployment, and also whether it has afforded them the security and enjoyment of their possessions. At times there may be trade-offs between various economic and social priorities. Thus satisfaction with system performance may depend on the balance between private and public gratifications that are produced and distributed. Regimes which repress and exclude large constituencies from political participation are more likely to ignore their demands; whether these may be for public amenities such as schools, hospitals, child care, or a more equitable distribution of income and welfare (typically resisted by right-wing authoritarian governments), for consumer goods and more private consumption (demands often resisted by Communist dictatorships), or for greater personal and political freedom (something opposed by all types of repressive regimes). While open, pluralistic systems are likely to maintain a better balance between public and private expenditure,[8] they nevertheless may respond very differently among themselves to practical policy questions involving the use of taxes (to reduce income discrepancies and encourage social equality or to stimulate investment and economic growth), economic policy (inflation versus unemployment), social priorities (social welfare improvements versus private investment), foreign and domestic considerations (the "guns or butter" question), and equality (equal opportunity for education and careers or an unwillingness to tamper with traditional social patterns based on status, class, ethnicity, or income).

The prospects for a political system may depend on how successfully it copes with these often conflicting priorities and the nature of the choices the system makes. The judgments people reach about a system's overall performance are likely to be important in determining its degree of legitimacy and acceptability. Ultimately the viability of the European political systems will be determined by how well they have met the needs of their population and by the extent to which these people feel a part of the political process and identify with it.

[8] On this theme, see Alexander J. Groth, *Comparative Politics: A Distributive Approach* (New York: Macmillan, 1971).

2

britain

2 BRITAIN

Britain has been the birthplace of industrialization, parliamentary government, the rule of law, and even the concept of impeachment. Its elements of shared language and history make it a fascinating object of study for Americans. Indeed, the British experience offers much that is relevant to contemporary life. Questions of political reform and political power, economic management and planning, business influence and trade union power, equality and merit, urbanism and the environment, education and health, nationalism and interdependence, and the nature of conservatism, liberalism, and socialism all find application in the United Kingdom.

Extraordinary comparisons and contrasts exist between Britain and America. The similarity of language, however, can be deceptive. In fact, those who readily discuss British politics sometimes fail to understand that country as well as they think they do. In recent years, American views of Britain have often displayed either a passionate and uncritical anglophilia or, more commonly, a certain hysteria. Thus, leading commentators have claimed that Britain's political and economic system is on the verge of collapse, and have compared the situation to the chaos of Weimar Germany (before Hitler took power). To be sure, there have been British voices in this chorus of cries about a "whiff of Weimar," a "smell of Argentina," "constitutional breakdown," "a left-wing Spain," and "our last democratic election." [1] But the British reality is far more elusive than these

[1] See, for example, *The Economist* (London), February 9, and September 14, 1974; *U. S. News and World Report* (quoted in *The Times*, London, October 9, 1974); Kingsley Amis (quoted in *Newsweek*, October 21, 1974); also see James Reston, *New York Times* (February 24, and August 30, 1974), and the television commentaries of Eric Sevareid on CBS news.

comments imply. An understanding of British political life is valuable not only in itself, but also for its relationship to the American experience.

background

The United Kingdom of Great Britain and Northern Ireland covers a remarkably limited and densely populated geographic area of some 94,000 square miles, which makes it smaller than the state of Oregon. Technically, "England" refers to the southern two-thirds of the island of Great Britain, in which some 49 million people live (approximately 3 million of whom are Welsh). Scotland, with 5.5 million people, lies in the northern portion of Britain; the population of British-ruled Northern Ireland numbers 1.5 million. Together, these 56 million British comprise a highly educated and, by American standards, relatively homogeneous population. Despite recent regional strains from Scottish and Welsh nationalism and an ugly level of communal violence in Northern Ireland, as well as regional residues of accent and tradition, these differences are less significant than what the British have in common. Overwhelmingly the British people are white, with about 1 million nonwhite Commonwealth immigrants from former British colonies (chiefly Pakistan, India, and the West Indies). They are also, since Henry VIII's break with Rome in 1534, mainly Protestant in religion (though there are 5 million Catholics and 0.5 million Jews), and they are mainly of common Anglo-Saxon and Celtic ethnic origins.

ENVIRONMENT AND INDUSTRIALIZATION

The constraints of geography, climate, and resources have conditioned much of Britain's internal political life as well as its relations with the rest of the world. The British isles, with their fertile soil and ample rainfall, enjoyed a thriving agriculture and early prosperity. Britain also possessed a favorable location on major sea lanes, with good natural harbors and no interior land more than 75 miles from the sea. These factors, together with huge resources of coal and some iron, enabled the British to produce a capital surplus. Partly because of their separation from the continent of Europe by the English Channel's 18 miles of water, the British never experienced the need to maintain a huge and costly standing army as a drain on national wealth. Protected instead by a large navy, which also opened major possibilities of foreign exploration and trade, Britain became the first country in the world to undergo industrialization. This process began in the late eighteenth century, and by 1850 the country had become predominantly urban and industrial. As late as 1870, Britain was the leading industrial power, producing, for example, more than half the world's steel. Yet its growth began to slow, and as Germany, America, and other countries intensified their own industrialization, Britain's relative position became less dominant. By 1910 it still had the world's most advanced navy but produced only 15 percent of the world's steel.

The causes of Britain's early industrialization are manifold; they include not only its advantages of insularity, maritime location, and agricultural surplus, but—in contrast to Germany and Italy—its long national unity and lack of cataclysmic internal warfare or upheaval during that period. Of perhaps equal importance at the time, Britain drew upon vast quantities of cheap grain in North and South America and Australia. As late as the 1840's Britain fed its own population of 24 million from locally produced foodstuffs. But by repealing its protective tariffs on agricultural imports (known as the Corn Laws), Britain encouraged the influx of cheaper food from outside to the detriment of its own agriculture. This intensified a vast population shift to the cities, which continued until World War I and provided the cheap labor for industrialization.

Britain and the International Economy   Lowering agricultural tariffs not only offered the opportunity to reduce the cost of living but it also allowed industrialists to reduce industrial wages. At the time, Britain could import cheap food and raw materials and find ready foreign outlets for its exports of manufactured goods. The logic of this pattern persisted until the turn of the century, but it contained the elements of longer term problems which would plague Britain in the twentieth century. One problem was that other countries also began to manufacture industrial goods and by 1900 these competed in price and quality with British exports and even inside the UK. Yet having run down its domestic agriculture, and without most raw materials other than coal, the country's survival depended upon its ability to earn enough from exports of goods and services to pay for these commodities. World War I, with the attempted blockade of British ports by German submarines, dramatically illuminated Britain's vulnerability. During and after the war, and again during the desperate struggle against Hitler's Germany in World War II, successive governments undertook to subsidize and modernize British agriculture. Within the limits of population and geography these efforts succeeded in increasing agricultural production so that with only 3 percent of its working population on the land—a figure far lower than that of its American and European neighbors—Britain could manage to provide two-thirds of its temperate zone food needs and half of the total food required by its population.

Nonetheless, this fundamental need to import vast quantities of food and raw materials remained an irrevocable fact of British life, making the country inextricably interdependent with the world economy. As we shall see, events outside British control, such as those resulting in sharply higher prices for food and oil, or in lessened opportunities to sell British exports, would have direct economic, social, and political effects within Britain itself. Thus the value of the British currency, the pound sterling, as well as the balance of payments (that is, the difference between Britain's foreign earnings and foreign expenditures), inflation, and other seemingly technical or economic matters would come to have the highest political importance for the British.

Involvement in Foreign Affairs A second and related consequence of Britain's pattern of geography and industrialization was its necessary involvement in foreign affairs. Since the sixteenth century Britain had become an important maritime power, its explorers navigating the globe and paving the way for settlement in North America, particularly in the seventeenth century, and the colonization of India. These and other possessions provided lucrative trade, and although the United States achieved its independence, Britain continued to maintain other colonies and a strong navy for protection of its increasingly important trade links as well as protection of the homeland from foreign invasion.

Britain continued to define its chief European security interest as preventing the domination of the European continent by any one great power. Britain therefore acted as a balancer, intervening whenever this interest appeared to be threatened: for example, against Spain in the late sixteenth century, against France, particularly Napoleon in the early nineteenth century, and later against Germany in the twentieth century. Although Britain remained a small, crowded island, its importance spread far beyond the British isles. The original colonial and trading interests in India, Canada, Australia, and South Africa were greatly expanded by the fruits of a successful race against other would-be colonial powers in Africa in the last quarter of the nineteenth century. By 1900, vast areas of the world were under either direct British Empire rule (India, the Caribbean, and much of Africa) or closely associated as Commonwealth Dominions (Australia, Canada, New Zealand, South Africa). These provided a huge market for British industrial products, a source of food and raw materials, and a basis of political and geographic influence. Altogether, more than half a billion persons resided within the Empire and Commonwealth. In World Wars I and II, these ties proved of immense value for the British, and in the aftermath of the war in 1945, Britain appeared, with the United States and the Soviet Union, as one of the three great world powers by virtue of sharing in the victory and by its status at the head of the Empire and Commonwealth.

Decolonization, however, came rapidly. First with India, Pakistan, and Ceylon in 1947–1948, then with a rush as Britain granted independence to its African and Asian dependencies in the late 1950's and early 1960's. Unlike France (in Indochina and Algeria), Britain did not by and large become involved in futile and bloody wars in an effort to retain colonies. But the largely voluntary transition, which converted direct Empire rule to loose association under the Commonwealth, preserved an illusion of British power and influence. For awhile, countries such as India, Pakistan, Nigeria, Cyprus, and the rest maintained close symbolic, commercial, and educational links to Britain. They patterned their governmental structures after those of London, put the Queen's image on their postage stamps, retained links to the British monetary system through membership of the sterling area, conducted their international business affairs through the institutions of the City of London, sent their élites for higher education at Oxford, Cambridge, the London School of Economics or Sandhurst (Britain's equivalent of West Point), and shared British language and customs.

Gradually, it became clear that these links were increasingly symbolic and decreasingly substantive. Over time, the less developed countries pursued their own paths and interests. Their institutions changed, many of their democratic governments were overthrown by military leaders (Pakistan, Nigeria, Ghana, Uganda) or by civilian officials (India). They increasingly followed the interests they held in common with other countries of their region or the less developed world, and they found Britain far too limited an outlet for all their exports and not necessarily the most advantageous or competitive source for technology, investment, aid, or imports. Even British ties with the old white dominions became less and less significant. Yet the illusion of the British Empire and Commonwealth role persisted long enough to delay British participation in European unity for many years. The British rejected opportunities to join the European Coal and Steel Community (1951), an abortive European Defense Community (1951–1954), and the European Common Market (1956).

Britain's failure to enter the European Community on the ground floor was not only the result of its Empire and Commonwealth role. In fact, leaders of both Labour and Conservative governments of Britain after World War II regarded their country as uniquely placed at the intersection of three geopolitical circles. The first of these "three circles" (as Winston Churchill and Anthony Eden termed them) was the Commonwealth, but a second one was Britain's "special relationship" with the United States. Here ties of history had been reinforced by alliance and shared victory in two world wars, collaboration on nuclear weapons research (including later privileged British access to U.S. nuclear technology) and a sense that the British could play a special advisory role to the Americans, who had become the world's leading superpower. Europe was only the third of the circles in which Britain found itself, and so the British were unwilling to give priority to this seemingly narrower regional interest at a time when the leadership of Europe could have been theirs. As Churchill had told de Gaulle during the war, if Britain were forced to decide between Europe and the open sea, it would always choose the latter.

In October 1956 Britain experienced a stunning debacle which shattered the illusion that it remained a truly major world power. In July of that year, President Nasser of Egypt dramatically seized control of the largely British-owned Suez canal and nationalized its ownership. Conservative Prime Minister Anthony Eden, who had succeeded Winston Churchill two years earlier, found this an outrageous affront to Britain and a threat to its sea lanes to the Persian Gulf, India, and Australia. Nasser's inflammatory rhetoric, as well as his threats to destroy the state of Israel, led Eden to draw a parallel between Hitler and Nasser. On October 31, after Nasser rejected proposals made by the principal countries using the Canal, the British and French launched an air and sea attack to occupy the Canal area. While the military operation succeeded, the British found to their despair that the action was strongly condemned by the United States government as well as the Soviets. In response to Soviet military threats and American pressure—particularly a refusal to support the pound sterling, whose value appeared jeopardized by the economic consequences and fuel shortage resulting from the Suez expedition and closure of the canal during the fighting—the British and French governments announced on December 3 that they would withdraw their forces.

Inside and outside Britain this was seen as a humiliation. A month later it led to Eden's resignation and replacement by Macmillan, and to a soul-searching public debate about Britain's world role. The choices commonly posed included a special stress upon Britain's Commonwealth leadership, emphasis on the special relationship with America, full participation in European unity, or a lessened involvement in world affairs and alliances and greater focus on internal matters in order to create a "super Sweden."

Ultimately, the European choice prevailed, if only because the Commonwealth role did not constitute a viable alternative and because the American government found the UK somewhat less important as a principal ally. The British government of Harold Macmillan finally decided to seek Common Market membership in 1961, but it found the way barred by the veto wielded by President de Gaulle in January 1963. The effect on Britain was demoralizing. As one Labour Party critic scathingly described it:

It was against this background of original hostility, then enthusiastic conviction, that the effect of President de Gaulle's *non* must be measured. It was as though an aging virgin who had resisted all advances in her youth had at last brought herself to the moment of delicious surrender: one by one the garments had been taken. Naked, defenseless and loving, she awaits the final embrace—only to be told that she is not yet ready or fit for union! [2]

Only in 1973, after successive vetoes and the death of de Gaulle did Britain finally gain entry to the European Community. In the meantime, its special links to the United States had grown far weaker and its position among the 32 member states and 900 million people of the Commonwealth had little more than symbolic significance. [3]

Industrialization and Social Hardship   A third major consequence of Britain's pattern of industrialization was the severe misery and hardship suffered by the millions of Britons who moved willingly or in desperation from rural areas to the cities. Mid-nineteenth-century urban conditions were marked by incredible squalor, desperately low wages, large quantities of cheap gin, severe crime and repression (children could be and were hanged for petty theft), disease and death. Conditions in the mines were no better; an 1842 report of the Royal Commission on Children's Employment spoke of widespread employment of seven-year-old children in coal mines and of women working as beasts of burden, pulling heavily laden rail carts along hazardous mineshafts. [4]

The response to this misery varied. Early British economic theorists such as Malthus and Ricardo argued that it would do no good to pay higher wages or otherwise alleviate suffering and early death of the laboring classes. Such actions would only result in increased population which —because of limits on food supply—could only be held in check by famine, pestilence, and war. Others, such as Karl Marx, predicted revolutionary change. Marx, writing in part on the British experience, produced the *Communist Manifesto* (with Friedrich Engels) in 1848, and the more detailed *Capital* (1867), which chronicled the extreme suffering and exploitation characteristic of British industrialization.

Over the next half century, both Malthus and Marx proved too pessi-

[2] Peter Shore, *Entitled to Know* (London: Macgibbon and Kee, 1966), p. 23.
[3] The 32 sovereign states of the Commonwealth are: United Kingdom, Canada, Australia, New Zealand, Bangladesh, Barbados, Botswana, Cyprus, Fiji, Gambia, Ghana, Guyana, India, Jamaica, Kenya, Lesotho, Malawi, Malaysia, Malta G.C., Mauritius, Nauru, Nigeria, Sierra Leone, Singapore, Sri Lanka, Swaziland, Tanzania, Trinidad and Tobago, Uganda, Zambia, Tonga, and Western Samoa.
[4] Arthur Bryant, *Pageant of England, 1840–1940* (London: Collins, 1941), cited in Aneurin Bevan, *In Place of Fear* (New York: Monthly Review Press, 1964), pp. 72–73.

mistic in their expectations. By the turn of the century, slow but significant improvements in the condition of the British working classes had taken place. Life was still poor and harsh, but the scale of suffering and squalor had notably diminished. Nonetheless, the enduring legacy of industrialization proved to be one of deep class divisions, particularly those between the working classes, on the one hand, and the propertied middle and upper classes, on the other. This theme would be found not only in British literature, as in Conservative Prime Minister Benjamin Disraeli's famous book, *Sybil, or the Two Nations*, but also in fundamental social, economic, and political differences that persist, in less dramatic form, to the present day.

THE CENTRALIZATION OF BRITISH POLITICS

Politics in Britain is predominantly national rather than regional or local. Elections for Parliament are fought largely on national issues, and swings in support for the major parties are remarkably uniform throughout the UK. Several factors account for this phenomenon. One factor is the compact size of the country (particularly of England, where four out of every five Britons live) and the scope of communications and the media. The press is predominantly national, in that the London newspapers circulate on a daily basis throughout virtually the entire UK. Similarly, radio and television are national in scope based on a public corporation (the British Broadcasting Corporation, the BBC) as well as commercial outlets. The educational system also follows more of a centralized than regional pattern, contrasted to the United States where school policy and curricula are totally controlled on a local or state basis. Another factor is the dominance of London. Not only is it the capital city and seat of government, but it also is the commercial, cultural, and media center of the UK. It thus combines the functions of a Washington, D.C., New York, and Boston, and without the rival attractions of a Los Angeles or a San Francisco. Some 8 million Britons live within Greater London, and many millions more are within an hour's train ride of the capital. Cities in England, such as Manchester, Liverpool, and Birmingham, or in Scotland, particularly Glasgow and Edinburgh, are important in manufacturing, shipping, or communications, but London dwarfs them all in importance. Next, the British parliamentary system with its unified and cohesive parties and unitary rather than federal government makes national politics dominant. There are no regional or state governments, no California or New York or Bavaria, with substantial independent powers. Instead the successive level of governmental authority is found only at the county or the local level. Finally, the British—and particularly the English—share a long common history. There has been no profound interruption in its continuity since the last successful invasion of Britain by the Normans in 1066 A.D. And the roots of the British Constitution can be found more than eight and a half centuries ago in the Magna Carta of 1215, which laid the foundations of the rule of law and of parliamentary government.

British political history in itself is a monumental subject but the origins of the present system lie in the Civil War between Parliament and King Charles I (1642–1649); the "Glorious Revolution" of 1688–1689 (actually a rather peaceful transition) in which Parliament succeeded in establishing limits on monarchical power; and the Reform Act of 1832 which extended the franchise to a part of the middle class male population and by doing so established the principle that representation in Parliament would be based on some relationship to numbers of voters. Even though hailed as a remarkable breakthrough, the 1832 Act created an electorate of no more than 7 percent of the adult male population and left significant powers in the hands of the king and aristocratic House of Lords (a largely hereditary parliamentary body).

Over a period of centuries there was a slow and sometimes agonizing movement away from the rule based on monarchical succession and aristocratic birth, and toward representative government and the supremacy of a popularly elected Parliament. The milestones in this progression include the second Reform Act (1867), which extended the vote to adult males in the urban working class, based on a modest property owning qualification, and the Reform Act of 1884, which enfranchised agricultural laborers so that for the first time more than half the adult male population could vote. During the nineteenth century, restrictions on voting and office holding were gradually removed from Catholics, Jews, and atheists. Only in 1918, at the end of World War I, was the vote finally given to all adult males and, prompted by the direct action tactics of the militant suffragettes, to women over the age of 30. By contrast, the United States had provided full voting rights to all white males by the 1840's, to black males in 1867, and to women in 1919. In 1928, the franchise was given to women over 21, and in 1948 a few remaining predemocratic vestiges were removed, including multiple votes for university graduates and businessmen. With the curtailment of the powers of the House of Lords (1911 and 1949), the democratizing process in the political realm had at last been largely completed (unless one adds the introduction of 18-year-old vote in 1969).

BRITISH COLLECTIVIST POLITICS: PARTY GOVERNMENT AND FUNCTIONAL REPRESENTATION

By themselves the details of extended franchise and a shift in effective control from monarchy and House of Lords to representative government and House of Commons provide only a starting point in understanding modern British politics. To appreciate the manner in which the system operates, it is essential to grasp the basic ideas of what Samuel H. Beer, America's most astute scholar of British politics, has termed *collectivist politics*.[5] Essentially, this differentiates two channels through which society and government interact.

Party Government   The first of these channels is the system of *party government*. Here, development of the welfare state as well as the realities of gaining power within the parliamentary system have required that the major political parties, Labour, Conservative, and to a far lesser extent the Liberals and Scottish and Welsh Nationalists, bid for the votes of consumer groups (blocs of voters). In several respects this presents a very different picture from that in the United States. First, even though the Labour and Conservative parties include a wide range of opinion and interests, each party is strongly influenced by its own distinctive conception of the common good, which, prior to each general election, finds expression in a specific party program or manifesto. This clearly contrasts with the deep fragmentation and lack of programmatic agreement within either the Democratic or Republican parties in the U.S. Next, a high degree of unity and discipline exists among the elected members of each party in the House of Commons. With a few important exceptions, the members of parliament vote in a solid bloc as directed by their party leadership and conveyed by the party whips. Thus British voters know that when they cast their vote for a party's candidate in their constituency, the person—if elected—will in fact support a very specific national party program and leadership. Here too, the contrast with American political life is enormous, since U.S. members of Congress customarily stress their independence or their ability to represent geographic interests, so that the pattern of party cohesion in the Senate and House of Representatives remains very loose.

Party government in Britain, assuring as it does responsible and programmatic government, grows in equal measure out of the parliamentary system and political ideology. Although both subjects are treated at greater length later in this chapter, we should note here some of these essentials. In the British parliamentary system the person who will head the government is not directly elected in the manner of an American or

[5] See Samuel H. Beer, *British Politics in the Collectivist Age* (New York: Vintage Books, 1969), especially Chapter 12, and *The British Political System* (New York: Random House, 1974). Also see, S. E. Finer, *Anonymous Empire*, 2nd rev. ed. (London: Pall Mall Press, 1966); and Robert J. Lieber, "Interest Groups and Political Integration: British Entry Into Europe," *American Political Science Review* 66, no. 1 (March 1972), especially pp. 53–54.

French president. Instead, the prime minister heads the majority party in the House of Commons. In effect, the members of each party in Parliament elect one of their number to lead their party and whichever leader can command a majority among the 635 members of parliament (MPs) becomes prime minister. It is as though the U.S. president were selected by the majority party in the U.S. House of Representatives and he or she then named a cabinet from among the leading figures of his or her party in the House and Senate. In Britain, the leader of the minority party becomes Leader of the Opposition, a post carrying a government salary and other privileges, and he or she either appoints (in the Conservative Party) or the parliamentary party elects (in the case of the Labour Party) a "shadow cabinet"—in effect an alternative government. This system places a premium on unity, since a majority party which failed to maintain cohesiveness would be unable to elect its leader as prime minister or else would risk being voted out of office if dissident members teamed up with the opposition to defeat government legislation or to muster a vote of no confidence. Conversely, a disunited opposition party would also appear less credible to the voters and thus jeopardize its electoral possibilities.

Ideology and tradition also have determined the evolution of collectivist politics and party government. Indeed, they may be more important than the parliamentary system as a cause since not all such systems in other countries (for example, Fourth Republic France) exhibit a comparable degree of unity and party government. In both Britain and America, the idea of conservatism commonly denotes a certain reverence for tradition and a resistance to radical innovation. However the substance of these traditions is very different. American conservatism tends to hold as its ideal a laissez-faire model of eighteenth and nineteenth century capitalist individualism. Its chief elements are a distrust of government intervention, a stress on individual activity and self-reliance, a highly favorable attitude toward private business, and a view (originating with Adam Smith) that the society's best interests will be served if individuals follow their own economic self-interest.

By contrast, British conservatism flows from an earlier, organic, and even aristocratic tradition in which society is viewed as a whole and those in positions of power are expected to act with a sense of paternalism or *noblesse oblige* in the interests of the entire society. In occupational and class terms the Conservative Party, although it includes the principal industrial and business élites, has its roots in a preindustrial ruling group based on land ownership and the aristocracy. Its best traditions are exemplified by Prime Minister Benjamin Disraeli in the mid nineteenth century, who successfully promoted policies of conservative reform in the effort to win the loyalties of newly enfranchised working class voters, and by the words of a leading mid-twentieth-century Conservative politician, Quintin Hogg (later Lord Hailsham), "If you do not give the people social reform, they are going to give you social revolution." [6] Thus British conservatism has been more committed to a collective notion of general welfare and gradual change in order to preserve than to any idea of "rugged individualism." There have been strands of British conservative thought and leadership which lean in the latter direction, but these do not dominate. The Conservative tradition has also emphasized continuity, hierarchy, and leadership, all of which work against any stress on political individualism or independence on the part of the individual legislator.

Within the Labour Party the collectivist ethos also runs strongly. In this case the party's democratic socialism calls for a kind of solidaristic brotherhood that is very different from the liberal individualism of the American politician. It has been said that the origins of the Labour Party are more Methodist than Marxist. This background of religious fellowship is oriented toward a shared comradeship or a banding together to seek improvement in the condition of the average Briton. The strong trade union component of the party also inclines it toward a collectivist orientation in which party leadership, a common program, and party unity are accepted as necessary or desirable. Only the weak and divided Liberal Party, out of power for more than half a century, at all embodies any of the liberal individualism that would bolster a legislator in taking an independent stance.

Functional Representation   The result of this system of party government is that British citizens are able to exercise their own influence as consumers or voters by means of the electoral process, in which they choose between distinctly different parties, each with its program and potential prime minister. Yet another channel links society and government: *functional representation.* In its most technical sense, this notion "finds the community divided into various strata, regards each of these strata as having a corporate unity, and holds they ought to be represented in government." [7]

In practice, functional representation emerged as a response to the development of the managed economy. Over several generations, government became more and more deeply involved in managing and controlling the economy to maintain or promote the well being of its citizens and cope with demands for prosperity, full employment, the needs of outlying

[6] 386 *House of Commons Debates* 1818 (February 16, 1943), quoted in Beer, *British Politics in the Collectivist Age,* p. 307.
[7] Beer, *British Politics in the Collectivist Age,* p. 71.

regions, consumer protection, the environment, equality, and other needs. However, Britain remains a free and pluralistic society in which numerous independent groups—businesses, trade associations, unions, farmers, professionals, and others—seek to protect and promote the interests of their members. While it may be possible for an authoritarian or totalitarian government to ignore or repress such groups, a democratic government finds it necessary to bargain for the active cooperation of the major interest or pressure groups. Indeed, a prominent political scientist has argued that these groups provide a more important means of communication than political parties for the transmission of ideas from the mass public to their rulers.[8]

Powerful groups such as the Confederation of British Industries, the Trade Union Congress and the National Farmers' Union achieve great influence and continual policy consultation as a result of government's need for their technical advice and cooperation. In the American context, some of the same pressures and processes apply but the interest group role lacks a comparable legitimacy and sometimes leads to excesses of corruption, influence peddling, abuses of corporate power, and the like. In the British setting, however, the collectivist ethos of the dominant Labour and Conservative parties legitimizes this kind of representation and partly as a result it has not involved so many of the excesses found on the other side of the Atlantic. A classic quote of Sir Winston Churchill about the House of Commons shows the openness of this interest group involvement:

> *Everybody here has private interests,* some are directors of companies, some own property which may be affected by legislation which is passing and so forth. . . . We are not supposed to be an assembly of gentlemen who have no interests of any kind and no association of any kind. That is ridiculous. That might apply in Heaven, but not, happily, here. . . .[9]

BRITISH POLITICAL CULTURE

The acceptance of functional representation and party government, as well as the long continuity of Britain's political history marked by 300 years of largely nonviolent political evolution and the peaceful alternation in power of competing political élites since 1715, contrasts vividly with the violence and upheaval that have characterized much political change elsewhere. Consider, for example, Germany, which since 1918 has experienced several opposing regimes: a conservative monarchy (the

[8] Robert T. McKenzie, "Parties, Pressure Groups and the British Political Process," *Political Quarterly* 29 (January–March 1958): 10.
[9] Quoted in Finer, *Anonymous Empire,* pp. 46–47. Italics added.

Hohenzollern Empire), revolution leading to the establishment of the ill-fated Weimar Republic (1918–1933), Hitler's Third Reich (1933–1945), and division into the Federal Republic (West Germany) and the German Democratic Republic (East Germany). Or we can compare Britain with France, which since 1789 has had five republics, two empires, a monarchy, and the collaborationist regime of Vichy; or Italy (a republic, fascism, and another republic); or the United States, with its rough and tumble, open, mobile and occasionally violent public life. To understand better the basis on which Britain's combination of stability and change has been possible we must explore the nature of the British political culture.

Stability and Change   To begin with, the term "political culture" denotes those aspects of national character that are political in nature, such as the attitudes of people toward their system and their participation within it.[10] In the British case, Gabriel Almond and Sidney Verba argue that a unique political culture has developed from a series of encounters between modernization and tradition. These have brought significant change, but not so abruptly as to create disintegration or polarization. In part they and others find that this has occurred because Britain's security as an island permitted it to tolerate more autonomy by aristocrats, towns, and corporate groups. Britain's separation from the Church of Rome helped to lay the basis for a later religious toleration, and the early emergence of a prosperous and confident merchant class widened the politically relevant strata. These merchants, together with religious nonconformists (that is, Protestant sects, particularly Methodists, outside the established Anglican Church), and aristocrats with independent local power bases all helped to transform Britain from its feudal tradition into a parliamentary pattern and to maintain this pluralism during an age of absolutism elsewhere in Europe.

Britain thus underwent industrialization in the eighteenth and nineteenth centuries with an élite political culture able to adapt to rapid changes in society without suffering disruptive shocks. The aristocratic elements were divided among themselves, and aristocratic Whigs formed coalitions with nonconformist merchants and industrialists. This contributed in turn to the victory of representative government and parliamentary supremacy. Meanwhile, the more traditional aristocratic groups reacted not by seeking to crush their opponents but instead by contesting against them for public support. Almond and Verba identify

[10] Gabriel Almond and Sidney Verba, *The Civic Culture* (Boston: Little, Brown, 1965), pp. 11–12. Also see pp. 5–6, 35, and 315.

the result of this evolution as a pluralistic culture which combined both tradition and moderation, and in which opposing groups employed communication and persuasion to protect or promote their positions. Working class Britons later became enfranchised within a civic culture that offered them a means to enter politics effectively within the political system and without having to seek its destruction or overthrow in order to improve their situation in life.

The result of this evolution was a tradition of representative government (within which conservative forces as well as those seeking change could operate), political parties which aggregated or combined the demands of various groups, a bureaucracy both responsible and ostensibly neutral in its operation, pressure groups willing and able to pursue their interests by bargaining, and a free press. More broadly there emerged a culture that combined both an older traditional culture which stressed obligations and rights as well as deference toward authority and a newer culture of active citizen participation. Perhaps the chief difference from the American political culture is the British sense of deference to authority, manifested, for example, in the continuation of the monarchy and other trappings and titles of tradition and ceremony.

In contemporary public life, the existence of a monarchy based on heredity and tradition might appear to be an outrageous anachronism. After all, if doctors, airline pilots, or even presidents achieve their station in life not by inheriting their positions but by some combination of talent, education, and skill—as well as an element of family background and perhaps a bit of luck—why should a person become head of state irrespective of personal abilities or training. In other words, we have here a contrast between modern notions of status based on achievement versus a traditional and premodern practice of ascribed or inherited status. Nonetheless, the British monarchy, as well as those found in Scandinavia, may in some sense be functional—that is, useful—for the political culture and possibly related to its past stability.

The British monarch embodies the formal sovereignty of the British people, but its powers are almost entirely symbolic. The prime minister and cabinet act in the name of the Queen, who must give "royal assent" to legislation, yet they are responsible only to the House of Commons and the British people. Real power lies with the head of government, the prime minister, even while the Queen carries out many of the ritualistic ceremonies we associate with the idea of an American President. Since 1688, parliamentary supremacy has existed in Britain, and since 1693, the monarch has automatically signed whatever bills Parliament has passed. In theory, the monarch has the authority to dissolve the House of Commons (in order to call new elections). In practice, this is an empty power since it is only done on the advice of the prime minister. Similarly, the power to choose the prime minister is in fact only a ratification of the choice made by the parliamentary Labour and Conservative parties, although the lack of a formal Conservative voting procedure until 1963 allowed Queen Elizabeth—on the advice of leading Conservative politicians—to invite Harold Macmillan to become prime minister in 1957 rather than R.A.B. Butler, who might have won an actual vote among Tory MPs. The Queen also creates peers—that is, members of the House of Lords—but (since 1911) only on the advice of the prime minister.

In every parliamentary system there is a head of state separate from the head of government, though not all heads of state are monarchs. By contrast, the United States president functions both as head of state and of government. In other words, the president exercises the formal sovereignty, authority, and ceremony of the American political system as well as the policy and governmental powers. At times, this can present political problems. Thus a Lyndon Johnson in Vietnam, or a Richard Nixon in Cambodia or in the abuses of Watergate, may present himself as the embodiment of the American political system, claiming that his policies are necessitated by reason of "national security" and implying that those who oppose these policies or the man himself border on treason against the state. Opponents of these presidential actions are thus at pains to defend themselves against accusations that their own views are not anti-American but instead are in opposition only to the policies of a specific government.

By contrast, the existence of a separate person, the monarch, as head of the British state helps to retain public loyalties despite shifts between various governments. A distinction formally exists between state and government, so that an individual, a group, or party may bitterly oppose the policies, whether radical or reactionary, of a particular government—and even villify a prime minister—and yet not be considered as "anti-British," nor be totally alienated from the British state. In sum, the monarchy is an important symbolic part of British political culture. While it is costly to maintain, and may disproportionately benefit the Conservatives because of the way it symbolizes tradition and deference to authority, it may also benefit Labour governments by enabling them to consider occasionally radical measures of change knowing that these are less likely to provoke opposition efforts to overthrow the political system than might be the case in another society.

AMATEURISM AND INSULARITY

All the same, this discussion of political culture, whether it reflects the highly favorable picture of stability and peaceful change painted by Almond and Verba, or focuses upon the blend of tradition and modernity reflected in the relation of monarch to government, should not cause us to accept a bland and uncritical view. In fact, some important faults in the British political culture have gone hand in hand with its virtues. One of these faults corresponds to the legacy of tradition and deference that is so often praised as quaint and supportive of stability. The problem is that of snobbism and a lingering aristocratic hangover of respect for style and prestige more than expertise, ability, or efficiency. This problem has become less acute with the spread of higher education, but it is nicely illustrated in the following account by the political journalist, Claude Cockburn, recounting an experience of his well-bred father just after World War I:

> A friend told him there was a good job going as chief of some inter-allied financial mission to look after the finances of Hungary. Perhaps he would like that? My father asked whether the circumstances of knowing almost nothing about Hungary and absolutely nothing about finance would be a disadvantage. His friend said that was not the point. The point was that they had a man doing this job who knew all about Hungary and a lot about finance, but he had been seen picking his teeth with a tram-ticket in the lounge of the Hungaria Hotel and was regarded as socially impossible. My father said that if such were the situation he would be prepared to take over the job.[11]

In the postwar period, the expression of comparable attitudes is evident in a preference for amateurism at the higher levels of civil service, government, and business. It is reflected in the jibe at a would-be Conservative Party leader, R.A.B. Butler, that he was "too clever by half." Only in the 1960's did this cult of amateurism finally come under sustained attack.

Next, although it is certainly true that British public life has historically preserved remarkable civility and lack of violence, there have been exceptions. To be sure, police and criminals tend not to carry guns and the murder rate in London is about one-fifteenth that of New York.[12] Yet there were occasions of real violence during the period of early industrialization; for example, 700 people were killed during the London riots of 1780, and between 25 and 40 civilians were shot and killed by British troops during an 1831 protest at the Welsh mining town of Merthyr Tudful.[13] In addition, Ireland has long been a kind of running sore on the British body politic. In the 1840's the British government failed to prevent the deaths

[11] *I. Claude . . . The Autobiography of Claude Cockburn* (Harmondsworth, Middlesex: Penguin, 1967), pp. 37–38.
[12] In a typical year, London had 113 murders, New York 1,691; *New York Times,* October 6, 1973.
[13] See *New Statesman,* London, (February 11, 1972), p. 176.

of approximately 1 million Irish people during the potato famine, and Ireland has been the scene of sporadic violence, sometimes spilling over into Britain, since the early twentieth century.

Although not a matter of violence, it is also true that the broadly peaceful evolution of British politics took place against a background of genuine suffering and deprivation. For example, prior to 1914, village people in Suffolk were virtually worked to death.[14] And as late as 1935, at least 10 percent of the population was malnourished to the point of retarded growth and 40 percent consumed a diet "demonstrably" too low in certain vitamins.[15] To be fair, these examples must be seen in a comparative light; there was nothing remotely comparable with American experiences of slavery and civil war, nor with the French revolution and Paris Commune, the Russian Civil War and the Stalinist agricultural collectivization and purges which murdered perhaps 10 million people, or the revolting and sadistic practices of Nazi terror and extermination.

Yet another intrinsic but often overlooked part of British political culture is its insularity and distrust of foreigners. Perhaps the British are no worse than others in this respect—and indeed far better than most—but their geographic location at the edge of Europe has left them reluctant to acknowledge the fact of being Europeans. Popular stereotypes and a residue of public sentiment continue to regard continental Europeans as "unclean, untrustworthy and over-sexed." Indeed, a British Labour Party MP could recently describe the West German social democratic Chancellor, Helmut Schmidt, as a "patronizing Hun."[16] Other even less salutary terms—one of the most common being "wog," (from "worthy oriental gentlemen")—are commonly used to denigrate non-Europeans and even non-Anglo Saxons. The common adage, "The wogs begin at Calais" (the French English Channel port), in a sense reflects this lingering but real sentiment.

Finally, it is crucial to understand that British political culture has coexisted, particularly in the twentieth century, with a continual record of political and economic disarray. In the years immediately prior to World War I, Britain experienced severe labor strife, an obdurate and conceivably anticonstitutional obstruction of legislation by the House of Lords, turmoil over the question of women's suffrage, and very nearly civil war over the question of quasi-independence (Home Rule) for Ireland. The war itself was marked by arrogant and often incompetent

[14] Ronald Blythe, *Akenfield: Portrait of an English Village* (New York: Pantheon, 1969), p. 38.
[15] Jean Mayer, "Coping With Famine," *Foreign Affairs* 53, no. 1 (October 1974): 100.
[16] John Ryman, MP, quoted in the *New York Times,* December 2, 1974.

military leadership and the appalling slaughter of nearly a million of Britain's best young men. This deprived the British of a generation of talent. After the war came the momentous General Strike of 1926, which posed a challenge to Britain's unwritten Constitution (though the strike was mostly peaceful, and in one celebrated incident policemen and strikers played "football"—actually soccer—together). In 1931 the country underwent a grave economic and financial crisis, which destroyed the Labour government. A year later the country suffered 22 percent unemployment. Throughout the 1920's and 1930's, the British experienced real economic and political mismanagement, culminating in the appeasement of Hitler, the celebrated and disastrous Munich Agreement of October 1938, which handed over Czechoslovakia to the Nazis in exchange for "peace in our time," the outbreak of World War II and the desperate escape of a surrounded British army from the port of Dunkirk on the Belgian coast in 1940. Victory in the war proved costly and was followed by economic crisis in the late 1940's, "stop-and-go" economics in the 1950's and 1960's, and frequent problems over the value of the pound sterling. In the late sixties, there was a resurgence of serious violence in Northern Ireland, followed in the early seventies by conflict between government and the trade unions, and an unprecedented rate of inflation.

Thus while it is no exaggeration to speak of historical continuity and a successful evolution marked by a melding of tradition and change, we need to be aware that this has not been an entirely smooth process; more often than not the British have only muddled through. In sum, we can best appreciate generalizations about British politics if we also consider the color, the turmoil, and the rough and tumble of real political and economic life.

policy agenda: problems, cleavages, and conflicts

The historic evolution of British society toward a managed economy and a welfare state, and of British politics toward the collectivist pattern of party government and functional representation, has by no means brought an end to the problems, cleavages, and conflicts that exist and that shape the policy agenda within Britain.

PROBLEMS

The agenda of policy problems in Britain has become more, rather than less, acute during the sixties and seventies. Problems with an economic component have been particularly central. In comparison with the United States, Britain has narrower room for economic maneuver: it possesses less in terms of domestic wealth and resources and it is far more dependent on the international economy. As a result, economic problems are often more important and "political" in Britain.

By the 1970's, Britain (as well as Italy) had become the economic "sickman" of Western Europe, a title which, as recently as the 1950's, had belonged to France. Economic problems are not new to the UK. Britain actually began to suffer the effects of the great interwar depression well before the United States did. As early as 1921, the country experienced an unemployment rate of 12.9 percent; for twenty years the figure only once dipped below 10 percent (9.7 percent in 1927), and it went as high as 22.1 percent in 1932.[17] Like the United States, Britain only recovered full employment during World War II. However, once postwar economic recovery had been largely completed, the British economy began to lag in the mid 1950's, experiencing a series of interruptions of economic growth. These foreshadowed the more severe problems of the sixties and seventies.

The past and present causes of these problems remain a matter of real dispute, but we can distinguish several factors which have played a significant part, even though there is little agreement on their relative weight. They include Britain's dependence on trade, the problem of poor governmental policy decisions, pluralistic stagnation among groups and parties, and the attitudes of both workers and management.

The Problem of Britain's Dependence on Trade   The first and in many ways the most crucial problem is that of Britain's historic dependence on trade. To earn the money to pay for the importing of half its food and most of its raw materials, Britain must export large amounts of goods (mostly manufactured products such as cars, aircraft, weapons, machine tools, chemicals) and services. Since the early nineteenth century, Britain has run a deficit in its *balance of trade* (that is, it has bought more abroad, in the form of imports, than it could sell in the form of exports). For the most part, however, it had been able to make up the difference through "invisible" exports, particularly in earnings from shipping, insurance, banking, and foreign investment, and in the willingness of foreign individuals, companies, and governments to deposit or to invest huge sums of money in Britain. Indeed, many countries of the Commonwealth tied the value of their national currencies closely to the pound sterling, using the British currency in their own foreign trading and as their hard currency reserve. These additional elements allowed Britain to maintain an

[17] London and Cambridge Economic Service, *The British Economy Key Statistics 1900–1970* (London: Times Newspapers Ltd., n.d.), p. 8.

adequate *balance of payments* (the difference between all inflows and outflows of money, of which trade is only a part).

The British thus maintained a viable economy, but one which remained profoundly dependent on foreign trade and payments, and which was also deeply penetrated and susceptible to factors beyond their domestic control. Not only was Britain thus involved in interdependence with other governments whose actions it could not fully determine, but it would become increasingly vulnerable to the actions of transnational actors, such as huge multinational corporations and bodies such as OPEC, whose decisions could affect its own economy.

As late as 1949, Britain remained one of the world's wealthiest countries; only the U.S., Canada, New Zealand, Switzerland, and Sweden enjoyed higher per capita income. But, during World War II (1939–1945) Britain had lost or sold off much of its overseas investments. With income from these sources significantly reduced, the British now depended increasingly on manufactured exports to earn the money necessary to pay for their essential imports. To the tune of such slogans as "Britain must export or die," successive British governments periodically encouraged the export industries and sought to restrain domestic consumption of consumer goods such as cars and appliances.

The crucial problem was that, throughout the fifties and sixties, whenever the economy began to enjoy a period of real growth and prosperity, the effect was to increase the demand for imports (whether of consumer goods such as foreign cars, or capital equipment such as machine tools which British factories needed and which were temporarily unavailable at home because of chronic bottlenecks in production). The surge in imports in turn threw the balance of payments into deficit, and governments responded by slamming on the economic brakes (through deflation, higher taxes and increased interest rates) in order to restrain the economy, decrease the demand for imports, and encourage British manufacturers to sell their products abroad. As the balance of payments situation slowly began to improve, the government would relax its constraints on the domestic economy, encourage a resumption of growth—and then run headlong into the same problems as before.

This stop-go cycle of alternating restriction and relaxation became a recurrent feature of British life, but the "stop" phases of the cycle became increasingly severe. Not only had Britain become more dependent on manufactured exports, because of its wartime loss of considerable overseas investment income, but it also began to increase its purchases of foreign manufactured goods (rather than just food and raw materials). In addition, the costs of its foreign policy had to be borne by its export earnings. Substantial expenditures abroad, for foreign aid, and for the maintenance of British military bases in Africa, Asia, and the Middle East created a further strain on the overall balance of payments. In addition, stop-go provided a very crude means of dealing with the balance of payments problem. It had the effect of discouraging productive investment and modernization of factories within Britain, so that even during periods of economic expansion, British workers, utilizing aging machinery, were less productive than their European or American counterparts and British goods were not always competitive in foreign markets. As we shall see later, lagging productivity was also due to labor and management attitudes. At older and less efficient steel plants, it required the work of twice as many men to produce a given amount of steel as were needed at the most modern plants in Japan. Not only did all these factors worsen the stop-go problem, but the delicacy of Britain's economic situation left it vulnerable to shifts in the world economy. Thus, during each of the United States' three recessions in the mid to late 1950's, demand for British exports was reduced and the British balance of payments suffered.

Despite these problems, the British economy managed a growth rate (about 2.5 percent per year) roughly comparable to that of the United States during the 1950's, though significantly lower than that of most Western European economies (4 to 7 percent). The problem became more acute, however, with the election of a Labour government in October 1964, after 13 years of Conservative rule. The outgoing Tory government had stimulated the economy prior to the 1964 election in a not quite successful effort to secure reelection on the basis of renewed prosperity. The incoming government was left with a huge balance of payments deficit and, in particular, with a "run" on the pound sterling. Since 1949 when a Labour government had been forced to devalue the pound from its previous value of $4.00, the price of sterling had been fixed at $2.80 (meaning that one British pound could be bought or sold for about $2.80 in American currency). By October 1964, the payments deficit had threatened this exchange rate as foreigners (and some British) sought to sell sterling for dollars (or other foreign currencies) expecting that the deficit would cause the value of sterling to fall. The government of Harold Wilson responded to the crisis with orthodox economic measures to constrain the economy and support the value of the pound.

This was only a prelude to a much more severe crisis. In March 1966 the Labour government was reelected with a large majority in the House of Commons. The Labour Party and Prime Minister Wilson had campaigned, in 1964 and 1966, on a program (faintly reminiscent of the 1960 John F. Kennedy campaign) to get Britain moving again. Wilson, particularly in the 1964 election, had pledged to unleash the "white heat of technology," and Labour had offered a model of economic planning, modernization, and increased social benefits (schools, housing, pensions, for example) to be paid for out of the revenues from increased economic growth.

All these hopes came to grief in July 1966. Faced with the worst crisis in nearly 20 years in the British balance of payments and the threat to the value of sterling, Wilson and several of his leading cabinet colleagues overcame the objections of the rest of the cabinet and the Labour Party and proceeded to impose drastic economic measures to deal with the crisis. These included both a "squeeze" and a "freeze"—specifically a classic deflation (a "stop") of the economy to reduce purchasing power, discourage imports and encourage exports, and a temporary freeze on wage increases. The effect of these measures was to destroy the program on which Labour had come to office as well as any hope for sustained economic growth and the elimination of the stop-go cycle.

The economic crisis proved to be Harold Wilson's "Vietnam." It bitterly divided the Labour Party and the trade union movement, damaged the country economically and politically, and cost Labour the next general election in 1970. Why did all this happen? In essence, Labour governments felt as sensitive to charges of being economically irresponsible as U.S. Democratic administrations have feared to appear being "soft-on-Communism." Major economic crises in 1931 and 1947–1948 had occurred while the two previous Labour governments of Ramsay Macdonald and Clement Attlee held office, and Wilson was determined to prove that Labour would not again be responsible for the sin of devaluation.

Despite proud and pious national television addresses by Prime Minister Wilson and his chancellor of the exchequer, James Callaghan, replete with invocations of the "Dunkirk" spirit and assurances that Britain was "paying her way in the world" and that the pound was "looking the dollar in the eye," the policy failed. In the autumn of 1967 the Labour government was forced to devalue the pound down to $2.40. Thus, three years of economic sacrifice had come to nothing, and the remainder of Labour's term in office proved difficult and almost anticlimactic.

The Problem of Poor Policy Decisions   The origins of Britain's economic (and ultimately many of its political) problems lie in its dependence on external trade. But the policies which successive governments followed do not automatically flow from this. Decisions made between 1958 and 1966 to support sterling at the cost of economic growth and a policy of stop-go seemed at the time to be virtually unavoidable, but alternatives did exist.

One alternative would have been to impose physical controls on imports and to introduce economic planning at home. Controls might have restrained the inflow of consumer goods and the outflow of sterling and allowed Britain to seek economic growth without seeing the value of sterling threatened. Economic planning at home would have permitted the channeling of scarce investment into the areas of greatest need and potential productivity. However, Britain had remained ideologically committed to a policy of free trade for more than a century; its international commitments, particularly in the General Agreement on Tariff and Trade (GATT), made it extremely difficult or even impossible for it to impose external controls. In addition, the Conservative obsession with ending the wartime and immediate postwar controls on the outflow of sterling (in investments, tourism, and the like) led a Tory government in 1958 to make sterling freely convertible. This threw away a major tool of policy and locked Britain into a situation where it would in the future face the unpalatable choices of devaluation or deflation. Direct domestic economic controls had proved difficult and unwieldy for the postwar Labour government and by the late 1940's, Labour had increasingly deemphasized their use. These controls were also anathema to the Conservative government (1951–1964), and so the much cruder and destructive tool of slamming on the economic brakes (that is, deflation and restriction of economic growth) was used to achieve the more delicate and limited objective of restraining imports. Even when a Labour government came to power in 1964, there was little readiness to adopt external controls or internal planning. The new government was caught largely unprepared to deal with a sudden foreign exchange crisis, and the permanent Civil Service officials at the Treasury were ready with orthodox measures to deal with the problem.

Another alternative would have been to reduce sharply the expenditures overseas for foreign and military policy. The substantial costs of foreign aid and the basing overseas of British troops placed a real drain on the balance of payments. But this alternative was also more or less unavailable. As we have seen, postwar British governments were very slow to come to grips with the question of Britain's world role. They persisted in viewing the UK as a major world power, whose seat at the "top table" was in part paid for by its nuclear weapons, foreign military commitments, and ambitious foreign policy. As late as 1966, Prime Minister Wilson could announce that "Britain's frontier is on the Himalayas." Until the late 1960's, the alternative of reducing these foreign expenditures was thus largely unavailable as a tool in dealing with Britain's economic problem.

If neither controls nor major reductions in foreign military expenditure could be employed, then one other major option remained: by allowing the value of the pound to fall, say by 15 percent, British exports would be made cheaper to foreign buyers. For example, a car costing £1,000 would have sold for $2,800 in the United States (based on £ = $2.80). But if the pound were devalued to $2.40, the same car would now sell for $2,400 and would be likely to find more buyers. Conversely, imports to Britain from the outside world would become more expensive and therefore—at least in theory—Britons would be less likely to buy foreign goods. In principle [18] devaluation would thus aid the balance of trade and payments and allow continued economic growth in Britain. As we have seen, however, the policy of devaluation was largely foreclosed. Indeed, discussion of it was regarded as almost illegitimate. In part, the unwillingness to devalue followed from the notion that to do so would be virtually immoral, and that the international economy (upon which Britain depended) relied on fixed exchange rates for its stability. Of course, the de Gaulle government had devalued the French franc by more than 20 percent in 1958 as part of a successful strategy of economic recovery, but Treasury officials and politicians were unwilling to emulate the French. In addition, maintaining a high exchange rate seemed a kind of international status symbol and devaluation could be regarded as a confession of failure.

To be fair, there were obligations and restraints which made it difficult for the British to devalue. As much as one-third of the world's trade was conducted in sterling, the pound was widely held abroad, and many Commonwealth governments maintained sizable sterling deposits in London. A 15 percent devaluation (such as that carried out in 1967, when the pound fell in value from $2.80 to $2.40) would mean that, overnight, foreign holders of sterling would see their money lose 15 percent of its international purchasing power. Not only would this stir resentment, but it might threaten sterling's role as a world reserve currency and London's place as a world banking center.

All these factors, as well as Labour's fears about seeming to appear soft on sterling, meant that devaluation could not be used as a tool of policy either. Indeed, it could scarcely be discussed (even in the cabinet!) for fear that word of such discussion would leak out and precipitate a run on sterling and the very devaluation that most policy-makers wished to avoid. Thus, throughout the fifties and sixties, successive governments found themselves locked into an unpalatable choice between devaluation and deflation. Since devaluation was forbidden, there was little choice but to deflate, thereby sacrificing future economic growth and prosperity for a short-run and precarious stability. Again, the parallels with the American experience in Vietnam are striking: a policy that few really welcomed but that policy-makers seemed helpless to avoid; alternatives that seemed

[18] This discussion simplifies the issue by disregarding the increased costs of imported food and raw materials, which are ultimately reflected in export prices.

unpalatable; an unwillingness or inability to comprehend that the policy would ultimately fail and that a decade or more of effort would be wasted.

In the end, devaluation occurred anyway. And by the 1970's, Britain allowed a "floating" exchange rate, whereby the value of sterling fluctuated (in a range between $2.60 and $2.00). Devaluation did not prove to be a panacea for Britain's economic and financial woes, in part because so much damage had already been done by more than a decade of stop-go. The reduction of foreign military expenditures also became a means of policy, but, ironically, withdrawal of troops from the Persian Gulf and other areas of the Middle East where Britain had maintained a military presence among former dependencies and Arab sheikdoms created new problems. Many of these areas are major petroleum producers and the departure of British influence left them more likely to become involved in the efforts of the oil producers' cartel, OPEC, to raise the price of oil by some 500 percent during the winter of 1973–1974—a cost which Britain would have to pay until such time as it could itself become self-sufficient in oil.

The Problem of Pluralistic Stagnation   Britain's economic troubles can be attributed in part to what Samuel Beer has called "pluralistic stagnation." [19] Thus, the low rate of new investment in manufacturing and the serious problem of inflation may result from the type of group politics found in Britain and the stagnation that it may entail. On the one hand, the closely matched competition between the Labour and Conservative parties, each relatively disciplined and programmatic, as well as the nature of party government, has caused these parties to bid for the votes of consumer groups at or in anticipation of each general election. Thus, the government of the day, as well as its opposition, tends to favor consumption expenditures, both private (for example, consumer goods, cars, appliances, private housing) and public (schools, transportation, welfare, public housing). Given the limited level of economic growth from which to pay for these things, such expenditures tend to take place at the expense of productive investment (which has a longer term payoff).

[19] Beer, *British Politics in the Collectivist Age,* p. 408. Also see Gerald Dorfman, *Wage Politics in Britain 1945–1967: Government versus TUC* (Ames, Iowa: University of Iowa Press, 1973); Andrew Shonfield, *Modern Capitalism: The Changing Balance of Public and Private Power* (London and New York: Oxford University Press, 1966); Jack Hayward, "National Aptitudes for Planning in Britain, France and Italy," *Government and Opposition,* Vol. 9, No. 4 (Autumn 1974), and Stephen Blank, "The Politics of Economic Policy in Britain: The Problem of 'Pluralistic Stagnation'," paper delivered at the 1975 Annual Meeting of the British Politics Group, San Francisco, September 1975. Also see the discussion of collectivist politics in Robert J. Lieber, *British Politics and European Unity: Parties, Elites and Pressure Groups* (Berkeley: University of California Press, 1970), pp. 4–10.

On the other hand, the nature of functional representation, in which organized and concentrated groups among labor and business pursue their self-interest and are accorded a virtual veto power over policies affecting them, contributes to inflation. Because of their strength and willingness to strike, trade unions are able to obtain substantial wage increases, almost regardless of the level of unemployment and the health of the economy. Trade unions have also been reluctant—and at times unable or unwilling—to accept governmental "incomes policy" (that is, the freezing of wages or the specific limitation of wage increases). For their part, business groups and firms have also exercised a near veto on government policies and have, typically, been free in raising the prices of their products at home and abroad, whether as a means of passing on rising wage and raw material costs or of maintaining their desired profit margins.

Although there may be some merit in the assumption that parties have failed to encourage sufficient investment because of their competitive bidding for votes, the widely heard criticisms that mainly blame veto groups, particularly the trade unions, may be seriously overstated. Far more serious as a cause of Britain's economic troubles are the policies followed by successive governments [20] (and already discussed above). What is more, Britain's deep dependence on the international economy has made it especially vulnerable to inflation resulting from increased world prices for food, raw materials, and oil. There is, however, yet another significant cause; it lies in the *attitudes* of both trade unionists and management.

The Problem of Attitudes   In recent years Britain has sometimes been described as being at the mercy of rapacious and disruptive trade unionists. Strikes have periodically disrupted production lines of important export industries and a number of spectacular interruptions of public services have caused the paralysis of public transportation and garbage collection as well as electrical blackouts and the closing of coal mines. Unions have pushed for and obtained high wage demands, which in turn contributed to high rates of inflation, and worker productivity has often been inefficient.

As we have seen, however, Britain's economic problems have other and perhaps more important causes, and even the record of trade union activity is more complex than might appear at first glance. Apart from a modest number of revolutionary activists, Communists, Maoists or Trotskyists, most British workers do not seek to destroy or overturn the existing eco-

[20] The latter point is made effectively by Blank, "The Politics of Economic Policy in Britain," p. 2.

nomic and political system. Many trade union leaders are willing and able to cooperate with government policy-makers and business leaders in efforts to promote the health of the British economy and to benefit the general public as well as their own members. Nonetheless, resentful and uncooperative attitudes and actions often exist. These may be traced—particularly among older workers—to very bitter memories of historic class cleavages and to the experience of the great depression of the 1920's and 1930's. In the interwar period, workers and trade unionists suffered the effects of severe unemployment, sadly inadequate and even reduced welfare and unemployment benefits, and unsympathetic treatment by government and business—both of which were unable to cope effectively with the economic depression or to alleviate its harmful human effects.

Throughout the postwar period, these memories of depression have proved enduring and important. In particular, trade unions have often bitterly resisted industrial modernization and efficiencies which would, in the short run, eliminate the jobs of any of their members. Despite the arguments that modernization would promote greater industrial productivity and thus greater international competitiveness, and that displaced workers would eventually find jobs in newer and more modern sectors of the economy where their labor was needed, British workers have reacted against any measures that would increase unemployment. By contrast, German trade unionists have retained far greater fears of inflation—the disastrous effects of which had helped to pave the way for Hitler's rise to power.

Negative working class attitudes may feed upon resentment at inept government economic policies, which have made them skeptical about repeated calls for belt tightening or sacrifices in the common interest. They also result from a chaotic, decentralized trade union structure in which, for example, as many as a dozen separate unions may be represented at an automobile plant and industry-wide agreements prove difficult to negotiate and to enforce. Finally, labor attitudes are a function of enduring class cleavages and resentments.

The attitudes of businessmen also constitute an important part of the British economic problem. In part, these attitudes reflect a legacy of certain premodern values. Thus, the personal ambition of more than a few industrialists and business leaders is to earn enough money to lead the relaxed life of a country gentleman, replete with a splendid country house, collections of fine art or of race horses, and the pursuit of aristocratic pleasures with perhaps a title thrown in. From a personal standpoint, the attraction of a relaxed and dignified life style—whether on this or a much more modest level—is readily understandable. However, it represents the legacy of values from a preindustrial age; in practice it often embodies a set of attitudes toward business which include a slowness to innovate or to modernize, a distrust or deprecation of technological expertise, and a cult of amateurishness. On occasion, it can also mean arrogance and snobbishness, which discourage modernization and efficiency and which provoke worker resentment. To be sure, some British enterprises and managers are highly efficient, innovative, and successful in their operations, but the legacy of older attitudes is prevalent enough to make a difference. Together with some of the negative trade union attitudes, it constitutes a problem for Britain's economy and polity.

The Problem of Dividing the Economic Pie   The attitudes of workers and businessmen reflect a sharp division over the classic political question of who gets what. At a time when economic growth has become slow or even stagnant, one sector of the population may increase its own income or wealth largely at the expense of other sectors, and such a situation is likely to heighten political conflict. The problem exists when we consider competing priorities of public (that is, government) versus private spending. It also concerns whether government spending will be channeled into social welfare and other immediate public needs or into longer term investment (transportation facilities, modernization of nationalized industries, scientific research, and the like). In addition, there are problems involving the distribution of income and wealth.

From the perspective of the political left, it is often argued that justice demands an effort to increase the incomes of poorer and working class people, whether or not at the expense of middle class or wealthier Britons, some of whom have achieved their advantages through the accident of birth. This redistribution may be achieved through wage increases that exceed productivity gains and by policies of progressive taxation that require higher income individuals to pay a larger percentage of their income to support public services for the benefit of all. The counter argument of the political right is that excessive taxation will reduce the incentive for people to work harder and to produce and earn more, thus depriving the society of the full efforts of its best citizens and even causing some (for instance, doctors) to emigrate to countries such as the United States where they are very highly paid.

These positions reflect differences of political values as well as disagreement over the meaning of equality (for example, equality of opportunity versus equality of condition). Nonetheless, the resolution of these differences presents a policy problem of how best to balance competing social needs and political demands.

Social Class   The most fundamental and important cleavage in Britain is that of social class. Though less dramatic than it once was, the difference between working class, middle class, and upper class Britons remains both visible and politically important. The variations of class accent and life style are much more striking than those in the United States. They also reflect traditions based on family background as well as on occupational status. In broad terms, we may say that nearly two-thirds of the British population is working class, one-third middle class, and about 1 percent upper class. These categories are not merely sociological labels but reflect the way people see themselves. (See Table 2-1.)

Whereas most Americans, even many with substantial wealth or of blue collar occupation, tend to regard themselves as middle class, most Britons are more self-conscious about their and others' class origins and status. While much of this rests on occupation, the basis goes deeper than that. It is reflected in such symbolic choices as whether a person enters the "saloon bar" or "public bar" sections of a local tavern or "pub." To enter the saloon bar leads one into a largely middle class environment, with carpeted floors and comfortable seats. To enter the public bar one often finds a wood floor, sparse furnishings, and slightly lower prices for alcoholic beverages served from the opposite side of the same bar to a largely working class clientele.

Class differences have tended to be perpetuated by the British educational system. Though it has always been possible for very bright and hard working children of working class families to become upwardly mobile socially and economically, and although the system of higher education expanded substantially in the fifties and sixties, diverse educational patterns still persist. Children of manual workers gravitate toward nonacademic secondary schools, either as a result of examinations or by choice, and they usually leave school at age 15 or 16. Middle class children are more likely to pursue an academic curriculum in the state-supported schools and then go on to a university education. Upper middle class and upper class youth often enroll in élite private schools, called (paradoxically) "public schools," the best known of which are Eton and Harrow.

TABLE 2–1   Class Self-Images in Britain

Upper Class	Upper Middle	Middle Class	Lower Middle	Upper Working	Working Class	Lower Working	Total
1%	3%	25%	4%	10%	53%	4%	100%

Source: David Butler and Donald Stokes, *Political Change in Britain* (New York: St. Martin's Press, College Edition, 1971), p. 49. Reprinted with permission.

Boys at the elite "public school," Eton.
Black Star

From there they tend to move on to Oxford and Cambridge universities and into positions of leadership in British business, government, and society. At each level, students mainly associate with others of their background and acquire the values, friendships, expectations, life style, and—most noticeably—the accents characteristic of their class.

With the general rise in prosperity after World War II, the establishment of the welfare state, expansion of educational opportunities, the spread of television, the growth of middle class occupations, the political predominance of the Labour Party, and even the effects of inflation, the most extreme vestiges of class differences have undoubtedly lessened. Yet class remains a significant factor. For example, one recent study of British universities found that only 2 percent of the children of unskilled and semiskilled manual workers obtained full-time higher education, whereas 45 percent of the offspring of higher professional workers did so. Overall, about one-fourth of university students had fathers who were manual workers (skilled, semi- and unskilled), yet this was virtually the same percentage as that prevailing during the two decades from 1928 to 1947.[21]

Working class children in Liverpool.
Black Star

[21] Robbins Committee Report, cited by T. Burgess, *New Statesman* (London), January 29, 1971, p. 138.

Class divisions are not exclusively a matter of income or wealth. Skilled manual workers, particularly those represented by strong trade unions, may earn more than some persons with middle class, white collar occupations, yet their life style, attitudes, and identifications will still set them apart. Similarly, a businessman or professional who becomes quite rich does not automatically become upper class even though his income may exceed that of some members of that privileged group. Membership of this élite is as much a matter of birth and even of inherited titles, and it is typically the children of the newly rich who gain access because of their parent's ability to purchase an élite "public school" education and sometimes through intermarriage, which brings an alliance of status on the one hand and wealth on the other.

Many of the most glaring disparities in earned income have lessened, yet differences in accumulated wealth remain enormous. Historically, inequalities of wealth and class divisions have been highly relevant to British political life and they underpin many of the principal differences among the political parties. In turn, the parties reflect a certain institutionalization of these cleavages. As Figure 2–1 illustrates, a definite pattern of voter alignment based on social class persists. For an understanding of this, we must now consider the political parties themselves.

Political Parties: The Conservatives   The British Conservative Party is a resilient and highly adaptable organization whose composition and policies make it far from identical with the Republican Party in the United States or American ideas of conservatism. Its adaptability, as well as the difference between British and American political spectrums, is reflected in a line from a British satirical review in which an Englishman seeks to explain U.S. politics by observing that the U.S. Republican Party resembles the Conservative Party and the U.S. Democratic Party resembles the Conservative Party. In any case, the parallels are not easy to draw. On some issues, for example, nationalization of industry and the National Health Service (socialized medicine), the Conservatives lie to the left of the Democrats; on others, education and monarchy for example, the Tories are to the right of the Republicans. While there do exist definable elements of conservative ideology, they are often less strong than the twin themes of preserving the best of tradition and of following the policies of the party leader.

Historically, Conservatives see more good than bad in things of the past; indeed, the party's roots lie in a predemocratic and aristocratic age in which its leadership was drawn mainly from the ranks of old privileged families. During the mid-nineteenth century, particularly from 1832 to the 1860's, the party was committed to preserving and protecting the mon-

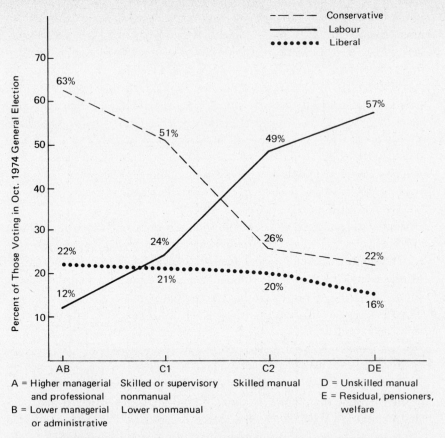

FIGURE 2–1 Voting on the Basis of Social Class in Britain

Source: Based on opinion poll figures in "Harris and O.R.C. Election Surveys," October 1974. London: Louis Harris International, p. 9.

archy, the Church of England, landed interests, and the privileges of the upper classes. By contrast, the other major party of that day, the Liberals, were more overtly the party of the rising business elements of society. In time, however, the Tories became increasingly attractive to the newly rich, especially as these acquired land of their own. During the latter part of the nineteenth century, the Conservatives began to accommodate both traditional landed and newer business interests, especially as the Liberals increasingly advocated social welfare legislation.

As the British electorate expanded, these Conservative interests would not have sufficed to keep the party within reach of political power. But in the 1860's, under the leadership of Benjamin Disraeli, the Conservatives successfully broadened their base by appealing to the new urban working class vote. Disraeli is said to have discerned the potential of "the Conservative working man as the sculptor perceives the angel imprisoned in a block of marble," [22] and he made use of his party's sense of *noblesse oblige* and Tory paternalism. These feelings stemmed from ideas about an earlier preindustrial age in which society was seen as an organic entity and different classes were to cooperate rather than compete, each having its special role to play in the interests of the whole. This conception predated the more laissez-faire, business-oriented philosophy of the Liberal Party. It also capitalized on deferential attitudes among workers who could be expected to look to their "betters" to govern. In essence, Disraeli employed a theme, which the Conservatives would use throughout the next century, that his was not a party based on a narrow class interest but one which would govern in the interests of the entire nation.

In practice, Disraeli gained working class votes by presenting a more generous mass suffrage bill than the Liberals had offered and by pressing an imperialist policy whose attraction cut across class lines. Working and middle class voters could take vicarious satisfaction in the extension of British nationalism overseas. Indeed, Empire became as emotionally important a word for the Tories as Socialism would be for Labour. The Liberals, who favored free trade, were less favorable to imperialism and the Conservatives reaped much of the electoral advantage from it. Throughout the mid to late nineteenth century, the Conservatives won sufficient votes to alternate in power with the Liberals. Despite their traditionalist and upper class foundations, they thus entered the twentieth century on a highly competitive footing.

Conservative ideology. The notion of Conservative ideology is almost a contradiction in terms since tradition, leadership, and flexibility are in practice more important. By contrast to parties of the left, ideological questions are hardly paramount among Conservatives. The party prides itself on pragmatism, a preference for whatever works. The eighteenth century philosopher and politician Edmund Burke (though actually a Whig in his day) embodies important themes of conservatism. In essence, man is seen as limited in his capacity for improvement; radical institutional innovation is distrusted because it may do more harm than good; change best occurs when it is very slow, natural, and organic; existing authority, whether in government or other social institutions, should be respected; governments should be strong and centralized as the embodiment of the society.

Conservative practice. In practice, Conservatives of the twentieth century inherited a party and an outlook that was flexible and responsive to at least some change. The paternalist tradition made the party willing to

[22] This widely quoted appraisal first appeared in *The Times* (London), April 18, 1883.

accept the idea of a welfare state in which the poor and deprived could receive state aid to alleviate their condition. Although the party has sometimes, as in the twenties and thirties, leaned more heavily toward a business-oriented laissez-faire conservatism not unlike that of U.S. Republicanism, the Conservatives have more often taken a wider perspective. Thus, their disagreements first with Liberals then with Labour on the welfare state have centered more on methods of administration than on the concept itself. In 1908, they opposed the national insurance scheme of Liberal Prime Minister Lloyd George because of its method of financing rather than because of the basic idea. Conservative governments of the 1920's and 1930's actually presided over the nationalization of telephones, broadcasting, and the airlines, and construction of some public housing; in 1945, their election manifesto advocated a comprehensive national health service covering the whole range of medical treatment.

To be sure, the two great surges of social welfare legislation took place under moderate leftist governments (Liberal in 1905–1911 and Labour in 1945–1950), but subsequent Conservative governments did not, by and large, repeal these innovations. Instead they maintained and occasionally extended programs of the welfare state and the managed economy.

Acceptance of the welfare state was feasible because of a paternalist tradition and a toleration of institutions and policies which were already established and working when Tory governments regained power. Nonetheless, the Conservatives remained stoutly anti-Socialist, thus flatly opposing the ideology to which Labour subscribed (at least in theory) after 1918. The Conservatives were content to preserve existing differences within society; they feared economic egalitarianism, public ownership, and the prospect of great social change. One innovation they did try to limit was nationalization. After their 1951 victory the Conservatives denationalized the steel industry, which Labour had brought under government ownership. This proved difficult and time-consuming, and the Conservatives did not try to denationalize other sectors (for instance, railroads). In any case, Labour renationalized steel after they regained power, and the Tories did not attempt a reversal during their 1970–1974 return to office.

The mix of tradition and change in the Conservative Party is well illustrated by the reaction of the Conservatives to their defeat in 1945 by Labour. Under the guidance of a leading Conservative, R.A.B. Butler, the party adopted in 1947 an *Industrial Charter*, which committed it to accept some nationalization, the essentials of the welfare state, and more economic planning and control than the Conservatives had ever considered prior to World War II. These policies were, however, not entirely new, having been foreshadowed by programs outlined during Churchill's wartime government. The rationale for this adaptation was expressed by leading moderate Conservatives such as Quintin Hogg, who reminded their Conservative colleagues that the party must follow the strategy of Disraeli in elevating the condition of the people. Over the years, the party thus accepted the large financial costs of the welfare state and the use of fiscal and monetary policy to manage the economy.[23]

"You've never had it so good." From 1951 to 1964 a pragmatic Conservative government ruled in Britain. During this time, the country saw some improvement of its social services and enjoyed the prosperity that the principal countries of the Western world were then experiencing. Thus, in 1959, the Conservative government of Harold Macmillan could win re-election on the slogan, "You've never had it so good."[24]

In celebration of this 13 year period, Quintin Hogg could proudly point to a doubling of the GNP, increased government spending on education and on research and development, peace and full employment, a foreign trade surplus, decolonization, and social legislation far in advance of the United States. Hogg summarized the Conservative success as due to the fact that in social policy the party was "two paces to the left of the Democratic Party in the U.S." and cited the Conservative commitment to a welfare state, affluent society, educated democracy, and pattern of consumer choice as providing an important example for the underdeveloped world and a precedent for the United States and Western Europe.

In fact, the Conservative government's performance was not a complete success. As we have seen already, British economic growth was lagging well behind that of most of Western Europe and the country experienced increasing balance of payments problems. The social services were seen by some as underfunded. Britain seemed to lag in its modernization and in the use of technology. The 1956 Suez fiasco had hurt Britain, and Macmillan's effort to gain Common Market entry had been blocked by de Gaulle's dramatic 1963 veto. In addition, the government proved vulnerable to Labour election pledges to unleash the "white heat of technology." Indeed, the Conservatives had even given the impression of shabby and bumbling amateurishness. The Macmillan government had muffed a number of major spy scandals, culminating in the lurid Profumo Affair in 1963, and had experienced some costly and humiliating failures in its aerospace programs. The Tories were defeated in 1964, although narrowly, and did not regain office until 1970.

---

[23] For a particularly insightful treatment of this period and the "New Conservatism" see Beer, *British Politics in the Collectivist Age,* Chapter XI.
[24] This slogan was later mercilessly parodied by the satirical magazine, *Private Eye,* when in response to a 1963 sex and spy scandal it coined the phrase, "you've never had it so often."

Conservatism out of power. The Conservative Party seemed to undergo a partial shift in policy prior to its victory in the 1970 election. In attacking the economic failures of the Labour government, the Conservative leader, Edward Heath, and his colleagues set out a policy less paternalistic and more competitive and business-oriented than before. The Conservatives pledged to free industry from excessive regulation, to encourage more free enterprise, to reduce trade union power, and to shift the social services to a pattern based more on need and on "means testing" than on universal availability. Unlike most of his twentieth century Conservative predecessors, Heath came from middle class rather than upper class origins. In part, he seemed to prefer a view of society which was more competitive than paternalistic. In fact, the Conservatives appear to have won the 1970 election by capitalizing on the rise in prices, particularly for food. In any case, although Heath's speeches were somewhat more laissez-faire oriented than those of his predecessors, his governmental actions were broadly comparable to those of prior postwar Conservative prime ministers.

Modern Conservative policy tended to stress a humane capitalism or at least the maintenance of a mixed economy in which elements of private enterprise and governmental intervention and control coexisted. Heath himself could criticize excesses of financial and real estate speculation as representing the "unacceptable face" of capitalism. One of Heath's leading cabinet members, Peter Walker, neatly summarized Conservative views of a "new capitalism." "Old capitalism" was weak because of its failure to generate ideological commitment and equality of opportunity. The Conservatives therefore must eliminate any traces of the "laissez-faire capitalist concept of master and man." The object of the new capitalism was to create a society in which all people share in happiness and the dignity of life—and in which British industry could be successfully competitive.[25]

Ironically, Heath's defeat in the 1974 elections was due in large measure to his bitter clashes with the trade union movement and in particular the coal miners. In the end, he failed to convey the Conservative image of a party that could govern in the interests of the whole country rather than as the embodiment of particular elements.

Heath's 1975 replacement as Conservative leader, Mrs. Margaret Thatcher, also tended to possess a view of society somewhat more competitive than Disraelian. As Education Minister in the Heath government she had abolished the provision of free milk in British schools, an action that earned her the enmity of many poorer voters and supporters of the welfare state. She had also expressed the slogan that "we must back the workers and not the shirkers." Like Heath, Mrs. Thatcher had come from

[25] See *The Economist* (London), October 13, 1973, p. 27.

All this is going to cost you a lot of money.

You may have a bill soon for thousands of millions of pounds.

It is going to cost vast sums of money for a Labour Government to take over and buy into many industries and companies. And the bill will be met by the taxpayer.

You will also meet the bill because nationalized industries tend to make a loss. And they are subsidised by the public.

All this means you will pay more and your money will buy less.

So what can we do about it?

We must make our voices heard.

Say 'NO' to the Elephants

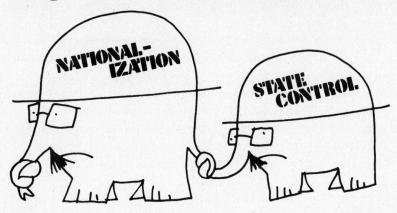

Issued by Aims of Industry against Labour's plans to take over British industry.

These Aims advertisements are paid for by free enterprise companies.

Aims of Industry

a hard working middle class family and had done well at Oxford. She chose to accentuate ideas of self-reliance and thrift, and to defend both equality of opportunity and the right to social inequality. These beliefs were explicitly stated in a speech by Mrs. Thatcher to an American audience several months after she had become Conservative leader:

> . . . the pursuit of equality is a mirage. What is more desirable—and more practical—than the pursuit of equality is the pursuit of equality of opportunity. And opportunity means nothing unless it includes the right to be unequal and the freedom to be different. . . .
>
> We must build a society in which each citizen can develop his full potential, both for his benefit and for the community as a whole. Ours must be a society in which originality, skill, energy and thrift are rewarded. . . .
>
> The promotion of greater equality goes hand in hand with the extension of the welfare state and state control over people's lives. . . .
>
> Government . . . must temper what may be socially desirable with what is economically reasonable.[26]

The rise to Conservative leadership of first Heath then Thatcher, two leaders of middle class background and nontraditionalist sentiment, had not completely changed the prevailing Conservative policy or ideology; yet by giving somewhat more emphasis to a competitive, business oriented, conservatism than to an older premodern and aristocratic tradition of Tory paternalism, this shift made it possible for the Conservatives to be depicted by their opponents as a party that could no longer claim to represent the interests of the nation as a whole but instead mainly those of the privileged. If this perception were to be shared by large segments of the electorate, it would lessen the ability of the Conservatives to obtain working class votes needed to gain victory (votes which Disraeli had first attracted). As a result, the Conservatives might be less likely to win elections on their own merits and would need to rely increasingly on gaining votes through the mistakes that Labour governments might make. If confirmed, this pattern would reflect the success of Labour Prime Minister Harold Wilson's aim of having made Labour the natural majority party in the way the Tories had previously been during most of the 1922–1964 period.

Conservatism and social class. The class aspect of Conservative Party leadership is evident when we examine the backgrounds of Members of Parliament. For example, from 1918 to 1935, 78 percent of Conservative MPs attended "public" schools and, indeed, 37.5 percent had gone to the élite schools of Eton and Harrow (see Table 2–2). By contrast, only 9

[26] Speech to the Institute for Socioeconomic Studies, New York, quoted in *The Sacramento* (California) *Bee*, October 5, 1975.

TABLE 2–2 Secondary Education and Occupation of MPs

| | 1918–1935 | | 1970 | |
	Conservative	Labour	Conservative	Labour
Secondary Education				
Elementary only	2.5%	75.5%	0.6%	20.6%
Grammar or other secondary	19.0	15.5	24.5	57.8
Eton and Harrow	37.5	2.5	22.1	0.7
Other "public" schools	41.0	6.5	52.8	20.9
Occupation				
Employees and managers (farmers)	32.0	4.0	39.7	7.7
Workers	4.0	72.0	1.5	31.0
Professionals	52.0	24.0	58.8	61.3
Others	12.0	0.0	0.0	0.0

Source: Adapted from R. W. Johnson, "The British Political Elite, 1955–1972," *Archives Européennes de Sociologie* 14 (1973): 40, 46.

percent of the comparable Labour group had gone to public school and 2.5 percent to Eton and Harrow.[27] Occupationally, 32 percent of the Conservatives were employers and managers, 52 percent were professionals, and only 4 percent rank and file workers. This contrasted dramatically with Labour, where just 4 percent were employers and managers, 24 percent professionals, and an overwhelming 72 percent workers.

By 1970, these figures showed some change among Labourites but little among Conservatives. Of the Tories 74.9 percent had attended "public" schools (although the number going to Eton and Harrow had fallen to 22.1 percent). Among Labourites, increased numbers (21.6 percent) had attended public schools but only 0.7 percent had gone to Eton and Harrow. On the basis of occupation there was almost no change among Conservatives over an entire generation: 39.7 percent were employers or managers, 58.8 percent professionals, and 1.5 percent workers. By contrast, the Labour group had become more professional and less working class: 7.7 percent were employers or managers, 61.3 percent professionals, and 31 percent workers.

Table 2–3 illustrates the differences in class structure between respective cabinets. During the decade from 1955 to 1964, nearly one-fourth of Con-

[27] Unless otherwise noted, these and subsequent figures are from R. W. Johnson, "The British Political Elite, 1955–1972," *Archives Européennes de Sociologie* 14 (1973): 41 ff. Johnson's figures are drawn in part from W. L. Guttsman, *The British Political Elite* (London: Macgibbon and Kee, 1968).

TABLE 2–3 Class Structure of Conservative and Labour Cabinets

	Total Conservative Cabinet Ministers 1955–1964		Total Labour Cabinet Ministers 1964–1970	
	No.	%	No.	%
Aristocrats	10	21	1	3
Businessmen	12	25	0	0
Professionals	26	54	23	62
Working class	0	0	13	35
Totals	48	100	37	100

Source: Adapted from R. W. Johnson, "The British Political Elite, 1955–1972," *Archives Européennes de Sociologie* 14 (1973): 51–52.

servative cabinet ministers came from aristocratic backgrounds, another fourth were businessmen and just over half were professionals; none were working class. By contrast, one-third (35 percent) of Labour ministers were of working class background, one was an aristocrat, none had been businessmen, and 62 percent were professionals. Thus, while both parties have become increasingly characterized by their professionals (typically lawyers—"solicitors" or "barristers"—in the Conservative Party, teachers and journalists in the case of Labour), each party retains a distinctive component that reflects the element of class: aristocrats and businessmen in the case of the Tories, workers and trade union officials in the case of Labour.

The occupation and background of MPs and cabinet ministers is, of course, only part of the picture of the relation between class and party. If we refer back to Figure 2–1, we can see that persons from the "AB" social classes (higher managerial-professional, and lower managerial or administrative), vote Conservative rather than Labour by a margin of more than five to one (63 percent versus 12 percent). Yet we must keep in mind that the Conservatives also draw substantial working class support. In the October 1974 general election, they received 26 percent of the vote of manual workers and their families and 22 percent of the vote of unskilled workers. Because nearly two-thirds of the British electorate is composed of manual workers and their families, these votes are crucial to the Conservatives. As a rule of thumb, nearly one-third of the working class has tended to vote Conservative. For example, a poll taken just prior to the February 1974 general election indicated that 32 percent of working class voters favored the Conservatives.[28] These votes provide roughly half the Conservatives' total electoral support. Thus, a century after it was first elaborated, Disraeli's strategy continues to attract essential working class support. However, it should be noted that the Tory share of this vote slipped to roughly one-fourth of this group in the October 1974 election, which may be one explanation of why the Tories suffered defeat. If the Conservative Party were to lose its ability to attract substantial working class support, its long term electoral prospects would be jeopardized.

Political Parties: Labour The British Labour Party (BLP) is widely regarded as perhaps the most successful democratic socialist party among the countries of the West. The party rests on a broad base and contains diverse groups and ideas; thus, it is a kind of umbrella party of the democratic left. By virtue of its explicit socialist ideology and self-conscious working class image it differs from the U.S. Democratic Party. Yet it is more widely based than its Italian or French counterparts, each of which has had to contend with other left-wing groups, including large Communist parties. In certain respects—both ideological and organizational—the BLP resembles the German Social Democrats (SPD) but unlike the SPD it has managed to gain a parliamentary majority on its own without having to accept a coalition government.

Why should the BLP and the American Democratic Party differ so distinctly from one another? The explanation for the more class based and ideological nature of the Labour Party lies in the different historical patterns of America and Europe. For one thing, Britain has a feudal past with sharp class distinctions and attitudes. By contrast, as Louis Hartz has argued, the United States is a kind of bourgeois (middle class) spin off from Europe without such a clear tradition of class cleavage and self-conscious class identity. Next, industrialism in Britain occurred in a less wealthy country than the United States, and class grievances were more marked. In addition, the broad extension of the franchise in Britain occurred after an organized working class had already developed its own institutions and solidarity. By contrast, in the United States expansion of the electorate took place largely prior to industrialization and the organization of strong trade unions. Finally, America experienced successive waves of immigrants whose ethnic affinities were often greater than their sense of class solidarity, and the expanding Western frontier operated as an escape valve for many of those dissatisfied or disadvantaged by industrialization. In all these respects, the United States differs from Britain, as well as from the rest of Western Europe.

[28] O.R.C. poll, cited by Richard Rose, *The Times* (London), February 23, 1974.

Origins of the Labour Party. During the late nineteenth century, British trade unions generally supported parliamentary candidates of the dominant, middle class based, Liberal Party. In some areas the Liberals allowed labor-oriented groups to select the Liberal parliamentary candidate, and by the 1880's about a dozen of these "Lib-Labs" had been elected to the House of Commons. This alliance was challenged, however, with the rise of political groups more avowedly working class or socialist in inspiration. In the 1880's, an explicitly Marxist group, the Social Democratic Federation, was established, as was the Fabian Society. Over a period of time, the Fabians became particularly influential. Based upon a group of middle class intellectuals which included H. G. Wells, George Bernard Shaw and Beatrice and Sidney Webb, the Fabians helped to make socialism respectable; they also shaped the elements of this ideology as a peaceful evolutionary method of democratic social change. This intellectual and literary element can hardly be underrated in its importance. As one contemporary Labour MP has wistfully commented: "Shaw, Wells and Orwell—and one or two other imaginative writers—did more to influence and encourage Socialism than *all* the textbooks. God, that we had their equal today." [29]

The Labour Party is fundamentally a combination of middle class intellectuals and a working class base. The ideas of the Fabians and others might have produced nothing tangible had there not been a burgeoning working class movement receptive to them. The establishment of the Independent Labour Party (ILP) by Keir Hardie in 1893 represented a crucial turning point in this development. Hardie, a staunch working class figure and a democratic socialist, had sought and failed to gain nomination as a Lib-Lab candidate for Parliament. His creation of the ILP makes him the founding spirit of the Labour Party. A few years later, Hardie was one of the first overtly working class representatives to sit in Parliament. His attire (a worker's cloth cap in particular) set him apart from Liberal and Lib-Lab MPs and his principles (Christian humanism, women's rights, a commitment to full employment) provided an enduring legacy for the BLP.

During the 1890's, the major trade unions, which possessed the greatest resources of organization and money, continued to support Liberal (and occasionally sympathetic Conservative) candidates. By contrast, the ILP succeeded in electing only a few MPs. In 1900, however, a key link was established among the ILP, Fabians, trade unions (via the powerful Trades Union Congress) and (briefly) the Social Democratic Federation.

[29] Quoted in S. J. Ingle, "Socialism and Literature, the Contribution of Imaginative Writers to the Development of the British Labour Party," *Political Studies* 22, no. 2 (June 1974): 167.

This new body was the Labour Representation Committee, which in 1906 changed its name to the Labour Party.

For a time, the infant Labour Party did not develop a constituency organization; it mainly provided support for ILP or trade union candidates and some Liberals. Labour made its first major parliamentary gains in 1906 at the time of a great Liberal victory. Twenty-nine Labour-supported candidates won election, mostly by arrangement with the Liberals in areas in which the parties agreed not to run competing candidates who would split the anti-Conservative vote. In addition, 25 Lib-Labs were elected.

As we shall see, the alliance with the Liberals did not remain permanent, and the Liberals would eventually lose out to a separate working class party as the major challenger to the Conservatives. A key event in this shift was the decision of the TUC to back the Labour Party because of a major anti-union court judgment, the Taff-Vale decision of 1901. Essentially, this decision had made unions liable for financial losses suffered by firms during labor strikes. The decision could only be reversed by legislation and the unions backed a separate party to achieve this. Many trade union leaders also felt uncomfortable within the Liberal Party; they had come from poor and working class backgrounds, which made them seem out of place among upper middle class Liberals. In any case, it is no exaggeration to restate the widely quoted words of Ernest Bevin that "The Labour Party has grown out of the bowels of the TUC."

The modern Labour Party. In 1918, the BLP finally organized itself on a constituency basis—that is, within electoral districts and with a party constitution containing a loose commitment to socialism. The party also produced a program, entitled *Labour and the New Social Order,* written by the Webbs, which advocated a policy of a national minimum living standard, democratic control of industry, and the use of surplus wealth for the common good. More broadly, Labour established itself as a loose coalition rather than a narrow sectarian party. This is well expressed in the phrase that the party was open to those who labored "by hand or by brain."

Socialism and the Labour Party. By contrast to Continental European parties of the left, the Labour Party is less absorbed in ideological questions. In comparison with American Democrats, however, the BLP exhibits far more interest in theoretical matters. The socialism of the Labour Party has received considerable attention both within and outside the party. The nature of Labour's socialism remains, however, a matter of intensive dispute. We can observe this by noting a series of conflicting definitions of socialism and social democracy offered by past and present British Labour Party leaders and socialist intellectuals:

"Socialism is about equality."—Hugh Gaitskell

"A broad human movement on behalf of the bottom dog."—G.D.H. Cole

"What the Labour Government does."—attributed to Herbert Morrison

"A wider social equality embracing . . . a redistribution of income . . . the distribution of property, the educational system, social class relations, power and privilege in industry . . . the age-old socialist dream of a more classless society."—Anthony Crosland

"A movement of conscience."—Roy Jenkins

"Nothing if not a crusade."—Harold Wilson

"The application through social engineering of the findings of the social sciences."—John Vaisey

"Anything that falls short of abolishing the wage relation has no claim to being described as socialism."—George Lichtheim [30]

The fact is that Labour's "socialism" is a uniquely British product, combining at least three divergent strands. The first comes from a kind of Puritan Methodist or nonconformist (in the British sense of non-Church of England Protestantism) view of power, wealth, class, and privilege. It dates back to the English Civil War of the mid seventeenth century and regards wealth and privilege as morally wrong. This strand of radical and religious egalitarianism, sometimes expressed in ideas of Christian brotherhood, is fundamental to British socialism.

A second component is that of a diluted Marxism. This strand, however, rejects the Leninist authoritarianism and the dictatorship of the proletariat typically advocated by Marxist-Leninists. While it has a relatively small following and is in practical terms the least important of the various socialist components, it has contributed one key element: the commitment to common ownership of the means of production. This is given formal embodiment in the famous Clause IV of the 1918 Labour Party Constitution. The commitment to nationalization has been extremely important as a symbol, particularly to the left of the Labour Party. In practice, however, Labour has been committed to nationalize only the "commanding heights" of the economy.

Finally, there is the crucial Fabian tradition of socialist administration, best expressed in the institutions of the welfare state. For intellectuals such as R. M. Titmuss and Brian Abel Smith, or social democratic politicians such as Roy Jenkins, the state must constantly intervene to facilitate real equality. Equality of opportunity alone is seen as insufficient unless

[30] Quoted in Peter Jenkins, "The Social Democratic Dilemma," *New Statesman* (London), September 20, 1974, p. 373, and Peter Jay, *New Statesman*, March 22, 1974.

the state acts to guarantee that people are not so deprived as to limit their opportunity. As expressed by Jenkins, the right to choose is meaningless without the power to choose.[31] A more classic definition of this kind of socialist view has been put by a Labour MP:

> If you have three children, you don't give them three different kinds of breakfast because of their different abilities. The one who is good at football does not get better clothes, or more pocket money than the one who is more keen on woodwork. And what mother would feed her children differently because some are girls and some boys. In spite of all differences in sex, ability, taste and temperament, they get the same start and the same treatment. That is the only way of running a family. And Socialists say it is the only way of running a country.[32]

Labour's socialism in practice. There has sometimes been a wide gap between Labour's ideology and the party's actual practice when in power. Labour first came to office in Britain as a minority government in 1924. In the General Election of December 1923 the party had offered a program comparable to that of the Liberals, stressing public works programs and increased unemployment compensation. Lacking a majority of the seats in the House of Commons, Labour was briefly supported in office for nine months by the votes of Liberal MPs although the Liberals remained outside the cabinet. The prime minister, Ramsay Macdonald, and the chancellor of the exchequer (equivalent to secretary of the treasury), Philip Snowden, continued to express socialist positions including a preference for the replacement of the capitalist system by a socialist system of public ownership and democratic control of the means of production and distribution, but they lacked a parliamentary majority to enact socialist measures. In practice, they actually followed social policies less imaginative than the Liberals on welfare and public works and pursued orthodox economic policies and a balanced budget despite high unemployment.

The first Labour government lasted less than one year, but once again in 1929 Labour returned to office as a minority government supported by Liberal votes. As before, Macdonald and Snowden espoused a vague socialism in theory but in practice pursued conservative policies. In fact, Snowden proved to be doctrinaire and intransigent on the principles of free trade, the gold standard, and a balanced budget. Labour had the misfortune to take office just as the worst part of the Great Depression began. Snowden reacted with economy-minded measures and a fierce hostility to socialist or welfare-state actions of any kind. Finally, in 1931

[31] See Roy Jenkins, *What Matters Now* (London: Collins/Fontana, 1972).
[32] Raymond Fletcher, *The Times* (London), October 23, 1974. These remarks were first published in 1955.

"WORKLESS"

PUBLISHED BY THE LABOUR PARTY, 33 Eccleston Square, London S.W. & PRINTED BY VINCENT BROOKS, DAY & SON, LTD 48 Parker St. Kingsway, London W.C.2

1920's Labour Party campaign poster.
"Workless," © *1971 The Labour Party. Reproduction Edition published by Motif Editions, 58 Frith Street, London W 1.*

Macdonald and Snowden responded to severe economic crisis by adopting major cuts in unemployment and welfare benefits and establishing a coalition "National Government" with the Conservatives and some "National Liberals." In Macdonald's view it was nobler to save the nation than to achieve socialism. In fact, there were other choices than those sanctimoniously put by Macdonald—for example, the kind of New Deal measures taken in the United States by Franklin Roosevelt and advocated by some British politicians and leading economists such as John Meynard Keynes (a Liberal). In any case, Macdonald's actions partially split the Labour Party (a small number of Labourites defected to support the National Government) and dealt it an electoral blow from which it would not recover until 1945.

During most of World War II Labour participated in the coalition government of Winston Churchill. Largely at the urging of Labour and the TUC, the government authorized major studies to propose solutions to the problems of welfare and unemployment that had plagued Britain before the war. In 1942, Sir William Beveridge presented his report on "Social Insurance and Allied Services" which effectively provided the basis for welfare state benefits: children's allowances, a health service, full employment, and a comprehensive "national minimum" (living standard). In 1944, a government report on "Full Employment in a Free Society" set out the essentials of planning for full employment while preserving individual liberty.

Shortly before the end of the war the Labour Party achieved a landslide general election victory over Churchill's Conservatives. For the first time they took office with a solid majority of the seats in the House of Commons. Over the next five years, under the ministry of Clement Attlee, they proceeded to enact a sweeping program of peaceful social reform: creation of a comprehensive welfare state, the National Health Service, nationalization of coal, railways, steel, and a number of other industries, and a host of related measures. In 1950 Labour was barely reelected, but in 1951 it suffered a narrow electoral defeat at the hands of the Conservatives and remained out of power for the next 13 years.

The experience of governing as well as the period of frustrating opposition from 1951 to 1964 led to a series of internal debates and disagreements about the fundamental purpose and ideology of the Labour Party. On right and center of the BLP, "revisionists" such as Hugh Gaitskell (the party leader from 1955 to 1963) and Anthony Crosland argued that the party must adapt itself to modern conditions of the mixed economy and welfare state. They stressed equality of opportunity, improved welfare and social services, economic growth, Keynesian policies of economic management, and a kind of liberal and humanitarian outlook at home and abroad. Their position, then and now, can be characterized as one of social democracy. By contrast, the left of the party, led until 1960 by the fiery and charismatic Welsh miner, Aneurin Bevan, argued for a policy of democratic socialism. By this they meant a continued emphasis on nationalization, and a determination not merely to manage better a predominantly capitalist economy but gradually to do away with capitalism and extend democracy from the political to the economic sphere. In practice, the left also put more weight on equality of condition (that is, equal treatment and benefits for all citizens) than on equality of opportunity.

While the left successfully resisted Gaitskell's effort to delete Clause 4 ("common ownership of the means of production") from the party Constitution, and continued to keep the terminology of socialism visible within the Labour Party and in its election manifestoes, it was the social democratic wing of the party which dominated the postwar Labour governments (1945–1951, 1964–1970, 1974–).

Is Labour a socialist party? If we consider George Lichtheim's definition that socialism means the abolition of the wage relationship, or if it implies a real commitment to eliminate the capitalist economy and create a socialist one, then the answer is clearly no. At one time, in the latter part of the nineteenth century, social democracy and democratic socialism were synonymous. Indeed, Marx himself became a German Social Democrat. With the passage of time, however, social democracy has come to mean something quite different, as exemplified by the revisionist or right wing of the Labour Party. This is not merely a matter of intellectual debate. For the most part the trade union component of the BLP has successfully urged the party to follow a policy which Lichtheim has called "labourism," or the political expression of union objectives (particularly higher wages and job security). Thus, despite the terminology and ritual references to socialism, the British Labour Party remains fundamentally reformist social democratic rather than socialist.[33] To be sure, the socialist left of the BLP remains an important force whose strength, as in Labour's period in opposition during the early 1970's, can nearly match or possibly exceed that of the social democrats, but—particularly while in office—the right and center of the Party continue to determine its policies.

Labour and social class. As we can see from Figure 2–1, Labour is preeminently the party of the British working class. Among skilled manual workers and their families (class C2), Labour enjoys a margin of nearly two to one (49 percent versus 26 percent) over the Conservatives, and

[33] These arguments are lucidly developed in Peter Jenkins, "The Social Democratic Dilemma," *New Statesman,* September 20, 1974, and in Mervyn Jones, "The Challenge to Capitalism," *New Statesman,* October 4, 1974.

in the lowest category (DE—unskilled manual, pensioners, etc.) Labour's advantage is 57 percent versus 22 percent. By contrast the BLP received only 24 percent of the votes of lower middle class Britons and a bare 12 percent of the upper middle class.

The organized trade union movement, embodied by the TUC, effectively dominates the Labour Party organization. Of Britain's 11.5 million trade unionists, 10 million belong to the TUC. The large majority of these unions also affiliate with the Labour Party. Their members also automatically belong unless they choose to "contract out," that is, refuse to pay the small annual subscription otherwise deducted from their union dues. Altogether, some 5.5 million trade unionists belong to the BLP. Their votes comprise 88 percent of the party's 6.5 million membership, and union votes are ordinarily cast as a bloc at Labour conferences. Thus the mammoth Transport and General Workers Union (T&GWU) casts 1.2 million votes and the Amalgamated Union of Engineering Workers (AUEW) disposes of another 900,000 votes. A minor switch in the balance of leadership within one such union can thus suddenly shift a union's entire bloc vote one way or another. In the fifties and early sixties, the major unions provided steady support for the right and center of the BLP leadership. In the late sixties and early seventies changes in several unions dramatically shifted the center of gravity to the left of the party, although after Labour's election victories in 1974, the weight of union votes once again began to reinforce the leadership of Prime Minister Wilson.

The unions' importance is not only numerical but financial. Union subscriptions bring in £1.5 million per year (more than $3 million), and unions also "sponsor" large numbers of Labour MPs by paying much of their election expenses.

As we have already seen, the class composition of Labour MPs and cabinet members differs from that of the Conservatives. Traditionally, the pathway of trade union and Labour Party activity has provided a means of social mobility for bright working class youth. Many of the most colorful figures in the leadership of the Labour Party and of Labour governments have come from trade union backgrounds. Thus Keir Hardie, Aneurin Bevan, Ernest Bevin, and George Brown have all made their mark in British politics. However, the Labour leadership has become increasingly less working class and more educated over the past generation. The percentage of Labour MPs with only a secondary education has fallen from about one-third to about one-fifth of the total, and the percentage of manual workers has fallen from more than one-third to about one-quarter. At the same time there has been a corresponding increase of those with professional backgrounds, particularly in teaching, journalism, and law.[34] Yet even when the party leadership included a higher proportion of working class and trade union figures its leader or prime minister frequently came from a middle or upper middle class background.

The class aspect of the Labour Party has often been diluted by the concern to gain respectability. Ramsay Macdonald, for example, who came from humble origins longed for social acceptance and there are some who explain his 1931 defection in these terms. The philosopher Bertrand Russell, for example, jibed that Macdonald preferred to be thought "a gentleman by his enemies than a comrade among his friends." [35] This element of deference was once assessed by Aneurin Bevan, who argued that the Tories were soft in their outside appearance and deadly hard on the inside but that Labour was often the opposite.[36] Nonetheless, as Labour has become less working class in the composition of its leadership it has also come increasingly to hold governmental power. Whether it can fulfill Harold Wilson's objective of making itself the natural party of government rather than of opposition is another matter. The BLP remains a broadly based umbrella party resting on a substantially working class electorate but reaching out to diverse groups of supporters and political opinions. At times this combination has seemed potentially unstable, but the marriage between the union movement and the BLP suits the needs of both parties and is not likely to be broken.

Political Parties: The Liberals   In effect, Britain has a two party system. Since 1922, Conservative or Labour governments have ruled Britain. Yet the Liberal Party was the major alternative force in politics until after World War I. Indeed, it continues to receive substantial support. In the October 1974 general election the Liberals managed to win over 5 million voters, or more than 18 percent of those voting—a total equivalent to more than half of that for the Conservative Party. But whereas the Conservatives won 276 seats in the House of Commons, the Liberals obtained a bare 13 seats. Why then has the Liberal Party fallen into political eclipse for more than half a century?

Until the late nineteenth century, the Liberals were a highly successful middle class and business oriented party, which regularly alternated in power with the Tories. By the early twentieth century they had adopted a reformist program of welfare state legislation, which caused them to

[34] For more information on this subject see R. W. Johnson, "The British Political Elite," *Archives Européennes de Sociologie* (1973), and Victor J. Hanby, "A Changing Labour Elite: The National Executive Committee of the Labour Party 1900–72," in Ivor Crewe, ed., *Sociology Yearbook: Elites in Western Democracies* (London: Croom Helm, 1974), pp. 122–158.

[35] Quoted in *New Statesman*, August 2, 1974.

[36] Cited by James Cameron, *New York Times Book Review*, February 10, 1974.

lose some of their business supporters to the Conservatives but which proved attractive enough to win them a great general election victory in 1906. The Liberal government proceeded to enact a vigorous reform program of legislation like that carried out in the United States nearly a generation later by President Franklin Roosevelt's New Deal. The party also enjoyed a large national organization and a healthy majority of seats in the House of Commons. Yet, at this Liberal high point, the Labour Party had already begun to make inroads. The 1906 Parliament contained 30 Labour MPs, many of whom had been elected after Liberals agreed not to run against them and thus split the anti-Conservative vote. There were also a further 25 Lib-Labs—Liberals elected with Labour support. In two successive elections, both held in 1910, Liberal support fell sharply and the Liberal Prime Minister H. H. Asquith presided over a minority government with occasional support from the Labour and Irish Nationalist parties.

Despite their vigorous reformist image and attractive leadership, the Liberals were increasingly caught in the middle of a twentieth century social and economic division between capital and labor. Their ideological commitment to free trade had served them well in the nineteenth century but the importance of this issue had begun to wane. For reasons we have seen, the Liberals failed to absorb the mass of the growing working class vote and the allegiance of working class leaders. They could not compete successfully with Labour's class image nor were they willing to adopt the kind of policies that the Labour Party advocated after 1918. Yet on their right flank, the Liberals could not make greater inroads against Conservative support. The traditionalist, paternalist and upper class strength of the Tories was not vulnerable to the appeals of Liberal reformism, and increasingly the business oriented and commercial strata of the population had drifted to the Conservatives in reaction against the Liberals' reform program.

The Liberal demise. A Liberal demise was not, perhaps, inevitable. The process of party realignment took place during a decade that saw deep splits and leadership crises within the Liberal Party and the ravages of World War I. Whether a unified party might, in a nonwar period, have survived as one of the two major parties can only be a matter of speculation.

From 1908 to 1916, the Liberal prime minister had been Asquith, who embodied the upper middle class and reformist aspects of the party. Asquith, who has been called the last of the gentleman politicians, proved to be insufficiently energetic as a war-time leader however. In 1915, nearly a year after the outbreak of the war, he had organized a coalition government that included Conservatives and a few Labourites. By the end of

1916, he was edged out of the prime ministership by his fiery and charismatic colleague, David Lloyd George. Lloyd George represented the more radical wing of the Liberal Party; he also came from a humbler Welsh background. In gaining his position, however, Lloyd George had had to rely not only on his own faction of the Liberals but on the Conservatives as well and this had the effect of splitting the Liberal Party.

In the divisive election of 1918, Lloyd George ran as head of one "Coalition Liberal" Party. The Asquith faction ran as a separate Liberal party, their candidates lacking the endorsement, or "coupon," of the coalition government. Lloyd George continued in office until 1922 but his coalition was dominated by Conservatives who actually enjoyed a majority of seats in Parliament.

In 1922, National Liberal and Liberal parties once again ran separately and for the first time won fewer seats (combined) than Labour. The Liberals reunited for the 1923 election, which confirmed that they had fallen slightly behind Labour as the main opposition party. A year later, the Liberals won only 40 seats compared to 151 for Labour. Henceforth, and despite a costly all out effort in 1929 on behalf of their reformist and Keynesian program (the "Yellow Book"), the Liberals never again came within serious reach of Labour or the Conservatives.

Liberal ideology. As a third party, the Liberals have continued to function, often appealing to defectors from the two major parties. At times, as in 1951, they have gained a mere 2.5 percent of the popular vote (see Table 2–4). More recently (February 1974) they have risen as high as 19.3 percent. The basis of Liberal appeal probably has more to do with voter dissatisfaction with Labour and the Conservatives than with the attractiveness of Liberal ideas and policies. Indeed, Liberal ideology is a heterogeneous mixture of divergent notions and beliefs. Nonetheless, several major elements can be discerned.

In general, Liberals have tended to espouse a liberalized capitalism with strong reformist flavor. They typically reject socialism (though in the late 1960's the party developed a young radical, more or less Trotskyist, wing). The Liberals are also differentiated from the Conservatives because of the latter's identification with big business, agriculture, and the status quo. There are echoes of an older laissez-faire and individualist Liberal tradition as well as a more widespread anti-bigness spirit which pits them against big business, big government, and big unions. The amalgam of Liberal ideas is broadly nondoctrinaire and opportunistic in the sense of being readily open to new ideas. Thus the Liberal Party was the first, in the late 1950's, to advocate Common Market membership. Some Liberals have also espoused ideas of co-ownership of industry, including greater worker participation in decision-making. Finally, they have sought to

TABLE 2-4 British General Election Results 1922-1974 *

Year	Total	Seats Con.	Seats Lib.	Seats Lab.	Seats Other	Votes % Con.	Votes % Lib.	Votes % Lab.	Votes % Other
1922	615	346	115	142	12	38.2	29.1	29.5	3.2
1923	615	258	159	191	7	38.1	29.6	30.5	1.8
1924	615	419	40	151	5	48.3	17.6	33.0	1.1
1929	615	260	59	288	8	38.2	23.4	37.0	1.4
1931	615	521	37	52	5	67.1		30.7	2.2
1935	615	431	21	154	9	53.6	6.6	37.8	2.0
1945	640	212	12	394	22	39.8	9.0	47.8	3.4
1950	625	298	9	315	3	43.5	9.1	46.1	1.3
1951	625	321	6	295	3	48.0	2.5	48.8	0.6
1955	630	344	6	277	3	49.7	2.7	46.4	1.2
1959	630	365	6	258	1	49.4	5.9	43.8	0.9
1964	630	304	9	317	0	43.4	11.2	44.1	1.3
1966	630	253	12	363	2	41.9	8.5	47.9	1.7
1970	630	330	6	287	7	46.4	7.4	43.0	3.2
1974 (Feb)	635	296	14	301	23	38.2	19.3	37.2	5.3
1974 (Oct)	635	276	13	319	27	35.8	18.3	39.3	6.5

*In 1922 National Liberal and Liberal are grouped together. In 1931 National Liberal and National Labour members are classed with Conservatives.

Sources: David Butler and Jennie Freeman, *British Political Facts 1900–1967*, pp. 142–144; *The Guardian* (London), June 20, 1970. *The Times* (London), October 10, 12, and 14, 1974.

change the electoral system, which has the effect of discriminating against them.

Not surprisingly the sources of Liberal support are very diverse. They lie among those who favor reformism but who are put off by the working class image and socialist rhetoric of Labour or who reject the status quo or business orientation of the Tories. Younger voters are a little more favorable toward the Liberals than are older ones; in fact, among 18 to 24 year olds the Liberals actually outdrew the Conservatives in the October 1974 General Election by a margin of 27 percent to 24 percent (Labour, however, attracted 42 percent of this group).[37] As Figure 2–1 illustrates, Liberal votes have recently come about equally from upper middle, middle, and lower middle classes and from the skilled working class (20 to 22 percent), but fall off (to 16 percent) among unskilled workers and pensioners. Geographically the Liberals have been strongest in outlying areas, the "Celtic fringe," in portions of Western England, Wales, and Scotland.

Liberal revival? The Liberal Party suffered a long decline from 1923, when it held 29.6 percent of the vote and 129 seats in the House of Commons, to 1955 when it won only 2.7 percent and 6 seats. Indeed, the Liberals were nearly eliminated in the 1950's. The Party then experienced a modest resurgence, to 11.2 percent of the vote in 1964 before falling back to 8.5 percent (1966) and 7.4 percent (1970). Suddenly, in the early 1970's it gathered renewed strength. Opinion polls during 1973 gave it a following comparable in size to that of the two major parties. In fact, the February 1974 election was a 50 year high point for the Liberals, even if it did fall well below their hopes for overtaking the Conservatives or Labour.

Part of the Liberals' problem lies in the nature of the British electoral system. After all, in October 1974, with more than half the votes of the Conservatives (18.3 percent versus 35.1 percent) the Liberals obtained less than one-twentieth the number of seats (13 versus 276). In effect, each of the Liberal MPs represented 411,000 Liberal voters, while the Conservatives enjoyed one MP for 38,000 votes and Labour one for 36,000. As we shall see, this maldistribution occurs because of the nature of Britain's electoral system, and it seriously impedes the Liberals' chances for becoming a major party.

The Liberals also face a problem of deciding where to focus their efforts. In February 1974, they gained roughly 1 million votes each from the Labour and Conservative parties, 1.5 million from those who had not voted in the 1970 election, and 750,000 from new voters. The party's

[37] "Harris and O.R.C. Election Surveys," Louis Harris International, London, October 1974, p. 9.

program and ideology remain diffuse; yet, to sharpen them might run the risk of alienating newly won adherents. In practice, any future Liberal gains of parliamentary seats would have to be largely at the expense of the Conservatives. Following the February 1974 election, 47 of the 49 seats in which the Liberals were within 15 percent of winning were held by Tory MPs. However, to appeal more directly to Conservatives might jeopardize gains among Labour voters.

In any case, it is difficult to see how the Liberals can gain additional support by their own actions and policies. Their periods of resurgence as reflected in opinion polls and by-elections have come during phases of voter disaffection from Conservative governments, as in 1963 and 1973. In fact, the Liberal Party exists as a halfway house for major party voters displeased with their regular party but unwilling to cast a vote for the other major party. The split personality and diversity of Liberal policies and supporters is reflected even among the 13 Liberal MPs, who frequently vote in divergent ways in Parliament and who display less party cohesion than Labour or Tory MPs.

Short of a surprising electoral result which gives the parliamentary balance of power to the Liberals, or the unexpected breakup of a major party—for example, the unlikely realignment of Labour's social democrats with Liberals and progressive Conservatives—Liberal fortunes are likely to wax and wane in response not to what the party itself does but in reaction to the failures and successes of the two major parties.

Regional Cleavages: Scotland From a distance, Britain has long appeared quite homogeneous in ethnic composition. Yet there have always existed regional cleavages. Until recently, these cleavages have been muted— indeed, manifestations of Celtic (Scottish, Welsh, Irish) nationalism were treated as a kind of vaudeville joke. Since the late 1960's, however, the regional divisions have become politically significant. For example, Wales, which has been unified with England since 1535, has seen the growth of a Welsh Nationalist Party, Plaid Cymru, able to gain 11 percent of the Welsh vote and three seats in Parliament. And the cleavage between Catholics and Protestants in British ruled Northern Ireland has produced years of inconclusive but bloody conflict. We shall examine Scotland, however, since it represents an unusual challenge to the unity of Great Britain.

Since the Act of Union in 1707, Scotland has been a unified part of the United Kingdom, governed from the Parliament at Westminster in London, where 71 Scottish MPs sit among the 635 members of the House of Commons. Yet Scotland has always retained significant institutions of its own. These include separate educational and banking systems, a Scottish legal system, and a different church (Presbyterian rather than Anglican). Since 1885 there has been a secretary of state for Scotland in the British cabinet and a Scottish administration under his direction has been based in Edinburgh (the capital of Scotland) since 1939. Nonetheless, there has been no Scottish Parliament nor the kind of internal self government characteristic of the American states or German regions (*Länder*).

Since the early 1930's the Scottish Nationalist Party (SNP) has campaigned for Scotland's autonomy. From 1935 to 1959, the SNP remained a largely irrelevant fringe party, never running more than eight candidates in the 71 Scottish constituencies, nor winning a seat in Parliament, nor capturing more than 1.3 percent of the Scottish vote. In the 1964 election, however, the SNP vote increased to 2.4 percent and has more or less doubled in each of the succeeding elections: 5 percent in 1966, 11.4 percent in 1970, 21.9 percent in February 1974, and 30.4 percent in October 1974.[38] The SNP also won its first seats in the House of Commons: one in 1970, seven in February 1974. In October 1974, it won 11 seats while campaigning on a program to create a completely independent Scotland with its own sovereign parliament, armed forces, UN membership, embassies, passports, and other attributes of nationhood. The only concessions to continued ties with England were to be membership in the Commonwealth and an association of British states to encourage cooperation between the various parts of the British isles.

Scottish nationalism is thus no longer to be taken lightly. The reasons for its recent upsurge are a matter of dispute, but several factors seem crucial. First is the demise of the British Empire. From 1707 until the early 1960's, membership in the United Kingdom meant belonging to a rich and powerful nation, whose Empire covered vast reaches of the globe. Talented Scots served the Empire all over the world and fought with distinction in its army units such as the Scottish Highlanders. Dissolution of the Empire not only closed off a major outlet for Scottish energy and imagination but turned Scottish attention inward to the less glorified and more confined setting of the British isles.

A second crucial factor is economic. Britain's difficulties over the past half century have been severely felt in Scotland. This has been particularly true among the 2.5 million people of the Glasgow area, where a city once prosperous during the industrial revolution and the nineteenth century has suffered high unemployment, poverty, slums, and demoralization.

Finally, there is a growing sense of disenchantment with the major

[38] Figures from Charles Lewis Taylor, "Why Vote SNP?", paper presented at the 1975 Annual Meeting of the American Political Science Association, San Francisco, September 2–5, 1975, p. 3.

British political parties. Both Labour and the Conservatives are seen as having neglected Scotland. More broadly, the United Kingdom has come to be regarded as an increasingly less attractive community—its standard of living, place in the world, future prospects, and sense of self-esteem are all seen as in decline.

Until the early 1970's, the brake on Scottish nationalism was its economic impracticality. Declining industries, Scotch whiskey, Harris tweed, and sparse farming would not have provided a viable economy for the 5.5 million Scottish people. Indeed, opinion polls indicate that by a margin of 91 percent versus 6 percent an improved standard of living is far more important to the people of Scotland than preserving their Scottish traditions and culture.[39] But virtually overnight the economic prospect has been transformed by the discovery of huge quantities of oil off the Scottish North Sea Coast. The oil from these fields will make Britain self-sufficient and a major oil exporter by the early 1980's, and the oil revenues will also provide a great boost to the British economy. To the Scots, who have already benefited from increased employment and economic recovery stimulated by the oil industry, control of this resource would mean great wealth and prosperity—for an independent Scotland.

The scene is thus set for a potentially serious conflict between British unity and Scottish nationalism. If support for the SNP (55 percent of whose voters favor secession)[40] continues to grow, such a confrontation may be inescapable. Both major parties included provision for a Scottish assembly elected either directly (Labour) or indirectly (Conservative) in their general election manifestoes. If the Labour government actually proceeds to create such an assembly to deal with subjects now controlled by the Scottish office (housing, health, education, local government), the result might satisfy Scottish demands for greater responsibility over their own affairs—but it could just as easily stimulate a greater appetite for autonomy. Indeed, such an assembly, if controlled by the SNP, could provoke a constitutional confrontation if it were to advocate Scottish independence.

In the short run, this cleavage has not yet produced any overt conflict. Only 17 percent of the total Scottish population favors independence, and 60 percent actually want North Sea Oil to benefit the entire UK.[41] Indeed, the SNP is not yet within reach of a majority; it attracts the support of just 30 percent of the Scottish voters. Labour retains 36 percent; the Conservatives 25 percent, and the Liberals 8 percent. And in the June 1975

[39] *The Scotsman* (Edinburgh), May 13, 1974, cited in Taylor, ibid., p. 6.
[40] O.R.C. poll, *The Economist* (London), May 18, 1974.
[41] Ibid.

referendum, the SNP suffered a stunning and unexpected reversal when Scottish voters cast their ballots decisively in favor of Britain's continued Common Market membership.

The future of Scotland and of Scottish nationalism is thus uncertain. In the long run, it is likely to depend on how successfully Britain can cope with the other problems, cleavages, and conflicts that beset it. An economically successful and politically coherent UK would be less vulnerable to fragmentation.

Racial Cleavages: Commonwealth Immigrants   Unlike the United States, which has been populated by successive waves of foreign immigrants, Britain has not had any truly large inward movement of population for nearly 1000 years. During this time the various Anglo-Saxons, Normans, Celts, Irish, Danes, Norwegians, and others have become intermingled and nearly indistinguishable ethnically. The exceptions have been modest: in total perhaps a few hundred thousand persons, including Protestant and democratic political refugees from Europe in the sixteenth century and after, Jewish refugees from Eastern Europe in the late nineteenth century, some Polish emigrés before and after World War II, and a wide though not overly numerous variety of others. There have been, however, two larger groups: Irish, from both the Republic of Ireland and Northern Ireland, seeking jobs and better economic opportunities in the cities of Britain, and nonwhite immigrants from the former British Empire.

Until the early 1950's there were perhaps no more than 50,000 nonwhite immigrants within Britain. Then, decolonization and a series of laws which embodied the idea that the entire population of the Commonwealth was in some sense British, made it possible for a citizen of India or Pakistan or the British West Indies to obtain a British passport and enter the UK with rights of citizenship. (This represented an extension of an opportunity previously accorded to the largely white populations of the old Commonwealth dominions such as Canada, Australia, and New Zealand.) Together with the desire of British employers to hire cheap labor at a time of relative labor shortage in the UK, and the desire of many nonwhite Commonwealth residents to flee the relative poverty of their own countries for greater opportunities in the UK, this stimulated a wave of immigration. By the mid 1960's, over 1 million nonwhites (all termed "colored" by the British) had entered the UK, and race had become a cleavage within Britain.

About half these immigrants were from Asia, particularly India and Pakistan. The remaining half were principally blacks from the West Indies (the Caribbean). In search of jobs they began to cluster in often decaying areas of Britain's cities such as London, Birmingham, Leeds, and Bradford. As early as the late 1950's there had been an outbreak of racial animosity in Nottinghill, a poor section of London. This brief outburst of anti-immigrant prejudice embarrassed many British but subsided without any wider consequences. By the mid 1960's, however, the racial issue had become increasingly visible. Enoch Powell, a fiery and mercurial Conservative politician, delivered a series of speeches against further nonwhite immigration and invoked the specter of a huge nonwhite population and growing racial conflict.

The leadership of the Labour, Conservative, and Liberal parties generally refused to cater to any anti-immigrant bias. Powell was ousted from an important (shadow cabinet) position in the Conservative Party by Edward Heath. Nonetheless successive Labour and Conservative governments responded by a stringent tightening of immigration laws, which sharply curtailed the nonwhite inflow. At times, this precipitated dramatic and poignant confrontations as in the early 1970's when the ruthless Uganda dictator, General Idi Amin Dada, expelled tens of thousands of Commonwealth Asians. Many of these persons were of Indian and Pakistani origins, but had lived in Uganda for three generations; some had even adopted Ugandan citizenship after Britain granted independence to Uganda in 1962. Although the British government was reluctant to admit many of these refugees, large numbers of them held British passports; ultimately many (particularly the large proportion with middle class and professional occupations) managed to enter the UK while others emigrated to India.

The growing nonwhite population in Britain began to face sporadic racial discrimination, particularly in housing, jobs, and private clubs. Having had little direct experience of racial division, and preferring to see the scope of the problem as minimal, British governments were slow to act. Eventually in the late 1960's the Labour government did enact a Race Relations Act barring certain forms of discrimination, particularly in public accommodations. These provisions were later extended (1975) to cover private clubs.

With further nonwhite immigration largely curtailed and with broad race relations laws finally in effect, the British nonetheless would continue to confront a racial cleavage. Roughly 1.5 million nonwhite immigrants had become a permanent part of British life. Their presence in the central cities, their problems of poverty, language, and discrimination, as well as issues of housing, education, assimilation, and of law and order all implied that the situation of the nonwhite Commonwealth immigrants would remain as a visible political cleavage.

Obviously, British politics are far from placid and the policy agenda contains numerous and significant political conflicts. Some of these are implied by the subjects we have already treated; others would find their place within a more encyclopedic examination of the subject. Here we will present several of the central conflicts of British political life.

Political Party Conflict   As we have seen, the political parties embody diverse interests and ideas. They express these most explicitly during the periodic general elections in which they seek to win popular support, elect MPs, and obtain control of (or at least influence) governmental power.

This clash between programmatic parties is exemplified with unusual sharpness and clarity when we examine the general elections held in February and October 1974. Although a British Parliament may last for a maximum period of five years, it is actually the prime minister who determines when to call the election (and who then advises the Queen to do so—advice which she is required to follow). Thus, in early February 1974 the Conservative prime minister advised the Queen to dissolve Parliament and call for a nationwide general election on February 28. Heath did so largely because of mounting public conflict and debate over a coal miners' strike to which he had reacted by placing Britain on a three day work week to conserve fuel.

The election campaign touched off dramatic cries of class warfare and of claims that Britain's economic and political system was about to collapse. This invective was widely presented in American reports on the election but by and large it reflected alarmist views rather than an accurate analysis of the situation. The February 1974 electoral contest has been called the "Reds under the bed" election.[42]

Prime Minister Heath and the Conservatives hammered away at the theme of "who rules Britain?"—the elected government or a group of powerful trade unions. Labour, in its turn, hammered away at Heath for unnecessarily precipitating a confrontation with the miners. The BLP pointed to Conservative economic mismanagement, including a gigantic balance of payments deficit, the three day work week, and unprecedented inflation. Foreign policy scarcely figured in the election except in that Labour's manifesto pledged to seek renegotiation of Britain's Common Market membership. Because of this issue, Conservative rebel Enoch Powell implicitly urged loyal Tories to vote Labour, on the grounds that

42 Peter Paterson, *New Statesman* (London), February 15, 1974.

this was the last election at which the British had the chance to avoid becoming "one province in a new European superstate." [43]

The confrontation with the miners reflected a strong undercurrent of class antagonism. Only two months prior to the elections, an opinion poll had indicated that two-thirds of the British felt there was such a thing as "the class struggle." A year earlier, nearly half (47 percent) of working class voters had agreed with the statement that it is the rich, the aristocrats, and civil servants who rule Britain and that "it doesn't matter what happens at elections." [44]

It had been widely anticipated that the confrontation between government and trade unions, expressed in the "who rules Britain" slogan would produce an anti-union backlash and a substantial Tory victory. Despite opinion polls forecasting a narrow Conservative victory, surprisingly Labour won. Evidently voters had found Heath at least partly to blame for the miners' strike, particularly after calculations by an official government Prices and Incomes Board had found a substantial (£5 per week) government overstatement of the miners' real wages.[45] In addition, the Conservatives had been hurt by increased inflation, worsening trade figures, and the anti–Common Market campaign of Enoch Powell.

The workings and paradoxes of the British electoral systems were neatly reflected in the results of the election. (See Table 2–4.) Although Labour candidates received fewer votes than the Conservatives (37.2 percent versus 38.2 percent) they nonetheless won a plurality of seats in the House of Commons, 301 versus 297. (This was not entirely unique: in 1951, the Conservatives had won fewer votes than Labour yet gained an actual *majority* of seats.) Labour, however, lacked a majority of the 635 seats. Despite calls by a few political figures for a coalition government of moderates of all parties and the suggestion of the Liberal leader, Jeremy Thorpe, for a government of national unity, both Wilson and Heath were unreceptive. Labour then succeeded in forming a minority government able to govern Britain for the next eight months.

At once, the somewhat heated language of political conflict subsided. Newspapers that had been villifying Wilson and the Labour Party once again painted them in more restrained and accurate terms. Britain's most prestigious newspaper, *The Times* of London, which had supported the Conservatives, nonetheless went on to admire Wilson's skill and judgment and offered its reassurances to "those in Britain or abroad who fear a Labour government":

[43] Quoted, *New York Times*, February 24, 1974.
[44] Gallup and N.O.P. polls, *New Statesman*, February 15, 1974.
[45] *The Times* (London), February 23, 1974.

This will not by any means be a government of wild men. Mr. Wilson himself is a political moderate, cautious in his political actions and conservative in his personal tastes and style of life. The principal members of his government . . . [are] thoroughly responsible and experienced moderate[s]. The Labour administration will include people of the highest ability.[46]

Nor was this resumption of a moderate political vocabulary confined to the media. In Parliament, Edward Heath, whose government had been more prone to confrontation than its postwar Conservative predecessors, nonetheless offered Prime Minister Wilson congratulations and understanding "due to any member assuming the immense responsibility of the first minister of the Crown." [47] Within a few weeks Wilson had made it clear that his government's policies would be moderate and low key: settlement of the miners' strike, resumption of a regular industrial work week, increased pensions, a rent freeze, subsidies to prevent price rises on bread, cheese, and milk, price controls, and modest price or tax increases on liquor, tobacco, fuel, and postage. These moderate actions neutralized the Conservative opposition, who feared that if they did manage to team up with Liberals, Nationalists, Ulster Unionists, and others in the House of Commons to force the resignation of the Labour government, the British electorate would not welcome an almost immediate repeat of the general election.

As if to confirm this pattern of heated electoral competition followed by practical moderation, the October 1974 general election presented a comparable pattern of events. Once again, journalistic accounts displayed an alarmist picture of British political conflict. One American newsmagazine report left an impression of British political power in the hands of the trade unions and the country on the verge of Communist revolution or military coup.[48] British novelist Kingsley Amis observed that he could not bring himself "to vote in what will probably be our last democratic election." [49] And newspaper columnist Bernard Levin found ". . . the chances of catastrophe are high," with "the probabilities of disaster . . . considerably higher if Labour is in power." [50] Even *The Times* of London wondered whether Britain's social democracy could survive. The paper pointed to a national crisis in which it found the trade unions too strong, taxes too high, incentives to invest too low. These constituted a system which lacked the rewards of capitalism and the disciplines of socialism.

[46] *The Times* (London), March 5, 1974. Italics added.
[47] *The Times* (London), March 7, 1974.
[48] The account appeared in *US News and World Report,* and is discussed in *The Times* (London), October 9, 1974.
[49] Quoted in *Newsweek*, October 21, 1974, p. 46.
[50] *The Times* (London), October 9, 1974.

The Times found a probability that the UK would be unable to maintain its present system: either Britain would become more socialist, like Yugoslavia, or more free, like the Federal Republic of Germany under its earlier Christian Democratic governments. It concluded by observing that "castrated capitalism" was ineffective. Yet Britain's political leaders remained committed to an "old consensus" which was based on an unstable combination of full employment, free collective bargaining, free elections, and reasonably stable prices.[51]

Labourites and Conservatives in conflict. While the governing Labourites and opposition Conservatives retained deep divisions within, each presented a distinctive program. The Labour Party manifesto projected a democratic socialist image and a commitment to fundamental change:

> We are a democratic socialist party and our objective is to bring about a fundamental and irreversible shift in the balance of wealth and power in favor of working people and their families.[52]

However, the specifics of the program were more limited. Among the most important was a "social contract" between the government and trade unions, which in effect meant voluntary wage restraint in exchange for improved social services, a more equal sharing of national wealth, and policies of full employment. Other significant provisions included nationalization of mineral rights, ports, shipbuilding and aircraft industries; an annual tax on wealth above £100,000; extra taxes on companies extracting oil from the North Sea; improved inflation-proof pension plans; the end of the "11-plus" examination and other means of selection in secondary education; public ownership of development land (except for owner occupiers); legislation to improve the status of women; elected assemblies for Scotland and Wales; and renegotiation of Britain's Common Market membership (the results of which would be put to the electorate for a binding decision within 12 months).[53]

The Conservative manifesto provided an alternative, elements of which might have fit a U.S. Democratic Party program. It accepted the existing welfare state and advocated a Tax Credit scheme ("the most advanced anti-poverty programme . . . in . . . any western Country"), providing cash automatically and without means testing, to pensioners, low income families, and families with children. The manifesto expressed particular concern that the mixed economy not be extended by further nationalization and that the existing private enterprise sectors be preserved. It

[51] *The Times* (London), October 8, 1974.
[52] *Labour Party Manifesto* (London), October 1974, pp. 29–30.
[53] Principal provisions of the Labour Party manifesto are summarized in *The Economist* (London), September 21, 1974.

sought to safeguard the existence of a free society, control inflation, avoid confrontation with the trade unions but reduce welfare payments to strikers and obtain a voluntary restraint on wages and prices (though it did not rule out legal restraint if this failed). It held out the possibility of cuts in public spending and of increased taxes and warned against a political challenge from the left to the balance between economic freedom and social provisions. It pledged to close tax loopholes on North Sea oil and to facilitate greater opportunities for trade union consultation by business firms. It advocated a Scottish assembly, equal pay for women, and the continuation of a selection process in secondary education in order to encourage brighter students. Finally, the party offered a coalition government—based on a Conservative parliamentary majority—and observed that "the Conservative ideal is a property-owning democracy." [54]

On election day, this contest produced a Labour victory and a Labour parliamentary majority of 319 of the 635 seats in the House of Commons. In the end the key factor was somewhat less the different programs of the parties than the voters' view of Wilson and Heath. While 44 percent of the public thought the Labour government was running the country well, only 32 percent felt the Tories could do so. Meanwhile, 54 percent believed Wilson was doing a good job as prime minister whereas only 33 percent believed Heath would do so. [55]

Economic Conflict: Government and the Trade Unions   The intimate relationship between economics and politics is well illustrated in the repeated conflict over the role of trade unions. Since the late 1960's this subject has been particularly salient. It finds expression in two closely related issues: free collective bargaining and wage restraint.

During the 1960's the British economy had experienced a substantial problem of unofficial strikes. Many of these were called by small groups of workers and shop stewards over minor disputes within a local enterprise. Typically the work stoppage lacked authorization of the national trade union headquarters, or even the vote of the majority of workers involved at the site. The number of working days lost was not extreme, but the effect on production was often disruptive since a sudden walkout by a small group of workers at an auto plant (for example, upholstery installers) could idle thousands of others and shut down an entire production line. These wildcat strikes accounted for roughly two-thirds of all working days lost through strike action.

[54] The Conservative manifesto is reprinted in *The Times* (London), September 11, 1974.
[55] Figures from Opinion Research Centre, cited in *The Times* (London), October 3, 1974.

In 1969, the Labour government sought to deal with this problem by proposing legislation to require registration of trade unions, cooling-off periods, and strike ballots (a system similar to that in the United States). But these proposals, outlined in a government report called "In Place of Strife," were bitterly resisted by the unions as infringements upon their freedoms. This caused deep divisions within the Labour government, which then backed down.

Inequities also developed because workers represented by powerful unions or those with strategic places in the economy could often succeed in strike actions while other workers, sometimes more deserving of increases, lacked the same bargaining power. This problem also threatened to produce higher inflation and ultimately a danger to full employment.

Lacking the trade union link that had restrained Labour, the Conservative government of 1970–1974 attempted to limit trade union bargaining power by allowing unemployment to increase and by passing an Industrial Relations Act.[56] This 1971 Act, which in part resembled the 1969 Labour proposal, also banned closed shops, made employer-union agreements legally enforceable, banned unofficial strikes, and increased the tax burden of unions that failed to register. It met with bitter opposition from the TUC and almost the entire trade union movement; in the face of a virtually complete refusal of unions to register, the Act's provisions became unworkable. Ultimately, the Labour government repealed the legislation in mid-1974 and the Conservatives did not even include its reinstatement in their October 1974 manifesto. More broadly, this conflict reflected the nature of British collectivist politics: in a free society, the willing cooperation of the major interest groups involved is usually essential if government is to succeed in its operation of the managed economy and welfare state.

The related problem of free collective bargaining versus wage restraint was also vividly illustrated when the Heath government clashed head on with the unions during several dramatic strikes. The most important was a miners' strike during the winter of 1973–1974. British coal miners had traditionally suffered from low pay, difficult working conditions, and serious risk of injury, disability, and death. Their case had been at the heart of the 1926 General Strike and their cause had deep emotional roots in the Labour and trade union movements; they also had some public sympathy. In any case, Prime Minister Heath sought to have the National Coal Board, which runs the nationalized coal industry, reject the miners' wage demand as excessively inflationary. The miners thereupon struck

[56] The circumstances surrounding this Act are lucidly treated in *The Economist* (London), April 27, 1974, pp. 78–79.

for considerably higher wages—at the height of the 1973–1974 energy crisis—and the Heath government responded by encouraging a three day work week, power blackouts, and other efforts to reduce coal use and defeat the miners' strike. Ironically, by one calculation, these measures cost 800 times more than the expense of meeting the miners' pay demands.[57]

Inside and outside Britain this confrontation was portrayed as a clash over the question of "Who Rules Britain?" Indeed, as we have seen, this clash was depicted in alarmist terms. Nonetheless, these descriptions may have been seriously overdrawn. The clash was avoidable and revised economic calculations—released during the February 1974 election—indicated that the miners' pay demands did not entirely exceed the government's own salary guidelines. In any event, Heath called a General Election to contest the issue and was narrowly and unexpectedly defeated by Labour. To some extent, the British electorate blamed Heath for having failed to avoid a clash with the miners.

Labour thus regained office facing what one observer described lucidly as the Social Democratic Dilemma:

> This dilemma, in its simplest form, is how to reconcile the maintenance of a full employment welfare state (the political objective of the trade union movement) with the maximization of money wages through free collective bargaining (the industrial objective of trade unions).[58]

For a time the Wilson government did its best to ignore this dilemma while inflation accelerated, the economy stagnated, and unemployment grew. Wilson was determined to avoid statutory limitation on collective bargaining yet his interim measures, such as a mid-1974 voluntary "social contract" between government and the TUC, failed.

Ultimately, in mid 1975, when the rate of inflation had reached a staggering 26 percent, Wilson acted to achieve an agreed limitation on wage increases. Crucially, he did so with the support of the TUC and of a key left-wing trade union leader, Jack Jones of the huge (1.8 million member) T & GWU, and of the leader of the left wing of the Labour Party, Michael Foot. In their view, a failure to act would threaten the British economy so seriously as to cause mass unemployment, social disruption, and the eventual election of a right-wing Conservative government committed to antisocialist and anti–trade union policies, probably involving not only wage freezes but cuts in social services as well. As

[57] The calculations were those of Professor Nicholas Kaldor, a Labour Party economist critical of the Heath government. See *New York Times*, December 19, 1973.
[58] Peter Jenkins, *New Statesman* (London), September 20, 1974.

Jack Jones told the TUC, "We can't afford the luxury of handing power over to Mrs. Thatcher." [59]

While the union's voluntary acceptance of wage restraint temporarily resolved the social democratic dilemma, the choices which this dilemma had posed were and are far more than technical and economic. What remained was a genuine question of authority between a democratically elected government and powerful institutionalized groups embodying concentrated economic power. The matter is as applicable to mammoth multinational business corporations as to powerful trade unions. The Labour prime minister, Harold Wilson, put the issue squarely when he appealed to the coal miners in July 1975 not to push for wage increases of 66 to 90 percent being advocated by a militant group of miners. Wilson termed the proposals "crazy, even suicidal" for the miners and the nation and argued for restraint in view of a larger political concern:

> The issue now is not whether this or any other democratic socialist govern-
> ment can survive and lead the nation to full employment and a greater
> measure of social justice. It is whether any government so constituted,
> so dedicated to the principles of consent and consensus within our
> democracy, can lead this nation. [60]

By American and Western European standards British trade unionists are by no means highly paid. And, trade union power has been a prime means of personal self-esteem against the influence and power of the upper classes as well as of protecting and promoting working class political and economic interests. Free collective bargaining has also been regarded as an inalienable right, which workers enjoy as one of the benefits of a free society. Thus the at least temporary acceptance of incomes policy by the TUC and leaders of the Labour left has not come lightly. The issue of voluntary compliance and the trade-offs among full employment, free collective bargaining and inflation are likely to ensure that conflict over the role of trade unions will remain of central importance.

Institutional Conflict: The Electoral System   By contrast with many other political systems—for example, France—Britain's political institutions are broadly accepted and are not called into question by competing groups or parties. In part this stems from a long and gradual process of constitutional evolution. However, at times there are calls for change, and in the early twentieth century these produced a curtailment of the powers of the then

[59] *The Economist* (London), September 6, 1975.
[60] Quoted in *The Economist*, July 12, 1975. Also see *New York Times*, July 8, 1974.

largely hereditary House of Lords and a sometimes bitter conflict over women's suffrage.

Recently, growing attention has been devoted to Britain's electoral system, which usually produces majority governments in Parliament but which also brings about a distribution of seats in the House of Commons that does not fully reflect the distribution of the popular vote. As we have seen, the Liberal Party has been particularly hindered by this system. Not surprisingly it is the Liberals, as well as a number of influential journals and newspapers, who have recently called for change.

This parliamentary maldistribution occurs because of Britain's *single-member district system* of election. The country is divided into 635 separate geographic constituencies, each of which elects one MP. In this sense it resembles the American system of electing the 435 members of the House of Representatives. In Britain each local party selects a candidate and indeed anyone can run for Parliament provided he or she pays a deposit of £150 (a little more than $300) which is later refunded if the candidate gains 12.5 percent or more of the vote. On the day of the nationwide general election, voters cast their ballots. The person who gains the most votes in each constituency is elected MP. There is no runoff—as in France—between the highest contenders if one lacks a majority (50 percent plus one) of the vote, nor is there any system of proportional representation (as in Germany). The result is that all votes for losing candidates are wasted. In practice, Liberal candidates frequently run third or even a strong second, but there are not many areas in which their votes reach a plurality.

One result of this pattern is that voters are reluctant to waste their votes on a Liberal candidate if he or she has little chance of election, or, indeed, if the party has no realistic chance to form a government. Opinion polls indicate that many potential Liberal votes are thus lost. Voters see the election as a contest between Labour and the Conservatives. In response to this, Liberals have begun to advocate a system involving some kind of proportional representation—that is, one which would give them representation in Parliament on a level roughly comparable to their share of the popular vote. They frequently point to the case of the comparable German liberal party (the FDP) which, by receiving between 5 and 10 percent of the German vote has been able to hold a position of major power within various coalition governments. Comparable instances exist in Italy and Scandinavia.

The prospects of electoral change, however, appear unlikely. In general, the British electoral system has tended to encourage the formation of stable governments based on one party in Parliament holding a majority of seats even though lacking a majority of popular votes. Not since 1935 has the governing party actually enjoyed a majority of the popular vote. Even the Labour landslide of 1945, which gained the party 394 of the then 640 seats in Parliament, was based on only 46.1 percent of the vote. Similarly, the big Conservative victory of 1959 (365 of 630 seats) rested on a less than popular majority of 49.4 percent. Indeed, in October 1974 Labour gained a majority of seats (319 of 635) with only 39.3 percent of the vote. (See Table 2–5.)

This system has been justified on the grounds that it provides stable majority government based on programmatic parties which voters can hold electorally responsible for the success or failure of their policies. By contrast the experience of continental European countries such as Weimar Germany (1918–1933), France under the Fourth Republic (1946–1958) and contemporary Italy are often cited as negative examples. In these cases a host of parties competed within a system of proportional representation and this often led to unstable coalition governments and a lack of programmatic and responsible parties.

In Britain, conflict over the nature of the electoral system has only become more noticeable with the rise of the Liberal vote and some expressions of concern over the possibilities of extremism. In the words of *The Times* of London, electoral reform in Britain is urgent "to make sure that the Allende disaster could not happen in Britain." Pointing to a situation in which a powerful extremist minority within a party might control a

TABLE 2–5 Relationship Between Votes and Parliamentary Seats Won—General Election October 1974

	Voter Turnout	% of Popular Vote	No. of Seats Won	% of Seats Won	No. of Votes Per Seat Won to Nearest Thousand
Labour	11,458,704	39.3	319	50.2	36,000
Conservative	10,458,548	35.8	276	43.5	38,000
Liberal	5,348,193	18.3	13	2.0	411,000
Scot. Nat. (SNP)	839,628	2.9	11	1.7	76,000
Welsh Nat. (Plaid C.)	166,321	0.6	3	0.5	55,000
Communist	17,426	0.06	—	—	—
Others	885,620	3.0	13	2.0	68,000
Total	29,174,440	100.0	635	100.0	46,000 *

* Average

Source: Computed from results of the election of October 10, 1974, in *The Times* (London), October 14, 1974.

government elected with a minority of votes but a majority of seats,[61] *The Times* has argued for change, as has the prestigious weekly news magazine, *The Economist*.

Despite these arguments, proposals for revising the electoral system are unlikely to be acted upon without the wholehearted support of either of the two major parties. Yet neither is likely to favor changing a system which they see as having worked successfully for generations and which gives them the chance of forming a majority government to carry out the policies for which they stand. Adoption of a system involving greater proportionality would essentially eliminate their hopes for majority government. Lacking majorities of the vote *and* majorities in Parliament, each of the major parties could hope for no more than a minority or coalition government. Indeed, even if a major party favored a change it could only carry this out if the proposal could obtain a parliamentary majority of passage. Yet a majority government would be unlikely to propose unilaterally a scheme almost guaranteed to eliminate its parliamentary majority at the next election.

Only if an election produced a stalemate—in which Liberals held the balance of power in the House of Commons and could bargain their support for a coalition government on the condition that electoral reform be adopted—could there be a change in this situation. Yet on the one occasion when this might have been possible (February 1974), when the Liberals held 14 seats and both Labour and the Conservatives were short of a majority, the leaders of the major parties were unreceptive to such a solution and it was never in fact a serious possibility. In the event, Labour established an effective minority government which remained in office until the party's subsequent victory in the October 1974 election.

Ethnic and Regional Conflict: Northern Ireland We have already seen how a regional cleavage made the subject of Scottish nationalism politically significant. But the conflict engendered by that cleavage has been minor compared to the turmoil over Northern Ireland. There, a recurrent and almost tribal conflict between Catholics and Protestants had, by the mid-1970's, produced a bloody confrontation, which periodically spilled over into England.

For centuries the English domination of Ireland has been the cause of sporadic conflict. From the mid-fifteenth century a religious dimension was added as most of the Irish remained Catholic while England became Protestant. In the mid-seventeenth century Cromwell suppressed the Irish and the British sought to cope with their Irish problem by settling

<hr>

[61] September 19, 1974.

large numbers of Protestant Scots and English in Northeast Ireland on land taken from the Irish. In 1689, an Irish uprising temporarily broke the English and Protestant domination of Ireland, but at the Battle of the Boyne (July 1, 1690), the English under King William III defeated the Catholics of James II and reimposed their control.

England maintained a relatively harsh rule of Ireland, partly out of fear that the Irish might ally with England's continental enemies. Ireland became part of the UK in 1800; then in the 1840's a serious potato famine hit Ireland. Millions of Irish emigrated to America, a million others died.

In the late nineteenth century, pressure for independence, in the form of "Home Rule" for Ireland, produced turmoil at Westminster as Irish MPs sought to obstruct parliamentary procedure until they achieved this goal. The pre–World War I Liberal government was committed to Home Rule, but during 1912–1914 Ireland came to the brink of civil war.

One million Protestants remained in Northern Ireland (an area known as Ulster) and by 1912, a 100,000 man Ulster Volunteer Force had armed itself to resist independence and Catholic rule. The outbreak of World War I intervened before a confrontation could take place. Finally, in 1921, Ireland gained virtual independence, with dominion status inside the British Empire. However, most of Ulster (6 of the 32 Irish counties) remained part of the UK. Civil war broke out in Southern Ireland between opponents and supporters of this partition. Ultimately, in 1948 the Irish Republic became fully independent but Ulster remained firmly British.

This lengthy historical record is important not only for an understanding of the contemporary conflict but because memories of this background remain very much alive. Thus each year the Ulster Protestants passionately celebrate the Battle of the Boyne of 1690.

In the late 1960's, conflict erupted in Ulster between Catholics and Protestants. The Northern Irish Catholic minority of a half million had endured a half century of discrimination in jobs, housing, and voting rights at the hands of the one million Protestants. These demands were first sought peacefully, and some of them were granted, but communal violence broke out. On the one hand, extremists of the Irish Republican Army (IRA) wanted to suppress the Protestants and achieve full union with the three million people of the Irish Republic (95 percent of whom are Catholic). On the other hand, Protestant extremist groups sought to protect their interests and subdue the Catholics. Both sides were caught up in a spiral of ethnic hatred, and bombings and murders began to take an increased toll.

Although Ulster had been governed by the Stormont, a regional— Protestant dominated—parliament of its own, the British government finally intervened in an attempt to restore order. In 1969 it used British troops to quell urban disturbances in Ulster and subsequently took over direct rule there. At first, British troops were welcomed by the Catholics as a defense against Protestant extremists, but a process of escalating violence, IRA provocation, and detention of IRA suspects without trial soon made the troops the target of Catholic hatred.

By 1975, a wave of shootings and bombings had destroyed many buildings and factories and killed 200 soldiers and 1000 civilians in Northern Ireland. The conflict seemed almost endless. Each side saw itself an embattled minority: the half million Catholics as a minority within Ulster, the million Protestants as a minority within a potentially unified Ireland. Each side was armed in secret parliamentary groups: such as the Catholic Provisional IRA and the Protestant Ulster Defense Association (UDA) and Ulster Volunteer Force (UVF). And for both sides it was a struggle continually played out between working class populations.

While the level of violence was not unendurable for the British army (the 24 army dead in 1973, for example, were far fewer than the 96 UK soldiers killed in traffic accidents elsewhere in Europe),[62] the IRA hoped to provoke Britain into withdrawing its troops from Ulster. Thus it launched a sporadic bombing campaign in cities such as Birmingham and London.

Because there was no major disagreement among the British political parties, conflict over Northern Ireland did not threaten the stability of British politics. Successive governments felt obligated to retain a presence in Northern Ireland in order to forestall a possible bloodbath between the Catholic and Protestant communities; nonetheless the violence and uncertainty placed an unwelcome burden upon the British political system as it sought to deal with other political issues.

Other Conflicts The analysis of conflicts involving party competition, the trade unions, the electoral system, and the Irish problem by no means exhausts the list of important matters which constitute the live substance of British politics. To these we could easily add conflicts over the educational system, income distribution (for example, the wealth tax), the debate between competing notions of equality of opportunity and equality of condition, and even disputes between divergent wings of the Labour Party. Internationally, we could consider the continuing issue of Britain's world role, particularly in its relationship to the Common Market and the United States. However, such a list would be too extensive to complete here. We will therefore turn to an analysis of the policy

[62] *New York Times*, June 25, 1975.

Youngsters throwing stones at British troops in Northern Ireland.
Transworld

process to illustrate how the vital problems, cleavages, and conflicts are resolved within the British political system.

policy process

In the previous section we have seen the wide array of issues on the British policy agenda. Now we must examine the formal and informal means by which these issues are resolved in the policy process and some of the institutions and methods by which this resolution takes place.

INITIATION OF ISSUES

Policy-making in Britain occurs within a relatively open, pluralistic, and democratic political system. As in the United States the initiation of issues can take place through many channels. Newspapers, interest groups, political parties, individuals, bureaucracies, the government of the day, and even transnational actors may, under varying circumstances, initiate policy proposals. These diverse sources have been reflected in such specific cases as a campaign by an individual member of the House of Lords against pornography, an ultimately successful drive by an MP (allied with a pressure group) to abolish capital punishment, and a spy case in which newspaper revelations were central factors in bringing the issue into the public realm.

Despite this diversity, most policy proposals originate either as a response to external events or as conscious choices of political party and governmental leaderships. In the first instance, the consequences of the Middle East war of October 1973 and the oil price rise achieved by the Organization of Petroleum Exporting Countries (OPEC) in effect forced the government to propose energy saving measures and increased energy taxes. More commonly, policy initiation follows general paths suggested by party programs and manifestoes and the specific proposals of the prime minister and cabinet. Measures to achieve greater equality and equal pay for women appeared in the 1974 Labour and Conservative manifestoes and led to specific legislative proposals. By contrast, the campaign by the Liberals and some of the press to secure a revision of the electoral system has not moved further into the policy process because it lacks the backing of a major party or of the cabinet. One or both of these would be necessary to formulate this proposal and bring it into serious parliamentary deliberation.

The response to some issues, particularly in the day to day conduct of foreign and economic policy, does not involve legislation but instead action by the prime minister, cabinet, or the various government ministries and the civil service. In these realms, initiation of policy falls within the hands of relatively small numbers of political and administrative élites, acting more or less in private.

DELIBERATION

In an official and literal sense, formal deliberation on policy proposals occurs in Parliament—at least for all proposals that take the form of legislation. The House of Commons, with its 635 elected members, provides the chief forum for this debate and deliberation. Legislation and resolutions introduced by the government and opposition leadership, as well as a small number of proposals put forward by individual MPs (private members' bills), are discussed and sometimes amended in committee (though these are far less independent, specialized, and important than their American counterparts). They are dealt with in successive stages or "readings" on the floor of the House of Commons. The House of Lords also deliberates on all legislation and may provide substantive amendments to improve or revise technical points in a bill, but the Lords' powers are very limited.

The process of parliamentary deliberation and debate receives attention in the press and can provide dramatic speeches and political jousting between the leaders of government and opposition. But, as we shall see, there are real limits on the autonomy of Parliament. Thus the parliamentary deliberation does not usually lead to amendment of legislative proposals unless these changes are accepted by the government.

Much of the effective deliberation takes place behind the scenes and in private. In particular, this occurs in the cabinet, or in cabinet committees, where the prime minister and other government ministers consider or debate government proposals before submitting them to Parliament or directing their civil servants to carry out the more important political actions that fall within their jurisdiction. Other nonpublic deliberation takes place within party caucuses of the House of Commons. These include the Parliamentary Labour Party (PLP) and the Conservative 1922 Committee (a caucus of all Tory MPs except those holding positions in government or—when the party is in opposition—the shadow cabinet). The party caucuses meet periodically to debate and sometimes to vote upon policies to be followed by their party in Parliament.

Deliberation also can take place outside government and Parliament. Debates at annual party conferences are important in shaping policies and manifestoes which later influence (although they do not determine) government actions.

Other major areas of deliberation, however, are nonpublic and yet highly significant. These include the upper echelons of the civil service where—for example, at the Treasury—significant deliberation shaping government economic policies may occur. Equally crucial are the private consultations between government and interest groups through the processes of functional representation. Leading officials of the TUC and of the CBI (Confederation of British Industries) regularly meet with high civil servants and government ministers to negotiate over policies in which the government requires their cooperation. Typically, incomes policy, or other agreements on price and wage restraint, are almost completely determined in these consultations. The results, if they require political endorsement or legislation, are presented to party conferences or to Parliament as a *fait accompli*. There is then little or no room for meaningful deliberation in these arenas.

APPROVAL

Before most policy proposals can become law they require the approval of both houses of Parliament and of the monarch. The popularly elected House of Commons is where the real, effective process of approval takes place. While the House of Lords also needs to approve legislation, its true powers are minimal and it possesses only a suspensive veto by which it can briefly delay certain kinds of legislation. Even these powers are rarely used. The House of Lords is a largely hereditary, partly appointive, and mostly aristocratic body whose members serve for life. In 1911 its powers were sharply curtailed and if—as a nondemocratic body—it were to abuse its remaining privileges, it would face House of Commons actions which would virtually reform it out of existence. On occasion, however, the Lords do serve a useful function in providing reflective debate and amendment of legislation. They have also initiated private members bills on potentially troublesome subjects (such as abortion, divorce, homosexuality) which the government of the day preferred to avoid introducing itself.

Final approval of legislation must also be granted by the monarch. The Queen is Head of State and government actions are largely taken in her name. Yet she has virtually no independent powers. Government legislative proposals are outlined on the first day of Parliament in the Queen's speech—which is written for her by the government—and thus one finds such anomalies as a monarch in royal attire speaking amidst ancient settings and procedures, yet saying that "my government" plans to re-nationalize the steel industry immediately. This disparity between formal and effective power has been described in the words of Walter Bagehot, a leading nineteenth century student of British politics, as the difference between "dignified" and "efficient" powers. Thus the ceremonial trappings of Lords and Queen are chiefly symbolic and the real, "efficient" power is held in the more low key, less celebrated realms of Commons, cabinet, and civil service.

The entire process of parliamentary deliberation and approval is less important and its outcome far more routine than is the case in the United States. Ironically, even though Parliament is constitutionally supreme, its decisions are usually predetermined by the government of the day. In Britain there is no constitutional separation of legislative and executive powers. The prime minister and his cabinet embody the leadership of the majority party in the House of Commons and govern because they can rely on the votes of a majority of MPs. Because of party discipline, and sometimes through decisions reached in caucuses of the parliamentary parties, MPs are not usually free to vote as they please. Instead they are expected to follow the decisions of the leadership of their parliamentary party. If they violate party unity by disobeying instructions from the party Whip (one of their party's parliamentary leaders) they may later face serious sanctions, including expulsion from the party caucus and non-readoption as their party's candidate for the House of Commons in the next general election.

Because of the lack of independence of most MPs it has been said that each party could manage nearly as well with a flock of sheep to drive through the House of Commons lobby to be counted in parliamentary votes. However, this exaggerates the situation. If a party's MPs strongly oppose specific proposals their leadership will often back down rather than risk an embarrassing party split or rebellion. Even so, one recent study has shown that MPs broke with party discipline on 586 different occasions during the period from 1945 to 1974.[63] While there was relatively little dissension in the 1950's, when as few as 2 percent of all parliamentary divisions involved violations of party unity, this figure climbed to a high of 20 percent for the 1970–1974 period. During this period, the ruling Conservative government of Edward Heath saw no fewer than two-thirds of its rank and file members of Parliament vote against it at least once.

In one particularly dramatic case in October 1971, the House of Commons approved British membership in the Common Market only because 69 Labour MPs broke party ranks and voted alongside the Conservatives and an additional 20 abstained. These votes more than offset the 39 anti–Common Market Conservative MPs whose votes, added to

[63] See *The Economist*, October 11, 1975. These and the following figures are based on Philip Norton, *Dissension in the House of Commons, 1945–74* (London: Macmillan, 1975).

those of the Labour opposition, would otherwise have caused the defeat of British entry.[64]

In theory, parliamentary approval is required to keep a government in office. In the event it loses the support of a majority of the House of Commons, as expressed in a vote of confidence or on an important piece of legislation, the government resigns and is replaced by another one enjoying a majority or else a new general election is called. *In practice*, no British government has lost a vote of confidence since 1924 (and that government was a minority Labour administration relying on Liberal support). The previous case before that dates to 1885. Even in the celebrated May 1940 case in which the Conservative government of Neville Chamberlain was replaced by one under Winston Churchill, the government was not actually defeated but instead suffered the embarrassing defection of 41 Tory MPs and the abstention of 60 others. More recently in 1969, the Wilson government was forced to withdraw legislation on reforming the House of Lords, because of the opposition and filibustering of left-wing Labourites and right-wing Tories. The same government also abandoned a bill on industrial relations because of bitter opposition from trade union MPs within the PLP. The Heath government (1970–1974) was defeated in the House of Commons on five different occasions and Wilson's minority government (March–October 1974) was on the losing end of several parliamentary votes. In each of these cases, the issue of approving or disapproving a specific policy proposal was simply not regarded as serious enough to cause the government's downfall and the government retained a working parliamentary majority or plurality.

The formal process of parliamentary approval should not cause us to ignore other formal and informal mechanisms. In an unprecedented procedure, Britain resorted to a June 1975 public referendum to decide on whether to remain in the Common Market. Labour's October 1974 manifesto had pledged an electoral decision after the terms of membership had been renegotiated and the Wilson government honored that pledge. In the end, the British electorate voted two to one in favor of remaining in the Common Market; this referendum approval more or less ended a bitter public debate as well as a sharp division within the BLP itself.

As we have seen, the processes of deliberation and approval may also be informal. Without the approval of the major interest groups involved, government policies may often fail, as was the case in the 1971 Industrial

---

[64] See especially, Uwe Kitzinger, *Diplomacy and Persuasion: How Britain Joined the Common Market* (London: Thames and Hudson, 1973), pp. 400ff.

Relations Act with the Conservative government's failure to secure trade union support. In addition, public opinion polls, the media, mass demonstrations, letter writing, petitions, lobbying, and other forms of public and private expression all constitute forms of approval and disapproval to which any government must pay serious attention if it is to maintain its effectiveness, keep the loyalty of its supporters, and face the next election with prospects of possible reelection.

APPLICATION

The implementation, or actual carrying out, of a policy proposal does not follow precisely and automatically after its approval. Almost invariably a certain amount of adaptation is required in applying general policies to specific cases. In addition, the judgments, preferences, and methods of operation of those administering policy will significantly shape outcomes. In the British case, a change in governmental power between the Conservative and Labour parties will bring into office a surprisingly small number of people. These comprise the prime minister, a cabinet of perhaps 20 ministers (almost every one responsible for the supervision of a vast administrative bureaucracy) and several dozen junior ministers and assistants—a total of no more than 100 politicians in all. They are drawn from among the majority party's ranks in Parliament and only a few of them will have had genuine expertise in the areas for which they are responsible (such as economics, trade, defense, education, welfare, technology, transport, health, and industry).

In order to carry out their mandate and policies, the elected political leaders of Britain must rely upon the civil service, a huge, well educated, and permanent corps of administrators and officials who carry out the actual tasks of operating governmental services and applying policy. Each of the major administrative departments of government is headed by a minister, who is a political figure and who sits in the cabinet, but his or her policies are implemented by an administrative hierarchy headed by a permanent secretary, deputy secretaries, under secretaries, and various lesser officials. In coping with the tasks of setting policy and directing a department that may have thousands of civil servants, the minister will be aided by no more than two or three junior ministers (who also sit in Parliament) and sometimes by several private assistants. Otherwise the minister is totally dependent upon the permanent civil servants.

The British civil service itself, particularly in its several thousand higher level personnel, is renowned for its qualities of diligence, honesty, self-confidence and unflapability. In particular, its élite officials are highly educated individuals, who are often described as having "Rolls Royce minds." Yet this civil service does not function as a wholly neutral instrument ready to be sent in whichever direction the political leaders of the day indicate. The politicians, after all, come and go, while the permanent civil servants remain. The bureaucracy builds up considerable momentum of its own and frequently limits the initiative of government ministers.[65]

Typically, only a minority of ministers establish mastery over the departments for which they are responsible. Accounts of the experience of the 1964–1970 Labour government by several political insiders bemoan the way in which the weight and power of the civil servants often dominated not only the application of government policies but also crushed or altered innovative proposals. Barbara Castle, a well known Labourite and former government minister, has reminisced:

> I thought, looking back at the Labour government, how effectively the civil servants impeded us by saying we could not do some of the things our successors are now doing with remarkable facility. Floating the pound: something we were told would bring total disaster. . . . Tax reform: we were told we couldn't have a wealth tax, the Inland Revenue wouldn't stand any more changes. . . .[66]

One means of dealing with this situation has been the recently increased practice of a new minister bringing several key personal assistants into office with him in order to extend his ability to plan and control. But even this procedure has its limits. As Richard Crossman, a leading Labour intellectual and former minister of housing and of social services commented, "You sit there with them [the assistants] and the Department makes sure nothing happens." [67]

To be sure, the civil servants can sometimes provide a handy alibi for politicians who seek to evade responsibility for governmental shortcomings. Indeed, the degree of civil service impartiality is often remarkable. More often than not, the bureaucracy's actions and preferences are dictated less by their political views than by a preference to maintain the organizational status quo. However, it is not necessary to employ a conspiratorial view of civil service machinations to appreciate that their natural inclination will be to frustrate innovative proposals. This resistance may be decisive unless there is strong political leadership by the minister and support by the cabinet. During his prime ministership, Wilson often failed to provide such support to his political assistants, and policy-making and application were often decisively shaped by civil servants in the cabinet office.

[65] On the power of the civil service, see the perceptive analysis by Michael R. Gordon, "Civil Servants, Politicians and Parties," *Comparative Politics* 4, no. 1 (October 1971).

[66] Quoted in the *New Statesman*, March 22, 1974.

[67] Richard Crossman, *Inside View: Three Lectures on Prime Ministerial Government* (London: Jonathan Cape, 1972), p. 69.

In part, the civil service operation and values are determined by the composition of its members. They are by and large middle aged, university educated, upper middle class, and male. As in the upper levels of the German and Italian civil services, some of them resent political pressure, disapprove of pluralism and political liberalism, are deeply skeptical about political equality and mass political participation, and define their role as guarantors of the permanent interests of the state. Nonetheless the British officials remain highly responsive to political authority.[68]

Civil servants have also been criticized for their characteristic lack of specialization. By one calculation, 96 percent of their leadership "has the classic arts background of the civilized amateur," [69] with little or no training in mathematics, science, or other technical subjects. Until recently, the rationale for this pattern has been that the best preparation involved cultivating powers of intellect and mental agility, which could then be turned to any specialized task whether economics, defense, or technology. Specialized training was seen as too narrow and unable to provide sufficient breadth of perspective and judgment. But the realities of dealing with highly complicated technologies and other subjects have compelled some effort to recruit a more varied group of civil servants.

Apart from the civil service, application of policy also depends upon the cooperation of those whose occupation is subject to public regulation. The National Health Service, for example, functions only with the active cooperation of doctors, nurses, and other personnel. In the absence of this cooperation, government health policies cannot be carried out. Even in the foreign policy realm, pressure groups may play a key role. For example, Britain's policy toward the Common Market in the period from 1956 to 1959 was deeply affected by actions of the Federation of British Industries and the National Farmers' Union. These two groups successfully influenced both the terms which the UK sought to obtain in efforts to become associated with the EC and the actual establishment of a seven country European Free Trade Association.

ADJUDICATION AND ENFORCEMENT

Almost invariably, disputes arise from the application or enforcement of any policy, and Britain has an ancient and elaborate rule of law with which to resolve these disputes. Yet much of the British policy process in these areas contrasts remarkably with American or continental European practice. Unlike the United States, France, or Germany—or even the

---

[68] Robert D. Putnam, "The Political Attitudes of Senior Civil Servants in Western Europe: a Preliminary Report," *British Journal of Political Science* 3 (1973): 268, 278, 284.
[69] Clive Irving, "Whitehall: The Other Opposition," *New Statesman*, March 22, 1974.

Soviet Union—Britain has no written Constitution. The UK has nothing comparable to the American Bill of Rights; instead, Parliament is supreme and there is no judicial review whereby a high court can declare a law unconstitutional. Neither police nor most criminals carry firearms, and there is no equivalent of the French paramilitary force (the CRS) to deal with civil disturbance.

The English legal system embodies ancient procedures and traditions. Judges and lawyers appear in court wearing white wigs and long black robes. In cases where the government is a party to a dispute, it is referred to as "the crown." Since 1689, parliamentary authority has been established as supreme and the courts respect this supremacy. Indeed, the supremacy of Parliament is reflected in the fact that the judges of the highest appeal court, the law lords, are themselves members of the House of Lords. The courts have no basis for declaring any act of Parliament to be unconstitutional. If a court upholds a challenge by a citizen or group to some government action, it may not do so on the grounds that the law under which the action has been taken is unconstitutional; instead it does so only if it finds the government has gone beyond its existing legal powers.

As a reflection of its supremacy it has been said that Parliament has the power to do anything it wishes. And in coping with emergency situations, Parliament has sometimes taken actions which would have transgressed notions of civil liberties prevalent in other free societies. For example, it has empowered the government to cope with terrorism in Northern Ireland by arresting and imprisoning suspects without trial.

Despite parliamentary supremacy, the nonexistence of a written Constitution, and the absence of a formal bill of rights guaranteeing individual liberties against actions of Parliament, Britons enjoy a relatively free and open society in which their liberties are rarely transgressed. In fact, they enjoy greater freedoms and are less often subject to abuses of official powers than the French, who do possess a written Constitution and explicit guarantees of individual rights. The explanation for this lies in what the British call their unwritten Constitution (a body of long standing tradition, law, and commonly accepted practice) and the shared popular consensus upon which this Constitution and British liberties ultimately rest.

By and large, the British political culture embodies a sense of compromise and fair play. Citizens are law abiding and there is little official corruption. To be sure, one can point to individual excesses such as widespread hooliganism by youthful spectators after many soccer games, or occasional instances of police brutality, but these are exceptions. Nor does the government usually abuse the powers that predominance in Parliament gives it. Again, there are excesses, but these are infrequent and on some occasions the courts can act as a counterweight. Thus in 1975 the attorney general, at the urging of the cabinet secretary (a high civil servant), sought to block publication of the diaries of the late Richard Crossman on the grounds that they violated cabinet secrecy and the tradition of cabinet confidentiality. In arguing their case before England's Lord Chief Justice, Lord Widgery, Crossman's publishers claimed that there was no violation of actual law, that previous prime ministers, including the head of the existing government (Harold Wilson) had repeatedly described cabinet meetings in their memoirs, and that the government had chiefly acted to suppress information which was politically embarrassing. The Lord Chief Justice rejected the government's effort to restrain publication, on the grounds that no legal statute existed under which the restriction would be justified and he allowed publication of the Crossman diaries.

In sum, the mix between a prevailing constitutional consensus and a degree of judicial autonomy permits a process of adjudication and enforcement which preserves the rights of citizens.

AUDITING AND MONITORING OF POLICY

To perform effectively, any decision-making system requires feedback.[70] Thus, if political systems are to accomplish their goals, they must obtain information on the differences between the way their policies have *actually* operated and the way they had been *expected* to perform. This information is essential so that, when necessary, actions or policies can be altered. Since Britain possesses a relatively open political system, monitoring of policy can take place through a variety of formal and informal means. These include reports and statistics collected by the civil service, Royal Commissions of inquiry, appraisals by government and private research units or "think tanks," the views of citizens expressed to their Members of Parliament, reports and requests from interest groups directly affected by specific policies, and the activity of the media, particularly the press.

Of these diverse sources of scrutiny, we shall pay particular attention here to the press. Typically, a certain healthy tension exists between government on the one hand and press on the other. The roots of this are centuries old and extend back to a period when the monarchy held great power. A prominent British journalist has expressed an historic example of this tension:

[70] See Robert J. Lieber, *Theory and World Politics* (Cambridge, Mass.: Winthrop, 1972), Chapter 4, and Karl Deutsch, *The Nerves of Government* (New York: The Free Press, 1966).

Royalty does not take kindly to the press. Elizabeth I resented the suggestion by one John Stubbs, in a pamphlet, that she was too old to marry, and that her proposed bridegroom had syphilis. She had Stubbs' right hand chopped off in Westminster Square.[71]

British newspapers combine several divergent traditions. One of these is "yellow journalism," which in the 1880's played to large numbers of newly literate readers with romantic and colorful tales of colonial exploits. Another tradition is that of a dignified and highly literate quality press. In addition, there are newspapers that maintain a large circulation mainly by titillation and reports of scandal. In short, Britain today possesses some very good and some very bad newspapers. On a daily basis, the "quality" press (*The Times, The Guardian, The Financial Times, The Daily Telegraph*) enjoys a circulation of 2.2 million, which is approximately 13 percent of the total daily national newspaper figure of 16.9 million copies. Of the Sunday papers, the quality papers (*Sunday Times, Observer, Sunday Telegraph*) have a circulation of 3.1 million, accounting for 14 percent of the more than 22 million copies sold.

Compared to America, France, or Germany, the British people read significantly more newspapers. Although there are a few important regional papers, most of the daily press is based in London and adopts a national perspective. Despite the wide circulation of the British press, it does not tend to follow the vigorous investigative reporting on which some American newspapers pride themselves. There are two reasons for this. One is the remarkable concentration of newspaper ownership. Four large companies (Reed International, Beaverbrook Newspapers, Associated Newspapers, and News International) control 87 percent of the national daily newspaper circulation and three of them control 86 percent of national Sunday circulation.[72]

A second, more important reason is the nature of British libel laws and judicial restraint upon the press. The editor of the *Sunday Times*, Harold Evans, has described Britain as having a "half-free press," and has observed that contempt of court procedures, which severely restrict newspaper reporting of matters in any way related to court proceedings, would have prevented a British newspaper from achieving what the *Washington Post* did on Watergate.[73] In a legal sense, the newspapers remain free to express their opinions—which they vigorously do—but where the subject in question is a matter of court proceedings they are often restrained from publishing the evidence on which their opinion is based. Unusually

[71] Paul Johnson, *New Statesman,* November 9, 1973.
[72] Calculated from figures in *The Economist,* March 23, and April 6, 1974.
[73] Harold Evans, "The Half-Free Press," *New Statesman*, March 8, 1974.

stringent libel laws also cause considerable caution in publishing charges about people in public life.

While there are thus limitations on the extent to which the press actually monitors public policy, great diversity of viewpoint and enormous freedom of expression remain. Although only one of the major daily newspapers, *The Daily Mirror*, adopted a pro-Labour stance in the 1974 elections, the remainder of the press is not exclusively Conservative. Some papers—for example, *The Guardian*—are pro-Liberal, and others, such as *The Sun*, sometimes shift in their allegiance. There also exists a daily Communist newspaper, *The Morning Star* (with a circulation of 50,000), as well as numerous weekly and biweekly newspapers and magazines which express radical, moderate, conservative, or satirical views of policy and politics.

The net effect of this press activity and of remarkably high quality television networks (one private, two public under the control of the British Broadcasting Corporation) is to give vent to a wide array of views on political questions. As a result, policies that fail to achieve their intended goals or that produce unwelcome or unanticipated consequences are subject to an onslaught of criticism. Whether the policy in question involves the economy, social services, education, trade unions, foreign affairs, or the environment, there is a steady barrage of public commentary and evaluation, as well as scrutiny by pressure groups, and ordinary citizens. In the end both government and public are thus presented with a continual assessment of the actual operation of public policy.

TERMINATION AND AMENDMENT

Sooner or later, some policies may need to be altered substantially or even halted. Because of the centralization of political power in Britain, such change ordinarily requires the decision of the prime minister and often that of the cabinet. At times, the pressure of events or the continuous inflow of information from the process of monitoring and auditing will cause the leadership to change or even reverse a policy. For instance, in 1960–1961 Prime Minister Macmillan and his Conservative cabinet decided to abandon Britain's aloofness from European unity and to seek membership in the Common Market. And, in 1967, the Labour government was forced by international financial problems to accept the devaluation of sterling, which it had bitterly resisted for more than three years.

At times, however, the prime minister and the leading members of the cabinet may refuse to change policy. If a determined member of the cabinet continues to disagree and is unwilling to accept the decisions of his or her colleagues, the minister may then choose to resign. The prevailing doctrine of *collective responsibility* holds that whether or not a minister agrees with an existing policy, he or she is expected to support it in public and in Parliament. The companion doctrine of *ministerial responsibility* holds that ministers are responsible for the actions of their ministries, regardless of whether or not they had direct involvement.

In practice, both these doctrines are often weakened. Individual ministers seldom resign because of a policy failure in the department for which they are responsible. If the prime minister is dissatisfied with a minister's performance, he will often shift that person to another position, or even remove him from the cabinet, but rarely is there an explicit connection with ministerial responsibility.

Cabinet responsibility also is weakened in other ways. At times, Britain has what Richard Crossman has termed prime ministerial rather than cabinet government. Frequently a prime minister, with a few key members of the cabinet and leading civil servants in the cabinet office, will effectively determine policy without the active involvement of the cabinet. The complexity of government, the pressures of time, personalities, and the political strength of the prime minister often determine this. On other occasions, the prime minister may play a more restrained role, as *primus inter pares* (first among equals), and the cabinet may well function in deciding policy on a more collective basis. Wilson, for example, tended to follow the first model from 1964 to 1967, and then the second from 1967 to 1970.

Public resignations over policy have played a far more important role in Britain than in the United States. In 1938, Foreign Minister Anthony Eden quit the Chamberlain government because of his strong disagreement over its policies of appeasing German and Italian fascism. In 1951, Aneurin Bevan and Harold Wilson resigned from the Labour government of Clement Attlee because they opposed cuts in the National Health Service at a time when Britain was rearming in response to the Korean War. In 1971, Roy Jenkins quit the Labour shadow cabinet because he disagreed with its increasingly anti–Common Market posture. Each of these resignations had some public impact and did not permanently damage the careers of those who resigned. Eden and Wilson both became prime ministers, and Jenkins regained a prominent role in the cabinet after Labour's victory in 1974.

On occasion, policy termination or amendment may be achieved as the result of a general election. Labour's policy of steel nationalization was reversed as a result of the Conservatives' 1951 victory—which in turn was reversed by Labour victories in 1964 and 1966. Prime Minister Heath's confrontation with the trade unions in general and the miners in particular was terminated by the defeat of his government in 1974. Reversals in educational policy, particularly at the secondary school level, have occurred because of the sharply divergent policies of Conservative and Labour governments. And foreign policy has also been altered as a result of elections: the 1974 Labour government, for example, was clearly less favorable toward European unity and more sympathetic to the United States than its Conservative predecessor.

conclusion: performance and prospects

PERFORMANCE

In assessing the performance of Britain, much is already implied by the previous discussion. What then can we add about the success or failure of the British system in meeting the needs of its people?

From an economic perspective, the performance has not been good when compared with that of the other advanced industrial societies of Western Europe, North America, or Japan. Since 1960, these countries have been growing at rates generally averaging above 4.5 percent per year, while Britain (and the United States) averaged about 2.5 percent.[74] As a result, Britain, which was once one of the world's wealthiest countries in per capita terms, has experienced a decline in its relative position and now ranks seventh among its Common Market partners, ahead of only Italy and Ireland.

Throughout the postwar generation, Britain has experienced not only a low economic growth rate but also low investment and productivity. Thus for every worker employed, the major British auto manufacturer, British Leyland, produces an average of six cars, yet the continental Europeans produce approximately 12 cars per worker and the Japanese Nissan (Datsun) firm turns out 37.[75] This relatively low British productivity occurs not only because of differences in worker efficiency and attitude but also because of lower capital investment. Volkswagen (Germany) and Renault (France), for example, utilize more modern and efficient machinery and techniques. For every dollar of fixed assets (that is, plant and equipment) per British Leyland worker, Renault has invested three and a half and Volkswagen four dollars per worker.

Technical figures such as these possess considerable social and political significance. They explain in part why Britain produces less national wealth and therefore has fewer resources available for the purchase of imports, for social services such as health and education, for other public spending (such as defense), for public or private investment, or for

---

[74] See UN *Yearbook of National Accounts Statistics* 1973, Vol. III, Table 4A, and James W. Howe, *The U.S. and World Development, Agenda for Action 1975* (New York: Overseas Development Council and Praeger Pubs., 1974), p. 206.
[75] *The Economist*, December 7, 1974 and October 11, 1975.

private consumption. The real standard of living of the British people has not risen nearly so fast as that of their immediate neighbors. Britain's economic performance has also involved serious problems of high inflation (double that of its Common Market partners) and unemployment.

Despite problems of economic performance, Britain's political system has had considerable success in allocating existing resources to meet public needs. Since the late 1940's, the British welfare state has provided its citizens a comprehensive range of services including health care, education, pensions, and other welfare benefits. Critics of British policy have argued that too many resources have gone into these services and not enough into productive investment. While Britain has nonetheless provided a generally decent standard of living for its population, its growing economic problems during the late 1960's and early 1970's meant that resources were increasingly scarce to meet major needs to the extent desired by the general public, pressure groups, and the government.

Compared with many other Western systems, there is less inequality of income distribution in Britain. For example, one study has found that, as measured by a *Gini Ratio* (by which complete equality would equal zero and the greatest inequality 1.0), Britain (with a figure of 0.38) had greater equality of income distribution than France (0.50), West Germany (0.45), or even Sweden (0.39). There was, however, even greater equality of income in Denmark (0.37), Norway (0.35), the United States (0.34), Australia (0.30) and Israel (0.30).[76] By different measures which stress accumulated wealth rather than annual income, inequalities in Britain are substantially greater. The response of the Labour government has been to propose a small annual tax on wealth over £100,000, while the Conservatives have opposed such measures on the grounds that they interfere with incentives and economic competitiveness.

It would be a mistake to focus exclusively on economic performance. Despite low growth, inefficiencies and the rest, the British political system provides a quality of life that most of its citizens find acceptable. According to a major opinion poll, most British are satisfied with their public services, including police, health, and education. Only in such areas as housing, pensions, and services for old people do majorities believe they

[76] Based on Felix Paukert, "Income Distribution at Different Levels of Development: A Survey of Evidence," *International Labor Review*, Vol. 108, No. 2–3 (August–September 1973). Pages 114–115, in Howe, *The U.S. and World Development*, p. 215. Actual figures are, variously, for 1957 to 1969. Measurements of wealth distribution vary, but tend to show greater inequality. One British source, the Bishop of Southwark (Mervyn Stockwood) argues that "the richest 7 percent of British taxpayers own 84 percent of the nation's wealth." Quoted, *New York Times*, February 22, 1974. Others calculate that inequalities are less pronounced if pension rights are included in measurements of personal wealth.

have not received "good value" for their tax money.[77] More specifically, the quality of life in Britain's cities and countryside is often excellent. Britain's system of mass transit in urban areas, railways, control of urban sprawl and pollution, health care (including infant mortality and life expectancy) crime rates, cultural attractions, parks and museums, higher education, radio and television programming, low levels of official corruption, and its standards of civility all compare favorably with those of Western Europe, North America, and Japan. Indeed, if we contrast specific cities such as London and New York, the contrasts can be highly favorable to Britain. The two cities each have populations of nearly 8 million persons, but London (which occupies twice as large an area) requires only one-third the number of firemen, less than two-thirds the number of uniformed police, and experiences far less crime (only one-fourteenth the number of murders and one twenty-fifth the number of rapes). Despite an occasional garbage or transit strike, London's public services function well, or at least adequately, and the city's financial stability is not in question.

Turning to political performance, there is, again, a mixed picture. Britain's institutions of representative government have functioned satisfactorily. Elections are openly and fairly conducted (at remarkably low cost, since television time is provided free to the political parties), the people enjoy a wide range of political rights and liberties, and there are no institutional roadblocks to effective government (such as can occur in systems where different parties control the executive and legislative branches of government). The actual policies of Britain's parties and political leaders have, however, been the cause of certain dissatisfaction. Neither the Conservatives nor Labour have satisfactorily dealt with some of Britain's principal problems while in office, nor have they proposed imaginative and effective solutions while in opposition. Thus the substantive performance of government in dealing with inflation, unemployment, trade unions, industry, energy, social services, the balance of payments, and even some aspects of foreign policy have often been regarded as ineffective or muddled.

In sum, if we are to attempt an overall assessment of the performance of the British political system, we can say that it has sometimes been inefficient but it has typically "muddled through" with its chief tasks and—except for the perennial Northern Ireland problem and the question mark of Scotland—it retains popular legitimacy.

[77] Social Surveys (Gallup Poll) Ltd., August 1973, in *Current Opinion* (Williamstown, Mass.: Roper Public Opinion Research Center), Vol. 1, No. 11 (November 1973).

The British experience reflects many of the central problems and dilemmas of politics in advanced or postindustrial democratic societies. These include resource distribution; pluralistic stagnation; the tensions between full employment, free collective bargaining and inflation; the role of trade unions and of private industry; the continuation of the mixed economy; and changes in political participation and in ideology. Thus the prospects of Britain in coping with these tasks are of considerable interest beyond the boundaries of the UK.

Britain's prospects in dealing successfully with its foreign and domestic economic problems, and the increasing political ramifications of these, are by no means entirely predictable. Despite generations of experience in coping with periodic economic difficulty and success in muddling through, there could come a point at which the existing economic and political system could no longer cope. Nonetheless, we must be wary of simplistic predictions and extrapolations which merely project existing trends into the indefinite future as though nothing would alter them. It may be helpful to recall that France in the 1950's was widely regarded as the political and economic sickman of Europe, but that within a decade the French situation had substantially improved.

No one can predict with certainty what the future will bring. Yet despite Britain's myriad difficulties, we can point to several crucial factors which may well presage a satisfactory outcome. These include a long and resilient tradition of political stability and representative institutions, a belated but real reorientation of Britain's world role from Empire and Commonwealth to membership in the Common Market and a more active European role, resolution of the perennial exchange rate problem by devaluation and the floating of sterling, and—most dramatically—the prospect of huge North Sea oil production which by the early 1980's will make Britain not only self-sufficient in oil but a major oil exporter as well and thus provide a real economic boost. The interplay among these various problems and strengths promises to make the future of British politics an exciting and relevant subject of attention.

3

france

3 FRANCE

background

If we contend that modern British political history began in 1688, we can place the beginning of modern French political history with the Great Revolution of 1789. But whereas British politics consolidated and extended the victory of parliamentary government over the old reign of feudal monarchy, French politics never permanently defeated the forces which had opposed the meaning of the 1789 upheaval and which therefore did not accept the basic principles of democratic government. For at least a century after the Revolution influential forces remained in France which favored an aristocratic (or at least privileged and élitist) government and the basic denial of political democracy, which supported the continued establishment of the Catholic Church as the official state religion, and which aspired to military dominance in Europe. Once the republican principle of government was finally settled in 1871, and the separation of Church and State achieved in 1905, the political and religious issues lived on in struggles over executive versus legislative forms of government, and over state aid to Catholic schools. Moreover, to these issues were added economic, social, and military disputes, which moved to the forefront in the twentieth century.

Most of the major ideological battles of modern European history have been fought out in France. In the century and a half since 1789 France has experienced a fitful historical development spawning more than a dozen different regimes. (See Figure 3–1.) Compared to Britain and the United States, the French unwillingness or inability to settle on the most fundamental charter of political authority is all too apparent. As each

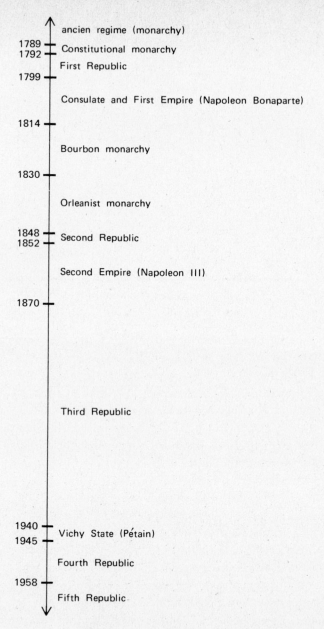

ancien regime (monarchy)

1789 — Constitutional monarchy
1792 —

First Republic

1799 —

Consulate and First Empire (Napoleon Bonaparte)

1814 —

Bourbon monarchy

1830 —

Orleanist monarchy

1848 — Second Republic
1852 —

Second Empire (Napoleon III)

1870 —

Third Republic

1940 — Vichy State (Pétain)
1945 —

Fourth Republic

1958 —

Fifth Republic

FIGURE 3–1 History of French Political Regimes

change of regime involved not only the government, but the nation's basic constitutional framework, political passions were inevitably inflamed, past memories recalled and evoked, and ideological persuasions further hardened. Let us look at the actual political evolution that affects

French citizens' political choices and principles, that jars so vividly their political memories, that divides rather than unites them.[1]

THE REVOLUTION OF 1789 AND THE FIRST REPUBLIC (1792–1799)

By the late eighteenth century, France had finally emerged from the feudal era; a succession of monarchs had forged a national entity out of former regional baronies, a growing but small middle class of traders and financiers had arisen to challenge the restrictive practices of mercantilism. But while the economic sphere thus began its transition from feudalism to capitalism, political, social, and clerical privilege remained.

In the decade before the French Revolution the French nation was divided into three "estates": the first estate was made up of the powerful and wealthy Catholic Church and its hierarchy of clergy; the second contained the nobility with the equally powerful and wealthy king at its head. The third estate was composed of the "commoners," 90 percent of whom were engaged in agricultural pursuits, and for whom life remained (in the words of the seventeenth century political philosopher Thomas Hobbes) "nasty, poor, brutish and short." Only the first and second estates held power, however, which meant that only 5 percent of the people actually held the legal and political status of "citizen." Traditionally, when privileged power becomes abusive, it has been challenged. In France before 1789, the king and his court filled much of their time "with the pursuit of pleasure or with intrigue," [2] which proved to be a great burden on the public treasury. Taxation in 1789 fell heavily on the commoners, because the very wealthy Church and the nobility enjoyed tax-exempt status. As in Great Britain and the United States, the immediate cause of the French Revolution was the issue of "taxation without representation."

Technically, the kings were required to get taxation approval from the representatives of the three estates, who met in an Estates-General. But the Estates-General had not been convened since 1614. When King Louis XVI tried to increase taxation in 1787, all three estates demanded an elected assembly to act on that decree. Originally, then, the representatives of the Estates-General did not intend to overthrow the monarch, unseat the Church, or abolish private property; they meant only to limit the king's prerogatives and to bestow increased powers on the representative parlia-

[1] For further reading on background to the Fifth Republic see David Thomson, *Democracy in France* (London: Oxford University Press, 1969), Gordon Wright, *France in Modern Times* (Chicago: Rand McNally, 1962), and Philip Williams, *Crisis and Compromise: Politics in the Fourth Republic* (Garden City, N.Y.: Doubleday, 1960).
[2] Gordon Wright, ibid., p. 17.

ments, as the British had done so successfully in 1688. But the king was unwilling to compromise on the structure of the assembly, and the moderate tone of the Third Estate soon gave way to an impatient mob's cry for total revolution. The Church and nobility retreated back into the king's camp, as the *ancien régime*'s reign of authority, tradition, and clericalism was overthrown in the name of "liberty, equality, fraternity" and "sovereignty to the people."

But these resounding precepts soon faded in the period immediately following the Revolution. Between 1790 and 1799, French politics degenerated into a series of violent and bloody power struggles that saw a brief attempt at constitutional monarchy terminated in 1792 with the beheadings of Louis XVI and Marie Antoinette, the Reign of Terror until 1795 of the "republican" Committee on Public Safety under Robespierre, the constitutionless three-year reign of the Convention, and the four-year moderate reign of the five-man Directory. This havoc was terminated in 1799 when Napoleon Bonaparte seized power and became "First Consul."

THE CONSULATE AND THE FIRST EMPIRE (1799–1814)

The aim of the revolutionaries in 1789 for representative parliamentary government had given way only a decade later to a new variant of executive dominated government, referred to thereafter as "bonapartism." Like the old kings, Napoleon ruled virtually as a dictator, but unlike them he ruled with the "consent of the governed." This "consent" was achieved by means of the plebiscite, or nationwide referendum. Napoleon's plebiscite of 1799, in which he asked the people to legitimize his role as First Consul, was ostensibly approved by 99.9 percent of those voting. The catch was that the electorate had been further limited (as compared to the early years of the First Republic) by property qualifications and income levels—in other words, to a privileged élite. In 1804, Napoleon proclaimed himself Emperor of France, and France became an "empire." So "bonapartism" was neither a return to the old rule of monarchs nor a fulfillment of the conditions of liberal democracy. Rather it maintained that one man, in a position of supreme political power, could interpret the will of the people and embody the aspirations of the nation as a whole; that one man, above conflicting and competing political movements, could somehow transcend those particularist choices and as such command the approval and respect of the great majority of the people. Since all this could be done without resorting to normal procedures of democratic selection, political liberties (which had been gained so recently in the Revolution) perished in the First Empire. In their place Napoleon substituted press censorship, a restricted franchise, the absence of parliament, and extensive police state practices.

As in the political sphere, the Revolution's gains were wiped out in the religious realm as well. The Revolution had revoked the Church's privileged position in society, confiscating the extensive Church lands and selling them to the peasants. It had also initially turned the Church hierarchy into a government bureaucracy, the clergy being salaried along with other civil servants. In this way the Church and State were still closely tied, but all important clerical decisions were made now by the State. In 1795, however, the Church and State were separated, leaving the Church completely on its own. Thus the extremely divisive religious issue might have been laid to rest had not Napoleon revived it by restoring the Church–State tie in 1801.

In contrast to these political and religious "regressions," Napoleon's economic and social policies in many ways carried on the intent of the Revolution. He completed the elimination of feudal regional barriers to commerce and trade, thus emphasizing the nationalizing aspects of the Revolution and reinforcing the burgeoning commercial, industrial, and financial interests. His expansion of the pre–Revolutionary centralized bureaucracy created a new class of privileged Frenchmen, whose status was based not on birth or class, but on meritocratic advancement. Napoleon backed his aim of "public careers open to talent" with an expanded system of public secondary education. Another of Napoleon's many contributions to the structure of French politics was the completion of reforms begun by the Revolution to codify, rationalize, and standardize French law. From the several hundred local legal systems existing before 1789, Napoleon forged one single Code which embodied the relatively modern notion that each citizen was equal before the law, regardless of wealth, birth, or occupation.

But Napoleon Bonaparte was not content to be Emperor of France alone. He was a soldier and his goal became the military domination of all of Europe. Military ambitions and territorial greed, however, proved his downfall, first in 1814 and again in 1815 at the hands of a European alliance in the battle of Waterloo. As the French Revolutionary era was ended by a military coup, Napoleon's First Empire fell in military defeat.

RESTORATION OF THE MONARCHY (1814–1848)

Monarchy again dominated French political life from 1814 to 1848. The Bourbon dynasty ("dethroned" in the French Revolutionary era) was restored and it reigned until 1830, when it was overthrown by the rival Orleanist dynasty. The Bourbon kings' tenure resurrected familiar questions. Would this latest experiment in constitutional monarchy provide the compromise and lasting precedent that Britain had achieved, or would the monarchy continue to insist on its supremacy over the representatives of the people in Parliament? Louis XVIII and his successor in 1824, Charles X, proved intransigent. They not only further restricted the apparently meaningless franchise (restricted to 0.4 percent of the entire population), but they refused to accept ministerial responsibility to Parliament (rather than to the king). In fact, they went so far as to insist on the old divine right of kings doctrine, totally rejecting the post–Revolutionary idea of popular sovereignty.

The Bourbon monarchs turned the clock back in terms of social and religious problems also. With the restoration came the return of many aristocrats who had fled the country in 1789. They brought with them a desire to regain their privileged positions—this time in the bureaucracy and advisory parliament—although that status was now shared with Napoleon's newly created peerage and the growing upper bourgeoisie of the business world. The Bourbon kings counted on the once exiled nobility for support, and they further strengthened their position by returning the Catholic Church to its pre–Revolutionary position in education. Napoleon, in an effort to create a meritocratic and élite civil service, had prohibited the Church from running secondary schools, but had allowed it to continue to provide the vast bulk of primary education. But under the Bourbons extralegal secondary Church schools flourished.

By 1830, the opposition groups in Parliament (a difficult status to maintain without democratic freedoms and with the political repression that characterized this period) were in a position to demand a true constitutional monarchy. But Charles X rejected compromise and responded instead with a coup d'état. He dissolved Parliament, altered the electoral system, restricted the electorate even further, and increased police repression. The people of Paris rose in insurrection, dethroned the king, and substituted in his place the Orleanist pretender, Louis Philippe. From 1830 to 1848 French politics settled into a comfortable pattern of constitutional monarchy, moderate bourgeois governments of élites, a final decline of the nobility's political influence, and (once again) the loss of special privilege for the Church.

REVOLUTION OF 1848 AND THE SECOND REPUBLIC (1848–1851)

This system might have survived longer but for the events of 1848, which produced a revolution and a republic almost by accident. Louis Philippe's opposition faulted him not on the broad philosophical grounds of monarchy versus republicanism, but on more immediate questions concerning the size of the electorate, corruption within the ruling élite, and the government's inability to handle increased labor unrest. Thus, the majority of the opposition wanted reform and the king's abdication, but not necessarily the revolution and republic with which they found themselves.

The Revolution of 1848 followed a pattern similar to other French "revolutions." In February 1848 students and workers in Paris clashed with police; barricades and street fighting followed in the working class quarters. A growing crowd then marched on the Chamber of Deputies. The indecisive king abdicated and the quickly appointed provisional government proclaimed a Republic. It had all happened fast, and with only several hundred dead—it was the least bloody of all the French Revolutions.

But the Second Republic proved as shortlived as the First. Although the new government proclaimed universal male suffrage, a unicameral (one chamber) assembly, and popular election of the president as head of State, it was obvious within two years that these very reforms would prove the undoing of the Republic. First, the December 1848 presidential election gave Louis Napoleon, the (supposed) nephew of Napoleon Bonaparte, an overwhelming victory over his pro-Republic opponents. Then in legislative elections of 1849, the monarchist forces displaced the moderate Republican majority in Parliament. But the most significant blow to future political development as well as to the Second Republic occurred within the alliance of Republicans and Socialists who had created the Republic.

The socialist movement in 1848 reflected the late and slow hold of the Industrial Revolution in France. Only since 1830 could the urban working class even be considered a force of its own. Karl Marx and Friedrich Engels, whose *Communist Manifesto* was published in the same year as the Revolution, did not have a formative impact on the French workers' movement until decades later. Thus, in aligning themselves with the liberal Republicans in 1848, the workers sought not necessarily a socialist revolution, but basic political and social reforms. In one sense they did seek economic reforms—reforms which would ensure them guaranteed jobs and a say in the running of those jobs. Their plan initially envisaged State financed "national workshops," or producer cooperatives owned and operated by those who worked in them. The Socialists had been accorded two ministerial positions in the new provisional government of 1848. One was held by Louis Blanc, the socialist theoretician and originator of the national workshop answer to job insecurity and unemployment. But instead of placing Blanc in charge of the creation of the workshops, an extremely anti-Socialist liberal Republican was given the job and he proceeded in such a way as to sabotage any success of the radical experiment. Throughout the spring, the working class increased its demands that political reform be accompanied by social and economic reforms. Their impatience ran out in June, though, when the government abolished the remnants of the disastrous workshop system. A three-day civil war in Paris followed, in which several thousand people were killed. By the end of the year, the Republican government had repealed virtually all of the reforms designed to satisfy the working class supporters of the Republic. The effects of the bloodshed and bitterness of 1848 were first, to alienate the working class movement from the assumption that a revolution leading to a democratic republic was the best way to achieve its aims and second, to strengthen the workers' belief in class conflict, in the inevitable gap between the interests of the liberal bourgeoisie and the growing proletariat.

Soon after its founding, then, the Second Republic's very existence was being challenged by opponents from the left and the right. By far the most significant and revealing example of antirepublican dominance was illustrated in the passage of the Falloux Bill of 1850. This Church and monarchist sponsored bill sought to go further than all previous attempts since the Revolution of 1789 to restore to the Church its crucial hold on the nation's educational system. Passed by the monarchist majority and signed by the president, Louis Napoleon, it provided that religious education could be taught in all public primary and secondary schools and that the Church could operate its own secondary schools. It further increased church influence on the public primary system by providing for clergy representation on school boards and for the hiring of ecclesiastical teaching personnel in public schools. The Falloux Bill marked the major clerical victory of the century. Its implementation meant that France was divided for generations into two opposing camps—those future leaders who had been educated almost exclusively in Catholic schools and those who had passed through the frankly anticlerical public schools.

Louis Napoleon and the monarchist majority went on to pass other "antirepublican" bills; one bill cut the electorate by one third, another restricted the right of political assembly and freedom of the press. Under these circumstances, the Republic could hardly withstand Louis Napoleon's next move, which was to change the constitutional provision that limited a president to a single three year term. Like his uncle, Louis Napoleon had aspirations to be Emperor for life, but the monarchists in the Assembly would not go along with his scheme. Louis Napoleon's response was a military backed coup d'état in December 1851. One year later, he converted his position from authoritarian president to Emperor Napoleon III.

THE SECOND EMPIRE (1852–1870)

Like the First Empire, the Second Empire qualified as a genuine police state. Napoleon III exercised one man rule, denied basic political liberties to his opponents, and controlled and censored the press. In this course, he enjoyed the support of the Church, the military, and the central bureaucracy. But again like his predecessor, Napoleon III sought to give some semblance of popular support to his regime. He revived the device of plebiscitory democracy with predictably astounding success. Each of his three plebiscites received over 90 percent of the vote. In addition, he sanctioned a parliamentary façade, consisting of a senate of loyal notables and a "legislative corps" which always met in closed session and had no powers whatsoever.

In the final years of his reign, Napoleon III appeared to be moving toward the creation of a quasiparliamentary political system. But that important development was crushed by the Emperor's military defeat at the hands of the Prussians in the fall of 1870. Once again the Parisian crowd's demands for a republic was granted—this time without bloodshed. It was to be a republic that surpassed everyone's expectations by lasting seventy years.

THE THIRD REPUBLIC (1870–1940)

The Paris Commune   The Third Republic was less than a year old when it experienced what was to become one of France's most vivid and divisive political memories—the Paris Commune of 1871. In the aftermath of occupation and defeat by the Prussians, most of provincial France and the new monarchist dominated Assembly voted to accept peace on the Prussians' terms. But the people of Paris did not agree. Outraged by national defeatism, and particularly by the provincial government's decision to establish a new capital in Versailles rather than in Paris, the working class population of Paris rose in arms, barricaded the city to outside forces, and proceeded to establish the democratic self-governing "Paris Commune." The 62 day life of the Paris Commune was a unique political–social–economic experiment. In the short time they had, the *communards* of Paris instigated direct election of municipal council representatives and judges (with provisions for their immediate recall), replaced the police force with a worker–civilian national guard, attempted to hold all wages to that of the average workman, set up free coeducational and secular schools, completely dismantled the Church, established worker-owned and run economic enterprises, and granted workers' demands for labor rights and improved working conditions. Some of the "radical" proposals of the *communards* were simply extensions of political democracy. This was because Paris, as the capital of France, had never been allowed its own mayor and city council. But the Paris Commune's plans went beyond self-government for Paris to the vision of a federation of free and self-managing municipalities throughout France. In this regard, the Paris *communards* were joined by similar uprisings in the cities of Lyon, Marseille, Saint Etienne, Toulouse, Narbonne, and Limoges. This conception of political authority was not particularly that of the 1789 Jacobins who wanted a strong central—but leftist—government. Rather, it was that of revolutionary trade unionists and socialists who favored a far more decentralized and participatory socialist system.

Whichever strand of the growing socialist movement predominated in the Paris Commune, its defeat created martyrs enough for all. Two months after the Commune's establishment, the new Republican government ordered military forces to Paris. A classic case of overreaction—on both sides—resulted. Retreating from their barricades, the *communards* set fire to many public buildings and executed their hostages, including the Archbishop of Paris. The army responded with the terrible slaughter of 20,000 to 25,000 people, and twice as many arrests. The scars from this, the bloodiest of French civil wars, were to remain deep. The working class movement had been devastated and deprived of its leaders for the second time in 25 years, and its philosophy had been radicalized into believing that the class struggle in France would always be violent.

In the course of the long Third Republic, two major issues dividing the French would more or less be resolved: the status of the French monarchy, and the status of the Catholic Church. While the monarchy finally gave way to the permanency of the republic, the political question of "bonapartism" or strong executive government versus "popular sovereignty" or legislative government was not completely solved. And while the Church was permanently disestablished in 1905, the debate over State aid to Catholic schools continued into the Fourth and Fifth Republics.

Monarchy or Republic? How did the Third Republic manage to resolve the political question of monarchy versus republic? The legislature elected in 1871 had returned a monarchist majority and a monarch was expected to be installed forthwith. But in their usual uncompromising way, the three French dynasties (Orleanist, Bourbon, Bonapartist) simply could not agree on which among them would fill the awaiting office. Temporarily, then, the new regime would remain a republic, with a provisional president at its head. But time and an over eager president worked in favor of the Republicans' cause. In the 1876 election, the

Republicans unseated the monarchists as the majority in the Assembly. Subsequently, when President MacMahon dissolved the Assembly in 1877 over a basic political disagreement, his legal, but too assertive, actions dispelled for many French people the desire for a strong monarchical head of state. Finally, in 1879, the Republicans captured the majority of seats in the traditionally conservative senate. Thus by 1879 the permanence of the republican concept of government had been secured.

The Third Republic and the Catholic Church The Republicans therefore turned to their second great cause—anticlericalism. The Third Republic had inherited from Napoleon III a situation in which the Church exerted great control over education. In 1875, in fact, the monarchical majority had further extended that control by authorizing what the Revolution and Napoleon I had prohibited: Catholic universities. But the Third Republic's famous Minister of Education, Jules Ferry, set about to remove finally the Church's influence. In a series of laws passed from 1879 to 1886, major educational reforms swept France. All primary schools became free, compulsory, and secular. The catechism being taught in these schools since 1850 was replaced by a civic and moral education stressing Christian ethics (but not religion), middle class values, and national patriotism. The state established schools in locales where none previously existed, including secondary schools for girls (previously for boys only) and departmental teaching colleges (to replace clerical teaching orders). Catholic universities were ordered to disband.

The Catholic Church seemed to be reading the handwriting on the wall; in 1892 the Pope issued an unprecedented decree declaring that the Church was henceforth "neutral to any particular form of government"; that is, it finally would accept the Republic. It seemed the clerical quarrel might have ended, but for the bitter and extremely divisive Dreyfus affair of 1896.

Alfred Dreyfus, a young Jewish captain in the French army, was accused of espionage and court-martialed by a military court. When the army turned up evidence that Dreyfus had been framed, it chose to cover up its mistake rather than admit error. The army's cover-up was then discovered and Dreyfus was eventually vindicated. But not before a searing battle consumed the nation's intellectual energies for almost a decade. The forces of the right insisted that order, national security, and the honor of the army had to take precedence over the civil rights of one "probably innocent" Jew. The forces of the left placed truth, justice, and individual political liberties above *raison d'état*. The Catholic Church entered into this extraordinary battle on the side of the aristocracy, the military, and the rabid anti-Semites, going so far as to urge the expulsion of all Jews and Protestants from the French army. So gratuitous was the Church's involvement that suspicions were once again aroused and public sentiment turned toward the complete separation of Church and State. In 1905, reversing Napoleon I's actions of 1801, the French Parliament disestablished the Catholic Church by cutting off all State financial support, reasserting the State's title to Church property (theoretically the case since the French Revolution), and attempting to democratize the Church by providing that committees of Catholic laymen administer Church affairs locally. The government's manner and actions were such that the Church and State were more "torn apart than separated neatly"; the Pope indignantly ordered all French Catholics to resist the new legislation and excommunicated every deputy who had voted for the Separation Law.

Between the Wars   In the period before World War I, the Third Republic's attention had been consumed by political and religious problems. Once these were "resolved," subsequent governments lapsed into a policy that would dominate the entire Third Republic. Rather than tackle the economic and social problems that had been building up in the late nineteenth and early twentieth centuries, the governments did nothing. They chose instead simply to "hold the fort" against all enemies and contenders for power. This they accomplished by placating their special interest and conservative peasant constituents by pursuing essentially noninterventionist, laissez-faire policies.

With no particular program to be enacted, the bourgeois politicians represented an oligarchy whose ministerial content changed—or more accurately revolved—frequently. Between 1870 and 1940 the French experienced 108 ministries (averaging eight months in duration); in the same period the Americans experienced only 17 changes of government and the British (in twice the time, 1801–1937) experienced 44 ministries.

Instability and ineffectiveness increased after World War I, a war that proved devastating to France in terms of manpower (10 percent of the country's active male population was slaughtered), resources (wide scale destruction of prime agricultural and industrial territory), and emotions (defeat, occupation, humiliation). In the early 1930's, the state of French politics was such that fascism was finding favorable terrain. In response to an attempted fascist coup in 1934, the French left formed a Popular Front coalition and went on to win power in the 1936 legislative elections. But the Popular Front government also fell victim to international forces and lasted less than a year.

Suffering from two decades of economic stagnation and deeply divided between the forces of left and right, the French failed to withstand the onslaught of Hitler's armies as they progressed through the low countries into France in May of 1940. For the second time since 1870, Paris was occupied by the foreign enemy. On July 10, 1940, the Third Republic deputies voted by a large majority to turn all power over to the aging hero of World War I, Marshall Philippe Pétain.

THE VICHY REGIME (1940–1944)

During the first two years of the war the Germans occupied only the northern half of France, with headquarters in Paris. Marshall Pétain and his entourage governed the rest of France from their headquarters in Vichy. After 1942, the Germans occupied all of metropolitan France, and the Vichy regime lost most of its independence. In the four year period of occupation, the French people were divided politically into several broad, and sometimes overlapping, categories. On the far right a small group of fascists actively welcomed and supported the Nazi's New Order for Europe (in which France was to be subservient to Germany). This group worked directly with the German authorities in Paris.

A second group, which included the Pétain government and its supporters of the army, Church, nobility, and business classes, placed nationalism above fascism, but also endorsed the establishment of non-democratic government. Thus the Vichy regime was a police state in which parliament, elections, politicians, trade unions, civil rights, a free press, and political parties were suppressed. Pétain ruled as a virtual dictator, surrounded by his court of generals, administrative bureaucrats, and royalists. In short, Vichy rallied all who had despised the revolutionary and republican traditions since 1789. The motto "Liberty, Equality, Fraternity" gave way in Pétain's "national revolution" to "Work, Country, Family." The Catholic Church was handsomely rewarded for its support. Public secondary schools were abolished and Church-run schools were substituted for them. In the social realm, the regime passed discriminatory laws against naturalized aliens, working women, Jews, and Protestants. The fate of the Jews in wartime France was determined by Pétain's prime minister, Pierre Laval. In his attempt to gain "French autonomy through collaboration," Laval agreed to turn over to the Germans all foreign-born Jews (including many refugees from Nazi Germany) in exchange for the safety of French-born Jews. The latter, while spared by and large, continued to be persecuted by the Vichy legal codes. Further, Laval agreed to the Germans' demands that French workers be sent to work the badly undermanned German industrial machine. Seven hundred thousand Frenchmen were conscripted and sent to Germany, thus strengthening the Nazis' military base.

A third group—passive and large—"sat on the fence" throughout the war, waiting to see what the outcome would be before acting. Finally, there was the Resistance movement, one of the most heroic, and therefore vivid, political memories of modern France. The Resistance movement was composed of two segments: the military, conservative, and Catholic anti-Pétainists who fled with General Charles de Gaulle to London and then to Algiers to set up a Free French Army and government in exile; and predominantly socialist and Communist civilians who joined the underground resistance within France itself. Many of these people met harsh death at the hands of the Germans. Torture, betrayal, assassination, random firing squads, eventually the purges and executions of collaborators—these were the cruel facts of political life in the time of occupation and resistance.

THE FOURTH REPUBLIC (1945–1958)

When the tide turned in June of 1944 with the allied invasion on the beaches of Normandy, France seemed to be perilously close to a vast social schism and possible civil war between the Vichyites and the Resisters. But the cautious fence-sitters changed the balance and with the liberation of Paris in August 1944, majority sentiment endorsed the sweeping economic and social changes drawn up by the National Council of the Resistance, an allied council of all the various resistance groups. A peaceful revolution appeared likely as the provisional governments of 1944 and 1945 moved toward establishing the Fourth Republic. In the euphoria of liberation, major legislation was passed to compensate for the stagnation of the past 50 years. This "revolution" included: economic reform (mainly through nationalizations) that sought to break the power of the often collaborationist industrial and financial special interests; social reform to expand basic welfare provisions to all citizens; a state planning commission to coordinate economic growth; and political reform to "undo Vichy" and restore basic political democracy.

The coalition of parties which ruled during this important period included the MRP (a progressive Catholic party), the Socialist Party (SFIO), and the Communist Party (PCF) and was presided over by the war hero Charles de Gaulle. But this tripartite coalition gave way over the next few years to familiar ideological divisions. De Gaulle resigned over the new constitutional provisions, the Communists left over foreign policy (with the advent of the Cold War in 1947), the Socialists left in 1951 over the issue of State financial aid to Catholic schools. More and more Fourth Republic governmental coalitions came to revolve around the Radical Party. The Radical Party once again found itself the "backbone of the Republic" because the situation was strikingly similar to the beginning years of the Third Republic. That is, the basic constitutional order was being challenged by hostile forces on the right and, this time, on the left as well. For by 1951, de Gaulle's RPF (a rightist and questionably democratic movement) and the French Communist Party (also hostile to the existing governmental provisions) together had garnered 45 percent of the votes in the legislative election of that year. This meant that possible ministerial combinations were restricted to the center-right, center, and center-left. It also meant that the resulting minority governments found their hands tied in governing actively in the name of the public interest or general will.

The result was another Republic that benefited primarily the special interests (especially business and agriculture) working through their lobbyists, another Republic that proceeded almost by default because of the workings of a centralized and efficient administrative bureaucracy. Such an unstable and immobilized system barely survived defeat in Indochina and the granting of independence to other colonies. It would not, however, allow the resolution of the Fourth Republic's final crisis. In May of 1958, events surrounding the Algerian war for independence brought down the Fourth and ushered in the Fifth French Republic under Charles de Gaulle.

ALGERIAN INDEPENDENCE AND THE FIFTH REPUBLIC

The effect of the Algerian war for independence on French politics and society was similar to the impact of the recent war in Vietnam on U.S. politics and society—only worse. For while Vietnam was never part of the United States' to lose, Algeria was considered by many French people to be quite literally an integral corner of France. The battle between those who sought to keep Algeria French and those who fought to establish an independent Algerian nation brought down one republic and dominated the first four years of the next.

The intensity of the conflict stemmed from the differing nature of Algerian colonization compared to French imperialist ventures elsewhere. The great era of colonization by the Western powers—France, Britain, Germany, Italy, Belgium—occurred in the 1870's and 1880's. By the turn of the century, the French Empire encompassed parts of North Africa, Indochina, Canada, West Indies, Equatorial and West Africa, and the Near East. The French intent in these colonies was not so much economic exploitation or emigration prospects for its citizens, but simply French cultural supremacy over the (combined) 100 million natives. French policy was therefore one of "assimilation" of the native élites (not populations) into French culture, language, and civilization so that they might become French citizens and administer the colonies as extensions of the central French State.

Algeria was an exception to this general rule in terms of time and degree. French people began to emigrate to Algeria as early as 1830. Once there, they put down roots, established farms and businesses, participated in the governing process, and achieved a feeling of permanence. By the 1950's, many more French had settled in Algeria than in any of the other colonies, though the one million French settlers were out-numbered by nine million Algerian indigents. After World War II, the great empires began to crumble. France, along with Britain, Germany, and Italy, lost out to native independence movements, which had generally triumphed by the 1960's. Most "new nations" (including neighboring Tunisia and Morocco) were given independence peacefully, but Algeria was granted independence only after a nine year struggle in which governments in Paris were caught between the demands of the Algerian National Liberation Front (FLN), the French settlers (who obviously feared native Algerian majority rule), the French army (which did not relish the prospect of losing yet another colonial war), the majority of French people who originally at least favored a French presence in Algeria, and a small minority whose sympathies lay with Algerian independence.

In May of 1958, it appeared that a new French government was likely to wash its hands of the entire difficult matter and begin negotiations with the FLN. At that point, the French settlers and French army officers in Algeria took the desperate steps of defying the public authorities and setting up their own governing Committees on Public Safety. They further threatened to carry their rebellion to metropolitan France by a coup d'état and civil war if necessary. To avert that disaster, the Fourth Republic politicians turned in June 1958 to General de Gaulle. De Gaulle was acceptable to all sides because, ironically, all sides thought he would handle the Algerian crisis as they wanted it resolved. Yet, the search for an Algerian solution dominated French politics for the next four years. It included secret, then open, negotiations with the FLN, sporadic episodes of French army and settler revolts (notably the April 1961 Generals' Revolt), two heavily endorsed referenda on Algerian self-determination and independence, atrocities on the part of both the French army and the Algerian insurgents, several attempts on de Gaulle's life, and OAS (Secret Army Organization) terrorism in Algeria and France. In the end, de Gaulle accepted "everything France had fought against—total independence, exclusive FLN rule, loss of the Sahara, evacuation of the whole

Street scene in Algiers, 1962.
Keystone

European population."[3] Yet, by 1962 the French public apparently was resigned to de Gaulle's decision to cut France's losses and liquidate the last major portion of its once great empire.

THE LEGACY OF THE PAST

Such were the developments that formed the ideologies, institutions, and movements of present-day French politics. Such are the highly divisive political memories that consciously subdue or inspire new courses of thought and action in the Fifth Republic. What are the patterns that persist and characterize French historical development? Obviously, the French people have continually grappled with a series of very basic questions regarding the nature of their national entity. Politically, the question has been whether France would accept democratic government,

[3] Philip Williams and Martin Harrison, *Politics and Society in de Gaulle's Republic* (New York: Doubleday, Anchor Books, 1971), p. 49.

whether it would be circumscribed by a monarchical authority or simply a strong executive, or whether it would allow full reign to "popular sovereignty" in a legislative oriented system.

In their quest for a political solution, the French had undergone uncanny "full circuits." The old monarchy (of 1788) gave way to a Republic (in 1792), which gave way to an Empire (in 1799). This cycle was then repeated as the restored monarchy (of 1814) fell to the Second Republic (in 1848), which gave way to the Second Empire (of 1852)! Twice around and back, in many ways, to where it had all started in 1789. Furthermore, it is striking to observe that each of the twelve changes of French regimes was due to either a military coup, a military defeat, or a revolution—and most were carried out in a bloody and traumatic fashion. Religiously, the battle in France has concerned the absolute position of the Catholic Church—first politically, then in the educational realm, finally in the spiritual realm, where the question boiled down to the acceptance or rejection of religious tolerance and religious plurality in France. Economically, the battle has continued over the "reformability" of capitalism versus the desirability and/or inevitability of it being surpassed by socialism. Socially, it has been a question of privilege versus a greater degree of equality among citizens. Finally, militarily, the question has been national glory and independence—but at what price?

The history of French political regimes has been a history of one combination of political–economic–social stances replacing another, with no single combination providing an acceptable resolution of the divisive issues. In the process, various factions learned not to give up completely, because their turn would undoubtedly come again. It was only necessary to survive until the next crisis, when once again the fundamental rules of the game could be changed to the victor's advantage. Such a pattern of historical development obviously excluded political stability, as it excluded compromise, confidence, and community. Above all, such a pattern only seems to have reinforced the age-old French observation that "plus ça change, plus c'est la même chose" ("the more things change, the more they stay the same").

policy agenda: problems, cleavages, and conflicts

We have seen that the problems plaguing French politics since 1789 revolve around major philosophical issues. In this section we shall discuss *who* tends to take positions on these issues and *why* they do so. For convenience sake the discussion will contrast the "right" with the "left."

Given the complexity of the problems confronting French politics, it should come as no surprise that its cleavages encompass a multitude of special interest groups and parties. The accompanying "multipartism" in France can be cursed—and praised. The disadvantages of the system lie in the weakness of organization and relatively small numbers of active members that stem from a surfeit of groups competing for the average citizen's time and attention. The advantages lie in the complete choice of options open to French voters. In the United States, for all practical purposes, the voter has to select from a reduced ideological spectrum—the capitalist part. In France the voter has a full range of political choices: conservatism, fascism, right-wing populism, Christian socialism, Gaullism, liberalism, socialism, communism, extreme-leftism. While many Americans might consider this a disadvantage in the political system, others might argue that the very precepts of democracy rest on the nonrestriction of political choices.

THE RIGHT

In general terms, to be on the right implies accepting the status quo, the existing political–social–economic order. By and large, people on the right feel that things as they are—however imperfect they may be—are preferable to the risks involved in conscious political change. While not going so far as the "reactionary right," which would prefer to restore old orders of society, those on the conservative right look to history and tradition as a source of wisdom and as a means of understanding the present. The past, they say, should be learned from and revered, not questioned or repudiated.

Naturally, many on the right are those who benefit from the status quo and who would have the most to lose from reform or revolution. Support for the right in France came initially from those groups which held positions of power before 1789—the aristocracy, the Church, the army. In the nineteenth century, they were joined by the expanding business interests, the middle class bourgeoisie, the wealthier agricultural classes.

What are some of the specific policy positions taken by the right in France?

Politics: A Strong Executive Politically, the right has usually supported an executive as opposed to a legislative government. In practice, the right moved from monarchism, to "bonapartism," even to support of a quasi-fascist dictatorship in World War II, and finally to Fifth Republic "presidentialism." Why has the right favored a strong executive? First, it has usually been far easier for the right to dominate the executive, rather than the legislative, branch. After all, the aristocracy's power did not lie with the force of votes, but with the force of habit, tradition, and deference. With the advent of republican government the representatives of the people tended to dominate the parliamentary bodies, and so forces on the right more than ever favored one man executive rule. In addition, as French history demonstrates, it is easier to capture and to legitimate power through a coup d'état backed by the army and sanctioned by a plebiscite than to win a majority of some 470 legislative seats in a democratic election. Then too it is not possible in a strong legislative system to wrap the chief executive in the mystical aura of "arbiter of the national will" or to evoke the heroic "man on a white horse" solution so reminiscent of the monarch's claims to rule by divine right.

A second reason the right has traditionally favored an executive system pertains to the advantages that accrue therein to special interest groups and to the administrative bureaucracy. France's central administrative bureaucracy has long been filled by élitist groups that sought to preserve their privileges by guarding the status quo and by working closely with like-minded interest groups. Such groups have usually included business and agricultural groups (winegrowers, small shopkeepers, artisans, farmers, industrialists), but also religious and veterans pressure groups. Since policy-making in an executive oriented government is more concentrated and secretive, the special interests and civil servants not unnaturally prefer that arrangement to the legislative oriented system that—theoretically at least—maximizes popular sovereignty and open representative government. Despite this preference, in practice the civil service and economic interest groups thrived in the rather stagnant Third and Fourth Republic parliamentary system.

The Role of the Military   Closely tied to the political division between right and left has been the division over the role of the military. While both left and right place the highest priority on the protection of France's independence and territory, they differ on the question of civilian control of the army versus granting the army considerable free rein to pursue national security. In this regard, the right has been more tolerant of the army's status as a state within a state, charged with a political role to play. The issue of the political role of the army in modern (republican) times exploded notably during the Dreyfus affair (1894–1906), then again during the decolonization process after World War II. From their (losing) vantage point in Indochina in the late forties and early fifties, then in Algeria during the following decade, French army officers believed that they had been betrayed by the republican governments in Paris and that partisan party politics had frittered away what remained of France's national pride and glory. Furthermore, the right has traditionally put high priority—with the army—on the concepts of "nationalism" and "patriotism"; these concepts consciously negate what the left sees as deep divisions or class conflicts within the national body politic. Finally, in terms of domestic politics, there is no question that it has been the left, not the right, that has borne the brunt of military repression, most notably in Paris in 1848 and 1871.[4]

The Catholic Church   Another division between left and right in France concerns religion—in particular, the Catholic Church. This may be surprising to Americans, who are accustomed to religious pluralism, the non-identification of political preference with various churches, and the non-political role in general of established religions. The clearcut division in France stems from the tendency of the Catholic Church to exercise an explicit political role in French history. We must distinguish, however, between the Church—or the formal hierarchy of clergy emanating from the Pope and the Vatican—and the Church's followers, or lay membership. In the twentieth century in particular the two segments have not always been in agreement.

The history of the Catholic Church in France has been one of a gradual loss of absolute power. At one time, the Church strongly influenced rules of acceptable economic behavior, sought to control intellectual developments through its conservative antienlightenment universities, ensured the spiritual predominance of Catholicism through its ruthless persecution of Protestant heretics and, in general, justified the existing social order as reflecting the "will of God." The Church, therefore, had a good deal to lose when the alliance of monarchy, aristocracy, army, and Church was swept away by the Revolution of 1789.

For the next century, the Church hierarchy remained hostile and unreconciled to the very idea of democratic representative government. It is easy to understand why, for the principles of the Republic challenged the very nature of the political practices of the Catholic Church. The Church organization was a rigid hierarchy, and all authority emanated from the Pope and proceeded downward. It was the heretical Protestants, not the Catholic Church, who had been so instrumental in bringing the democratic process to modern society. In its disagreement with democratic principles, the Church not only was slow to accept the Republic, but went on to side with the reactionaries in the Dreyfus affair and even to accept fascism (in Spain and Vichy France, and—initially—in Germany and Italy). As we shall see, on that stand in particular the Church hierarchy was not joined by many of its followers.

A succession of Popes in the twentieth century issued instructions to their subjects forbidding certain political preferences: Pope John's *En-*

[4] See John S. Ambler, *The French Army in Politics, 1945–1962* (Columbus: Ohio State University Press, 1966).

cyclical Mater et Magistra in 1961 finally lifted the threat of excommunication to all those who voted socialist (but not to those voting Marxist or Communist). It was precisely the Church's power of excommunication that led many on the left to believe that a good Catholic could never be a good democrat—that he or she would not act as a free agent in the political process, but would ultimately act in consort with the Church's consistently conservative position.

As political power slipped from its control, the Church turned to the realm of education to maintain at least its spiritual power. The Third Republic's onslaught of public and civic education threatened to undermine the totality of the Catholic message by replacing the catechism with the scientific method of questioning and testing. It took the long experience of the Third Republic to convince the Church that its own preservation could be secured through family and religious ties alone. Once the Church accepted that parochial schools would henceforth serve a small minority of French students, the Church's aim became one of winning State financial support for the Catholic schools. With Gaullist pressure, in 1951 and in 1959 the French Assembly voted to give State aid in exchange for some degree of control (usually to bring the parochial schools up to public school standards).

Though much diffused compared to the nineteenth century, the religious question has not entirely been laid to rest in French politics. The left favors the termination of all State aid to private schools and these schools' absorption into the public sector (minus their ecclesiastical teaching staff). Finally, while the Socialist Party has recently experienced an influx of left-wing (and anticlerical) Catholics, and while the French Catholic Church is itself in a period of possible progressive change, the clerical–anticlerical cleavage among French people remains prominent in political terms. In the United States, the single most important factor today in determining how a person will vote is how that person's parents voted. In France, the primary factor is the voter's degree of religious commitment—the more practicing the Catholic, the more certainly he or she will vote on the right.

The Economic Question The mainstream right in France strongly defends the capitalist system. A system which is based on private ownership of productive, distributive, and financial facilities quite naturally will be supported by industrialist and big business interests, small shopkeepers and artisans, farmers, and the independent professions. But important splits exist within those constituencies which impede a homogeneous right in France. The divisions have to do with "small" versus "large," and State intervention versus laissez-faire economic policies.

Until World War II, the largest single class in French society was that of the peasantry, or all those involved in agricultural pursuits. As a result, the farmers were a predominant electoral force in the Third Republic, and the governments of that period were beholden to their demands. One of the farmers' chief demands was that infringements by the public authorities be kept to an absolute minimum and that a policy of laissez-faire economic (as well as political and social) individualism not give way to the "collectivist" trend of Great Britain and other European countries.

In this respect the farmers were joined by the small shopkeepers and artisans of France—the "Mom and Pop" stores, the strictly family businesses that still characterize French commercial practices. Although the small business classes continued to vote on the right, because they feared the left's stress on public ownership, a more immediate threat to them came from big business—from monopolies and large companies whose scale permitted them to drive out competition and swallow up small concerns. In France today, the small shopkeepers increasingly see their struggle for survival to be against the supermarkets, discount houses, and chainstores, as well as against the assumed collectivist aims of the left.

The division on the right between small and large private economic interests is exacerbated by their division over the role of the State in the economy. Unlike the peasants and small commercial classes, big business and industrialists do not necessarily want to be left alone. Traditionally, in fact, they have benefited from working hand in hand with the State. Napoleon I, the restored monarchs, and Napoleon III in particular, presided over France's expansion of private enterprise in the nineteenth century by using the powers and monies of the State directly to stimulate growth. Thus the concept of state intervention itself was not regarded as undesirable; the practical question was, state intervention for whose benefit? After World War II, business–State relations became increasingly institutionalized (as we shall see in the section on policy process) and the close cooperation between the French government, administration, and business interests continues in the Fifth Republic.

The Traditional Right Despite certain broad principles and the strong support of the aristocracy, military, Church, traditional business classes, and the peasants, a single, unified, conservative party did not emerge in France until after World War II.[5] Rather from 1870 until 1948 a series of disparate groups, parties, and movements came and went, thereby characterizing the right more for its discontinuity than for its effectiveness in

[5] On the right in France see René Rémond, *The Right Wing in France from 1815 to de Gaulle* (Philadelphia: University of Pennsylvania Press, 1969), and Malcolm Anderson, *Conservative Politics in France* (London: Allen & Unwin, 1974).

the political party sphere. One of the reasons for this development was that, in contrast to the left parties, the right was at a disadvantage when it came to building coherent, continuous party organizations. The various parties on the left could anchor their tendencies on clearly enunciated party programs for active change. But because the right offered a "program" of status quo maintenance, it could only stress its candidates' qualities of leadership, judgment, and ability to respond in a responsible manner to situations and crises as they arose. Thus notables, or people recognized for their personal merits, not their ideological positions, predominated in rightist politics; in place of national political uniformity, local and regional diversity was the rule. This in turn produced rightist party organizations quite unlike the left's disciplined and mass parties. With the emphasis solely on elections—not mass membership, programs, or militant participation—those on the right organized periodically around local or constituent electoral committees, leaving more regular coordination to the deputies at the parliamentary level. As a result, personal rivalries and regionalisms plagued the various groups on the right in the Third Republic.

Following the demise of the three competing royalist groups by the turn of the century, the traditional right found itself split in the 1920's and 1930's among such groups as the *Fédération Républicaine, Alliance démocratique,* and *Action libérale populaire.* The right in general was compromised and discredited by its ties with the Vichy regime. After the war, therefore, many on the traditional right supported the MRP, or the Catholic Resistance party (to be discussed below). But the leadership and philosophy of the original MRP was left of center, and by 1948 the traditional right regained its autonomous existence by grouping some (but not all) of the existing smaller parties into the National Center of Independents and Farmers (*Centre national des indépendents et paysans,* or CNIP) of July 1948. The CNIP represented par excellence rural, small-town and Catholic France which used so effectively the immobilized State in the Fourth Republic to protect its vested economic and social interests and to prevent someone else from wresting similar privileges at its expense. In this course, the CNIP was joined by active pressure groups such as the National Council for French Employers (CNPF), the National Council of Small and Medium-sized Businesses (CNPMF), and the National Federation of Farmers (FNSEA).

As in the case of the Third Republic, the traditional right did not survive the Fourth Republic intact. Although the CNIP reached its peak in the 1958 legislative election (See Figure 3–2), it could not withstand the Gaullist tidal wave. But the traditional right did not wish to join the Gaullist right because the two parties differed on several philosophical

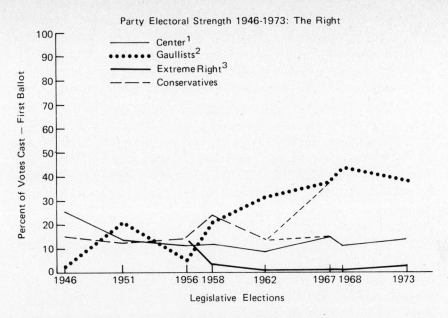

Party Electoral Strength 1946-1973: The Right

Center[1]
●●●●●● Gaullists[2]
Extreme Right[3]
– – – Conservatives

Percent of Votes Cast — First Ballot

Legislative Elections

[1]MRP until 1962; CD in 1967; PDM in 1968; Reformateurs in 1973
[2]Includes Independent Republican allies
[3]Poujadists in 1956

FIGURE 3–2 Party Electoral Strength—1946–1973: The Right

points. First, the CNIP members had grown to appreciate the stagnant and immobilized parliamentary regime that served their economic interests so well in the Fourth Republic. In this regard they distrusted the bonapartist quality of de Gaulle's presidency. Second, the CNIP constituents were oriented more toward laissez-faire economic policies and less toward business–State collusion than the Gaullists were to be. Third, many in the CNIP bitterly opposed independence for Algeria. Lastly, those in the CNIP had usually supported Pétain—not de Gaulle—in the war years.

By 1962 it was clear that the CNIP would split. One faction dwindled to relative unimportance in the center-right Christian Democratic (formerly MRP) movements of the Democratic Center (CD) and Progress and Modern Democracy (PDM); the other faction, the Independent Republicans (RI) accepted a parliamentary alliance with the Gaullists but maintained its organizational independence. The main aim of the Independent Republicans seemed to be to gain access to ministerial positions and to wait for the day their leader, Giscard d'Estaing, would accede to the presidency.[6]

---

[6] See Jean-Claude Colliard, *Les républicains indépendents: Valéry Giscard d'Estaing* (Paris: Presses universitaires de France, 1971).

The Gaullist Right De Gaulle accomplished in the Fifth Republic what no one had previously been able to do: by his very presence he created a unified conservative party in France. With and without its allies, the Gaullist party (the UDR) has held unprecedented majority status in the French Assembly since 1962.[7] The unquestionable success of the Gaullist movement is all the more remarkable given the movement's earlier setbacks in the Fourth Republic, setbacks which had seemingly ensured de Gaulle's political retirement in 1953. Following his resignation as head of the post–Liberation tripartite government of Socialists, Communists, and Christian Democrats (MRP), de Gaulle attempted a comeback through his Rally of the French People (*Rassemblement du peuple français* or RPF) of 1947. The RPF was considered to be extreme right-wing because of its questionable commitment to the Republic and to democratic government. Like the later Poujadist movement, the RPF experienced a rapid rise in popularity (40 percent of the vote in the October 1946 municipal elections). It gained enough seats in the 1951 National Assembly to resurrect the age-old religious battle by assuring the passage of the Barangé Bill which restored State aid to private education. But because of the diversity of its supporters on most questions other than the personality of de Gaulle, the RPF disintegrated and then disappeared in 1953.

De Gaulle was brought out of retirement in June 1958 by an Assembly incapable of handling the Algerian rebellion, which involved the Algerian nationalist liberation front and the opposing French settlers backed by a mutinous French Army. As de Gaulle had "saved" France in World War II, he once again returned in 1958 as the "savior." The Gaullist party, formed just weeks before the November 1958 legislative election, swept in on the coattails of de Gaulle's success. From 18 percent of the vote on the first round of that election, the party climbed to 32 percent in 1962, 38 percent (with allies) in 1967, 44 percent in 1968. (See Figure 3–2.)

What is the philosophy of this party that is so unique in the politics of the French right? Who supports it and how is it organized? First and foremost a commitment to the UDR meant a personal commitment to Charles de Gaulle.[8] Mainly because of his patriotic role in World War II, de Gaulle enjoyed a true "cult of personality." In terms of de Gaulle's own philosophy, his most explicit commitment was to the restoration of the

[7] The Fifth Republic Gaullist movement began in 1958 as the Union for the New Republic (UNR), became the UNR-UDT by the time of the 1962 legislative election, then the Union of Democrats for the Fifth Republic (V République) in 1967, finally the Union of Democrats for the Republic (UDR) since 1968.

[8] On de Gaulle see Alexander Werth, *de Gaulle* (New York: Simon and Schuster, 1966).

grandeur of France and to his mystical belief in France's future "destiny." To achieve this, de Gaulle proposed—and the Gaullists endorsed—a return to the executive tradition of government which permitted him to govern almost singlehandedly. In terms of economic and social philosophy, de Gaulle was considerably less explicit. He often spoke of achieving "something between capitalism and communism," something along the lines of the old Catholic idea of corporatism. This entailed a rejection of laissez-faire capitalism for a system in which the State coordinated economic life in pursuit of the public interest and in which private property and social or class distinctions nevertheless remained. It differed therefore from the socialist alternative, which stressed public ownership and the eventual elimination of social inequalities. This aspect of de Gaulle's philosophy appealed much more to the left-wing or "social Gaullists," who originally grouped in a Gaullist splinter group called the Democratic Union of Work (UDT). These Gaullists had constituted the core of de Gaulle's war-time and resistance supporters, but in the Fifth Republic they were to be continuously frustrated by de Gaulle's inattention to economic and social reform. At any rate, the "big business" philosophy of most Gaullist leaders, such as Georges Pompidou, proved much more pervasive within the party ranks.

In terms of party organization, the UDR remained a relatively loose movement.[9] It did not stress membership totals, although it claimed 100,000 members in 1968 (more than the French Socialist Party at that time and down considerably from the one million members in the RPF of 1947). Stripped of the function of policy initiative (which lay solely with de Gaulle), the party existed mainly as an electoral machine, active only in selecting candidates and in raising money and management skills for campaigns. Recruitment was facilitated because little more was required of the party clientele than the acceptance of de Gaulle. What mattered was to hold onto the power already gained through de Gaulle's presence. As such the party did not bother with enunciating what it would do with its power. This approach appealed spectacularly to the French. In a rare feat achieved only by previous "bonapartist" personalities, the party of de Gaulle gathered support from almost all segments of the population— businessmen, farmers, technocrats, middle classes, even one-quarter of the working class—but especially from women, the elderly, and rural France.

Since the 1973 legislative and 1974 presidential elections, however, certain weaknesses in the party's voting clientele have emerged. (See Table 3-1.) The UDR finds one of its greatest proportional strengths with the liberal professions, high level management, and independent business

[9] See Jean Charlot, *The Gaullist Phenomenon* (London: Allen & Unwin, 1971).

TABLE 3–1 Voting Intentions in March 1973 Legislative Elections by Socio-Demographic Categories

	PCF	UGSD	PSU	Reformers	Majority	Other Right	Total	Adult French Population
Overall	19%	23%	4%	15%	36%	3%	100%	
(Actual vote)	(21.3)	20.4	3.3	12.4	38.5	2.8)		
Sex:								
Men	22	25	4	16	30	3	100	48
Women	16	21	4	14	43	2	100	52
Age:								
21–34	21	24	7	17	27	4	100	29
35–49	17	27	3	16	34	3	100	29
50–64	21	21	4	15	37	2	100	22
65+	17	18	1	10	52	2	100	20
Occupation of head of household:								
Professional, top level management, and civil servant	11	20	10	20	39	–	100	6
Industry, merchants, small business	12	22	2	22	36	6	100	9
White collar employees	17	29	9	19	23	3	100	17
Workers	33	27	4	12	22	2	100	32
No occupation	17	20	3	14	44	2	100	24
Farmers	8	19	1	16	49	7	100	12
Residence:								
Rural Communes	13	21	2	14	46	4	100	30
Under 20,000 population	22	24	2	10	40	2	100	14
20–100,000 population	15	29	4	18	32	2	100	14
100,000+	21	24	5	15	32	3	100	25
Parisian population	28	18	8	19	25	2	100	17
Religious Practice:								
Practicing	1	10	2	16	70	1	100	17
Occasionally	14	22	2	13	47	2	100	42
Nonpracticing	32	31	4	11	20	2	100	41

Source: Adapted from *Sondages*, no. 1, 1973, p. 21.

classes, who nevertheless make up only 15 percent of the overall population. The party is also disproportionately represented in the categories of the old and the retired; it does not attract the youth vote as does the left. It is strong among practicing Catholics, in a time of declining religious commitment, as well as with the farmers, whose numbers continue to decline in proportion to other producer groups. Finally, the Gaullist inroads into the working class were swept back significantly in the 1974 presidential election.

The Extreme Right An extreme right had always existed alongside the more respectable traditional right. Originally royalist in nature, these groups actively entered the Dreyfus affair on the side of the army and Church. Charles Maurras' extreme-right wing *Action française* of 1905 grew out of that bitter battle, and the *Action française* philosophy prefigured the fascist groups of the 1930's with its anti-Semitic, anti-Republic, antiforeign, proauthoritarian elements. But the vituperative and reactionary nature of Maurras' group was too much even for the Pope and the Bourbon pretender (the Count of Paris), both of whom denounced the *Action française* in the 1920's. By then the fascist leagues were gaining prominence. Colonel de la Rocque's *Croix de Feu* (Iron Cross) and even more extreme groups with names like National Volunteers, French Solidarity, and Patriotic Youth presented a potential threat to French democracy in the mid 1930's. Their attitude (shared by many in the traditional right) was "better Hitler than Blum." These groups were all banned by the socialist Léon Blum's Popular Front government of 1936, but they were subsequently welcomed and active in the Vichy authoritarian interlude. The more purely fascist of those groups, in fact, staffed the *Milice française* (the French equivalent of Hitler's SS troops) and were responsible for the repression and death of many fellow French men and women.

There arose in the mid 1950's a revival of right-wing extremism, this time known as *Poujadisme*. Pierre Poujade's protest movement of "little people"—shopkeepers like himself, bar and café proprietors, small farmers, artisans—was not truly fascist, since its aim was not to abolish the Republic but to call for a new one. Closer to the right-wing populism of the Third Republic peasant constituency, the Poujadists espoused "individualism" or less interference by politicians and the State authorities. The immediate cause of the Poujadist revolt in 1954 was a bill passed by a traditional right government providing for a more careful scrutiny of income tax returns. Small businessmen in France have long been notorious tax-evaders, and stricter tax enforcement threatened to drive their incomes down even closer to the level of the working class. If traditional independent middle classes had one fear, it was that of "sinking into the ranks of the proletariat." This great economic and social fear was compounded because the larger, more modernized business interests on the traditional right were squeezing them to the economic margins. The Poujade movement swept the French countryside from 1954 to 1956, and while it was not immediately clear what they were *for,* it was very clear what the Poujadists were *against:* against taxes, big business, politicians, civil servants, bureaucrats, technocrats, officials, the rich, the powerful, the State—to say nothing of Jews, financiers, academics, intellectuals, decolonizers, and cosmopolitans! The Poujadist party (the Union and French Fraternity or UFF) enjoyed momentary success in the 1956 legislative election (with 12.5 percent of the vote), but the party dissolved two years later, subsumed by the Gaullist and the reactionary *Algérie Française* ("Keep Algeria French") movements.

The *Algérie Française* camp was the last significant manifestation of right-wing extremism in French politics. Its supporters fought against granting independence to Algeria, sometimes literally with the OAS (Secret Army Organization).

Small extreme-right groups exist in the 1970's in France. The *Ordre Nouveau,* for instance, has recently acquired attention in its street confrontations with Trotskyist groups. But the near demise of the extreme right as an independent political force (assuming many of its supporters have found a home in the Gaullist party) is evident when its recent paltry electoral performances (see Figure 3–2) are contrasted with its support in the first two decades of the twentieth century, when, between 1893 and 1919, the extreme right parties averaged 20 percent of the vote!

THE LEFT

The idea that people should live in community and own most things in common is an ancient one, ranging from the times of Moses and then the early Christians on to the primitive communism of some medieval groups and societies. But "modern socialism" did not arise until the nineteenth century, when it emerged in direct response to the effects of the rise of capitalism and the Industrial Revolution. One of the Industrial Revolution's primary effects on the social sphere had been to replace the old class of independent artisans and craftsmen with a new and expanded class of urban factory workers. In Britain, where the benefits and ravages of the industrial age were felt earlier and with greater intensity, the working classes had become conscious of their tenuous relationship to the capitalist (private owner of the productive facilities). They subsequently had formed organizations to maximize their strength, to emphasize their indispensability, and to demand basic reforms of the system.

In France, however, industrial development was slow, producing isolated and small-scale production units in which the lack of anonymity and the close contact between owner and worker tended to subdue open class conflict. Nevertheless, early French socialist spokesmen enunciated a vague and popular moral condemnation of a system that, in 1830 for example, worked the workers 15 hours a day, paid them even less than subsistence wages (the remainder coming from charity), kept them overwhelmingly illiterate, denied them citizenship as well as the right to form labor unions, and controlled their movement through a system of internal "work passbooks." Saint-Simon, Fourier, Proudhon: these French utopian socialist writers predated Karl Marx in identifying private owner-ship as the source of human exploitation. In their own differing ways they presented the case for a socialist society: that is, that the productive, distributive, and financial facilities of a society should be owned, con-trolled and run by the very people who work in them. Public (also called common or collective) ownership was the only way to achieve "produc-tion for service not profit" and cooperation was to replace competition as the motor force of society.

In the Revolution and Republic of 1848, the socialist movement had put aside its utopian vision and had entered the world of practical politics, only to be "betrayed," then physically devastated. Persecution of the socialist movement continued throughout the Second Empire, culminating in the debacle of the Paris Commune. In the early decades of the Third Republic, the movement gained several important rights—in 1874 the right to vote for all males over 21, in 1884 the legal right to form trade unions, in 1890 the abolishment of the work passbook system. Some at-tempt was made prior to World War I to alleviate with social legislation the generally abysmal lot of the workers (public assistance to the destitute in 1893—enacted in Britain in 1601; the ten-hour day for women and children in 1900; Sundays off in 1906; and optional social insurance in 1910), but these measures fell far behind provisions made for the labor force in most other industrial states. Even then it was too late. The French working class movement had long since moved beyond the British work-ing class position of reform and was demanding instead the complete overthrow of the capitalist system.

While most French socialists agreed on the goals of a socialist society which embodied Marx's visionary slogan "from each according to his abilities, to each according to his needs," they were plagued continually by rifts over the tactics and strategies needed to achieve that elusive end. After the events of 1848 and 1871, French socialists were skeptical about the British Labour Party tactic of alignment with bourgeois liberal parties. Another successful British option was foreclosed to the French socialists in the last two decades of the nineteenth century as the trade union movement asserted its independence from socialist politics. Finally, the most cruel split of all occurred in 1920, as the Communists branched off from the Socialist Party in pursuit of Lenin's Soviet experiment. The history of the French socialist movement has been a history of disunity. One major result has been that, since the establishment of modern democratic government in the Third Republic, the French left has held power for only six of the last 100 years. To reverse that trend, the French left in the Fifth Republic has been forced to confront the classical divisions between liberalism and socialism, trade union and socialist party politics, and democratic socialism and communism.[10]

Syndicalism   In Britain and Germany, the direct links between powerful trade unions and the socialist parties have contributed to the relative political strength of the left. In France, the trade union–political party split was formalized almost from the beginning. Syndicalism, or revolutionary trade unionism, grew out of the same workers' movement as the socialist party organizations and it shared the philosophy that the capitalist system had to be undermined and then overthrown. But in place of a political revolution, the syndicalist movement counted on an economic transformation through direct action by the workers themselves. Boycotts, sabotage, finally the complete and simultaneous withholding of workers' services—the general strike—would suffice to transfer the private ownership of the mines, factories, and railroads into worker ownership and management. The syndicalists thus rejected all political party activity that aimed at the conquest of the State by parliamentary electoral activity. Furthermore, the syndicalists opposed the very notion of the centralized State based on representative democratic government. Instead, they envisaged a decentralized socialist society in which semi-independent local groups would voluntarily federate to achieve some direction of social–economic–political purpose, and in which the State (whether on a regional, national, or even European level) would be reduced to the vague role of coordinator.

In the pre–World War I years, the trade union movement consolidated and grew, as did the socialist movement. The still largest union, the General Confederation of Labor (or CGT), was established when several large federations, themselves uniting many local labor exchanges, merged in 1902. Then in 1906, the CGT wrote its guiding *Charte d'Amiens,* a document which spelled out the principle of trade union independence from all political parties. This principle ruled trade union practice for many

[10] For background on the left in general, see Georges Lefranc, *Les Gauches en France* (Paris: Payot, 1973); for the 1965 to 1973 period, see the two volumes of Jean Poperen, *La gauche Française* (Paris: Fayard, 1972 and 1975).

decades. By 1945, however, the CGT leadership was overtly sympathetic to the French Communist Party. In protest over this violation of the *Charte d'Amiens* a minority of trade unionists broke from the CGT in 1947 to form the *CGT-Force Ouvrière*, which was a more social democratic body with links to the French Socialist Party and to American trade unions.

The third main trade union group in France today is the French Confederation of Democratic Labor (CFDT). It was formed originally in 1919 as an explicitly Catholic trade union body, but underwent a "desecularization" process in 1964. The CFDT is closest to the French Socialist Party in terms of ideology and militant overlap, and in many ways is the most politically radical of the trade unions. The CFDT currently has 800,000 members, the CGT-FO 600,000, and the CGT claims over 2 million. These totals are small compared to the British TUC's 9.5 million and the German DGB's 6.5 million; in fact, the rate of unionization in France is around 20 percent of eligible workers, whereas in Great Britain and Germany it is 44 percent and 37 percent, respectively. The net effect of the historical division between party and trade union and the present divisions within the syndicalist movement itself have been primary sources of weakness in the French working class movement.[11]

French Socialists   Trade union independence not only undercut the Socialist Party's potential organization, but it left unchallenged the party's commitment to a kind of socialism called *state socialism.* In the late nineteenth and early twentieth centuries, proponents of state socialism—such as the Fabians in Britain and Eduard Bernstein in Germany—argued persuasively that the advent of universal male suffrage, freedom of association, and parliamentary democracy would allow the socialists of Europe to come to power through a peaceful, electoral route. Once the socialists achieved power, argued the state socialists, they could create a more egalitarian society through state-provided social services and by nationalizing, or placing under State control, key industries and services. The French Socialists thereupon entered the electoral battle in earnest (though disunited) and gained 40 seats in the 1893 election. In 1905 the five socialist factions united to form the French Socialist Party (SFIO). Under leaders such as Jean Jaurès and Léon Blum, the SFIO couched its stringent Marxist analysis in reformist programs and actions that led it to accept, like the British Labour Party, a mixed economy and welfare state.

[11] See Val R. Lorwin, *The French Labor Movement* (Cambridge: Harvard University Press, 1954) and Jacques Capdevielle and Rene Mouriaux, *Les Syndicats ouvriers en France* (Paris: Colin, 1970).

The period from 1936 to 1945 marked a high point in the life of the SFIO. In 1936, the Popular Front alliance of Socialists, Communists and Radicals gained an unprecedented majority of seats in the Assembly. With Léon Blum as prime minister, the Popular Front government proceeded to enact a political–economic–social reform bill that was similar to the American New Deal and the British Labour "revolution" of 1945. For the first time workers were granted the right to collective bargaining. Their working conditions were considerably improved by provisions calling for wage increases, a forty-hour week, four weeks paid vacation, measures to reduce unemployment through public work projects, and more progressive income taxation. The Popular Front government also nationalized the Bank of France, armament industries, and insurance companies. But the Socialist–led coalition did not withstand the growing international crisis presented by German fascism. A year later, it gave way to a more centrist coalition. The Socialists and Communists would not find themselves together again until the years of the underground war Resistance movement.

After the war new opportunities for the left were frustrated by multipartism, an overly legislative oriented government, and—after 1947—the Cold War. The SFIO, under the leadership of Guy Mollet since 1946, became a closed and aging party whose principles seemed to have been reduced to electoralism, anti-communism and self-perpetuation.

The Fifth Republic brought new problems. The existence of a united right behind de Gaulle forced the left to grapple with problems of realignment and unity as they never had before. The SFIO tried three differing strategies in the pursuit of unity. From 1963 to 1965, Gaston Defferre (Mollet's major rival in the Party) sought an alliance with moderate groups on the SFIO's right: the Radical Party, the newly arisen political club movement, and the Christian Democratic MRP. By fusing these groups into one large *Fédération,* Defferre hoped to create a strong third force that might shake lose the PCF's mordant hold on the left. But Defferre's innovative plan for a federation of the center-left was drowned in a torrent of anticlericalism from the Radical Party, antisocialism from the MRP, and stubborn party patriotism from all sides.

Having survived this first attempt to unseat his leadership, Mollet soon faced a second attempt in the form of François Mitterrand's Democratic and Socialist Federation of the Left (FGDS). Formed during Mitterrand's unsuccessful presidential race in 1965, the FGDS combined the SFIO, the Radical Party and the Convention of Republican Institutions (CIR), a major club grouping to which Mitterrand belonged. For three years Mitterrand sought to fuse the parties, write a more left-leaning socialist program, and from a position of strength effect an electoral and governmental coalition with the ever powerful French Communist Party. This time basic personality rivalries rather than ideological divisions caused the FGDS to collapse in the fall of 1968. There remained only one option to those who sought democratic socialist realignment: to unseat Guy Mollet and his supporters and capture the SFIO itself. This was accomplished in the Socialist Party congress of 1971 by a secret alliance comprised essentially of all "anti-Molletists" in the old SFIO and in the about-to-be-merged CIR. Under the leadership of François Mitterrand, the French Socialist Party (now called the *Parti Socialiste* or PS) went on to renovate its ideology, clientele, and strategy.[12]

In terms of ideology, the PS of the 1970's stands for a more radical democratic socialism. In addition to familiar nationalization, other forms of public ownership are endorsed by the French Socialists; such forms include municipal, cooperative, and mutual society ownership. The party also insists that common ownership be coupled with community and workers' control; if not, it says, the goals of economic (and especially industrial) democracy will remain unfulfilled. In this sense the French Socialists have refound their original syndicalist base, which had for so long been covered over by the more prominent "state socialists."

The structure of the PS remains that of an open, democratically run (though faction-ridden) mass party. Its 150,000-strong membership in 1975 represents twice that of 1969. The PS has also experienced a change in the nature of its expanded clientele. The former SFIO was characterized by certain sociological categories, such as lower level civil servants and functionaries, workers, pensioners, and some petty bourgeois artisans and merchants. The new PS appeals increasingly to youth and intellectuals, workers, lower and middle white collar workers, and to the growing numbers of technological personnel in government and industry (see Table 3–1). The PS, in fact, counters the French Communist Party's "traditional working class" notion with its own "new working class" concept that includes all *salaried* workers, a group that makes up 80 percent of the French work force. This concept stresses the common cause of traditional workers and new technological personnel because, while the latter may enjoy middle class standards of living and expectations, they too remain excluded from the decision-making process in their place of work. Finally, in a development never paralleled by the former SFIO, the PS has experienced an influx of trade union activists (mainly from the CFDT), Catholic leftists, and young people (who have no prior party affiliation).

[12] See Frank L. Wilson, *The French Democratic Left: 1963–1969* (Stanford: Stanford University Press, 1971) and Pierre Guidoni, *Histoire du nouveau parti socialiste* (Paris: Tema-Action, 1973).

The French Socialists have begun a new lease on life in the 1970's. One explanation of this—besides the personal leadership qualities of Mitterrand—is the relative success of its "union of the left" strategy. Beginning in 1969, the Socialists decided to go beyond the legislative electoral alliances they had maintained with the French Communist Party since 1967 and to agree on a common governmental program of action. Mitterrand and the post–1971 party leadership pursued that course, signing in 1972 a Common Governmental Program with the Communists. Eight months later, in the March 1973 legislative elections, the Socialists nearly equalled the Communists' electoral strength for the first time since the war (see Figure 3–3).

French Communists   A far worse blow than the syndicalists to the development of a united left in France occurred in 1920 with the creation of the French Communist Party.[13] In that year, all of the mass socialist parties of Europe voted on whether or not to join Lenin's recently established Third International. To qualify as an official Communist Party, however,

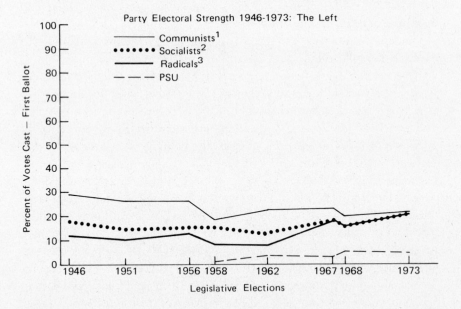

¹PCF

²SFIO until 1967; FGDS in 1967 and 1968; UGSD in 1973

³FGDS in 1967 and 1968; Minority Radicals in UGSD in 1973

FIGURE 3–3 Party Electoral Strength—1946–1973: The Left

[13] On the French Communist Party, see Jacques Fauvet, *Histoire du parti communiste francais*, Vol. I and II (Paris: Fayard, 1964 and 1965) and Ronald Tiersky, *French Communism: 1920–1972* (New York: Columbia University Press, 1975).

the socialists had to accept Lenin's list of 21 conditions. When summarized, these conditions give us an idea of the general nature of Communist, as opposed to socialist, parties. The conditions fall into three categories: the recognition that the USSR, as the first socialist country, deserves absolute loyalty; the necessity to organize the party along "democratic centralist" lines, actually meaning control from top to bottom through secret procedures and strict, internal discipline that does not tolerate "factions"; the immediate aim of establishing a "dictatorship of the proletariat" or the need for the party of the working class (the Communist Party) to capture political power. In contrast, socialist parties (then and now) totally reject the notion of loyalty to the USSR. They reject democratic centralism in favor of maintaining (what the Communists call) "bourgeois democracy," with its provisions for the secret ballot, free and open discussion, the right to protest and to challenge decisions. Socialists also reject the absolute primacy of the working class, seeking instead a numerical majority drawn from the population as a whole. Despite Léon Blum's presentation of these positions at the Socialist Party's 1920 Congress of Tours, the majority of delegates accepted Lenin's ultimatum, and the body formally became the French Communist Party (PCF). The minority delegates regrouped under Blum, retaining the name SFIO.

Immediately following its victory at the Tours Congress, the new PCF's fortunes began to drop precipitously. Disillusioned by factionalism and the expulsion of dissidents and resentful of Moscow domination of the party, many members (including the top leader) returned to the SFIO. In three years, the PCF's membership fell by half. To compound the problem, Lenin's answer to the party's precarious condition was complete "bolshevization" of the party, a tightening of democratic centralist discipline in the organization. This was followed by the instigation of a "class versus class" electoral tactic for the 1928 and 1932 elections, a tactic which only brought on the defection of a great number of PCF voters. By 1934, however, the PCF changed tactics in the face of rising concern over the specter of fascism in Germany and its possible spillover into France. With the Comintern's approval, the PCF joined with the Socialists, Radicals, and other leftist groups in forming the *Front Populaire* of June 1935. As a result, PCF membership rose spectacularly, from 32,000 in 1932 to 340,000 in 1937. In 1939, however, the party alienated many of its new members by lauding the temporary Nazi–Soviet Pact. But by 1941 it recovered its dynamism when its members entered in full force the French underground Resistance movement.

As a result of the party's identification with the Popular Front and Resistance movements, it emerged from World War II as the largest political party in France. Accordingly, de Gaulle allotted the Communists three ministries in his postwar government, and members remained in the tripartite government until the onset of the Cold War. After 1947, the PCF entered a bleak decade characterized by isolation, unrespectability, and Stalinist sectarianism. One of the major causes of the Fourth Republic's immobilism was precisely the effective removal from the political sphere of those one-quarter to one-fifth of the French voters who stayed with the PCF in its political ghetto.

In 1959, pondering the onslaught of Gaullist candidates who eroded even the normally stable Communist electorate, the PCF reached the same conclusion as the rest of the left: they could all stand united or remain fallen divided. As the SFIO's social democratic program evolved into the PS's democratic socialist philosophy, the PCF moved in 1959 from its previous isolationist posture toward an alliance with the Socialists in pursuit of a "peaceful road to socialism" in France.

First, to persuade its allies of the party's new image, the French Communists, in effect, consciously lessened their commitment to the general thrust of Lenin's original conditions. Thus the party showed slight signs of reduced submissiveness to the USSR. It publicly questioned the manner in which Khrushchev was ousted in 1964, disagreed with the Soviet invasion of Czechoslovakia in 1968, and criticized the Prague political trials of 1972. But at the same time the full effect of this "independence" was undercut by the PCF's continuing tendency to hold up the USSR as a society well on its way to achieving "true socialism."

Second, the party decided to commit itself formally to the rules of "bourgeois democracy." Since the late 1960's, the Communists have formally endorsed the notions of plurality of parties in a socialist France, sovereignty of universal suffrage and thus the alternation of power, and protection of basic individual and collective liberties. But again, the commitment is obscured since the model country, the USSR, does not follow these democratic practices and since the PCF's own internal politics remain based on strict democratic centralism. While the Communists have modified the first two conditions, they continue to insist, however, that the march toward socialism must be led by the party of the working class—the PCF.

It is essential to understand the PCF's appeal to the working class in France. Just over half the party's votes come from the working class electorate—and one in three working class electors votes for the PCF (see Table 3–1). Most of these voters support the party not because they want a revolution, a Communist society, or have read Marx and Lenin. Rather, it is because they want to register a protest against the status quo—a status quo which, after all, gives the working class the longest work hours, the lowest pay, the least interesting jobs, and the least access to national political power. In addition, they feel the Communists have done—or at least want to do—the most for the working class at the level of daily life. Many municipal councils and mayoralities in France are controlled by Communist party members and party cells make sure they are visible in places of work and in local community affairs.

To emphasize the working class nature of the organization is one thing; to quote Marxist–Leninist doctrine that the party must be predominant in the march toward socialism lest it fail is another. In fact, the accomplishment of left unity in 1972 (with the signing of the Common Governmental Program of Socialists and Communists) *did* bring about a strengthening and a realignment of the forces of the left, but it was the electorate and membership of the Socialist Party which rose. The PCF's percentage of the vote remained stagnant at 21 percent (see Figure 3–3), its membership equally stagnant (though large) at 425,000.

By the mid 1970's then, after fifteen years in pursuit of leftist unity, the PCF had to take stock of the price it had paid for its political reintegration through leftist unity. That is, if the PS succeeded in reversing the postwar situation in which the PCF was the predominant party of the left, was the price not too high to pay?

The PSU The historical span of the Unified Socialist Party (PSU) is short (it originated in 1960), its electoral importance minimal (less than 4 percent of the votes in most elections), its structure diffuse and dwindling (never more than 15,000 members). Yet, in terms of its theoretical probings and leadership personnel, this party has contributed much to the renovation and resurgence of the new PS.[14]

In 1958, two issues caused splinter groups to break away from the Radical, Socialist, and Communist parties. One issue was support or rejection of the Algerian independence movement; the other was initial support or rejection of de Gaulle's Fifth Republic. Alongside these splinter groups was a "new left" current from the Fourth Republic which rejected both the reformist "social democracy" of Guy Mollet's SFIO and the Stalinist model of socialism of Maurice Thorez's PCF. In 1960, a number of these small groups merged to form the PSU, whose goal was to define and to achieve an "authentic socialism" for France. The PSU struggled for eight years to change the rest of the left simply by (in the words of a former leader) the "quality of its intellectual and theoretical contributions." [15]

When the FGDS and PCF failed to join the PSU at the forefront of the

[14] See Michel Rocard, *Le PSU et l'avenir socialiste de la France* (Paris: Seuil, 1969).
[15] Michel Rocard, cited in *Tribune Socialiste*, November 15, 1972, p. 9.

May 1968 student-worker riots (to be discussed below), the PSU changed course, moved closer to the extreme left groups of Trotskyists, Maoists, and anarchists, and all but gave up on unity of the entire left. But the French Socialist Party had been affected by the post–May 1968 resurgence of a revolutionary democratic socialist model, and after 1969 a number of former PSU members were elected to the PS governing boards. Most importantly, the PS' 1972 ideological statement and program drew heavily from previously unorthodox PSU concepts. These included the general notion of *autogestion* (self-management) and its economic application as workers' management and control in industry; democratic planning or the arrival at national economic and social priorities with public participation in local, regional, and national elected assemblies; regional decentralization or the dispersal of power from Paris into the hands of people whose lives are most closely affected by those decisions; the notion of the *couches nouvelles* or new working class of technological and scientific personnel in advanced industrial society and their relationship to the development of socialism; environmental and ecological concerns and the limits of continued economic growth; and the notion of socialist party pluralism in a democratic and socialist France. Because of the rapprochement of the PS to the views of the PSU, the PSU's independent existence no longer made much sense by 1975. While the majority of the now tiny organization chose autonomy, many of the PSU's militant Catholic and trade union members went over to the PS. Most importantly, the minority was led by the PSU's most outstanding asset, its leader Michel Rocard.

French Radicals The *Parti républicain radical et radical-socialiste*, or French Radical Party, dates from 1901, technically making it the oldest party on the left. But since its evolution in the 1970's, it would be more accurate to move the party to the liberal center. The Radical Party was originally considered on the left not because a majority of its supporters were socialists (although as the name indicates, the party has always balanced two factions of liberals and socialists), but because in the 1870's, mere support for the Republic placed one on the left. Led by famous leaders such as Thiers, Gambetta, and Ferry, the Republicans' battle from 1869 to 1905 was in the name of such radical ideas as political democracy (or the "indispensable liberties" similar to those contained in the U.S. Constitution's Bill of Rights) and social democracy (equality of opportunity and the abolishment of privilege based on wealth or birth).

Most but not all Radicals, however, did not accept the idea of economic democracy, instead preferring a laissez-faire, but resolutely antimonopolist, capitalism. Then a curious thing happened to the Radical Party. The bulk of its famous 1869 "Belleville program" had been fulfilled by 1905! Republican governments had succeeded in defeating the monarchist cause, in abolishing press censorship, in providing free education, in separating the Church from the State, and in passing a mildly progressive income tax. From that time on, the party's "program" became one of simply holding on to governmental power in order to protect these achievements from erosion by either the extreme right or extreme left. The Radical Party's philosophy in the Third and Fourth Republics became that of electoralism, governmentalism, and (inescapably) opportunism.

The Radical Party as an organization very much resembled the notable dominated structures of the traditional right. This was because all these groups evolved out of parliamentary cadres, not out of long-excluded mass movements as did the Socialist and Communist parties. Hence the Radical Party's active clientele drew heavily from the professional, management, and business classes. In the Fourth Republic, the former Radical Prime Minister, Pierre Mendès-France, tried and failed at the first of what was to become a series of attempts to build a tighter, mass-supported party structure and to reinforce the socialist wing of its philosophy.[16] In the Fifth Republic, with its old route of ministerialism foreclosed by the Gaullist majority, the Radical Party joined in the trend toward left realignment and unity, first willingly supporting Defferre's *Grande Fédération* plan, then more begrudgingly supporting Mitterrand's FGDS. The Radical Party split definitively from the Socialists, however, in the late 1960's over the strategy of a governmental program with the PCF. While a small group of left-Radicals endorsed the 1972 Common Governmental Program, most of the Radicals turned toward the center and temporarily allied with the Christian Democrats in the *Movement Réformateur*. The move allowed the controversial head of the party, Jean-Jacques Servan-Schreiber, briefly to gain entry to the first cabinet of the Giscard d'Estaing presidency. By then it was obvious that the Radicals' time on the left had long since come and gone.

The Center   In a sense, the Radicals' problems in the Fifth Republic were shared by the center parties in general. What place was there for them in an increasingly bipolar political situation? The hour of the centrists clearly had been in the multipolar days of the Fourth Republic, when powerful antisystem groups to the right and to the left narrowed the field and therefore enhanced the indispensability of centrist coalitions in government. Along with the center-left Radical Party elements, the other postwar centrist party, the Popular Republican Movement (MRP)

[16] See Francis deTarr, *The French Radical Party from Herriot to Mendès-France* (New York: Oxford University Press, 1961).

grouped the "social Catholics" otherwise known as Christian Democrats.[17]

The history of practicing Catholics who rejected their Church's authoritarian, even reactionary, stand in political–social–economic questions goes back to the turn of the century and to the *Sillon* movement of Marc Sangnier. This movement of progressive Catholics believed that the economic counterpart to a social system based on justice and brotherly love was socialism, not capitalism. For their beliefs, these Catholic socialists were ordered to disband their political movement in 1912. Citing the Tenth Commandment as divine sanction of private property, the Pope ruled that Catholicism and socialism were obviously incompatible.

Consequently, progressive Catholicism lay dormant until World War II. While the Church hierarchy supported the Vichy regime, there were many Catholics who did not. These Catholics joined the Socialists and Communists in the underground Resistance movement and formed their own party, the MRP. After the war, the MRP emerged as the largest non-Communist party in France, and became one of the three governing parties in the left-oriented tripartite era of 1945–1947. MRP notables continued to play a significant role in many Fourth Republic ministries. By 1950, however, many MRP supporters had placed political considerations over religious preference and the party's support rapidly dispersed. Some MRP voters were drawn to the once-again respectable traditional right (the CNIP), others were swept up in the arch-Catholic Charles de Gaulle's RPF (and later, the UDR). The more militant of the progressive Catholics joined the revolutionary but insignificant "new left" of the 1950's, moved through the PSU in the Fifth Republic, and most recently have found a home in the new PS of François Mitterrand, who himself embodies a lingering Christian socialist aura.

The main body of the MRP managed to limp on into the Fifth Republic. After rejecting a role in Defferre's federation, it eventually merged with other centrist groups to form the Democratic Center (CD), then the Progress and Modern Democracy (PDM), then the *Movement Réformateur.* (See Figure 3–2.) All had not been in vain, however, because following Giscard d'Estaing's election as president, several centrist notables, led by Jean Lecanuet, were accorded key positions in the government of Prime Minister Jacques Chirac.

POLITICAL CONFLICTS IN THE FIFTH REPUBLIC

Given the unresolved issues and the contending forces or cleavages, what are some of the notable conflicts of the Fifth Republic? We shall examine the substance of several of these conflicts, which include the legislative

[17] See Mario Einaudi and François Goguel, *Christian Democracy in Italy and France* (South Bend, Ind.: University of Notre Dame Press, 1952).

and presidential elections, the events of May 1968, the Socialist–Communist Common Governmental Program of 1972, and the economic debate kindled by that document.

Elections　History shows us that contending political forces in France have not hesitated to change the rules of the game (that is, the Constitution) once they attain power. One of the key rules subject to change has been the electoral system.[18] This seemingly mechanical question masks a highly political nature; namely, incumbents can manipulate the electoral system to their advantage and to undercut their opponents' actual strength.

Since 1919, France has used five different electoral laws, all based on some variant of two basic systems. The first system, the single member winner-take-all (*scrutin majoritaire*), was utilized in the Third Republic and is now used in the Fifth. The second, proportional representation (PR), was in effect throughout the Fourth. To an American, the most logical (indeed, only) way to decide an election is to declare as winner the candidate who receives the most votes in a general election, as, for example, in the case of the selection of U.S. senators and representatives. To a French voter, who is accustomed to seeing many parties and candidates on the ballot, this system makes better sense if there is a second ballot (usually a week later) that allows for realignment and withdrawals—in short, that allows a second chance to express a clearer voter preference.

Opponents of the single member system (for example, the current French left) hold up PR as a much more just system of representation. In the PR system, the proportion of seats in the elected body is meant to be more or less equal to the proportion of votes. Thus, if a party receives 20 percent of the vote, its candidates would be allotted 20 percent of the seats. In a single member system that same party would receive no representation and its voters, goes the argument, in effect would be unrepresented. Perhaps PR is a fairer electoral system, but there are many who put efficiency above fairness. Because a single member system tends to force small parties out of existence or into larger coalitions and alliances, it increases the likelihood of returning a majority party to power. The result is stable and efficient government, and that, goes the argument, is preferable in the end to a detailed representation of the peoples' voices which results in a multitude of uncompromising parties and an ungovernable political system.

When de Gaulle began to draft a new constitution for the Fifth

[18] For a history of French electoral systems, see Peter Campbell, *French Electoral Systems, 1789–1957* (New York: Praeger, 1958).

Republic, he rejected the PR system because he felt that it had doomed the Fourth Republic to multipartism and immobilism. Instead he resurrected the Third Republic system of single member constituencies with provision for a second ballot, which he felt would prove more beneficial to a newly established Gaullist national movement. He was right, of course, and the unprecedented Gaullist majorities in the Fifth Republic have resulted from the advantages that accrued to the Gaullist candidate in second ballot run-offs against a Communist candidate. The statistics alone confirm the rewards to be gained by a carefully selected electoral system. (See Figure 3–4.) With the PR system in 1946, a party's electoral percentage translated into a similar percentage of Assembly seats. With the *scrutin majoritaire* in 1958, however, the Gaullist candidates managed to translate their 18 percent of the first-ballot vote into 40 percent of the Assembly seats; the Communists saw their 19 percent of the first ballot vote transformed into only 2 percent of the Assembly seats. But the system favored the Gaullists only as long as the left remained divided. By cooperating on the second ballot (as the figure shows in 1973, for example), the Socialists and Communists managed to secure a somewhat fairer share of Assembly seats.

The period from 1958 to 1962 proved a strong one for de Gaulle and the Gaullists, and the elections of that period went far to legitimate the new Republic. With a simple platform of support for de Gaulle, his constitution, and his future reign, the Gaullists and their allies racked up impressive scores in the 1958 and 1962 legislative elections. The four referenda—1958 on the new Constitution, 1961 and 1962 on Algerian independence, 1962 on presidentialism—proved effective and fast means to approve major institutional and policy changes. The French voters endorsed them by scores of 80 percent, 76 percent, 91 percent, and 62 percent respectively. Their plebiscitory nature, however, resurrected the charge of "bonapartist" one man rule and fueled the left's growing rejection of de Gaulle's regime. Indeed, the October 1962 referendum (which provided for the direct popular election of the president) met with much stiffer opposition than the three previous referenda, because by 1962 the left had finally reassembled in total opposition to de Gaulle. The November 1962 legislative elections saw the first signs of electoral cooperation between the long feuding SFIO and PCF and forced the once aloof de Gaulle to intervene directly on behalf of Gaullist candidates.

In the period from 1965 to 1969, de Gaulle and the Gaullists met with continued success, but their invincibility began to wear thin. In the 1965 presidential election, the single candidate of the left, François Mitterrand, forced de Gaulle into an unexpected and humiliating run-off on the second round. De Gaulle won that race, but only by a score of 55

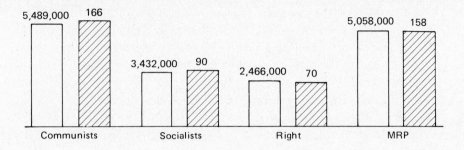

(a) 1946: Proportional Representation

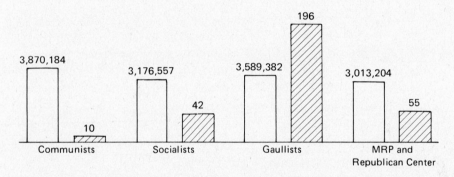

(b) 1958: Single Member Constituency with Run-off

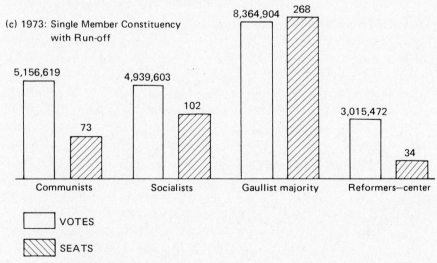

(c) 1973: Single Member Constituency with Run-off

FIGURE 3–4 Effect of Electoral Law on Assembly Seating Strength

Source: Data for 1946 and 1958 from *Le Monde*

percent to 45 percent, which was down considerably from the 80, 75, and 90 percent totals on de Gaulle's first three Fifth Republic referenda. Mitterrand's candidacy marked the beginning of the left's formal electoral alliance. By agreeing to combine votes behind a single left candidate on the second round, the left managed to double its share of seats in the 1967 legislative elections, but it still did not unseat the (reduced) Gaullist majority. The revolt of May 1968 (to be discussed below) gave the Gaullists a temporary respite, but in the longer run May 1968 marked a turning point in the Fifth Republic. In the hastily called June 1968 legislative elections, the electorate proved receptive to the relatively dirty campaign and scare tactics of the Gaullists. The left's electoral alliance was deserted by many Socialist and Radical voters who refused to endorse the second ballot Communist single candidate, and for the first time in French history, one party alone (the UDR) gained an absolute majority in Parliament.

The calm observed by de Gaulle to be reigning in France in early 1968 had been deceptive; so had been, it turned out, his loyal support. In April 1969 de Gaulle chose to submit for approval by referendum a proposal to decentralize the power of the state from Paris to the regions and to change the Senate into an advisory body of representatives of economic and social groups. The reform proposals were major ones. Yet by combining them into one consultation, de Gaulle seriously underestimated the rebelliousness of even his own supporters. For while decentralization was a popular idea, Senate reform (abolishment, in effect) was not. Furthermore, the proposal was long, extremely detailed, and complex. To top off the matter, de Gaulle made clear that rejection of the referendum would bring about his resignation. Yet on April 28, 1969 the French voted *no* by 53 percent to 47 percent; de Gaulle promptly resigned (and he died a year and a half later). The post–de Gaulle period and a new presidential election, so long awaited by the French left, had arrived—but just at the time the left was divided the most. Instead of a single candidate as in 1965, the left was represented by four candidates—a Socialist, a Trotskyist, a Communist, and a PSU candidate. As a result, the second ballot run-off slots were gained by the centrist Alain Poher and the former Gaullist prime minister Georges Pompidou. Due in part to the Communists' call for abstention (motivated by their implied preference for a right-wing Gaullist rather than a moderate centrist), Georges Pompidou—ex-English teacher, ex-banker, and long-time Gaullist associate—became President of France in June 1969.

The post–de Gaulle period from 1969 to 1974 saw personality and leadership maneuverings in the Gaullist majority as it became apparent that Pompidou was no de Gaulle and that the president was in fact very ill. The March 1973 legislative elections presented the first real challenge to Gaullist hegemony. In the months prior to these elections, opinion polls were indicating the possibility of a left majority in Parliament. While the elections returned a Gaullist majority (again reduced), the party was definitely on the defensive. Then, when Pompidou died suddenly in April 1974, the Gaullist candidate, Jacques Chaban-Delmas, was edged out on the first round of the presidential race by the Independent Republican, Valéry Giscard d'Estaing. Giscard d'Estaing was a former Minister of Finance, known for his brilliant economic expertise and aristocratic demeanor. He had been supported on the first round by a contingent of Gaullists, led by the eventual prime minister, Jacques Chirac. In an extremely tight race two weeks later, Giscard d'Estaing beat François Mitterrand, again the candidate of the united left, by a vote of 50.8 percent to 49.2 percent, to become the third president of the Fifth French Republic.[19]

In the Fourth Republic, ten to twelve parties regularly ran candidates in elections, and as a result no one party gained more than a plurality of votes. For a while in the Fifth Republic, the net effect of the Gaullist tide and the left's unity response was to create a general bipolarization of electoral life. But given historic patterns, it would be wrong to assume that bipolarization will become a permanent feature in French politics. André Malraux, a prominent Gaullist, used to (perhaps wishfully) say that there was "nothing between the Gaullists and Communists." But the Gaullist movement's "glue" was the person of de Gaulle. Not only is he dead, but the movement has lost the presidency. The new president, Giscard d'Estaing, relies on the support of the Gaullist legislative majority, but the Gaullist deputies have disagreed among themselves over recent legislative issues. Furthermore, Giscard is intent on resurrecting a "liberal" center-right coalition to free him from Gaullist dependence. Finally, the current "union of the left" could be broken by the PCF if the alliance continues to operate to the Socialists' advantage. In sum, the balance on the political spectrum remains fluid and Malraux's prophecy is less accurate today than ever.

Events of May 1968 The "events" of May 1968 stand as the most serious threat to the Gaullist Fifth Republic to date. In the course of several weeks, large numbers of citizens (over 10 million) participated spon-

[19] On French elections, see Philip Williams, *French Politicians and Elections, 1951–1969* (Cambridge: Cambridge University Press, 1970), Jean Charlot, *Quand la gauche peut gagner* . . . (Paris: Editions Alain Moreau, 1973), and Howard R. Penniman, ed., *France at the Polls: The Presidential Election of 1974* (Washington, D.C.: American Enterprise Institute for Public Policy Research, 1975).

taneously in a revolt that challenged the political, economic, and social status quo. The "events" included student occupation of university buildings, police repression, workers' occupation of factories, general system paralysis, and final defusion of the "revolution" through concessions and an eventual Gaullist electoral triumph.[20]

Tension had been building up in the universities since March, as students increasingly took to demonstrations and strikes. The students, influenced by the international student protest movement of the 1960's, held grievances in three basic areas. First, they had their own particular grievances: overcrowded educational facilities, an élitist and authoritarian university administration which shunned student input, and a lack of prospective jobs for degree-holders. Second, the students were protesting against the Vietnam war (as former students had done against their own Indochina and Algerian wars); third, they were expressing their general protest against the idea of all hierarchical authority, of "undemocratic" social relationships that pervaded social, political, and especially economic French life. Thus the protest took on a revolutionary, anarcho-syndicalist meaning, as the old ideas of direct democracy, economic self-management, and egalitarianism came to the ideological forefront.

The students were not alone in their grievances. The workers also were unhappy with Gaullist policies, and their grievances centered on low wages for long working hours (compared to the German workers, for instance), the prospect of increased unemployment, a lack of confidence in the stability of the economy, few trade union rights in the workplace, and regressive legislation concerning social security benefits. As the students' demands had gone beyond "bread and butter" issues into demands for participation in governing university affairs, so too did the demands of workers, employees, and many professionals. Thus workers and personnel in over 100 factories and business firms occupied their place of work and took over management responsibilities during the accompanying prolonged strikes.

The Pompidou government was in a precarious position. There was a question as to whether the Gaullist regime itself would survive. The government's initial response to the students' occupation had been the standard one of police repression. Special CRS riot police "cleared" the Sorbonne, students set up street barricades in the Latin Quarter, and the two sides clashed in bloody skirmishes (several dead, thousands injured) for over a week. Ten million striking workers could not be repressed so easily, however, so the government tried concessions. But when representatives of government, employers, and trade unions

[20] See, out of many, Daniel Singer, *Prelude to Revolution* (New York: Hill & Wang, 1970).

hammered out a comprehensive package of concessions and compromises, the workers—in a revolutionary, not conciliatory, mood—turned down the offer and continued their strike.

It was then that de Gaulle conceived of the unbeatable strategy of new legislative elections and a "threat of Communist takeover" campaign. A good scheme as it turned out, but a disingenuous one. For the realities of May 1968 presented as much a challenge to the Communist conception of a socialist revolution as it did to the Gaullist regime. If anyone led the fairly spontaneous events, it was the extreme-left groups (the *gauchistes*) joined by PSU and CFDT militants. As such, those at the forefront represented the Communists' "enemies to the left"—the Maoists, Trotskyists, anarchists, and syndicalists. Their rejection of hierarchy included the rigid, disciplined, centralized hierarchy of the PCF and the USSR; theirs was a literal interpretation of Marx's dictum that "the emancipation of the workers shall be accomplished by the workers themselves." No "representative party" of the working class for them; what was crucial was the politicization that would result when workers spontaneously took matters into their own hands. The PCF and CGT (trade unions) saw this course as "adventurist" (that is, doomed) and their initial position had been one of caution. They only later jumped aboard the movement rather than be dangerously out-flanked on their left. But the PCF and CGT's obvious stalling only served to earn them the extreme-left's contempt; their eventual participation only served to sway people into accepting the Gaullist line of a "red totalitarian takeover."

The call for a legislative election had effectively defused the extra-parliamentary course of events and channeled most energies into the more traditional electoral game. The "revolution" evaporated, but a disquieting degree of popular discontent had been revealed. After May 1968, and despite a resounding electoral victory in June 1968, the Gaullists could no longer be sure of their long-term dominance.

Common Governmental Program of the Left Like the events of May 1968, the formation of the 1972 Common Governmental Program of the Socialists, Communists, and left-Radicals presented a basic challenge to the political, economic, and social policies of the Gaullist regime. Unlike May 1968, this challenge took the form of an electoral–governmental battle led by the established parties of the left. As such, the threat to the status quo has been more enduring and more realizable.

The memory of the Popular Front of 1936 is a vivid one for the French left; one reason is because it was one of the very few times the left actually held power. But more important for the left in the Fifth Republic, the Popular Front experience had shown that by creating an electoral alliance for second round run-offs, the left could—with only a 1.5 percent increase in voting strength between the 1932 and 1936 elections—capture the majority of seats and proceed to enact substantive reforms. For much of the Fifth Republic, then, the Communists and some Socialists strove to create a second Popular Front, which they hoped would allow the left to go beyond reform to the transformation of the capitalist system into the socialist alternative.

By June 1972 the PCF was willing to make many programmatic concessions to demonstrate its commitment to democratic principles, and the Socialists had moved to the left under Mitterrand, particularly concerning the extent of nationalizations. The Common Governmental Program, signed in the summer of 1972, was unprecedented in the left's history. It consisted of 100 pages of proposed legislation to be undertaken by the left should it win a majority in the legislative elections due in 1973.[21] The program pertained solely to the five-year legislative term, and as such entailed an "advanced democracy" transition period on the "march toward socialism." Thus in the social realm, the program called for an extension of public services (concerning health, social security and pensions, jobs, housing, transportation, education, leisure and culture, and child care and women's emancipation). In the economic realm, the main provisions of the program spelled out the triple axis of workers' self-management in industry (*autogestion*), collective ownership, and democratic planning, plus fiscal and monetary policies to encourage socially beneficial investment and redistribution of income through more progressive taxation. Concerning institutions and liberties, the common program assured the indispensable personal and collective liberties of political democracy and specified a half dozen revisions to the Constitution designed to curb the abuse of presidential power. On foreign policy, the Communists gave in on most of their pro-Soviet stands. Thus, a French left government would remain in NATO, retain some kind of nuclear striking force, encourage a system of European collective security, and continue to participate in the European Community (EEC).

Aside from the question of whether the united left with its common program would gain a majority in the 1973 legislative elections (which it did not), there was a second, more implicit, question: which partner, PCF or PS, would benefit the most from the governmental alliance? For while a united left obviously stood to gain as a whole, each partner hoped to "use" the other in the race to secure senior partner status. The answer to that question is that since 1972 Mitterrand and the Socialists have predominated on the left in several ways.

[21] Published as *Programme commun de gouvernement* (Paris: Flammarion, 1973).

First, the Common Program itself emerged as a result of mainly Communist programmatic concessions. Second, in the cantonal and by-elections since then, the PS has continued to gain in voting percentages while the Communist votes have stabilized or even dropped. Third, the manner in which Mitterrand was selected and campaigned as the common candidate of the left in the May 1974 presidential race clearly confirmed his role as leader of the left. Fourth, the PS has almost doubled its membership since 1971, established roots in previously inactive departments (thereby taking on a national character), taken a strikingly wide lead over the PCF in opinion polls, and in general appears as a rejuvenated and prospering competitor to the defensive and stagnant PCF. Under these circumstances, the Communists might be tempted to break the alliance rather than to continue. Yet to break the alliance risks the alienation of many of its voters who supported the PCF's long search for unity of the left. In the long run, it might also enable the Socialists to govern without the Communists, which would only be fulfilling the Socialists' ultimate goal.[22]

ECONOMIC CONFLICTS IN THE FIFTH REPUBLIC

Opposition to the Gaullist political regime brought together more than just the socialist and Communist left. The Radical Party and many elements in the centrist parties criticized what they considered to be the excessive powers granted to the French presidency by de Gaulle. In addition, the Radical Party accepted the left's general critique of what it saw as the maintenance of social inequality (of opportunity as well as of reward) in the Fifth Republic. But on a third point, the Socialist–Communist coalition separated itself from the broader opposition to the Gaullist regime: that point concerned the economy. As long as the French Socialists had continued to endorse a "mixed economy" (as did most Western European social democrats) and as long as the French Communists insisted on a centrally planned and executed socialist economic model (as in the USSR), there did not exist a strong opposition alternative to the prevailing state-directed capitalist economic system in France. With the signing of the Common Program of 1972, however, the capitalist–socialist debate came to the forefront of French politics. In its Common Program, the united left went farther than the 1945 program (which came out of the general Resistance movement) in the detailing of specific governmental measures to be taken, and, more importantly, in presenting innovative socialist economic policies for the 1970's.

We shall examine several of the issues that currently characterize left–

[22] See Nancy I. Lieber, "Politics of the French Left: A Review Essay," *American Political Science Review*, December 1975.

right economic conflict in France. They include the extent of the public or nationalized sector, management of economic enterprises in general and formulation of the national Economic Plan. We shall also examine the long-standing conflict over the system of taxation in France.

The Public Sector The existence of public enterprises does not necessarily denote socialism. If that were the case, King Louis XV (who nationalized French tobacco and match industries) could qualify as France's first prominent socialist. Charles de Gaulle presided over the wave of postwar nationalizations put in force by the Resistance movement because he felt it would better ensure the "public good." Running the public industries and services soon fell to the status quo oriented civil service and center to center-right governments in the Fourth and Fifth Republics, and the French right learned it could live with the existing nationalizations. It did not want, however, further public ownership and therefore vehemently opposed the nationalization list drawn up by the Socialist–Communist Common Governmental Program. That program specified the extension of public ownership to natural resources (steel and petroleum), finance, armaments, space, aeronautics, nuclear power, pharmaceuticals, electricity, chemicals, transportation, and telecommunications. The Socialists endorsed the list because they felt it would be sufficient to break the hold of "feudal economic interests"; from there most Socialists envisage nonstatist, decentralized ownership alternatives such as cooperatives and the municipalization of goods and services. The Communists originally pushed for a much longer list of enterprises "ripe for nationalization." While downplaying the Soviet model of state socialism, they nevertheless speak of "progressive nationalization."

Economic Democracy Like the issue of nationalization, there is a related issue which splits the right and the left in France, and also divides the left itself. This issue is economic democracy, the idea that each person should be counted equally in the decision-making process in his or her place of work. As political democracy was the aim of progressive movements in the eighteenth and nineteenth centuries and social democracy the challenge of the twentieth century, economic democracy has recently become a fundamental issue in European politics in general.

The capitalist economic system, based on private ownership, proceeds on the principle of hierarchical decision-making. However, as the labor movement has grown, become legal, and achieved collective bargaining rights, owners of productive facilities have experienced an erosion of their powers of command. Legislation passed in Europe throughout the twentieth century reinforced the rights of labor by putting into law provisions concerning a minimum wage, retirement age, number of work hours per week, paid vacations, and trade union organizational rights. But workers are still dependent on the employer in three major areas: salary schedules (what pay for what job), shop-floor work conditions (health and safety, eating provisions, breaks), and hiring and firing (unemployment and discrimination by age, sex, race).

In France the small but ideologically influential PSU brought to the forefront in the 1960's the old ideal of workers' control. As we noted earlier, the concept spread throughout much of the left after May 1968 as *autogestion* or economic self-management. *Autogestion* means that those who work in an enterprise should be responsible collectively for its management and general direction. In this sense, it parallels the notion of direct political democracy. Currently the French Socialists accept *autogestion* more readily than do the French Communists, because the Socialists value the participatory, politicizing nature of the process that contrasts with the bureaucratic centralist—and dictatorial—nature of the Soviet economic system. Nevertheless, both Socialists and Communists want to see an extension of workers' decision-making powers to the levels of physical work conditions and personnel policies, then to business decisions concerning investments, profits, salaries, contracts, and finally, in short, to all aspects of management. If the workers would not actually fulfill the management positions themselves (on a rotating basis), they would hold ultimate control with veto power over their elected management boards.

Numerous practical examples of workers' self-management exist; the Yugoslav economy is the main case of pervasive (though not ideal) economic self-management, and legislation in Sweden has recently accorded workers extensive de facto control over private industry. Similar trends are growing in Belgium, Germany, and Norway. This being the case, what could the French right offer to counter this movement? The response of first de Gaulle and then Giscard d'Estaing has been "worker participation," or the co-sharing of power in industry by workers, owners, and management. Drawn from a policy practiced in the German coal and steel industry since World War II, workers' participation means that workers would elect representatives to sit on management and directing boards. In this way, workers' concerns and demands would be threshed out, heeded, or ignored. To the French right, "participation" offers a fair and consensual solution to the problem of workers' discontent. It ensures the maintenance of a highly desirable economic system based on private ownership; at the same time it corrects the total (and potentially dangerous) exclusion of the work force from decision-making. To the French left, however, "participation" is cooptation; it is a situation tilted 51 percent to 49 percent to the side of private owners. It is another "too-little, too-late" crumb for the workers' table. But whether the Chirac government enacts "participation" legislation or whether a future socialist government implements a form of self or democratic management of the economy, it is likely that capitalism in France will resemble even less than before its American counterpart.

Democratic Planning   A third current economic issue concerns who shall formulate the Economic Plan and who, therefore, shall benefit from it the most. The first six economic plans in France were decided by selected representatives of various socioeconomic groups. But the Planning Commission's advisory bodies have been heavily weighted toward business, employers, and civil servants, or those forces that lean to the right, rather than toward trade union representatives. The left would be likely to draw up national plans differently, and again the key word is *democratization*. In the case of the plan, workers councils, citizens in their locales, and consumer groups would elect representatives to local, regional, and national assemblies, whose purpose would be to deliberate and to set economic and social priorities. As voters currently designate their political bodies, they likewise would vote directly on economic decision-making bodies. In this way, the left would try to secure economic priorities that favor the individual and collective needs of its constituency, the *masses populaires*.

Taxation   A fourth and final economic issue that is the subject of political debate in France is that of taxation. There are two basic characteristics of the complicated French system of taxation. First, the French are notorious tax-evaders, and second (as a result) the French pay taxes on a predominantly regressive—not progressive—scale.

The income tax came to France in 1917, just after it came to the United States. It came against the wishes of the Republicans' staunchest constituency, the farmers, who foresaw that public funds would accrue more to the benefit of the rising working class than to themselves. Legislation passed, therefore, only because it set low rates, contained many loopholes, and was to be weakly enforced. The law soon became openly abused. Intruding tax collectors were tarred and feathered by the peasants, independent small businessmen and artisans eschewed basic bookkeeping methods (which made compliance difficult to enforce), self-employed professionals such as doctors and lawyers took to declaring only half their income. With employers' records, however, tax evasion has been more difficult for the large numbers of salaried personnel. It has been estimated that in 1974 the rate of tax evasion for workers was 3 percent, for independent professionals 47 percent, for farmers 78 percent.[23]

In the United States there exists a remarkable degree of voluntary compliance with income tax laws. Knowing that the IRS audits only a small percentage of returns and having certain escapes in the various loopholes, the American taxpayer nevertheless pays up. As a result, 33 percent of U.S. government revenue is furnished from the direct income tax. But in France only about 10 percent of public revenue comes from the direct income tax. How is the difference made up? To a great extent it is made up through heavy and unavoidable indirect taxes on goods and services (called VAT), or the French equivalent of the U.S. state sales tax. The crucial political difference between these two manners of taxation is that income taxes are much more progressive (that is, those who have more, pay more) and sales taxes are regressive (the worker and the company director both pay the same 7 percent tax on food, for example). The indirect sales tax and social security monthly contributions (which have recently become more regressive) together account for almost 80 percent of government revenue. The overall effect is that the less well-off citizens pay a higher percentage of their income for public goods and services than those who can afford more. Clearly, the French tax system in the Gaullist Fifth Republic has not been used as a tool for income redistribution, as it has by both socialist *and* conservative governments in so many modern European states.

policy process

By what means and through what channels are policy questions decided in the Fifth Republic? As in all democratic systems, the policy process in France involves formal channels such as the executive-administrative, legislative, and judicial branches of government, and informal—but equally crucial—channels such as political parties, interest groups, and the media. Again, because France is a democracy, it is the force of public opinion, registered primarily in elections, that at least in part allows a particular policy process or resolution to be continued or that causes its termination. Nevertheless, within this general framework, the French system does not operate in a manner entirely like the British or American governmental process. The differences point up that some democratic

[23] Cited in "La France des Inégalités," *Nouvel Observateur*, April 22, 1974, p. 35.

systems are more open, some—as in the French case—are more closed than others.[24]

INITIATION, DELIBERATION, APPROVAL

We know that the Fifth Republic marked a return to the tradition of strong executive government. Thus to answer the primary question of who initiates, deliberates, and approves of policy in France today, we must look at the executive branch of government. And within that branch—which is composed of the president, prime minister, cabinet, civil service or administrative bureaucracy, Planning Commission, and nationalized industry and social security administration—by far the most important power position is the presidency.

The President According to the 1958 Constitution, the primary role of the president is that of a national "arbiter," or "mediator," who stands above partisan politics and particularist constituencies, who represents the nation as a whole and who protects its independence and stability. The vagueness of this task is reflected in the relevant constitutional articles which state, "the president shall ensure by his arbitration the regular functioning of the public powers, as well as continuity of the State," and "he shall be guarantor of national independence, of the integrity of the territory." The tone is reminiscent of the bonapartist notion that a leader, by "wrapping himself in the flag," can somehow represent all the people in a divided nation. But as two Empires and recent Gaullist governments have shown, bonapartist leaders inevitably represent only a majority at best, and a rightist one at that.

The president's important *specific* duties and powers listed in the Constitution are as follows: he appoints the prime minister; can dissolve the National Assembly; approves and promulgates the government's statutes and decrees; makes judicial, administrative, and military appointments; exercises the power of pardon; negotiates and ratifies treaties; can rule with emergency powers in the face of a national emergency (Article 16); and can submit certain legislation to a national referendum for approval by the electorate (Article 11). On the face of it, most of these powers deal with *execution* of policy, not primarily with its initiation, deliberation, or approval. Nevertheless, de Gaulle asserted his primary role in all four stages of the policy process. From the beginning he made

---

[24] On the Fifth Republic system see Philip Williams and Martin Harrison, *Politics and Society in de Gaulle's Republic* (Garden City, N.Y.: Doubleday, 1973), Gilles Martinet, *Le système Pompidou* (Paris: Seuil, 1973), Roy Macridis, *French Politics in Transition* (Cambridge, Mass.: Winthrop Publishers, 1975), and Jack Hayward, *The One and Indivisible French Republic* (New York: W. W. Norton & Co., Inc., 1973).

it clear that foreign policy and defense matters fell into a domain reserved exclusively for him. Thus he alone—without consultation or cabinet input—made a series of key policy decisions concerning the independence of France's African colonies, Algerian independence, the establishment of a French nuclear striking force (the *force de frappe*), the vetoing of Britain's entry into the Common Market, and withdrawal from the NATO integrated command. After the 1962 dismissal of his prime minister, Debré (a constitutional purist), de Gaulle expanded this reserved domain to include government policy in general.

How did de Gaulle manage to assert presidential prerogatives that were not clearly spelled out in his own Constitution? First and foremost, he did so on the basis of his mystique and assumed indispensability to the security of the nation. Simply put, no one wanted or was in a position to challenge the man who had averted a civil war in 1958: not the loyal prime minister, hand-picked for his utter loyalty to de Gaulle; not the judiciary, appointed by de Gaulle himself and confronted with an unfamiliar, untested Constitution; not the Gaullist majority in Parliament, whose members owed their election solely to de Gaulle. While there were cries of abuse of personal power from the left, the Socialists and Communists remained disunited and weak for the first decade of the Fifth Republic.

De Gaulle further consolidated his power because throughout his tenure in office (and particularly in the early years) he was accorded virtual dictatorial powers. In June 1958 the Assembly passed enabling legislation granting the government "full powers" for six months (while a new Constitution was being drawn up). In January 1960 de Gaulle (invoking Article 38) asked for and was accorded full powers to deal with the Algerian crisis; the full powers remained in effect for a full year. In April 1961 de Gaulle put into effect the infamous Article 16 and ruled with emergency powers for five months, even though the immediate crisis (a French Generals' attempted putsch in Algeria) lasted for only a matter of days. De Gaulle then improperly invoked Article 11 when he presented the April 1962 referendum, and its passage once again gave him full powers to implement Algerian independence over the next few months. Finally, Article 38 was invoked in 1967 when the government wanted to obtain enabling powers to put through unpopular economic and social reforms (mainly raises in social security contributions to make the system solvent); the powers were granted for a six-month period.

At times de Gaulle overstepped his authority in such a blatant manner that public authorities felt obliged to register protests. The October 1962 and April 1969 referenda dealt with matters that would have amended the Constitution. But to amend the Constitution required the use of

Article 89, not the "referenda" Article 11. Since Article 89 required Parliament's as well as the president's approval of the proposal, de Gaulle chose to ignore his own Constitution to secure his policy of direct election of the president, reform of the Senate, and decentralization. In both cases, the Council of State and Constitutional Council rendered judgments that de Gaulle's proposals were unconstitutional; de Gaulle did not let those judgments hinder his assumed powers and went ahead with the referenda.

In the October 1962 referenda de Gaulle went far to institutionalize the French president's enormous power and prestige. In the original Constitution of 1958, the president was to be elected by an electoral college of 80,000 notables or elected officials at various governmental levels. If the president received a direct mandate from the people, however, his formal legitimacy would be elevated to that of the directly elected Assembly. Obviously de Gaulle wanted to assure future presidents every means to predominate over the legislative branch. He certainly succeeded, because Pompidou continued and Giscard d'Estaing still continues to exercise great personal power. But Pompidou and Giscard d'Estaing did not work in such arrogant isolation as de Gaulle. There is an increasingly large president's staff which initiates policy proposals, deliberates on them, and works closely with a variety of advisory committees (often filled by lobbyists), experts from the civil service, and the staffs of the various cabinet ministers. And here we enter another ambiguous area of the policy process: the relationship of the president to the prime minister.

The Prime Minister According to the Constitution it is the government (the prime minister and his cabinet) which "shall determine and conduct the policy of the nation." This would seem to put the prime minister in a key position. But we have seen that in practice it is really the president who determines policy. Not only does the president name the prime minister, but he selects the prime minister's cabinet ministers as well. Thus in the meetings of the council of ministers, the presiding president's broad policy outlines are usually discussed with individual ministers and their staffs, who in turn work closely with the president's office. In many cases, therefore, the prime minister is completely by-passed. If the prime minister has been stripped of what is usually considered the "normal" role (as in Great Britain), what is his function in the Fifth Republic? Essentially he supervises the day-to-day functioning of government and acts as a buffer between the president and the National Assembly. The French president is responsible to the people, but the government is responsible to Parliament. Therefore, the prime minister presents to the Assembly what is really the president's program; he defends it and assures its passage, yet is himself sacrificed if a vote of no confidence is passed in the Assembly. The prime minister is clearly the precarious middle man in this mixed presidential–parliamentary regime.

Parliament According to classical democratic theory, the role of Parliament in the policy process is to initiate, deliberate, and approve, while the executive exists to see that these policies are applied or administered. If, in the Fifth Republic, the bulk of all those powers resides in the executive branch, what is left for the French Parliament to do? Essentially, the task of Parliament is to give rubber-stamp approval to the government's (that is, the president's) proposals. In particular, the impotence of the National Assembly (compared to its heyday in the Third and Fourth Republics) has been carefully assured by the 1958 Constitution. The most important article in this regard is Article 34, which lists explicit areas in which Parliament can make "laws" and places all other areas under the executive's prerogative to govern by "regulation" through executive decress and orders. Thus Parliament's approval is not even required for all government action. A further means by which the Constitution limits Parliament is the stipulation that the government's bills get priority in the parliamentary timetable. The result is that the vast majority of bills in the Fifth Republic are the president's; private members' (deputies') bills have been reduced to a mere 10 percent of legislation. Another device is the government's right to declare a bill subject to "block passage," or a "take it or leave it" vote. Government sponsors also have the right to refuse certain amendments, or to put a piece of legislation to a vote of confidence. These last measures actually are intended to prod recalcitrant or independent-minded majority members into submission to their government. On matters dealing with finance and the budget, the government has great powers; for example, if Parliament has not acted on the budget within 70 days, it automatically becomes law. And the Parliament can never by itself propose a law that would either cut public revenues (taxes) or increase public expenditures (goods and services). Obviously these measures would bring Parliament much greater popularity than the opposite measures (which Parliament *may* initiate) of raising taxes and cutting public expenditures! Other devices meant to curtail the initiative and deliberative powers of the Parliament are: (1) reducing Assembly committees from 19 to 6 in number, which tends to make them too unspecialized and unwieldy to be effective challengers to the executive staff; (2) shorter working sessions (cut from 7 to 5½ months each year); (3) rules making a vote of censure more difficult (by counting all abstentions and absences as promajority), and (4) curtailment of the weekly question period between the prime minister and Parliament.

With its most important function reduced to that of pro forma approval, the Parliament as a whole nevertheless continues to fulfill its function of public deliberation and advisory consultation. The Senate, for example, has never been dominated by the Gaullists. It continues to reflect the traditional right and center which stands for legislative supremacy. The Senate provides an annoying thorn in the executive's side (which is why de Gaulle sought to abolish it in 1969); yet its rejection of a bill can be overruled by the Assembly if the president so chooses. Besides the Assembly and Senate, there is a third legislative organ, the Economic and Social Council (ESC). The ESC had existed informally since the 1920's, but was written into the 1958 Constitution by de Gaulle. In the ESC, elected representatives of trade union, business, professional, and social organizations debate and advise on major economic and social policies. The level of debate and expertise is high in the ESC, yet its efforts tend to be ignored by both the government and the general public.

APPLICATION

Who is responsible for executing or applying a policy that has been either "legislated" by the Parliament or "regulated" by the executive? In theory and in practice it is the government that is responsible for seeing that official policies are carried out, and it is the vast civil service, or administrative bureaucracy, that actually applies policy.

The Civil Service   The first thing that needs to be said about the French administrative bureaucracy or public service is that its role is enormous. We know that increasingly large governmental bureaucracies have been a major postwar development in the United States and most of Europe, but a powerful administrative apparatus has long been a French tradition. Kings of the *ancien régime,* to consolidate monarchical power over feudal baronies, established the centralized bureaucracy. It was not swept away in 1789 because the Jacobin revolutionaries found the system compatible with their wish to implement standardized (and therefore egalitarian) policies for all citizens. The administrative bureaucracy was consolidated under Napoleon I and has remained virtually unchanged ever since.

The size and importance of the French civil service stem from institutional and sociological factors. Institutionally, the French political system is a unitary, not a federal, system. This means that all decisions are made in Paris, and policies are equally applicable to the entire nation. Hence the all-encompassing role of the State proceeds right down to the 37,700 "communes," or lowest units of administration. The Minister of the Interior is responsible for applying all national policy and services. In this regard he directs the *corps préfectoral,* which provides the field services of the central administration. In each of the 95 French departments, a prefect (or head civil servant) oversees operations and the prefect in turn works with subprefects, departmental councils, and local authorities. The system diffuses power from top to bottom, except at the last juncture. At this point a popularly elected municipal council selects a mayor, but the mayor is still officially considered an arm of the State authorities. As such, the tradition of local autonomy, local government, and local initiative does not exist in France. Instead, regulations and practices concerning local schools, roads, building construction, police, social services, public facilities, and the like, are made centrally and standardized throughout France.[25]

The second institutional reason for France's large civil service concerns the State's intervention in the economy. Laissez-faire economics has never been prevalent in French (big) business practices. After World War II, the State took on two additional economic responsibilities: planning and nationalized industries.

In an effort to coordinate and stimulate postwar economic recovery, the French government, inspired by Jean Monnet, turned to state planning (called *"planification"*). That is, a General Planning Commission representing business, labor, agriculture, industry, commerce, banks—and, of course, civil service experts—consults and draws up a five-year plan designed to establish desirable growth rates, production and consumption priorities, social welfare provisions, and other key economic developments. Unlike the Soviet five-year plans, the French plans are only indicative and do not carry the force of law. Successive French plans have presided over impressive French economic recovery, growth, and modernization since the war. French plans have also been a boon to French big business, which not only is privy to governments' short and long term intentions because of its place on the Planning Commission, but receives subsidies, incentives, and tax breaks in exchange for better voluntary compliance with the Plan.[26]

The existence of a large nationalized sector in the French economy has also increased the scope and size of the civil servants' role. The French government owns and controls the nation's railroads and airlines, oil, electricity, coal, gas, ore and armaments industries, central banks, communications (radio, TV, telephone, telegraph, post office), and some of the nation's sea transport, automobile manufacturing (Renault, for example), lesser banks, and insurance companies. In fact, some 25 percent of capital investment in France passes through State-owned concerns, a

25 See Mark Kesselman, *The Ambiguous Consensus: A Study of Local Government in France* (New York: Alfred A. Knopf, 1967).
26 See Stephen Cohen, *Modern Capitalist Planning: The French Model* (Cambridge: Harvard University Press, 1969).

very high rate in Europe. If the State owns these industries, it must run them. While ultimate control theoretically resides with Parliament and the appropriate minister, permanent civil servants staff the highest echelons of the nationalized industries, utilities, and services and as such are engaged in key decision-making.

A third institutional factor responsible for the greater importance of the French bureaucracy lies in a tradition of parliamentary delegation of its legislative authority to the executive branch.[27] Despite their disavowal of such delegation of power, French Parliaments frequently (and especially in terms of crisis) passed enabling legislation that either held the executive to a general policy area (as in the Third Republic) or stated the objectives and proper means to accomplish a specific purpose (as in the Fourth). Governments of the Fifth Republic not only practice, but the Constitution preaches, delegative powers. First, much legislation passed by Parliament is in the form of an organic law, whose specific details are only filled in later. Second, any area of rule-making not covered in Article 34 is open to government regulatory decree or order. Third, Article 38 permits the government to take through ordinances measures that are normally within Parliament's domain of law. Ordinances are assumed to deal with unpopular aspects of a governmental program—as in the 1967 social security reforms—and apply for a limited duration. What do organic laws, regulations, and ordinances all have in common? Their details have been developed at some time or another by civil servants in the appropriate ministries. In a sense, the bureaucrats write some of the laws they are then responsible for applying.

In the United States and elsewhere, criticism has been raised concerning the size of government bureaucracies. In France, it is not only—or even—that particular issue that has politicized the debate surrounding the civil service. Rather, it is the structure and sociological make-up of the *grands corps* that invite charges of a "ruling élite." [28]

From Figure 3–5 we see that the main avenue into the French government and bureaucracy élite is through the *grandes écoles*, or great training schools. By far the most important among these approximately 150 schools are the National School of Administration (ENA) and the Ecole Polytechnique. The top graduates of these schools enter influential posts in the *grands corps* or civil service, or into the national services and industries. They are in turn recruited into the various appropriate ministries,

[27] This argument is developed by William G. Andrews in a paper interestingly entitled, "Constitutional Dictatorship in Gaullist France: A Study in Constitutional Theory," prepared for delivery at the 1975 Annual Meeting of the American Political Science Association, San Francisco, September 2–5, 1975.
[28] See John Ardagh, "The French Corps d'Elite," *New Society*, London, March 20, 1975.

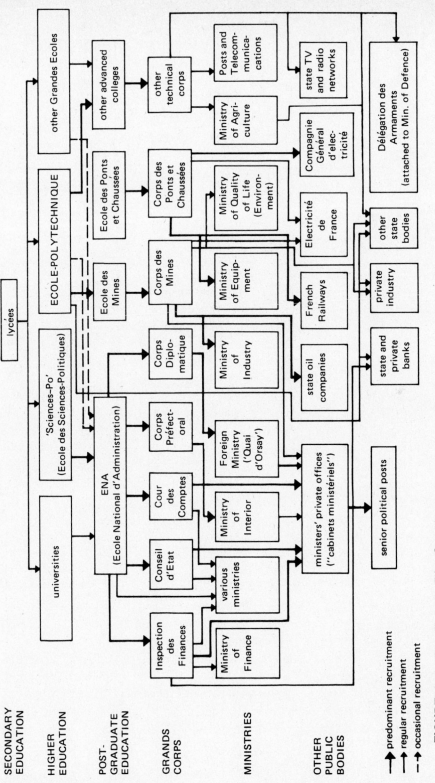

FIGURE 3-5 The French Elite Structure

Source: *New Society*, March 20, 1975, p. 712.

as either staff members or consultants, perhaps one day to emerge as ministers, or even prime minister or president. Of the Fifth Republic's six prime ministers to date, five were members of one of the *grands corps:* Debré and Pompidou in the Council of State, Couve de Murville and Chaban-Delmas (as well as President Giscard d'Estaing) in the Finance Inspectorate, and Chirac in the Court of Accounts. For those who do not quite reach these pinnacles of power, the figure indicates that there are other secure and powerful posts to be had in private industry. There is a distinct tendency for younger civil servants to leave public service (after serving their required four years) for more lucrative positions in private corporations; this constant crossing over has cemented the close ties between business and government in the Fifth Republic. Thus we can say that the "industrial/bureaucratic complex" in France is similar to the American "military/industrial complex" regarding the configuration of power.

Entry into the *grands corps* is limited, and the common characteristics of those entering the *grandes écoles* make the French ruling élite resemble more the British "old boy network" than the more openly recruited American governmental administration. Although admission to these schools is based on meritocratic exams, the exams have a built-in bias toward classical education and background. In practice this has meant that the (predominantly male) recruits for ENA and Polytechnique come almost exclusively from upper middle class, Catholic Parisian families; working class students make up only 1 percent of each entering class. The result has been a "mandarin" class of super-bureaucrats who claim to act for the public interest by shunning the "politics of men" for the mere "administration of things." Yet in the Fifth Republic these mandarin civil servants administer (and make) policies of basically rightist governments, in close cooperation with the business, industrial, and agricultural interests that support those governments. Ultimately, then, this support of the status quo is not in fact a "neutral" administrative position but instead reflects a specific political position and set of values.

ADJUDICATION AND ENFORCEMENT

The Courts   The judiciary in France resembles that of the United States and Great Britain more than it differs, but it has some interesting characteristics that reflect French heritage and political culture. The regular, or ordinary, court system handles civil and criminal cases, offering an appeal system and stressing decentralized facilities which administer uniform justice to all citizens. The uniformity of French law stems from one of several administrative reforms attributable to Napoleon I. In Anglo-Saxon law, all adjudication proceeds on the basis of an interpretation of specific precedents or prior court rulings. In French law, adjudication rests on the interpretation of general principles of justice enunciated in the Napoleonic Code.

What interests us more, however, are the French "administrative" courts. As the State modernizes and the bureaucracy grows, it is important that the individual citizen has channels to seek redress from this omnipotent—and sometimes arbitrary—authority. The administrative courts, headed by the prestigious Council of State (*Conseil d'Etat*), deal exclusively with cases in which the State is a party; they are looked upon increasingly as the guardians of individual liberties versus bureaucratic usurpations of power.

In addition to the ordinary and administrative courts, there is a third judicial body, the Constitutional Council, whose function is basically a supervisory one. According to the Constitution, the duties of the Constitutional Council are to supervise elections and declare their results, to arbitrate in contested elections, and to rule on the constitutionality of pending bills and standing orders of Parliament. This really means that it is up to the Constitutional Council to determine if proposed legislation is within the Assembly's prerogative, or whether it is subject to simple executive "regulation." In practice, the Constitutional Council has almost always ruled on the side of presidential power. The Constitutional Council does *not* provide a "judicial review" process in which controversial economic, social, and political questions are ruled upon, a process which gives the U.S. Supreme Court a crucial role in the policy process.

The regular courts judge the citizens, the administrative courts judge the bureaucrats, the Constitutional Council judges legislative–executive relations. There remain two judicial bodies which judge the president, the government, and the judges themselves. The president of France can be removed from office prior to the end of his term only if he is indicted for "high treason" by a majority in Parliament, then tried and convicted by the High Court of Justice (itself elected by Parliament). The same High Court of Justice tries members of the government for "criminal actions performed in the exercise of their office." Finally, the High Council of the Judiciary nominates judges to higher posts and rules on disciplinary matters relating to the judiciary.

The Police When voluntary compliance with the law is not forthcoming, State authorities turn to the police for enforcement. The police in France are decidedly unlike those in Britain. Historically, the French police have been used for and motivated by political purposes, and their methods reflect a definite military training and instinct.

The political role of the French police is tied to its status as a national police force. As we have noted, local communities do not control or administer their own peace-keeping forces; instead the minister of the interior has several forces at his disposal: a force serving larger provincial towns, one for Paris alone, and the CRS, or mobile reserve units associated with "riot control" functions. Peace in small towns is kept by *gendarmerie* units (under the control of the minister of defense). The *gendarmerie* also fulfills a domestic military role and is armed with weapons (such as tanks and helicopters) that are usually not associated with police forces.

Why this overlap between police and military, which keeps France virtually under "armed forces"? The answer is—tradition. We should not forget that the First and Second Empires were ahead of their times as virtual police states. Protection of the citizen's existence, property, and civil rights was subservient to the protection of the political regime; law and order could only be maintained by repression of the left opposition. Even Republican France carried on the tradition of a "politicized" police-military establishment. The victims ranged from the Parisian working classes in 1848 and 1871, rebellious natives in a host of colonies (notably during large-scale war in Indochina in 1954 and guerrilla warfare in Algeria in the late fifties, early sixties), the Fourth Republic itself when the French Army in Algeria threatened civil war in metropolitan France, and,

CRS police blockading the entrance to the Sorbonne, 1968.
Keystone

most recently, the students in May 1968. Since 1968, the police (with government approval) have continued to concentrate on the domestic extreme left. Agencies akin to the American FBI and CIA collect intelligence through wiretapping, bugging, and spying (though the victims are by no means exclusively on the extreme left, and though the government has acknowledged that most buggings are illegal, and that they are not solely in the interests of national security). CRS units are daily amassed in the student Latin Quarter of Paris and there are frequent clashes with student demonstrators. Political arrests continue without benefit of habeus corpus (bringing formal charges within 48 hours), without evidence, and with a certain degree of brutality.

AUDITING AND MONITORING

Inspectorate Corps   One way to avoid adjudication battles involving the State and bureaucracy is to institutionalize certain supervisory bodies in the policy process itself. The French "inspectorate corps" are predictably important because of the extensive nature of the State apparatus. Their members constantly audit proposed legislation and subsequent execution of policy; they advise and/or confront the government and administration when appropriate. Though most ministries contain inspectors who watch over day-to-day work, the Ministry of Finance is closely supervised. The most important supervisory body is the Finance Inspectorate (or *Inspection des finances*), whose members help prepare and execute the budget, audit all public accounts and matters of taxation, enjoy wide investigatory powers, and, in general, seek to ensure the best use of public funds. Similarly, a second body of accountants, the Court of Accounts (or *Cours des Comptes*) supervises the legality of expenditures and scrutinizes the disbursement of public funds. In addition, its members are frequently involved in the actual running of the nationalized public enterprises.

The Council of State, already discussed for its key judicial role between citizen and State, also performs an important auditing function. Its members spend a good deal of time advising various ministries concerning the wording, legality, and possible unintended results of drafted legislation. As with the Finance Inspectorate and Court of Accounts, the Council of State's "audit through consultation" role often means that it takes on important, though inadvertent, decision-making powers as well. Finally, these three auditing bodies have become all the more indispensible as the ability of Parliament to act as watchdog over the executive branch has diminished in the Fifth Republic.

If we consider "auditing" to be a technical, nonpublic function and "monitoring" to be a more general and open process of checking the executive branch's policy process, then the Parliament still plays both an auditing and monitoring function. Some legislation, after all, requires the formal approval of Parliament; its committees still meet and confer, and questions are still posed to the government at designated times in the Assembly agenda. But more importantly, Deputies and Senators funnel information back to their respective parties, who in turn serve as information links to the electorate. In fact, a well-organized opposition, acting through its representatives and party organizations, is probably a more effective policy monitor in France today than another customary monitoring institution: the press and media.

The Press and Media   Traditionally, the status of the French press has alternated between freedom in republican times and repression, censorship, and "official" newspapers only in dictatorial times. Even so, republican France's record is unadmirable. In the Third Republic, press freedom was so great that extreme right groups could print not only calls for the overthrow of the Republic, but for the assassination of leftist opponents as well. In the Fourth Republic, nationalized radio and TV came under (limited) government control, and there was an attempt to have the press operate within guidelines designed to ensure greater reporting responsibility. In the Gaullist Fifth Republic, however, government manipulation of the press and media became blatant. The Gaullists' assumption was expressed by André Malraux when he observed, "How can one govern a country where the government does not have a TV monopoly?" [29]

As the Constitution and electoral system were used as tools of political power, so too were the media. Thus, until the 1965 presidential race, opposition speakers simply were not heard or seen on French TV. After the government decided in 1964 to create a public but independent Radio-TV corporation (such as the admirable BBC), it proceeded to sabotage these efforts by putting the new ORTF in the political hands of the (Gaullist) minister of information. For the next ten years, pro-Gaullist forces inevitably triumphed in the continual struggles over TV news content and coverage. French TV consciously reflected a news bias in the government's favor and its board of directors continued to censor controversial (usually political) programs.

The monitoring role of the printed press has also declined in the Fifth Republic. At one time, a variety of political parties published their own (partisan) newspapers. In this sense, the press was engaged in the initiation and deliberation of policy as well. In the Fifth Republic, however, the trend has been toward a less politicized, uninformative—and significantly more profitable—press, with muted (if any) criticism of the government.

[29] Cited in Hayward, *The One and Indivisible French Republic*, pp. 148–49.

The most notable exception to this rule remains the world-renowned independent Paris daily, *Le Monde.* Another notable exception is *l'Humanité,* the French Communist Party daily newspaper. Other political parties (mainly for financial reasons) have resorted to weekly partisan newspapers.

One explanation for the nonparty press' docility lies in a French tradition of overt government harassment of opposition newspapers. The final ministries of the Fourth and early ministries of the Fifth Republic together seized several hundred specific issues of newspapers whose columns were too critical (or too revealing) of French government and army policies in Algeria. After May 1968, Gaullist governments condoned outright police harassment of extreme left newspaper street sellers, thereby exacerbating existing police–journalist hostilities. Finally, the Gaullist governments used extensive wiretapping and bugging to harass the press (as well as over 1,500 "enemies" in the Paris area alone). In 1973 listening devices were discovered planted in the recently refurbished headquarters of *Le Canard Enchaîné* (a satirical, muckraking antigovernment journal). It seems that the government had reversed the process and was doing its own monitoring of the press.

Despite certain limitations that are apparent when compared to the press in the United States and Great Britain, the French press remains a free and pluralistic one. And though French radio and TV are a government monopoly, French citizens can always tune in foreign radio and TV stations, which broadcast a broader range of political and other viewpoints. Then too, President Giscard d'Estaing has sought to disassociate himself with past Gaullist practices concerning the media and press. One of his first promises in office was to end political wiretapping and to refrain from seizing specific newspaper issues, "even when they attacked him personally." He also promised to work toward greater radio and TV autonomy. But given past government intimidation of the press and control of the media, and the technical nature of the policy process, nongovernmental monitoring forces in Fifth Republic France probably will never reach the same level of effectiveness as their British and American counterparts.

TERMINATION AND AMENDMENT

How can a policy be terminated or amended in a system that concentrates vast decision-making powers in the executive branch? As we have seen, Parliament has been left with very few means to prevail over executive authority. Typical American recourses are also foreclosed; the nearest French equivalent of our ballot initiative is the referendum, but while Parliament may propose one, it requires the president's approval to proceed to the ballot box. Another American recourse—impeachment—is severely restricted in France to grounds of "high treason." If the opposition in Parliament cannot terminate or amend executive policy, it must defeat the majority in the next election. This explains the left's preoccupation in the Fifth Republic with electoral alliances and the programmatic alliance of the Common Governmental Program. But Assembly elections occur every five years (compared in the United States to congressional elections every two years), and the presidential term runs a full seven years. Furthermore, unlike the United States and Great Britain, there has not been an alternation of power between government and opposition in the Fifth Republic.

"Direct Action" With the right in power since 1958, another course has been taken by dissatisfied groups on the left (and elsewhere) in pursuit of more rapid policy termination and amendment. This course, again a French tradition, is called "direct action." It holds that if one's elected representatives are unable to affect governmental decisions, regular channels have to be circumvented by citizens who take matters into their own hands and act in a way that literally forces the government to act. French trade unions have usually won wage increases *not* through routine collective bargaining procedures, but after staging one-day strikes—strikes which are symbolic since they are preannounced and limited in time, but which remind everyone of those particular workers' strength. May 1968 was an obvious example of the students', workers', even professionals' attempts to force the government's attention to pressing economic and social problems.

Since then, isolated cases abound. In June 1973 workers at the Lip watch factory in Besançon occupied the factory and continued to operate production lines themselves rather than accept mass layoffs because of impending bankruptcy. These workers presented a vivid example of workers' self-management, although their intention was simply to protect their jobs, not cooperatively to own the factory. The several hundred workers, supported by PSU and CFDT militants in particular, held out for several months, only to be forcefully evicted by a mass of CRS troops. Nevertheless, the workers' point had been made; the government interceded and supervised the eventual sale—not collapse—of the enterprise. In the summer of 1975 winegrowers in southern France, threatened by the importation of cheap Italian wines, showed their discontent by storming the (purely symbolic) public buildings in the town of Montpelier. In response, the Chirac government acted by placing restrictive tariffs on the Italian wine, an action that violated Common Market free trade provisions. Also in the summer of 1975, prostitutes, protesting police harassment and seeking to have their incomes taxed so that they too could collect social security benefits, made their point by occupying local church buildings (for shock value but also to avoid police arrest). A government official was immediately appointed to look into the prostitutes' situation. Finally, high school students in Paris and the provinces began street demonstrations in the spring of 1975 to register their rejection of Education Minister Haby's school reforms (which the students considered to be regressive). Unlike the winegrowers, workers, and prostitutes, however, the students met not with the government's stated good intentions, but with the familiar CRS teargas.

conclusion: performance and prospects

How have the governments of the Fifth Republic fared in terms of economic, social, and political performance? Have they assured French citizens a decent standard of living and favorable economic prospects? Have they continued the European tradition of providing social welfare benefits to citizens in the form of public goods and services? Have French citizens enjoyed protection of their individual and collective political rights as well as basic territorial security? After answering these questions regarding performance, we shall conclude with observations regarding the overall stability of the Fifth Republic political system and the direction French politics is likely to take in the future.

THE ECONOMY

In the economic realm, the Gaullist governments of the Fifth Republic have delivered by and large on their promises to continue to raise the standard of living and to ensure a stable economy—in short, to deliver a sense of economic security to the nation.[30] The roots of French economic prosperity in the Fifth Republic were established after World War II with American assistance (in the form of the Marshall Plan) and with the success of French five-year plans that concentrated heavily on assuring economic growth (rather than social services, for example).

Economic Security   As citizens of a developed industrialized nation, the French are among the richest in the world. In terms of per capita income (GNP, or gross national product, divided per person), France comes eleventh after a number of other West European and former Commonwealth nations. It is, for example, less wealthy than the United States, West Germany, or the Scandinavian countries, but richer than Italy or Britain. Another way of measuring the French standard of living is to

[30] For an excellent (and recent) discussion of economic and social progress in France, see John Ardagh, *The New France* (Harmondsworth, England: Penguin, 1973).

ascertain if peoples' shares of per capita income go mainly for food, clothing, and shelter, or if they can move beyond basic necessities to "luxury" items. As Table 6-6 in chapter 6 shows, French citizens own large numbers of automobiles, TV sets, and telephones; other data confirm large numbers of washing machines, refrigerators, and other items that make life comfortable, rather than just tolerable. The standard of living can also be judged on the basis of infant mortality and life expectancy rates. (See Table 3–2.) These measurements reflect much more than material consumption, since they depend on health care, eating habits, literacy levels, and the nature of daily work. Thus the infant mortality rate for France is 12.9 deaths for every 1,000 babies born, which is about average for Western Europe. In contrast, the rate for Egypt is over ten times the French rate and for Zambia over twenty times. The life expectancy rates for the industrialized nations as opposed to the developing world also point out vast differences in the standard of living. Women in

TABLE 3–2 Quality of Life as Measured by Infant Mortality and Life Expectancy Rates

Country	Infant Mortality Rate (number of deaths per 1,000 one year old or less)	Life Expectancy Male	Female
Sweden	9.5	72.0	77.4
Norway	11.3	71.1	76.8
Netherlands	11.6	70.8	76.8
France	12.9	68.5	76.1
Britain	17.5	68.9	75.1
United States	17.6	67.4	75.2
West Germany	20.4	67.2	73.4
Italy	25.7	67.9	73.4
Spain	15.1	67.3	71.9
Greece	27.8	67.5	70.7
Portugal	43.3	65.3	71.0
Yugoslavia	44.8	65.3	70.1
Brazil	170.0	60.7	
Egypt	114.0	51.6	53.8
South Vietnam	100.0	50.0	
India	60.6	41.9	40.6
Zambia	259.0	43.5	
Guinea	216.0	26.0	28.0

Source: Adapted from *The New York Times*, September 28, 1975.

France can expect to live on an average of 76.1 years, men 68.5 years. In this regard, only three Western European countries (Sweden, Norway, the Netherlands) do better than France concerning women and nine countries do better concerning men. By contrast, women and men in India can expect to live only about half as long, and those in Guinea (West Africa) a third as long.

Prospects From a worldwide perspective, the French are economically secure. But what matters from the standpoint of domestic political debate is the nation's relative economic stability. By 1974, new economic problems had arisen in France—as in most of the world—because of the effects of a world recession and the energy crisis. Among other things, this has meant for France a high inflation rate of 14 percent (normally 6 percent), a decline in total economic growth (down to 4.5 percent per year instead of the usual 6.5 percent), and a rise in unemployment (to 4 percent from an average of 1 percent).

While these problems were recognized as worldwide, and thus not necessarily "solvable" by a French government alone, the economic debate came to center on the classic right-left division of "who should sacrifice" in the face of economic difficulties, or "how should the burden be shared"? The left replied, "equally by all citizens"; the right placed more emphasis on "not killing the goose that lays the golden egg." Specifically, the left favored anti-inflation measures such as wage and (especially) price controls, coupled with increased public spending to create jobs as private industry laid off workers to reduce rising costs. Obviously, these measures would soften the blow to people who were most vulnerable to economic difficulties: the poor, the working classes, the "marginals" in society who counted on social security for survival. The right advocated combatting inflation by cutting or holding down government spending and by tolerating a higher unemployment rate (the logic being that if people lose their jobs, they will not have so much money to spend and inflation therefore will be slowed). As in the case of the left, these were political choices, since the business constituency of the right obviously preferred no price controls. Also, the more well-to-do in society were less vulnerable to unemployment and not, at any rate, the prime beneficiaries of increased social services.

Thus the economic difficulties of the mid seventies served to refuel the debate—ever-present even in earlier times of economic prosperity—over capitalism versus socialism. Many of the French left (mainly those Marxist-Leninists in the PCF or Marxists in the PS) believe that while the capitalist system may experience temporary reprieves, its inherent contradictions will inevitably cause its downfall. Thus they are not really interested in shoring up the present troubled system with reforms. To many others on the left, the demise of capitalism is morally desirable. They feel that the system is an inherently exploitative one and thus, in good times as well as bad, does not serve the public interest. The defenders of the present French economic system reply to their critics that priority must go to stimulating economic growth, while at the same time holding down inflation, and that can be accomplished only by helping and protecting the nation's business and industrial interests. The healthier and wealthier those elements are, goes the argument, the greater will be the benefits that "trickle down" to the workers and *masses populaires*.

SOCIAL WELFARE

Like most Western European governments, the French State provides and coordinates an extensive system of public goods and services. These range from the realm of social insurance (welfare-state provisions) and collective goods (such as schools, parks, theaters, transportation, housing) to measures designed to integrate certain social groups more equally into society (especially a "majority" group, women). For many French citizens, a government's performance is measured by the difference these services make to everyday life, and in the social realm in particular the prospects offered by the opposition can greatly influence votes.[31]

Social Security   Always slower to enact economic and social reforms than most other European industrialized nations, France nevertheless passed legislation in 1928 that set up a comprehensive public insurance scheme to protect against the social and economic devastations of sickness, disability, and old age. Greatly expanded after World War II, the French social security system remains a vital ingredient in determining the quality of life of the average French citizen. The system covers payments to the disabled and to widows; it provides social aid in the form of orphanages, old-age homes, and hospitals. But most importantly, it provides for old-age pensions and complete health insurance.

Since every citizen faces the prospect of retirement, old age pensions are high on the list of social priorities. But health care is equally vital in the sense that sickness concerns are present throughout a lifetime. The French health care system is not like the British National Health Service, which salaries doctors and provides free health care through tax revenues. Instead, the French system operates on the principle of reimbursement by the State of medical and pharmaceutical costs. Thus a French patient goes to any doctor he or she chooses (as in Great Britain), pays for the

[31] See Peter Coffey, *The Social Economy of France* (London: Macmillan, 1973).

health care received, and then submits a form to the health authorities which enables the patient to recover 70 percent of the costs of the illness (under President Pompidou the health care reimbursement was lowered from 80 percent). At one time doctors' fees were fixed at levels negotiated by the Social Security Administration and the French Medical Association. Presently, French doctors can charge what they want, but reimbursement by the State continues to be based on the official set fee, not the doctor's actual fee. Doctors who agree to charge no more than the official fees are referred to as *conventionné*, and lists of these cooperating doctors are available to the public at large. The French health system, while not nearly so coordinated as the British, does provide comprehensive health care, and in this respect, the French are much freer from the medical anxieties that plague many Americans.

Women's Role   Another aspect of the social security system brings us into the economic–social–political realm of women, children, and the French family.[32] If there is one social aim that has dominated most French regimes, it has been, simply, to increase the population. In the minds of French politicians, more French people meant a stronger nation, better able to hold its own against its European neighbors. Following the great loss of life in World War I, the French legislature in 1920 passed an extremely repressive bill prohibiting not only abortions and the use of contraceptives, but providing for the prosecution of those who advocated their legalization. Nonetheless, the birth rate failed to rise, and in 1932 the government instituted the "family allowance" provision, or a generous cash payment upon the birth of each child after the first. In addition, maternity costs were subsumed under health insurance provisions and childbirth became practically without cost to French families.

In addition to the denial of birth control devices and the provision of cash incentives for large families, French governments ensured the population growth by making it difficult for women to enter the male-dominated working world. In fact, until the twentieth century, women were treated on the same level as their children—as minors! The French Revolution did little for women directly, and Napoleon's contribution was a legal code that is said to have codified the "rights of men and the wrongs of women." Public secondary schools did not admit girls until 1880, and it was not until 1938 that a new Family Code gave full legal capacity to women with regard to the family (meaning women no longer had to be "obedient" to their husbands). Equal rights for women suffered a tem-

[32] For the prewar perspective on women in France see relevant sections of Theodore Zeldin, *France: 1848–1945*, Vol. I (London: Oxford University Press, 1973) and for a postwar perspective, see relevant sections in John Ardagh, *The New France*.

porary setback under the Vichy regime. To emphasize that women's place was in the home with (hopefully, many) children, the regime went so far as to restrict legally the right of married women to work. France was among the last of European countries to grant women the vote; this it did (under de Gaulle) in 1945. Despite the good intentions of those in the Resistance and subsequent progressive legislation, women did not achieve equal status with men in the working world. As in the United States and elsewhere, women in France today earn considerably less pay than men. Sometimes this is because they hold more menial jobs, but in some cases they earn less pay for doing the very same job.

As the women's movement grew in the 1960's throughout Europe and the United States, proponents of birth control specifically and equal rights in general challenged the prevailing and traditionally Catholic notion of women's role in society. François Mitterrand shocked many people by including in his 1965 presidential platform a provision to rescind the birth control laws of 1920. By 1967, a dissident Gaullist deputy sponsored and got through a ground-breaking bill legalizing birth control devices and providing for contraception information centers. A final step was taken in 1974 by Giscard d'Estaing's Minister of Health, Madame Simone Veil, when she achieved passage (by a wide margin) of a bill that legalized abortion.

With regard to equal rights for women, the Giscard presidency has proved more sensitive than previous Gaullist governments. One of Giscard's first moves in office was to create a new position, "Secretary of State for the Condition of Women." Its head, Madame Françoise Giroud, announced her intention of securing legislation concerning equal pay for equal work, flexible and part-time working hours, prohibition of sex discrimination, complete legal equality for women, and a more liberalized divorce law.

Hence the "women's issue" has opened up a new field of government endeavor, because if the old ways of encouraging child-bearing are no longer acceptable, there is another, more humane and rational way. It goes on the assumption that if the prospect is made attractive enough, substantial numbers of French women will continue to choose motherhood. A full 38 percent of the French work force is made up of women, some of whom work by choice, others out of necessity. Many of them have children. Yet any working mother will confirm that the most essential service needed to combine work and family is adequate child care. Compared to the United States, that battle by and large has been won in France. For included in the "public goods and services" sector are neighborhood pre-schools (*écoles maternelles*), nurseries (*crèches*), and day-care centers (*garderies*). These tax-supported, open-to-all child care centers have existed (in theory) since the Jules Ferry educational reforms of the early Third Republic—over 100 years ago! In practice, though, the system has expanded only since World War II and remains inadequate to the demand. Nevertheless, the idea that "public schools" should begin earlier than age five is only beginning to be discussed in the United States. In France, no one questions the State's role in offering women the option of combining family-rearing with a career.

Public Goods   Generally, social security provisions are thought of as "public services"; "public goods" refer to what the French call "collective equipment." These are principally municipal facilities such as schools, parks, playgrounds, recreational and sport facilities, theaters and other cultural centers, transportation, housing, even family vacation centers and summer camp facilities. As in many aspects of social policy in France (and in Europe), the role of the State is assumed and it is deemed necessary and appropriate. What is questioned is the scope of the State's endeavors. Thus the French left continuously urges the expansion of the public goods

French day nursery.
Keystone

and service sector, while the right wants to hold the line or make such facilities available through the private sector as well. Why, specifically, is the provision of collective goods a subject of political debate? The topic is political because public facilities and services entail a fundamental means of income redistribution. Open and accessible to all, public facilities nevertheless are established, financed, maintained—and often subsidized —through general taxation into which those with more money pay progressively higher rates. Thus a poor user of free parks, in effect, has had his fee paid for by a wealthy user. And the one-franc bus ride is available to the poor rider because a wealthier rider has paid, through taxation, a good deal more for the same ride.

There are other reasons for the political nature of the debate surrounding public goods and services. Governments have traditionally provided goods and services in areas in which private concerns have not acted to meet the public need or interest. Thus, the nationalized railroad and postal services were taken over from private concerns and extended to sparsely populated, out-of-reach areas because it was felt that service, not profit, had higher priority. But there exist areas which are highly profitable to private concerns, yet have social significance as well—one of these is housing. How does the housing question epitomize the conflict between private and public priorities?

Housing   Housing is a problem for a large portion of the French population. French housing is in short supply, it is old, and it lacks basic amenities. For example, one-quarter of French homes lack a shower or bath. During World War I, 11 percent of all French housing was destroyed; yet between the wars, practically no new housing was built, as private concerns sought other outlets. After World War II, public housing became an understandable priority, resulting in the establishment of the HLM (*Habitations à Loyer Modéré*), or low-rent public housing. This housing is financed, constructed, and managed by semipublic building societies, and the five-year plan sets targets for the number of units to be built per year. Because the HLM house predominantly working class families, housing policies of the left and the right differ. The first, and more predictable, difference is that the left favors greater State budget allotments to the HLM construction. The second difference is more subtle but equally political in nature. If a commune or neighborhood is selected as a new site for HLM construction, that constituency's voting pattern is likely to change with the influx of working class voters. Therefore a center or right-controlled commune is likely to appeal to the State authorities (Gaullist dominated since 1958) in order to prevent the construction of public housing in its particular area. And the more marginal the constituency, the more political becomes the housing policy process.

In a way, the case of Paris (in whose broad contours 18 percent of French people live) epitomizes the broader social implications of housing patterns. Paris has experienced a reversal of American housing trends. Instead of seeing the middle classes moving to suburbia, the French capital over the last century has seen an eviction of the working classes to the near suburbs, coupled with an inflow to the central city of the rich, the cosmopolitan, and the commercial interests. This process began with Napoleon III's famous city-planner, Haussmann, who demolished large sections of the Right Bank working class quarters to construct wide and beautiful boulevards leading out from the Arc de Triomphe. The process accelerated with the steady influx of the farming population, which joined the working class in the industrialized areas of the Paris agglomeration. As a result, Paris proper is now surrounded by a "red belt" of working class Communist-voting communes, many of which are characterized by their enormous, crowded HLM apartment buildings. Finally, the process has further spiraled in the Fifth Republic as real estate speculators continue to build high-rent luxury apartment buildings in Paris itself. The demand for them exists—from the rich, international business concerns, and diplomats, for example—but fulfilling speculators' profit needs has not fulfilled the Parisian public's need for decent yet affordable housing.

THE POLITICAL REGIME

Civil Rights The French Constitution of 1958 clearly postulates the principles of liberal democracy. It says, "France shall be a republic, indivisible, secular, democratic, and social. It shall ensure the equality of all citizens before the law, without distinction of origin, race or religion. It shall respect all beliefs. . . . The motto of the Republic shall be 'Liberty, Equality, Fraternity'. Its principle shall be government of the people, by the people, and for the people." There is no question that French citizens enjoy many of the basic freedoms that characterize the other Western European liberal democracies. They have freedom of speech and association, freedom of the press, freedom of religion, free elections, competing political parties, provision for orderly and legitimate transition of government, and freedom to travel. In fact, the number of French citizens choosing to emigrate has always been comparatively low; on the contrary, France (along with Britain) has traditionally provided a welcome haven for exiles the world over.

At the same time—and while no liberal democracy can be perfect—French politics presents a basic paradox. The promise of freedom and democracy is great (and even greater if we consider the legacy of the French Revolution); yet the French experience has been less ideal than many of its Western European neighbors. As we have seen, a succession of French regimes has tended to abuse (in varying degree and with varying methods) their basic political powers. This abuse cannot be attributed solely to the Gaullist Fifth Republic, nor necessarily only to regimes on the right. But precisely because the French left has been in power for so very few years, it is difficult to judge whether its actions would continue to reflect what seems to be a particular French attitude toward authority or whether its own ideals and program would cause it to exercise political responsibilities differently. At any rate, we know from studying the policy process in the Fifth Republic that the Gaullist regime in many ways opted for a closed, efficient, and stable system of government over an open and responsive system, one that would be sensitive to citizens' individual and collective rights. President Giscard d'Estaing, in contrast, has promised reforms to strengthen French citizens' basic rights, but always within an ever-powerful presidential system. To date this has meant a lowering of the voting age to 18, assurances that political exiles would find safe asylum in France, an end to politically inspired wiretapping, and preliminary steps to forming a judicial review process.

Governmental Stability If Giscard d'Estaing offers the prospect of enhancing the civil liberties of individuals in France, what of the prospects for his assuring the continued stability of the political system? Here the post–Gaullist prospects are not clear. We know that the president in the Fifth Republic holds great power supremacy in practice, but not necessarily in theory—therein lie further difficulties. Let us consider what would happen if a hostile majority were voted into the Assembly, as nearly happened in March of 1973. It would not be long before the government would be censured or would receive a vote of no confidence. Assuming the president named a new prime minister and in time he too was rejected, the president would be likely to dissolve the uncooperative Assembly and call for new elections. If the same hostile majority were returned, a stalemate would become inevitable, since (according to the Constitution) the president can only dissolve the Assembly once a year. In that case, the president would be compelled to select a prime minister from the opposition's ranks. But, ironically, if the president and prime minister were not compatible, it would be the prime minister who would predominate. This is because while the president can appoint a prime minister, he cannot fire him. (De Gaulle changed prime ministers three times only through persuasion.) So at that point the prime minister and his cabinet could proceed to initiate policy, send it to the now receptive

Assembly for deliberation and approval, and, through public opinion, force the president either to promulgate such legislation or to offer his own resignation.

This possibility could happen because the Fifth Republic Constitution is unclear as to who ultimately governs, the president or the prime minister. The trouble stems from de Gaulle's modernization of the concept of executive dominated government. Previously, strong executive governments in France were all one-man dictatorships: the monarchs, two Bonapartes, Pétain. For de Gaulle to create an executive dominated system that was nevertheless *democratic* required some sort of provision for the National Assembly. Yet by providing for a dual executive (with one branch, the president, responsible to the people and the other, the prime minister, responsible to Parliament), de Gaulle only further complicated the political process. It seems possible then, that the present mixed presidential–parliamentary system, like the previous dozen regimes, may eventually fail to provide a workable compromise between efficient and representative government.

There are other reasons to believe that the present regime in France very well may be provisional. Both the left opposition and some elements on the right and center advocate constitutional changes, including a shorter presidential term, reduced presidential powers, and a return to a PR electoral system. Coupled with the fact that the apparent political bipolarity in France rests on two potentially unstable multiparty coalitions, these institutional changes could very well lead toward a legislative oriented system reminiscent of the Third and Fourth Republics, or on to something fairly different, perhaps even a Sixth French Republic.

Foreign Affairs From protection of the individual to protection of the regime, we now move to protection of the nation itself. Located in the strategic center of Western Europe, France for centuries has fought for self-survival, if not for European domination. The nation frequently has been embroiled in the principal European conflicts, and it is likely to remain at the center of the European political stage.

The foreign policy of President de Gaulle was perhaps the most controversial aspect of his reign, controversial because de Gaulle was not content simply to ensure the nation's security from external aggression.[33] He went far beyond that into the realm of seeking grandeur and glory for the French nation. This foreign policy priority ultimately led to de Gaulle's downfall, because in pursuit of this course he left unattended more pressing domestic needs of the French people.

[33] See Alfred Grosser, *Foreign Policy in the Fifth Republic* (Boston: Little, Brown, 1966).

Once de Gaulle had withdrawn the French presence from Algeria, he was free to turn his attention to asserting the French presence in the world. For if de Gaulle's foreign policy was based on one goal, it was that of establishing France as an independent, neutral, and indispensable actor in world politics. French independence meant being able to defend itself alone, without its European and American allies in NATO, through bilateral defense agreements. Neutrality meant establishing France as an arbiter between the two superpowers of the USSR and the United States. Indispensibility meant establishing (largely economic) ties to the developing nations of the Third World. To secure an adequate defense for France without relying on the American nuclear umbrella, de Gaulle proceeded to develop a French nuclear striking force, the *force de frappe*. France had tested nuclear weapons in 1960, thereby becoming the fourth nation to hold such devastating power, and by 1966, de Gaulle had withdrawn France from the NATO integrated military command (although France remained a member of the Atlantic Alliance). At the same time, de Gaulle continued to thwart the European Community's aim of greater cooperation and integration. Then too, de Gaulle profited from the polycentrist situation resulting from the Sino-Soviet split, and his "opening to the East" policies (to China, USSR, and Eastern Europe) set France on a more independent course. Through a generous foreign aid program, de Gaulle asserted the French presence in the developing world, and his "active neutralism" gained France economic advantages after the Middle East war of 1967.

The costs of maintaining a nation's own defense system—especially when it is a nuclear one—are extremely high, as Americans and Russians know. And when those costs are coupled with inattention to pressing domestic concerns, troubles arise. In France, a turning point in foreign policy was reached in 1968. After the events of May 1968, de Gaulle was no longer able to convince the people that national glory and an enhanced French role in international politics was a sufficient substitute for socioeconomic measures that related directly to their daily lives. Between 1968 and 1969, the defense budget dropped faster than any year since the wind-up of the Algerian crisis; conversely, the budget for ministries concerned with health, education, and welfare rose.

Presidents Pompidou and Giscard d'Estaing oriented their foreign policy increasingly away from de Gaulle's vision of an independent France and toward the goal of France as the senior partner in the European Community. This policy is much more in keeping with French public opinion, which favors political—as well as economic, monetary, and defense—integration in Europe. In addition, a high military budget is no longer easily justified to a public that perceives the threat of a Soviet invasion as increasingly unlikely.

Thus the French are becoming more aware of the classic "guns versus butter" dilemma. That is, to what extent should the government's budget for "nonproductive" defense measures be cut in order to increase measures that affect the quality of citizens' daily lives? To a great extent, the degree of modernization of a country can be measured by the explicitness with which its citizens insist that the government serve their domestic needs and aspirations as well as secure their basic defense requirements. This leads us into one remaining political problem that has recently moved to the forefront of political debate in France. It concerns the way in which citizens can make their demands known and acted upon, and entails the decentralization of decision-making into the hands of citizens at the regional, departmental, and local levels.

The "Blocked" Society   Commentators on French politics and society have long lamented the "blocked" nature of the political process.[34] The administrative apparatus in Paris, by leaving no initiative or autonomy to lower levels, has produced apathetic, "incivic" French citizens. In the Fifth Republic both the left and the right have broached the previously unbroachable subject of "dismantling the Napoleonic State"—their solutions, however, are not the same.

To the ruling Gaullists, the answer to an over-loaded central State lay in "regionalism." In 1960, the Debré government grouped the 95 French departments into 21 regions, complete with a "super-prefect" to oversee each region. In 1964, these regions were endowed with Regional Economic Development Councils (CODER), whose purpose was mainly to assist with the formulation of the National Plan. In response to the May 1968 challenge to the omnipotent State authority, de Gaulle proposed in the 1969 referendum that these regional structures be given constitutional status, thereby introducing an element of federalism into the rigidly unitary French system. The result of the referendum was a defeat for de Gaulle's proposal (though it was defeated not because of the regionalist question, but because the Senate would have been abolished). The CODER were then abolished under the Pompidou presidency in 1970, and replaced in 1972 with regional assemblies.

The "regionalist" Gaullist answer has been criticized for several reasons. First, the purpose of regionalism seems to have been more one of rationali-

---

[34] See Michel Crozier, *The Stalled Society* (New York: Viking Press, 1973) and, more generally, Stanley Hoffmann, *Decline or Renewal? France since the 1930s* (New York: Viking Press, 1974).

zing the administration to achieve greater efficiency rather than of expanding the decision-making arena. Thus there has been *deconcentration* of decision-making, not decentralization. Decisions are still made under the auspices of and with the assistance of representatives of the central authorities, not by the regional assemblies themselves. Second, those who sit on the assemblies are not directly elected representatives of the people; they are indirectly elected officials (such as deputies and senators) and local representatives selected by departmental and municipal councils. Third, the duties of the regional assembly members are advisory only and limited for the most part to consultations regarding the National Plan.

The left has quite another idea of what constitutes decentralization of the State. True decentralization, says the left, entails not just further delegation of middle and lower level administrative powers down the line, but a redistribution of power so that it flows from the bottom up. Hence the Common Governmental Program calls for local, departmental, and regional decisions to be made democratically by all involved, with the State (through the prefect) exercising *a posteriori* legal power only. Considerably more autonomy would be granted to various governmental levels, including the all-important powers to *tax* and *spend* according to the area's needs and priorities. In addition, representatives on the ruling assemblies and councils would be directly elected by the people.

The left has not always urged decentralization—on the contrary. Since 1789, the term "Jacobin" has meant someone on the left who favors the unitary Napoleonic state and explicitly rejects federalism. Until recently, the SFIO and PCF were resolute Jacobins. But in the 1960's the PSU began to espouse the notion of decentralization as a means of getting around the grip of the Gaullist regime; the events of May 1968 then spread the demand to break down the omnipotent powers of the central State. Finally, separatist movements in Britanny and Corsica, for example, have joined the left's demand to "decolonize the provinces" and see regional autonomy as a political prerequisite in the struggle to preserve their identity, language, and cultural uniqueness.

If society is "blocked" by the power of the centralized State, many commentators see the other side of the coin as the "anarchic individualism" of the French people. While perhaps characteristic of French society at one time, such an analysis does not really reflect postwar, and even more so, Fifth Republic, social realities. The French body politic is no longer dominated by large numbers of self-sufficient farmers, tradespeople, or professionals, who can and do operate individually and independently. On the contrary, as France approaches the status of post-industrial society—defined as a situation in which the majority of the work force is engaged in the delivery of services, not the production of food and goods—this modernization process has brought the rise of certain socioeconomic groups such as technological and scientific salaried workers, white-collar tertiary workers, and public (government) and private management personnel. These people do not work in isolation, but are engaged in collective endeavors characterized by interdependency and interaction. With increased politicization these groups seek to participate in deciding matters that traditionally have been entrusted to the State. "Anarchic individualism" implies a position of anti-State, anti-collective political endeavor. Yet these new politicized strata demand just the opposite. The feminist, consumer, environmental, cultural regionalist, trade union, and salaried groups who are politically active seek to operate on the collective level through established public authorities; they do *not* endorse a course of hands-off rugged individualism.

Finally, many commentators have argued that modernization of French society has brought citizens and groups to take on an increasingly "nationalized"—as opposed to particularist—political outlook, and that this has resulted in a more pragmatic approach to politics. Yet, it is actually the opposite that prevails. As politicization increases in the sense that citizens demand to know, to understand, and then to determine the business of government, political-economic-social cleavages tend to harden if the system remains closed and insensitive to those demands. Thus the political process in the Fifth Republic, calculated to exclude the more than 40 percent of French people who vote on the left, has only served to reinforce the opposition's resolve for major change, even peaceful revolution. Many people in the early 1960's thought that the intensity of political debate in France would diminish, that somehow "progress" implied middle-of-the-road consensus. But knowing the development of French political history since 1789 and the kinds of issues still in political contention, we may conclude instead that it would be illusory to declare the "end of ideology" in France.

4

the two germanies

NORTH SEA

BALTIC SEA

SWEDEN

DENMARK

POLAND

CZECHOSLOVAKIA

AUSTRIA

NETHERLANDS

BELGIUM

LUX.

FRANCE

SCHLESWIG-HOLSTEIN

Kiel

Lubeck

HAMBURG

BREMEN

ROSTOCK

NEUBRANDEN-BURG

SCHWERIN

LOWER SAXONY

Hannover

MAGDE-BURG

Berlin

Potsdam

FRANKFURT (ODER)

GERMAN DEMOCRATIC REPUBLIC

COTTBUS

Dresden

GERMAN FEDERAL REPUBLIC

NORTH RHINE-WESTPHALIA

Essen   Dusseldorf

Cologne   Bonn

Kassel

HESSE

Frankfurt

HALLE

ERFURT

Weimar

Leipzig

GERA

SUHL

KARL MARX-STADT

RHINELAND-PALATINATE

SAAR

Heidelberg

BADEN-WUERTEMBERG

Stuttgart

Nurnberg

BAVARIA

Munich

4 THE TWO GERMANIES

background

West Germany is economically the most powerful member of the European Common Market. It is both actually and potentially one of the most important world powers. Its 62 million people operate the fourth largest economy today—after the United States, the Soviet Union, and Japan. East Germany is the most technologically and economically advanced state in the whole Communist orbit. Culturally and politically, the Germans have left a major imprint on the development of world civilization in the twentieth century.

Yet, today's Germany may be likened to a verdant slope on Mount Vesuvius. Its calm, peaceful, and prosperous exterior has been created upon such a volcanic political foundation that many have wondered if it can long survive. If people are influenced by what they have been, then the trauma of German political history raises extraordinary uncertainties about the German present and future.

FROM MIDDLE AGES TO MODERN TIMES

Though the German people have inhabited central Europe for centuries —even before William the Conqueror sailed for England in 1066—they had not achieved common statehood until comparatively quite late. Like the Italians, the Germans formed a series of many separate principalities well into the 1800's. At the time of the French Revolution in 1789 there were actually more than 300 principalities. None possessed or developed substantial democratic institutions of self-government. Long after Russia, France, England, Spain, and Sweden had achieved strong national monarchies, Germany stagnated in disunity and weakness. In the mid-nineteenth century the impulses of nationalism, stimulated by the French Revolution and Napoleonic conquests, finally asserted themselves. Germany became a nation-state in 1871. It did so, however, under the leadership of the most authoritarian and militaristic of all its principalities —Prussia. The German state was brought into being by the crafty and ruthless policies of Prince Otto von Bismarck, the chancellor of Prussia, and it emerged as the end-product of wars that asserted Prussia's undisputed supremacy in Germany. In 1866, Bismarck's Prussians, in a lightning war, defeated Austria, a rival for all-German leadership; in 1870, they defeated France of Napoleon III, the principal foreign opponent of a strong and united Germany.

As soon as unity was achieved, the new German empire (as successor to the ninth century empire of Charlemagne, it was titled the Second Reich) proceeded to establish itself as a foremost industrial, military, and diplomatic world power. The militarism of Prussia and its grandiose European and worldwide aspirations were reinforced by the still larger population and resources of the rest of Germany. The growth of German might was formidable, and it created widespread anxieties abroad. On the home front, Bismarck interpreted Prussian success in unifying and strengthening Germany as proof of the virtues of authoritarian and militaristic government. While a German parliament (Reichstag) had been created, it was never allowed to operate as anything more than elaborate window-dressing, and to some extent, a ventilator of grievances for the regime. Bismarck personally reminded the German parliamentarians that in the lives of nations "it is not speeches and majority resolutions but iron and blood" that are the decisive factors. Germany had adopted some of the external trappings of a parliamentary democracy between 1871 and 1918, but the substance of power lay largely with the King of Prussia as Emperor, and with his advisors drawn from the upper rungs of the landed nobility (the Prussian Junkers) and the military.

On the whole, until the outbreak of World War I, this regime did bring Germany power, international prestige and, perhaps most importantly, great prosperity. It was Bismarck who had introduced in Germany, earlier than anywhere else, such measures as compulsory health and accident insurance for workers (1883, 1885), and disability and old-age pensions (1891). These factors combined to give Germany's feudal-military rulers a high degree of legitimacy and popularity, even though there were many suppressed and persecuted elements in Germany at that time. Much of the conflict centered on the repression of three major forces: the German Catholic minority, whom Bismarck and other Protestant Prussians suspected of disloyalty to the new German state; the workers—trade

FIGURE 4–1 History of German Regimes

unionists and socialists—whose claims were not only opposed by the wealthy but who were also suspected of subversive revolutionary designs; and finally, the ethnic minorities, particularly the Poles in Silesia, Pomerania, Poznania and East Prussia, and the French in Alsace-Lorraine; they, too, were considered either actually or potentially hostile.

WORLD WAR (1914–1918) AND WEIMAR REPUBLIC (1919–1933)

The First World War, which in the course of four years brought on great suffering and millions of casualties to the German people, finally resulted in the defeat of the Second Reich. Amidst riots and mutinies, the Emperor fled to Holland. With tacit approval of military leaders, field marshals von Hindenburg and Ludendorff, a Republic was proclaimed. All those forces which had opposed the autocracy during the days of the Empire—the Social Democrats, the Catholic Center Party, and the liberal Progressive Democrats—came to the fore. The pendulum of German politics swung to the left-center. An ultraliberal Constitution for a new German republic was drafted in the city of Weimar in 1919. It provided a very extensive bill of rights—even longer and more detailed than America's famed first ten amendments. It also provided for a scrupulously fair and accurate system of elections based on thoroughgoing proportional representation. The Germans chose their parliamentary representatives in multimember electoral districts, and through nationwide party lists. This meant that if a group received, say, 15 percent of the popular vote nationally, it was likely to get about the same percentage of seats in the parliament. Under the American electoral system, where only one senator or representative is chosen at a time, the winner "takes all"; the votes cast for candidates who fail to get a plurality are "wasted," even if very close to the winner's vote. Only in later years was it realized that even this very liberal Constitution contained loopholes that eventually would prove useful in establishing a dictatorship.

From its very beginnings, the Weimar Republic seemed ill-fated. In 1919, coincident with its foundation, the Peace Conference at Versailles —dominated by the victorious Western allies, Britain, France, and the United States—imposed its terms upon Germany. To millions of Germans, the terms seemed surprisingly harsh and vengeful. The Versailles Treaty officially saddled Germany with responsibility for starting the World War, a proposition considered dubious even by many non-Germans. It called for huge reparation payments to be made by Germany to the victorious states. It deprived Germany of large portions of territory (Alsace-Lorraine, part of Pomerania, Silesia and Poznania); it sanctioned French occupation of the western bank of the Rhine as a guarantee of reparation payments; and it limited the size and quality of Germany's military forces, as if Germany were a singularly suspect criminal among the nations. This was particularly disappointing to those Germans who had hoped that a democratic Germany would be treated more fairly by states which, in President Wilson's words, fought to "make the world safe for democracy."

The diplomatic-military humiliation of Germany was combined with severe economic difficulties. Runaway inflation destroyed the savings of the German middle class and brought havoc to the whole economy. By the mid-1920's the inflation was finally brought under control and Germany enjoyed a few years of recovery from the ravages of the war. Its statesmen, particularly foreign ministers Stresemann and Rathenau, busily worked to restore the country's international position through negotiation and conciliation. But all this soon ended with the United States stock market crash of October 1929. A world depression ensued, and it hit Germany particularly hard. By 1931 some 6 million Germans were out of work; misery and want once again afflicted the Weimar Republic. The shock proved too strong for the new system to absorb.

THE RISE OF EXTREMISM

Among the most important political consequences of the Depression were the phenomenal rise of the Nazis (National Socialist German Workers Party) led by Adolf Hitler on the Right, and a more gradual but substantial increase in the strength of the Communist Party on the Left. Hitler, an obscure corporal in the imperial army, who had joined with just six other political adventurers in the so-called Nazi Party in 1919, became the foremost politician in Germany. In 1923 he had tried, unsuccessfully, to seize power by a march on Berlin. He and a few hundred of his followers were stopped by a handful of policemen. Hitler was tried for attempting to overthrow the government; he was imprisoned for less than two years. While in jail, he wrote his blueprint for the future, a book titled *Mein Kampf*. In it he outlined such subsequently infamous principles as the German racial superiority over all the peoples of the earth, his vitriolic hatred of the Jews, his adamant opposition to both Marxism and democracy, his worship of violence and expansionism, and his dreams of revived German power and foreign conquests.

Until the Great Depression, not many Germans seemed to take Hitler seriously. As late as 1928 Hitler's party had obtained a mere 12 seats out of more than 600 in the German Reichstag. But the Depression changed things both for Hitler and for Germany almost overnight. By 1930 the Nazis increased their vote almost tenfold. As the economic and social crisis deepened, middle class German voters fled from their moderate party allegiances into the fold of the Nazis. By 1932 Germany had become profoundly polarized. The Nazis drew one-third of the national vote; the Communists upwards of 16 percent. A so-called negative majority had come into being. About 50 percent of the electorate was turning its back on the democratic-parliamentary system of Weimar, giving support to two extremist parties, each advocating opposite types of dictatorial regimes: one allegedly on behalf of the proletariat, one allegedly on behalf of all true German people. Hitler's appeal to German nationalism, to the traditions of authoritarianism, militarism, unity, order, and power in the midst of the bitter divisions engendered by the Depression proved attractive to millions. His impassioned demagogical oratory and mass propaganda techniques were also becoming increasingly effective.

THE FALL OF WEIMAR

Since no solid parliamentary majority could be found to rule Germany as the Constitution had anticipated, President von Hindenburg resorted to rule through an emergency clause of the Constitution: Article 48. This article enabled him, with the concurrence of a chancellor whom he could name, to issue decrees that would have the force of law, subject only to post facto repeal by parliament and without any initial legislative approval. Coupled with the president's power to dissolve parliament and call for new elections, this meant that Germany could be ruled for relatively long periods under executive discretion alone. Yet, successive elections in the early 1930's did not bring about any real coalescence of German public opinion. In January 1933, President von Hindenburg finally called on Hitler, leader of the largest party (the Nazis), to form a coalition government with the more moderate Nationalist Party, ostensibly in the hope that these two parties might obtain a parliamentary majority in the next election. Considering all the things that Hitler had had to say publicly about parliamentarianism in *Mein Kampf* and elsewhere, and his past conduct, we have good reason to second-guess President von Hindenburg's judgment and motives.

In any event, once invested with the chancellorship, Hitler almost immediately proceeded to destroy the existing republican-parliamentary regime by force and fraud. Taking advantage of a mysterious fire that broke out in the Reichstag building in February 1933, Hitler promptly blamed it on the Communists and called for emergency measures to save the state from a Communist insurrection. The aged President von Hindenburg obligingly provided him with special powers under the provisions of Article 48. Thus, with the assistance of Goering and Himmler and the Nazi Party's brown- and black-shirted storm troopers, Hitler proceeded to harass and terrorize all possible opposition. Communists as well as other people whom Hitler disliked or who dared oppose him fell victims to this anti-Communist campaign which, conveniently enough, coincided with the election campaign for a new Reichstag. In March 1933 the German people cast their ballots. Despite all of his violent measures, Hitler failed to obtain a majority. The Nazis received about 44 percent of the vote. Still, together with their Nationalist allies, who got about 8 percent, Hitler could count on the support of 52 percent of the German parliamentarians. This might have been enough for an "ordinary" politician, but Hitler vowed to rule in virtual independence of parliamentary scrutiny. To achieve this with any pretense of constitutional legality, he needed a so-called Enabling Act. The Weimar Constitution provided that under circumstances of national crisis, the Reichstag could—by a two-thirds vote—vest legislative powers in the cabinet for a maximum period not exceeding its own term, that is, four years at the most. It also specifically forbade the cabinet to change the Constitution during any such emergency period.

HITLER'S DICTATORSHIP

Since Hitler and his allies stood far short of a two-thirds majority, the Nazis proceeded to arrest about 100 opposition deputies, most of them Communists. They were thrown into concentration camps. Together with assorted pressures and cajoling of the other parties, Hitler managed to put together the necessary votes for his Enabling Act in March 1933. Only the Social Democrats dared vote against him, while hundreds of armed storm troopers surrounded the Reichstag building chanting "This bill, or fire and murder!" For all practical purposes, the Weimar Republic had ceased to exist. When President von Hindenburg died, Hitler unconstitutionally merged the offices of chancellor and president into one new position—that of the fuehrer, or Leader, with himself as incumbent. On August 4, 1934, the German Army was asked to take an oath of loyalty, not to the Constitution or to the state, but to the fuehrer personally, Adolf Hitler.

All parties other than the Nazis were declared illegal. All the personal and political rights guaranteed by the Weimar Constitution were nullified by the institutions of the secret police (Gestapo—*Geheime Staats Polizei*), concentration camps, and centralized censorship and propaganda through all the media, under the direction of Dr. Joseph Goebbels. Hitler turned the Reichstag into a one-party, purely ceremonial body, convoked for the sole purpose of applauding his speeches before the whirring cameras of Dr. Goebbels' Propaganda Ministry. He also resorted to plebiscites, asking the German voters, among other things, to ratify post facto by a "yes" vote his decisions to become fuehrer and to have Germany leave the League of Nations—but all this only after opposition had been outlawed and terrorized. Within three years of his accession to the chancellorship, Hitler also dispensed with the cabinet as a collective body meeting to discuss and approve policies. The government of Germany thus became, by early 1936, a virtually private affair at the fuehrer's court.

NAZI POLICIES

Hitler pursued three principal policies: (1) massive rearmament of Germany which violated the provisions of the Versailles Treaty; (2) territorial expansion embodied in the annexation of the Rhineland, Austria, Sudeten-

land, ultimately the rest of Czechoslovakia, and culminating in the demand for Danzig and a corridor through Poland; and (3) a policy of
Nazification at home. Nazification consisted of jailing and killing opponents, expelling and persecuting racial enemies (Jews) and killing misfits
(malformed or mentally defective persons) as well as other "positive"
mobilizational measures: inducting millions into paramilitary, Nazi mass
organizations.

Hitler's rearmament program brought back full employment to Germany, and while his regime killed or imprisoned thousands of opponents
in concentration camps, the streets were once again made tranquil. The
demonstrations, marches, and protests of Weimar days were all gone;
and so were the political brawls among opponents (particularly among
Nazi stormtroopers and their targeted victims, of course).

In Hitler's Germany, not only the Communists but also the Socialists
and all working-class parties were dissolved; the trade unions were taken
over by the Nazi government and staffed by Nazi party officials. Left-
wing press, schools, and associations were all suppressed, and the leaders
and members of what might be called the Left in Germany—the Communists, the Socialists and those who in the American context might be
loosely termed "liberals"—numbered highest in Nazi prisons and concentration camps as well as among firing squad victims.

The conservative Nationalist party dissolved itself, too, but most of its
leaders moved over into substantial leadership positions in the Nazi system—political, administrative, economic, and cultural. The Center party
was dissolved also but the infrastructure of the Catholic church and its
various auxiliaries remained.

Generally, those groups and interests which had been allied with the
Nazis or had maintained a benevolent neutrality toward them—business
groups, landlords, army officers, upper levels of the bureaucracy, well-
to-do farmers, and so on—received much more considerate treatment.
Some of these groups not only maintained considerable integrity and
autonomy in their internal organizations—the German Chamber of Industry, for example, continued under its old leadership after 1933 as
before—but thanks to Nazi support, and the collapse of the Leftist
competition, they were able to enhance their positions beyond the wildest
dreams of the Weimar period.

Big business no longer worried about strikes because the Nazis effectively and totally forbade them. Many firms received iron-clad monopoly
rights from the state; they had no competition to worry about. In due
course, Hitler even provided businesses with slave-labor imports from
the conquered countries, and with windfall profits from his massive re-

armament programs. The Prussian Junkers and many other bankrupt and inefficient landowners were bailed out by the Nazi regime. The military, who had been subject to severe budgetary stringencies under the Weimar regime, became the beneficiaries of stupendous largesse under Hitler's expansionist policies. The budget for war purposes had jumped more than tenfold between 1932 and 1938!

Workers clearly benefited by high employment and overtime pay; they obviously welcomed the end of the Depression, the dole, and the bread lines. But their wage rates actually fell in the 1930's relative to Weimar levels; their share in the national income fell; they were subjected to considerably greater tax burdens as compared with Hitler's affluent big business and landed friends. By the end of the 1930's inequality in Germany substantially increased. Workers' freedom to change jobs and residences was sharply curtailed. The upward mobility of all the poorer strata of German society suffered a severe setback in Hitler's educational policies. Compared with Weimar, the Nazi period was one of drastic cutback in the German people's access to an education, particularly secondary and higher education. Hitler's antirationalist bias, his jingoism, and his contempt for the common people—all unchecked by competitive political processes—led to a great reversal of Weimar's cultural and social achievements. A few illustrations may suffice here.

The number of university students under Hitler's rule declined from 95,807 in 1931 to just 39,236 in 1939. The number of students in higher technical and professional schools fell from 23,749 to 10,307. In fact, even the elementary schools, their staffs, and their students, all declined substantially during the Nazi years, population increases notwithstanding.

Similarly, in the field of social welfare, the Nazis managed to decrease the share of national wealth devoted to the care of the poor, the sick, and the elderly over what it had been in the Weimar era. Old age pensions and industrial sickness benefits were substantially reduced. Despite an increase in the population, total spending of all kinds under the various provisions of social insurance was 4 percent less in 1938 than in 1929.[1]

By 1936, the Nazis had managed to increase the national income by about 70 percent and the total tax burden of the people by 120 percent. At the same time, they shifted this burden from only 30 percent in regressive indirect taxes to 41 percent. The profits of large corporations soared, and the index of inequality in income distribution rose from .649 in 1931 to .721 in 1935.

[1] Maxine Y. Woolston, *The Structure of Nazi Economy* (New York: Russell and Russell, 1941), p. 227. See also Jurgen Kuczynski, *Germany: Economic and Labor Conditions Under Fascism* (New York: Greenwood Press, 1968).

While Hitler's policies led Germany directly into the Second World War, even that ordeal had had its high moments. The years 1939, 1940, and most of 1941 were, on balance, years of overwhelming victories purchased at low cost in manpower and material. Germany had attained virtual mastery of Europe. Britain was an obstreperous but seemingly hopeless hold-out in 1940. The prospect of German primacy in the whole world was not farfetched as the Nazi war machine closed, swiftly, and to all appearances irresistibly, on Moscow in late 1941.

The tide against Hitler did not begin to turn decisively until 1942, following the unsuccessful winter campaign in Russia, and the defeats suffered by field marshals Rommel in Africa and von Paulus at Stalingrad.[2] With the entry of the United States into the war, Germany became subjected to large scale and more intensive allied bombing of its cities and centers of production. Throughout 1943, 1944, and 1945, German armies retreated with great losses, pursued into the very heart of Germany by the armies of the Soviet Union, United States, Great Britain and other allies, including French, Poles, Canadians, Australians and New Zealanders.

In 1944, a group of high-ranking German officers participated in a plot to kill Hitler, to bring peace and restore a more benevolent and internationally acceptable domestic order for the German nation. On July 20, 1944, Colonel Klaus von Stauffenberg placed a bomb in a brief case under the table of Hitler's conference room. But the bomb killed and wounded several of his aides, while only slightly wounding Hitler himself. Hundreds of German officers were rounded up by the Gestapo and executed in reprisal for this act. The plot failed.

Until the last day of the war, when Hitler's successor Grand Admiral Doenitz signed the document of unconditional surrender in the face of destruction and defeat, not one Germany military unit—regiment, battalion, or even company—mutinied against the Nazi command. Nor were there any civilian defections. Not one town or village in all Germany acted to depose its Nazi leaders before the arrival of Allied armies. Rank-and-file Germans, soldiers and civilians, remained far more steadfast behind Hitler than they were behind the Kaiser in the First World War. What mix of loyalty, fear, resignation, or doubt accounted for their behavior can only be a matter of speculation today. But the fact of obedience to Hitler is of great significance for subsequent developments in Germany.

[2] See William L. Shirer, *The Rise and Fall of the Third Reich* (New York: Simon and Schuster, 1960).

The regimes established in 1949, both in West and East Germany, did not stem from the initiative of the German people. Unlike the Americans in 1776, the British in 1689, and the French in 1789 or 1871, the Germans did not spontaneously bring into being some new form of rule for themselves. They set up regimes which were, more and less rigidly in the two cases, called for by the occupying powers, Russians in the east, Americans, Britons, and French in the west. In the case of West Germany, there was much more leeway for the elected representatives of the German people than there was in East Germany. Here, Stalin's hand was heavily felt; the rule of the German Communists, the so-called SED (Socialist Unity Party), was virtually from the beginning based on police terror and the de facto exclusion of all anti-Communist political forces from the public arena.

In West Germany, the allied imperative to the Germans was more broadly for some form of parliamentary-democratic regime, and for excluding former Nazis from public life. Beyond this, the three occupying powers—United States, Britain, and France—were at odds on what the Germans ought to do. Diverse views among Germans themselves were both tolerated and encouraged. In creating the West German Federal Republic (FRG) of 1949 the Weimar and Nazi experiences played an important role. The Constitution adopted in Bonn may be said to have been organized on the principle: "How can we avoid the pitfalls of Weimar that made it possible for a Hitler to seize power?" In large measure the Constitution was aimed at preventing the possible repetition of the Nazi experience.

Some of the features of the new system directed toward this end were:

1. Greater emphasis on federalism, with more power to the 11 constituent *länder,* or states, than was the case with Weimar. This change may be more fully understood by analogy to a ship with several watertight compartments: the flooding of one chamber would be less likely to cause damage to the whole ship. Under Weimar, the control of the Reichstag would enable anyone (including, as it happened, Hitler) to gain power in all of Germany. In the Federal Republic of today, an upper chamber, called the Bundesrat, made up of the representatives of the 11 states, can exercise absolute veto over the decisions of the popularly elected lower house, the Bundestag. Thus, a sudden electoral victory for any party in the Bundestag could not be converted into as much national power as quickly as it could under Weimar.

2. The provision of judicial review in an explicit scheme of checks and balances. In this respect, the Federal Republic had imitated the United

States. It set up a Constitutional Court which can invalidate laws and acts of the executive if, in the Court's judgment, they clash with the Basic Law. Under Weimar, Germany had operated on the doctrine of political-parliamentary supremacy. Courts had no power to invalidate laws that parliament had sanctioned, and in practice the courts shied from imposing any check on the outwardly proper acts of "lawfully constituted authority." The actions taken by von Hindenburg or Hitler, pursuant to Article 48 or the Enabling Act, were never judicially questioned.

3. The modification of proportional representation (P.R.) to a new "half-and-half" formula, combining single-member electoral districts to the Bundestag with a nationwide proportional representation system. Thus, the single-member districts in Germany today elect representatives in the same way as is done in the United States and Britain. Whoever gains the most votes, not necessarily a majority, wins the seat in the legislature. Obviously, if many candidates split many votes among them, the result might not be very democratic. The winner could receive a small percentage of the total vote cast, so long as it was more than the vote of any other candidate. The advantage of the system, however, is that it favors large, well-established parties. Voters are more likely to assume that only these parties have a chance of winning and presumably are less likely to "waste" their votes on the chancy prospects of new, marginal, radical entrants into the political arena. Under pure P.R., they would be more likely to back esoteric choices because it is not necessary to gain a plurality in order to gain some representation. After all, the vote is not likely to be "wasted." To be sure, half of the lower house of parliament (Bundestag) is still chosen by proportional representation but small parties (see 4 below) have been deprived of any share in this.

Many political analysts have concluded that without proportional representation, Hitler's Nazis would not have been able to stampede the German electorate as quickly and thoroughly as they did during the Depression. Under Weimar, parties offered many candidates in each electoral district, thus enabling them to get at least *some* seats in parliament even if they won only a small percent of the vote. There were also nationwide lists of party candidates serving the same purpose of reflecting voter preferences faithfully. By its very nature, proportional representation faithfully reflects divisions in society. Where these divisions are—or become—serious, it may be difficult to create a working majority in parliament to govern the country. This problem also made itself felt in Germany of the 1930's, with the emergence of a "negative majority" described earlier.

4. The so-called "threshold law" which has been adopted to buttress

the stability of the electoral system. Parties receiving less than 5 percent of the national vote do not receive any representation under the present system. We may note, parenthetically, that had it not been for the concern of the German Socialist Party (SPD)—with some Western concurrence—that without proportional representation they might be completely submerged by the Christian Democrats (CDU), the P.R. system might have been scrapped completely.

5. A provision for outlawing political parties and organizations judged to be incompatible with the democratic order. This new feature in German constitutional law was invoked in 1956 by the Constitutional Court to dissolve the German Communist and the neo-Nazi parties.

6. Safeguards on the use of emergency powers by the executive. The new Constitution recognized that there might be a need for decisive and discretionary action by the cabinet or chancellor in cases of special public urgency or national crisis. But it has made it harder for such power to be obtained and set more limits on its use. For one thing, the Constitution requires the agreement of three agents—president, chancellor, and, above all, the Bundesrat—for the power to be granted. And it provides that such emergency powers cannot be exercised for more than six months without explicit approval by the Bundestag under the same government. Thus, a cabinet would have to face the choice of abandoning emergency powers after six months' use or resigning, unless specifically authorized by the Bundestag to continue.

7. Provision for a so-called positive vote of no confidence. This measure in the Basic Law also addresses itself to the bitter experience of Weimar when Communists and Nazis regularly voted against the government without, of course, the least disposition to agree on some commonly acceptable alternative. The present Constitution provides that a chancellor and his cabinet need not resign from office even if a majority in parliament (Bundestag) votes against them, *unless* that majority, or any majority of the Bundestag, can designate an alternative chancellor. If it cannot, the cabinet remains in office, although the president of the Republic may call for new parliamentary elections to resolve the impasse.

8. The power of the president of the Republic has been substantially reduced in two important ways. He can no longer name the chancellor, subject to a post facto vote of no confidence by parliament as under Weimar. The president may still submit his *candidate* for chancellor to parliament for its explicit approval (presumably upon consultation with the party or parties having a majority in the Bundestag). In any case, he cannot singlehandedly put such a person in office. And, also, he no longer

has the power to grant a chancellor emergency powers. The concurrence of the Bundesrat is now mandatory. The chancellor's powers vis à vis the president's are enhanced. The latter now more closely resembles a constitutional monarch on the British model: the dignified head of state who routinely signs public laws and appointments. There is less likelihood of another von Hindenburg.

No one can be sure that all these constitutional provisions, established in the 1940's by an élite of German anti-Nazi politicians, such as Konrad Adenauer, Kurt Schumacher, Ludwig Erhard, and Willy Brandt, can really save West Germany from another Hitler. Obviously, much depends on evolving popular attitudes and future circumstances, including the kinds of crises to which Germany may be subjected.

In East Germany, the Soviet Union and indigenous Communist elements have created a regime which is designed to forestall the repetition of Nazism in still another way. Marxist–Leninist ideologists believe that the root cause of fascism, including Hitler's Nazi fascism, is the decay and degeneracy of a capitalist society seeking to stave off revolution against itself. The need of the oppressive bourgeois and feudal elements to stifle, more effectively and more desperately, the demands of the oppressed workers and peasants during economic crises is said to lead inevitably to the kind of brutal and dangerously aggressive regime that Hitler had established in Germany in the 1930's. The bourgeoisie discards democracy when economically "pressed to the wall." The cure is seen in abolishing capitalism and in creating an egalitarian, socialist society. Presumably, such a society would in due course abolish both want and all exploitive, oppressor classes. Even official Communist organs, however, would agree that the task of "construction" is still very much in progress, and its impact on German attitudes, in the absence of open monitoring devices, is subject to considerable doubt. With some variations, the structure of power which has been adopted by East Germany is patterned on the dictatorship-of-the-proletariat model of the Soviet Union, with great power concentrated in the hands of the bureaucracy of one political party. Many observers argue that the "cure" is not really better than the "disease."

ORIENTATIONS

It is appropriate to point out that ideologically and even logically, judging from their respective constitutions, the two Germanies are headed in different directions. The aims of the FRG are basically those of a Western liberal democracy, seeking to guarantee sufficient freedom and security to its citizens so that they may fashion their destiny and happiness as their collective judgments would incline them. The democratic process, however, by which policies may be fashioned is held out to a higher judicial protection, even against the will of a possible popular majority in the country.

In East Germany, however, both the process of politics and its objectives are prescribed, with a de facto deemphasis on the popular will and people's idiosyncratic judgments as to what constitutes "happiness." The state is directed to the achievement of the higher stage of Marxian socialism—the classless equality of those who contribute what they wish and receive what they need—after an appropriate preparatory transition under the leadership of the Socialist Unity Party (the SED), leader and teacher of the proletariat. In the East German (official) sense, freedom, peace, and justice could only be lastingly achieved by rejection and destruction of West German type "bourgeois freedom." The latter, in the Marxian view, allows for the exploitation of humans by humans and is incompatible with true freedom, in which no one works for another. The path to true freedom requires increased production for material abundance. It also requires discipline, vigilance, and an all-out struggle against bourgeois ideology, culture, morality, and subversive influences. Socialist people must be created by great organizational and ideological efforts. They will not, in the Party's view, emerge simply by being left alone.

policy agenda: problems, cleavages, and conflicts
WEST GERMANY

The Participants   The basic issues of German politics in the post–World War II period have been articulated by many different, autonomous parties, interest groups, media, and institutions.

The principal political parties have included the Christian Democrats (the CDU and its Bavarian affiliate, the CSU), who have dominated West German politics since the beginning of the Federal Republic, from 1949 until 1972. The Christian Democrats have provided West Germany with its first three chancellors: Konrad Adenauer, Ludwig Erhard, and Kurt Kiesinger. We should note that the CDU and the CSU are successors to the old Catholic Center Party of pre-Hitler days. Although the CDU is a nonsectarian organization, its following is, in fact, heavily Catholic. As a result of the loss of largely Protestant eastern German territories to Poland, the Soviet Union, and the German Democratic Republic after the war, the population balance in the West has become more Catholic than ever before in German history (about 48 percent). This has strengthened the mass base of the CDU/CSU. Still, the Party has never achieved a solid majority of the German electorate; its high water mark came under Adenauer in the 1957 election, when it obtained 50.2 percent of the popular vote. Between 1949 and 1972, the Christian Democrats relied on a coalition of forces with the small, middle-class Free Democratic Party (FDP) to stay in power.

Since 1972, the Social Democrats (SPD) have replaced the CDU/CSU as the ruling party, under the successive chancellorships of Willy Brandt and Helmut Schmidt. The SPD polled 41.5 percent of the vote in the 1972 election. Between them, the two major parties had garnered almost 82 percent of the vote. Interestingly, both have relied on the same "third force" as a coalition partner to enable them to keep power: the Free Democratic Party. This group had received about 8.5 percent of the popular vote in 1972. The party's membership has been drawn from relatively well-to-do business and professional elements with an eighteenth century liberal laissez-faire but secular, and anticlericalist, orientation.

Because of the "threshold law," which excludes all parties with less than 5 percent of the popular vote from parliamentary representation, these three parties—CDU/CSU, SPD, and FDP—have now achieved sole control of the Bundastag. There are, however, many other parties, including the neo-Nazi NPD and the Communists, which participate in the elections and which conduct a wide variety of activities throughout West Germany between elections.[3]

The agenda of West German politics is set in the context of one of the world's most highly developed, diversified, and autonomous communication networks, as well as elaborate judicial safeguards of political and individual freedoms. In the late sixties West Germany had more than 1400 daily newspapers, from far Right to far Left with a circulation of 318 copies per 1000 persons. West Germany had a multimillion public of attentive readers with the world's highest levels of literacy, educational attainments, and political information.[4]

Party Clienteles Somewhat on the American model, the two major parties in Germany have become big, umbrella-type organizations, representing a variety of interests, often at odds with one another. The parties have tried to appeal to the broadest possible strata of the electorate and

[3] The Communist Party was active in West Germany from 1949 until 1956, when the Federal Constitutional Court outlawed it on the ground that the Party's undemocratic objectives and methods violated the provisions of Article 21, section 2, of the Bonn Basic Law of 1949. Until 1965, the Party operated as an underground organization directed from East Berlin. In 1965 a German Peace Union, combining ex-Communists and other Leftist elements, was formed. It polled 1.3 percent of the national vote. In 1968 a German Communist Party (DKP) was founded in the FRG to replace the outlawed Communist Party of Germany (KPD). Thus far, its legality has not been challenged. Its membership was self-reported at 39,344 persons in 1973.

[4] See Leon N. Lindberg, "The Political System of the European Community," in Martin O. Heisler, ed., *Politics in Europe* (New York: David McKay, 1974), pp. 221–228. Among Europeans, only the Dutch exceeded the Germans in information relevant to their common European concerns.

have thus tended to be more indecisive than extremist in terms of their programs or collective positions. In 1959, the SPD abandoned its last pretense to the socialist legacy of Karl Marx and to the class war image that it had inherited from its pre-Hitler predecessor. Rather, the image of pragmatic, middle-of-the-road type of politics has been characteristic of both parties. As in the United States, some of the real differences on public issues have been articulated not so much *between* the parties as *within* them, and in some cases by groups and individuals standing outside the major parties.[5] Even so, the major parties—just as in the United States—have tended to aggregate somewhat different clienteles and different, even opposite, tendencies on some of the basic national issues. Public opinion polls have shown significant divergencies between the parties even if these are not always openly articulated by their national leaders.

The CDU/CSU draws its support, disproportionately, from the upper-middle and middle class elements of German society; from entrepreneurs and managers; from the ranks of farmers and the self-employed; from the older rather than the younger people; from among churchgoers rather than agnostics; and from women rather than men. Its general tendency is to draw upon the more affluent and the more traditionalist elements in the country, and in this sense the party may be said to have a right-of-center orientation.

The SPD, on the other hand, draws its support disproportionately from blue collar workers; trade unionists; clerical and government employees; the younger and the less religious elements; nominally from among Protestants rather than Catholics; from men rather than women; from the urban-industrial rather than from the rural and self-employed categories. It is the party of the economically less well-to-do, and of those aspiring to changing and redistributing resources and values within the society. It is thus a left-of-center party in comparison with the CDU/CSU. Because of its urban-industrial mass base, it may also be seen as a more modern party than the Christian Democrats.

Nevertheless, it is useful to bear in mind that the clientele distinctions between the two great parties are only relative. To a significant degree, virtually all the elements of German society have found representation within both of these parties. And there are some deviations from the patterns, too. The leaders of Germany's big business, for example, over-

---

[5] In the 1960's, the consensus between the major parties seemed outwardly so overwhelming that one SPD official defined the difference between the parties in that "some are in and others are not." Another story which circulated in West Germany was that the "SPD is the best CDU we ever had." See Karl W. Deutsch and Eric A. Nordlinger, "The German Federal Republic" in R. C. Macridis and R. E. Ward, eds., *Modern Political Systems: Europe,* 2nd ed. (Englewood Cliffs, N.J.: Prentice-Hall, 1968), p. 420.

whelmingly support the CDU/CSU against the Socialists but are predominantly Protestant in their religious affiliations.

In a late sixties analysis, among Catholic voters generally 40 percent were found to be CDU/CSU supporters; 28 percent SPD supporters; the balance was distributed among those with no preferences (15 percent), the no responses (14 percent), and 4 percent supporting other parties. Protestants favored the SPD by a margin of 40 to 21 percent.

Interestingly, however, among people identifying as strongly Catholic, the preference for the Christian Democrats over the Socialists was 58 to 16 percent; among those identifying as strong Protestants, the CDU/CSU had an edge of 33 to 26 over the SPD. However, among people who reported weak religious identifications, the SPD drew 37 percent of the Catholics and 43 percent of the Protestants, while Christian Democrats received the support of only 29 and 20 percent, respectively, from these categories of voters. Among independent farmers 45 percent favored the CDU/CSU and only 9 percent favored the SPD. Among men, 26 percent opted for the Christian Democrats; 42 percent for the Socialists. Among women, however, 33 percent preferred the Christian Democrats and 29 percent the Socialists. Among professional people the preference for the CDU/CSU over the SPD was 41 to 35 percent; among the self-employed, it was 33 to 26; among pensioners, it was 41 to 28; and among those over 60 years of age it was 34 to 27 percent in favor of the Christian Democrats. In the category of rural laborers—that is, farm employees as distinguished from operators—the CDU/CSU held a 39 to 26 margin over the Socialists.

On the other hand, the SPD drew the support of 54 percent of West Germany's skilled workers as compared with only 18 percent for the Christian Democrats; 48 percent of the unskilled workers as compared with 20 percent for the CDU/CSU; it held a somewhat narrower margin among white-collar employees, 36 to 31, and civil servants, 39 to 26. Its support among people under the age of 30 was 36 percent compared with the Christian Democrats' 30 percent; its biggest lead was in the 30 to 39 year old bracket, 45 to 26 percent.[6]

Leaders and Followers A characteristic that has been observed in the United States also prevails in West Germany: the backgrounds and attitudes of the leaders and activists in the respective major parties tend to be different from what they are among their followers. A study of the respective élites of the CDU/CSU and the SPD in the late fifties showed that two-thirds of the Christian Democratic cabinet ministers and Bunde-

---

[6] See data for early 1960's from the surveys of the D.I.V.O. Institut, *Umfragen: Ereignisse und Probleme der Zeit im Urteil der Bevolkerung* (Frankfurt: Europaische Verlanganstalt, 1959–1962).

stag committee chairmen were Catholic; nearly 90 percent were born in West or South Germany; almost half had received doctorates, and two-thirds had had some university education; about three-quarters could be classified as having middle class backgrounds. Almost 40 percent had anti-Nazi records, though none had been in exile during Hitler's rule; 40 percent had past military service and 20 percent had served in the Nazi armed forces during World War II; 4 percent were actually ex-Nazi officials!

In contrast, the élite of SPD political-parliamentary leaders showed *no* former Nazi office-holders; a third had been in exile during the war, and 70 percent had had anti-Nazi records. Only 38 percent of the Socialist leaders came from West and South Germany, with 41 percent from areas currently under Communist rule and the rest from the industrial North; in terms of education, 59 percent of the Socialist leaders never went beyond secondary school, and only 14 percent held doctoral degrees. More than half of the Socialist leaders reported blue collar worker family backgrounds.[7]

The Issues: Facing the East   Even though many issues do not necessarily produce clear-cut divisions *between* the major parties, there are significant conflict and tension areas in German public life. First, there are those problems that involve Germany's relations with the world. These include, first, the legacy of the Cold War and West Germany's relations with the East European countries. As much as 40 percent of the area which constituted Germany *before* Hitler had begun his conquests was taken over by Soviet armies in 1945. Part of this territory beyond the Oder-Neisse rivers, including Silesia, Pomerania, and East Prussia, was incorporated into the People's Republic of Poland and the Soviet Union. Several million Germans either fled from these lands to West Germany or were expelled from them. In the remainder of the Soviet-occupied territories, the German Democratic Republic (GDR) was established by members of the old Communist Party of Germany who had fled Nazi persecution to the Soviet Union in the 1930's. Within this area was also a special enclave: the former capital city of Berlin, made into a four-power zone of control by the Soviet Union, United States, Great Britain, and France in a conference

[7] See K. W. Deutsch and L. J. Edinger, *Germany Rejoins the Powers: Mass Opinion, Interest Groups and Elites in German Foreign Policy* (Stanford: Stanford University Press, 1959), particularly pp. 66–73. And Juan Linz, "The Social Bases of West German Politics," Ph.D. dissertation, Columbia University 1959 Mic 59-4075. Ann Arbor, Michigan: University of Michigan Microfilm, 1959. Compare with findings of Herbert McClosky, "Consensus and Ideology in American Politics," *The American Political Science Review* 58, no. 2 (June 1964): 361–82; and also E. Costantini, "California Party Elites" in J. R. Owens, E. Costantini, L. F. Weschler, *California, Politics and Parties* (New York: Macmillan, 1970), pp. 219–236.

at Potsdam in 1945. Berlin had had a population of nearly 4 million before World War II. And, as the imperial capital of Germany since 1871, it also had considerable symbolic and psychological, as well as economic and human, significance. As the relations between the Soviets and the West worsened in the period from 1945 to 1948, contacts between Germany's eastern and western lands were severed. In 1948, the Soviet Union imposed a land blockade on the western sectors of Berlin which might well have starved the city out, or forced the Allied powers (Britain, France, United States) to withdraw, had it not been for the huge United States airlift of food and other vital supplies.

The practical consequences of all these developments for West Germany involved the seemingly permanent loss of substantial territory with all its agricultural, mineral, and industrial wealth; a huge refugee burden; the severance of contacts among millions of German people who could not be reunited with families and friends on the other side of, in Winston Churchill's phrase, the "Iron Curtain." It also meant separation of the German economy from markets and sources of supply in Eastern Europe which for many years, long before Hitler and even in the nineteenth century, were significant factors in its operations and well-being.

The position toward these problems taken by the Christian Democrats under Adenauer might be described as "tough anticommunism." To a large extent, anticommunism is still a distinguishing feature of the Christian Democratic Party. In Adenauer's day, the CDU took the view that the German Democratic Republic (GDR) was merely a Soviet puppet state; for years its spokesmen referred to the GDR as the "Soviet zone of occupation." The CDU/CSU refused to recognize Polish acquisition of German lands, and refused to maintain diplomatic relations with any country which recognized the GDR as a sovereign state (under the so-called Hallstein Doctrine). The CDU/CSU advocated close collaboration with the United States and other Western countries aimed at the containment and even the eventual rollback of Communist expansion in Europe. It looked toward a unification of Germany, with free elections and an end to Soviet influence.

The SPD has, from the earliest, advocated a more accommodating approach which culminated in Willy Brandt's *Ostpolitik:* a recognition by the Federal Republic of the status quo in Eastern Europe, including the annexations of pre–1939 German territories by Poland and the Soviet Union, as well as the sovereign independence and territorial integrity of East Germany. Increased trade, relaxation of tensions, access rights to West Berlin, and, it was hoped, greater East-West contacts, were the advertised—and to a certain extent realized—advantages of the policy. In 1974, both the FRG and the GDR were admitted to the UN. In large part,

Willy Brandt kneeling before Ghetto memorial in Warsaw, 1970.
UPI

the socialist attitude has been based on an assumption of futility of confrontation between East and West. Neither the Soviet Union nor East Germany was likely to disappear; neither seemed particularly weakened by a policy of Western belligerency. Moreover, there were grounds for hope, the Socialists believed, that in the wake of Stalin's death the Soviets would grow more flexible and pragmatic in their attitude toward the West.

The CDU/CSU has, for the most part, either opposed this Socialist policy of recognition and reconciliation with the East, or at least has serious reservations about it. Many Christian Democrats have attacked *Ostpolitik* because of the immorality of the West German concessions ("sealing the fate of our German brethren in tyranny"), and the lack of genuine reciprocity by the Communist side, particularly the GDR. During the 1950's and 1960's, the position of these Christian Democrats was reinforced by various organizations of people who were expelled from or fled the eastern territories and were opposed to the "sell-out" of their homelands, and by smaller political groupings, among them the FDP and the still smaller neo-Nazi NPD. In the 1970's the positions of many segments of the CDU and even the expellee groups have softened. In the 1969 elections, the FDP was the main spokesman for *Ostpolitik*. The climate of

German public opinion on this issue has thus shifted from Right to Left over the years.

Considering the continued maintenance of the Berlin Wall (erected in 1961), the shootings of escapees, and the stringent limits on travel by people out of East Germany, *Ostpolitik* continues to be justifiably controversial for millions of people in West Germany.[8] This is true notwithstanding a number of treaties concluded by the Soviet Union, Poland, and the GDR with West Germany in the 1970's. For many people in West Germany the attempt to establish better relations with East Germany seems a prudent facing up to the realities of power in East Central Europe. The GDR, they think, is here to stay. One must deal with it as best as one can. For many others (probably a sizable minority), this policy still seems humiliating, futile, and compromising.

Facing West Another problem for Germany is the Atlantic issue, or West Germany's relationship to the United States and NATO. The Christian Democrats have traditionally supported the principle of a political-military alliance with the United States and with other Western nations as a deterrent to possible Soviet aggression in Europe.

In the 1940's and 1950's, the SPD opposed an alliance on the ground that it would tend to jeopardize the eventual reunification of East and West Germany. The Socialists argued that the Soviet Union could not be expected to agree to hand over any German territories to a hostile West German state but it might be induced to hand such territories over to a Germany that had adopted some form of neutrality or disengagement. In the 1960's, partly in response to Soviet actions, statements, and denunciations of the idea of German reunification, the SPD finally gave up hope of ever persuading the Soviets to dismantle the East German Communist regime. It became a "me, too" party, supporting West German membership in NATO and adopting a pro-American stance during the Brandt and Schmidt administrations. Still, on such issues as the desirability of West German possession of nuclear weapons, and on appropriate levels of military expenditure, or even U.S. involvement in Indochina, the SPD has been consistently more "dovish" than the CDU, to use an American term. In both parties, there have been sizable factions dedicated to greater independence from the United States, and a more significant international role for a united Europe in which, by the early seventies, West Germany had clearly reached economic primacy.

[8] On the shifts of German public opinion between the 1940's and 1970's and the remaining differences between the followers of the major parties, see K. Deutsch, G. Schweigler, and L. Edinger, "Foreign Policy of the German Federal Republic," in Roy C. Macridis, ed., *Foreign Policy in World Politics*, 4th ed. (Englewood Cliffs, N.J.: Prentice-Hall, 1972), pp. 119–141.

A perennial issue has been German contributions for the support of some 200,000 American troops stationed as part of the NATO shield in West Germany. While prevalent German opinion has supported this U.S. presence, even thirty years after World War II, understandably there have been many controversies about it. Interestingly enough, with a population of more than three and a half times that of East Germany's, the Federal Republic maintained an army of just under half a million; the East German forces numbered almost seven hundred thousand troops.[9]

Facing Europe   A third problem is West Germany's relationship to the Common Market countries of Western Europe. On this issue, there have been some differences between and within the major West German parties, but not nearly as much as on *Ostpolitik* and earlier on NATO. The Socialists were initially (in the forties and early fifties) skeptical and apprehensive about European integration, largely because they feared permanently splitting Western and Eastern Europe (and Germany . . .) and antagonizing the Soviets. The SPD's early leader, Kurt Schumacher, while staunchly anti-Communist at home, believed that a neutral stance would more likely serve the ultimate cause of peace and reunification of Germany. The European Community was seen as a reinforcement of NATO. Some Socialists looked with suspicion upon Gaullist France and Christian Democratic Italy as reactionary forces. In the late 1950's, coinciding with the Party's general deradicalization, the Socialists became more Europeanist in outlook. Their support of European integration, originally laced with doubts, gradually became as warm as that of the CDU/CSU. Both parties could be currently described as generally pro-European; that is, they favor Common Market participation by West Germany and even the goal of eventual supranational integration.

In this respect, the two big parties have reflected a remarkable national consensus. The German people have shown, in repeated polls over the years, their strong support for the ideal of West European cooperation and even amalgamation. Since the beginnings of the FRG in 1949, only relatively minor splinter parties, including the Communists and the neo-Nazis, have fundamentally quarreled with West Germany's integration

[9] See Aidan Crawley, *The Rise of Western Germany, 1945–1972* (London: Collins, 1973), pp. 118–157, on early differences between Konrad Adenauer and Kurt Schumacher. On foreign policy conflicts between and among the German parties, see also Wolfram F. Hanrieder, *West German Foreign Policy, 1949–1963* (Stanford: Stanford University Press, 1967); Peter H. Merkle, *German Foreign Policies, West and East* (Santa Barbara, Cal.: ABC Clio, 1974); Alfred Grosser, *The Federal Republic of Germany* (New York: Praeger, 1964), pp. 114–125; and his *Germany in Our Time* (New York: Praeger, 1971), as well as the early work by Hans Speier, *German Rearmament and Atomic War* (Evanston: Row, Peterson, 1957), and Hans W. Schoenberg, *Germans From the East* (The Hague: Nijhoff, 1970); and Willy Brandt, *A Peace Policy for Europe* (New York: Holt, Rinehart and Winston, 1969).

into a larger European framework. But there have been more serious divisions even among the mainstream parties about certain aspects of this policy.

Thus, Konrad Adenauer, for example, shared the fundamentally anti-British attitude of General de Gaulle and tacitly supported de Gaulle's conception of Western European cooperation in the EEC more as a confederacy of sovereign states than as a prelude to a single European superstate. Yet, many West Germans, within and without the CDU/CSU, have always wanted to move toward a closer form of European integration and a more universal membership in it.[10]

The Issue of Equality A further problem is the redistribution of wealth, influence, and power in the German society. The Federal Republic has made great strides in assuring to the people of West Germany one of the highest living standards in Europe, a dynamically expanding economy, and a great expansion of various social and cultural public services as contrasted with the Hitler era. But highly unequal distribution of wealth, monopolistic control of the economy, and rigid class structure have remained serious problems.

One can point to many indices; one illustration is the distribution of incomes. In 1964, according to a recent study, West Germany's top 10 percent of income earners received 41.4 percent of the total national income before taxes. This compared with an estimated 27 percent in the United States; 29.3 percent in Great Britain; 36.8 percent in France; about 27 percent in Sweden and Denmark; and 25 percent in Norway. West Germany's income distribution was somewhat more equitable, to be sure, than in Hitler's day but it lagged behind most other European democracies.

Germany's educational system, though considerably expanded since Hitler's time, reflected continued upper class domination of higher education. Thus, in 1963–1964, the children of blue collar workers constituted only 5 percent of university students although workers and their families accounted for nearly 49 percent of the population. Only 2 percent of university students had peasant origins while farmers accounted for almost 15 percent of the people. On the other hand, 34 percent of university students were children of public officials, who comprised only 5 percent of the population; and 26 percent were the sons and daughters of white collar workers whose share in the whole population was 18 percent.

---

[10] See Richard Hiscocks, *The Adenauer Era* (New York: Lippincott, 1966), pp. 108–112, on how the SPD "swung around" to basic acceptance of CDU positions on both EEC and NATO between 1959 and 1961. In the late sixties, the reverse occurred, with CDU moving considerably closer to the SPD's *Ostpolitik* stand.

Finally, 15 percent of all university students came from the professional classes, a mere 2 percent of the whole people.

In the 1970's, the demand for higher education among the less privileged strata of society grew so far in excess of West Germany's existing facilities that it resulted in offers by American colleges to absorb excess West German applicants!

By the mid-seventies, the traditionally monopolistic structure of German economy—barely touched by allied efforts to break up pro-Nazi cartels after 1945—survived and prospered to an amazing degree. Big firms, such as Thyssen and Krupp, became bigger than ever. By one estimate, 2 percent of German industry accounted for more than half the total output and 60 percent of all West German exports.[11] Efforts to halt the domination of monopolies thus far have been tepid and ineffectual. The 1957 so-called Erhard law did not prove a serious brake on monopoly power in German economic life. Organized business has been an extremely important influence in West Germany's political life, with particular impact on the Christian Democrats and the Free Democratic Party. Prior to the 1957 campaign finance law, which shifted the basic costs of electioneering to the state, German business organizations, particularly the BDI (Federation of German Industry), heavily supported the CDU/CSU and the FDP. As a result, the Christian Democrats and their allies have at sometimes outspent their Socialist opponents by as much as four to one. In fact, the CDU/CSU supported the reform for financing campaigns at public expense to make itself somewhat freer of its excessively demanding big business clientele.[12]

The Socialists have traditionally demanded a more egalitarian society in Germany, while the Christian Democrats have tended to emphasize freedom—that is, status quo—albeit with a measure of social responsibility by the haves toward the have-nots (Ludwig Erhard, for example). Nevertheless, the issue has produced sharp division within the forces of the Left, not simply between Left and Right. Some members of the SPD, particularly the more militant Jusos, or young Socialists, have viewed the rest of the Party as apathetic, acquiescent, and even opportunistic in its effort to end inequalities in Germany. The Party's alliance with the middle

[11] See John H. Herz, *The Government of Germany* (New York: Harcourt Brace Jovanovich, 1967), pp. 120–128; also T. H. Tetens, *The New Germany and The Old Nazis* (New York: Random House, 1961); and particularly Walter Stahl, ed., *The Politics of Postwar Germany* (New York: Praeger, 1963), pp. 171–277, on the survival of Nazi and other undemocratic or antidemocratic elements in West Germany.

[12] On this subject see Arnold J. Heidenheimer, "German Party Finance: The C.D.U.," *American Political Science Review* 51, no. 2 (June 1957): 369–385, and also his *The Governments of Germany*, 3rd ed. (New York: Crowell, 1971), as well as U. W. Kitzinger, *German Electoral Politics: A Study of the 1957 Campaign* (Oxford: Clarendon Press, 1960).

class FDP has moderated the SPD's stance in parliament and is widely perceived as a trade-off between "principle" and "power." The issue has also attracted much attention from the more radical or new Left elements, including the APO, or extraparliamentary opposition, as well as the several splinter Marxist parties.[13]

Economic Health   The management of the economy is still another whole complex of issues between and among the parties. In recent years, West Germany has experienced substantially lower inflation and unemployment than either the United States or most of the advanced European countries. Inflation has run at a rate of about 7 percent here but between 15 and 20 percent in Britain and Italy and above 10 percent in the United States since 1973. Unemployment has never reached 7 percent of the work force, as it has in Great Britain and the United States. Still, there have been some serious problems.

Recession, or stagflation, has produced a pinch unequalled in many years in the West Germany economy. Workers have been laid off. The Volksvagen company ran into "red ink" for the first time since World War II. One effect of the hard times has been to revive and augment ideological schisms among the parties in Germany. Some Socialists have been reaccepting the nationalization of industry, an idea which had been for practical purposes scrapped by the Party in 1959. The more conservative FDP allies of the Socialists, however, have been increasingly restive with such SPD ideas, as well as with the notions of new worker profit-sharing and still more deficit spending to stimulate the economy.

Responding to their different clienteles, the parties have sought divergent solutions. The CDU has advocated greater frugality in welfare programs, restraint in wage claims by unions, and less government expenditures as means of checking inflation and of promoting the expansion and competitiveness of Germany industry at home and abroad. The CDU has been leery of expensive reforms in education and environmental controls. The SPD has been reluctant to check the inflationary pressures by sacrificing the social benefits of the lower strata and becoming a "cut, trim and squeeze" party. It has sought instead to continue to stimulate the economy by government expenditure on the Keynesian "pump-priming" model, preferring tax cuts to budget reductions.

In the 1960's West Germany had been so short of labor that it had imported over 2 million immigrant laborers from southeastern Europe,

---

[13] On the views and activities of APO, see the excellent article by Kurt L. Shell, "Extraparliamentary Opposition in Postwar Germany," *Comparative Politics* II, no. 3 (July 1970): 653–80, reprinted in H. S. Albinski and L. K. Pettit, *European Political Processes*, 2nd ed. (Boston: Allyn and Bacon, 1974), pp. 486–506.

mostly Turkey, to work at a whole range of unskilled and low-paying jobs for which West German applicants were hard to find. In the seventies, with mounting business recession, these immigrants have become an issue, as "foreign competitors to German workers." Also, the immigrants have begun to make demands of their own for better housing, social services, and living conditions. Currently, one out of ten workers in the Federal Republic is a resident foreigner. Recently, a series of strikes by Turkish assembly plant workers dramatized their plight and brought the issue to public attention. It exacerbated feelings of doubt and guilt among the more humanitarian elements on the Left and it caused unease among the West German trade unions; it was fuel for the fire of latent nationalism on the Right.

Energy In 1973, the Arab oil embargo on countries trading with and otherwise supportive of Israel presented West Germany with another crisis. In a nation with nearly 16 million automobiles for about 60 million people and no domestic oil reserves, a shortage of gasoline posed some unpleasant choices.[14] The United States, West Germany's NATO ally, was supplying Israel weaponry by air during the so-called October War (1973) with Egypt and Syria. The Soviet Union was supplying the Arab side in the war. If West Germany allowed the United States to use its airfields for the supply operation, its economy might be crippled by an Arab oil boycott. If it refused U.S. landing rights, it would be showing lack of support for its principal ally and shield against possible Soviet aggression; it would be implicitly cooperating with U.S. adversaries. Finally, however, Germany refused the landing rights, and the United States resorted to new types of long range aircraft and the Portuguese base in the Azores for its airlift to Israel. West German accommodation to the oil embargo was looked upon with diplomatic indulgence in Washington. When the Arab countries increased the price of their oil for all buyers, friend and foe, West Germany was able to adjust with a Sunday driving ban and a relatively mild gas-conservation program.[15]

Strengthening Democracy Participation and democratization of German public life may be said to involve another set of issues. In part, these are

[14] In 1969 West Germany depended on imports for 42.4 percent of its total energy needs, compared with only 6 percent imports by the United States. See Guy de Carmoy, "The Politics of European Energy Policy," in M. O. Heisler, *Politics in Europe*, p. 372. Contemporaneously, the Soviet Union enjoyed a 10 percent energy surplus! The GDR, the world's third largest coal producer, imported its rather modest oil supplies almost wholly from the Soviet Union.

[15] On party differences relating to economic issues, see Geoffrey K. Roberts, *West German Politics* (London: Macmillan, 1972); and Kurt Sontheimer, *The Government and Politics of West Germany* (New York: Praeger, 1973).

bread and butter economic questions, what German trade unionists call "codetermination." The German Trade Union Federation (DGB) with some six and a half million members in the mid-sixties now contains about one-third of the workers and employees of the Federal Republic. They have demanded and substantially realized the right of representation on work councils in all the larger units of German industry and a voice in the management of enterprises. Workers are involved in decisions on work and safety regulations, the hiring and firing of personnel, and even more general policy affecting the viability of the business operation. Currently, there is a struggle underway over the extension, and the enhancement, of the idea of codetermination in other types of enterprises and to other areas of life, including schools, hospitals, retail establishments, and cultural and public institutions.

In some respects, the issue is not just economic but broadly cultural. The structures of German society, economy, and family have long been authoritarian—the legacy of Prussia, the Bismarckian Empire, and Hitler's Reich. The ethos of blind obedience to the orders of superiors characterized not merely the military but many German national institutions, with the remarkable, if partial, exception of the 1919–1933 Weimar Republic period. Under the Bonn regime there has been a profound revulsion from this long-established tendency to manipulate and order people about in a hierarchical fashion. There has been a movement to democratize German schools, family life, business, bureaucracy, and the military. Part of the effort has gone into de-Nazification, removing officials who had served in the Hitler regime. Also, there has been increased concern with the procedures of public institutions with more emphasis on popular participation and individual rights. Among the achievements of this movement has been the establishment of a Civilian Commissioner for the German Armed Forces, which enables soldiers to appeal officers' actions and official regulations to an independent authority, who in turn reports and may appeal to the parliament, public opinion, and the courts.

Without confining it narrowly to the CDU and the SPD, participation is a Left-Right issue in the sense that those who support increased and changed methods of public participation, responsibility, and involvement in Germany come mainly from the ranks of Socialists, liberals, trade unionists, and the so-called new-Left elements such as the Jusos and the APO. The opposition, in the name of maintaining traditional social organization and legality, is generally identifiable with conservative right-wing forces.[16]

[16] On the problems of democratization of German life, see Herbert Jacob, *German Administration Since Bismarck* (New Haven: Yale University Press, 1963); Carl Landauer, *Germany: Illusions and Dilemmas* (New York: Harcourt Brace Jovano-

Environment Another emergent issue in West Germany today is the quality of the environment. The problems of urban blight, overcrowding, congested highways and, above all, pollution of air and water have now become manifest. While to some extent the concern with environment is a non-party issue, in which all profess a stake and an interest, it has taken on some ideological-partisan aspects similar to those evidenced in the United States. Some of the more conservative, right-wing elements, and also many trade unionists, are concerned about balancing environmental policies against the possible loss of jobs and business opportunities. The conservatives don't want to see economic expansion checked by zealous environmental measures. They also do not welcome another extension of a governmental-bureaucratic role related to environmental controls. Yet, many people on the Left and Center see an inescapable government obligation; they do not share the ideological qualms about the role of the state. The SPD is generally bolder than the CDU.

What Kind of Germany? The final major issue is one of the system itself. There are both cultural and political forces in West Germany, some overt and some latent, which are arrayed against the existing constitutional order, opposed to the democratic "game" and the "rules of the game." On the Right is the relatively small neo-Nazi Nationalist Party (NPD) led by Dr. von Thadden, a former official of Dr. Joseph Goebbels' Nazi Propaganda Ministry. The Party has never received more than 4 percent of the national vote, and a minuscule 0.5 percent in 1972. But many Germans remember how Hitler's Nazis had jumped from just a few seats to a plurality in the parliament of the 1930's. Moreover, the themes articulated by the far Right are shared by many people not currently involved with the Party.[17] The Right is alarmed and dismayed by the very openness of the Bonn regime, by its tolerance and support of social and political conflicts and various shades of radicalism. The far Right is opposed to the regime on grounds familiar in the context of American politics: zealous anticommunism; the support of "law and order"; and

---

vich, 1969); Stanley Radcliffe, *Twenty-five Years on: The Two Germanies, 1970* (London: Harrap, 1972).

[17] See Linz, "The Social Bases of West German Politics," pp. 114–16. When a sample of the West German electorate was asked to express views about Communists and right-wing extremists, 80 percent of the respondents expressed some negative views about Communists, but only 42 percent did so about the Right extremists. Only 9 percent of the respondents were indifferent or unknowledgeable about Communists, and only 11 percent evidenced positive attitudes toward them. On the other hand, 46 percent of the people questioned showed neutrality or indifference to Right extremism, with 12 percent expressing positive attitudes.

opposition to dangerous social experiments, ferment, and loss of German identity.[18]

On the other side is the far Leftist opposition, which views the democratic system as largely a game manipulated by capitalists and their stooges for their own selfish ends. The Left, particularly the antiparliamentary APO, opposes the basic cultural values of the present order. They see the social system as materialistic, corrupt, and dedicated to the dehumanizing goals of acquiring goods and perquisites. The many are exploited for the benefit of the few. They see the political system as a deceptive and more or less subtly coercive screen for the domination and manipulation of the masses by the corporate and bureaucratic élites. In both cases, the implication is that violent revolution or at least a very serious and fundamental restructuring is necessary and inevitable. The far Left is alienated from the social as well as the political realities of West German life. Much of its following is drawn from university students, professors, and youth.[19]

In fact, one can speak of two kinds of fundamental Leftist opposition to the political and social system in West Germany today. The old opposition, represented primarily by Moscow and GDR-oriented Communists, and led by veteran Herbert Mies, continues the traditions of the Weimar KPD. It opposes bouregois democracy at home on traditional Marxist grounds (exploiting workers) and it points to the Soviet Union (as the KPD did) and to the GDR (which, of course, did not exist in the 1930's) as models of "progressive social development" in which workers have seized control from capitalists. The "new" Left in Germany, influenced by the teachings of U.S. professor and philosopher Herbert Marcuse, generally takes a "plague-on-both-your-houses" position. The New Left detests bourgeois democracy as oppressive and hypocritical, just as the old fashioned Communist does, but it also sees the Soviets and the GDR as examples of oppressive, bureaucratic, and dehumanizing regimes which should be abolished or at least fundamentally "loosened up." It sees new bureaucratic élites replacing the old. The background of the New Left opposition may be identified with the so-called postindustrial, or at least highly industrialized, society, in which the great accumulation of wealth, technology, and education is combined with a general shift of the work force from production and agriculture to services; with urbanization of life and bureaucratization of work; with increasing and shifting differen-

18 On extremist politics of Right and Left, see Stahl, *The Politics of Postwar Germany;* Helga Grebing, *Konservative gegen die Demokratie* (Frankfurt, Main i Europaische Verlagsanstalt, 1971); and Gieselher Schmidt, *Hitlers und Maos Sohne: NPD und Neue Linke* (Frankfurt: Schaffler, 1969).
19 See Shell, "Extraparliamentary Opposition in Postwar Germany."

tiations of group identities; with sharply increased awareness of mal-distributions and inequalities; and also with increased sense of alienation from one's surroundings, of depersonalization, and loss of one's sense of purpose and meaning in this contemporary, bureaucratic-industrial-corporate life. The anger, frustration, resentment, and anxiety generated by the social tensions of change often find political, authority-related outlets. In Germany, as in the United States, most of the New Left politics in the sixties and seventies has been student politics, and it has been fueled by the surviving traditional rigidities and restricted access to German higher education. To some extent, this opposition has identified itself in West Germany, as in other European countries, with the Maoist brand of communism. In all its varieties, however, the opposition on the far Left may be counted in thousands rather than millions. Yet, it is highly vocal, visible, and potentially very influential—culturally, economically, and politically. The New Left is given to tactical alliances, particularly welcomed and sought out by the Communists, based on the formula that common enmities and at least partially shared outlooks can be exploited with mutual advantage: for more successful opposition to the status quo.

The far Left has greater strength among university students and teachers than among the population at large. It has more influence in the media than mere membership and voting figures would suggest. The Communist Party of West Germany, the DKP, shows how extreme elements can use the media. With a membership of about 40,000 in 1974, the Party issues a daily paper *Unsere Zeit* (Our Time) with a circulation of 60,000 copies, and several regional supplements; it also publishes monthly a theoretical journal of some 8.5 thousand circulation. Its youth organization publishes a weekly journal of about 20,000 circulation; the university youth organization, in which the Party shares influence with other radical groups (MSB-Spartakus), publishes an estimated 200,000 issues of newspaper copies per semester. Moreover, the Party produces a large volume of industrial and trade papers, even including Turkish-language factory newspapers, as part of its campaign to appeal to West Germany's substantial foreign work force. By some estimates, the circulation of the Party's trade, industry, and military press (that is, circulated to the soldiers of West Germany's Bundeswehr) is about 200,000 copies per month.

EAST GERMANY

The agenda of public problems in the East German Democratic Republic may be presented somewhat differently and more summarily because the rules of the game preclude open conflict over questions of government policy. If such conflict were accorded legitimacy by the regime, the issues of East Germany's relations with the West and the Soviet Union, the right to emigrate, and the right to pass judgment on party policy, among many other questions, would be publicly debated. The agenda of problems in the GDR would be a very short one, indeed, if one tried to establish it solely on the basis of what is being fought over in the public media. A more realistic construction of the agenda may be based on certain themes articulated prominently in the Party-controlled press, on inferential disagreements which appear from time to time, usually concerning technical aspects of broader policy issues. And all of this may be supplemented by inferences from events and the testimony of exiles. Thus, the question of "Should East German citizens be allowed to come and go as they please?" as a major preoccupation of the East German public could not be inferred directly from published controversy in the GDR. It may be inferred, however, from other evidence: the volume of escapees over the years, and the stories which do appear in the official media of alleged Western provocations and subversion involved in the "removal" of individuals to the West.[20]

A *Mobilized System* The GDR is a highly organized or "mobilized" political system. People are drawn in great numbers into all sorts of politically significant group memberships and activities. At the apex of political organization stands the SED, Socialist Unity Party, which is an amalgam of segments of the old Communist Party of Germany and the left-wing elements of the Social Democratic Party of Germany merged in 1946. In 1974 the SED had over 1.9 million members. In addition, there are several mass organizations represented in a so-called National Front. Among them are four parties, carefully "coordinated" and controlled by the SED and representative of certain strata which are said to be distinct from but allied with the proletarian vanguard, the SED. These are the Christian Democratic Party (CDU); the Liberal Party (LDP); the National Democratic Party of Germany (NDPD); and the Democratic Peasants' Party of Germany (DBP). These groupings are supposed to organize the Catholics, the middle-class secular liberals, the ex-Nazis and officials, and the peasants, respectively. Although the memberships of these parties are relatively small and not publicly revealed, each of the

---

[20] During 1974 at least 4,800 persons are known to have escaped to the West. In 1973 some 6,000 escaped. At least 164 persons have been killed trying to escape from East Germany since 1961 and 2,668 GDR military have defected to the FRG. See Eric Waldman in R. F. Staar, ed., *Yearbook on International Communist Affairs 1975* (Stanford: Hoover Institution Press, 1975), p. 33. Between 1945 and 1961 (before the erection of the Wall in Berlin and other fortification improvements by the GDR), the net flow of population from East to West was 2,789,000 persons, an average of 165,000 a year. Deutsch and Nordlinger, "The German Federal Republic," p. 341.

four parties is allotted 52 seats in the People's Chamber on the one National Front ticket which voters are asked (and for practical purposes required) to approve, usually by 98 percent plus margins. The SED arrogates 127 seats directly to its own members, and additional representation through the following non-party mass organizations which it controls: the Free German Trade Union Federation (FDGB), 68 seats; the Free German Youth (FDJ), 40; the Democratic Women's League of Germany (DFD), 35; the German Union of Culture (DK), 22.

The FDGB has some 7.8 million members out of about 12.5 million adults in East Germany, a far greater percentage of the working force than is unionized in West Germany. The FDJ comprises 1.9 million youths; a Pioneer Organization for preteen age children enrolls about 1.2 million; the DFD has some 1.3 million members. The military organization including security troops, combat troops, and people's police number about 690,000. And another .5 million are enrolled in the paramilitary Society of Sport and Technic (GST). According to official information, 47.1 percent of the SED members in 1970 were drawn from the ranks of workers; 5.8 percent were farmers; 28.1 percent were classified as officials and intelligentsia, with 19 percent in the enigmatic (and probably regrettably bourgeois) category of "others." [21]

Détente In the last few years, GDR's official concerns have emphasized, above all, the "extension and strengthening" of the détente between East and West. The process has involved diplomacy, trade, military preparedness, as well as disarmament, the status of West Berlin, the issue of contacts between East and West Germany, and GDR support of various Soviet initiatives in global policy.

The milestones of that process were, first, the nonaggression pact between West Germany and the Soviet Union in August 1970 and a similar treaty between West Germany and Poland in December 1970; in 1971, a four-power agreement on the international status of West Berlin; and the GDR–FRG pact of the same year concerning surface traffic and communications with West Berlin; and finally the "Treaty on the Basis of Relations" between East and West Germany of June 21, 1972.

The result of all these arrangements was the recognition of the territorial identity and sovereignty of two German states by each other and by most other members of the world community of states. The notion of reunification of the German people, except as it might conceivably result from the initiatives of the two separate, independent, and sovereign states,

[21] See Richard F. Staar, *The Communist Regimes in Eastern Europe,* 2nd rev. ed. (Stanford: Hoover Institution Press, 1971), pp. 95–100.

was scrapped. In effect, two German peoples were recognized. West Berlin was officially proclaimed a city with a special international status, belonging neither to the West Germans nor to the East Germans, although West Germany was granted the right to represent the city in certain aspects of external relations, such as consular matters involving West Berliners travelling abroad. The rights of access by West Germany to Berlin—through East German territory—were explicitly recognized. Détente produced a number of high-level diplomatic meetings between East and West German officials, all unprecedented in post–World War II history. The most dramatic were the two summits in 1970 between Chancellor Willy Brandt and East German Premier Willi Stoph in Erfurt and Kassel. These dealings have resulted in a considerable upsurge in trade between the two Germanys (including indirect utilization of Common Market tariff preferences for East German goods exported to West Germany). Also, numbers of West German citizens were allowed, for the first time in decades, to visit East Germany.

Underlying Tensions Nevertheless, since 1973 the East German leadership has coupled calls for the extension of détente with accusations aimed at West Germany for seeking to undermine it and to "exploit" normalization. East Germany has steadfastly supported Soviet initiatives for European security and disarmament conferences, with the avowed objectives of neutralizing and disarming both sides in the historic NATO-WTO (Warsaw Pact) confrontation. But, simultaneously, it has reduced the flow of persons coming from West to East Germany between 1973 and 1974–1975 by doubling the requirements for the purchase of East German currency by visitors in the latter part of 1973. It has also discouraged travel to West Germany by East German citizens, reducing such travel to a mere trickle. In 1973 over 1 million West Germans visited East Germany; in 1974 about 900 thousand did. In contrast, only 20,000 East Germans, most of them elderly people, visited West Germany. Execution as punishment for fleeing the East, and security precautions against such "desertion" from East to West, have not only been retained but strengthened. West Berlin access routes have been subjected to intermittent harassment by East Germany on the grounds that the West German authorities have attempted to exceed their legitimate rights of presence in West Berlin. The SED leadership has taken the view that détente is an opportunity for *intensifying* the ideological struggle against the imperialist forces in West Germany and elsewhere. Accusations of *revanchist* (that is, revenge seeking) attitudes in West Germany have been coupled with massive East German outlays and organizational measure for military preparedness.

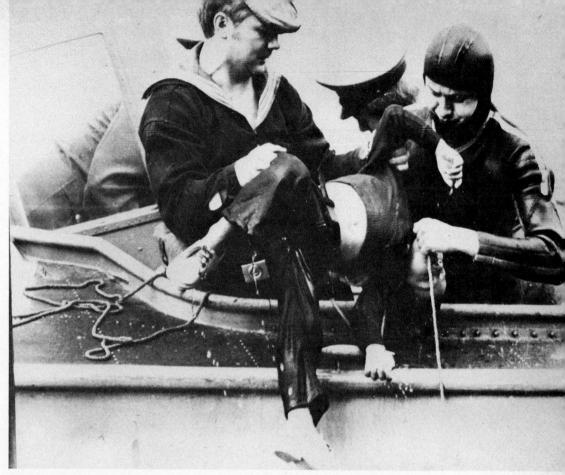

East German naval border guards pull aboard their vessel the body of a five-year-old Turkish boy who drowned in the River Spree after East German authorities refused to let West Berlin firemen save the child after he fell into the West Berlin side of the river, which separates East and West Berlin.
UPI

Facing East In its overall foreign policy, East Germany has acted as the most dedicated auxiliary of the Soviet Union, both within the CMEA (Council of Mutual Economic Assistance), and the WTO (Warsaw Pact), as well as in relation to other Communist states. Unlike the Romanians, the Yugoslavs, the Albanians, the Czechoslovaks (before the Soviet invasion of 1968), and sometimes even the Poles and the Hungarians, the East Germans have faithfully adhered to the slogan of Soviet leadership of all Communist parties. They have denounced the Chinese for their "splittism" and "slander" of the Soviet Union; and they have otherwise supported all the major initiatives of Soviet foreign policy, including the proposal to convene a world Communist conference for the ostensible purpose of censuring or even reading the Chinese out of the international movement. They also strongly supported the 1968 invasion of Czechoslovakia, as in 1956 they supported the invasion of Hungary.

In large measure, this attitude of the GDR has stemmed from the Party's insecure footing in its own environment and the urgent need for Soviet support. The SED regime has been in many ways the most artificial creation of the postwar Communist world. To begin with, the area within which East Germany was created had never existed as a national state. Strictly speaking, that could also be said for West Germany, but that state at least included a majority both of the territory and of the people who in modern times have been identified as Germans. Moreover, the German Communist Party, the forerunner of the SED, had had very little indigenous popular support in the 1944–1945 period when a Soviet-type regime was being established throughout East Germany.[22] And with its more attractive Western neighbor just across a long land border, the historic outflow of refugees has emphasized the insecurity of the GDR regime, and led to the adoption of singularly coercive, watchful, and punitive methods of rule. These have earned the East German Communists the unenviable distinction of remaining more Stalinist than anyone but the Albanians in Eastern Europe.

Controls and the Economy   The regime's more "domestic" concerns in recent years have centered on issues similar to those confronting the Soviets. There have been efforts to reform economic organization to increase productivity and improve consumer satisfactions: all bedeviled by the same dilemma of reconciling reliable party controls with a sufficient measure of flexibility and initiative for managers, producers, distributors, workers, farmers, and consumers.

By all indices, considerable progress has been realized in the economy during the 1970's, although East Germany still lags far behind the very advanced consumer society achieved in the Federal Republic. (See Policy and Performance section for some comparisons.)

The Search for Legitimacy   The most fundamental East German problem has been that of the system itself: the task of creating a legitimate foundation for SED rule in the eyes of the 17 million East Germans. The same problem in West Germany has involved relatively small extremes of

22 On the shallow roots of East German communism, see Andrew Gyorgy, "East Germany," in V. Benes, A. Gyorgy and G. Stambuk, *Eastern European Government and Politics* (New York: Harper & Row, 1966), pp. 100–139; also M. Seton-Watson, *The East European Revolution* (New York: Praeger, 1951), pp. 360–368.

Right and Left, both opposed to "the system." In East Germany, though obviously no competitive election results can be cited, the opposition appears to be much more massive, even if it is largely muted. It lacks access to the media and the opportunity of lawful expression. But, judging by the violent uprising of workers and students in East Berlin in July 1953, the number of escapees from East Germany over the years, and the persistent reports of visitors to the East, there appears to be a profound current of passive opposition and nonacceptance of the regime in the GDR. In terms of the regime's activities, the problem resolves itself into a question of how the SED can convert attitudes of resignation and muted hostility toward itself into genuinely enthusiastic and voluntary support. How can it make the people stay and work in East Germany without a Wall? This, in the Party's eyes, is a manifold task. It involves propaganda; the proper socialization or education of the people; the inculcation in the masses of a properly supportive ideology; the manipulation of information; the adequate provision of rewards and incentives to "loyal" and cooperative citizens; and an effective system of surveillance, coercion, and retribution designed to thwart those who evidence opposition and disloyalty. Despite an enormous organizational effort by the East German regime, the performance of this task is still very much in the balance. With the presence of over 60 million West Germans, equipped with powerful television, radio, and news media across the frontier, it has been a formidable task.

Links with the Soviet Union   The Soviets themselves have attached great strategic importance to East Germany, as a gateway to and from Western Europe, as a resource to themselves, and also as an important element of power to be withheld from West German control. Such power, if added to the present great population and economic capacity of West Germany, would push it toward an unwelcome (from the Soviet point of view) super power direction. Thus, because of both Soviet and East German requirements, the Soviet Union has maintained larger military forces in East Germany than in any other foreign country. And it has also monopolized East German trade to a higher degree than anywhere else.

More than 500,000 Soviet troops—the equivalent of some 40 divisions—are believed stationed on East German territory as the main spearhead of any offensive or defensive Soviet operations against the NATO countries. And East Germany's economy is more closely integrated by far with the Soviet and the CEMA economies than that of any other East European state.[23]

[23] See Staar, *The Communist Regimes*, pp. 240–260.

In both East and West Germany, the issues of what is usually called "domestic policy" and what is usually called "foreign policy" are closely, even inextricably, linked. As far as East Germany is concerned, on the one hand, the massive presence of Soviet troops on its territory as well as economic dependence on the Soviet Union set limits to how "open" and "pro-Western" East Germany *could* be even if its leaders really wished it. On the other hand, even if Soviet soldiers may seem hostile intruders to ordinary East Germans, they are bound to be seen as saviors to the leaders of the SED as long as the great majority of the East German population cannot be relied upon to support the regime freely and voluntarily.[24] To achieve greater independence of the Soviets, however, the East German regime would need, above all, to increase its domestic support. This has certain economic aspects requiring, for example, expansion and diversification of East German trade volume and consumer technology so as to be able to offer the people a more satisfying way of life. This brings us full circle back to such dilemmas as "How can we improve conditions and satisfy popular demands without more contacts with the West?" And at the same time, "How can we risk greater contacts with the West given the attitudes of our people as they are now?" Winning more popular support might also call for decreased investments in the military-police sectors of the economy and for modifying some traditional Marxist-Leninist stands on such issues as collectivization of agriculture, for example. But if reforms should bring about at least short-run unrest, and the alienation of Soviet support, how could the regime afford to undertake them?

Similar problems of policy or issue interdependence are also evident in West Germany. Obviously, the prosperity and well-being of West Germany owe a great deal to foreign trade and investment. West Germany has benefited substantially by the destruction of tariff barriers in the Common Market trading zone. It has also benefited by the indirect subsidy of its NATO allies, particularly the United States, providing it thus far with a framework of military and nuclear defense that costs West Germany far less than going it alone would. West Germany, unlike East Germany, has not invested heavily in a garrison state. But, the ability to minimize defense costs has depended above all on the good will of other states based on their perceptions of West Germany as a peaceful and

[24] Adam B. Ulam, "The Destiny of Eastern Europe," *Problems of Communism*, vol. 23, no. 1 (January–February 1974), pp. 1–12. As Professor Ulam observes: "How could even the most popular and progressive Communist regime ever feel secure unless it assumed that the Soviet Union would not tolerate its overthrow?" p. 11. See also Robert Legvold, Ibid, "The Problem of European Security," pp. 13–33.

democratic nation. A Germany which succumbed to a revival of a Nazi-type nationalism would not be compatible either with NATO or with the EEC. Thus, Germany's domestic developments such as de-Nazification, democratization, internal stability, the weakening of extremist political movements, rising affluence, the diffusion of more cosmopolitan and co-operative attitudes among the people, and the like, have always been closely watched abroad. These developments have encouraged foreign traders, investors, politicians, and publics. Political changes have contributed to and supported the domestic "economic miracle." Setbacks in *either* sphere—political, international, or economic—would likely be mutually reinforcing.

policy process

INITIATION OF ISSUES: THE FRG

The West German system, like the American, is highly diffuse and inter-dependent. New initiatives can, and do, originate at many different points in the system. There is no requirement for a central "clearance" to legitimize new proposals.

Within the formal structure of government, the chancellor is considered the policy spokesman for the whole federal cabinet. But even within the cabinet, ministers are considered constitutionally autonomous in managing their departments. And in practice, they can usually initiate actions and policies whenever these are not inconsistent with the agreed-on policy of the chancellor and the cabinet together.

In the federal legislature, the members of both houses are free to initiate new measures, and to offer significant amendments to the cabinet's proposals. Although the West German parliament, particularly the Bundestag, has been a less frequent originator of bills than the U.S. Congress, it has generated many important legislative initiatives and amendments. There are also state governments and legislatures in the 11 *länder*, and the Constitutional Court; all of these exercise de facto policy initiatives.

Media Role   Outside the formal structure of government are the interest groups and the media. The importance of the power of independent initiative outside the government structure itself has been illustrated by two great scandals in West German politics.

In 1965, the then Minister of Defense, Franz Joseph Strauss, ordered the arrest of a newspaper publisher. Rudolf Augstein, publisher of the magazine *Der Spiegel*, was arrested on charges that he had unlawfully revealed state secrets. The police seized Augstein, and the files contained in his office, in a midnight raid and carted them off without any court warrant. If this had happened "quietly," there might have been no political consequences. But both *Der Spiegel* and other German newspapers took the position that Augstein's arrest (and the seizure of his papers) constituted an assault on the constitutionally protected freedom of the press; that it smacked of the methods of Hitler's Gestapo; and that it was an act of political revenge by Franz Joseph Strauss against a political opponent, and not a legitimate legal action. Augstein's arrest became a political issue against the government on the initiative of the press, and shortly after its disclosure, by the parliamentary opposition, and various other segments of public opinion, too. In the end, not only was Augstein freed and his possessions restored, but the cabinet of Chancellor Adenauer resigned and underwent a reshuffle. Franz Joseph Strauss was dismissed, and his otherwise promising political career was effectively shadowed.

In 1974, in a series of events reminiscent of the Watergate crisis in America, the German press and parliament jointly developed two issues which culminated in the resignation of one of the most popular and successful federal chancellors—Willy Brandt. The first of these issues (discussed here later) related to allegations of bribery which Brandt denied. The second related to a compromising association. According to stories published in the West German press, an assistant and a close confidante of the chancellor's, Gunther Guillaume, was, in fact, a spy for the Communist East German regime purposely planted in his office. An investigation ensued. Brandt eventually acknowledged the truth of the charges. The spy was arrested, and Brandt resigned.

INITIATION OF ISSUES: THE GDR

In East Germany the function of policy initiative is lodged with the Politburo of the Socialist Unity Party (SED); this party, a Marxist-Leninist equivalent of the Soviet Union's CPSU, is organized on the same basic pattern. The Politburo (15 to 20 members) is elected by the Central Committee; the Central Committee (135 full members and 54 candidate members in 1975) is chosen by the Party Congress; the Congress (about 3000 persons) is elected indirectly by the constituent territorial and functional party units, which ultimately reaches down to the rank-and-file. Total SED membership is about 2 million of which perhaps 100,000 constitute the core "apparat" of the Party. The rank-and-file never elect the leaders directly.

Between meetings of the Congress, the Central Committee speaks for the Party; between meetings of the Central Committee it is the Politburo which speaks for the SED. In prevailing practice, elections are not what they seem. The Politburo and the SED Secretariat *designate* candidates for all elective posts—from the top down to the grassroots. The meetings and procedures of the SED's Politburo are secret, like the CPSU's. No one knows what is discussed, when, or how, and what the positions of the various members and reasons for decisions may be. Since the East German system operates on the same "interlock" principle as the Soviet—that is, that both the governmental structure and the society as a whole are supposed to be guided by the Party—there is no right of policy initiative independent of the Party leadership anywhere in the system. No direct proposal for new policies or actions in East Germany can surface in the party-controlled media, in the legislature, or in any public forum unless it is endorsed by the SED leaders.

Organizational Structure East Germany, like the USSR, possesses two pyramids of government ruled by a third. At the apex of the legislative power of government is the Council of State, created in 1960, and composed of 24 members elected by the Volkskammer (People's Chamber) for a four-year term. The body is equivalent to the Russian Presidium of the Supreme Soviet. The Council of State can issue decrees with the force of law and, in effect, preempt its parent legislative body, the 500-member Volkskammer. From 1961 until 1973 Walter Ulbricht served as the chairman of this Council. In 1973 upon his death Willi Stoph succeeded to the post.

As in the Soviet Union, parliament—formally, that is—controls the executive. Thus, the Council of Ministers is theoretically responsible to the Volkskammer, and to the Council of State when the latter is not in session. The Council of Ministers, like its Soviet counterpart, is headed by a Presidium composed of a premier and several deputy premiers. It too has extensive legislative powers. The premier since 1973 has been Horst Sondermann. The Presidium is believed to be the only portion of the Council of Ministers which actually meets as a body to discuss policies and pass instructions to the individual ministries.

While the general subservience of the government pyramid to the party pyramid is as true in East Germany as it still is in the Soviet Union, there has been some diversification of personnel lately. The Party Politburo and Secretariat have been headed since 1971 by Erich Honecker, who replaced Walter Ulbricht. Interestingly enough, between 1961 and 1971 Ulbricht had outdone Stalin himself by simultaneously holding all the leading jobs in East Germany: First Secretary of the SED, Chairman of the Council of State, and Premier.

In West Germany deliberation is a process that is fragmented and, at many of its junctures, public. Legislative proposals are generally drafted by the bureaucracy—at the request of cabinet ministers—and submitted to parliament only after consultation with a variety of affected interest groups and the so-called *Fraktionen,* or caucuses of different party groups in the Bundestag. Nevertheless, all such proposals are first scrutinized by the Bundesrat—that is, by state (*Land*) officials and their particular bureaucratic chiefs. They are then transmitted to the Bundestag and debated generally in its specialized legislative committees before receiving formal approval of the whole house. Controversial measures are debated on the floor. In addition, the media, in all their partisan varieties, are likely to thrash out the pros and cons of whatever policy or legislation may be under way. There is also wider public participation on many measures, similar to American practices.[25] Citizens assemble, demonstrate, and write or call upon their officials as well as the media. Vociferous grass-roots opposition and noisy demonstrations are virtually routine.

Curbing Big Business An illustration of the deliberative process on a very controversial issue is afforded by West Germany's anti-cartel legislation.[26] It was first submitted by the cabinet to the Bundesrat in March 1952 and enacted into law in January 1958. This measure was originally favored by some elements in the CDU and had even more enthusiastic and solid backing by the SPD and a majority of the FDP. The measure was opposed, however, by the powerful Federation of German Industry (BDI) which argued that cartels promoted economic stability and that the proposed legislation was really anti-business. Within the CDU Ludwig Erhard espoused a free trade, laissez-faire position directed against monopoly practices in general, and restrictive cartel agreements in particular. Others, including Konrad Adenauer, were more ambivalent. The original bill died in the Bundestag's Economic Affairs Committee. In 1954, the cabinet reintroduced the bill in the Bundesrat where conservative interests succeeded in attaching a number of amendments to it. By 1955, when the second version of the bill finally reached the Bundestag, the government and the BDI agreed to several exemptions for

[25] See Deutsch and Nordlinger, "The German Federal Republic," pp. 431–434 and William G. Andrews, *European Political Institutions,* 2nd ed. (New York: Van Nostrand, 1966), pp. 409–410; and particularly William Safran, *Veto-Group Politics: The Case of Health Insurance Reform in West Germany* (San Francisco: Chandler, 1967).

[26] As discussed by Gerard Braunthal in his "Struggle for Cartel Legislation," in James B. Christoph, ed., *Cases in Comparative Politics* (Boston: Little, Brown, 1965), pp. 240–255. See also the excellent account of group struggle over policy by David Schoenbaum, *The Spiegel Affair* (Garden City, N.Y.: Doubleday, 1968).

various industries; this had the effect of watering down the proposed legislation.

On the one hand, Erhard had compromised his earlier stand. On the other hand, public support for some form of anti-cartel legislation, and the division among businessmen themselves, prompted the BDI to accept the principle of anti-cartel legislation while still seeking to water down its content further. Big business seemed to have a greater hold on the CDU's rank-and-file deputies than upon the Party's top leadership in the cabinet. The cabinet felt that some form of anti-cartel legislation would help them prevail nationally over the Socialists. Nevertheless, the process of negotiating and bargaining in and out of parliament finally led to what some observers called "a piece of Swiss cheese" and a "sieve with mighty big holes." Finally, the SPD voted against the ultimate version of a law that the Party had originally strongly supported. Business has continued to proclaim its dissatisfaction, albeit more moderately, and the whole process still continues to receive public attention through the rulings of a Cartel Agency empowered to levy fines on monopolistic firms.

DELIBERATION: THE GDR

In East Germany, the process of deliberation of policy and legislative decisions is virtually as closed as the process of initiation. For the most part, there is no more than a pretense of public deliberation involving short, perfunctory debates by the Volkskammer—East Germany's unicameral parliament or people's chamber. In the entire history of East Germany—that is, since 1949—there has been *no* oppositional discussion in any public forum of proposals submitted by the SED leadership for legislative approval. Again, as in the case of the Soviet Union, there have been a few issues, notably economic decentralization in the 1970's, on which the SED has asked for and encouraged a debate among its experts: economists, managers, planners, party officials, trade unionists. Such debates may occur when the leadership is uncertain about the course it wishes to pursue, or when it wants to sound out lower echelon attitudes.

The real debate usually takes place in the Politburo (and occasionally the Central Committee) in utter secrecy. The extent of that debate—how real and lively it is—depends not only on the issues but probably also on the splits in the SED leadership; and these are usually hidden as much as possible from the world at large.

An Exception? In 1973, for the first and only time in GDR history, there was a genuine debate, with dissenting voices and ultimately even votes, on an issue which the SED leadership decided to submit to the Volkskammer for a "free-for-all." The issue was women's right to free abortion.

After a debate that involved the opposition of several church groups and even produced some division within the SED itself (some Party members believed that unrestricted abortion would undermine socialist morality; most saw the issue in terms of Party ideology in relation to equality and freedom for women), the bill passed the Volkskammer. It provided for abortion on demand within the first 12 weeks of pregnancy and it authorized distribution of contraceptive pills to 16-year-olds on demand. For the first time, 14 deputies voted against a measure and 8 abstained.

APPROVAL: THE FRG

In West Germany approval is almost inevitably an extended process. *No* decision taken by the chancellor even in the field of foreign affairs, if it has any domestic repercussions, can be put into effect without the approval of both houses of parliament. Some decisions also, in fact, require the approval of still another official who is independent of the chancellor: the president. Some decisions or policies require the approval of the states (*länder*), if they touch upon areas of state control or state rights. *All* decisions and policies may, in any case, be appealed in the West German political system to the Constitutional Court—even before approval—if any citizen wants to argue that a proposal is unconstitutional and asks for an advisory ruling. The Court may render a judgment that could doom the particular proposal even before it is formally approved and put into effect. Many measures and policies require a great deal of parliamentary "haggling" before they are enacted. In most instances, admittedly, the problem of getting approval for bills that are proposed by the chancellor is not very difficult. They are usually supported by the same majority of parties, or party, that forms the chancellor's cabinet. The government can usually count on party discipline to help it. But the need to obtain approval in a public forum, subject to the scrutiny of one's opponents and the possibly adverse consequences of any publicity, usually makes the government prudent and cautious. What is routinely approved, after all, has generally been cleared with various affected parties and has received careful drafting by a nonpartisan bureaucracy. If a measure is attacked in parliament, the government must be prepared to defend it publicly. The last thing that it wants, or can stand, is a scandal that reveals corruption or incompetence on its part.

West German Parliamentarians The 496 members of the West German Bundestag are directly elected by the people, half from single-member districts and half from nationwide party lists allocated in proportion to each party's total national vote. They are elected by secret ballot without any trace of police terror, and with relatively effective controls, including public subsidy, on the expenditure of campaign funds by the candidates. Virtually anyone can run for a district seat.

Yet this system, too, has developed its contraints because of the discriminatory effects of the electoral laws on small parties, the attitudes of German voters and politicians, and the centralistic tendencies of party organizations. These factors may be considered serious defects in the German parliamentary system—from the standpoint of how open and democratic it is. The same factors, however, may also be considered virtues.

The first of these factors, the discriminatory effects on small parties, is shown in the decline in the representation of minor parties in the Bundestag. Since the 1965 election, West Germany has had a so-called "two-plus" party system, with the CDU/CSU and the SPD as the major parties and the Free Democrats as the minor party. No other parties have had representation among the Bundestag's 496 deputies. In 1949, 1953, 1957, and 1962 the Bundestag still contained at least some representatives of other groupings, including those from a Refugee Party, the German Party, the Communists, and some right-wing deputies. From the middle 1960's, none of these was able to gather enough votes to overcome the obstacles of the electoral law with its 5 percent threshold clause.

How They Act   Party discipline within the three parties that have been continuously represented in the Bundestag has been extremely tight. Past studies suggest that deputies of a party are likely to support it on between 95 to 99 percent of the votes taken in the Bundestag. However, Party policy positions are determined, in considerable detail, by the meetings of all deputies in each Party, with a majority binding the rest. Considerable discussion and bargaining thus takes place within each Party's Bundestag delegation. German voters, like the British and unlike the Americans, have shown that they are more interested in choosing among different party programs and orientations than among different personalities. This attitude has tended to strengthen discipline within the parties.

Moreover, a great deal of the Bundestag's work, even more than in the United States, is done by the specialized committees whose deliberations are sometimes secret, although always subject to the access of civil servants and cabinet ministers, and to disclosure of proceedings by minority and majority reports post facto.[27]

[27] See Gerhard Loewenberg, "Parliamentarism in Western Germany: The Functioning of the Bundestag," *American Political Science Review* 55, no. 1 (March 1961): 87–102; see also his *Modern Parliaments: Change or Decline?* (Chicago: Aldine Atherton, 1971). See also Andrews, *European Political Institutions*, pp. 421–432.

The Bundesrat is not a people's chamber. It is a house of delegates made up of ministers of the *Land* governments, often represented in discussion by their senior civil servants. Each of the 11 *Lands* has at least three votes in the Bundesrat with the largest *Lands* (those with at least 6 million inhabitants) having six votes. The votes of each *Land* are cast as a unit based on positions taken by those whom they represent—the state or *Land* governments. Ultimately, of course, these governments derive from state elections. Here, too, much of the work is done in specialized committees. On any legislation that requires the involvement of *Land* governments, the Bundesrat can exercise an absolute veto. Usually, this means that all controversial measures have to be worked out by a Joint Coordinating Committee of the two houses. On legislation that is strictly in the federal domain, the Bundesrat may exercise suspensive veto—that is, subject any measure to a reconsideration by the Bundestag, with the proviso that if two-thirds of the Bundesrat had opposed it, at least two-thirds of the Bundestag must vote to override the veto.

Legislation   Between 1949 and 1965, 80 percent of all legislation originated with the federal government, 19 percent with the Bundestag and only 1 percent with the Bundesrat. Nevertheless, bills originating with the government require first consideration by the Bundesrat before they go to the other house; and even so, 9 percent of all legislation finally reported from the Bundestag has been amended by the Bundesrat.

APPROVAL: THE GDR

In East Germany, approval for proposals, whether legislative or policy (and all emanating through one source—the Politburo of the SED), is publicly largely perfunctory. If the Politburo can agree on a course of action, the legislature, the press, the judiciary, the various adjuncts of the SED all sing its praises. Just as there is no recorded argument opposing Party proposals in the history of the East German parliament, so there is no record of any oppositional votes or even abstentions, not even one (the 1973 abortion bill involved a "free vote" by the Party leadership).

The Volkskammer has been very much like Hitler's Reichstag—an enthusiastic claque for an authoritarian regime. Approval occurs *in camera* by a handful of the principal leaders of the SED. In a variation on Soviet themes, the SED has brought into being a number of adjunct political parties—not to constitute competition for itself but to help appeal to and organize the people more effectively on behalf of the Party's programs. This is now done through a so-called National Front dominated by the SED. The SED allows the other parties a certain percentage of candidates on the single (National Front) list presented to the voters in the quadrennial national elections. The adjunct parties are allotted a percentage of seats in the 500-member parliament or Volkskammer: not enough to make a decisive difference *even* if these parties were truly oppositional but enough to create an appearance of heterogeneity.

Elections East German elections usually produce turn-outs of 98 or 99 percent of the eligible voters (men and women over 18 years old); and the National Front never fails to get at least 99 percent of the votes cast. Since crossing out the names of its candidates requires the use of a special booth, under constant police surveillance, it is not a realistic choice for the East German voters. Elections are not concerned with choices but rather with outward imagery and Party campaigns to mobilize people into political activism.

Interestingly enough, the SED has participated in several genuinely free elections in the city of West Berlin; in 1954 it polled 2.7 percent of the vote; in 1958 1.9, and in 1963 1.3 percent. In 1972 it did not elect even one representative to the Bundestag.

APPLICATION: THE FRG

In West Germany application involves the cooperation of political-governmental, bureaucratic, and frequently voluntary organizations of the community. The powers of Germany's central government are about as extensive as those of the U.S. federal government. Constitutionally, some powers are "reserved" to the center or the states; most powers are concurrent. However, the bureaucracy which the central (or federal) government uses in Germany is overwhelmingly under the direct pay, supervision, and orders of *state* governments—not the center.[28] The practical implication is that in most fields the power of the central government can only be used indirectly—through the states. And if the states fail to carry out directives of the central government, the chancellor cannot fire the bureaucrats or directly carry out any kind of administrative reprisals against them. They are not, after all, his employees. He and his cabinet could act only indirectly—that is, by such relatively more cumbersome procedures as new fiscal measures, new legislation, and, of course, appeal to the Constitutional Court. Another element that fosters the bureaucracy's relative independence of the federal govern-

[28] Lewis J. Edinger estimates that only about 14 percent of the nearly 2 million government employees in the Federal Republic are federal officials. See his *Politics in Germany* (Boston: Little, Brown, 1968), p. 312.

ment is its civil service status. Not even the *Land* governments can fire or punish their bureaucrats without a substantial legal cause that can be sustained in court. The bureaucracy's status is carefully protected from the day-to-day interference by politicians.

The cooperation of autonomous nongovernmental organizations is necessary in the case of many policies, as, for example, in the social welfare and health insurance fields. Here the trade unions, whose own leaderships are often at odds with that of the government, and the physicians' and nurses' associations, play the roles of partners to the government in implementing various policies.

APPLICATION: THE GDR

In East Germany, the bureaucracy is effectively centralized; the Party's control over it is direct, and there is no civil service concept—as in West Germany or the United States—to give the bureaucrats a measure of independence, nonpartisanship, or detachment of judgment. The least displeasure felt by the SED leadership can be translated into drastic punitive action against the bureaucracy. Similarly, all the so-called mass organizations, trade union, student, youth, farmer, professional, and so forth, are Party controlled. They do not really bargain with the government as independent entities. The leaders of these groups are usually designated by the SED to act, in Stalin's phrase, as "transmission belts" of Party policy.

There is also recourse to significant extralegal coercion in the process of applying policy decisions. While terror has markedly declined from the "bad old days" of Stalin and Ulbricht—that is, from what it was like in the 1940's, 1950's and even early 1960's—the presence and intervention of the secret police are factors that are still (for good reasons) taken into account. The leaders of the SED do not have to wait for time-consuming court injunctions to help them enforce their decisions— as in the United States or West Germany. They can fire, demote, and jail virtually anyone who stands in the way of their will.

The problems the leaders face, therefore, are not usually with overt opposition, particularly from their own state apparatus. It is rather with the more subtle, but nevertheless serious, difficulties of implementing policies which for one reason or another may be unrealistic or unpopular at the grassroots level. The policy results may be disappointing, and the bureaucracy can be ineffective, without it ever being overtly oppositional.

Bureaucrats and Media One of the ways in which the application of policy differs in East Germany from the Federal Republic and the United

States is in the relationship of the bureaucracy to the media and to the people. In East Germany, the bureaucrats don't have to worry as long as the Party leaders are pleased with their performance. Only an unlikely revolution would translate popular discontent into reforms of or reprisals against the bureaucracy. Since all the media and the rights of expression, assembly, and association are preempted by the Party, ordinary people cannot attack the bureaucrats for their abuses. Only when the Party leaders allow this to happen do we find instances of irate citizens having their letters printed in the newspapers attacking various abuses and official mistreatment. In West Germany, as in the United States, no official—elective or appointed—is shielded from the right of citizens to complain about his actions and to criticize them. Thus, there is little likelihood of any independent, grassroots reform of the bureaucracy in East Germany while the Party maintains its political monopoly.

ADJUDICATION AND ENFORCEMENT: THE FRG

In West Germany, as in the United States, courts play a significant role in deciding how policies may be invoked in particular cases. Courts sometimes rule against the government or its agencies if they conclude that legal powers have been exceeded, misused, or improperly applied. Thus, whatever the chancellor or the federal legislature or one of the states may decide, citizens and interest groups have a very important power of appeal to the courts. The judiciary is both highly professional and politically independent in the Federal Republic.[29]

The Federal Constitutional Court has had even broader jurisdiction than the U.S. Supreme Court and it has exercised its powers with vigor and independence. The Court decides disputes between the federal government and the states, as well as among the states; it can also hear appeals by individuals who believe that their constitutional rights have been abridged. It may also render judgments on the constitutionality of laws, apart from any litigation, when asked either by the federal government, by one of the states, or by one-third of the members of the Bundestag. In 1961, the Federal Constitutional Court denied the Adenauer government the right to establish a nationwide television network on the grounds that such action infringed upon states' rights. In 1952, the Court outlawed the neo-Nazi so-called Socialist Reich Party as an antidemocratic and anticonstitutional organization; and it did the same to the Communist KPD in 1956. The police is a state force, maintained

[29] On the political role of the court, see Donald R. Reich, "Court, Comity and Federalism in West Germany," *Midwest Journal of Political Science* 7, no. 3 (August 1963): 197–228; reprinted in Albinski and Pettit, *European Political Processes*, pp. 364–390.

by each of the 11 *länder;* it is not a central, national agency such as Hitler's Gestapo.

ADJUDICATION AND ENFORCEMENT: THE GDR

In East Germany, the courts play a much more limited, subordinate role. They dispense "socialist justice" which, in accordance with the tenets of Marxism–Leninism, means that they are obligated to serve the interests of the Party as formulated by its leaders, and not to oppose or thwart them for any reasons whatever. The judiciary is professional, but it is strictly subordinate to the Party in the same way as the bureaucracy. Conflicts of policy, conflicts in administrative jurisdictions, and the misconduct of state officials are not matters seriously appealable to the courts. They are resolved by the political leaders. The courts confine themselves to administering the criminal and civil codes; individuals may pursue their claims in the courts, according to the laws, so long as these claims do not infringe, or even adversely reflect upon, the regime. The secret police (SSD) or state security service is still a very feared agency in East Germany.

MONITORING: THE FRG

In West Germany the media, the individual citizens, parliament, state legislatures and interest groups, all participate in a never-ending process of policy observation and evaluation.

There has always been a great deal of diversity among the German media, with all of the major interest groups putting across their points of view in different types of publications and news programs. The media represent a significant force on behalf of democracy and constitutional government in West Germany. According to a study made by Karl Deutsch and Lewis Edinger in the late 1950's, newspaper editors and the communication élites of West Germany have tended to be much more anti-Nazi and anti-authoritarian in their orientations than the élites of the bureaucracy and business. Forty-two percent of the editors of the largest newspapers and periodicals had had "major anti-Nazi records"; 38 percent had been imprisoned by the Nazis and another 5 percent were exiled by them. In contrast, Deutsch and Edinger reported that only 2 percent of the top civil servants and 4 percent of the military among their sample populations reported any anti-Nazi records. Similarly, an inquiry into the backgrounds of 47 leaders of the principal German business organizations in 1956 yielded only two replies that claimed some sort of anti-Nazi activity.[30]

---

[30] Deutsch and Nordlinger, "The German Federal Republic," p. 428.

In East Germany, the monitoring function is narrowly circumscribed by censorship and by Party control of the media. Therefore, the question "How are things going?" which is so characteristic of public discussion in the Western world—the speculation about what, if anything, is wrong, where, and how it might be changed or improved—is handled very gingerly in the German Democratic Republic. With the exception of occasional public relations campaigns launched by the regime itself (and usually designed to deflect blame from the leadership or to exhort people to greater efforts and vigilance), one has to read between the lines of official organs to detect any inkling of national difficulties. The general tone of the media is "upbeat." The average reader or listener who takes the usual media output at face value can only conclude—in East Germany as in the Soviet Union—that the zone of happiness and righteousness is at home; the zone of calamity and wrong-doing is abroad. Many subjects—such as the alliance between East Germany and the Soviet Union, the issue of one party control at home, the validity and fruitfulness of Marxism–Leninism, the public ownership of the means of production and distribution, the pernicious character of West German institutions—are forbidden as critical themes in the official media. And so is any explicit criticism of Party officials. On the other hand, one can occasionally find seemingly innocuous discussions on the efficacy of incentives in industry and agriculture which *imply* the failure or the unsatisfactory character of certain policies and perhaps of those connected with them, or calls for increased efforts in certain endeavors which also imply "shortcomings." Such stories may often require the same kind of Kremlinological translation—guessing who in the Party bureaucracy is really attacking whom—that occupies the expert students of the Soviet Union.

TERMINATION AND AMENDMENT: THE FRG

The chief difference between East and West Germany in this aspect of policy is the existence of what might be termed organs of interposition in the Federal Republic. Whatever actions or policies are undertaken by some government organs in West Germany can always be legitimately revoked or modified by others. In this respect, the Federal Republic is analogous to the United States. The Constitutional Court can invalidate or, in fact, amend parliamentary legislation and federal policy. And, parliament can override the Court's objections by redrafting "objectionable" laws or by constitutional amendment. The *Land* governments and their bureaucracies can interpret federal regulations to amend them— subject to Court appeal—if the federal authorities should object to these interpretations. Even those actions which seemingly fall wholly into the discretion of the executive—speeches, declarations, and other symbolic acts, as well as policies which do not take the form of legislation—are all subject to parliamentary interposition. The Bundestag may remove the chancellor and his cabinet from office by the so-called constructive vote of no-confidence; that is, by agreeing on a successor. In addition, however, even a simple vote of no-confidence in the government, carried by a majority of the Bundestag deputies, could conceivably lead to the same result. The president could under such circumstances exercise his prerogative of dissolving parliament and calling for new elections. This would reduce the incumbent chancellor to a caretaker pending the outcome of the elections.

Actually, the executive in West Germany has been reconstituted several times in response to parliamentary and public pressures short of a special election. The reshuffles of the Adenauer cabinet, the resignation of Ludwig Erhard and the succession of Kurt Kiesinger as well as the change from Willy Brandt to Helmut Schmidt, all took place without special elections or no-confidence votes.[31]

TERMINATION AND AMENDMENT: THE GDR

In East Germany there have been some top level reshuffles, too, though not nearly as many as in the Federal Republic. East Germany has had essentially two principal leaders since 1949: Walter Ulbricht until the 1970's (first in partnership with Wilhelm Pieck, then alone when Pieck died in 1952) and currently Erich Honecker. Far more important, however, has been the lack of any organs of interposition in East Germany. No body of officials or citizens in the country has been able to exercise a veto on the actions of the SED leadership. And, appropriately enough, there is no record of any attempt at it in the entire history of East Germany. A motion of no-confidence in the government would be as unthinkable in the Volkskammer as would an oppositional vote or a critical remark. Consequently, the amendment or termination of any policy is up to the people who initiated it in the first place. From time to time, of course, the rulers do decide to change or modify their course. What prevails in the GDR, as in the USSR, however, is not amendment or revocation of policy by those who are independent of the policy initiators but rather occasional policy distortion and surreptitious noncompliance

---

[31] Peter H. Merkl shows that on each of seven occasions, from 1949 to 1966, when coalition cabinets were formed in West Germany, a significant number of deputies even from the participating parties cast their votes *against* the government. The lowest figure was 12 deputies out of 286 in the CDU-DP (Conservative German Party) coalition in 1957; the highest was 87 out of 447 in the grand coalition between CDU and SPD in 1966. Albinski and Pettit, *European Political Processes*, p. 279.

which is, to some degree at least, inevitable in all complex, bureaucratic systems.

AUDIT: THE FRG

An important phase of policy-making relates to a post facto accountability of those people who make decisions and carry them out. It is a sobering thought to all officialdom to realize that whatever they may do could be the subject of an independent inquiry long after the fact. Skeletons are apt to fall out of the closets. The anticipation may sometimes encourage prudence and restraint among the power holders. In this respect, too, the West German system is like the American, and the East German like the Soviet. In the Federal Republic, the press and the media can generally exercise an audit function as do all sorts of government and private agencies.

Early in 1973, a bizarre incident surfaced in the West German press, occasionally referred to as Bonn's Watergate affair. A former deputy of the CDU in the Bundestag, one Julius Steiner, alleged that he had been paid 50,000 marks (about $16,000) to abstain on a crucial vote of confidence against SPD Chancellor Brandt in April 1972. He claimed that the money was given to him by a prominent SPD deputy and Brandt associate, Karl Wienand. Steiner also claimed to have acted as a spy both for the Federal Republic and (presumably as a double-agent) for the GDR. A Bundestag investigating committee was convoked to look into the matter. Although Steiner's assertions were found to be contradictory, and raised the possibility that Brandt was being "framed" by foreign and/or domestic opponents, the proceedings (together with "stagflation") helped undermine Brandt's position. The subsequent disclosure of the Guillaume affair appears to have been the final blow.

AUDIT: THE GDR

In East Germany the past, like the present, is a forbidden zone to unauthorized trespassers. Audit agencies are strictly governmental and are controlled by the Party. Even subjects of relatively academic, historical nature, such as the history of the SED or its KPD (Communist Party of Germany) predecessor, the early years of the GDR, German-Soviet relations, the abuses of the Stalin era, and countless others, cannot be pursued without official authorization and approval of the Party. What East Germany has in terms of a watchdog is a Party Workers' and Peasants' Inspectorate, which together with the Prosecutor General and the secret police monitor and audit the "correctly socialist" performance of all state functions.

Taken together, the decision-making processes discussed above produce a much more open political system in the West German Federal Republic than in the GDR. That is not to say that the process is *completely* open in West Germany; or even that it is as open as *all* the participants in it might want it to be. Similarly, the East German system must not be seen as wholly insulated from and oblivious to its social environment. What we have here, however, is divergent patterns of institutions and decision-making processes, with markedly different tendencies.

conclusion: performance and prospects

THE FRG

The current West German system has been a relatively *sensitive* one—that is, one which has allowed a great variety of societal interests, from Left to Right, to make demands on the political mechanisms. There have been strong unions and farmer organizations; there have been consumer advocates, political parties, exile associations, business and professional groups. In sum, there have been all sorts of interests voicing their demands for policy "outputs"—through the legislature, through the media, by the exercise of the rights of free speech and association, by mass organization, by lobbying the central government, the states, the bureaucracy, and the judiciary.

If we look for comparisons in terms of the impact on policy, it is useful to keep in mind Hitler's Germany of 1933–1945, on the one hand, and the Communist-ruled German Democratic Republic, on the other. Both of these regimes could be described as dictatorships, sharply curtailing the spontaneous right of citizens or groups to make "inputs," or to voice their particular, idiosyncratic demands on the respective political systems.

The Federal Republic, quite apart from the political issues of freedom and individual security, has displayed far greater balance between goods and services provided in the private and the public sectors, than either of these dictatorships, with consequent—apparent—greater satisfaction for more people.

It is important to note that the Bonn regime of 1949 has thus far been aided by three important factors that Weimar lacked. First, this time, the Western powers gave Germany massive economic aid through the Marshall Plan, instead of claiming and collecting reparations as they did after World War I. Second, the period since World War II has been one of generally ascending recovery and prosperity for Germany, unlike the runaway inflation and depression, with mass unemployment, experienced in the twenties and thirties. Finally, notwithstanding all the bitter memories of Nazi crimes and persecutions in Europe and throughout the world, Germany has succeeded in gaining full international acceptance in the European Economic Community, in the North Atlantic Treaty Organization and, finally, in 1974, by membership in the United Nations. All of these factors have helped new and old generations of Germans to associate the relatively new democratic regime with prosperity, success, and a measure of international prestige.

West Germany has reversed the trends which Hitler had inaugurated. It has greatly expanded educational and cultural facilities of the nation. It has enacted one of the most comprehensive, advanced—and expensive —social welfare programs in Europe and the world. It has reduced many of the inequalities of the Third Reich. Admittedly, as one prominent German scholar has shown, some of its reformist work had been done for it by others.[32] World War II and Soviet occupation of Germany's eastern territories brought about the demise of the landed Junkers. The aristocratic military caste suffered by the natural consequences of the war; Hitler himself began the process of their liquidation after the failure of von Stauffenberg's plot. Junker lands in East Prussia, Pomerania, and Silesia passed into the control of the Soviet Union, East Germany, and Poland in 1945. The traditional dominance of Catholics by Protestants was virtually destroyed by the separation of the largely Protestant east from the rest of Germany.

West Germany's foreign policy has given impetus to European economic and political integration, with a consequent submergence of traditional German nationalism, and with many important economic, social, and cultural consequences for all of Europe. It has sought, and succeeded to a considerable degree—particularly through Willy Brandt's *Ostpolitik* —in easing relations with the Soviet Union, East Germany, and the Warsaw Pact nations as a whole. Again, there has been great tangible impact on the Federal Republic's trade and investments abroad, and upon its domestic prosperity.[33] (There have also been increased personal contacts for many West Germans with friends and relatives in the East, and behind the Berlin Wall.)

West Germany has sought a generally low military profile, consistent with its *Ostpolitik* aspirations, Europeanness (that is, cultivating confidences among EEC partners), the reliance on the American "nuclear umbrella," and military presence in Europe, as well as the enhancement of prosperity at home. It is precisely this relatively internationalist,

[32] Ralf Dahrendorf, *Society and Democracy in Germany* (Garden City, N.Y.: Doubleday, 1969), Chapter 26.
[33] See *Basic Statistics of the Community*, 12th ed. (Luxembourg: Statistical Office of the European Communities, 1972), pp. 78–83.

Rubble of a German city: 1945
Courtesy E.C. Photo Library

peaceful posture of German foreign policy that has allowed the Federal Republic to cultivate its humanistic "economic miracle" of the postwar years and extend German economic influence abroad—particularly among the less developed nations.[34]

THE GDR

The results are strikingly reflected in a comparison with East Germany's heavy military expenditures, garrison-state internal organization and atmosphere, much greater isolation and highly *undiversified* trade. Even in

[34] See Claude E. Welch, Jr. and Arthur K. Smith, *Military Role and Rule* (N. Scituate, Mass.: Duxbury Press, 1974), p. 278. In 1971, the percentage of GNP spent on military purposes was still 6.8 in the GDR and only 3.3 in the FRG.

Germany rebuilt—West Berlin in the 1970's.
Robert Lackenback/Time-Life Picture Agency © Time Inc.

the case of the EEC, West Germany's open door policies have resulted in much *less* dependence by the Federal Republic on the rest of its Common Market partners than GDR's on the COMECON (Communist) bloc. In 1970, about 80 percent of GDR's trade was accounted for by other Communist states. In the case of the Federal Republic, only 42 percent of its trade was in the EEC. Overseas industrial countries, the so-called Third World states, Communist nations, and the European Free Trade Association were all involved in substantial shares of West German business. In 1971 the total volume of West Germany's foreign trade was nearly seven times as large as that of East Germany.

Frontier a Prison Wall?   If the earlier synopsis indicated the orientation of Germany's Nazi dictatorship, the record of the still extant German Democratic Republic gives evidence of the Communist orientation. The GDR, with its 42 thousand square miles and 17 million people (as compared with about 96 thousand square miles and about 62 million people in West Germany), faces its larger German neighbor across a barbed wire border and lethally protected wall in Berlin. Although East Germany has some considerable accomplishments to its credit, the Wall and the barbed wire have been explicitly built and maintained to prevent East Germans from escaping to West Germany. Even so, the East German regime has not succeeded in stemming the outflow of people to the West. Between 1949 and 1961 when the Berlin Wall was built, one out of six East Germans is estimated to have fled to the West! One of the consequences of this exodus has been that the population of the Federal Republic had *increased* by 23.4 percent from 1950 to 1971 (from 49.8 to 61.5 million); the population of East Germany had actually *declined* over this period by 7.2 percent— from 18.4 to 17.04 million persons. There are now—relative to population —more pensioners and fewer working adults in East Germany than in West Germany. There are more women than men. One consequence of this has been that West Germany's labor force utilizes about 54 percent of women of working age; East Germany almost 79 percent.

Communist Objectives and Accomplishments   Historically, the main interests of the powerful East German Party bureaucrats have been in the destruction of the old social class structure; collectivization of agriculture; the primacy of industrial development; an emphasis on communal as opposed to private-individual services and enterprises; the pursuit of internal security and political reeducation of the masses; and faithful support of Soviet-international policies. Given these orientations, East Germany has not been hospitable to individualism, to private farmers and entrepreneurs. It has, in fact, expropriated both. As of 1970, only 6.9 percent of all the farm land in East Germany was under private cultivation —in marginal strips of land worked by the farmers employed on collective state cooperatives and estates. Industry, wholesale and retail trade, as well as various forms of services, are publicly owned and operated.

In this system, there has been a great disproportion between the relatively few goods and services made available to the consumers, and those more generously devoted to industrial development, armaments, and exports by the state. In terms of the quality of life, this has meant less food of less variety in the diets of the people of East Germany. It has meant various degrees of deprivation with respect to clothes, shoes, appliances, automobiles, furniture, housing, and cosmetics. It has also meant serious restrictions on the ability of people to move about, to travel and communicate both within Germany and, above all, abroad.

Some Yardsticks An example of the different priorities of West and East has been the construction of private dwellings. In 1950, for example, housing constituted 48.1 percent of all construction in West Germany but only 10.2 in the GDR; in 1970, it constituted 39.8 percent in the West and still only 19.5 percent in the East.

East German agriculture, subjected to forcible collectivization and low investment priorities, has not produced as abundantly as the West German. Yet, between 1935 and 1938, the very areas now comprising East Germany produced more grain and potato crops per acre than the areas currently comprising West Germany. But as of 1950, 1960, and 1970, West Germany's private farms consistently and substantially out-produced East Germany in these and most other crops.

As in the Soviet Union, one of the larger difficulties of the East German economy has been poor customer service. Since here, as in other Communist states, it has not been the customer but the Party which has been regarded as "king," retail and service personnel have been notoriously indifferent to customer preferences and convenience. The problem is compounded by the traditionally scarce allocations made to the service sector by the Party leaders.

Perhaps most important have been problems which cannot be easily quantified. In East Germany, quite apart from the material issues, there has long been an atmosphere of oppression, fear, and despondency generated by SED inspired coercion, surveillance, persecution, forced collectivism, and incessant propaganda.

Admittedly, there have been some improvements in the 1970's, but considerable differences between the Germanies still remain. Censorship and police surveillance in East Germany still continue to be more prevalent and more characteristic of everyday life than virtually anywhere in Eastern Europe, with the possible exception of Albania. Despite détente and *Ostpolitik*, escape to the West is still no less severely punished than it was four or five, or even ten years ago. Contacts with West Germans and travel outside the Warsaw Pact area are still, in practice, very severely restrained.

Let us, however, return to the more tangible indices of economic satisfactions provided in the two German systems. The figures in Table 4-1 indicate some of the differences in estimated working time required to

TABLE 4–1   Comparison of Purchasing Power in East and West *

Clothes

Man's suit, 50 percent wool	1.5
Dress, 50 percent wool	1.5
Man's shirt	5.0
Man's tie	6.0
Women's stockings	4.5
Men's shoes	2.0
Women's shoes	1.7

Food

Sugar	2.3
Butter	4.6
Eggs	3.0
Milk	1.3
Pork chops	8.0
Coffee	7.0
Brandy	3.0
Chocolate	9.0
Cigarettes	2.5

Appliances

Bicycle	3.0
Portable typewriter	3.2
Man's watch, stainless steel, shock resistant	3.4
Vacuum cleaner	1.9
Refrigerator	6.5
Washing machine	2.6
TV table/model (b/w)	5.1
Automobile	4.9

* The amount of time that one has to work, at average wages, to buy an item in the GDR, as compared with the FRG index of 1.0.

purchase a particular item in East Germany as compared with West Germany in mid-1971.[35]

A similar picture may be gleaned from Tables 4–2, 4–3, and 4–4.

Some GDR Successes   East Germany, however, has done rather well for its people in providing such public goods as education, whether general, technical, or higher; and cultural services, ranging from the provision of

[35] The comparisons of the next few pages are based in part on *United Nations Statistical Yearbooks* for the years 1966–1971, and Helmut Arntz, ed., *Facts About Germany* (Wiesbaden: FRG Press and Information Service, 1966–1971). Compare with the excellent and extensive account by Arnold Heidenheimer, *Governments of Germany*.

TABLE 4–2 Consumption (1970–1971)

Foods	(Kgs per capita) West Germany	East Germany
Fresh fruit	91.7	37.0
Meat	78.5	68.5
Poultry	8.5	5.9
Fish	11.2	8.0
Cheese	10.1	4.6
Eggs (no.)	276	246

TABLE 4–3 Appliances and Transportation (1971)

	West Germany	East Germany
(per 1000 people)		
Automobiles	225	72
Telephones	232	129
Air passengers		
carried on domestic airlines	350	50
Buses	.75	.98
Motorcycles	21	175
Railroads (in km.)	.54	.85

TABLE 4–4 Production (1972–1973)

Industrial Goods	West Germany	East Germany
(Kgs per capita)		
Coal	337	1,452
Crude steel	777	370
Cement	659	647
Electrical energy	4,431	4,284
(KWH per capita)		
Appliances		
(per 1000 people)		
Television sets	414	241
Refrigerators	398	241
Washing machines	257	164
Automobiles	602	79
Trade		
(Volume in marks per capita)		
Exports and imports	3,787	2,088

books, libraries, and museums, to theaters, cinemas, exhibits, and the refinements of opera and ballet. The regime has also provided considerable social welfare and public health facilities, and also relatively cheap, subsidized, public municipal transportation, rents, and utilities (for such scarce housing as may be available).

In 1970, the GDR had placed some 600,000 children out of 953,000 eligible in kindergartens, thus accommodating 63 percent of its eligible school population in comparison with the Federal Republic's 37 percent. East Germany maintained significantly better student-teacher ratios in its elementary, secondary, and technical schools. West Germany had a slight edge in the percentage of youths over 18 enrolled in higher education (10.1 percent as compared with the GDR's 9.8). But East Germany produced significantly more college graduates in relation to population (12 per 10,000 persons) than did West Germany (8.7 per 10,000). In each state there were 65.1 students in all of the various fields of higher education for each 10,000 inhabitants. But in East Germany a larger percentage of these students was made up of women (45.6) than in West Germany (31.4); a far larger percentage was recruited from among those with working class parents (38.2 percent in the East and only 5.7 in the West). Ninety-one percent of East Germany's full time students received grants subsidizing their education, as opposed to about 44 percent in the West. Since the two states did not employ identical classifications for a survey of their respective labor forces and student bodies, official statistics merely suggest different class biases between the two systems. One has favored sharp change from past social patterns; the other at best incremental modifications.

GDR and FRG: Health and Welfare   East Germany has managed to develop one of the finest public health systems in the world. There are about as many physicians, dentists, and hospital beds per capita here as in West Germany; for example, there are 112 beds for each 10,000 people in the West and 110 in the East. The GDR has actually succeeded in reducing the levels of infant mortality and tuberculosis below those achieved in the more affluent West Germany. In the social welfare field, the two German states are rather closely matched and both are highly advanced. Considering the disparity in national incomes, these are substantial achievements for East Germany.

Since incomes are lower in East Germany, all pensions and welfare benefits based on wages and incomes are, of course, correspondingly lower. Most of the rates of remuneration, however, are set to the same scale. One important example that illustrates some differences is sickness benefits paid to employees. West Germany's system pays much more generous benefits to persons suffering long-term occupational illness or injury (beyond 13 weeks) than does East Germany. On the other hand, East Germany, eager to encourage population growth, pays substantial maternity bonuses (500 marks for the first child; 600 for the second; 700 for the third; 850 for a fourth; and 1,000 for each additional one). West Germany gives only 50 marks for each hospital confinement. Both East and West Germany have increased their allocations of funds to social services and to pensions between 1964 and 1970; the GDR by about a third, the FRG by about a half. Considering, however, that the population of the Federal Republic has substantially increased while that of the GDR has been relatively constant, neither side has drastically overtaken the other.

Some Cross-National Comparisons We should add that among the EEC's original six—France, Belgium, Netherlands, Luxembourg, West Germany, and Italy—West Germany, on the whole, has the most extensive and generous social welfare system. In West Germany alone, for example, are family allowances fully covered by the federal budget rather than by individual contributions, and sickness benefits are granted for a much longer period than elsewhere.[36]

Among the chief differences between American and German (both East and West) social policy patterns have been: (1) far more universal access to education, particularly higher education, in the United States. In fact, the United States has achieved the world's highest ratio of university and college students to population; (2) lack of universal medical insurance systems in the United States which both West and East Germany have developed; (3) considerably less generous benefits to most individuals and families under the American social welfare systems. Thus, the United States does not provide any subsidies to self-supporting families with children (that is, family allowances), unless the families become indigent and "go on welfare." Nor do American social welfare programs provide for minimum paid vacations to all workers and employees.

In both East and West Germany people are guaranteed at least 15 working days' vacation during a year. Industrial insurance and sickness benefits are also both more uniform (that is, unlike the United States, they are set on a single national standard throughout the whole country) and actually are more extensive. For example, West German miners are entitled to compensation not only for injuries sustained on the job but for

[36] See Commission of the European Communities, *Comparative Tables of the Social Security Systems in the Member States, etc.* (Seventh edition, 1972); also *Report on the Development of the Social Situation in the Community* (Brussels: Commission, 1974), pp. 214–235.

diseases, like "black lung," likely to be contracted in the course of employment.

The "Miracle" of the GDR   On balance, from the standpoint of ordinary Germans, was the disciplined sacrifice demanded by East German party leaders from the people worth it? What could they show for it? Well, even here one can speak of a "miracle," all the suffering notwithstanding.

The fact remains that East Germany was a basically agricultural area before World War II; that it was plundered by the Russians in the mid-forties (unlike West Germany which was highly industrialized before 1939–1945 and was generously supported by Western aid); and that it has become a great industrial power—by some accounts the eighth most important industrial state in the world. It has also become the richest, in

East German troops in East Berlin celebrate the twenty-fifth anniversary of the founding of the GDR.
UPI

per capita terms, member of the Soviet-led Warsaw Pact; a crucial supplier of sophisticated hardware to the Soviet Union and other Communist states; and finally it has one of the foremost military arsenals in Europe, far surpassing in proportion to both income and population the corresponding effort of West Germany.

Outlook for the Future The question frequently posed by political analysts has been "How durable are these new German political systems?" Would they buckle and fold under the impact of the first severe crisis, domestic or international, that might develop? The answer depends in large measure on the values and attitudes of the masses of German people. How much, for example, if at all, do they value the democratic system in the West? What do they really think of the GDR in the East?

A number of public opinion polls taken in West Germany in the early 1950's brought disturbing results. They seemed to indicate that West Germany was, or had been made into, a political democracy without having many democratic believers. According to one such poll in 1948, 57 percent of the German public believed that Hitler's Nazism was a basically good idea but badly carried out; in 1952, only one out of four Germans was willing to condemn Hitler without any qualifications; in polls taken in 1953 and 1956, only one out of four declared a willingness to do all he or she could to prevent the return of a Nazi-type party to power; in 1954 only one out of four unequivocally endorsed the role of the anti-Hitler German resistance movement. This one-fourth of the German public constituted what Karl Deutsch called the "all-weather" supporters of democracy. Interestingly enough, as late as 1956, only 29 percent of the public expressed support for the Bonn Constitution, and even as late as 1960 only the "usual" 25 percent approved the idea of naming a public school in honor of one of the heroes of resistance to Nazism.

Changes in Attitudes Nevertheless, there are some indications that many of the attitudes have been changing with the passage of time. Where in 1951, for example, only 32 percent of the people put the principal blame for the outbreak of World War II on Nazi Germany, 47 percent did so in 1956 and 62 percent in 1967; also in 1967, 83 percent of the public expressed the view that, given the chance again, they would vote *against* "a man like Hitler," while 67 percent had said so in 1953. There was also a remarkable decline in support for militarism and the military. In 1958, 71 percent opposed equipping the German army (Bundeswehr) with nuclear weapons. In 1961, 29 percent were willing to see the army abolished altogether; and in 1966 only 8 percent approved of policies aimed at reunification of Germany which might involve the risk of war. In 1951, 45 percent of the German people named the Bismarckian Empire as the period when the country enjoyed its finest period, but by 1970, 81 percent identified the current era as the finest yet, and only 5 percent harked back to the pre–1914 days.[37]

West Germany's Political Culture in Comparative Perspective   In a 1963 study, two political scientists compared some of the more basic German orientations toward democracy with those in the United States and Great Britain, as well as in Italy and Mexico. The comparisons with the first two are particularly interesting because in these countries democratic political systems presumably have operated, without interruption, for a very long time.[38] The researchers classified people's attitudes toward politics in terms of three principal types: (1) parochials, persons who have very little knowledge about and involvement, active or emotional, in the political process; (2) subjects, those who may know a good deal about politics and have strong feelings but who do not believe that it is proper for them to make the policies and laws under which they live; (3) participants, those who are the prototypes of the involved democratic citizens—concerned, involved, and committed to a policy-making role for themselves and all their fellow citizens.

Interestingly, the German sample in the study displayed some solid, subject qualities but also considerably fewer participant attitudes than its American or British counterparts. The Germans, with the benefit of many years of universal public education, highly developed technology, and information media, easily ranked first among the five nations studied in the level of their political information. They also scored high in their reports of attention to public affairs in the various media. Sixty-nine percent of the German respondents could name at least four leaders of political parties, compared with 65 percent in the United States and 42 percent in Great Britain. Forty percent could name at least four ministries in the cabinet, compared with 34 percent in Britain and the United States. Also, 53 percent of the German sample reported reading about political affairs in the press at least once a week compared with only 49 percent in the United States, 43 percent in Britain, and 16 and 31 percent respectively in Italy and Mexico.

Yet, only 7 percent of the Germans took pride in their political system compared with 85 percent in the United States and 46 in Britain! Only

[37] See K. Deutsch, G. Schweigler, and L. Edinger, "Foreign Policy of the German Federal Republic."
[38] Gabriel Almond and Sidney Verba, *The Civic Culture* (Boston: Little, Brown, 1966).

Italians, with a mere 3 percent, ranked lower. Fewer Germans expected *equal* treatment for all from their bureaucracy and their police than did British or Americans (although not nearly as few as Italians and Mexicans).[39]

Interestingly, however, when asked if they expected *serious* consideration from these agencies, more Germans than Americans thought so; only in Britain was there an even greater expectation of considerate treatment by the bureaucracy and the police than in Germany. This finding has an historical explanation in the so-called Prussian "*Rechtsstaat* tradition." In the practice of the Prussian bureaucracy, carried over into the Bismarckian Empire, Weimar, and even through the Nazi period into the current era, the officials were supposed to act according to rules and orders of duly authorized superiors. While these rules and orders may themselves have been unjust and capricious, the officials were expected to carry them out with scrupulous adherence to duty—neither more nor less. Bribery and individual willfulness have been conspicuously rare among them.

In terms of strictly political-partisan attitudes, however, the researchers found the Germans much more reserved and skeptical about various democratic processes than their American and British counterparts. Even though Germans were better informed about politics than the others, 39 percent said they *never* talked about politics with other people compared to only 24 percent in the United States and 29 in Britain; 16 percent refused to divulge how they voted in the last national election compared with only 2 percent in Britain and the United States. There was generally greater hostility between opposing partisans in Germany than in either of the long established democracies. Feelings about elections were substantially less positive in Germany than in Britain and the United States. Above all, there were great differences on the idea of popular participation.

Fifty-one percent of Americans and 39 percent of Britons believed that ordinary people should be active in their local communities; but in Germany only 22 percent thought so. Seventy-five percent of the American and 62 percent of the British respondents believed that, if necessary, they could do something about an unjust local or national regulation. But only 38 percent of the Germans thought so.[40]

There were also significant differences in social trust, with fewer Germans willing to believe in the good will and disinterestedness of other people in their own society. When respondents were asked to agree or disagree with the statement, "No one is going to care much about what

39 Ibid., pp. 71, 72.
40 Ibid., p. 142.

happens to you, when you get right down to it," only 38 percent of the Americans and 45 percent of the British agreed with it; but 72 percent of the Germans agreed, compared with 61 and 78 percent, respectively, in Italy and Mexico.[41]

For obvious reasons, no comparable surveys have been taken in East Germany.

A recent survey of élite attitudes, comparing senior bureaucrats in Great Britain, Italy, and West Germany, seems hopeful. It suggests that an appreciable extension of democratic norms and a narrowing down of differences between British and German (but not nearly as many Italian) civil servants has occurred in the post–World War II period.[42]

Stability or Upheaval? Obviously, the legacy of past political life and institutions has influenced the character and dispositions of the German people. Even in relatively recent years, the attachment to the values of democracy has not been quite as profound as in some of the older and more successful world democracies.

American and British heroes have been democratic politicians—men like Washington, Jefferson, Jackson, and Lincoln, William Pitt, Disraeli, Lloyd George, and Churchill. Until the recent era, when Konrad Adenauer first combined the practices of democracy with lasting prosperity, most Germans looked back to Prussia's Frederick the Great, Otto von Bismarck, and even Adolf Hitler as prototypes of successful leaders.[43]

The future will tell if this time, unlike Weimar, German democracy is here to stay. Much depends on the course of international and domestic political, economic, and cultural changes now sweeping the world. Is German nationalism dying, or is it merely dormant? Could an international crisis revive German militarism? Would an (unlikely) Soviet withdrawal from east-central Europe "collapse" the structure of the GDR? Have détente and the more liberal, consumer-oriented policies of the SED in the 1970's increased the legitimacy of the Communist regime? Is there still a realistic prospect of future German reunification? What would

[41] Ibid., p. 213.
[42] See Robert D. Putnam, "The Political Attitudes of Senior Civil Servants in Western Europe: A Preliminary Report," *British Journal of Political Science* 3 (September 1974): 257–290. Asked if it was proper for the state to "carefully regulate" the use of political propaganda, 78 percent of British respondents rejected the idea with lesser or greater reservations; and so did 67 percent of the Germans. But only 43 percent of the Italian bureaucrats rejected it. See also David P. Conradt and Dwight Lambert, "Party System, Social Structure and Competitive Politics in West Germany," in *Comparative Politics* 7, no. 1 (October 1974): 61–86. These authors show greater recent balance in the social followings of the major parties.
[43] Cf. Cordon Craig, *German Statecraft from Bismarck to Adenauer* (New York: Harper & Row, 1965).

happen if German prosperity declined, perhaps in response to European and worldwide economic disorders? Could an authoritarian government return to West Germany despite the tragedies of Hitlerism and the recent apparent changes in popular attitudes? Would the GDR be strengthened or weakened?

5

the soviet union

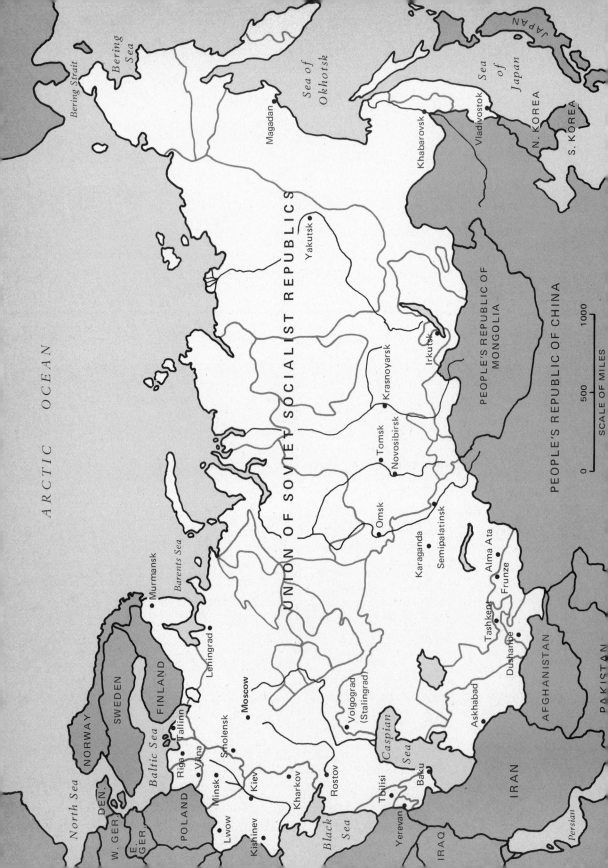

ARCTIC OCEAN

Bering Strait

Bering Sea

Sea of Okhotsk

JAPAN

Sea of Japan

N. KOREA

S. KOREA

Vladivostok

Khabarovsk

Magadan

UNION OF SOVIET SOCIALIST REPUBLICS

Yakutsk

PEOPLE'S REPUBLIC OF MONGOLIA

PEOPLE'S REPUBLIC OF CHINA

Irkutsk

Krasnoyarsk

Tomsk

Novosibirsk

Omsk

Semipalatinsk

Karaganda

Alma Ata

Frunze

Tashkent

Dushanbe

Barents Sea

Murmansk

Leningrad

Moscow

Smolensk

Volgograd (Stalingrad)

Askhabad

AFGHANISTAN

PAKISTAN

Tallinn

Riga

Vilna

Minsk

Kiev

Kharkov

Rostov

Tbilisi

Baku

Caspian Sea

Yerevan

IRAN

IRAQ

Persian

Black Sea

Lwow

Kishinev

POLAND

E. GER.

W. GER.

DEN.

North Sea

NORWAY

SWEDEN

Baltic Sea

FINLAND

1000

500

0

SCALE OF MILES

5 THE SOVIET UNION

background

Thanks to a complex but fortuitous combination of circumstances, a very small political party, the CPSU or Communist Party of the Soviet Union (known in 1917 as the Bolsheviks), dedicated to the most far-reaching program of change, came to power in a vast, heterogeneous, and largely hostile land. The CPSU, under the leadership of V. I. Lenin (1870–1924), established its rule in what had been the tsarist Russian empire at the outbreak of World War I in 1914. On the eve of the Revolution in 1917, the Party was a force of only about 23,000 members in a country of nearly 140 million people occupying one-sixth of the whole land area of the world. Its victory occurred despite many clearly adverse circumstances. The CPSU was recruited predominantly from among workers and middle class intellectuals (most of the latter non-Russian) in a country whose population was almost 80 percent rural. The majority of the people were Russian; however, perhaps as many as 40 percent represented ethnic minorities in various stages of sociocultural development and hostility to Russian rule. The Party was dedicated to principles of economic, political, and social revolution which had been developed in the industrial West for advanced capitalist countries by German-born Karl Marx (1818–1883) and Friedrich Engels (1820–1895). That Lenin's Marxist followers won power in such an unlikely environment as Russia was because of several interrelated factors: among these were the heritage of brutal cultural, religious, and political oppression by the preceding tsarist regime, and consequent mass alienation from it; a legacy of striking inequality and privation, particularly among the peasantry; the strain and trauma, as well as the greatly increased mass suffering, caused by the first years of World War I (1914, 1915, 1916); the consequent weakening and disruption of the Old Regime which led to the tsar's abdication in April 1917; the mutual hostility and indecisiveness among the anti-Communist forces, first under the rule of liberal premier Prince Lvov, and finally under the moderate socialist, Alexander Kerensky.

Even so, the Communist Party did not succeed without a protracted civil war which followed the October Revolution itself (1917–1922). The victory owed much to the skill, energy, and zealous dedication of the Party's leadership, particularly that of Lenin, a man who managed to combine a fanatical devotion to the cause of the Revolution with a great deal of shrewd pragmatism and political acumen.

THE IDEOLOGY: FOUNDATIONS

Lenin may be said to have established the government of the Soviet Union on two basic, interrelated principles which survive to this day: the unchallengable supremacy of one political party and of one political doctrine—the Communist Party of the Soviet Union (CPSU), and the ideology of Marxism-Leninism as defined and applied by the Party. These principles were not accidental occurrences of the Revolution or pragmatic responses particular to post–1917 events. They were essential elements of Lenin's thoughts in various writings completed and developed between the 1890's and the end of 1917. Over the years, Lenin adapted the ideas of Marx and Engels both to justify and to bring about a Marxist revolution in Russia, and simultaneously to make this Russian revolution a harbinger of a universal, worldwide revolution against the rule of capitalism.

In borrowing from Marx and Engels, Lenin retained many of the concepts and all of the phraseology of his masters; indeed, he always professed the utmost fidelity to their ideas, and generally accused all those who disagreed with his interpretations of betraying and falsifying Marxism. Lenin cast his ideology in terms of the grand vista of history that Marx and Engels had already established in their *Manifesto* of 1848.

The history of mankind, thus far, had been a history of class struggle, of "haves" against "have-nots"; its conduct and outcome were governed by socioeconomic conditions. The nature of the means of production and distribution, and the relationships of the various classes to production and distribution, determined the course of the struggle. As material conditions changed, so did the class structure, and so did the relationships of power among the various classes. In the broadest and ultimate sense, economics shaped politics. Specifically, for Marx, political, legal, social, and cultural institutions and ideas were a superstructure resting on an economic foundation or substructure. Economic power conferred political power. To gain the one was to gain the other; conversely, the loss of economic power inevitably led to the loss of political power. In the course of history different economic conditions had produced different class systems and different political relationships. What they all had in common was a scarcity of resources so that however different in the particulars, these relationships had always been exploitive. In antiquity, masters were arrayed against slaves, in the middle ages nobles against serfs, in more recent times landlords against peasants and finally, capitalists against workers or proletarians.

The dynamic of social change was cast by Marx and Lenin (and continues with their heirs) in a framework of *dialectical materialism*. History is seen as a series of spiraling conflicts in which opposing trends and forces emerge, clash, and produce ever new solutions, or plateaus of social development—giving way to new conflicts (new theses opposing new antitheses) and new solutions or temporary equilibria (syntheses). The "trends" or "forces" are impersonal ones; they arise from material conditions in society, and the adaptation of the class structure to it. They are not the results of willful acts of individuals, whether they are ordinary human beings or the so-called great heroes of history. Individuals may act out, in various roles, the larger impulses of universal history; but these impulses are rooted in the socioeconomic environment. Individuals do not create them.

In the vision of Marx, the march of history is basically predetermined by the socioeconomic forces, and the dialectic of conflict reaches its most significant peak with the triumph of capitalist accumulation and technology. As forecast in the *Manifesto,* the progress of capitalism was bound to simplify the class structure of all societies which succumbed to it. A relative handful of capitalist owners would gradually obtain all the means of production and distribution. A vast mass of people working for them, erstwhile peasants, artisans, merchants, and craftsmen would be herded into the operation of mass-production centers, urban and rural, with no significant property of their own. Subjected to exploitation and the vagaries of wolfish competition among profit-seeking capitalists, these propertyless workers, the proletarians, would eventually revolt. Having acquired the common consciousness of their new class situation, they would unite and overthrow capitalist rule. Thenceforth, the great accomplishments and possibilities of capitalist industry, its vast energy and resources, would be put under the control of the proletarians and used for the benefit of the whole of society and ultimately all of humankind. This would occur because, save for the relatively few capitalists, everyone else would be a proletarian. And it would occur because the technology and methods of capitalism were so superior, in the Marxian view, to the earlier, more primitive economic systems that by the sheer force of their competitive power they were bound to conquer the whole world.

The seizure of economic and political power by the workers would be, according to the *Manifesto,* the last independent act of the state. For, after all, the state was but the expression and tool of the exploitation and oppression of one class, or some classes, by others. In the wake of the proletarian revolution, there would be no class left to oppress. And, for this reason, the historical form of social organization—the state—would disappear or "wither away." Coercive and punitive types of organization would be replaced by cooperative and voluntary organizations. A whole phase of human history would come to an end with the beginning of a classless society, characterized by abundance, equality, and real freedom.

After a transitional (and presumably brief) period of "socialism," in which people would work according to their abilities and be paid according to their work, there would ensue full-fledged "communism." People would work according to their abilities and inclinations but receive rewards according to their self-perceived needs. In this stage, not only the division of humankind into classes, but also the division of labor and the very fact of scarcity (which accounted for the rise of classes in the first place), would disappear. True freedom would reign.

IDEOLOGY AND REVOLUTION

Lenin accepted the Marxian formula with certain important modifications. Interested in giving Marxism an unequivocally militant, revolutionary stance and in applying the doctrine to the Russia of his time, Lenin sought to take into account two problems. One was the apparent failure of Marxian prophecy in the industrialized world; the other was the seeming irrelevance of Marxian revolution in a largely backward, agrarian society such as Russia still was in the 1880's and 1890's, and, relatively speaking, even in 1917.

What had occurred in Western Europe was that, contrary to the Marxian prediction, the development of capitalism was not bringing about worsening immiseration of the proletarians. Rather, capitalist development coincided with higher wages and better working conditions, as well as social welfare programs established peacefully, gradually, and without the overthrow of capitalism. These developments tended to promote *reformism* among the socialist, Marxist parties of Europe, the belief that revolution was unnecessary or impractical and that ordinary, within-the-system type of political activity could eventually yield all those objectives of better livelihood, freedom, and equality that Marx associated with revolution.

As for Russia, how could one urge a workers' revolution in a land so overwhelmingly peasant, in which the industrial workers and the bourgeoisie alike were still seedlings of the future, and in which modern technology was just beginning to take root?

Most Russian Marxists (of whom there were relatively few) accepted the apparent limitations of their environment. They recognized Russia's economic and social backwardness and saw a proletarian revolution far in the future. The revolution they sought was against tsarism, which was oppressive to all sorts of elements in Russia: the peasantry, the workers, the bourgeoisie and, of course, the non-Russian peoples. Following this revolution, these reformist Marxists, writers and political activists like G. V. Plekhanov, Julius Martov, P. B. Axelrod, were prepared to follow parliamentary democratic methods to achieve further reforms. Socialism and communism—the rule by the workers—would come only in a further perspective of history: when capitalism matured in Russia, the peasantry diminished and the proletariat grew. All this seemed quite a ways off in the late 1890's and early 1900's.

But Lenin prepared a different scenario for Russia; its milestones were his essays, *What is To Be Done?* (1902), *Imperialism* (1916), and *State and Revolution* (1918). Lenin telescoped the Marxian process of history, and endowed the revolutionary Communist Party with an active mission of hastening the arrival of Marx's inevitable future. Lenin argued that the capitalism that Marx knew had become transformed—into a more international and predatory form of *imperialism.* It was now a system of international monopolies and cartels which exported capital from highly developed industrial nations to the less developed ones in order to exploit cheaper raw material resources and labor and assure itself, through force when necessary, protected markets and sources of supply. The various segments of this system were viciously competitive. For Lenin this situation was conveniently highlighted by the great power rivalry (British, French, and German) in Africa and Asia toward the end of the century. Domination of the relatively backward colonial peoples abroad made it possible, Lenin argued, for the imperialists to keep up greater prosperity at home, and grant some concessions in the form of higher wages and better conditions to domestic workers, precisely because of more efficient exploitation of the peasants and miners in the underdeveloped areas. This accounted for a deceptive, temporary, and in any case very uneven, European prosperity. But Lenin held that the imperialist system was inherently unstable, that competition over the spoils, fueled by the desire to lower costs and increase profits, as well as to protect against the intrusions of other monopolists, would inevitably lead to power struggles and cataclysmic wars among the imperialists. In these wars, all the poor and working people would be the losers—as well as the "cannon fodder" of the imperialist armies. Thus, Lenin maintained that there was reason for a mutual alliance between all the workers and the peoples of the under-developed or colonial world against the exploitation and deception of imperialism. Having become a worldwide system, imperialism developed a worldwide vulnerability. The chain was likely to break in its weakest link, industrialized or not. The conflagration would spread. Capitalism, or imperialism as Lenin now called it, suffered from three incurable "contradictions": the conflict among the several imperialist blocs; the conflict between the imperialists and the working class; and finally, the conflict between the colonial peoples and the imperialists. After the Revolution, a fourth contradiction was added, between imperialism and the first state of workers and peasants: the USSR.

Lenin also argued, however, that given the uneven nature of modern capitalist (or imperialist) development, one could not expect workers, or other oppressed elements, spontaneously to appreciate the nature of their situation and to act on it. What was needed was a vanguard of skilled, knowledgeable, and professional revolutionaries. Such people, on the basis of their true understanding of Marxism, would be able to organize and lead the working class and its various potential allies to a revolutionary victory over imperialism. Left to themselves, Lenin argued, workers could only develop a "trade-union mentality" based on their immediate local conditions and circumstances. They might clamor for marginal improvements in terms of higher wages and shorter hours, but they would not by themselves realize the necessity of an all-out struggle against their imperialist masters. The role of leadership, which objective world circumstances dictated, could only be fulfilled by a Communist Party led by revolutionary experts, appropriately disciplined and highly organized for the task. Lenin sought to move the rank-and-file, not to be moved by them. This concept of the Party, as of the Revolution itself, was an élitist one. The Party would not wait upon history to happen; it would not wait for cues from any particular clientele or set of conditions. It would actively apply its Marxist knowledge and its leadership skills to build revolutionary consciousness among the masses and to strike at the appropriate hour.

IDEOLOGY AND REVOLUTIONARY POWER

Although Lenin envisioned a wide coalition of social forces potentially arrayed against imperialism, he maintained the Marxian "place of honor" for the working class as the leading and most revolutionary of all classes. Unlike peasants, craftsmen, and the petty bourgeoisie of the developing world, the workers were free of any attachment to property in the means of production and distribution. Moreover, their association with industry made them the technological leaders of the present and the future.

In his later writings, Lenin addressed the tasks of the revolution once it had succeeded in seizing power. What he sought to establish was a dictatorship of the proletariat, under the leadership of the Communist Party. On this point, he parted company with virtually every other Russian political leader, including the more moderate Social Democrats or Marxists, who sought to replace tsarist autocracy with some form of democratic regime. Lenin argued that the Party must lead the proletariat and the rest of the potentially revolutionary elements in society—in Russia mainly peasants and working intellectuals—toward four basic objectives. These objectives, which were to develop simultaneously, were: cooperation with other revolutionary elements in overthrowing imperialist-bourgeois rule throughout the whole world; an intensive effort at the economic and technological progress of backward Russian lands to create that indispensable abundance and vast reservoirs of proletarians, without which the Marxian vista of a classless society was impossible; to reeducate and uplift the masses, away from the heritage of feudalism, nationalism, religious "prejudices," and other traditional and bourgeois values, and toward a new social, cultural, and political consciousness of socialism and ultimately communism; and finally, to provide instruments of vigilance and repression to deal with, in Lenin's view, the inevitable attempts of world imperialism to "nip the Communist regime in the bud" by attack or subversion, and to fight ruthlessly against all the remnants of defeated social classes at home, noble or bourgeois, who sought to destroy the Red regime and who were often in natural "cahoots" with foreign imperialist powers and their agents. These objectives have been, and still are, of considerable significance for an appreciation of Soviet domestic and world policy.

BEGINNINGS OF SOVIET POWER

How did Lenin and his comrades succeed in imposing this rather complex and esoteric philosophy upon the great masses of the people of Russia? At a moment when the country lay exhausted from war and famine, Lenin offered the Russian people his tactical slogan of "Bread, Land and Peace." Where others felt qualms or hesitated to act on nationalistic-patriotic or constitutional "due-process" grounds, Lenin boldly promised the Russian peasant immediate relief from war, and the seizure and redistribution to the poor of the nobles' lands and granaries.

Lenin's program of 1917 almost certainly lessened the Russian people's resistance to the claims of the Bolsheviks. It also made them preferable to the so-called Whites, who wanted to continue the war against Germany "until victory" and who refused to redistribute the land, either altogether, or at least until authorized by a duly elected Constituent Assembly, with appropriate safeguards and compensation for those who would lose the land.

Yet, notwithstanding the probable attractiveness of Lenin's program to many of the people, the Communists could not muster a majority—even a plurality—for their cause. At the November 1917 election to a Constituent Assembly, Lenin's party, together with its leftist socialist revolutionary allies, polled only 25 percent of the vote. Almost 60 percent of the popular vote went to the more moderate agrarian Social Revolutionary Party, which espoused democratic methods and gradual reforms. Lenin's reaction to this popular rebuff was promptly to dissolve the Constituent Assembly, arrest many of the members, and suppress dissident political views as well as all other political parties.

An important advantage to Lenin's cause was the Russian people's relatively scant experience with self-government. Until the abortive revolution of 1905, no national parliament had ever existed in the Russian empire; what the tsar allowed after 1905—the so-called Duma—was a very weak parliamentary body with no real power to compel the government or the tsar to do its bidding. Censorship and police terror inhibited the development of lawful organizations, trade unions, and political parties. The Russian political tradition combined enormous political inertia of the illiterate peasant masses with sporadic outbursts of revolutionary violence, channeled into riots, strikes, and assassinations. Even though the Russian people clearly showed a preference for a democratic political order in the 1917 elections to the Constituent Assembly, their traditional attitudes, capabilities, and expectations helped those who sought to replace one type of autocracy with another.

COMPARING THE REVOLUTIONISTS

Here, we may usefully note some of the basic differences between the Russian and American revolutions. In the 13 American colonies, the revolution was directed against foreign rule and taxation—by King George III of Britain, by the British parliament (in which Americans had no representation), and by British royal governors and military commanders. It was not directed against the internal social and economic organization of the colonies; it was not a revolution on behalf of the poor against the rich. In fact, the American Revolution left undisturbed the institution of slavery, at least where it had existed before the War of Independence.

In Russia, however, the revolution was directed primarily against

Russian rulers and Russian privileged classes. Its basic thrust was not toward independence from abroad but rather toward redistribution of wealth and power at home. The distinction is not an absolute one, to be sure, because Lenin and the Communist Party always sought to identify their noble and bourgeois opponents with foreign imperialism. They argued that the overthrow of tsarism and the expropriation of the land and property of Russian landlords and capitalists would simultaneously free Russia from the web of imperialist financial and political influences. These were conveniently symbolized by French, British, and American bankers and diplomats who urged the Russians to keep up the apparently hopeless war against Germany for their own benefit. Later, the imperialist influences were symbolized by the detachments of foreign troops sent in support of the Whites.

In 1776, the American revolutionists, unlike the Russians, did not challenge such basic customs, values, and institutions as religion, property, law, social hierarchy, or even local political arrangements (legislative elections, modes of representation, roles of governors and mayors, and so on). Thus, it was possible for Edmund Burke to look upon the American Revolution as one fought not *against* but *on behalf* of the traditional rights of Englishmen—to self-government—rights which England itself denied to the Americans.

On the other hand, the Russian Communist revolutionists, more like the French Jacobins of 1789, sought drastic changes in the whole fabric of the society around them. They were not content to let the Russian *muzhik* (peasant) worship as he had for centuries; they were unwilling to tolerate the accumulation of property in the hands of peasants and merchants, let alone large landowners and manufacturers. They were opposed to traditional nationalistic loyalties, professing a world proletarian revolution as their goal and beacon. They advocated a sharp break with the past, not a more (or even completely) autonomous continuation of the society's course. The Leninist revolution was directed simultaneously against Russia's heritage of feudalism and the open possibilities of a democracy.

The abolition of tsardom in Russia, in the wake of the voluntary abdication of Tsar Nicholas II in April 1917, commanded overwhelming public support, as may be judged by the reactions of the various political parties at the time. Lenin's overthrow of the Kerensky regime,* however, and the dissolution of the Constituent Assembly, the suppression of opposition, the attacks on religion, and the reign of terror unleashed by the Bolsheviks in the ensuing Civil War were not consensual measures. They

* In October 1917 according to the Russian calendar, and November according to Western reckoning.

provoked deep hostility, bitterness, and division among the Russian people. Thus, Lenin's revolutionary regime was unlike George Washington's not so much in the degree of voluntary support it received (the loyalists and those indifferent to the American Revolution probably outnumbered the revolutionists for most of the 1775–1783 period), but in the suppression of differences among the revolutionaries as to the course that was to be pursued *after* the Revolution. Where Washington welcomed the free discussion of the nation's agenda, Lenin suppressed such discussion, drove the opposition underground and, in large numbers, liquidated it.

THE IMPACT OF WAR ON REVOLUTION

It is important to take note of the transnational aspects of the Russian Revolution—that is, the extent to which this was an event shaped by external forces and the reaction to such forces.

Even though it was the personal decision of the tsar to mobilize Russian armies that precipitated German declaration of war, the causes of Russian involvement in World War I were much more complex. To begin with, the assassination of Austria's Archduke Ferdinand in Sarajevo, Serbia, prompted "unacceptable" demands on Serbia by Austria. Thereupon, a network of far-flung treaty obligations came into effect. Germany rushed to the side of Austria-Hungary, Russia to the defense of Serbian sovereignty, and France and Britain to the aid of Russia. The bloody conflict between Germany and Russia, which exhausted Russia's resources, strained the social fabric beyond endurance, and meant the doom of the tsarist regime, was thus brought about by events far beyond the border of the Russian empire.

Naturally, while the war continued, substantial German forces were involved in the struggle against the Russians. If the battle against Russia could be concluded quickly, these German forces might be shifted to the West and conceivably enable Germany to defeat the French and the British. Alternatively, as long as the Germans were busy fighting the Russians in the East, France and Britain had a better chance to defeat Germany in the West, and certainly more cheaply in terms of lives and other costs to themselves. As a consequence of this basic international situation, the Western allies—France, Britain, and, after 1917, the United States—all urged the Russian government to continue to fight Germany, both before and after the tsar's abdication, even though the domestic consequences for Russia were clearly catastrophic and grimly foreboding. Inasmuch as Germany succeeded in capturing large chunks of Russia's territory, both the tsar and his successors, Lvov and Kerensky, were loath to negotiate a peace that would almost certainly leave Germany in possession of Russian lands. On the one hand, if the French and British won, all would be regained by Russia: if only it remained a faithful ally, that is. On the other hand, separate peace with Germany would compound treachery to the allies with the likelihood of enormous territorial losses.

It is interesting to speculate whether Germany could have achieved peace with the tsar, defeated the Western powers, and averted the Revolution by offering generous terms to Russia. Actually, though, Germany was interested in keeping its territorial acquisitions *and* in seeing Russia leave the war. Thus, in 1917 the German Imperial government facilitated and even subsidized the return of Lenin and some of his associates from their Swiss exile. Lenin, they hoped, would divert Russia from war to revolution. Ironically, the Bolshevik seizure of power came too late to help Imperial Germany win the war, even though Lenin did conclude peace with the Germans at Brest Litovsk in March 1918.[1]

REVOLUTION TRIUMPHANT

From 1921 until 1928, the victorious Communists figuratively took a breather. Beginning with the New Economic Policy (NEP) initiated by Lenin, the Party sought to restore a degree of normality to the economic life of the country, wrecked by years of war and revolution, with concessions to the peasantry and middle class private enterprise. Between 1924, when Lenin died, and 1929, Joseph Stalin (1879–1953) outmaneuvered other aspirants for Lenin's mantle. Utilizing the then obscure office of General Secretary of the CPSU, Stalin gradually eliminated all of Lenin's principal associates and consolidated preponderant and heretofore unprecedented power in his own hands. Coincidentally with his own victory over all the oppositional forces within the Party, Stalin terminated the "breather," and launched the CPSU into a headlong and thorough transformation of Russian society. He sought to industrialize the Soviet Union as rapidly as possible, changing the country from its rural-agrarian backwardness to urban-industrial modernity. He relied heavily upon coercion and terror both against those who opposed him (or even against those whom he thought merely *potential* opponents) within the Party and those in the society at large. Medium and small landholders as well as commercial and industrial entrepreneurs were ruthlessly destroyed financially, and, in millions of persons, physically as well. Those who were not killed or exiled to harsh labor camps were relatively fortunate.

Stalin's period of rule contributed basic terms to Soviet and communist

[1] See Donald G. Treadgold, *Twentieth Century Russia* (Chicago: Rand McNally, 1972). Also, W. H. Chamberlin, *The Russian Revolution, 1917–1921,* 2 vols. (New York: Macmillan, 1935).

political vocabulary. Those whom Stalin accused of appeasing popular demands and wanting to "ease up" on the revolutionary mission of the Party—like Nikolai Bukharin and Aleksei Rykov—were labeled "right-wing deviationists." Such people were "liquidated" in Stalin's time. Nowadays, the Chinese apply the label to Tito and, ironically, to the Russian leaders themselves, whom they see as bourgeois liquidators of revolutionary militancy in the USSR. Those whom Stalin accused of reckless adventurism—that is, those advocating more or faster change than what he was momentarily prepared to accept—were, like Leon Trotsky, Gregory Zinoviev, and Lev Kamenev, labeled "left-wing deviationists." They, too, suffered extermination. Ironically, the phrase currently used in the USSR to describe the deviation of being a die-hard Stalinist is "dogmatism."

Stalin's rule institutionalized fear in Soviet society. His ubiquitous secret police became unpredictable and without pity or scruple. By recent Soviet as well as Western accounts, Stalin trampled upon the rights of individuals and the principles of law and federal autonomy of the peoples of the USSR to which he had paid propagandistic lip service in his Constitution of 1936 (still in force in the USSR today).

Yet, though the costs were great, Stalin had managed to achieve spectacular goals of economic and social development as well as national power. During the course of the first two five-year plans (1928–1933, 1933–1938) the USSR became one of the great industrial nations of the world, capable of supporting a huge military establishment. This, Stalin argued, was indispensable for defending the USSR against imperialist enemies that surrounded it.[2]

THE "GREAT PATRIOTIC WAR" (1941–1945)

Notwithstanding all the Soviet preparations, and Stalin's apparent determination to "sit out" World War II as long as possible "letting the imperialists bleed each other to death," the Nazi attack on the USSR in June 1941 caught the Soviets by surprise. It took four years of devastating war, fought largely on Soviet territory, an all but unbelievable sacrifice of 20 million Soviet lives, and massive American aid, for the USSR ultimately to prevail over the Nazis. The epic struggle of 1941–1945 has come to be known in the Soviet Union as the Great Patriotic War. In the last year of the war, Soviet armies penetrated most of east central Europe, occupying Poland, Hungary, Czechoslovakia, Rumania, Bulgaria, and the eastern

[2] See Roy A. Medvedev, *Let History Judge: The Origins and Consequences of Stalinism* (New York: Alfred H. Knopf, 1971) and Robert Conquest, *The Great Terror* (New York: Macmillan, 1968). See also Aleksandr I. Solzhenitsyn, *Cancer Ward* (New York: Farrar, Straus and Giroux, 1969).

Monument to heroes of the Battle of Stalingrad, 1942–1943.
NOVOSTI from SOVFOTO

portion of Germany. In all these areas, communist regimes were set up under Soviet auspices.

The entire story of Soviet politics from 1953 to the present is substantially one of reform and modification of Stalin's regime of domestic and international domination: with more accommodationist policies toward the West; relaxation of controls over the East European satellites; loosening of police measures at home; and more allocations to consumer welfare, among others.

policy agenda: problems, cleavages, and conflicts

The Soviet Union is the world's third most populous state. Its nearly 250 million inhabitants place it behind China (with about 800 million people) and India (at over 500 million persons). The peoples of the USSR are a heterogeneous mix of nationalities, cultures, religions, and levels of development. The USSR is geographically the largest state in the world, encompassing about one-sixth of all the earth's land surface and virtually all its climate zones. In area, the USSR is two and one half times as large as the United States. The Soviet economy as a whole ranks second only to the United States in the total annual value of goods and services produced.

Naturally, one might expect that a society of such great size and complexity would have a very large agenda of problems occupying the public's attention. This impression may be reinforced because the Soviet Union is one of the most highly organized (or mobilized) societies in the world, and it possesses one of the largest and most developed communication and information networks in existence.

Since the Revolution of 1917, when the Soviet regime was established under the leadership of Lenin, the people of the USSR have become a nation of "joiners" in a great variety of political, social, cultural, professional, and trade organizations. Illiteracy has been virtually eliminated. Vast numbers of schools, training institutes, universities, libraries, museums, theaters, and cinemas have been constructed. Radio, television, newspapers and magazines have all achieved some of the world's highest circulation and diffusion figures.

The membership of the various Soviet mass organizations, some of it overlapping, considerably exceeds the total population. In 1917, there were only 1.5 million people belonging to trade unions, roughly one out of every hundred people. In 1966, there were 80 million persons in Soviet trade unions, or roughly one in three people for the whole population. In addition to the (then) 16 million Party members, there were 23 million members in its young people's apprentice branch, the Komsomol (those between ages 15 and 26); 19 million in the Pioneers (ages 10 to 15) and, finally, 12 million Young Octobrists, aged 7 to 10. Thirty-five million Soviet citizens belonged to various athletic organizations; 56 million belonged to the Red Cross and Red Crescent paramedical units; and over 40 million were members of the paramilitary DOSAFF—Voluntary Society to Aid the Army, Air Force and Naval Fleet.[3]

[3] Ellsworth Raymond, *The Soviet State* (New York: Macmillan, 1968), pp. 273–291.

Nevertheless, the agenda of legitimate public concerns in the USSR is a severely limited one largely because of the directing and coordinating role of the CPSU (the Communist Party of the Soviet Union). The CPSU consists of some 16 million persons, or just under 7 percent of the total population of the country. The Party's professional apparatus—that is, those persons who are full-time employees of the Party organization directed by the Party's central Secretariat in Moscow—are estimated to number only about 200,000.

Both by the terms of the Soviet Constitution of 1936 (especially Article 126) and the Statutes of the Party, the CPSU is invested with the leadership, not only of the entire government of the USSR, but of the whole society. This leadership is grounded in the Party's task of building a communist society, according to the tenets of Marxism-Leninism, the official doctrine of Party and State in the USSR since the Revolution.

The official vision of this "goal-society" is one of freedom, equality, and abundance for all. But the ideology also teaches that this society is to be achieved only through a long and hard struggle for massive economic and cultural development, and against the enemies of communism, both within and without the country. In practice, this means that the Party organization strongly controls the function of agenda setting in the USSR, which is its legally permissible concerns. Public media are carefully controlled and coordinated by officials of the CPSU. The information that is legally printed and aired in the USSR is subject to censorship and is an important part of the Party's programs to mold the attitudes of Soviet citizens. Facts and interpretations of events which are made available to the general public are very carefully screened by Soviet television, radio, newspapers, and other official communication networks.[4]

PUBLIC DISCUSSION OF ISSUES

One practical consequence of this is that the official media all tend to develop the same Party-directed themes with generally "upbeat" and bland interpretations of official policies. They screen out all criticisms of

[4] See Mark W. Hopkins, *Mass Media in The Soviet Union* (New York: Pegasus, 1970), pp. 236–264, and Harold Swayze, *Political Control of Literature in the USSR, 1946–1959* (Cambridge, Mass.: Harvard University Press, 1962); also Emily C. Brown, *Soviet Trade Unions and Labor Relations* (Cambridge, Mass.: Harvard University Press, 1966); Harvey Fireside, *Icon and Swastika: The Russian Orthodox Church Under Nazi and Soviet Control* (Cambridge, Mass.: Harvard University Press, 1970); Allen Kassof, *The Soviet Youth Program: Regimentation and Rebellion* (Cambridge, Mass.: Harvard University Press, 1965); Abraham Brumberg, ed., *In Quest of Justice: Protest and Dissent in the Soviet Union Today* (New York: Praeger, 1970); Zhores A. Medvedev, *The Medvedev Papers: The Plight of Soviet Science Today* (New York: St. Martins Press, 1971).

Party and Government leaders, and exhort the populace to the support of various programs and policies officially adopted by the regime, such as the latest five-year plan, or solidarity with the "just struggle of the Vietnamese people against U.S. imperialist aggressors," or of the "Arab peoples against Israeli-Zionist-U.S. aggressors." Even in the letters-to-the-editor columns of Soviet newspapers, one cannot find any expressions of opinion that dispute and challenge these official positions.

Occasionally, there appear articles even in the mass circulation media such as *Pravda* (central CPSU newspaper) and *Izvestia* (central government newspaper) deploring and condemning bureaucratic red tape; or shortcomings in the execution of the economic plan; or "hooliganism" among youths; or poor quality of consumer products. Generally, however, the news of bad accidents in industry and transportation and of national disasters, let alone strikes or prison riots, is withheld or minimized in these media—along with information and commentary about such symptoms of social malaise as alcoholism, suicides, divorces, dishonesty of Party officials, or favoritism toward and maltreatment of various segments of the public.

Thus, much of the criticism of social conditions in the USSR or of official policies appears in an oblique and indirect way: by implication occasionally in specialized journals such as the *Krasnaya Zvezda* (Red Star) of the Soviet armed forces; or the *Voprosy Ekonomiki* (Economic Problems) of academicians and technocrats; or *Trud* (Labor), the official organ of the trade unions; or it appears privately and illegally. The hand-typed publication, *samizdat,* circulated underground to perhaps 20 or 30 thousand Soviet intellectuals and clandestine oppositionists, illustrates the latter. In addition, some Soviet citizens, either the relatively few who travel abroad or those more numerous who may hear foreign broadcasts and read Western newspapers or magazines, do achieve exposure to some of those more negative facets of Soviet life which the regime chooses to ignore.

Still, many of the problems which seem to be acutely felt by millions of Soviet people in their private lives are almost never aired publicly. What we know about them is based on information supplied by foreign news media, gleaned by visitors to the USSR, and occasionally supplied by defectors. Let us examine some of the principal problems of Soviet politics in recent years.

ETHNIC CONFLICTS

One of the biggest problems in Soviet politics involves cultural, religious, and political freedoms as well as economic and social opportunities of non-Russian peoples in a Russian-ruled system.

A recent example, which dramatizes this larger and long-standing issue of Soviet politics is the effort by hundreds of thousands of Soviet Jews (out of an estimated population of 2.5 million) to emigrate. Subjected to cultural persecution and discrimination by the regime in jobs, housing, and education, many Jews have expressed the wish to leave the USSR, to go to Israel, the United States, or elsewhere. The regime has discouraged and opposed emigration. It has imposed enormous "exit fees" on Jewish professionals, such as scientists or engineers, arguing that the Soviet Union was giving up substantial educational investments in allowing them to leave. In 1975, Jewish sources outside the USSR estimated that as many as 130,000 Soviet citizens of Jewish descent were prepared to leave the Soviet Union immediately if granted exit visas by the Soviet government. In 1971, 1972, and 1973 considerable numbers of Jews were allowed to leave. During this period, the Soviet government was pursuing favorable credit terms for expanded trade with the United States and importation of advanced U.S. technology. For at least three years, the Soviet government appeared at least partially responsive to pressures by U.S. officials and public opinion. In 1974, coincident with the passage by the U.S. Congress of the Jackson amendment to the U.S.–Soviet trade

A demonstration of Soviet Jews protesting the government's denial of exit visas for Israel.
UPI Photo

pact,* with terms the Soviet government did not like, the Soviets reverted strongly to past policies. Jewish emigration ground to a trickle. Drastic reprisals against Jews expressing the desire to emigrate were intensified; they were frequently fired from their jobs and sometimes imprisoned for "parasitism" because of their joblessness.[5]

In the case of Jews, the problem of language and culture has been intertwined with religion. Not only has the regime banned virtually all Jewish (Yiddish or Hebrew) language publications and schools; it has closed down synagogues and prohibited Jews from running religious seminaries, which would enable them to maintain cultural-religious existence. Stymied in their aspiration to leave the USSR, Jews have been subjected to discriminatory quotas in and exclusions from certain types of employment and education.

According to the latest Soviet census, nearly half of the 246 million people in the Soviet Union are non-Russian. The largest "minority" component are the Ukrainians, inhabiting most of the southwestern reaches of the USSR and numbering more than 45 million people. In addition, there are more than 30 other major ethnic groups, which by 1980 may well constitute a *majority* of the total population. Indirectly, the Party admits the existence of a problem in this area by occasionally condemning what it calls "bourgeois nationalism" or "chauvinism." The line it has taken since Lenin's time has been that all nationality groups in the USSR —Ukrainians, Byelorussians, Estonians, Latvians, Lithuanians, Georgians, Jews, Tatars, Tadjiks, and others—are entitled to cultivate their particular languages and cultures. But they may do so only within the context of a larger and more important interest—maintaining and strengthening the dictatorship of the proletariat in the USSR under the leadership of the CPSU. Another way of stating this position, from the Marxist-Leninist point of view, is that national considerations must always be subordinated to class considerations. According to Lenin, and other CPSU leaders, class solidarity must prevail over national solidarity.

Within this general framework of values, Party leaders used to attack and deplore the oppression of non-Russian peoples under the tsars, while at the same time insisting that, in the eventual communist future, people would naturally get over their basically infantile national identifications. In the classless society of the future, national particularisms would be dissolved and effectively lost. Meantime, they argued, there ought to be

---

* Formally conditioning trade exchanges on Soviet permission for Jews to emigrate freely from the USSR.

[5] See Lionel Kochan, ed., *The Jews in Soviet Russia Since 1917* (New York: Oxford University Press, 1970); Salo W. Baron, *The Russian Jew Under Tsars and Soviets* (New York: Macmillan, 1968); and Robert Conquest, *The Nation Killers: The Soviet Deportation of Nationalities* (New York: Macmillan, 1970).

freedom for people to express and cultivate their ethnic personalities provided that this did not interfere with the higher interests of the proletarian revolution; in some cases, it might even be helpful, if the Party could harness the wrath of indigenous nationalists against their imperialist masters.

The Gap Between Claims and Achievements   Ironically, the Party managed to secure some very significant gains for the non-Russian peoples as compared with what they had enjoyed under the tsars. But it has fallen short, almost necessarily, of meeting some of their most basic demands. These demands include, in part, complete independence of Russia, full equality, genuine autonomy, and unrestricted pursuit of their cultural, linguistic, spiritual, as well as social and economic, identities within the framework of the USSR.

The ethnic achievements of the regime are evident in the extension of native-language schools, from kindergarten through university levels, for virtually all of the so-called territorial minorities in the USSR—that is, those historically clustered in particular geographic regions. Another important area of achievement has been recruitment of minorities into important government, administrative, economic, and cultural positions in their regions and, to some extent, throughout the USSR as a whole. In both areas one can argue considerable, even striking, improvement over the record of the blindly repressive and autocratic rule of the tsars.

Illustratively, of the 14 Soviet republics outside Russia itself, only two—the Ukraine and Georgia—possessed institutions of higher learning under the tsarist regime. Already by 1927, all but four possessed such institutions. In 1966, the record was as follows:

Ukraine	132	Lithuania	11
Byelorussia	27	Latvia	10
Uzbekistan	32	Estonia	6
Kazakhstan	39	Moldavia	7
Georgia	18	Tadzhikstan	7
Armenia	11	Kirgizstan	8
Azerbaidzhan	11	Turkestan	5

Yet, because of both the numbers of people involved and their claims, the USSR faces a far more serious problem in its ethnic relations than, for example, does the United States. Between the two world wars, the three Soviet Baltic republics—Estonia, Latvia, and Lithuania—were actually three separate, fully independent states. In 1940 Soviet armies invaded and seized these countries. When Hitler attacked the Soviet Union in

1941, the three states were overrun by the Nazi armies and then reconquered by the Soviets in 1944–1945. It is thus very difficult for the USSR to quash the living traditions of independence in these areas merely by allowing the people to use their native language in schools and in local media. Such a concession may actually do no more than help keep alive the spirit of Baltic nationalism. Similar aspirations—to sovereign statehood—have long persisted in the Ukraine and Caucasus (Georgia and Armenia) and in other parts of the USSR. Since some of the territories now comprising the Soviet Union were seized from other states at the end of World War II (from Poland, Rumania, Czechoslovakia, Finland, and Germany), there is also the problem of some continuing allegiances to other states.

Finally, much may be said about the essentially unsatisfactory nature of Soviet response to those ethnic groups in the USSR whose claims cannot be classified either as "independence" or as "ultramontanism," and about official persecution of minorities on the suspicions of disloyalty and separatism. In Stalin's time, in fact, numerous minorities were subjected to such mass mistreatment—executions, confiscations, deportations—that in some cases it approached genocidal extermination. More recently, persecution and discrimination have taken more subtle forms. One example has been Russification—that is, the favored use of the Russian language and culture as being the official language and the common culture of all the Soviet people, and particularly of the federal, all-Soviet agencies of the USSR. Another has been confinement of minority-ethnic schools to areas largely inhabited by those particular groups. As a result, a Ukrainian or Byelorussian who moves to another part of the USSR, say Moscow or Leningrad, is no longer able to send his children to a school in which instruction is given in his native language, and in which his culture can be preserved. Participation in ethnic cultural activities has been generally circumscribed and suspect.

Minorities have been subjected to discriminatory treatment in the distribution of career or educational opportunities, rewards, jobs, honors and perquisites in the Soviet Union. With about 55 percent of the population in the late 1960's, Russians accounted for 62 percent of the socially and economically favored intelligentsia. According to data gathered in 1959 there were three Russians for every Ukrainian but four Russians with higher education for every Ukrainian, and six Russian scientists for every Ukrainian scientist. Similarly, there were 14 Russians for every Byelorussian, but more than 40 Russian scientists for every Byelorussian one. Only Jews, Georgians, and Armenians, out of 16 major non-Russian nationalities, had a higher share of the intelligentsia than their share in the population. And Jews were being steadily whittled down in Soviet institutions of higher learning.

Most ethnic minority groups have been significantly underrepresented in the apparatus of the Party. At the Central Committee level of Party leadership, the Russians have at times had representation close to the 80 percent figure.[6] While no recent figures are available, a historical tabulation of Politburo members shows that 51 of 86 persons who have served on that body from 1917 to 1967 were Russian—that is, slightly under 60 percent.

Trends and Implications   In recent years, there has been a moderate tendency to open up the CPSU to more minority representation. Still, in the mid 1970's, the Soviet regime was singularly vulnerable to the charge that the Great Russians, with a little "tokenism" here and there, were ruling and exploiting a vast non-Russian empire. Thus, there are at least two major struggles involving minorities in the USSR: one is for greater equity in the distribution of values, including greater freedom and autonomy, within the system; and another, deeper, underlying struggle is for complete independence from it by a number of peoples. It is difficult to judge the magnitude of the forces behind these diverse aspirations, largely because of censorship and persecution. But, by all indications, they are historically and currently very considerable. The problem they present for the Party may be stated in terms of a dilemma. To grant independence to all those who want it would without any doubt greatly weaken the industrial-military power of the USSR. Should the Ukraine and Caucasus with their vast resources of energy, food, raw materials, population, and highly developed technology be lost to Russia, the remnant of any remaining Soviet or Russian state might well decline to the level of a middle-rank power. Not granting this demand, however, implies indefinite continuation of serious internal tensions and requires the maintenance of a large, expensive, and unpopular machinery of coercion that includes the secret police, rigid censorship, and the like. More realistic options for the Party lie in the area of the lesser concessions: more autonomy and greater equity in resource distributions to the minorities. Demands in this direction could be expected, tacitly at least, even from within the CPSU itself—its minority segments, that is. The problem with such concessions, however, is that they arouse fear that agreeing to more

[6] See Vernon V. Aspaturian, "The Soviet Union," in R. C. Macridis and R. Ward, eds., *Modern Political Systems: Europe*, 2nd ed. (Englewood Cliffs, N.J.: Prentice-Hall, 1968), pp. 560–562; and John S. Reshetar, Jr., *The Soviet Polity* (New York: Dodd, Mead, 1971), pp. 170–172.

of the seemingly innocuous claims—more freedom, more schools, more native-language publications, more autonomy—may strengthen the "sinister," unacceptable claims (from the CPSU point of view), rather than weaken or erode them. Concessions may have the benefit of reducing social tensions and the costs of control, but they are not without dangers.

US/USSR Parallels? There are some similarities in the Soviet and American "minority problems." In both cases, there has been some progress for many of those who, for centuries, have lived as the "disinherited." In the United States such groups include the American Indians, Blacks, Chicanos, and Asians. In both cases, there is reason to believe that recent progress has led to further demands by minority groups on their political systems. Perhaps partial equality is better than no equality, or slavery, but full equality for such groups still lies ahead and is increasingly demanded in the United States as in the USSR. Yet, the official treatment of Jews and certain other groups (Volga Germans and Tatars in World War II, for example) under the Soviet regime has markedly deteriorated since Lenin's time. And the problems of irredentism (that is, the desire to regain lost territory) and separatism have been much more serious in the Soviet Union than they have been in the United States.

CIVIL RIGHTS AND POLICE RULE

Another important problem has been the struggle for civil rights on the part of people seeking greater freedom and security of self-expression in the arts, sciences, literature, and history, as well as in their daily lives. This struggle has centered on the abolition of the remaining legacies of the Stalinist police terror of the 1930's, 1940's and early 1950's. During that period, often without apparent cause, people were widely subjected to massive, arbitrary imprisonment, violence and death by the secret police.

In Stalin's day, it was estimated that one out of every two families in the USSR had had some relative either executed or in prison. As late as 1953, more than 6 million people out of 190 million were believed held in Soviet camps and prisons. (There were only about 200,000 prisoners in all the prisons in the United States in a population in the late 1960's of over 200 million.) Stalin used stark terror to change the character of Soviet society quickly and against the wishes of millions of people.[7] Collectivization was such a process: from nearly zero to about 95 percent

[7] Cf. Raymond, *The Soviet State*, p. 264; See also Simon Wolin and Robert M. Slusser, eds., *The Soviet Secret Police* (New York: Praeger, 1957); Alexander Dallin and G. Breslauer, *Political Terror in Communist Systems* (Stanford: Stanford University Press, 1970); Ronald Hingley, *The Russian Secret Police: Muscovite, Imperial Russian and Soviet Political Security, 1565–1970* (London: Hutchinson, 1970).

of the land was collectivized in a period of about six years (1929 to 1935) in a country where 78 percent of the population were peasants.

In the course of all these traumatic upheavals the secret police—progressing under different names from the GPU, NKVD, MVD, and, today, KGB—grew, in effect, to a multibillion dollar bureaucracy, administering a vast network of camps, prisons, intelligence networks, military installations, and surveillance units. The secret police also developed into a powerful political interest group—with a vested interest in maintaining the huge apparatus of "vigilance and deterrence" that it had acquired. In the late sixties, the bureaucracy of the KGB together with various police auxiliaries was still estimated at about 2 million persons.

After Stalin's death, Lavrenti Beria, NKVD leader, is widely believed to have attempted a seizure of power as Stalin's successor. His execution (briefly announced post facto) signaled a decline for the secret police, but hardly its demise. It continues to be an important component of the Soviet political system, supportive of tough measures at home and wary of any relaxation of tensions abroad. Such relaxations, after all, could rob the KGB of its "raison d'être." Interestingly, and ominously perhaps, only twice in the history of the USSR has the chief of the secret police sat on the top policy-making body of the CPSU: Lavrenti Beria was a member of the Politburo from 1946 until his "liquidation" in 1954; and currently, Yuri Andropov has been a member since 1972. He is joined there by Marshal Andrei Grechko, the first representative of the Army since Zhukov in 1957, and a likely spokesman for Russia's equivalent of the Pentagon.

Yet, over the years Soviet society has also greatly changed and in many respects stabilized. It is difficult to argue for continuing terror when the Kulaks and other more or less obvious "class enemies" have been eliminated, and the revolutionary regime has endured almost sixty years.* The Soviet population is now made up of more relatively well-educated managerial and technocratic elements, who are more likely to resent, some believe, and perhaps more effectively oppose, heavy-handed police controls.

Since Khrushchev's time there has been an abatement in the power exercised by the secret police, and growing efforts to strengthen the status of the regular courts with their somewhat greater due process. Soviet intellectuals, historians, and writers were temporarily emboldened by Khrushchev's policy of de-Stalinization in the late 1950's and early 1960's. At the CPSU's 20th Congress in 1956, Khrushchev had denounced

* Between 1928 and 1936 several million peasant proprietors and their families are believed to have been killed, resisting collectivization or in the process of Siberian expulsion.

Stalin as a paranoic tyrant who had isolated and abused the ideals of communism. Some of Stalin's deeds—particularly the murder of many innocent persons and capriciously autocratic methods of rule—were exposed and denounced. In 1958 Khrushchev permitted the publication in the USSR of a book by Aleksandr Solzhenitsyn, *A Day in The Life of Ivan Denisovich,* which was an exposé of Stalinist prison camps. Soon quite a few Soviet writers, academics, and Stalin's erstwhile generals, began to write critical accounts of various periods of the Soviet regime.

But this permissiveness soon gave way to renewed repressions, which became enhanced under the 1964 Brezhnev-Kosygin regime. In 1966, a critical Soviet writer, Valeri Tarsis, was stripped of his Soviet citizenship while visiting Britain. Two other writers, Andrei Sinyavsky and Yuli Daniel, were sentenced to long prison terms for works published abroad, as was Andrei Amalrik, author of *Will The Soviet Union Survive 1984?* The protests of Westerners and some distinguished Soviet intellectuals, such as physicist Andrei Sakharov, proved to no avail.* In 1974 the expulsion of Solzhenitsyn dramatized the turn to repression. The regime seemed to be acting on the principle that even a little freedom might be dangerous. And, above all, the frank disclosure and criticism of the past seemed too full of foreboding for the present and the future.

Implications of More Freedom   The hard-line CPSU conservatives may see relaxation of controls as a prelude to the disintegration of Party rule in the Soviet State. To loosen or erode the secret police apparatus might embolden various dormant opposition forces within the society, and destroy the restraints induced by fear. The opposite course, however, might promote greater initiative on the part of people, particularly administrators and intellectuals, who could be made to work more creatively, more freely and independently because they would be less fearful of the consequences of offending ideological orthodoxy. In this view, relaxation of police controls is part of the price of continuing economic and technological progress.

This also relates to the Party's policy toward science, long restrained by Marxist-Leninist dogmas. Currently—in sociology, for example—efforts are being made to use research survey methods to improve information relating to labor productivity, consumer preferences, and even other potentially more "delicate" questions. One of the difficulties for the Party conservatives has been the uncomfortable possibility that people

---

* The protests of Soviet intellectuals are generally contained in letters addressed to the Soviet leadership with copies shown to Western newsmen. They are never made public in the USSR.

may be discovered to be thinking not what they are supposed to be thinking. This is one of the dangers of survey research. Are Soviet workers really more dedicated to proletarian solidarity or, perchance, to some particularistic bourgeois chauvinism? Are Soviet farmers restive or accepting of life in collective agriculture? Obviously, free inquiry has its risks for the maintenance of dogmatic beliefs even if it improves the nature of information available to the CPSU.

In Stalin's day, the biologist Lysenko argued that it was feasible to change hereditary qualities of plants by environmental adaptations. Stalin regarded this view as singularly Marxist, and in consequence Lysenko "ruled the roost" for quite a few years in Soviet biology. No one could question the Lysenko position without being branded a "bourgeois deviationist," with high risk not only of being fired but of being jailed as well.

Since Soviet leaders generally regard Marxism-Leninism as a universal doctrine—relevant for science and nature as much as for society—its heavy-handed application to such fields as physics, chemistry, biology, astronomy, as well as economics or sociology, could obviously have important adverse consequences for the development of Soviet scientific disciplines, at a time when science and technology are increasingly important.

AGRICULTURE

There has also been the persistent "bottleneck" of Soviet agriculture, the underutilization of land, which causes chronic undersupply of foodstuffs (particularly proteins, fruits, and vegetables) to the Soviet consumer. This problem is related to the rigidity and ineffectiveness of central planning and lack of local autonomy, as well as lack of adequate incentives for people engaged in the production and distribution of goods and services. In the case of agriculture, the difficulties have been often attributed (by Western observers) to the collectivization of land by the Soviets. In the USSR, however, such speculation is publicly "taboo."

The Soviet agricultural system as a whole is relatively backward. It suffers from low productivity and is notoriously unable to provide adequate food supplies for the Soviet people. Nearly 30 percent of the population is involved in farming—a considerably larger share than in most industrial nations of the world. In part, this situation results from the legacy of past policies. Stalinist collectivization, with its ruthless attack on the landholding peasant, resulted in such enormous destruction of livestock and other agricultural capital that the damage has never really been fully undone. Moreover, Stalin's investment policy grossly favored industry over agriculture. The legacy of Stalinism is reflected today in the Soviet people's low protein diets and in the continual need to import foodstuffs from other countries, as in the 1972 $2 billion grain purchase from the United States.

Apart from the irrevocable legacy of the past, however, all current output indicators show that the most productive sector of Soviet agriculture is the very marginal private sector. It is the tiny, private plots and small herds of private livestock cultivated by individual farmers that account for an amazingly disproportionate share of the food available in the USSR. By some estimates, Soviet farmers derive about half of their income from what they can raise and sell out of such small plots (an acre at most) which the state allows them to keep. These tiny plots, amounting to less than 3 percent of all cultivated soil in the USSR, produce almost 50 percent of Soviet potatoes, vegetables, meat, and eggs. Thus, food is raised very effectively by individuals for their own private use and profit in the USSR. However, the large public farms—state and collective— even though benefiting from official aids in the form of tractors, machinery, fertilizers, transport, and so forth, have been extremely unproductive.

Implications of Change In strictly economic terms—that is, to provide the most food at the lowest cost to the Soviet people—it would seem that the encouragement of private farming is all but imperative. But the ideology of the CPSU cannot be readily reconciled with such a change in official policy. Private ownership and production are seen as classically bourgeois institutions, the very antithesis of communism and socialism. If the Party agreed to the expansion of private farming, it would be turning its back on the heralded achievements of collectivization: the public, communal and cooperative cultivation of land. It would be retreating to capitalist institutions and confessing the failure of socialism. Moreover, the change would restore the private cultivator—the landholding class enemy—to a position of importance in economic life and, by Marxist logic, clearly and ultimately in political life as well. It would mean shifting at least part of the control over the economy from Party leaders and bureaucrats, as under the present system, to the private judgments and decisions of profit-seeking land entrepreneurs.

If on these grounds one can appreciate the reluctance of the CPSU to adopt economically desirable changes in agricultural policy, it is nonetheless evident that the failure has its costs—to society and to the Party itself. Famines, queues, shortages, and the embarrassing need for imports from presumably decadent and hostile foreign states do not make the Party popular. Such developments maintain an element of dissatisfaction and tension throughout the society, which the CPSU must constantly counteract. Moreover, they make the USSR, ironically, vulnerable in a strategic-military sense. A nation controlling one-sixth of the world's land surface and one of the two largest military establishments on the face of the globe cannot assure itself the security of adequate food supplies against the exigencies of occasional drought, crop failure, and, conceivably, the refusal by potential foreign suppliers to sell.

One of the current conflicts in Soviet politics—on a much lesser scale than the choice between "collectivism" and "private enterprise"—relates to the scale of investments by the CPSU in agriculture. For many years, under Stalin, heavy industry so dominated Soviet investment policy that the land—even the collectivized farms—received relatively little by way of machinery, fertilizers, building supplies, transport, tools, and the like.

Interestingly enough, immediately after Stalin's death, his successor as Premier, Georgi Malenkov, advocated more generous allocations to agriculture; Party First Secretary Khrushchev opposed them. After Malenkov's ouster in 1956, Khrushchev changed his course and sided with those party leaders and state bureaucrats who favored more liberal investments in agriculture and consumer goods generally. The general direction of this policy has been maintained by the Brezhnev regime since 1964. Nevertheless, most "kremlinologists" agree that this allocative issue continues to be a source of conflict among the top leadership of the Party and the state.

Heretofore, the CPSU leadership has looked upon substantial concessions to popular pressure in these areas as "right-deviationism" (associated in the 1930's with the purged Nikolai Bukharin). Those resisting pressures for concessions to popular demands, even if and to the extent that the CPSU leadership grants them, are usually labeled "dogmatists" or "left-deviationists," an appellation that was once reserved for Zinoviev, Kamenev, and Trotsky. In Western parlance, the seemingly more responsive, pragmatic, and reform-minded leaders of the CPSU are generally referred to as "liberals." Those who adhere to the Stalinist legacies of policy and are suspicious of change are usually termed "conservative." [8]

CONSUMER PRODUCTION

Another conflict involving a liberal-conservative cleavage in the Party is the struggle over the management of industry and the supply of consumer products. Historically, the CPSU, under Stalin's leadership in the 1930's, 1940's, and 1950's, opted for centralized Party control at the top enforced through rigid national plans. Production goals had been set

[8] On all these themes, see Roy D. Laird and Betty A. Laird, *Soviet Communism and Agrarian Revolution* (Baltimore: Penguin Books, 1970); and R. D. Laird and E. L. Crowley, eds., *Soviet Agriculture: The Permanent Crisis* (New York: Praeger, 1965).

mainly on quantitative considerations according to the priorities of the CPSU leaders. Consumer choice, let alone sovereignty, in terms of producing what people will buy, and not producing what they will not buy, was explicitly rejected. The central planners would decide—typically, for every segment of five years—what the Soviet people would get by way of industrial products: what kinds of things and how much, or how many of them. If people did not like what they were offered through the state retail stores, this had virtually no significance for the industrial managers of the USSR. All they had to worry about was the fulfillment, and preferably even overfulfillment, of the quotas assigned to them by the Party's economic plan. This policy resulted in the frequent production of some things which no one really needed or wanted; in the disregard of quality, assortments, and general appeal of products; and in the failure to manufacture and distribute many things which people really needed and demanded. It caused considerable unhappiness, grumbling, and frustration among Soviet consumers.

A truly radical remedy for all this might be a market-oriented system of supply and demand. Not a central plan, but the volume of sales and other tangible indications of consumer demand at different times and places would dictate what and how much would be actually produced. Again, however, such a system would shift power of economic decisions away from the Party leaders and bureaucrats to the millions of consumers. It would also certainly divert energies away from the Party's cherished ideal of progress toward various grand economic goals, above all progress in heavy industry, and channel them toward an unpredictable, helter-skelter, consumer free-for-all.

Trends of Change Yet, the failure to make any response to consumer demand is certain to maintain both wasteful use of resources and deep popular dissatisfaction. The Party might not want to give up power, or even its ideological orientation, but it would clearly prefer to minimize frictions in the political system, increase its support, and also benefit by better returns on the large investments made in industry and trade. If, for example, labor productivity could be increased by the more adequate satisfaction of workers' consumer needs, the Party would stand to profit both economically and politically.

It is these considerations which have led to the adoption of a "modified centralism" under the Brezhnev-Kosygin regime. The Party planners still decide, on a nationwide basis, how much is to be allocated to the different economic sectors; but now the industrial managers are rewarded, in part, by how well their products sell in the state's distribution centers and how good they are qualitatively. This introduces an element of competition among production units, not just on how much they can turn out but how successfully they can sell it. The factory whose bicycles sell better will get bigger bonuses for its employees than one whose bicycles don't sell, or require more repairs.[9] What is at stake is the achievement of greater economic efficiency and productivity, with improved provision of consumer amenities, including more and better housing, appliances, clothing, and services available to people in publicly-run stores and establishments.

THE SOVIET STATE

Another issue is power in the state itself and how it might change. In the Soviet Union, this issue is faced only obliquely in Party, press, and media discussions prevalent since Khrushchev's day about the need to "observe Leninist norms of public life" and "overcome the harmful consequences of the cult of personality." Such terms generally refer to Stalin's high-handed dictatorship and imply a repudiation of it by subsequent leadership. But a vigorous debate has gone on (openly) in the West and possibly behind the scenes in the USSR on just how and to what extent the Soviet regime has been changing and what its future direction may be.

Until Stalin's demise, the Soviet system was generally interpreted in the Western world as an extreme form of dictatorship, or *totalitarianism*. The characteristics of such a system were said to consist of (1) a supreme leader; (2) a political mass movement headed by the leader; (3) an official ideology, sanctioning both the leader and the movement, and espousing their all-important joint "mission" on behalf of the whole society and even mankind; (4) a system of police and propaganda controls; (5) a monopoly of armed force by the leader and the movement; (6) an analogously monopolistic control of the economy.[10]

In the aftermath of Stalin's death, several leaders fought for Stalin's power and control of policy: Khrushchev, Malenkov, Beria, Molotov, Kaganovich, Bulganin, and others, until at least 1957 when Khrushchev appeared to consolidate the reins in his own hands. The losers in the power struggle against Khrushchev (except for Beria) did not lose their lives. The new Party line emphasized greater sharing of responsibility in Soviet decision-making and greater responsiveness to popular needs and wishes. When Khrushchev himself was ousted by Brezhnev in 1964, he, too, was allowed to live out his life in obscure retirement. In the post-Stalin years, police terror was visibly relaxed, and there was an increase

[9] See G. R. Feiwel, *The Soviet Quest for Economic Efficiency: Issues, Controversies and Reforms* (New York: Praeger, 1967); H. J. Sherman, *The Soviet Economy* (Boston: Little, Brown, 1969); and Janet G. Chapman, *Real Wages in Soviet Russia Since 1928* (Cambridge, Mass.: Harvard University Press, 1963).

[10] As presented by Carl J. Friedrich and Z. K. Brzezinski, *Totalitarian Dictatorship and Autocracy* (Cambridge: Harvard University Press, 1956).

both in the consumer amenities available to the people, and in the degree of freedom of expression in the arts and sciences, and particularly in the fields of history and literature.

These changes seemed to call for a reexamination of what the Soviet regime was and where it was headed. The picture of Stalin's totalitarianism did not seem to fit anymore. Was the Soviet Union currently an oligarchy rather than an autocracy? Was the Soviet system becoming more responsive and less coercive? More pragmatic than ideological in nature and direction? Would secret police rule and ideological conformity be gradually replaced by bargaining, accommodation, and consensus among the various bureaucratic hierarchies of the Soviet state? Would there be an eventual democratization of the regime analogous to the situations of the economically developed Western countries? [11] These issues not only preoccupied Western analysts of Soviet affairs, but they have also been of great concern to Marxist theoreticians inside the USSR and elsewhere, and, indirectly at least, to millions of Soviet citizens and people in all parts of the world.

What does "Marxism" demand of the Party and the Soviet government by way of organizing and controlling decision-making power? As seen by Karl Marx? As seen by V. I. Lenin? By both? Is the USSR, as it has historically evolved, a corruption of the Marxist (and even perhaps Leninist) ideal? Or is it, as the Party officially proclaims, a triumphant fulfillment of the Marxian ideals? To what extent, for example, should a Marxist party be controlled by the workers and be open to the demands of the masses? To what extent can it legitimately delay the abolition of the state itself and sanction widespread inequality? These issues are of great concern not only to theorists but to ordinary Soviet citizens. They relate to the personal freedoms, security, and amenities that people may enjoy.

One practical concern for top decision-makers as well as the rank-and-file in the USSR has been the question of succession. Thus far, the Soviet system has not provided for a routine transfer of power. Great uncertainty and conspiracy still accompany such transitions, with traumatic consequences for losers and bystanders—even if heads no longer roll quite as they did in Stalin's day.[12]

Much of the conflict over power in the Soviet state involves the role of

[11] Useful summaries of divergent views are contained in Chalmers Johnson, ed., *Change in Communist Systems* (Stanford: Stanford University Press, 1970); Roger Kanet, ed., *The Behavioral Revolution and Communist Studies* (New York: Free Press, 1970); Allen Kassof, ed., *Prospect for Soviet Society* (New York: Praeger, 1968); and Leonard J. Cohen and Jane P. Shapiro, eds., *Communist Systems in Comparative Perspective* (Garden City, N.Y.: Doubleday, Anchor Books, 1974).
[12] See Myron Rush, *Political Succession in the USSR* (New York: Columbia University Press, 1965).

the new technocracy—the large stratum of managers, technicians, administrators, scientists, and engineers. These people are becoming increasingly important in the Soviet's expanding, modernizing economy. Will they remain—indeed, are they today—docile instruments in the hands of the Party bureaucracy? Is it likely that over a period of time they may challenge the ideologues of the Party for leadership from new positions of power—the dominance of technology and industry and services?

REDISTRIBUTION OF RESOURCES

A significant area of contested policy in the USSR—notwithstanding the official protestations of class harmony and end of exploitation—is social redistribution of resources, which involves the regulation of status and perquisites of different classes of people in Soviet society. When in 1958 Khrushchev introduced wide-ranging school reforms, the purpose was to redress the balance between a predominant and favored intelligentsia on the one hand, and the children of workers and peasants for whom ostensibly the Revolution had been fought, and whom the CPSU supposedly represents, on the other.

Clearly, the reality of Soviet life and the ideology have seriously diverged on this point. The CPSU today is predominantly a middle-class organization, in terms of status, income, and education generally associated with "middle-classness" in the West. And it is particularly so the higher one moves in the Party pyramid.

The CPSU is only in its minority made up of blue collar workers. Least of all is it representative of the peasantry. The regime as a whole has never quite gotten over its suspicion of the peasant with his bourgeois, love-of-the-land attitude. Until 1965, the farm population was not even included in the coverage of Soviet social security and old age pensions established for workers and intellectuals. Agricultural employees were left to the charity of the particular farms on which they happened to have spent their years of productive labor. In most cases, where the collective farms were quite poor, this meant lives of hardship and penury in the farmers' old age. The 1965 reforms improved the pension system for farmers by including them, but the level of benefits has not yet been equalized between them and other nonagricultural employees.

The most important distinction between the privileged middle class of the USSR and the other strata is not ownership of the means of production and distribution: it is use and control. There is use of all the perquisites of affluence for some people—private automobiles, private villas, expensive clothes, foreign holidays, and even jewelry (Brezhnev-style, for example). Control relates to official power to make decisions affecting and manipulating the lives of other people, and all the pomp and pride associated with that kind of status. It also appears that the Soviet's class system, based on use and control, has an element of inheritance in it. Those who achieve high status and power in Soviet society tend to pass them on to their children. As is clear from occasional references in the Soviet press, the privileged use influence on behalf of one another to gain university admissions, preferred positions, and other favors for their children, relatives, and friends.

In 1917, the still minuscule CPSU was made up of 61.7 percent workers; 4.7 percent peasants, and 33.6 percent "intelligentsia," or persons with higher education. In 1920, the Party expanded from 23.6 thousand to more than 600 thousand members. Its worker component declined to 33.2 percent; the peasants, whom Lenin counted as allies in the Revolution against the "Whites," rose to an all-time high of 36.9 percent, while the intelligentsia declined to 22.1.

By 1932, the Party was vastly enlarged, to about 3.2 million members. Stalin had driven the peasant membership down to 27.8 percent and reduced the intelligentsia to just 7.7 percent. The workers constituted an all-time high of 64.5 percent. In the intervening twenty-odd years, with the impact of Soviet economic growth, the CPSU's composition drastically shifted. The 1956 census showed a clear majority of its 7.1 million members (50.9 percent) to be the intelligentsia *; the peasantry declined to 17.1 percent and workers to 32 percent. And the CPSU, through all successive membership increases, has basically adhered to the 1956 profile. The intelligentsia has constituted close to half the membership, workers only a little more than a third, and the peasantry about one-sixth. Taking official Soviet population figures as a whole, however, the intelligentsia constituted only 24.3 percent of the people; peasants 28 percent and workers 47.7 percent, respectively.

Yet although the role of the intelligentsia has been preponderant in the Party as a whole, it is more so in the upper rungs of its power mechanisms. Thus, it represented 65.7 percent of the delegates to the Twenty-third CPSU Congress in 1966, while peasants and workers acounted for 11.2 percent and 23 percent, respectively. The Central Committee elected by that Congress included only 4 percent of persons *outside* the intelligentsia. Neither workers nor peasants had any representation at all in the Politburo or the Secretariat.[13]

* Those with university and higher technical training.
[13] *Partiinaya Zhizn*, No. 7, April 1967, pp. 7–8; See also T. H. Rigby, *Communist Party Membership in the USSR, 1917–1967* (Princeton: Princeton University Press, 1968).

An important challenge to the political system has been the nature of Soviet policy in the world at large, particularly in the following specific respects: 1. Establishing a détente with the United States to avoid war and possibly achieve a neutralization or disintegration of anti-Soviet alliances (such as NATO). Should the USSR shift its priorities from expensive military hardware and dangerous confrontations with the United States to satisfying more consumer demands at home? Should it modernize and improve its economy by trade exchanges with the United States and by importing American computers, machinery, and technical know-how? What steps should be taken toward these objectives? What risks and costs does détente, or specific measures of détente—such as, for example, people-to-people exchanges—pose for the Soviet regime? Can détente be used, and should it be used with only feigned reciprocity, to lull and weaken traditional enemies? 2. The Soviet relationship to the Warsaw Pact states of Eastern Europe. Should it be based on Stalinist-type Russian domination? Or should it allow for autonomy among the once satellite states, or perhaps even complete freedom for them? 3. The role of the USSR vis à vis world Communist parties, particularly in Asia, Latin America, and Western Europe. Should the USSR continue a revolutionary role in behalf of these parties? Should it do so at the expense of better relations with, and influence upon, local governments? Can it jeopardize or risk détente? Should it compete for support of local Communists against the Chinese? 4. The Soviet relationship to the People's Republic of China. How can the USSR regulate its relations with the People's Republic of China, consistent with the national and international claims of each side?

In terms of foreign policy, the legacy of Stalinism was an expectation of eventual all-out war with the Western capitalist states; extreme hostility and vigilance toward the non-Communist world—that is, sharp polarization of the world into "ours," a peaceful sphere, and "theirs," a warlike sphere ruled by imperialists or dominated by imperialist influences; rigid control of the Communist regimes of East Europe by Moscow; and the expected subordination of the whole international Communist movement (including Mao's Chinese) to Moscow's leadership; above all, highest possible preparedness at home militarily and also in terms of domestic-political security in support of this foreign-military policy.

Psychologically, one could probably better understand Stalin's policies by recalling his view that the USSR was completely surrounded by ruthless, rapacious imperialist wolves. Only extreme measures of vigilance, defense capability, and determination could counteract this predicament.

This attitude justified not only Soviet belligerence toward the West but, above all, the garrison state at home. One had to curtail freedoms, demand maximum discipline from the people, subordinate consumer preferences to defense needs and industrial priorities, keep a wary eye on individualistic peasants, and lean heavily on the secret police, the military, and the managers of heavy industry.

Trend of Change In the wake of Stalin's death, Khrushchev attempted to move Soviet foreign policy—and by implication all the other policies—away from this rigid Stalinist model. He provided certain attenuative formulations which are still of current relevance. The "fatal inevitability" of war was discarded. Khrushchev proposed that war could be, and certainly should be, avoided. War was not fatally inevitable, he argued, although its danger could not be completely ruled out as long as there were any imperialists left. Khrushchev publicly recognized that a thermonuclear holocaust would be as destructive to the USSR as to the so-called imperialist states, and could possibly destroy all human life on earth. Moreover, he argued, imperialist encirclement of the USSR, which he implied did exist before World War II, was now ended—by the establishment of Communist regimes in Eastern Europe and, ironically, in view of later quarrels, of People's China. According to Khrushchev, the USSR had been strengthened and was not as vulnerable as before the War.

Khrushchev discarded Stalin's colateral thesis that the more successful Soviet "socialist construction" was at home, the more determined attacks would be made against it by all the imperialist forces—foreign and domestic. He also rejected Stalin's polarized view of the world, recognizing for the first time in Soviet politics that there was a Third World. Thus states like India, Egypt, Indonesia, and Ghana were no longer seen as imperialist stooges, even if they were not Communist states. Khrushchev began a very substantial effort—diplomatic, economic, cultural, and military—to woo these so-called neutralist nations into a Soviet sphere of influence. This policy has continued under his successors.

Khrushchev also moved in the direction of *polycentrism* both with respect to East Europe and to the whole worldwide international Communist movement. This has been termed "desatellization" by Professor Vernon Aspaturian. This policy was opposed, we now know, by the conservative Stalinist forces of the Politburo in the 1950's—by V. M. Molotov, Lazar Kaganovich, and to some extent also by Georgi Malenkov. Among those opposed to such policy may have been the Party's leading theoretician, Mikhail Suslov, Aleksandr Shelepin, and possibly still others. After Stalin's death, there appeared to be growing recognition in Moscow that the CPSU could not simply go on issuing orders to foreign Communist

Russian tanks in Prague, 1968. A Czechoslovak student waves his nation's
flag while standing on a Soviet tank.
Wide World Photos

parties. "Brotherly equality" of all the parties and the right of each to
determine its own course became new Soviet slogans. However, the military intervention of the Brezhnev regime in Czechoslovakia in June 1968,
and, with little publicity, the visible readiness of the Soviets to intervene
in Poland in December 1970, showed that many continuities of outlook
and policy still connected the past and the present in the USSR.[14]

[14] See William Zimmerman, *Soviet Perspectives on International Relations, 1956–
1967* (Princeton: Princeton University Press, 1969) on how Soviet writers view the
different problems of foreign policy; see also Alexander Dallin, *The Soviet Union and
Disarmament* (New York: Praeger, 1964) and Z. K. Brzezinski, *The Soviet Bloc:
Unity and Conflict* (Cambridge: Harvard University Press, 1967); and Michael P.
Gehlen, *The Politics of Coexistence* (Bloomington: Indiana University Press, 1967);
see also J. F. Triska and D. D. Finley, *Soviet Foreign Policy* (New York: Macmillan,
1969). Among more recent assessments, see Raymond Garthoff, "SALT and The

Currently, the USSR experiences some problems that are common to most industrialized or rapidly industrializing societies: problems of social and environmental dislocation. Shifting millions of people into urban areas in a relatively short period of time, and intensive utilization of mineral and natural resources, have had psychic as well as physical consequences. Crowding, delinquency, pressures on traditional values and institutions, including those of marriage and the family, the inadequate adaptation of public services to new patterns of human use and habitation: all these, and the increasing impersonality and bureaucratization of life in the so-called modern, urban-industrial sector of Soviet society, are current problems. They create tensions as well as alienation among people who feel frustrated and unhappy in highly unstable and unsatisfactory social and physical environments. Unlike West Germany or the United States, the Soviet Union does not allow its disaffected youths to organize and advocate political change against the existing "irrelevant," "ineffective," or "inhumane" institutions. But the repression and inhibition of political responses to advanced industrialism does not dispose of the underlying problems. The need for new policies, new planning, and new environmental controls are now, increasingly, openly recognized by Soviet officials, bureaucrats, and scholars.[15]

In the process of rapid industrialization in the thirties, forties, and fifties, the Soviet leaders were not overly concerned about the human impact of moving great masses of people from the countryside to the cities. When the proportion of people involved in these migrations was only 15, 20, or even 25 percent of the population, this unconcern was something that the leaders could readily afford politically. Soviet planners simply did not worry about aesthetic aspects of urban living or about industrial pollution. Today, with an urban population in excess of 60 percent, the problems are far more serious. Just as in the United States, West Germany, Britain, and other technologically advanced countries,

---

Soviet Military" in *Problems of Communism* 24, no. 1 (January–February 1975): 21–37; the author sees a Soviet recognition that a nuclear balance between the U.S. and USSR has been reached with a dangerous and costly confrontation for both sides. The Soviets, in this view, wish to reduce and balance nuclear forces on both sides. The problems of Soviet control over restive erstwhile "satellites" are discussed by Adam B. Ulam in "The Destiny of Eastern Europe" *Problems of Communism* 23, no. 1 (January–February 1974): 1–12. See also the earlier Adam B. Ulam, *Expansion and Coexistence: The History of Soviet Foreign Policy, 1917–1967* (New York: Praeger, 1968); and Thomas B. Larson, *Disarmament and Soviet Policy, 1964–1968* (Englewood Cliffs, N.J.: Prentice-Hall, 1969).

[15] See David E. Powell, W. A. Douglas Jackson, and Murray Feshback, "Soviet Society in Flux," *Problems of Communism* 23 no. 6 (November–December 1974): 1–33. See also Zhores A. Medvedev, *The Medvedev Papers: The Plight of Soviet Science Today* (New York: St. Martins Press, 1971).

there is now in the Soviet Union a far greater diffusion of education than ever before; there is greater affluence; there is more leisure time; there is greater exposure to all types of media; and there is a significant shift of the labor force from agricultural and industrial to service occupations. The problems of a whole new population with new ways of life have acquired a greatly increased importance. The regime and its Marxist-Leninist ideology must somehow maintain their relevance to the newly emergent Soviet society, or failing this, perish. Both Soviet and Western reports indicate that crime, and particularly youthful crime, appear to be increasing; tensions associated with urban crowding are blamed for the 30-fold increase in divorce rate as compared with prerevolutionary Russia; there are indications that Marxism-Leninism no longer elicits the kind of enthusiastic support and commitment from the youth as it did for hundreds of thousands in earlier times. New material, cultural and political choices are called for in order to cope with these social changes.

THE LINKAGE OF ISSUES

Having enumerated some of the major issues of the Soviet polity in recent years, let us reflect on their interrelatedness. It is clear that the different ways in which problems of Soviet foreign policy may be solved must also affect all of the domestic concerns that we have outlined. What the USSR can do for the consumer, the farmer, and the new urban "postindustrial" society depends largely on resources that can be made available. Thus, détente with the United States in general—and particular settlements on such issues as strategic arms limitation, reduction of conventional forces, or the demilitarization of Europe—all have a direct bearing on what the Soviet Union can afford to spend on its people at home. It also affects the Soviet capability for attracting trade, capital, and technology from outside to develop the various "people-oriented" branches of the Soviet economy, all the way from Swedish hotels to automobiles.

Pressures and demands in the United States for détente have an analogous rationale. It is time, some people say, to turn the funds now spent for missiles, tanks, and nuclear submarines toward the reconstruction of decaying cities, more adequate health care, better educational systems, more generous social welfare provisions, and a better lot for disadvantaged minorities.

But détente poses certain dangers, too. Some degree of trust and confidence may be required in attempting mutual concessions. From the standpoint of the Soviet leaders, there is risk in any agreements or concessions which open their political system to external penetration and influence. If Soviet citizens get to know Western ways better, they might end up preferring them to the Soviet. Some analysts see the 1968 Dubček reforms in Czechoslovakia as, from the Soviet point of view, a by-product of excessive "opening-up-to-the-West." Czechoslovakia illustrated a basic Soviet dilemma. How much autonomy could the East European regimes be allowed so as to ensure their internal harmony and interests, but without losing for the USSR valuable buffers in the West and without creating politically infectious examples? The Soviets saw too much autonomy in Czechoslovakia and intervened by force.

One of the key issues in Western misgivings about continuing the present disengagement course with the Soviets is the suspicion engendered by the "garrison state." Extreme secrecy, and, among other things, the surveillance and harassment of people having contacts with foreigners are taken as signs of evil intent; so is persecution of domestic dissenters. In fact, these phenomena are taken as proof by some Westerners that détente is actually a Soviet "set-up," an attempt to lull, deceive, and conquer an unwary West.

Any significant change within the USSR, in terms of the values, attitudes, and expectations of the Soviet people, is likely to have some consequences for the conduct of Soviet foreign policy. If people are no longer taught to regard the United States and other Western governments as hopelessly malevolent imperialist entities, this may very well undermine, in the long run at least, much of Soviet hostility and intransigence in dealing with the West. We should note also that Soviet problems have their Western analogies. Some people in the United States (for example, AFL-CIO leader, George Meany) believe that détente is dangerous because it so undermines public hostility and vigilance toward communism that it makes effective foreign policy responses in crisis situations involving Communist countries either impossible or at least very difficult. For some people in the West, what happened in Portugal in 1974–1975—that is, since the military take-over—demonstrates Western erosion spawned by détente analogous to Communist erosion in Czechoslovakia in 1968. Whatever assessments we may make as decision-makers and participants in a political system, and however we may see the trade-offs between different values and concerns, it is impossible to separate modern policy issues into air-tight compartments.

Few of these long-standing policy issues have been openly debated in Soviet mass media. Occasionally, dramatic events have served to highlight the Party's grip on the system's public agenda. In early 1974, an illustrious Soviet citizen and writer, Aleksandr Solzhenitsyn, 1970 winner of the Nobel prize for literature, was hustled by armed guards onto a waiting airliner at Moscow's Vnukovo Airport and sent into permanent exile abroad. A cryptic, post facto announcement was made by the official Soviet news agency, Tass, while Solzhenitsyn was still in flight to Zurich,

Switzerland. He had been stripped of his Soviet citizenship and sentenced to exile by a decree of the Presidium of the Supreme Soviet of the USSR for his anti-Soviet activities, the announcement said. Although Solzhenitsyn had sharply criticized the Soviet regime (in publications smuggled to the West, and in the underground press), and his views and work had been attacked by the Soviet media, the deportation occurred with an autocratic abruptness. There had been no official indication whatever in the days and weeks preceding the expulsion that it was being considered; there was no public trial; there was no discussion of the pros and cons of this action afterwards. No Soviet citizen since Leon Trotsky in 1929 had been so dramatically exiled or generated greater worldwide public attention on the issues of dissent in the Soviet Union.

Yet, the tragedy and drama of Aleksandr Solzhenitsyn, nearly 60 years after the Great October Revolution of 1917, did not produce even one (published) letter of protest or anguished doubt in even one Soviet newspaper! In fact, the case of Solzhenitsyn was but the tip of an iceberg of secrecy, large-scale repression, and muted opposition which have historically characterized the Soviet regime.

Soviet View of Conflict The official Soviet theory of political conflict, so far as it regards the USSR, is simply that it does not exist. In the United States and other Western democracies conflicts are taken for granted and "politics" is seen as a legitimate process by which conflicts are resolved— through negotiation, debates, bargaining, elections, and majority rule. In the USSR, however, Marxist-Leninist ideology assumes that harmony exists on the basis of a class alliance between workers, peasants, and a working class stratum of intellectuals—all united in the pursuit of socialist construction leading to the development of full-fledged communism. In the present, all are said to believe in the maxim, "From each according to his ability; to each according to his work." In the future, when the stage of pure communism is reached, this will be replaced by the formula, "From each according to his ability; to each according to his needs."

The one organization which, above all others, leads the Soviet society in the direction of this goal is the Communist Party of the Soviet Union. It has, in the official view, full support of all the people of the USSR, who recognize and welcome its great revolutionary role. This is the regime's view about Soviet society, at least as it has existed since the late 1930's— that is, since the "liquidation" of the landholding Kulaks, who along with the pre-1917 noble landlords, merchants, and other middle and upper class elements, were recognized as necessarily (out of economic interest) hostile to the revolution and the CPSU. Opposition to the Party since that time—to the extent that it has even been acknowledged—has been pictured by official organs as a kind of aberration. It has been viewed as an archaic cultural lag from the prerevolutionary past; a product of foreign-inspired bourgeois influences; as treasonous or corrupt collaboration by particular individuals with foreign enemies to which no "honest Soviet people" could possibly stoop; or, as actual mental aberration, appropriately, from this point of view, treated like mental illness in psychiatric institutions. According to the official ideology, there is no reason for conflict and opposition in the USSR because there is no basic class cleavage, no oppressor and oppressed. In the Soviet Union, officially, such a situation does not exist. Underneath this official posture, however, conflict and cleavage have always existed although, unlike the United States, they have been expressed only in an ubiquitously indirect fashion, or simply illegally and clandestinely.

policy process

INITIATION OF ISSUES

Appearances notwithstanding, the initiation of national policy in the Soviet Union is the prerogative of relatively few leaders of the Party. To be sure, the government of the USSR is a large, dual structure; it consists of two pyramids. There is the parliamentary legislative pyramid beginning with small local councils, or Soviets, and culminating in the bicameral Supreme Soviet of the USSR in Moscow. The Supreme Soviet consists of some 1500 deputies, headed by the Presidium of the Supreme Soviet of 33 members with Nikolai Podgorny as chairman. There is also a vast bureaucracy of government officials, from the local militia and sanitation workers to the Council of Ministers of the USSR, headed by a Presidium of the Council of Ministers. There are more than 50 ministerial departments and more than 20 interdepartmental state committees. The Presidium consists of 12 members with Aleksei Kosygin as chairman.

According to the Soviet Constitution, the apex of the legislative pyramid controls the apex of the administrative pyramid. The Supreme Soviet can hire and fire the Council of Ministers, and can call it to account. It has supreme legislative powers.

On the face of it, this is the classic parliamentary model of government: there is a popularly elected legislature, which constitutes and controls the executive. And we might add that in the Soviet system, as in the British (but not in the American, German, or French), the legislature is constitutionally superior to any and all courts; its decrees cannot be overturned by any judge on the grounds of alleged unconstitutionality, and it can freely regulate the structure and the workings of the judicial system. In the USSR, a prosecutor general formally responsible to the Supreme

Soviet oversees the work of all the courts. Both the legislative and administrative (or bureaucratic) pyramids, however, are subject to the control of a third: that of the Communist Party of the Soviet Union.

Politburo and Secretariat Any new departure from past national policy, or any discussion of new themes of national concern, is the prerogative of the highest level of CPSU leadership, the Politburo. In recent years this body has been composed of between eleven and sixteen (as of 1975) full members and between six and nine candidate or alternate members. The alternate members may participate in the discussions of the Politburo, but do not have voting rights. Sometimes the alternate members advance to full membership after a period of time; occasionally, they may be demoted, never to be heard of again. All members of the Politburo are elected by the Central Committee of the CPSU, which in turn is chosen by a National CPSU Congress that meets, according to Party statutes, every five years. In 1971, this Congress was composed of nearly 5000 delegates who, in turn, chose 241 persons to full (voting) membership and 155 to candidate membership in the Central Committee of the CPSU. In prevailing practice, Party bureaucrats at the top of the power pyramid decide who shall be elected by making official nominations extending all the way down to local Party organization.

The Politburo is closely linked to several of the top supervisory bodies convoked by the Central Committee; the most important of these is the Secretariat. The Secretariat is run by five or six top leaders, or Secretaries, headed by the General Secretary (currently Leonid Brezhnev). Its professional staff numbers hundreds of thousands, reaching into every area of life in the USSR. This body collects information from all the sources available to the Party, and is the principal conduit of information upon which the Politburo makes its decisions.

The leadership of the CPSU Secretariat was successfully used by Stalin in his bid for supreme power in the USSR. Stalin became General Secretary of the Party in 1922; he consolidated power in his own hands about 1929, maintaining the position of General Secretary without interruption from 1922 until his death in March 1953. Within a week of his death, G. M. Malenkov, who succeeded to the post when Stalin died, yielded it to Nikita S. Khrushchev. Khrushchev maintained it continuously, under a slightly altered label of First Secretary, until his own downfall in October 1964. The subsequent incumbent has been, again under the name of General Secretary (as in Stalin's day), Leonid Brezhnev. The memberships of the Politburo and the Secretariat have substantially overlapped. That is, the General Secretary and several lesser members of the Secretariat have usually served on the Politburo as well.

It is in this small body, whose proceedings and procedures are very much a mystery to the "outside world," that the most vital policy initiatives are taken, and passed as directives to all the organs of Soviet state administration, as well as to all nongovernment institutions staffed and led by CPSU members. Here the Party sets down its general policy line. Here is where the decisions to intervene in Hungary in 1956 and invade Czechoslovakia in 1968 were made. Here, all the conflicts over industrial, military, and consumer priorities are authoritatively sorted out.

The only instance in which a major decision might be taken outside the Politburo appears to be in case of serious disagreement among its members. In 1957 Khrushchev split with V. M. Molotov, Lazar Kaganovich, and Nikolai Bulganin, and convoked a plenum (or full-fledged meeting) of the Central Committee—nominally the parent body of the Politburo—to resolve the dispute. The Central Committee upheld Khrushchev, and his opponents, subsequently labeled the anti-Party faction, were ousted from the Politburo and banished to obscure retirement.

In prevailing practice, the Central Committee meets rather infrequently and takes its cues from the Politburo. Central Committee membership denotes élite status in the Party, and although the Central Committee's interventions in policy decisions *against* the Politburo are probably rare, there are strong indications that at least since Khrushchev's time some real and lively debates have taken place among Soviet leaders in this forum.

No one knows when the Politburo meets or what it deliberates. There is no public access to its meetings and no summaries of proceedings or minutes are ever published. No public hearings are held before this body. There is some uncertainty as to whether voting is actually employed in the Politburo's decisions or whether informal consensus prevails. It is not even certain that the Politburo meets with regularity or that all of its members participate in the deliberative process.

We do know, based upon revelations made by Khrushchev and others subsequently, that Stalin often acted in place of, as well as in the name of, the Politburo. For some twenty years, in Stalin's heyday, membership appears to have connoted no more than the highest status in the Party hierarchy—next to Stalin himself—and the "right" to serve the Leader as he wished. The consensus of Western scholarship is that the leadership has become considerably more collegial since Stalin's time. But we have virtually no "hard" information on the relationships among Brezhnev, Kosygin, Podgorny, and other principal Politburo leaders. Does Brezhnev really consult these men before he acts? Are they his equals or subordinates in the councils of the Politburo? Do they quarrel among themselves? How do they differ in outlook and positions on issues? On all these questions, the curtain of secrecy in Soviet political life makes possible only some very indirect and speculative answers.

Soviet/U.S. Differences   Secrecy itself is one substantial difference between the Soviet Union and the United States. In the United States, a good portion of the policy initiation process is publicly visible—in the Congress, in party meetings and conventions, in public proceedings before courts, regulatory agencies, and, above all, in the media. The main differences between Soviet and American systems in policy initiation are that in the USSR (1) the circle of initiators is much more narrow; people wait for initiative to come from the "top." And (2) the process of initiation is all but totally secret.

An issue which illustrates the importance of a wide circle of issue and policy initiators in the United States was Watergate. The Nixon administration obviously did not *seek* to make the break-in at the Watergate Democratic headquarters in June 1972 a top public issue. But the issue surfaced largely because independent media doggedly pursued it in the face of administration denials that there was any wrong-doing, or that the matter was really worth any public attention. An inquiry launched by the Senate Watergate Committee led to further exposures and to the appointment of independent prosecutors (Cox, Jaworski, and Ruth); the launching of an impeachment process against the president; some far-reaching proposals for election reforms by Senator Sam Ervin's Committee in 1974; and, eventually, the president's resignation. None of this would be remotely possible in the Soviet political system as it has evolved to our day. Attacks on the state's leaders can only come from within their own top circle and, in fact, occur publicly only post facto, as when Khrushchev deplored Stalin's crimes three years *after* his death, and Brezhnev condemned Khrushchev's "hare-brained schemes" *following* his ouster.

CPSU Controls Over Political System   Not only has the Party laid claim to the control of "government," but of virtually *all* the institutions and social organizations in the USSR. Since many crucial decisions in modern societies are made by nongovernmental organizations, whether they are corporations, universities, trade unions, or perhaps professional associations, the Party's claim to supremacy over all of them is obviously a very important one.

Practically speaking, how is this claim realized? After all, constitutions and party statutes are not self-enforcing. The first method of securing de facto Party control is by overlapping élite membership. Thus the leadership of all those organizations and bodies regarded as important by the Party—whether they are governmental or not—are numerically dominated by high-ranking, trusted members of the CPSU. These are people who have served many years in the Party and who have achieved relatively senior status in it. In the most crucial positions—that is, among persons who are ministers or members of the Presidium of the Supreme Soviet, top trade union leaders, military and police officials, and the like—the incumbents are likely to be full or candidate members of the Central Committee of the Party, the Politburo, the Party Secretariat, or one of the equivalent bodies in one of the subordinate federal (Union) republics or the autonomous regions. Among the 57 ministers of the USSR in 1971, only one—the Minister of Medical Industry, P. V. Gusenkov—was *not* a member or candidate member of the Central Committee of the CPSU.

This method of overlapping control is combined with intensive indoctrination or civic training for virtually everyone in the political system. People in all walks of life are constantly being told—through their schools, their media, and also very importantly through face-to-face political information meetings—that the CPSU is and ought to be the leader of the whole Soviet society, the heroic builder of socialism and communism, the repository of all the finest talents and virtues among the people. Of course, the schools, the media and the propagandists are all Party-controlled. What the indoctrination does is to create an ethos, a general climate of opinion, in which both the Party members and other, ordinary citizens see the directing roles played by the CPSU members as being proper and rightful ones.*

Another method of control stems from the power of superior information. CPSU members are expected by their leaders (and Party statutes) to divulge all they learn in their various activities to the Party organization. However, they are expected to observe strict secrecy concerning their knowledge about what transpires within the Party. Thus, members of the CPSU who fail to "tell all" about their work and their associates in, say, a trade union, may be expelled from the Party. If members tell their trade union associates about the inner workings or "politics" of the CPSU, they face not merely expulsion but, in all probability, severe punishment usually meted out to political criminals. The result of this practice is that the leadership of the Party has built up the widest, most extensive and diversified information network in the country, very likely exceeding even that developed by the KGB (secret police). The Party has millions of informers throughout the society. All its cells are required to make periodic reports to higher organs, culminating eventually at the very top, with the Secretariat and the Politburo. But secrecy and censorship make it impossible for people outside high echelons of CPSU leadership to

* The indoctrination is not always successful, of course. See concluding section.

gain even remotely equivalent knowledge of what is really going on throughout the USSR and the world.

Still another method of control stems from the Party's manipulation of rewards and punishments. No person in the USSR can ascend to any job of managerial importance—for example, supervising the work of a large number of people, heading up an organization, a research institute, or a journal—without the explicit approval of the appropriate party secretary. Alternatively, the Party's displeasure is just as certain to cost a person his or her job, and possibly bring about more severe punishment in terms of jail, exile, demotion, confinement in an asylum and, occasionally, even death by firing squad.

Crisis Management and Democratic Centralism   There is also what might be termed "crisis management." This is the periodic assertion of the Party's power to intervene extraordinarily in various domains of life— overriding all the usual channels. This "right" or "power" serves to remind everyone of the Party's supreme authority: permanent stand-by emergency power to deal directly with crucial issues. A recent example of it is the summitry of Leonid Brezhnev, General Secretary of the CPSU, in pursuit of détente. During the last several years, Brezhnev has travelled and signed treaties between the Soviet Union and the United States as well as France and West Germany, although he holds *no* formal position in the Government of the Soviet Union, and the Constitution of the USSR does not even acknowledge the existence of his particular (Party) office. Nevertheless, his role is well understood in terms of the Party's historically exercised discretionary right to direct all those activities that it deems particularly important. During the Civil War, the collectivization campaign, the first five-year plans of the 1930's, and the Second World War, Party leaders were frequently assigned special tasks, whether in military or economic activities, supervising all the established bureaucratic authorities and agencies, army or civilian.

Granted that the Party dominates Soviet political life, why is this control exercised by so few individuals at the top of a pyramid of power? After all, the Party consists of some 16 million people. The foundations of Soviet oligarchy, if not one-man dictatorship, rest on the practices of democratic centralism—the principles of party organization first advocated and introduced by Lenin. To begin with, the Party is not an open organization. One can only join it on the recommendation of at least two current members, of relatively senior standing, having provided evidence of one's suitableness in terms of political and social background and attitudes. Moreover, each prospective member must serve a probationary period of at least one year before attaining full membership.

Once admitted, the Party member never directly votes either on the leadership of the CPSU or on its policies. Elections are indirect and generally controlled by leadership nominations from above. Such elections are actually a form of cooptation by a hierarchy of professional Party secretaries. The vote of the rank-and-file members in a local Party cell or grassroots organization is thus filtered upward. Members vote for the nominees of the local Party secretaries to a district meeting; these nominees, in turn, elect delegates to a regional meeting, until the whole process culminates in the all-union national Party Congress.

The Party rules, which embody Leninist democratic centralism, require that all Party officials be elected by those directly below. However, the rules also require the unconditional (and even enthusiastic) subordination of those below to those above *between* the convocations of electing bodies. Hence, the members of the Central Committee, even though they elect the Politburo, are individually fully subject to the Politburo's directives unless convoked into plenary session.

The power of convocation is carefully safeguarded so that without the concurrence of at least several top leaders it is practically impossible to assemble the various electing bodies. Since the tenth CPSU Congress of 1921, the Party has operated under a rule banning the existence of any "factions" or "interest groups" within the Party. Those outvoted in Party elections are not entitled to associate with others of similar persuasion to overturn these decisions at a subsequent meeting; nor are they allowed to attempt to win over still other Party members to their particular point of view. Leninist democratic centralism requires the unconditional subordination of the (losing) minority to the (winning) majority. Observance of secrecy and disciplined obedience to Party directives are among the principal virtues of the Communist. These are enforced internally by the CPSU and also backed up by the instruments of coercion.

Checks on Party Power The above summarizes the ways in which the Party has dominated policy initiatives in the Soviet Union. But "domination" is not quite an all-or-nothing relationship. The Party's power of initiative is not total and absolute and that of other sectors of society simply nil. There are overt as well as covert powers involved in the process of decision-making. And while no one in the Soviet Union in the last 50-odd years has had the audacity to suggest publicly that the power to make national policy ought *not* to belong to the Party, the Soviet political system is, in fact, subject to the pressures of many conflicting claims outside the CPSU. To develop policies, or to order actions to be taken, the leaders require a certain amount of information and often technical advice of experts. The more complex, technologically advanced, and interdependent a society is, the more likely the need for such advice and information.

Much of this information and advice is likely to be, in some degree at least, self-serving and permeated by the biases, or points of view, particular to those sectors of the larger society from which it emanates. This is likely to be the case even though most of the people at the top of each of those organizational echelons that is providing the information and advice are CPSU members. This paradox can be explained partly in terms of role conflicts and tensions, and partly in terms of the problems of cooptation.[16]

Obviously, even long-time CPSU members who have spent many years, sometimes a lifetime, in a particular line of work develop professional interests, perspectives, and associations. A CPSU leader who is also a manager of a large factory or a commander of an army may well feel that he understands the problems pertinent to these institutions better than his Party colleagues who have never shared the experience. More than that, he may feel that he must protect his interests in terms of what his institution is called upon to do—as in the fulfillment of an economic plan or military preparedness. Obviously, no one wants to be saddled with a job he cannot do, and so a factory manager or a military commander is likely to pass on information to his Party superiors which will reflect the technical and professional requirements of a task as he sees them—in light of his experience, the likely consequences for him and his associates, and the feasibility of it in terms of his professional knowledge of the problem. And, of course, "leaders" must work with "non-leaders," managers with workers, officers with soldiers, Party members with non-members. The demands, expectations, and performance of the rank-and-file are likely to be important to the ease and efficiency with which the people at the top can carry out their plans of action.

Role conflicts and strains—in terms of pressures from segments of the Party leadership opposed to the demands of different technical and bureaucratic sectors of society—are likely to grow particularly serious as the society develops technologically. Jobs and careers tend to become more and more specialized, and subdivided into various esoteric offshoots. The old saying that experts are people who know more and more about less and less has political implications. It gets harder to understand their work, and thereby to control them, but at the same time it is also increasingly difficult to do anything without them. The Party is now less likely to succeed with generalist-type troubleshooters who can merely say, "You, you and you, do this and that, and be quick about it." In some

16 See Frederick C. Barghoorn, *Politics in the USSR* (Boston: Little, Brown, 1972), pp. 58–86.

areas, it is only possible for the Party to acquire expertise and control by cooptation, that is, by extending membership to mature persons who have already achieved some considerable measure of status and recognition in a particular activity—in various branches of science and technology, for example—without having displayed any great political zeal toward the Party.

DELIBERATION

At least since the time of Stalin, who had tended to neglect it as a collective consultative body, the Politburo of the CPSU has been the main deliberative organ of the Soviet Union. As related in the previous section, this is the forum in which the ultimate questions of policy are discussed, decided, and passed on, in effect, to subordinate organs as binding directives. According to statements made by some of its recent members, including Leonid Brezhnev and Anastas Mikoyan a few years ago, the Politburo may actually meet at least once a week. Presumably, its voting members (currently 16) and candidate members (six in 1975) all gather together. In Mikoyan's version, the group decides issues not by a show of hands but by consensus, with the postponement of those questions on which consensus seems unattainable. It appears that when the Politburo somehow fails to agree, it may ultimately refer the disagreement to its larger parent body—the Central Committee of the CPSU. Inasmuch as the Central Committee does not meet with any particular regularity, presumably the Politburo is where all the issues of policy are (if anywhere) frankly and fully debated. In fact, lacking public, verifiable information, the only thing which can be said with *certainty* about the Politburo is that official Soviet sources have persistently identified it with the overall leadership of Soviet affairs.[17]

Beyond the Politburo To be sure, there are quite a few deliberative organs in the Soviet political system, all presumably subordinate to the Politburo. All of them are working out of the public view. The most important of these are:

1. The Secretariat of the Party, which is also the apex of the CPSU bureaucracy. It is led by ten senior secretaries headed by the Party leader, the General Secretary, and it has a large staff. Almost certainly it deliberates on all issues which are put forward before the Politburo, with particular emphasis on Party control of and Party implementation of

[17] See Vernon V. Aspaturian, "Soviet Foreign Policy," in Roy C. Macridis, ed., *Foreign Policy in World Politics,* 4th ed. (Englewood Cliffs, N.J.: Prentice-Hall, 1972), pp. 193–216.

policies. There is no direct information of any kind on the process which occurs in this "inner sanctum" of the Party organization. Usually, at least half of the secretaries of the Central Committee of CPSU are also members or candidate members of the Politburo.

2. On the government side, there is the 12-member Presidium of the Council of Ministers which issues decrees with the force of law on behalf of the whole Council of Ministers. The Presidium is believed to be a body which actually meets collectively to consider its actions, while the Council of Ministers is simply a term for a large group of government departments (57 most recently) whose chiefs never interact personally in one ministerial forum. Virtually nothing is known of the procedures employed by the Presidium of the Council of Ministers. There are no public hearings before it, no indication of how its deliberations are conducted, when, or how frequently, and how the members may participate—for example, with respect to what constitutes a quorum—or whether votes are taken.[18]

In all likelihood, this Presidium, granted its subservience to the directives of the Politburo, deliberates both on the recommendations of the various ministerial departments and on its own initiative as to how broad policy principles may be best carried out. It also considers issues of administration on which policy recommendations may be made to the Politburo. There is, of course, a significant overlap in membership between the two bodies, with at least three or four of its members also sitting on the Politburo. The chairman of the Presidium has always been a member of the CPSU's top policy organ.

3. There are also several interdepartmental ministerial committees, headed by senior Party officials, such as the State Planning Committee (Gosplan), led in 1975 by N. K. Baybakov, a Central Committee member. Here, privileged discussion of economic policy presumably takes place.

4. Finally, the 33-member Presidium of the Supreme Soviet of the USSR stands at the apex of the Soviet parliamentary pyramid. This body also overlaps the Politburo in its membership, and it, too, is invariably headed by a Politburo member. The Presidium exercises, theoretically, the most extensive legislative, executive, and judicial powers in the USSR. It has the full jurisdiction of the whole Soviet parliament when the latter is not in session. In Stalin's time, this meant virtually all year, every year. The role of the Supreme Soviet as a whole had been for many years merely symbolic and token. The Supreme Soviet assembled for a few days during the year, to hear speeches by Party and government leaders and to give wholesale and routine approval to decrees issued in its name by the Presidium.

[18] Cf. Reshetar, *The Soviet Polity*, pp. 208–215.

In the 1960's and 1970's the role of the Supreme Soviet has been somewhat upgraded. It stays in session several weeks longer. It approves directly more laws than it used to do (though still less than half of the total parliamentary output). Its standing committees seem more active in their closed door deliberations of government proposals.

But the substance of change could be readily exaggerated. Thus far, in its 40-year history—that is, since the adoption of the 1936 Constitution—not *one* of the 1500-odd members of the Supreme Soviet has been publicly heard to say a single unkindness about government policy or leadership. A clue to the kind of politically bland deliberation that the Supreme Soviet has engaged in is that there is as yet *no* record of a single vote cast either against or in abstention on any government proposal. About three-fourths of the membership of the Soviet parliament has been traditionally drawn from the ranks of the CPSU; one-fourth has been generally recruited from obviously reliable, though non-Party, people.

Acting in the name of the whole Supreme Soviet (and subject to its eventual approval) the Presidium can promulgate any laws it wishes; change the Constitution; appoint and dismiss government ministers, lesser officials, and the chief legal officer of the USSR, the prosecutor general. It can also declare a state of war and approve treaties. All these enormous powers are exercised in the most obscure manner imaginable. The Presidium appears to possess a large staff but the mystery of its proceedings—including even the question of how many of its statutory members actually participate in its work—is at least as profound as that which attaches to the deliberations of any of the bodies discussed here.[19]

Thus, the Soviet Union is ruled by organs whose deliberations are somewhat less open than those of the court of King James I in Stuart England.

In Soviet political practice, public deliberation is usually displayed by post facto exhortation—in the form of newspaper, radio, and television announcements and word-of-mouth messages telling the people what the Party and government have decided, appealing for all-out support, usually with no more than oblique references to the rationale of why the decision was made.

Public "Debates"   Occasionally, however, the leaders call for more public debate. In the last few years this has been the case with certain aspects of educational and economic reforms. Once the leaders have given approval to such discussion, letters from various persons, particularly technical experts, are printed in the newspapers and also in the more specialized professional journals discussing how the relevant problems—more effi-

[19] Ibid., p. 210.

ciency in industrial production and consumer satisfaction, for example—might be dealt with. One such "debate" was launched during Khrushchev's time on his 1958 proposal to reform Soviet education, and another under the Brezhnev regime with respect to decentralizing Soviet economic planning and abandoning or modifying crude quantitative goals that are set for factories and farms.

Such debates, rare as they are, never involve what might be termed political "rough stuff" that one would almost always encounter in the United States and other Western systems. No one says that the incumbent leaders or the "system" have been at fault, as such. It is this peculiar covertness of the Soviet political system which gives rise to the Western art of "Kremlinology." Journalists and academics study obscure and subtle clues for indications of nuances and changes in Soviet behavior and perceptions: the rise and decline of individual leaders and the disagreements among them. Sometimes this may involve close comparisons of speeches made by certain leaders to notice whether subjects mentioned by one are also mentioned, in the same order and with the same emphasis, by another. Occasionally, much is made of omissions or different wording in basically similar speeches or articles. Other favorite themes of speculation and analysis include the order of names in certain official announcements, the order of appearance by CPSU leaders at the Moscow May Day and October Revolution parades, the amount of applause accorded to different personages (and officially reported) at various party conferences, and similar esoteric pastimes. All these may be related to the consideration of certain issues in the official media, however cryptic and bland. Still another technique involves the use of public information about the past associations of CPSU functionaries; the knowledge that Comrade A served in the same district as Comrade B or even as B's subordinate is sometimes interpreted as meaning that A is "one of B's men" and, therefore, likely to share his attitudes on policy questions. Sometimes the inferences turn out strikingly wrong, as when Western analysts saw Leonid Brezhnev as a principal pillar of Khrushchev's support shortly before Khrushchev's ouster and replacement by none other than Brezhnev.[20]

We do know, through the institutional identifications of some of the members, what interests have direct representation in the Politburo. In recent years there has been some broadening in this interest representation with the elevation to full Politburo membership of Marshal Andrei Grechko, Foreign Minister Andrei Gromyko, and secret police chief, Yuri

[20] See Jerry Hough on the issue of just *how* debates may be waged in the Soviet media, "The Soviet System: Petrification or Pluralism?", *Problems of Communism* 21, no. 2 (March–April 1972): 1–17. And also Alex Simirenko, ed., *Social Thought in the Soviet Union* (Chicago: Quadrangle Books, 1969).

Andropov. Thus, Soviet military, police, and foreign policy specialists now for the first time find simultaneous representation in the Party's highest council. The heaviest representation continues to be drawn, however, from the professional CPSU organization men and from the government bureaucracy, with much emphasis on industrial managerial expertise, as in the case of Aleksei Kosygin, who is also Premier or Chairman of the Council of Ministers.

APPROVAL

Elections Looking at the Soviet decisional system as a whole, one is struck by its central paradox. On the one hand, the regime has mobilized vast numbers of people into organized political, social, economic, and cultural activities. On the other hand, it has confined meaningful participation in decisions to relatively few persons. For the past 40 years—that is, since the Stalin Constitution of 1936—the USSR has had the largest national electorate in the world.

All persons over the age of 18 have the right to vote. Voter turn-out, vigorously encouraged by the Party, is nearly always close to 99 percent of those eligible. But there has never been a choice in all these elections. Voting for the Party list is open and public. Those who do not wish to vote for the CPSU slate can step into a special booth to cross out the names of the official candidates. According to the law, if a candidate's name is crossed out by at least half of the voters, he fails to get elected. In the past 40 years—with secret police presence at the polling places and other, more indirect, ubiquitous sanctions—not even *one* candidate to either house of the Supreme Soviet, with its 1500-odd deputies, has failed to achieve election. Nor has even *one* of these deputies either voted *against* or *abstained* on a measure proposed by the Government—not even once. (Some defeats or nonelections are believed to have occurred in local Soviet elections.) There are no referenda in the USSR in which the people as a whole could vote "yes" or "no" on specific measures. As indicated earlier, even rank-and-file CPSU members never vote directly on leaders or policies.

The function of Soviet elections appear to be principally mobilizational and symbolic. Every election affords the Party apparatus a chance to carry the message about the Party's program to every single district and hamlet in the nation. From the Party's point of view elections thus serve educational, informational, and, broadly speaking, socializing functions. Elections draw the masses into Party activities, and they help familiarize the people with the Party's policies and values. In addition, the results of elections are cited (however implausibly in some Western eyes) as proof of the moral-political unity of the Soviet people and their support of the regime.

The position and status of a Supreme Soviet deputy appear to be largely honorific; the job is only a part-time occupation. To the extent, however, that deputies are elected from districts in which they work and reside, and inasmuch as they may receive communications from their constituents (never made public), it is likely that from time to time they funnel at least some information about local conditions, attitudes, and problems to the central authorities in Moscow.

Decisions Actual approval of policies is generally given by the Politburo; occasionally by the Central Committee of the CPSU, either when the Politburo is divided or simply in concurrence with the Politburo when the Party leaders wish to dramatize their decisions. Approval is converted into legal sanctions—in the form of either laws or decrees—by one or both of the two small presidia. The Presidium of the Supreme Soviet issues "laws"; the Presidium of the Council of Ministers issues "decrees." The most important, dramatic, and solemn Soviet decrees (such as war mobilization, for example) are issued in the name of the CPSU Central Committee as well as the two presidia—of the Supreme Soviet and of the Council of Ministers. For practical purposes or binding effect, there are no differences between laws and decrees. In the total volume of Soviet legislation both by law and decree only a small fraction, probably less than 5 percent, is enacted directly by the Supreme Soviet at the initiative of the Party leadership in the Politburo.

APPLICATION

Bureaucracy The most important component of application is the state bureaucracy, although the CPSU's own organization, the rank-and-file, various voluntary organizations such as the trade unions, and millions of ordinary people—workers, farmers, consumers—are also involved in policy application.

The Soviet bureaucracy is large, specialized, and frequently unwieldy. It also has its own special interests depending on its function, objectives, location, internal organization, and the like. These interests can be asserted in various *indirect* ways, despite the overall control by the CPSU. What is especially different about Soviet bureaucracy, particularly unlike the American or other Western (British, French, West German) bureaucracies, is its total lack of legal independence from the Party leadership.

Western bureaucracies operate under what might be termed in American usage Civil Service rules. People are appointed to jobs by meeting certain entrance requirements, as in competitive examinations; thereafter, they are likely to be promoted on the basis of years of service and the quality of their performance based on generally nonpartisan considerations and applied or supervised in practice by other civil servants. Above all, no bureaucrat can be fired without legal cause or even demoted without resort to judicial or at least quasi-judicial proceedings, such as those of the French Council of State or hearings before the U.S. Civil Service Commission.

The relationship of the entire Soviet bureaucracy to the CPSU is more like that of the American bureaucracy to the politicians in the heyday of the spoils system. Opposing the Party is likely to be very costly. An offending bureaucrat—that is, one who has displeased the Party leaders even if he did not break any laws or regulations—may be summarily fired. In Stalin's day the offender could be quite readily executed or imprisoned. Neither laws, rules, nor his fellow-professionals could save him. Pleading that he was only doing his job—to the best of his ability—and within the laws did not suffice.

Soviet bureaucrats are not supposed to be "neutral" and "impartial" in dealing with *all* citizens and *all* problems that come before them. Party directives may not be (openly) flouted or disregarded. Bureaucrats cannot display "bourgeois objectivism"; they must show ideological-political vigilance, which means that their ultimate allegiance is not to the laws but to the Party. Laws are seen as significant tools of the Party, serving but not hampering its cause. One practical consequence of this relationship is that illegal, if not simply objectionable, orders to the bureaucracy cannot be openly resisted.

Comparison with U.S. In many of the Western countries, including the United States, the situation is significantly different. In case of conflicts, or worse yet, "irregularities" committed by the politicians against the bureaucracy (say, by ministers of the government) the bureaucrats can appeal to the courts, to the legislature, and, above all, through a variety of independent media, to public opinion outside the "government." Thus, politicians may be resisted, challenged, flouted, and exposed to public criticism and pressure if they offend the bureaucrats. All this is evident in the United States with some frequency in bureaucratic testimony before congressional committees. What the president says and what the bureaucrats say in public hearings are often quite different. Watergate was a case in point, as the testimony of CIA's General Walters and FBI's Patrick Gray demonstrated. In the Soviet Union, Party control of government and communication channels makes it impossible for Soviet bureaucrats to find such recourse against their rulers.

Soviet government workers cannot sue their bosses in courts for breach of law or procedure. The Soviet press sometimes publishes articles which selectively criticize the bureaucracy and, in effect, use it as a scapegoat for failures of policy. The press *never* publishes articles in which either the bureaucracy, or some outside defenders of it, castigate the Party for its misuse or abuse of the bureaucrats.

The regime controls the trade unions. There are no special civil service associations in the USSR—as in the United States or Britain (Whitley Councils)—which routinely bargain over wages and working conditions with the government. There is no right to strike for any employees, let alone government employees. Political advocacy by bureaucrats would be similarly regarded as treasonable, counterrevolutionary activity.

Bureaucratic "Slippage" Granted these important differences, even in the Soviet political system great distortions from the leaders' commands are still likely to occur in the process of policy implementation. Inevitably, much is left to the discretion and the good or bad judgment of all kinds of bureaucrats. And if these people, however surreptitiously, choose to interpose their idiosyncratic interpretations on the leaders' commands, if they lack appropriate information, if they lack the will or the capacity to carry out their directives, or if they work at cross-purposes, then the policy may fall apart in the process of application.

Latent Interests Moreover, Soviet administrators, planners, and politicians, even if they are CPSU members or selflessly dedicated to the CPSU, must take into account the effects of what Gabriel Almond calls *latent* interest articulation by millions of ordinary Soviet citizens.[21] An economic plan, for example, cannot succeed if workers, consumers, farmers, and bureaucrats all fall behind in meeting the targets. And this may happen because of high incidence of absenteeism, industrial sabotage, carelessness and inefficiency of employees, theft and collusion among managers, and possibly even through (illegal) strikes. In turn, all of these phenomena may reflect the unhappiness of people outside the Party with what the Party is doing to them. Inasmuch as planners and administrators want to be successful—other things being equal—the grievances of Soviet workers, farmers, and consumers may occasionally at least have

[21] G. Almond and G. B. Powell, Jr., *Comparative Politics: A Developmental Approach* (Boston: Little, Brown, 1966), pp. 218-241.

some indirect impact on Party-initiated policy. The need for accommodation sometimes may lead to modification.

Propaganda and Coercion   The uses of persuasion (or propaganda) and coercion are important elements, too, in the application of policy. To be sure, in *all* political systems leaders who launch policies usually embark on public relations campaigns to "sell" these policies to the people. In the United States, the president may use television, invite congressional leaders, tour the country making speeches, and send other members of his administration on nationwide speaking tours. Newspapers and other media friendly to the president may well give him additional support through their news coverage as well as through editorials. If the president's policies arouse misgivings from substantial segments of the population, however, this kind of campaign is always accompanied by a counter-campaign. Some public figures and some media are likely to attack the policy, to produce information intended to discredit it, and to dwell on reasons why it ought to be rejected. American readers may recall President Ford's pardon of former President Nixon; the proposal for more military aid to South Vietnam; and the abortive proposal to restrict oil imports by taxing gasoline at the pump.

In Soviet political practice, application of policies is invariably accompanied by well-orchestrated media and word-of-mouth propaganda campaigns. Party members throughout the country are alerted to their duty of exhorting and persuading the people among whom they live and work. The Agitprop (agitation and propaganda) section of the Central Committee Secretariat coordinates these media and word-of-mouth campaigns. Meetings of factory workers and collective farmers may be held throughout the country. Newspapers report the enthusiastic attitude of people toward the policy, as well as praise its intrinsic merits and virtues. The whole process is generally a movement down a one-way street. There is no consideration of other points of view, no reports of objections, or elucidations of doubts and qualms or any factual discouragement in any of the media, or in any public forum.

The momentum for the policy is also reinforced by coercion, both in its actual application and in terms of a credible threat. In Stalin's day, Soviet citizens generally knew that opposing or even appearing to oppose the Leader's policy risked their lives. The credibility of secret police deterrence was established on the basis of the gigantic purges conducted by the GPU and NKVD since the thirties under such merciless chieftains as Henry Yagoda, Nikolai Yezhov and, finally, Lavrenti Beria. Since the 1960's, mass terror is no longer characteristic of secret police operations in the USSR. But the devices available to and used by Soviet leaders to assure compliance are still sufficiently arbitrary, severe, and formidable to instill fear and caution in most people. Arrest, interrogation, and detention on mere suspicion (political or security related) of the secret police; assignment to a psychiatric hospital ward for "abnormal behavior"; summary loss of one's job; banishment to a remote exile: all of these are current realities. And it must be remembered that the secret police, even if used much more sparingly in the last two decades, continues to be an enormous, ubiquitous, and ominous force in Soviet society. Its operations have not yet been hampered by any public, political-legal inquiries: whether it has acted abroad, or at home, and whether it has lived up to constitutional guarantees and statutory limitations or not.[22] In fact, the KGB has acted both at home and abroad to link espionage and anti-espionage activities with far-reaching "anti-subversive" vigilance at home; wiretapping places of residence and work; shadowing and following suspected individuals (often those having contacts with foreigners) investigating, arresting, interrogating and intimidating—all of this in complete absence of any scrutiny by press, media, or political opposition.

ADJUDICATION AND ENFORCEMENT

As in other political systems, the Soviets need to perform three basic tasks: (1) resolution of jurisdictional conflicts among different state agencies; (2) resolution of disputes among ordinary citizens and claims by them against state agencies; and (3) enforcement of rules within the whole political system, or the observance of authoritatively promulgated norms.

In the Soviet Union, these functions are, in part, carried out by courts. Much more substantially, however, than in Britain, Germany, France, or the United States, they are carried out by nonjudicial political agencies. Specifically, the Presidium of the Supreme Soviet constitutes the ultimate tribunal for any conflict of laws or jurisdictional quarrels in the Soviet political system. It is also the highest tribunal of appeal; in fact, most of the judicial work associated with both conflict resolution and appeals is exercised on its behalf by two agencies formally responsible to the Presidium: the Procuracy, headed by a procurator general of the USSR, and the Supreme Court of the USSR, with many different panels of judges depending on areas of jurisdiction.

Jurisdictional conflicts in the Soviet system are resolved either directly by "private" Party instructions, or by appeals to the procurator general.

---

[22] See Elizabeth K. Poretsky, *Our Own People* (Ann Arbor: University of Michigan Press, 1970); Oleg Penkovsky, *The Penkovsky Papers* (Garden City, N.Y.: Doubleday, 1965); and particularly David J. Dallin, *Soviet Espionage* (New Haven: Yale University Press, 1955).

In this case, too, such conflicts are settled in a virtually private fashion, not by court cases, as so often in the United States, where, for example, state agencies of different jurisdictions can sue the federal government, or vice versa. Similarly, claims by citizens against the officials of the state may be referred to the procurator general. These, too, are never tried in the courts, pitting citizen against state or party official. They could, however, result in independent proceedings by the procurator general against an offending official if he chooses to press the case. We must hasten to add that first, Soviet citizens do not themselves have the right to sue agencies of the state (no Soviet citizen or group of citizens can use the courts to block or compel governmental action—as had happened with the Alaska oil pipeline a few years ago in the U.S.); and second, the fusion of membership between the Party and the judiciary, capped by the overlapping membership of the Politburo and the Presidium of the Supreme Soviet, assures extremely close and reliable Party control of the judiciary. It is as if top White House staffers, president included, ran the U.S. Supreme Court. (The president thus would not have experienced any anxiety about those tapes back in 1974.)

Most Soviet judges are "elected" Party nominees, through processes quite as "reliable" as those governing the elections of Supreme Soviet deputies. Party nominees are never challenged, and they never lose. They may be "recalled," according to the laws on the books, which in fact means that they serve at the pleasure of the Party. Cases involving private citizens among themselves, civil and criminal, are tried routinely in the courts. With respect to non-criminal cases, such as divorces or domestic disputes, the processes of Soviet justice are reasonably cut-and-dried; they follow statutes and are not much less equitable or open than most Western practice.

The Political Cases   There are various differences between Soviet and other European, as well as American, courts, to be sure,* but these pale into insignificance as compared with cases in which the private citizens are objects of special official accusation, the so-called political cases. These may be tried by military tribunals, even where the accused are civilians in time of peace; they may be wholly or virtually secret. As in all Soviet criminal practice, legal defense is available to the accused only *after* he has been confined and investigated by the authorities, and put on trial. Failure to answer procurators' questions carries a six-month statutory

* Including the conception of courts as ideologically and morally educational institutions and use of lay assessors as judges.

jail term. Above all, judicial personnel are alerted to their own important political responsibilities where state-Party interests are involved.

In the Soviet political system, the judiciary stands in virtually the same relationship to the CPSU as does the bureaucracy. Conviction in open court is not necessary for removal of a judge from his office, or for expulsion from the Party. The judges are as vulnerable to the Party's displeasure as the rest of the bureaucracy. Moreover, by requirements of statutes, ideological training, and every day practice, the judiciary continues to operate on the basis of "socialist legality" or "socialist legal consciousness" as opposed to "bourgeois objectivity." Judges are expected to take into consideration the interests of the Marxist-Leninist state before all else, so as to serve in behalf of the class-conscious vanguard of the working people—the CPSU. Judges must actively serve the cause of Marxism-Leninism, the proletariat, and the Revolution. They may not "play into the hands of imperialism." Treating all interests, all persons, and all problems with the blindfolds of impartiality—even as an ideal—is seen as impermissible and treasonous capitulation before hostile class interests. In deciding cases, the Soviet judiciary cannot take the position of letting the chips fall where they may. The judiciary is explicitly required to concern itself with the political and social consequences of its verdicts. It is regarded as an arm of the proletarian dictatorship and is expected to advance its objectives. It would be officially regarded as a scandal if Soviet judges took instructions from the private defendants before them, but certainly not from the Party.

The practical consequence of such a judicial system is that no individual can expect to win a case against the Soviet government in court. The Party's box score of judicial victories against those charged with political crimes is a virtually perfect 100 percent. Very often, defense lawyers assigned by the court vie with the prosecutors in asking for tough punishment of persons tried in political cases—that is, those regarded as sensitive for itself by the CPSU. It also means that no one can use the courts in the USSR as a means of countervailing the Party's policy, as is often the case in the United States and other Western systems. No environmentalists, or civil rights advocates, or consumer protection societies, or employees can sue in the Soviet courts to stop or modify official policies and decisions. Cases of sabotage, treason, espionage, and attempted assassination are usually handled by special military tribunals, often with no media coverage of the proceedings and tremendous latitude to the prosecutor and police officials with respect to detaining and interrogating suspects.

It is especially worth noting that the enforcement of policy by the Party receives great support from the notorious vagueness of Soviet codes that pertain to political offenses, and the great latitude and resources accorded to the police apparatus, and above all, the KGB.[23]

MONITORING

In many political systems, the United States included, the press and the media perform much of the monitoring function. They report on what goes on, offer commentary, sometimes in a general way and often by focusing on various specific cases or human interest stories. In the United States, we have periodic exposés of such matters as misuse of government contracts, high costs of medical care, neglect of the aged, malnutrition among some strata of the population, mismanagement of resources, pollution of the environment, lack of safety in the manufacture of various products, and so forth. Much of this monitoring goes on outside the structure of government, and is both independent and critical of it.

Party control of the media in the USSR makes monitoring a wholly "in-house" operation. Occasionally, critical reporting is evident when the leadership launches a campaign against some segment of the bureaucracy —casting them as scapegoats for the failure to meet the objectives of an economic plan; or when statements appear which, by exhorting people to greater efforts in certain areas of activity, imply more or less serious "shortcomings" in them. As far as the genuine mass media—press, television, and radio—are concerned, criticism of policy is rare, and where it occurs it is usually veiled and indirect. Criticisms are never laid at the door of the Politburo or the Party. The monitoring of policy in public is most likely to be either laudatory or nil. Generally speaking, Soviet media are dedicated to a "what's right with our society" approach. The coverage of news emphasizes official announcements and "upbeat" kinds of stories: the successes of socialist construction at home and the policy of détente and peaceful coexistence abroad. There are stories of official celebrations and speeches, exchanges with friendly foreign visitors, and periodic reports of achievements in the various official organizations and activities. Muckraking and reports of social malaise—including cases of accidents, disasters, strikes, riots, crimes, suicides, and the like—are very rare, as are reports on juvenile delinquency, divorces, alcoholism, and other serious problems which might reflect on the failures of the "Socialist Society."

Much of the more candid monitoring of what really happens to and in the USSR, and how policies are really working out, occurs in the *private*

---

[23] On Soviet judicial system see the comparative work by K. Grzybowski, *Soviet Legal Institutions* (Ann Arbor: University of Michigan Press, 1962); and Glenn G. Morgan, *Soviet Administrative Legality* (Stanford: Stanford University Press, 1962), on the procuracy.

channels of several official bureaucracies. It also occurs to some extent, still obliquely but nevertheless with greater candor and interest than in the mass media, in some of the more specialized periodicals of various functional groups, legal, military, economic, scientific, and cultural.[24]

One of the main practical consequences of this closed and oblique monitoring process is that apart from a few experts in a particular area people have very little critical information about official policy. The real problems and the possible alternatives to official policy remain hidden below the surface of public discourse.

When an American president visited China in 1973 to reverse a traditional U.S. policy of quarantine toward the Chinese, this came in the wake of years of public discussion. For more than two decades such discussion was symbolized by the perennial high school debating topic: "Resolved, that Red China be admitted to the United Nations. . . ." The State Department was by no means the only agency considering the practical impact and consequences of *not* recognizing Maoist China as a bona fide member of the world community of nations. Lacking this widely diffused monitoring function, the Soviets' policy changes often occur as if out of a void. It is done because the leadership says it ought to be done. The public lacks the means for any substantial, active, and conscious involvement in policy changes.

TERMINATION AND AMENDMENT

Although some policies may be informally modified in application by the bureaucracy, amendment and termination in the Soviet political system are only within the powers of those organs which initiate policy—the Politburo with simple formal ratification by one or both of the two Presidia discussed earlier. Amendment and termination are subject to the same secret and summary proceedings as are initiation, deliberation, and approval. What is worth pointing out, moreover, is that in the Soviet Union—unlike the United States and other Western systems discussed in this book—formal amendment or termination of a policy cannot be *interposed* upon those who initiated it.

In some systems, regardless of who may have originated a policy, still other organs may legitimately cause that policy to be abandoned, curtailed, slowed down, modified, or put in abeyance. This may be done both directly and indirectly. It is done directly when a parliamentary assembly formally amends or repeals a particular piece of legislation, or when a court strikes it down as "unconstitutional," or indeed issues a restraining

---

[24] See Hopkins, *Mass Media in the Soviet Union,* and. Hough, "The Soviet System: Petrification or Pluralism?"

order that delays the implementation of the measure; or it can be done by popular referendum as, for example, in France in 1969 when President de Gaulle's decentralization proposals were rejected by the French electorate. It may also be done indirectly, where a parliamentary body votes to censure the government rather than a particular policy, but with the effect of bringing a demise to both. Interposition may also be achieved by an open and competitive election process itself: for example, in Great Britain in 1974 when the Conservative government staked its fate on intensifying a "get-tough-with-the-unions" policy and lost out to Harold Wilson's Labour party. In the United States, the Congress and the Supreme Court can cause either the abandonment or the modification of presidential policies and actions. In 1951, the Supreme Court declared President Truman's seizure of the steel industry to be illegal and caused its abandonment. Also, during the U.S. involvement in Cambodia in the early 1970's, Congress voted to cut off funds for what it regarded as an illegal presidential war, and in 1973 it voted against further U.S. military intervention in Indochina. In Britain, the cabinet is sometimes forced into amendments of its legislative proposals in parliament; an adverse vote on government policy or legislation would generally bring the government down; ministerial actions may be declared *ultra vires* (that is, beyond the bounds of law) by the courts. In West Germany, the Federal Constitutional Court and the parliament, and in France, the Constitutional Council and the parliament, also could act either to quash or to modify policy. The Council of State may also rule against specific applications of government measures as being illegal.

This power of legitimate interposition—by one or some organs of the government against another, or others—is wholly lacking in the USSR. The power of the Party leadership is unchecked by any legitimate institutional pluralism. The blockage of policy which exists in the Soviet system stems either from the inability of the officialdom to carry out directives (because of such factors as inefficiency, lack of information, lack of means to carry it out, misunderstanding, lack of coordination, environmental constraints, and so on) or from *covert opposition*. There is no sanctioned right of refusal to the directives of the Party.

AUDIT

An important phase of policy is the examination, post facto, of what has been done, how and why, with a view to controlling the policy-makers and the policy-implementors, and bringing about changes and improvements. In the United States and other Western states, the media frequently uncover the muddy tracks of past government actions, launch exposés, and sometimes even succeed in toppling high officials in the process. In each of the Western parliamentary regimes there are interesting histories of official scandals, involving illegal and improper government activities, uncovered and publicized by the press and recently, also, by television. In addition, there are formal government organs, independent of those who may initiate and carry out policies, to check into their activities. One such agency in the United States is the General Accounting Office, a watchdog of the Congress upon the executive. Of course, the Congress itself can and often does investigate past actions by the executive. Such famous inquiries include those in the aftermath of the stock market crash in the 1930's, and the Pearl Harbor disaster in the 1940's, as well as the Senate inquiry into the Watergate scandal in 1973.

This power of independent public inquiry and exposure, from whatever source or sources, is wholly lacking in the Soviet political system. The investigation or even mention of past abuses is always very carefully controlled and manipulated by the CPSU leadership of the day. In the 1950's and early 1960's, Khrushchev chose to single out certain acts of Stalin for official condemnation. These included, for example, the physical liquidation of 70 percent of the members of the CPSU Central Committee elected in 1934. But many parts of the Stalinist record have remained strictly "taboo" in the USSR. The assassination of Leon Trotsky and the liquidation of such Party oppositionists as Bukharin or Kamenev, let alone the killing of millions of Kulaks and others, have gone both unmentioned and unmentionable in official media. Under Brezhnev the limits of criticism of the Stalin era have been narrowed down even further. Any Soviet citizen who would challenge the Party by digging up the forbidden past would likely face the fate of Aleksandr Solzhenitsyn, and possibly much worse (if he or she were not well known internationally and actually "watched over" by Western reporters stationed in Moscow). Officially, much of the past in the USSR continues to consist of "unpersons" and "unsubjects."

To be sure, there is no lack of auditing agencies under the Soviet regime, including especially the secret police, the ministries of state control and finances, under the supervision of the Presidium of the Council of Ministers; the Procuracy under the supervision of the Presidium of the Supreme Soviet; and above all, the Party itself, particularly its Party-State Control Committees, subsequently (since 1965) the Committee of People's Control, and the CPSU's Central Auditing Commission. But all these agencies are Party-controlled and Party-supervised. Their records are never made public, though there are some perfunctory speeches given by their leading officials at Party congresses. The CPSU deliberately rejects the idea that non-Communists, or anti-Communists, should be allowed access to facts and disclosures that might weaken or jeopardize the Party's power. The Party's whole view of its power is not compatible with the kind of "let-the-chips-fall-where-they-may" attitude that would be required for a truly effective auditing system. This has been seen as simply too risky. The Party is well aware of the great shadows which the past can so often cast upon the present, and it is consequently most "Orwellian" and sensitive about controlling the social image of the past.

conclusion: performance and prospects

STALINIST LEGACY

In the USSR the political process, as described in the preceding pages, has tended to emphasize the power of the CPSU leadership, and to impair the capability of many elements in the society—whether farmers, consumers, ethnic dissidents, or just ordinary rank-and-file citizens—to pursue their interests as they see them, not as the Party sees them. Ideology, CPSU-control, police and administrative measures, censorship and propaganda—all these have imposed restraints on the power of people to make their own preferences "count" in the policy process. These factors have impeded, on the one hand, the ability of many people to get what they want, while on the other they have added to the power of some other people in the system (for example, Party leaders, bureaucrats to achieve their preferences.

The effect has been to create a "command economy": one in which tremendously disproportionate weight, in terms of effort and investment, has been given to targets selected by the party leadership. In effect, there has been single-minded pursuit of some objectives to the overwhelming, even spectacular, neglect of others. What has had the greatest bearing upon life in the USSR today is the historic transformation of Soviet society from agrarian to industrial, supported by rapid and massive collectivization of farming. (See Table 5-1.) Stalin began this process in the 1920's. When he launched the first five-year plan in 1929, the Soviet Union's per capita income was only about one-sixth that of the United States, and only about one-fourth that of Britain, Germany, or France. (See Table 5-2.) Seventy-one percent of the Soviet labor force was involved in agriculture, making it comparable in this respect to India, China, and South Korea in our own time. By the late 1960's, however, the USSR emerged as the second largest world economy (after the United States). The Soviet GNP surpassed Germany, France, and Italy combined. The USSR changed from a largely rural nation to a predominantly urban one. Most of the work force shifted from agriculture to industry. In 1926, before the first five-year plan and collectivization, there were only three cities in the Soviet Union with over 500,000 people (Moscow, Leningrad, and Kiev).

TABLE 5–1 U.S./USSR Agricultures Compared c. 1973

	U.S.	USSR
Percentage of labor force in agriculture:	6.6	31.9

Yields in KG/HA:		
Potatoes	25,575	13,428
Cereals	3,680	1,774
Wheat	2,136	1,737
Barley	2,169	1,871
Maize	5,735	3,334
Oats	1,596	1,532
Roots and Tubers	24,274	13,428
Sugar beets	45,011	24,418
Peaches and nectarines	1,265	355
Tomatoes	35,873	15,556
Cabbage	18,354	28,493
Cucumbers	10,672	14,941

TABLE 5–2 Total Per Capita Consumption and Per Capita GNP of the USSR as a Percentage of U.S. and other Western States' Equivalents

USSR as % of	*1955*		*1968*	
	Total Per Capita Consumption	*GNP*	*Total Per Capita Consumption*	*GNP*
U.S.	27	36	33	47
Great Britain	41	53	52	72
France	47	59	—	—
West Germany	48	57	49	63
Italy	79	94	75	98

In 1966 there were 30 such cities. The number of cities between 100,000 and 500,000 rose from 28 to 162; those with populations between 50,000 and 100,000 from 60 to 183. The total urban population rose from 26.3 million (less than 20 percent) to 124.7 million (54 percent), solidly reversing the rural predominance of Russia.

The Stalinist method of achieving this transformation involved (1) central planning by an organization called the Gosplan under close Party direction; (2) massive use of coercion and summary punishment for plan-fulfillment failures; (3) expropriation of private property in land and other means of production; (4) differentiated income and bonus incentives for

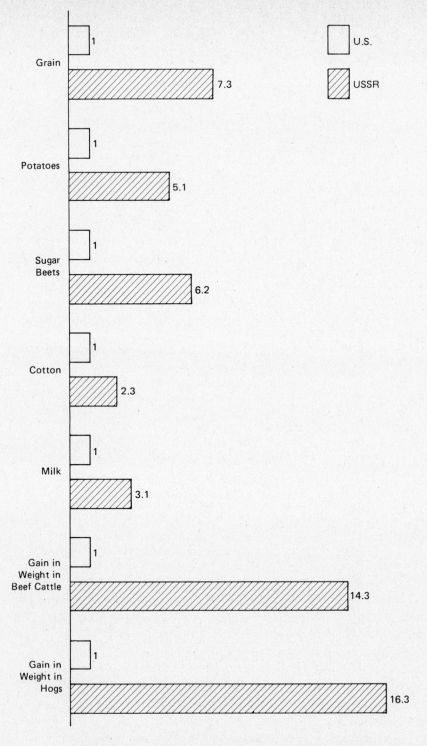

FIGURE 5–1 Soviet and American Labor Requirements per Unit of Agricultural Output (U.S. = 1)

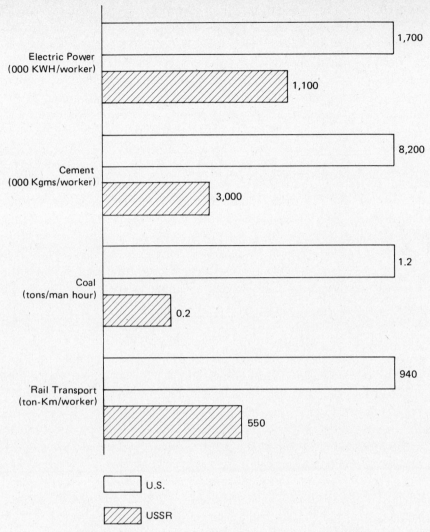

FIGURE 5–2 Output per Worker in U.S. and USSR

employees; (5) propaganda and agitation techniques; (6) autarky—that is, mobilization of domestic resources without any substantial reliance on foreign capital; (7) sacrifice of the consumer sector and agricultural production to heavy industry and capital investment; (8) emphasis on military over civilian production, particularly beginning with the second five-year plan in 1933–1938.

The Stalinist model led to the development of high priority economic sectors: in defense and defense-related industries; in manpower training for industrial and technological tasks; in the development of cultural, social welfare, and economic programs that emphasized public-communal activities—controlled by state-Party bureaucracies—as opposed to private-individual activities that emphasized personal and family controls; in the massive, rapid, and frequently coercive redistribution of statuses and benefits in the society; in extreme under-consumption; and in morbid concern with surveillance and control of the population, aimed at inhibiting easy, autonomous flow of persons and ideas throughout the country.

THE CONTINUING INFLUENCE OF STALINISM

In various respects, the Stalinist legacy has been enduring. One illustration of this is in the allocation of resources. Consider defense. Even though the USSR has had a total GNP still less than 60 percent as large as that of the United States in the early 1970's (and only about 45 percent as large in per capita terms), its allocations on defense were at least on a par with, and in all likelihood larger than, those in the United States. In terms of certain crucial items, singled out for development by the Soviet leadership, the Soviet Union has actually achieved substantial leadership over the United States.

According to estimates of the International Institute for Strategic Studies, by the end of 1972 the Soviet Union had accumulated 1,530 ICBMs (intercontinental ballistic missiles) while the United States possessed 1,054. The U.S. had 522 bombers in its strategic offensive force; the USSR, 840. In total armed forces personnel, the Soviet Union exceeded the United States, 3,375,000 to 2,391,000. The U.S. Air Force had some 6,000 planes to the Soviet's 9,000. The USSR had a huge lead in armor and artillery. Even with respect to naval strength, traditionally a weak spot in Russia's defenses, the USSR mustered 231 major surface combat ships while the U.S. had 243, and 300 attack and cruise missile submarines against 91 for the United States. The USSR had 560 submarine-launched missiles on 61 ships; the U.S. had 656 on 41 vessels.[25]

Naturally, the above figures do not consist of a complete inventory of forces; nor do they take into account *qualitative* aspects of military strength. They are, however, indicative of the disproportionately heavy effort made by the USSR in the military preparedness field.

CONSUMER DEPRIVATION

Since the total American economy is much larger than the Soviet (and the population smaller), what do the Russians give up in relation to the Americans for their spectacular military performance? In fact, we can

[25] *The Military Balance, 1972–1973* (London, 1972), pp. 2–9.

broaden this question to virtually all other states, because with the possible exception of modern Israel, no state has invested quite as heavily of its resources on military purposes as has the USSR. What has been sacrificed in the process is largely consumer goods and services. The USSR has been outspent and outperformed by all of the comparably advanced nations of the world (that is, those with similar GNP's per capita) for such purposes as housing, clothing, appliances, automobiles, many categories of food, travel and tourism.

For ideological-political reasons, the Soviet regime has discouraged private house building and private farming, while it has subsidized relatively low rents (in such housing as it has provided) and directed the bulk of agricultural investments into notoriously inefficient state and collective farms.

According to latest available data, there were 2.8 rooms per dwelling in the USSR, with 1.5 persons living in each room. In the United States, the average dwelling had 5 rooms and 0.6 occupants per room. Even in considerably poorer countries of the world and in this sense more comparable to the USSR, there was much less crowding. Virtually all the West European states, including Austria, Ireland, Italy, Portugal, and Spain—with per capita GNP's *lower* than the Soviet Union—provided more ample housing space to the population.[26] Even in crowded Japan the average dwelling had 3.6 rooms with 1.1 inhabitants in each. In the USSR there were few bathtubs, flush toilets, running water, and central heating facilities in housing, notwithstanding some new promises and new plans by the Brezhnev-Kosygin leadership for more such amenities.

The relatively low level of investment in services to the consumer is partly reflected in the number of persons employed in wholesale and retail trade. The USSR, with more than 246 million population, claimed only 3.9 million persons engaged in this branch of the economy in 1970. The United States, however, had 12.3 million so employed for a population of only about 200 million (in 1967); Britain had 3.3 million wholesale and retail employees for a population of about 52 million; France, 2.4 million for a somewhat smaller population in 1966; West Germany, 2.8 million in 1968 for a population of about 57 million.[27]

More striking still are figures on the availability and costs of certain types of goods in the USSR. According to U.S. Department of Labor estimates in 1971, given Soviet and American wage levels, a Soviet worker must work six times as long as the American to buy a pair of shoes or a shirt; ten times as long for a pair of nylon stockings; six and a half times as long for an ordinary cotton shirt. In fact, the Soviet worker must work

[26] United Nations, *Statistical Yearbook, 1971* (New York: 1971), pp. 716–733.
[27] Ibid., pp. 360–371.

four times as long as the American even for a fifth of Vodka! Average consumption of meat and fish is about one-third that of the United States; consumption of sugar, vegetables, fruits, and fats is only about 60 percent of the U.S. figure. The situation is even more unfavorable with respect to most consumer durables. In 1971, the Soviet Union produced 60,000 color television sets—for the first time. In the same year, the United States produced 4,650,000 color TVs. Most appliances in the USSR are so scarce, and consequently are priced so high, that an average worker must work about ten times as long as his U.S. counterpart to buy one. This lop-sided comparison applies not only to the United States, but to all industrial nations of the world. With only 1,650,000 passenger automobiles in the whole country, the USSR ranked an incredible eighty-first in world per capita automobile use—far behind all Western European and even most Latin American nations. With about 12 million telephones, the USSR ranked an even more abysmal eighty-seventh among some 120 nations surveyed by the UN in 1970.[28] There are still very few dishwashers, toasters, freezers, clothes dryers, and food mixers in the USSR.

As of 1971, the Soviet Union produced only 500,000 cars as compared with 8.6 million in the U.S.; 8 million radios compared with 18.6 in the U.S.; and a somewhat more respectable 4.6 million refrigerators and 4.1 million washing machines as compared with 5.7 and 4.6 million, respectively, in the U.S. Still, not only was the Soviet population larger, but the American consumers, unlike the Russian, continued to augment their supplies with large foreign imports. We can better appreciate the disproportion if we keep in mind that Soviet consumer deprivations were sustained in an economy which until the 1950's had produced only handfuls of these durables, but in 1971 outproduced the U.S. in pig iron 90 million to 84 million tons; in steel 121 million tons to 109 million; in coal 641 to 505 million tons; in cement 100 to 72 million tons.[29]

SOME ADVERSE IMPACTS

Tight security and management policies have made it very difficult for the Soviet people to move about their own country, to travel abroad, or to change jobs. In 1967, according to UN information, fewer than 800,000 Soviet citizens out of the then 237 million travelled abroad—the lowest percentage in any even remotely comparable nation of the world! In contrast, almost 50 million American tourists were recorded in various foreign countries. In fact, more persons travelled overseas from Greece in

[28] See A. J. Groth and William C. Potter, "Personal Mobility and Communication in the Warsaw Pact States," AAASS paper, Banff, Canada, September 4–6, 1974.
[29] Based on data presented by William Ebenstein, *Today's Isms*, 7th ed. (Englewood Cliffs, N.J.: Prentice-Hall, 1973), pp. 51–54.

1967 than from the Soviet Union. In 1970, the situation was about the same—less than 1 million out of 246 travelled abroad.*

All of this has meant a more drab and parsimonious existence for millions of ordinary Russian people: crowded living conditions, with little or no privacy in poorly furnished and poorly equipped apartments; starchy diets with fewer protein meals and fewer fruits, vegetables, and imported delicacies than in any Western country. It has meant major expenses and relatively little choice in the purchase of clothes and shoes, and extreme difficulty (bordering on impossibility) in acquiring an automobile or enjoying the stimulation and excitement of travel abroad. It has also meant queuing up in front of stores and receiving notoriously poor and surly service from the state bureaucracy running them.

SOME POSITIVE IMPACTS

Where the USSR has done very much better for its citizens, in relationship to the outside world, has been in two areas relevant to the Party's special interests: cultural and communal services. Education and culture have always had a double significance for the CPSU: first, as vehicles of political indoctrination and therefore, ultimately, control, and second, as means of training the necessary labor force, or cadres, for the technological, industrial, and military tasks set by the regime. Communal services also have had a similarly dual function. Partly, they have served ideological-political purposes to reorient people away from private and traditional institutions, such as individual enterprise, the family, and the church, and toward the State as provider of important service values. Partly, they have been economic in purpose—that is, designed to maintain the welfare and morale of the labor force engaged in what the CPSU broadly calls "socialist construction."

Education The Soviet regime has made great achievements in the fields of science, technology and, above all, education. It has created virtually universal literacy in a land where, under the tsars, the overwhelming majority of the people could neither read nor write. It has provided universal primary education to all children. It has also provided high quality secondary, vocational, and higher education to its people, although more selectively.

The Soviet regime raised the literacy rate from 24 percent in 1914 to almost 99 percent in the 1970's. In 1914, only 127,000 persons out of some 150 million in all of Russia attended universities; in 1966, 3.9 million out

---

* In all cases multiple entries may be involved—one tourist going to six countries counts for more than two going to one or two countries.

Moscow schoolchildren on a field trip to visit the Kremlin.
Keystone Press Agency, Inc.

of a population of 246 million did so. This meant that while the population increased less than two-fold, the number of students in higher education increased more than thirty-fold. During the same period the total number of students in primary, secondary, and technical schools rose from about 10 million to nearly 65 million. The regime extended educational opportunity in the USSR not only far beyond anything attained in tsarist days, but also in comparison with the achievements of most other nations today. Between 1917 and 1939 Soviet primary and secondary school enrollments rose from 7.9 to 34.6 million—that is, by almost 450 percent—while the population of the country increased only from about 150 to 183 million—that is, less than 25 percent. By 1967, the Soviet Union had surpassed in total school enrollments most of the West European states. Its university enrollments per thousand people were among the highest in the world. And a far higher proportion of Soviet university students were majoring in the sciences and in engineering than in any Western nation, including the United States.[30]

Popular Culture In terms of cultural services, with all their indoctrination and propaganda uses, the Soviet Union has been one of the world

[30] See Stanley H. Cohen, *Economic Development in the Soviet Union* (Lexington, Mass.: D. C. Heath, 1970), pp. 77, Table 16.

leaders for at least two decades. The USSR has provided its people with more cinemas, theaters, museums, exhibits, libraries, opera, and symphony ensembles, among other things, than any economically comparable world state. It has also supplied more books, magazines, newspapers, movies, and translations of (carefully screened) foreign works per capita than has the overwhelming majority of the world community of nations.

In 1965, there were 73 million radio sets in the USSR; almost half of them were wired speakers capable of transmitting only official programs. In 1973 the USSR had accumulated some 40 million television sets—one for every six persons. Thus, with respect to centrally controlled and disseminated information flows, the USSR has been undeniably generous.

Health The Soviet Union has also made major advances in the fields of public health and medicine, providing more physicians, nurses, dentists, hospitals and hospital beds per population than most economically comparable (and many considerably richer) Western states. It has been very effective in controlling epidemics and in assuring generally good health and medical care to the Soviet population. It has also been particularly effective in providing medical and social welfare benefits to the industrial, managerial, and technological components of the population: the very people on whom the thrust of Soviet economic policy has thus far depended.[31]

Enhanced Role of Women The Soviet regime could also claim that it has given women greater opportunities than have most other regimes thus far in the world. As of 1959, women made up 54 percent of the Soviet intelligentsia; 52 percent of those with higher education in 1965 were women, and 62 percent of those with specialized secondary education were women. Seventy percent of Soviet teachers and 73 percent of all physicians in the mid-1960's were women. Ninety-two percent of medical specialists in the USSR were women. It is certainly true, however, that despite all Soviet achievements, women have not yet reached equal status with men in the USSR. It is also true that generally they have been "thinned out" in the upper rungs of most professional hierarchies, and above all in positions of political power.

Twenty-eight percent of the deputies to the Supreme Soviet of the USSR in 1966 were women (compared with 3 percent in the U.S. Congress); 23.3 percent of delegates to the CPSU's Twenty-third (1966)

[31] Cf. George Hyde, *The Soviet Health Service* (London: Lawrence and Wishart, 1974), and Bernice Madison, *Social Welfare in the Soviet Union* (Stanford: Stanford University Press, 1968); and Robert J. Osborn, *Soviet Social Policies, Welfare, Equality and Community* (Homewood, Ill.: Dorsey Press, 1970).

A medical team at work.
NOVOSTI from SOVFOTO

Congress were women, although they constituted only 20.9 percent of the Party's membership. In 1966, however, only five women (2.5 percent) were members of the Party's Central Committee; only one woman, Ekaterina Furtseva, has served on the Politburo and as a Minister of the USSR. Yet, in the less politically sensitive local, regional, and republic soviets, women have had more substantial representation. They have had 42.7 percent of the membership in the 48,770 local and regional soviets; 34.9 percent in the 20 soviets of autonomous regions and 33.7 percent in the 15 union-republic soviets. Given, however, that most countries of the world still incline to male supremacy (not many women have held ministerial rank in France, Germany, Britain, or the United States, for example), and particularly in view of the singular backwardness of the tsarist regime in this area, the Soviet achievement has been impressive.[32]

32 See Samuel Hendel, ed., *The Soviet Crucible*, 4th ed. (N. Scituate, Mass.: Duxbury Press, 1973), Chapter 24, pp. 364–378.

A major change in social stratification has taken place in the USSR since the Revolution. In 1913, the bulk of Russia's people—about 67 percent—were poor peasants with little or no land. The Kulaks, peasants with substantial holdings, amounted to 11 percent; workers comprised 13 percent of the population; the middle class (shopkeepers, small-scale manufacturers) and intelligentsia (professionals, teachers) 6 percent. At the very top of tsarist Russia's social pyramid stood the nobility, upper bourgeoisie (bankers, large manufacturers), clergy, and military officers. These elements constituted only 3 percent of Russia's population.

The disparities in incomes and life styles were enormous. At the top of the pyramid many of the nobles lived lives of such luxury that not even Hollywood's wilder extravaganzas could do them justice. Palaces, vast estates, thousands of servants, priceless art collections, sumptuous banquets, silver, gold, and china, the most extravagant of luxuries foreign and domestic—all these were part of a pattern of life at the top. Figuratively, and sometimes literally, the prerevolutionary Russian nobility and upper bourgeoisie could be said to have bathed in champagne.

At the bottom of the pyramid were millions of poor peasants. Their lives were usually spent in utter poverty, often starvation, in an environment that lacked the most fundamental amenities; they lived in mud huts, prey to disease and epidemics, with little hope or opportunity for education and self improvement.

The Soviet regime not only destroyed the upper stratum of the old Russian society, it also created in its place a new pyramid of wealth, privilege, and power. In this new pyramid, however, more people share the wealth at the top. The upper stratum has become broader; and the distance in perquisites and life styles between the top and the bottom, while still quite substantial and distinctly unegalitarian, is not nearly as vast as in the prerevolutionary period.

The privileged group of Soviet society consists in part of the intelligentsia, with about 26 million persons out of a work force of 76.9 million (the latest estimate in 1965). This group includes occupations which usually require or are associated with higher education, such as scientists, engineers, bureaucrats, artists, teachers, physicians, lawyers, higher clerical personnel, and party workers. These people currently account for about one-third of the total labor force, and with their families about one-third of the Soviet population. They are augmented by several million highly skilled and well paid blue collar workers. These two strata are thus considerably larger than old Russia's nobility, middle class, and even Kulak categories put together. As for differentials in means, we find the incomes of the poorest peasants at about 60 rubles a month ($74); office clerks at about 100 rubles ($123); and significantly, skilled workers with wages between 100 to 250 rubles a month ($123-$308), enjoying incomes comparable to and in some cases greater than those of physicians, teachers, engineers, or accountants. Top party and state officials might make as much as 1800 rubles ($2206) a month.

Vernon Aspaturian recently observed that:

> The maximum Soviet *annual* income, which is about $26,400, from which about $3000 is deducted in taxes (those earning less than 60 rubles pay no income taxes), allows the *highest* members of the Soviet élite to live at a level only comparable to that of the American or Western European upper middle class. This income is very modest compared to that for top American executives, and there are no Soviet citizens whose income or standard of living even approaches that of the big executive, the successful performing artist, or the large entrepreneur and investor in America.[33]

Thus, the top of the Soviet socioeconomic pyramid has grown larger, while the distance between it and the bottom has somewhat shrunk.[34] Another aspect of change is that the Soviet "privileged class"—particularly the intelligentsia—has been created substantially and deliberately from those strata of the population which constituted the disinherited elements under the tsarist regime. It has been recruited predominantly from among the sons and daughters of workers and peasants. In cutting down the old order and creating a new one, Lenin, and Stalin particularly, adhered to the old Machiavellian maxim that he who wishes to rule a state with absolute power must make the rich poor and the poor rich. A new stratum of people was thus created who would look upon the Soviet regime as their principal benefactor: the source of their opportunity, status and income. As some Western studies have confirmed, it is among this intelligentsia (notwithstanding all the problems of dissent among its individual writers, artists, and scientists) that the regime has found its most solid support and enthusiastic commitment. The greatest resistance appears to be found precisely among those most mistreated thus far—the peasants. They have benefited the least from the regime's policies, and they continue to espouse precisely those values of property-mindedness, religiosity, and skepticism toward the official ideology of which the leaders

---

[33] Vernon Aspaturian, "The Soviet Union," pp. 518–519.
[34] An interesting value question is whether the Soviet's narrowing down of income and status differentials—similar to the process taking place in other industrializing societies —was really worth the price in lives and suffering incurred through the Revolution and its aftermath.

have always suspected them. It is among these people, and among the "ethnics," that the opposition to the regime is still most substantial. It remains to be seen whether further relaxation and change of the Stalinist model of development will alter this situation.

SOME LINKAGES OF IMPACTS

In examining the quality of life in the USSR, we must consider the linkages of different policies. In particular, the connection between domestic and international policies have reinforced the deprivations among Soviet consumers and the limitations on the freedom of individuals. As long as the regime operates on the expectation of imminent conflict, whether with the United States, the NATO countries, West Germany or China, Soviet resources must continue to flow preponderantly into the military sector. Contacts with the potentially hostile countries, whether in terms of tourism or trade, are likely to continue to be limited. Moreover, international security considerations reinforce domestic ones. This had been a familiar pattern of policy in Stalin's time. Vigilance, secrecy, and unquestioned subordination toward the Party at home have been seen as patriotic necessities against foreign enemies, who are constantly seeking to subvert the USSR from within, recruiting Soviet citizens for their nefarious espionage and sabotage projects. Such alleged threats, which Stalin associated with "the imperialist encirclement" of the USSR, sanctioned the massive uses of the secret police, rigorous censorship, and persecution of dissenters. These people, in Stalin's view, wittingly or unwittingly played into the hands of the enemies of the Soviet Union. Collaboration with foreign enemies was, after all, the main theme of the Great Purge of the 1930's against Kamenev, Bukharin, Rykov, Tomsky, Tukhachevsky, and countless others.

If the "peaceful coexistence" policy, inaugurated by Khrushchev and continued by Brezhnev, under the theme of détente, should convert former mortal enemies—the Western capitalists—into peaceful and acceptable competitors in Soviet eyes, this could weaken much of the rationale of the police state at home. In turn, the decline in policies such as surveillance, censorship, persecution of dissent, and restrictions on movement in and out of the USSR, not to mention the use of terror and slave labor camps, would "uninhibit" the demands of the Soviet people. Many long unsatisfied wants would come to the surface, and the momentum for changes, thus far only gingerly indulged in by the CPSU leadership, would in all likelihood be greatly and, from the official point of view, dangerously, accelerated. Naturally, Party officialdom may not exactly welcome the prospect of its own demise.

The Party's capacity to make lop-sided allocations has given it, thus far, some advantages in areas of particular concern to modern Americans. The ability to *deny* consumers what they want—for example, automobiles—has had favorable consequences for the Soviet energy situation. There has been no energy crisis in the USSR, and there has been a steadily increasing output of oil, electrical energy, coal, natural gas, and other sources of power. Automobile emissions do not threaten the air of Soviet metropolitan areas on the scale that they do in the United States or Western Europe (although with quite a few very old cars, pollution has been a problem in many Soviet cities). Soviet decision-makers, however, need not be nearly as concerned with environmentalist interests in constructing their nuclear power plants as are their American and Western European counterparts. Yet, if the Soviet regime *were* to become convinced of the need for drastic environmental protection measures—against water pollution, for example—its power to deal with the problem(s) sweepingly, comprehensively, and, if need be, brutally, should not be underestimated. No local or commercial interests are as likely to thwart it.

One area in which the Soviet experience has compared quite favorably with the American and Western European—precisely because of the regime's capacity to say "no" to its constituents (including its Party-run trade unions)—has been price stability. Although there have been *some* officially imposed price increases in the USSR over the last five or six years, the general rate of inflation has been remarkably low; probably closer to the 2-3 percent annually than the 7-18 percent experienced in Britain, Italy, Germany, France, and the United States over the same period. To be sure, the advantage of price stability was itself purchased at a price (as discussed here earlier). Controls have hampered not only consumer freedom of choice and the diversity of available goods and services, but also efficiency in the use of labor and resources. Still, they have produced a trade-off in terms of certain kinds of stability and predictability of economic development that, for all their faults, many people could regard as advantageous.

FUTURE PROSPECTS

Toward Liberalization? Hopeful interpretations of Soviet politics in the United States and the West—looking toward convergence with Western constitutional systems—have generally revolved around the theme of modernization.[35] Socioeconomic needs and constraints have been used to

[35] "Modernization" is taken here to mean change in, and diffusion of, technology and economic and cultural resources, with destabilizing effects upon the organization of society and the needs or wants perceived in it. Sometimes the terms "development"

determine the character and the future possibilities of the Soviet political system. Thus, Stalin's regime has been explained in terms of meeting the need for rapid industrialization. In this stage, the CPSU acted as an agent of economic growth; it promoted the socioeconomic mobilization and development of the country. Post–Stalin regimes have been seen as political adaptations to a more mature Soviet economy and society. The Party under Malenkov, Khrushchev, Brezhnev, and Kosygin has been viewed as gradually settling down to routine administration of a largely modernized, increasingly affluent society, its epic struggle and zealous ideological commitments largely spent. The future is often pictured as the inevitable, though perhaps uneven and fumbling (and more or less remote), adjustment of obsolescent political institutions to the full social and economic requirements of modernity.[36] Dictatorship is now gradually relaxed and will eventually disappear, as it has among the wealthiest industrial nations.

CPSU rule has been pictured as a means for a basically traditional, backward society to catch up rapidly with dynamic modern societies; and once economic and social convergence have been brought about, a political convergence must also ultimately follow. The nature of the truly "modernized" political system—toward which convergence occurs—is generally inferred from the current (and recent) orientations of the ten or fifteen wealthiest members of the world community of nations. Most of these are in the scope of Western European and Anglo-Saxon culture. The Middle Eastern country of Kuwait constitutes (still) a somewhat uncomfortable exception to the rule "high development—representative and/or participatory democracy." But presumably incipient changes can already be discerned even in Kuwait. The recent, pre-1945 "aberration" of Germany is usually explained by the peculiar, still unmodernized, circumstances of that country in the 1930's.

Industrialization is usually associated with urbanization. Similar living conditions develop everywhere so that eventually, it is claimed, "industrial life [becomes] the same in Sverdlovsk and Detroit." [37] Specialization and differentiation, both stemming from the application of complex technology, lead to the rise of ever new and more specialized interest groups: thus greater social pluralism. Industrialization also produces affluence and

---

and occasionally even "mobilization" seem to be used to the same effect by social scientists.

[36] In the words of Professor Frederick Barghoorn: "I think that perhaps within two decades, or even sooner, substantial reforms in the structure of the Soviet political system are almost inevitable." *Politics in the USSR*, p. 316.

[37] Samuel H. Huntington and Zbigniew K. Brezezinski, *Political Power: US/USSR* (New York: Viking Press, 1963), p. 10.

this in turn destroys adherence to dogmatic, millenarian ideological beliefs in any society—such as Marxism-Leninism in the USSR.[38] The more Russia approximates the economic development of the United States and Western Europe, the more likely the demise of Communist dictatorship.

These arguments for convergence—and simultaneously for the impact of the social environment upon political institutions—are buttressed by still another thesis. We may call it the *interdependence-fragility theory*. The more technologically complex a society becomes, the more vulnerable to disruptions and malfunctions. Like a delicate Swiss watch, it can't be made to work by a beating. The failure of any one part to perform correctly is likely to undermine all the rest. Therefore, it is necessary in such a society to respect carefully functional expertise, promote incentives, disseminate adequate information to all those involved in societal decisions, and above all, coordinate the activities of all members on the basis of voluntarism. These functional requirements would point any and every industrializing society in the direction of participatory democratism. Indeed, in the words of Alvin Toffler:

> . . . under superindustrialism, democracy becomes not a political luxury, but a primal necessity.
>
> Democratic political forms arose in the West . . . because the historical pressure toward social differentiation and toward faster paced systems demanded sensitive social feedback. In complex, differentiated societies, vast amounts of information must flow at ever faster speeds between the formal organization and subcultures that make up the whole. . . .[39]
>
> . . . as interdependency grows, smaller and smaller groups within society achieve greater and greater power for critical disruption. . . . This suggests that the best way to deal with angry or recalcitrant minorities is to open the system further, bringing them into it as full partners, permitting them to participate in social goal setting, rather than attempting to ostracize or isolate them.[40]

[38] Ibid., pp. 10–11. See also W. W. Rostow, *The Stages of Economic Growth* (Cambridge: Harvard University Press, 1960) for the argument that high mass consumption society is incompatible with either Marxism or dictatorship. The more Russia approximates the economic development of the United States and Western Europe, the more likely the demise of Communist dictatorships, pp. 133, 162. For much more modest assessments of technocratic claims see Jeremy R. Azrael, *Managerial Power and Soviet Politics* (Cambridge: Harvard University Press, 1966), particularly Chapter 6.
[39] Alvin Toffler, *Future Shock* (New York: Random House, 1970), pp. 420–421.
[40] Ibid., p. 422. For the view that Hitler's dictatorship, like Stalin's, occurred not in a "modernized" socioeconomic system but in a "transitional" one, see Manfred Halpern, "The Revolution of Modernization in National and International Society" in C. J. Friedrich, ed., *Nomos VIII, Revolution, Yearbook of the American Society for Political and Legal Philosophy* (New York: Atherton Press, 1966), pp. 192–193, 210. Such arguments continue to be made, explicitly and implicitly, even though Germany

None of the processes usually associated with modernization are really new. Obviously, "differentiation" and "specialization" of functions have occurred to some degree and in some areas of economy and culture even in ancient societies. "Secularization" or "rationalization" would not have been altogether inapplicable terms in referring to the life of Rome, Greece, or Phoenicia. "Interdependence" was surely an important fact of life in medieval times, not only since the industrial revolution. Communication—with "feedback"—could undoubtedly have been found in the ancient Indian empires of Latin America, as would have been "technology," "mobility," and all the rest. Presumably, however, in the industrial world we have much greater complexity, speed, power, and scope in these processes, as well as greater magnitudes of people involved, distances travelled, types and quantities of information conveyed, goods processed and moved, and so forth.[41]

Recently, two Sovietologists have written:

> During the early stages of Soviet rule the party preempts interest articulation not only because it wants to but also, to some degree, because it *has* to. The society which the Bolsheviks inherited was largely composed of an undifferentiated mass of peasants who had traditionally played a politically passive role. Thus the task of identifying and articulating interests fell to the party by default.
> . . . functionally specialized groups with political experience . . .

---

of the 1930's could be readily identified among the then top ten industrial powers of the world through virtually any number of indices. Moreover, Germany's development was much more homogeneous than that of some of the other industrial powers: the United States, for example, with its southern "pocket." As John Gunther observes in his *Inside USA* (New York: Harper, 1947), p. xi, 13.9 percent of U.S. army draftees in 1943—one out of seven—were found to be illiterate. The figure in Germany was in all likelihood virtually nil. Moreover, nowhere in Germany—not in Pomerania, East Prussia, Silesia, Bavaria—could one find the abyss of cultural backwardness contemporaneous in, say, Mississippi, Georgia, and many other American states. Cf. Bertram D. Wolfe, "The Convergence Theory in Historical Perspective," *An Ideology in Power* (New York: Stein and Day, 1969), p. 394. Interestingly, Gabriel Almond and Sidney Verba in their *Civic Culture* (Princeton: Princeton University Press, 1963) found that in postwar "modern" Germany, increased levels of education corresponded with increased alienation from democracy, not attachment to it. Thus, "educated Germans have higher political information scores, more frequently follow discussions of public affairs in the media . . . but wherever political feelings are concerned, the educated Germans show greater alienation and negativism than the less well educated." Pp. 111–112. See Table IV.12. Among Germans with primary education, 35 percent reported a sense of satisfaction in voting but of those with university education only 26 percent did; 43 percent of persons with primary education or less reported sometimes getting angry during political campaigns; 73 percent of the university educated did; 37 percent of those with little education reported that they found political campaigns pleasant at least sometimes; only 27 percent of the highly educated agreed.
[41] See Karl W. Deutsch, "Social Mobilization and Political Development," *American Political Science Review* 55, no. 3 (September 1961): 493–501.

existed but they were far fewer and far less significant than in the present period.[42]

The authors go on to argue that all these groups lacked political legitimacy, unlike current groups whose "counsel cannot be ignored" because they are "the products of the Soviet period," and because expertise has now allegedly become too costly to be wasted or destroyed.[43]

Notwithstanding imprecise knowledge, "modernization" has been elevated in some quarters to the level of an all-purpose myth. Through it various cherished preferences, hopes, and hunches (not to say illusions) are held to be guaranteed, as if by a deity. The myth is analogous to eighteenth century rationalist and utilitarian faith in the progress of science and education; it is also similar to the beliefs of nineteenth century Victorians. How could humanity fail to grow more cooperative, humane, prosperous, and peaceful, as learning conquered ignorance and scientists mastered the secrets of nature?

Admittedly, the saints have not yet everywhere prevailed, but they cannot be held off much longer. Somehow, somewhere, modernization will achieve a quantum leap that will make all the disappointing experiences of the past utterly irrelevant and inapplicable. What no previous technology could effectively constrain, future technology must and will bring about. Though the message of ever increasing education has not yet turned the tide against dictatorial "irrationality" around the world, eventually it must—somehow. In such a perspective, the thorough democratization of the USSR (with or without the agency of revolution) is simply a matter of a few years or at most decades. A theoretical possibility, opposing the prevalent view, may be suggested here.

Toward More Authoritarianism? With rising affluence the Soviet Union may begin to experience more and more of the problems felt in some of the most advanced Western nations, including decline in labor discipline and productivity; an upsurge in ethnic and regional strife; the displacement of more inclusive civic loyalties by increasingly more specialized ones; a flux in terms of hitherto prevailing social values and standards; a decline or collapse of all sorts of authority structures and their concomitant ability to command deference and sacrifices; increased demands for personal goods and services as well as greater opportunity for asserting

[42] Joel J. Schwartz and William R. Keech, "Public Influence and Educational Policy in the Soviet Union," in Roger E. Kanet, ed., *The Behavioral Revolution and Communist Studies* (New York: Free Press, 1971), p. 180.
[43] Ibid.

idiosyncratic, nonconformist life styles; and even more generally perhaps a disturbing problem of enervating boredom and aimlessness throughout society; increased drug consumption; increased incidence of crime; irrational violence; alienation and unrest among youth.

Some of these negative aspects of modernization are likely to be perceived in the external world by members of the various Soviet élites, and some are already being experienced, at least to an appreciable extent, in the relatively advanced Soviet society of the 1970's. In connection with both external and internal perceptions, there is some likelihood of a reinforced political coalition in the USSR between the Party *apparat* (that is, CPSU bureaucracy) and various other publics, particularly from among the relatively successful and prosperous new Soviet middle class of managers and technocrats, who have much to lose from open-ended upheavals. The CPSU's now traditional capability for repression and manipulation could acquire a new functionality: more analogous to the historic dictatorships of the Right than of the Left.[44]

In abstract terms, political institutions can be at times seen as "useful" and "functional" by various publics because they are *sensitive* and *responsive* to all the shades and currents of a society's public opinion. At other times, however, and in the perceptions of different observers (or from the standpoint of different interests) they may well be seen as "useful" and "functional" precisely because they are *insensitive* and *unresponsive* to some of these currents. Much depends not merely on the values of the observers but on their intuitive, or rationally calculated, perceptions of outcomes, of benefits and costs in these situations. If increased pluralism should bring about increased conflict, stalemate, or chaos, the political result of its occurrence may be opposite to what optimistic modernizers expect: that is, as social pluralism increases, the governmental function may become more insulated and monistic to cope with resultant crises.

[44] See Barrington Moore, Jr., *Political Power and Social Theory* (Cambridge: Harvard University Press, 1958), p. 7, for the view that hopes of change stirred by Khrushchev could not be laid to rest now. Since the hopes of various publics were disappointed by NEP in 1921, and the abandonment of NEP in 1929, one has to go back to the alleged uniqueness of "modernity" to justify this argument. Some current and recent indications of how the Party cultivates the values of authority, hard work, dedication to duty, and the like, are apparent in its press organs. See, for example, *Partiinaia Zhizn'* "Vospitanie sotsialisiticheskoj discipilny truda," May 1972, No. 10, pp. 3–7, on the need and virtues of iron discipline in socialist construction; also, on the traditional role of party as nucleus of all social organizations, see Ibid., "Komunistii v obshchestviennich organizatsiach," No. 12, June 1972, pp. 39–43; see also "Tschlenstvo v KPSS," Ibid., No. 2, January 1973, pp. 22–29, emphasizing toughness in the face of adversity and unfailing dedication to duty. Cf. the conclusions of Carl A. Linden, *Khrushchev and the Soviet Leadership 1957–1964* (Baltimore: Johns Hopkins Press, 1966), p. 279 on CPSU attitude to socioeconomic changes, and Robert G. Wesson, *The Soviet State: An Aging Revolution* (New York: John Wiley, 1972), pp. 211–215.

In fact, if modernization in the United States, Britain, and France is relevant, it seems to enhance ethnic and regional differentiation. This may be profoundly alarming to Russian nationalists.[45] Thus, change and growth, if unchecked by the Party, could produce (for some, for many) unmanageable or unacceptable conflicts, turmoil, and strife, as well as other undesirable "output" consequences. Differentiation may imply division; specialization a decreasing sense of mutual identification among groups and individuals. Secularization may mean the erosion of all, or most, cherished values, standards, and ideals: the sense of unity and self-discipline in a society. Indeed, the basic ability to maintain order under *any* set of rules may seem under attack by headlong, ever accelerating technological and social change. It is possible that in the case of the USSR the introduction of some genuinely responsive forms of government (demanded from "below") could enhance strong secessionist movements—in the Ukraine, Byelorussia, the Baltic states, Caucasus, and throughout Soviet Asia.

Most people readily agree that the frustrations attendant upon rapid change are likely to have political consequences. There is, however, a tendency to see political defenses against "technology" and "modernization" or the human demands associated with them, as, ultimately at least, exercises in futility. The viability of coercive alternatives often is not seriously considered. It may be readily granted that any kind of economic, technological, and social change creates new and changing political demands. But, generally, only *some* of these demands are likely to be toward further change. Others are likely to be in the opposite direction, toward cooling, stabilizing, and even reversing new relationships in the sociopolitical system, and thwarting further demands for change.

The capability of the present Soviet decisional system to resist environmental pressures, to manipulate the environment ("creatively" or "capriciously," depending on the point of view) must be duly valued. For it could well turn out to be an asset on behalf of continuing CPSU power if the impact of modernization proves to be more abrasive and disruptive than much Western theorizing would allow. The Party may rally to its support a number of publics seeking to escape the conflicts, turmoil, and even disintegration which continuing modernization may bring. Quite apart from its historic ideology, the CPSU may be seen by its own cadres, and

---

[45] Andrei Amalrik's *Will the Soviet Union Survive Until 1984?* (New York: Harper & Row, 1971) is actually a spelling out of these fears. See also Boris Lewytzkyj, *Polityka narodowosciowa ZSRR w dobie Chruszczewa* (Paris: Instytut Literacki, 1966) and Michel Garder, *Agonia rezymu w ZSRR* (Paris: Instytut Literacki, 1965) on the Soviets' ethnic "pressure cooker."

various external publics, particularly the bureaucratic and technocratic élites, as capable of defending the continuity, order, and cohesion of Soviet society ("the gains of the Revolution") in the maelstrom of change and social ferment.

6

the european community

6 THE EUROPEAN COMMUNITY

On March 23, 1971, 80,000 European farmers from six countries gathered in Brussels, Belgium to press for changes in European agricultural policies. Ultimately, their protest march led to a clash with police in which a 38-year-old farmer was killed by an exploding tear gas grenade, 50 police and 100 demonstrators were injured, and substantial property damage occurred. It is symbolic that this demonstration was directed not at the individual governments of France, West Germany, Italy, Belgium, the Netherlands, or Luxembourg but at the Commission of the European Economic Community (the Common Market). In effect, the action of these European farmers, organized by a European agricultural pressure group (C.O.P.A.), was based on a recognition that the crucial bread-and-butter decisions affecting their livelihood are taken by a European organization which transcends the individual governments of the member states.

Clearly, the traditional frame of reference in which European politics and government have been perceived on an exclusively national basis is now obsolete. Some observers already identify—and not always approvingly—the European Community as a superpower in the making, potentially comparable to the United States and the Soviet Union.[1] Indeed, this view of the European Community as a power to be reckoned with is not confined to scholars or farmers. Former president Richard Nixon, in a widely noted *Time* magazine "man of the year" interview in 1972, endorsed the emergence of a new five-sided world balance of power in

[1] For a very critical view along these lines, see Johan Galtung, *Europe: A Superpower in the Making* (London: Allen & Unwin, 1973).

Angry European farmers introduce a cow to disrupt a meeting of the Commission of the European Community.
Courtesy E.C. Photo Library, Photographer J. L. Debaize

which Europe was a full-fledged player alongside the United States, the Soviet Union, China, and Japan.[2] And, Western European leaders in government, politics, business and labor have discovered in encounters with their foreign counterparts that the rest of the world really has come to view the European Community as a distinct and major entity in world politics and economics.

There are valid reasons for seeing Europe in this light. Following the formal admission of Britain, Denmark, and Ireland to the European Community in January 1973, the nine-member [3] group could be regarded as having a population and economic strength in roughly comparable magnitude to that of the United States and the Soviet Union. Based on the 1970 census, the Nine have a population of 253 million, slightly larger than the Soviet Union's 242 million and the United States' 207 million. The Europeans also hold a slight lead over the two continental superpowers in steel production and fall roughly midway between the U.S. and USSR in terms of computers and overall gross national product. (See Table 6-1.)

[2] "I think it will be a safer world and a better world if we have a strong, healthy United States, Europe, Soviet Union, China, Japan, each balancing the other, not playing one against the other, an even balance." *Time,* January 3, 1972.
[3] The original six members were France, Germany, Italy, Belgium, The Netherlands and Luxembourg.

TABLE 6–1 Europe, United States and Soviet Union Compared

	The "Nine"	United States	Soviet Union
Population (1970)	253 mil.	207 mil.	242 mil.
GNP (1973, approximate)	$1,076 bil.	$1,400 bil.	$700 bil.
Steel (metric tons) (1970)	139 mil.	132 mil.	138 mil.
Computers (1970)	21,000	60,000	5,000

The weight of opinion from farmers and presidents as well as the evidence of economic strength would seem to mark the European Community as a genuine world power by now, but the reality of Europe is not so straightforward. Indeed, there are some who see Western Europe as composed exclusively of traditional nation-states and who regard the European Community as no more than a narrow customs union, restrictionist and bureaucratic in nature, and inconsequential outside the commercial realm.[4] And even a former EEC Commissioner laments that the world expects Europe to act as though European unity were fully completed when the reality is much more limited.[5]

What then is the European Community? Does it constitute a major world player or is the achievement of European unity in fact a more modest and elusive phenomenon? To comprehend the present reality one must begin with an understanding of the European background.

background

The present achievements of European unity can be fully appreciated only when set against a background of centuries of division, conflict, and warfare. Indeed, until the end of World War II, Europe had for hundreds of years been the center of world conflict. Despite elements of a common civilization dating back 2,000 years to the Roman Empire, Europe had periodically torn itself apart in bloody conflict which, if anything, intensified with the rise of centralized nation-states in the seventeenth, eighteenth, and nineteenth centuries.[6] Ironically, substantial commercial,

[4] See, for example, John Newhouse, "Stuck Fast," *Foreign Affairs* 51, no. 2 (January 1973): 353–366; Edward L. Morse, "Why the Malaise," *Foreign Affairs* (January 1973): 367–379; and Raymond Vernon, "Rogue Elephant in the Forest: An Appraisal of Transatlantic Relations," *Foreign Affairs* 51, no. 3 (April 1973): 573–587.
[5] This is particularly the view of Ralf Dahrendorf.
[6] For a lucid discussion of the historical antecedents of European unity, see Lord Gladwyn, *The European Idea* (New York: Praeger, 1966), especially pp. 1–40.

social, and intellectual interchange coexisted with sporadic fits of warfare. In 1913, travel throughout Western Europe often took place without the requirement of passports, and visitors could go by rail and ferry between London and Paris in a slightly shorter time than is possible by the same means today.

World War I (1914–1918), a disastrous interwar period (inflation, depression, the rise of fascism, autarchy, and economic warfare), and then World War II (1939–1945) represented the catastrophic culmination of international conflict in Europe. Although the label "World War" is used to describe the successive cataclysms, there exists another perspective from which these wars may be seen as European Civil Wars, since the brunt of the fighting took place on the European continent and among European peoples.

Whatever the perspective, the disastrous experiences endured by Europeans from 1914 to 1945 acted as a catalyst for change. Fundamentally, traditional nation-states became discredited by war and economic collapse, either because their nationalism had become so virulent as to metamorphose into fascism and Nazism, or because no European state alone could cope with the economic disaster of the 1920's and 1930's, or because individual states alone could not provide sufficient security to protect their citizens from the devastation of war. World War II, with its tens of millions killed, genocidal slaughter, destruction of cities and industries, and real suffering and hardship inflicted on the vast majority of families and individuals, thus made the political and intellectual leaders of Europe, as well as the mass publics, ready to contemplate new and unprecedented measures to achieve unity among their countries. Indeed, in the resistance movements which developed during World War II, there grew a commitment to seek real European integration in the postwar world. To be sure, the idea of a United States of Europe was not new; it had been put forward after World War I by an Austrian aristocrat, Count Coudenhouvre-Kalergi, and occasionally supported by European leaders, but only after the traumatic experience of World War II did widespread support develop.

While most of the states of Western and Central Europe thus shared a horrendous experience, Britain alone among the major European powers had not suffered invasion at the start of the war (as had France), or defeat at the end of it (Germany, Italy). Thus Britain's own independent national existence had not been called into question. Despite air attacks and heavy battle losses, Churchill had rallied the British people and at the end of the war the country remained at the head of its huge Empire, standing with the United States and the Soviet Union as one of the Big Three victorious powers. In addition, an ambitious social reform program preoccupied the postwar Labour government, and many Britons viewed the entire European unity enterprise with distrust, even regarding the continental Europeans themselves as—variously—Catholic, Communist, Fascist, conservative, capitalist, over-sexed or unclean,[7] Britain thus seemed to have little to gain by becoming involved. It tended to remain aloof from successive European unity efforts or else attempted to weaken their supranational character.

INITIAL STEPS

With or without the British, the Western Europeans sought to construct some kind of common federal system in the aftermath of the war. It is a sign of the depth of this commitment as well as of the lessening sanctity of the nation-state that the postwar constitutions adopted for the Fourth French Republic (1946), the Italian Republic (1947), and the German Federal Republic (1949) each made provision for the transfer of sovereign state powers to a future United States of Europe.[8] Initially, two important postwar conferences took place,[9] the first in September 1946 in Zurich, Switzerland, the second at the Hague in 1948. Addressing the Zurich meeting, Winston Churchill endorsed the creation of a United States of Europe; his ringing and vague declaration made no place for Britain as a member, but only as a friend and sponsor. Though Churchill spoke not as Prime Minister but as a leader of the opposition Conservative Party, his views of European unity foreshadowed the positions of both Labour and Conservative governments over the next 14 years. Had Britain instead taken an aggressively pro-European unity position at this time, it would have ensured itself not only the determinant role for the entire European unity enterprise but also helped to propel Europe farther and faster along the path to both economic and political integration.

While the Zurich meeting resulted in few tangible results, the Hague Congress of May 1948 led to the establishment of the Council of Europe a year later. Despite attempts to provide this new organization with limited but real federal authority, the British succeeded in eliminating the Council's supranational elements (that is, those features which would have allowed the Council to exercise powers above the states or formerly held by them, in a manner analogous to the relationships between the U.S. federal government and the American states). Instead, the Council of Europe became a strictly intergovernmental body, in which no basic

[7] Polls reported widely held views such as these prior to Britain's actual entry in 1973.
[8] Roger Morgan, *West European Politics Since 1945: The Shaping of the European Community* (London: B. T. Batsford, Ltd., 1972), p. 5. Morgan provides an excellent and lucid discussion of this period.
[9] Even prior to the war's end, a European Federalist Congress met in Paris in March 1945. Participants included Albert Camus and George Orwell. Morgan, p. 78.

authority was given up by the members and unanimous approval was required for any major undertaking. The Council of Europe thereby became little more than a useful forum for discussion of European affairs among a membership which grew to 15 states. Its parliamentary assembly did, however, develop a pattern which was to be repeated in successive European organizations; in effect, parliamentarians began to sit and divide less on national lines than on a crossnational partisan or ideological basis. Thus, French, German, and Italian democratic Socialists began to vote together against French, German, and Italian Christian Democrats, rather than dividing by nationality. This characteristic, as well as deep divisions between conceptions of Europe as supranational or intergovernmental, were to appear repeatedly during the next two decades.[10]

Efforts to create European unity did not take place in a vacuum and they cannot be understood without reference to the role of the United States and the impact of the Cold War. In the late 1940's the growing sense that much of Western Europe faced both internal breakdown, with the possibility of domestic Communist parties coming to power in France and Italy, and an external threat of Soviet political or even military pressure, contributed to the sense of urgency and willingness to seek new and unprecedented solutions. To this situation, the United States brought its increasingly manichean anti-Communism and the weight of its immense political, economic, and military power. What is relevant about the American involvement is that in tandem with its growing military commitment, the United States sought to reconstruct and reinvigorate Western Europe by providing enthusiastic support and promotion for European unity.[11] For example, the United States stipulated that its huge Marshall Plan program required the Europeans themselves to establish the planning and coordination for the best use of this economic aid. In response, 16 European states established the *Organization for European Economic Cooperation* (OEEC) in April 1948. Like the Council of Europe, which it preceded, the OEEC was a strictly intergovernmental body, and although it performed its economic functions effectively and later evolved into the broader *Organization for Economic Cooperation and Development* (OECD) with the United States and Canada as members, the OEEC was never provided with real supranational powers.

European cooperation was not confined to matters of economics. In March 1948, France, Britain, Belgium, the Netherlands, and Luxembourg

[10] The British orientation during this immediate postwar period is set out in Robert J. Lieber, "Britain Joins Europe," in Alan M. Jones, Jr., ed., *U.S. Foreign Policy in a Changing World* (New York: McKay, 1973), pp. 149–162.
[11] See, for example, Max Beloff, *The United States and the Unity of Europe* (New York: Vintage, 1963).

signed the Brussels Treaty, aimed at providing military defense against Germany. However, increasing concern about a Soviet threat, particularly after the start of the Russian blockade of West Berlin in June 1948, led to the involvement of the United States and the signing of the North Atlantic Treaty in April 1949. Although the resultant North Atlantic Treaty Organization (NATO) achieved substantial military integration, and ultimately grew to 15 members including Germany in 1955, it too provided no real structure for European unity. NATO also signaled the priority that Atlantic defense matters would often have above other values, for while the NATO Treaty Preamble stated that member countries were "determined to safeguard the freedom, common heritage and civilization of their people, founded on the principles of democracy, individual liberty and the rule of law," this provided no obstacle to the membership of the repressive Portuguese dictatorship or, between 1967 and 1974, to the presence of Greece whose military forces had overthrown a democratically elected government and installed a dictatorship of their own.

Five years after World War II, and despite European desires, economic and political necessity, and American pressures, no fundamental step had been taken toward real European unity. To be sure, the Council of Europe, OEEC, and NATO each proved useful and important in individual areas, but there had been no transfer of sovereign state powers to any kind of European body and the traditional authority of the nation-states had nowhere given way to new forms of European organization.

A BREAKTHROUGH: THE EUROPEAN COAL AND STEEL COMMUNITY

The first real breakthrough came in May 1950 with the proposal by French Foreign Minister Robert Schuman for a *European Coal and Steel Community* (ECSC) as the initial step toward a federated Europe. The inspiration for this plan came from a formidable behind-the-scenes actor, Jean Monnet. Monnet, who had had an extraordinary career in French government, the League of Nations, American banking, Chinese railways, and wartime Anglo-French-American arms coordination, had been the author of a 1940 offer by Winston Churchill for immediate union between Britain and France, and in the late 1940's had brilliantly directed economic planning and modernization in France.[12] Monnet was now determined to work for the establishment of a United States of Europe and toward this objective he employed a formidable array of political, business, and personal contacts. Monnet and his associates aimed at tying together the coal and steel industries of Western Europe, particularly

[12] See the brief but insightful portrait of Monnet drawn by Anthony Sampson, *Anatomy of Europe* (New York: Harper & Row, 1968), pp. 6–9.

those of Germany and France, so closely that neither side would be able to prepare independently for war against the other. In addition to eliminating the political friction which had already begun to reemerge over control of the Ruhr and Saar, the Schuman Plan would also offer real economic advantages. To ensure the solidity of this linkage, the ECSC would have an executive High Authority whose members would be appointed by the participant states but who would make binding decisions having the force of law in the coal and steel sectors of France, Germany, and the other member states.

The Schuman Plan benefited from the extremely influential support of the United States, and membership in it was formally made available to the countries of Western Europe including Britain. Monnet, however, feared that British participation would cripple the ECSC because of Britain's opposition to supranationalism and European federation, and the proposal was presented in such a way as to lessen the chances for a favorable British response.[13] In any case, the Labour government, then in the process of nationalizing its own coal and steel industries, distrusted the conservative, Christian Democratic sponsors of the ECSC: German Chancellor Konrad Adenauer, Italian Premier Alcide de Gasperi, and French Foreign Minister Robert Schuman, all of whom had grown up as German-speaking Catholics, Adenauer in the Rhineland, Schuman in Alsace-Lorraine, and de Gasperi in a portion of the Austro-Hungarian Empire. Despite the endorsement of important European democratic socialists, the Labour government refused even to negotiate because of the proposed federal powers for the High Authority. Soon after the British refusal, Italy, Belgium, the Netherlands, and Luxembourg joined France and Germany in signing the ECSC treaty in May 1951. The ECSC, with its High Authority, parliamentary assembly, and European Court of Justice, came into operation in July 1952 and proved to be a major success in modernizing and coordinating European coal and steel during the period from 1953 to 1958; moreover, its six-country membership and institutional pattern of supranational exercise of powers formerly held by national governments constituted an historic breakthrough and set the outline for the subsequent establishment of the European Common Market. The ECSC also firmly entrenched the split between the Six's approach to European unity and that of the British together with the Scandinavians, European neutrals, and a number of other states who preferred looser intergovernmental arrangements.

[13] Merry and Serge Bromberger, *Jean Monnet and the United States of Europe* (New York: Coward, McCann, & Geoghegan, 1969), p. 106.

To a substantial extent, European unity depended not on the actions of European states alone, but also upon the impact of external events and of outside powers such as the United States and the Soviet Union. Barely one month after Robert Schuman's proposal (June 1950), the outbreak of the Korean War had an immediate effect in Europe, where it was feared that war in Asia foreshadowed an immediate Soviet threat. In organizing their own defense, the Europeans faced agonizing choices: on the one hand, Europe was scarcely defensible without the participation of German troops (especially since the French army had become mired in an Indo-China war); yet, on the other hand, the genuine horrors of World War II were only five years past and memories of Germany's role in war, occupation, and genocide remained so intensely painful that few—even in Germany itself—could welcome German rearmament and the re-creation of a German General Staff.

Once again, Jean Monnet seized an opportunity to provide a dramatic thrust toward European unity. In October French Prime Minister Pleven unveiled a plan (fathered by Monnet) for creating a European army in which national units would be merged into a unified *European Defense Community* (EDC). The proposal closely paralleled the Coal and Steel Community in its institutional structure, and together with the ECSC it would have provided another basis for substantial European integration. Adenauer supported the idea; indeed, he himself had proposed a European army in December 1949, because he abhorred the re-creation of a German General Staff. The United States also backed EDC as a means of rearming Germany against the Soviet Union as well as offering an improved method of military coordination through the prospect of dealing with one European General Staff instead of six or more national ones. Yet, although Churchill himself had in August proposed a European Army, the British rigidly refused to take any part in EDC. In refusing, they doomed any real chance for the plan's success: the French, Dutch, and Belgians particularly feared being locked into EDC with a rearmed Germany and without a substantial British role.

For four more years the EDC struggle was played out to its inevitable failure. Monnet had hoped to use its institutions as a building block toward an eventual United Europe, but it took until May 1952 to achieve agreement on a treaty among the Six. Once again the impact of events outside Western Europe proved significant. As time passed, the perceived urgency of the Soviet threat receded and the death of Stalin in March 1953 coupled with the ending of the Korean war a few months later removed much of the pressure for ratification. In turn, severe difficulties arose over ratification in each of the member states. France in particular provided the chief obstacle; there, opposition from Gaullists (who opposed this transfer of national sovereignty), from Communists (who viewed the EDC as anti-Communist and anti-Soviet), from those who could not support German rearmament (half the Socialists) and from opponents of the imperfectly drafted Treaty finally defeated ratification in August 1954.[14]

Ironically, Germany was soon rearmed within the loose auspices of the misleadingly named *Western European Union* (in effect a successor to the Brussels Treaty grouping of 1948) and of NATO, and with a British pledge—previously withheld from the EDC—to maintain troops on the European continent. These arrangements placed restraints on Germany, mainly in forbidding it to develop nuclear and biological weapons, but provided no integration of forces. With the defeat of EDC, there also died a proposal for a *European Political Community* (EPC) which would have functioned as the governing body for both ECSC and EDC. The abortive plan included a European Executive Council responsible to a bicameral parliament, a Council of Ministers, and a Court of Justice. Thus by late 1954 the quest for European unity appeared to be on the verge of failure. The EDC and EPC proposals seemed the high water mark of the European movement; nearly a decade after the end of World War II the postwar impetus appeared completely spent and all the energies, necessities, and ideals of a United Europe had brought into being little more than the infant Coal and Steel Community.

RÉLANCE: THE COMMON MARKET AND EURATOM

The European dynamic proved remarkably resilient, however, and there soon occurred a European *rélance* (relaunching), leading to the establishment of the *European Atomic Energy Community* (EURATOM) and the *European Economic Community* (EEC or Common Market). In retrospect the time for such a breakthrough appears to have been ripe and the genesis of these institutions appears swift, smooth, and almost inevitable. But in reality they came into existence against wide resistance in diverse political, labor, and business sectors and amidst government instabilities, economic difficulties, and serious personal and institutional differences. The European *rélance* succeeded only because of intricate and semi-secret planning, intense lobbying and negotiation, and the tenacity of Jean Monnet and the Belgian Socialist Foreign Minister, Paul Henri Spaak.

In late 1954 and early 1955, operating behind the scenes while still president of the ECSC High Authority, Monnet and a close group of

[14] Italy never ratified the Treaty either. On the French case see Raymond Aron and Daniel Lerner, eds., *France Defeats EDC* (New York: Praeger, 1957).

associates hammered out plans for a series of European ventures. The failure of EDC and EPC had convinced them that a political United States of Europe could not be achieved through the straightforward presentation of a plan acceptable to all the prospective participants and the leading political parties and pressure groups within the member states. Instead, the most promising path to an eventual European political unity might be indirect, via *economic* integration. The pro-Europeanists would no doubt have preferred a more direct approach, but a European federation, unlike that in America of the late eighteenth century, was not being attempted against the background of 13 weak and newly independent colonies with a common language and colonial past but instead among ancient and powerful nation-states with long histories and deep emotional and institutional roots.

Using his influence, Monnet succeeded in convincing Spaak to present a plan for both an atomic energy community comparable to the ECSC and a wider European customs union. In turn, the Belgian government together with those of the Netherlands and Luxembourg presented these proposals to all six ECSC member states in May 1955. A month later, high level representatives of the Six met in Messina, Italy, to appoint a successor to Monnet (who had resigned from his ECSC position to devote full time to his behind-the-scenes campaign for European unity), and to discuss the Benelux proposals. Despite some differences, the Six agreed to appoint a committee headed by Spaak to explore these possibilities for European unity. The Spaak Committee, in turn, met in Brussels for several months and in April 1956 presented a full-fledged report calling for establishment of EURATOM and for a supranational customs union and free trade area (the EEC).

Britain, meanwhile, had been invited to participate in these negotiations and, in fact, sent a representative to observe the discussions. This time the Europeans displayed more serious interest in having Britain take part, particularly in view of Britain's ten-year lead in nuclear technology and the greater importance which many European leaders attached to EURATOM as the possible source of revolutionary breakthrough in the energy field. Yet Britain's damaging postwar European policy continued. Unlike the Labour government which had sought to preserve its freedom of action to nationalize industries and carry out economic planning and had distrusted the more conservative continental governments, the Conservative government of Anthony Eden opposed European supranational ventures as a threat to national sovereignty and preferred to give priority to Britain's Commonwealth and Atlantic relationships. The British government became critical of the new proposals, expecting them to fail just as the EEC had done, and it withdrew its observer in October 1955.

The Spaak Report, which had been accepted by the six foreign ministers in May 1956, contained a provision for the possible association of other countries in a free trade area. While the Spaak Committee drafted the actual EEC and EURATOM Treaties, the OEEC Council began to explore this free trade area proposal. And in November the British government, now inclined to seek a limited accommodation with the EEC, decided to negotiate for such an association.[15] Britain proposed a loose free trade arrangement in industrial goods between the six-member EEC and a larger number of other Western European states. But while the British regarded this as an adventurous proposal, the French and a number of other officials within the Six saw it as too little and too late. Unlike the Common Market, it made no provision for agriculture (which was crucial for France), nor for economic integration and strong supranational institutions. While *Free Trade Area* (FTA) negotiations dragged on under OEEC auspices, the Six put the finishing touches on the EEC and EURATOM, and in March 1957 signed the Rome Treaties which established these organizations.

Monnet, meanwhile, had established a small but extremely influential group of several dozen of the most powerful political leaders in Western Europe; this Action Committee for a United States of Europe proved helpful in promoting support for the treaties and in pressuring for their successful ratification. Once again, events outside Europe proved important: the disastrous British-French Suez expedition against Egypt in October 1956 highlighted the weakness of these two former imperial powers and their vulnerability to Soviet and American pressure. It thereby strengthened the case for a new supranational grouping that would give the Europeans greater economic and political weight. The combination of Christian Democratic and Socialist support (particularly the cooperation of Adenauer in Germany and Premier Guy Mollet in France) proved decisive, and the twin institutions of the EEC and EURATOM formally began operation in Brussels on January 1, 1958.

To be sure, this was only a Europe of Six. Britain was left out, and the FTA negotiations bogged down. The EEC states were unwilling to accept Britain's loose intergovernmental proposal, which seemed to provide it with all the advantages of industrial free trade but without participation in the long-term political commitment to create a supranational Europe. Ultimately, General de Gaulle (who had come to power with the collapse of the Fourth French Republic in June 1958) administered the *coup de grace*. In November he vetoed the Free Trade Area—the first of several

15 For a detailed discussion of the British role during this period, see Robert J. Lieber, *British Politics and European Unity: Parties, Elites and Pressure Groups* (Berkeley: University of California Press, 1970), pp. 32–36.

vetoes with which he was to shock Britain and Europe. The British countered by establishing the *European Free Trade Association* (EFTA) to their own requirements, including in it Norway, Sweden, Denmark, Austria, Switzerland, and Portugal. EFTA was to prove a modest economic success but this loose intergovernmental association achieved little political importance.

The new EEC quickly became the foremost European organization. Its general scope, growing economic success, and long-term political aims gave it primacy. By contrast, the ECSC, although quite successful, had been limited to a specific *functional* sphere—that of coal and steel—and began to encounter problems after 1958 as national governments sought to intervene more directly in dealing with a growing coal surplus. As for EURATOM, the almost romantic hopes which had been placed upon it were soon disappointed, principally because important areas of atomic energy remained under national control, because no dramatic breakthrough to huge quantities of cheap atomic power occurred, and because Britain, with its more advanced atomic technology, remained outside.[16] In 1967 the institutions of both functionally specific European Communities (ECSC and EURATOM) were merged with those of the broaded gauged EEC to create the European Communities, but the term "Common Market" remained in wide use as a label for the entire enterprise.

The EEC itself possessed institutions closely resembling those of the ECSC, but with a slightly greater national government role. The executive body, a nine-man *Commission*, was less powerful than its ECSC counterpart. It was responsible for the day-to-day operation of the Common Market and for making proposals to the *Council of Ministers*, a body of top officials who represented national governments and met several times per year to make major political decisions (potentially by a system of weighted majority voting). There were also a *Committee of Permanent Representatives* of ambassadorial rank, to represent national governments on a day-to-day basis in looking over the Commission's shoulder, as well as an enlarged parliamentary assembly (later named the *European Parliament*) and a *Court of Justice* to judge disputes under the Rome Treaty. More important than its institutions was that the EEC was committed to achieving full economic integration, embodied in a long list of specific and general measures and objectives to be realized over a 12 to 15 year period. While these provisions and the issues to which they gave rise will be analyzed later, it is well worth noting that the Treaty represented a balance of national and supranational decision powers and that the

[16] Morgan, *West European Politics Since 1945*, p. 145.

participants and their governments often held deeply divergent conceptions about the EEC.

THE BRITISH STRUGGLE FOR MEMBERSHIP

From the start, regardless of national divergences, the EEC made rapid economic progress and began to attract growing political attention from the outside world. Gradually, Britain's opposition to full membership began to change. Its Commonwealth ties proved of lessening economic and political importance despite symbolic ties to former colonial states (many of which retained the queen's picture on their postage stamps and a link between their currencies and the British pound sterling). In addition, Britain's special relationship with the United States had weakened over time, and the European connection appeared to hold out to Britain a new political role as well as economic advantages. In July 1961 the Conservative government of Prime Minister Harold Macmillan formally applied for EEC entry. Even though abandoning Britain's insistence on intergovernmental arrangements, the Macmillan government pressed for a series of safeguards and made slow progress in the negotiations, which began to bog down on major matters as well as on trivial questions (such as the tariff on canned Australian kangeroo meat). Political opposition within Britain grew and suddenly, in January 1963, President de Gaulle vetoed Britain's attempt at entry on the grounds it was not yet European enough. De Gaulle viewed Britain as too closely tied to the United States. He appeared to have particularly resented the Nassau agreement between Macmillan and President Kennedy in December 1962 in which the United States agreed to provide Polaris missiles for British nuclear submarines and thereby tied the British nuclear deterrent intimately to its own. Once again external events had proved crucial; in addition, the differences between Macmillan and de Gaulle on whether Britain and Europe ought to maintain close ties with the United States or instead seek a far more independent world position foreshadowed a continuing disagreement within the European Community.

Had it not been for the de Gaulle veto, Britain might eventually have negotiated Common Market entry in 1963.[17] Four years later in 1967, the Labour government of Harold Wilson applied for membership, but this time de Gaulle issued a veto even before negotiations could begin. Matters then stagnated until the French President resigned in April 1969. His successor, Georges Pompidou, proved willing to see Britain bargain for

[17] A report by the Commission argued that with the help of additional concessions by Britain, negotiations would probably have succeeded. See European Economic Community Commission, *Report to the European Parliament on the State of the Negotiations with the United Kingdom* (Brussels: February 26, 1963), pp. 110 ff.

President de Gaulle says "No," January 1963.
Photo by Raymond Depardon-Gamma, E.C. Photo Library

entry—at a stiff price. Pompidou welcomed the prospect of British membership as a counterweight to the growing economic and political strength of Germany and as a means of strengthening Europe's weight vis à vis the United States and the Soviet Union. Negotiations between the EEC and the Conservative government of Edward Heath began in mid-1970, and in May 1971, Heath and Pompidou achieved a major breakthrough. In the dramatic press conference that followed, ironically held at the ornate Elysee Palace where de Gaulle had announced the previous vetoes, President Pompidou stated:

> Many people believe Britain was not and did not wish to become European and that she wished to enter the Community only to destroy it. . . . Many also thought France was ready to use all pretexts to put up a new

British Prime Minister Edward Heath and Foreign Minister Alec Douglas Hume arrive to sign treaty establishing Britain's membership in the E.C.
Courtesy E.C. Photo Library

Heath is doused with ink by an irate woman.
Courtesy E.C. Photo Library

veto to the entry of Britain. . . . Well, ladies and gentlemen, you see before you this evening two men who are convinced of the contrary.[18]

policy agenda: problems, cleavages, and conflicts

UNRESOLVED ISSUES IN THE EC BACKGROUND

Although the European Community has taken on a relatively definitive membership and organization after an evolution covering an entire postwar generation, several sets of increasingly crucial questions remain unresolved. These can be summarized as: (1) how closely unified can or should Europe become; (2) what relationship ought Europe to have to the United States and the Soviet Union as well as to Eastern Europe; (3) what kind of economic and social pattern should Europe follow; and (4) how is an increasingly united Europe to be governed and by whom? Thus the long and historic struggle leading up to the present development and membership of the Community does not in any sense represent a coming to rest of an historical or political process. Controversy over these unresolved issues becomes more prominent as prior questions of membership recede; the character of the European Community and more broadly of European unity itself thus remains in a dynamic and political evolution.

1. What Kind of Unity?   The first and in many ways the principal unresolved question is what degree of unification Europe should have. The struggle over this issue began immediately after World War II with the British preference for intergovernmental rather than supranational arrangements. Even though France in effect accepted a degree of supranationality by its membership in ECSC, EEC and EURATOM, the French position sometimes leaned closer to that of Britain than of its EEC partners. At the time of de Gaulle's 1963 veto, it was observed ironically that France really preferred *Europe à l'Anglaise sans les Anglais* (Europe English–style but without the English). These differences led to bitter struggles and in 1965–1966 to a constitutional confrontation between de Gaulle and the other members of the Six. To a degree, they still persist in the expanded European Community despite the death of de Gaulle and of his heir Georges Pompidou. This continuing tug-of-war, previously embodied in the opposite positions of Charles de Gaulle and Jean Monnet, shapes the resolution of critical institutional questions that involve the Commission, the Court, the European Parliament, common foreign policy, and a broad array of pressing institutional matters.

In the most straightforward terms, one can say that Monnet, together

[18] Quoted in *The New York Times,* January 21, 1972.

with many other deeply motivated proponents of a united Europe, emerged from World War II determined to construct a united Federal Europe similar to the United States of America. In their view, this was the most promising means of ending intra-European warfare, harmful economic rivalry, and the wasting of Europe's political energies and influence. After all, had the continental United States remained divided first into 13 and later 48 separate states, its fate might well have been one of continued conflict and instability, underdevelopment of its full resources and potential, and far less political influence in the world. Not surprisingly, Monnet's influential pressure group, established in 1955, called itself the Action Committee for the United States of Europe. Monnet's definition of the Committee's role was to ensure unity of action among the 33 participating political and trade union leaders (representing 67 percent of the total electorate in their respective countries) in attaining "by concrete achievements the United States of Europe." As Monnet put it, "mere cooperation" between governments would not suffice; it was indispensable that the states delegate real power to federal European institutions.[19]

Initially, the partisans of a federal Europe had sought, through the Council of Europe, the EDC and the companion European Political Community, to achieve major constitutional and political advances in one great stride. But the weakening of the Council of Europe and the failure of EDC and EPC reflected the inherent national antagonisms (particularly in Britain and France) to an immediate frontal assault on national sovereignty. In recognizing these practical obstacles to their *federal* approach of directly unifying governmental and political institutions from the top down, Monnet and the European unity movement moved to a more *functional* approach. This meant the creation of European integration in specific economic sectors, such as coal and steel (the ECSC), atomic energy (EURATOM), and a customs union and free trade area with broad commercial and economic unification (the EEC). Governments were more willing to accept the transfer of sovereign powers in these specified economic areas; but Monnet's objective, and one which is set out in the Rome Treaty, was to create eventual *political* unity via an economic route. There exists an elaborate and sophisticated body of regional integration theory, federal, functional, and neo-functional, which provides an intellectual basis (as well as criticism) a priori and a posteriori of this approach.[20] In practice, proponents of a united Europe have

[19] See *Statements and Declarations of the Action Committee for the United States of Europe, 1955–67* (London: Chatham House, PEP, 1969), p. 11.
[20] See, for example, Leon N. Lindberg and Stuart A. Scheingold, eds., "Regional Integration: Theory and Research," special issue of *International Organization* 24, no. 4 (Autumn 1970); Lindberg and Scheingold, *Europe's Would-Be Polity: Patterns of*

sought to strengthen the independent supranational authority of European institutions to propose new initiatives, to exercise powers once held by national governments, and to proceed on the basis of majority rather than unanimity among participant states. It is here that they have clashed repeatedly with those holding a totally different conception of European unity.

Charles de Gaulle, president of France from 1958 to 1969, best embodied this opposing stand, but many key elements are represented in the earlier Gaullist movement, by de Gaulle's successors, and in limited respects by other European governments, particularly that of Great Britain. In the British case, a constant theme of both Labour and Conservative governments has been to retain the maximum degree of national sovereignty and to minimize the transfer of authority to European supranational institutions. As we have seen, this initially took the form of outright insistence that all organizations in which Britain participated be exclusively intergovernmental in nature. Thus, they would be limited to actions initiated and agreed upon by all member-states, with the activities being carried out by a staff that lacked independent authority of its own. While the British found it necessary to modify their position to seek and ultimately gain entry to the European Communities, successive British governments nevertheless tended to accept only the minimum amount of supranationality consistent with their treaty obligations and to oppose proposals that would extend powers of the European Commission. Many British officials—for example, in the Foreign Office and those who became permanent employees of the European Community—favored much greater steps toward European unity, but the Conservatives have tended to resist transfers of power based on their sense of nationalism and the maintenance of Britain's historic sovereign institutional powers, embodied especially in parliament and the monarchy. The Labour party, although deeply divided, shared the reservations; in addition, many of its leaders were concerned about democratic control of Europe's institutions and feared interference with democratic socialist economic measures (especially nationalization and economic intervention) which Labour might wish to carry out within Britain. They also embodied more than a touch of antiforeign and anticontinental bias.

In practice, the Gaullist orientation has favored intergovernmental cooperation rather than supranational integration, but there are important differences of style and substance. For one thing, the French position has

Change in the European Community (Englewood Cliffs, N.J.: Prentice-Hall, 1970); and Robert J. Lieber, *Theory and World Politics* (Cambridge, Mass.: Winthrop, 1972), Chapter 3.

long been draped in elaborate and almost mystical pontification about the essence of statehood and national identity; that is, it embodies a large dose of romantic (though not particularly virulent) nationalism and a desire for maximum freedom of action. In addition, France has had a greater inherent geographic place as well as a more inescapable economic involvement with its neighbors in the Six, and both Gaullist and non-Gaullist French governments have found it advantageous to take part in the successive integrated European ventures. Indeed, there was considerable surprise in Europe that after coming to power in 1958, de Gaulle did not refuse to have France carry out the initial tariff cuts required by its role in the newly begun Common Market. An important factor here was de Gaulle's determination that the peace of Europe—as well as the world role of France and Europe—required a conclusive end to the historical animosity between Germany and France. De Gaulle thus favored the establishment of a unified Europe, but along different lines from those of the supranationalists. In his view a unified Europe would have to be built upon a strictly national base, since the nation was where patriotic loyalties, emotional ties, and legitimacy inhered after centuries of national and international history. His conception of a united Europe was that of a Europe of States (*"Europe des Patries"*)[21] where countries would cooperate while maintaining their institutions, powers, individual cultures, and national identity. This idea was characteristically reflected in an observation of de Gaulle's:

> Dante, Goethe, and Chateaubriand belong to Europe only insofar as they are respectively and eminently Italian, German, and French. They would not have served Europe very well had they been men without a country, or had they written some kind of Esperanto or Volapuk.[22]

In practice, this Gaullist view meant a constant opposition to the authority and initiatives of the European Commission, to any expansion of its independent budgetary authority, to any movement for greater power or direct election of the European Parliament, and to all efforts at majority voting within the Council of Ministers. Indeed, de Gaulle launched a series of abortive counterproposals, such as the Fouchet Plan of 1960–1961, to weaken the Community's supranational character and to create a European political union based on regular institutionalized consultation among the participant governments.

The antagonism between these two divergent ideas of Europe reached

[21] The phrase itself comes from a Gaullist disciple and former French prime minister, Michel Debré.
[22] Quoted in Bromberger, *Jean Monnet and the United States of Europe*, p. 175.

a peak in 1965 and nearly destroyed the Common Market; they were partially resolved in the "Luxembourg Agreement" of January 1966, but a kind of stalemate persisted. Ironically, the clear victory of either the Monnet or the de Gaulle conception might have permitted more decisive and far reaching steps, but their stalemate slowed much of the momentum toward enhanced European unity. The integration that has taken place and that ultimately may develop in Europe will almost certainly be *sui genesis*—that is, unique to the European situation, resembling neither the federal model of the United States nor the Gaullist *Europe des Patries*.

2. *What Relationship to the United States and Soviet Union?* The second unresolved theme concerns the relationship of Europe to the United States and to the USSR. It again pits Monnetist against Gaullist conceptions, though with some importantly different allies. For Monnet and his associates, European federation was to proceed hand in hand with the Atlantic Alliance. Monnet's Action Committee went so far as to endorse the ill-conceived and abortive United States plan for a multilateral nuclear force (MLF) to provide nuclear weapons to a European naval contingent manned by mixed national crews under a joint U.S.-European veto.[23] The idea of the Atlantic relationship expressed by President Kennedy epitomized a view widely held by advocates of European unity on both sides of the Atlantic. Kennedy's celebrated Philadelphia speech of July 4, 1962, rested on three basic premises. The first of these was that for the moment the Europeans must "go forward in forming the more perfect union which will some day make this partnership possible." [24] Second, and following the Europeans' achievement, the United States would then be ready for a "Declaration of Interdependence" and would be prepared to discuss with a united Europe the ways of forming a concrete Atlantic partnership— an idea expressed elsewhere by reference to "twin pillars" of America and a unified Europe—as the ultimate goal. Third, and in a manner which seems almost archaic in view of intervening events such as the Indochina War and détente with Russia and China, President Kennedy drew upon the ambitious universalism of his 1961 inaugural address, transferring it to an Atlantic context by observing that although the United States alone could not establish justice throughout the world, nor ensure tranquility, the common defense, welfare and liberty, it could if joined with other free

[23] Walter Yondorf, "Monnet and the Action Committee," *International Organization* 19, no. 4 (Autumn 1965): 900. The following discussion is elaborated upon in Robert J. Lieber, "Expanded Europe and the Atlantic Relationship," in F.A.M. Alting von Geusau, ed., *The External Relations of the European Communities* (Farnborough, Hampshire: D. C. Heath, Ltd., 1974)), pp. 45 ff.
[24] President Kennedy's speech is reprinted in Edmund S. Ions, ed., *The Politics of John F. Kennedy* (London: Routledge and Kegan Paul, 1967), p. 116.

nations "do all this and more." Together we would thereby aid the developing nations to throw off the yoke of poverty, balance our trade and payments at the highest growth level, provide a powerful deterrent against aggression, and ultimately create a world of law and free choice. The Atlantic partnership would be the "nucleus for the eventual union of all free men." [25]

In shaping the goal of Atlantic partnership, Monnet's Committee placed greater emphasis upon equality for the Europeans. For example, in June 1962, the Action Committee adopted a resolution calling for equal partnership between the United States and a united Europe (including Britain) in economic, political, and military affairs. More generally, European élites tended to support Atlantic partnership, or at least did not regard European integration and a close Atlantic relationship as mutually exclusive. Indeed, if there had been a perceived conflict between these two goals, the Atlantic tie might well have been the one accorded priority. Thus, in 1963 and 1964 major opinion surveys found that French and German élites regarded their countries as likely to share common interests with the United States for a longer period than with each other. (See Table 6–2.) Similarly, the European mass publics of France, West Germany, Italy, and Great Britain were found to have greater trust for the United States than for each other.[26]

TABLE 6–2   French and German Elite Perceptions of Long Term Common Interests

(*Question:* With which countries will France (Germany) continue to share common interests for a long period?)

	France	*Germany*
EEC countries	88%	35%
United States	87	72
Great Britain	52	28
France	—	28
Germany	37	—
Western Europe	—	14
Russia	5	—
Other, don't know or not ascertained	7	64

SOURCE: Adapted from Karl W. Deutsch, Lewis H. Edinger, Roy C. Macridis, Richard L. Merritt, *France, Germany and the Western Alliance: A Study of Elite Attitudes on European Integration and World Politics* (New York: Scribners, 1967), pp. 71 and 150.

[25] Ibid., p. 117.
[26] Lindberg and Scheingold, *Europe's Would-Be Polity*, p. 54.

Despite this weight of opinion and the position of many proponents of European unity, maintaining an intimate tie between Europe and the United States has not been and is not a foregone conclusion. At its inception, the European idea was neutral between the options of Atlantic partnership and a third force (meaning a position tied neither to the U.S. nor to the USSR but somewhere between them).[27] For General de Gaulle and his supporters, Europe could only be created in its own identity, separate from the domination of the United States. Thus de Gaulle opposed the various proposals for Atlantic partnership, wherever they came from, and he sometimes expressed a desire for the creation of "Europe from the Atlantic to the Urals," [28] though this remained a vague conception, dependent upon a fundamental change of ideology and orientation within the USSR. To a substantial extent, de Gaulle's desire for Europe to play an independent world role rather than be tied to Atlantic partnership reflected continuity in French policy. His predecessors as well as the successive governments of Pompidou and Giscard d'Estaing clearly favored a less Atlanticist and more independent policy for Europe than did any of France's other European partners. This orientation has been closely shared by the French Communist Party (not least because it proves useful to Moscow) and by portions of the Socialist Party. To be sure, French élites in the early 1960's were broadly sympathetic to the United States and there was actually greater élite support for strengthening both NATO and Europe (49 percent) than for strengthening the EEC alone (40 percent). Nonetheless, third force sentiment has been consistently higher in France than elsewhere within the European community, and in recent years while approval of European unity has increased, élite support for a close Atlantic relationship has weakened. Among French élites there now exists a clear priority for strengthening European unity exclusively (77 percent) rather than both the Atlantic Alliance and Europe.[29] Moreover, French public opinion favors a third force Europe, independent of both the United States and the Soviet Union by a margin of two to one.[30] Ironically, while this third

27 See Uwe Kitzinger, *Diplomacy and Persuasion: How Britain Joined the Common Market* (London: Thames and Judson, 1973), p. 26.
28 The Urals are a mountain chain dividing European from Asiatic Russia.
29 Question: "Do you feel that France should rather endeavor to strengthen NATO or European Unity (EEC), or both?" Answer: NATO—4 percent, EEC—40 percent, both—49 percent. Karl W. Deutsch, *Arms Control and the Atlantic Alliance* (New York: Wiley, 1967), p. 122. Responses to a comparable question a decade later were: Atlantic Alliance—0 percent, European unity—77 percent, both—18 percent. See Robert J. Lieber, "European Elite Attitudes Revisited: the Future of the European Community and European-American Relations," *British Journal of Political Science* (July 1975): 331.
30 *Sondages: Revue Française de l'Opinion Publique.* No. 1–2, 1972. "L'Opinion Française et l'Union de l'Europe, 1947–1972," p. 115.

force view has been prevalent among the French public for twenty years, it coexists with a dominant opinion that regards the United States as one of France's best friends. (Fifty-nine percent express great or rather great confidence toward the Americans compared to 29 percent toward the Russians.) [31] Some of this same inconsistency is reflected in public opinion polls among the original six EEC countries, where a two-thirds margin agree with the idea that a United States of Europe should become a third force equal to that of the United States or the Soviet Union [32] even while continuing to express greater confidence toward the Americans than toward each other. (See Table 6–3.)

The explanation for this seeming incongruity of opinion as well as the ultimate limitation upon the European Third Force conception lies in the realm of defense. As long as the Soviet Union is perceived as militarily or politically threatening by the Western Europeans, the Atlantic Alliance and resultant close European–American relationship is inevitable. Only the United States and the Soviet Union are full-fledged nuclear super-powers with the ability to withstand an all-out nuclear attack and retaliate by inflicting unacceptable damage upon the attacker. France and Britain possess modest nuclear forces of their own, but both lack this

TABLE 6–3 Degree of European Confidence Towards Foreign Peoples

Express great confidence or rather great confidence towards the following peoples:	The EEC Six	Germany	Belgium	France	Italy	Netherlands
The Swiss	78%	86%	77%	77%	70%	84%
The Americans	69	77	69	59	67	75
The British	61	72	70	55	49	66
The French	52	58	74	—	43	51
The Germans	45	—	52	48	39	60
The Italians	31	26	41	34	—	32
The Russians	23	17	20	29	25	24
The Chinese	9	7	8	9	10	8

SOURCE: Adapted from Rabier, "Europeans and the Unification of Europe," in G. Inonescu, ed., *The New Politics of European Integration* (London: Macmillan, 1972), p. 157. (Figures for Luxembourg have been omitted.)

[31] See Jacques-René Rabier, "Europeans and the Unification of Europe," in Ghita Ionescu, ed., *The New Politics of European Integration* (London: Macmillan, 1972), p. 157.
[32] Sixty-seven percent favor this idea. Ibid., p. 168.

crucial capability of mutual assured destruction ("M.A.D.", for short), and cannot provide effective deterrence without the support of the United States. Although Europe has the resources to develop its own nuclear capability, this is unlikely to take place because of the un-acceptability of the costs involved, the lack of European cooperation, the political unpopularity of such an action, the political problem of Ger-many, and the unresolvable difficulties of nuclear decision-making. Thus the defense question has and continues to set limits upon the European freedom of movement. For example, during the 1973 French legislative election campaign, French President Georges Pompidou stressed that France's security depended upon its remaining within the Atlantic Alliance and he criticized the Communist Party for its view that France should not permanently remain a member.[33] However, Europeans can and do differentiate between the sphere of defense and those of politics and economics. Defense may constrain Europe's drift away from America, but it does not prevent major differences and even conflicts in such areas as foreign policy toward the Middle East or in energy policy.

Overall, the question of Europe's world role remains unresolved, and the lines of division over this issue cross-cut those regarding the degree of unity Europe should have. (See Table 6–4.) Some of those who favor the Atlantic Partnership are staunch proponents of a federal Europe or of enhanced powers for the EC. These views are prevalent among many

TABLE 6–4 European and Atlantic Priorities—Cross-cutting Cleavages

		View of Europe's World Role	
		Atlantic Partnership	Third Force
Preferred degree of European unity	Supranational	Many German Officials Christian Democrats and most Social Democrats Many EC Officials Some British Conservatives	Many Democratic Socialists Some EC Officials
	Intergovernmental	Majority of British Labour Party	Gaullists Some Democratic Socialists European Communists Some British Conservatives

[33] *Le Monde* (Paris), February 9, 1973, and *The Economist* (London), February 17, 1973, p. 30.

German officials, and exist widely in Brussels and elsewhere. Others (for example, much of the British Labour Party leadership) are favorable to the United States connection yet oppose European supranationalism. Conversely, the proponents of a more distant or even third force position for Europe (particularly in political and economic questions) include some ardent advocates of European unity (many European democratic Socialists, some Common Market officials in Brussels), but also many who are cool to a federal Europe (Gaullists, many British Conservatives) or even totally opposed to European unity (the European Communist Parties and some Socialists).

3. *What Kind of Economy and Society?* Unlike the sometimes grandiosely political and even philosophical question of Europe's unity and its international alignment, the third unresolved theme, that of the social and economic nature of Europe, is as much a matter of day-to-day contention as it is of general principle. Even after the broader structural and international questions may be resolved, the issue of the content of this Europe will remain. The fundamental contest, described by political scientist Harold Lasswell as who gets what, when, and how, is the essence of politics, whether on a national or a European scale.

To begin with, there exists a fundamental split between economic outlooks. Some, particularly German officials, prefer a certain amount of laissez-faire, or free market economics, while others, especially the French, have a tradition of massive state intervention, planning, and direction (*dirigisme*) in the economy. From an American perspective, this can be seen as a division between two historic views. One view is a conservative, business-oriented policy of a minimum governmental economic role, posited upon the assumption (whose lineage extends back to the late eighteenth century and Adam Smith) that an invisible hand operates whereby the result of each individual and business pursuing its own economic self-interest will be to provide the maximum benefit for the entire society. The alternative, reformist, socially oriented view is identified with parties of the moderate left, and the achievements of the managed economy and the welfare state. This view holds that government can and must intervene in the economy to encourage nationally, politically, or socially desirable objectives (national power or sovereignty, regional development, efficient use of resources, full employment, fair wages and working conditions, protection of the environment, and so on). These distinctions, however, may be only partially applicable in the European context, and German and French national views of these questions tend to transcend any such right versus left distinctions. Thus, in Germany, a less economically interventionist orientation has been held tenaciously by both Christian Democratic and Social Democratic governments (for example, that of Willy Brandt's successor, Helmut Schmidt). Business-oriented French governments of the moderate right, however, including those of Presidents Georges Pompidou (1969–74) and Valery Giscard d'Estaing (1974–) have held to a traditional *dirigiste* and interventionist policy whose roots run back to the seventeenth century and King Louis XIV.[34]

For Europe, this is not merely a debate over economic philosophies. The initial measures taken within the EEC aimed at removing barriers to European trade so that national industries could compete without the interference of state obstacles or favoritism. The objective was to create a full scale Western European economy in place of a series of six (later nine) compartmentalized national economies. This process of integration by removing barriers was relatively easy and was also underpinned by theoretical views (functional and neo-functional) which saw economic unity growing as integration in one area created pressures which spilled over into adjacent economic sectors, inevitably bringing about eventual political integration. But as we shall see, political unity has not followed automatically. Agreement was easier to reach on removing barriers than on creating subsequent positive measures to hammer out willful and sometimes interventionist policies in such areas as economic and monetary union, regional policy, business competition policy, energy policy, and social policy.

Differences on questions of economic intervention and the development of common European policies also overlap those between business and labor. Those who have adapted most successfully to the European Community's opportunities for freer movement across traditional borders have been the huge multinational corporations (MNC's) and in particular American-owned firms, which have tended to make greater profits than their European counterparts and to provide disproportionately important investment in the most technologically advanced modern industries. To be fair, this is not entirely a new phenomenon; in 1901, a British writer could complain:

> In the domestic life we have got to this. The average man rises in the morning from his New England sheets, he shaves with "William" soap and a Yankee safety razor, pulls on his Boston boots over his socks from North Carolina, fastens his Connecticut braces, slips his Waltham or Waterbury watch in his pocket and sits down to breakfast. . . . From shaving soap to electric motors, and from shirt-waists to telephones, the American is

[34] The German case is further complicated by the fact that major welfare state measures were initiated by the conservative and monarchist government of Bismarck in the late nineteenth century.

clearing the field . . . these in-comers have acquired control of almost every new industry created during the past fifteen years . . . the telephone, the portable camera, the phonograph, the electric street car . . . the typewriter and the multiplication of machine tools.[35]

In any case, European firms have also prospered and modernized as the overall success of economic integration has brought substantial growth and prosperity to the countries of the EEC. It is here, however, that social questions begin to arise, for trade unionists, democratic socialist leaders, and others who supported European unity have done so as part of the initial understanding that the practical pathway to political unification would be by economic integration. With the relative economic success, these leaders note that political progress has been much more limited and that businesses have done particularly well; they therefore intensify their own pressures for better regulation of the MNC's and especially for labor to get its share of the expanded pie, both within national borders and inside the Common Market itself. As far as the EEC's institutions are concerned, this means pressure for harmonization (to the highest existing levels) of social welfare policies, minimum wage laws, and other such policies throughout the Community. Thus, from an American perspective, the standardization and transferability of employment and welfare benefits can be understood as a kind of European social security system. In the United States workers retain their Social Security credits and benefits when they move to take a job in a different state, and the Europeans have begun to put into effect this kind of harmonization. For the present, trade union pressures on EC institutions are limited because unions have not achieved the degree of cross national integration enjoyed by business. (For example, during the 1972 Belgian coal miners strike, Belgian mine owners succeeded in importing German coal because of the absence of effective cooperation among European coal miners.) Trade unionists have established a European Confederation of Trade Unions, representing 35 million workers, but its resources and coordination remain weak. Moreover, from 1973 to 1975 it was hindered by the initial failure of the British Trades Union Congress (along with the British Labour party) to participate in EEC institutions. On a broader political basis, the competing social and economic visions of Europe are reflected by the two largest blocs in the European Parliament, the Christian Democrats and the Democratic Socialists. In the event that powers of this parliament ever become significant, their political contest is likely to exercise a major

---

[35] Fred Mackenzie, *The American Invaders*, quoted in Anthony Sampson, *Anatomy of Europe* (New York: Harper & Row, 1968), p. 161.

role in resolving these questions. But in any case, these differences will also be played out within national political systems.

4. Who Governs Europe? The fourth major unresolved issue within the European Community is, to use Robert Dahl's phrase, "Who Governs?" With the creation and rapid evolution of new and often unique institutions, democratic and responsible governments have not kept pace. A sprawling bureaucracy has grown up in Brussels to administer the European Community, but the European Parliament has been prevented from developing into an effective political institution as its counterpart. On the one hand, the member states, particularly France, have resisted proposals that enhance the Parliament's powers so that it might begin to resemble a genuine European federal parliament with the ability to pass upon legislative and budgetary measures and to appoint as well as to dismiss the European executive. On the other hand, the same sources, including the British government, have blocked efforts to achieve the *direct* election of European parliamentarians in place of their indirect selection from national parliaments. Thus constrained, without substantial institutional power or the effective political influence and legitimacy which would stem from direct elections, the Parliament can do little more than question the EC Commission, pass resolutions that have only limited influence, and occasionally threaten to invoke its one limited power—the ability to dismiss (but not to appoint!) the EC Commission by a two-thirds vote.

Control of the Common Market's Eurocrats (a 9000 member staff) rests with the 13 EC Commissioners, who are themselves appointed for a four-year term by the nine national governments. The Commissioners have in practice respected their oaths to act on a European basis and not as national representatives nor to accept national instructions, and at times this independence has irritated national governments, especially France's. The Commission presents proposals to the Council of Ministers for decision, and while these form the required basis of the Council's agenda, the fact that final approval rests with high national government officials means that the major outlines of European policy remain under the veto power of individual governments. The Council exercises little detailed control because it meets only a few times per year, in contrast to the permanent day-by-day operation of the Commission. But a growing national supervision is exercised by the *Committee of Permanent Representatives,* a body of national representatives in Brussels who maintain a steady watch on behalf of the Council of Ministers. As for the *European Court,* composed of nine judges, one from each member state, it decides disputes arising under the Community treaties and thus functions on a limited but real supranational basis, although it has been hesitant in trying to assert the kind of right to judicial review which the U.S. Supreme Court adopted under John Marshall. There are, in addition, other bodies, both formal and informal, which govern or influence the European Community: for example, the 144 member advisory body known as the Economic and Social Committee provides an institutional basis for pressure group access by farmers, trade unions, business groups, and professional organizations.

What emerges from this overall structure is a tension between national and supranational elements, in which democratic control through the electoral process is far removed from the center of decision, but where rudimentary checks and balances do exist among the various organs. Clearly, the U.S. federal government could not have established its own role vis-à-vis the state governments if the Congress were appointed by state legislatures and the president, vice president, and cabinet chosen by state governors. To be sure, the European Community does not and will not resemble the U.S. model, but effective European unity is only likely to develop if greater popular democratic control comes into operation; in its absence, the balance of authority will remain heavily lop-sided toward national control.

OPPONENTS AND SUPPORTERS OF THE COMMUNITY

If cleavages among the participant *states* do not result in challenges to the EC itself, there do exist cleavages between those *groups* who oppose the Community and those who support it. Here we find a mixed picture. Among organized political movements, the Communist parties of Western Europe are the most consistently anti-Europe. They have tended to oppose the EC as embodying imperialism, German militarism, or strengthening "Europe of the Trusts." [36] The French Communist Party (PCF) opposed the expansion of the EEC and in the April 1972 French referendum attacked it as "the Europe of poverty." [37] More recently the PCF has modified its hostility somewhat by taking its seats in the European Parliament, although it is still deeply divided from the French Socialists on the issue. The chief exception here is the Italian Communist Party (PCI), the largest such party in Western Europe. It is relatively pro-European while it favors major changes in the Community, including direct election of the Parliament, the ending of NATO ties, closer links to the East, and a

---

[36] Neil McInnes, "The Communist Parties of Western Europe and the EEC," *World Today* 30, no. 2 (February 1974): 82–83.
[37] Ibid., p. 85.

Europe from the Atlantic to the Urals.[38] With the exception of the Communists, there is little organized opposition to the Common Market in the original Six. In Britain and Denmark, however, vocal opposition exists among young people, inhabitants of outlying regions, farmers, right-wing nationalists, and some elements of the democratic left. These are very diverse elements, though to some degree their position may be characterized as pre- or anti-industrial, traditionalist, or embodying a preference for smaller and decentralized units of government as opposed to larger and centralized ones. However, those who oppose the EC on ideological grounds remain deeply divided. Many on the British and Scandinavian left oppose it because they believe the Community would interfere with the achievement of internal socialist measures or because they regard the EC as a capitalist and conservative enterprise benefiting multinational corporations and ignoring the third world. Others, on the right, see it a threat to traditional national institutions and to sovereignty. And some oppose the Community as bureaucratic or undemocratic. Younger voters have been a vocal part of the opposition, although opinion studies indicate that within the Six and in Britain, they are actually slightly more pro-European (from 5 percent to 8 percent more) than their elders.[39] In Britain, for example, prior to that country's actual entry, 38 percent of those aged 18–24 favored joining the Common Market, compared to 33 percent of those aged 25–44, 30 percent of the 45–64 age group, and only 20 percent of those over 65.[40]

In Britain, more than half the Labour party's members of parliament and a large majority of the powerful Trades Union Congress opposed membership in the European Community. They refused to participate in the Community's institutions (for example, by refraining from taking their seats in the European Parliament for the Labour party and on the Economic and Social Committee for the TUC). On the British right, extreme nationalists such as Enoch Powell attacked the Community as a threat to British sovereignty and political institutions. The effect of this opposition, particularly within the Labour party, forced Prime Minister Harold Wilson to renegotiate the terms of Britain's membership. The outcome—as much a matter of appearance as of substance—was put to the British electorate in an unprecedented referendum. After a campaign in which the Liberal party, most of the Conservatives and the right and

[38] Ibid., p. 97.
[39] See Ronald Inglehart, "An End to European Integration?" *American Political Science Review* 61, no. 1 (March 1967): 92, and Opinion Research Centre, *Britain and the Common Market: A Summary of Research* (London: February 1972), ORC/1152, p. 11.
[40] ORC, p. 11. These figures, from a July 1971 poll, are consistent with other results.

center of the Labour party supported continued British membership, the outcome of this June 1975 vote was a resounding endorsement (67 percent voting yes to staying in). Given this margin of support and pro-European majorities throughout the United Kingdom (even in Scotland and Wales) much of the hostility may begin to fade over a period of time—as was the case in France and Germany during the late 1950's. Opposition cannot, however, be completely ignored. In Norway, a 1972 referendum actually rejected entry after it had been negotiated by the government, and a similar referendum in Denmark produced a bare majority for approval. Apart from Britain and Denmark, there exists a broad consensus of support or at least acceptance of the Community; most of those who are critical of its shortcomings do not question the EC's existence or their country's continued membership but instead seek reform or improvement of it.

REGIONAL CLEAVAGES

Regional cleavages within the European Community have also become a significant source of division, but one which cuts across national lines. The Common Market has brought or will further stimulate great prosperity and development in a relatively central area bounded by London on the Northwest, Amsterdam and Frankfurt in the North and Northeast, Munich and Turin in the Southeast and South, and Paris in the East. These administrative, business, or industrial centers are closely linked by geography, transport, and communication ties. In outlying regions, however, the pattern is sometimes less favorable—for example, in declining industrial and mining regions of northern England, Scotland, and Wales, and in rural areas of southern Italy and southwestern France. High unemployment, lack of investment, and an absence of opportunities make these depressed regions. It is sometimes argued that the EEC has worsened these regional problems by diverting national attention and resources toward the center of the Community. In some cases, political movements have arisen (for example, Scottish and Welsh Nationalist parties, Bretton nationalists) which seek greater regional autonomy or even independence. Initially, regional movements often looked favorably upon the EEC. It has, for example, been widely argued by separatists (for instance, in Belgium) and by many European federalists that existing European nation-states are simultaneously too large to pay adequate attention and to be responsive to the concerns of peripheral regions and too small because broad economic and political problems require an overall European perspective.[41] Thus with the passage of time one might see an erosion of

[41] Belgian parties such as the Flemish-speaking People's Union (*Volkunie*) and the French language Walloon Assembly (*Rassemblement Wallon*) and Democratic Front

national authority in two directions: to smaller subnational regions on the one hand, and to a wider supranational Europe on the other. However, as the political strength of certain regional movements has grown, they have —at least in the British case—displayed narrowly regional nationalism and growing hostility to the European Community.

One European response to the problem of depressed regions has been to seek a massive *regional policy* which would transfer huge amounts of resources from the Community's revenues to stimulate economic activity in peripheral regions. From an American perspective, comparable programs are commonplace, whereby federal tax revenues are used to transfer resources from relatively wealthier portions of the United States to aid poorer regions such as Appalachia or the rural South. In the European case, as much as several billion dollars per year in revenues collected from customs duties and a percentage of the Value Added Tax ("VAT," comparable to a sales tax) could—at some future date—be appropriated by the EC to aid depressed regions. The commitment to develop backward regions of the Community and to lessen the gap between them and the richer areas exists in the 1957 Rome Treaty and has been strongly reaffirmed at the summit meetings of EC government leaders; for example, at Paris in October 1972 the endorsement of regional policy was meant to reinforce the establishment of Economic and Monetary Union (including a common currency) by 1980, as well as to alleviate difficulties which Britain might face in carrying a disproportionate share of Community burdens. However, only a huge program (comparable in size to the yearly $5 billion of the Common Agricultural Policy) would make any impact, and national objections have arisen to such a program. The most tenacious difficulty results from a frequent national insistence on "just return," in essence the idea that each state should receive a closely proportionate return on any national contributions made to the Community. In the United States, for example, the insistence that New York State must recoup exactly in federal expenditures what it contributes in federal taxes would doom any redistributive efforts. In essence, wealthier states need to pay a disproportionate share. But in Europe, Germany is reluctant to do so unless greater progress toward political and economic union can be made to justify such a step. Despite these reservations, one opinion poll has indicated that Germans would strongly favor by a margin of more than four to one (60 percent versus 14 percent) the idea of taxes to help poorer areas in the EEC. The Six as a whole were almost as favorable (55 percent

of French-speakers (*Front Démocratique des Francophones*) have sought regional self-government for their language groups but also strongly support a European government as a logical extension of the Belgian federal system they advocate. The *New York Times* (March 10, 1974).

versus 18 percent), and even the French supported such taxation by more than two to one (56 percent versus 27 percent); only in Britain did a plurality (35 percent for, 47 percent against) object to the idea.[42]

THE COMMUNITY AS REALITY OR ABSTRACTION?

Apart from the above cleavages, there is yet another between those who see the Community as somehow relevant or significant and those who see it as a distant abstraction. Here there are elements of class cleavage, since businessmen, bankers, and professional people often find the EC to be part of their daily professional concerns, whereas working class families may find little direct reason to pay attention. Of course, these divisions are not absolute: the Community's involvement in agriculture, social policy, and transport policy has a direct impact on farmers, trade union officials, and truck drivers, and the Commission's actions often determine the prices people pay for food and other necessities. Yet the fact remains that many Europeans do not perceive the EEC as having a direct impact upon them. In one survey among persons aged 16 and over in the Six, less than half (42 percent) believed the Common Market had had a favorable effect on the living standard. Only 18 percent believed the impact had been unfavorable, but 40 percent did not know or did not answer.[43] Perhaps as a result of this, a majority (56 percent) would be unwilling to make certain personal sacrifices to achieve European unification, whereas only 35 percent would agree to do so.[44] From these figures we can conclude that while a large minority of perhaps one-third is deeply committed to European unity, the Community has not yet made sufficient impact among the remainder of its population to elicit more than vague support.

EUROCRATS VERSUS BUREAUCRATS

A final, institutional cleavage often divides the Brussels Eurocrats from national officials. On the one hand, several thousand European civil servants are actively employed in carrying out the Community's duties; most of them have become strongly and personally committed to the achievement of European union and regard themselves and their mission as European-oriented rather than nationally-oriented. The chief embodiment of this drive lies in the 13-man Commission, whose members have taken an oath to discharge their responsibilities as Europeans. But on the other hand, government officials of the individual states tend to orient themselves as French, Italians, or British in their interaction with the

[42] Source: Reader's Digest Association, *A Survey of Europe Today* (London: 1970), pp. 174–175. (The survey was conducted in 1969.)
[43] Rabier, "Europeans and the Unification of Europe," p. 170.
[44] Adapted from Rabier, Ibid., p. 172.

Community; this difference of views is probably inevitable given the shorter range political considerations which national governments and bureaucracies must heed. This cleavage often comes to a head in conflicts between the Commission and the Council of Ministers (or the Committee of Permanent Representatives). Even under the best of circumstances a cleavage based on different European versus national perspectives is inevitable. What is remarkable is that the European outlook prevails more often than we would expect. Because of the Commission's right to formulate the proposals which the Council meets to consider, and because the Commission can exert its influence through the press, pressure group contacts, the European Parliament, and a vague but substantial popular support for European unity, the Commission is often surprisingly effective. One inside participant has termed this tension a "natural expression of a federal or pre-federal system which is constitutionally characterized by the struggle between the federation, eager to increase its powers, and the states which form it, which are anxious to retain as much as possible of their autonomy," and he notes in particular the effect of the Commission:

> . . . There are very few instances of the Council simply rejecting one of the Commission's proposals. Thus one can count on one's fingers the proposals which the Council has modified to such an extent that they have differed substantially from the one put forward by the Commission. Normally, the Commission adapts its proposal to make it acceptable to the Council without going so far as to abandon any of the principles upon which it is based.[45]

THE PROBLEM OF EXTERNAL FORCES

Just as the politics of the individual European countries cannot be understood apart from the international, political, and economic context, so the European Community itself is profoundly affected by events outside its own boundaries. One of the most dramatic illustrations of this interrelationship can be found in the aftermath of the energy crisis. Thus, although the Community had periodically reaffirmed its commitment to establish a Common Energy Policy, the events following the October 1973 Middle East war not only obstructed the development of such a policy but, in addition, produced profound conflicts among its nine member states. Because of their differing energy needs and foreign policies toward the United States, Israel, and the Arab world, the Nine pursued three overlapping and often contradictory policies: first, cooperation with the United States and other oil consumer countries (resulting in formation of the International Energy Agency); second, a policy of bilateral deals with oil

[45] Luxemburgensis, "The Emergence of a European Sovereignty," *Government and Opposition* 9, no. 1 (Winter 1974): 86.

producing states; and third, largely unsuccessful measures to maintain a common EC energy policy, despite support for such efforts by Germany, Italy, and the smaller EC members. Britain and France pursued nationalistic policies which engendered a sense of *sauve qui peut* (every man for himself) among the Nine; at one point during the winter of 1973–1974 this disunity reached such a level that Britain and France expressed a willingness to honor an Arab oil boycott of Holland—their Common Market partner—in potential violation of the Rome Treaty.

In other spheres, international and external pressures have also created internal strains within the Community. Thus, efforts to achieve economic and monetary union have so far proved abortive because the international monetary and trading patterns have affected the economies of the Nine in different ways. And the international inflation and recession of 1974–1975 produced severe economic and political problems in several member states, causing Italy and Denmark to impose temporary restrictions against imports from their Common Market partners, and creating severe problems within Britain, thus jeopardizing its performance in the Community.

These and other cases reflect the pervasive political and economic interdependence of Europe with other developed industrial states such as the United States and Japan, as well as with raw material producers in the less-developed world. Because of Europe's need to import vast quantities of energy, food, and raw materials, to sell its exports on world markets, and to cooperate in seeking solutions for world monetary, economic, and political problems, the internal agenda of the Community is inescapably affected by external forces.

policy process

A great deal could be written about the intricacies of the European Community's institutions and labyrinthine bureaucracy, but, even more than in the case of the individual states, this would prove disproportionate to the amount of understanding conveyed about the political dynamics of decision-making. To be sure, the Community does possess legislative, executive, and judicial branches, but they are unequal in power. The significant political conflicts tend to take place *within* the executive organs between those elements representing or advocating Community-wide interests and those with a predominantly national perspective, as well as between advocates of different national interests. In an American context, it is as though Congress and the judiciary remained weak and the principal political struggles were played out within the White House and Executive departments. We would see repeated conflicts between advocates of state primacy and those favoring a stronger federal system, and among larger state interests (such as California, New York, or Texas), each seeking to minimize its own contributions to the national budget and to maximize the benefit it received from existing programs while preserving substantial autonomy in both its internal and international affairs.

By contrast with its Eastern European counterpart, Comecon, the European Community is also polyarchic in nature since no single member within it plays a dominating role comparable to that of the Soviet Union. To be sure, the larger EC members (West Germany, France, Britain, and Italy) exert a major influence proportionate to their strength and population (all in the 50 million plus range), but the smaller states (the Netherlands, Belgium, Denmark, Ireland, and Luxembourg) are able to make themselves heard and their interests are taken routinely into account.

As we have seen, transnational forces also shape the problems and politics of the Community, and any treatment of the EC system which narrowly focused upon the Community and its institutions to the exclusion of these influences would prove inadequate. The nature of the Community's institutions, the participant national interests, and transnational influences will become evident as we treat each of the specific decision-making stages in turn.

INITIATION OF ISSUES

The raising of issues for discussion and decision comes through a multitude of channels, and in this respect bears comparison with the way in which issues are placed on the agenda in national political systems. Thus the press, interest groups, political parties, the European Parliament, external or transnational influences (such as the United States and Soviet Union, associated external states, MNC's, the oil-producing countries, unexpected events such as the October 1973 Middle East war), and the desires of major institutional and national government elements can all cause issues to come to the foreground.

The mere fact, however, of an issue becoming publicly visible does not ensure that a decision on it will necessarily be made. For example, despite the wide attention generated by the media over the unusually low prices on butter and beef sold to the Soviet Union (tantamount to the embarrassment of the U.S. Department of Agriculture over its Soviet wheat deal), or by the perennial demands made by the European Parliament for enhanced legislative powers and direct election of its members, no substantive action has been forthcoming in changing on-going Community policies. In the case of the Parliament, for example, although it is officially mandated as a forum for discussion and criticism of Commission proposals, there is no requirement that this discussion be acted upon. Formally, the 13-member EC Commission makes most of the routine decisions about Community matters and submits major proposals to the Council of Ministers for decision. Unless the Commission chooses to address a given issue, or a national government determines to raise the matter within the Council of Ministers or at one of the crucial European summit meetings, there is no way in which a matter will actually become a subject for decision.

Formally, initiation of policy comes from the Commission, which also has the responsibility for administering policy that has been defined by the Council of Ministers. As a rule of thumb, it may be said that the Commission proposes; the Council of Ministers enacts.[46]

The Commission runs the Community on a day to day basis. Although its 13 members (two each from Germany, France, Britain and Italy, one each from the remaining states) are appointed by the national governments for four-year terms, they are pledged to carry out their duties in the interests of the Community as a whole, and neither to seek nor to follow instructions from any national government. In fact, it is the Commission which gives the Community its supranational character. Although the decision power of the Council is fundamental, the Commission derives real authority from the fact that it alone is mandated to initiate policy and to provide the proposals upon which the Council makes its decisions. In some important areas, however, which were unspecified or ambiguous under the Rome Treaty, the Council has dominated, even in policy initiation, through the establishment of intergovernmental mechanisms for policy coordination. Thus in the foreign policy field, the "Davignon Committee" has been established as a body to coordinate the foreign ministries of the Nine and their diplomatic representatives in foreign countries. It has been relatively successful in developing common European positions on such matters as the Conference on Security and Cooperation in Europe and—in part—the Middle East, but it mostly bypasses the supranational organs of the Community.

DELIBERATION

If the European Community were in fact a full-fledged federal union, a discussion of the European Parliament would probably encompass the decision-making functions not only of deliberation and monitoring of policy, but of the decisive approval phase. It is symptomatic of Europe's present status that the Parliament's primary role is one of deliberation, criticism, and consultation but not of decision.

The Parliament itself is composed of 198 members from the nine coun-

---

[46] See European Community Information Service, *Questions and Answers about the European Community,* 2nd ed. (Washington, D.C., 1973), p. 11.

The European Parliament at Strasbourg.
Courtesy E.C. Photo Library

tries. Germany, France, Britain and Italy each have 36 seats, the Netherlands and Belgium 14, Denmark and Ireland 10, and Luxembourg 6. As noted previously, seating is by political groups rather than by nation. Traditionally, the Christian Democrats have been the largest block, although since 1975 the Socialists have been more numerous because the British Labour Party finally took its allotted seats. The European Socialists thus have 67, Christian Democrats 51, Liberals 23, Conservatives 20, Gaullists 17, Communists and independent left 13, independents and independent right 7.[47]

Members are not popularly elected but instead are chosen by their own national parliaments. For a long period, Communists did not take part, but since 1974 all major groups are now represented. Any political group with 14 or more members receives special facilities and appoints one of the eleven vice presidents of the Parliament. These, together with a president, organize the Parliament and its flow of work. The Parliament also is divided into twelve standing committees: Political Affairs; Legal Affairs; Economic and Monetary Affairs; Budgets; Social Affairs and Employment; Agriculture; Regional Policy and Transport; Public Health and

[47] Figures as of late 1975.

Environment; Energy, Research and Technology; Cultural Affairs and Youth; External Economic Relations; and Development and Cooperation. Although these are comparable to congressional committees in their subject matter, they lack most of the comparable powers: there has been, in short, no EEC equivalent of a William Proxmire, a Frank Church, or a Peter Rodino.

Parliament's main task is to discuss policy with the Commission and to provide opinions on Commission proposals before these are taken up for decision by the Council of Ministers. This is done through the Committee system and plenary debate of the full body. The completed reports are sent to both the Commission and the Council. Members of the European Parliament also have the authority to ask formal written questions of the Commission and occasionally of the Council of Ministers. Following the entry of the United Kingdom in January 1973, the Parliament adopted a more lively British-style oral question period to which members of the Commission respond. This process of questioning is best considered under the heading of monitoring of policy, but the Parliament does possess two rudimentary but real powers which ensure that its opinions cannot be altogether neglected.

Formally, Parliament has the authority to dismiss the European Commission through a censure vote by two-thirds of its members. The impact of this power is in certain respects comparable to the impeachment authority held by the U.S. Congress: it is an unwieldy and unselective weapon, analogous to a nuclear deterrent in the difficulty of its use. Nonetheless, it lends credibility to the parliamentary opinion even though a new Commission would be appointed by the Council of Ministers without a formal role for the Parliament in the selection process. On only one occasion has the European Parliament actually passed such a censure motion. In November 1972, angered by the Commission's failure to meet its April 1970 commitment to propose a strengthening of parliamentary controls over the Community budget, the Parliament voted no confidence in the Commission. Shortly thereafter the motion was withdrawn because of a procedural dispute, because events had overtaken the original commitment, and because of an agreement to entrust the new Commission, then on the verge of taking office upon the expansion of the EC, with the responsibility for suggesting reforms.[48]

The Parliament's attention and authority focus mainly upon the Commission, but its chief differences are usually with the Council of Ministers. The Commission responds to parliamentary questions and opinions by modifying its proposals, and both bodies have sought to increase the pace

[48] *The Times* (London), December 13, 1972.

and scope of European integration as well as to expand the Parliament's authority. But in confronting the Council of Ministers, the Parliament has little authority and the Council has jealously guarded its own prerogatives. Apart from one formal yearly meeting (a "colloquy") the Council is scarcely obligated even to heed the opinions of the Parliament.

The one formal power Parliament does have relates to the Community's budget. Since 1975, Community financing has depended no longer on direct national contributions (an area where at least a degree of national parliamentary scrutiny existed), but comes directly from the EC's "own resources." These resources include all customs duties and all levies on agricultural imports (less a 10 percent "fee," which the individual nations are allowed to deduct for their service as tax collectors), plus a small part of Value Added Tax (which all the member states utilize). Since the Community's budget comes to more than $8 billion, there are substantial stakes involved, yet Parliament's authority is limited to that portion of the budget which deals mainly with administrative costs and information services—a paltry 3 percent of the total. During the early 1970's, there was much pious discussion of expanding the Parliament's budgetary authority, but the Council and national governments—particularly the French—successfully forestalled any real increased authority. The summit meetings at Paris in 1972 and Copenhagen in 1973 produced little tangible result and the Council in effect retained control of all major expenditures, particularly those for agriculture and the social fund; it also succeeded in confining the Parliament's role to an extremely complicated and restrictive framework.[49] In sum, the position of the Parliament vis-à-vis the Council is weak.

Some limits on Parliament's authority are more narrowly institutional. As a body, it meets approximately twelve times per year, part of the time in Luxembourg, where its secretariat is located, and part of the time in the highly inconvenient location of Strasbourg, France. Its proceedings must be translated simultaneously and then published in six languages (French, English, German, Italian, Dutch, and Danish), and its debates and procedures are often rigid and inflexible. The European Parliament's chief needs are for enhanced powers and for direct election to endow it with greater legitimacy—and full-time members. Remarkably, section 138(3) of the Rome Treaty (Europe's Constitution) requires that proposals ultimately be drawn up for "elections by direct universal suffrage in accordance with a uniform procedure in all member states." Several major proposals and numerous minor ones to implement this commitment

[49] For a lucid discussion of Parliament's role in this budgetary problem, see Roy Pryce, *The Politics of the European Community* (Totowa, N.J.: 1973), pp. 75–86 and especially pp. 91–96.

have been made during the past decade and a half,[50] and seven of the nine member governments favor direct election of the Parliament.[51] None of the proposals has been approved by the Council of Ministers, yet if the formal commitment to achieve "European Union" by 1980 made at the Paris Summit meeting in October 1972 and reaffirmed by the European heads of government at Copenhagen in December 1973 is to be achieved, it will necessarily require a dramatic breakthrough in powers granted to the European Parliament; otherwise the powers of this European Union would be substantially unregulated by democratic control. In the interim, the Copenhagen summit did call for a strengthening of the Parliament's powers without waiting for direct election, but the extremely narrow scope in budgetary authority actually relinquished to the Parliament contradicts this sentiment. Europe's parliamentary dilemma is likely to intensify as the Community's budget comes principally from its own resources. Either the Parliament's powers will have to increase or the Community's further development may well stagnate; in the meantime, the European Parliament has a visible role to play but one that is primarily consultive and advisory, while the real legislative authority of the EC continues to inhere in the Council of Ministers.

Apart from the European Parliament, other important arenas of deliberation also exist. Perhaps the most important is the Economic and Social Committee, which has consultative status. Provisions of the Rome Treaty require the Commission and the Council of Ministers to consult this body before they take actions on economic and social questions. Like the Parliament, its opinions are chiefly advisory, though it lacks any formal powers. The Committee includes 144 members: 24 each from Germany, France, Britain, and Italy, 12 from the Netherlands and from Belgium, 9 each from Denmark and Italy, and 6 from Luxembourg. Its members, whose names are provided by individual governments in consultation with the Commission, are appointed by the Council of Ministers in such a way that roughly one-third represent workers' interests, one-third employers, and the remaining one-third other interests and the general public. The Economic and Social Committee thus provides a formal, though often diffuse, means of pressure group influence on Community decisions. The influence of these groups is more often felt informally through contact with the Commission and its large staff.

One of the significant consequences of European integration is that,

[50] Major formal proposals were made in 1960 and 1971; among recent informal proposals see Federal Trust, *Electing the European Parliament* (London: 1972), as well as the discussion of potential political alignments by Richard Rose, "Could Europe Elect a Parliament?" *European Community* 166 (June 1973): 20–21.
[51] *The Economist* (London), June 14, 1975. Britain and Denmark remain reluctant.

especially since the inception of the EEC and EURATOM in 1958, interest groups in the individual states have found it essential to form European-wide organizations to express their interests in Brussels. Indeed, the Commission has even encouraged the process, partly to facilitate its own business in having coherent voices available to provide information and speak for the various economic sectors and partly to foster further European unity by making the major occupational groups more European oriented rather than exclusively national in focus. Over the years, such bodies as C.O.P.A. (*Comité des Organisations Professionnelles Agricoles*), U.N.I.C.E. (*Union des Industries de la Communauté Européenne*), and the E.C.T.U. (*European Confederation of Trade Unions*) have sprung up to coordinate agriculture, business and labor interests; hundreds of other more specialized bodies have also established themselves. As the Commission prepares proposals it thus considers both the formal and informal views of these groups. Significantly, group influence during this deliberative stage is not confined to Brussels, and national representatives of, say, the farmers also aggressively assert their views within their own political systems in an effort to influence the decisions that governments will ultimately take within the Council of Ministers.

Finally, the European Community does not operate in a vacuum. Many of the same political processes found in Germany, France, or Britain also apply to the Community setting, both directly and indirectly via the press, radio and television, national parliaments, and by other means of public expression. In sum, deliberation within the Community is often a lengthy, bureaucratic, and untidy process, but it ensures that the views of competing interests are fully heard and frequently taken into account. Perhaps the chief difference from the American pattern is that interest groups in Europe are accorded formal status and legitimacy, whereas in the United States these groups lack the same degree of legitimacy, although they have a comparable impact on policy.

APPROVAL

Harry Truman once said in reference to his presidential office, "the buck stops here." In the European Community, the buck stops with the Council of Ministers, the Community's principal decision-making body. Significantly, the one major Community institution in which member states are directly represented is also the one in which the greatest power lies. The limits of supranationalism within the EC inhere in the fact that the fundamental decision-making authority—in effect, the power to legislate for the Community—rests not with the Commission or the European Parliament but with the nationally oriented Council of Ministers. In short, the "okay" in Europe remains a national one.

The Council of Ministers itself is drawn from ministers of the national member governments. Customarily this involves the individual foreign ministers, but on specialized and technical matters it may include ministers of finance, transport, agriculture, or others. Voting within the Council is supposed to be based upon a weighted majority: Germany, France, Britain, and Italy each have ten votes, Belgium and the Netherlands five, Denmark and Ireland three, and Luxembourg two. Of the 58 vote total, a majority of 41 is officially required by the Rome Treaty. Thus the four larger states cannot push through a decision against the wishes of the smaller members.

In practice, majority voting is seldom used. As a consequence of the "Luxembourg Compromise" of January 1966, countries are not outvoted on matters which they consider to be of vital national interest. Since each country effectively determines what is "vital" to it, the Council has essentially adopted the French preference for a unanimity rule, or, in effect, a national veto power. Viewed from another perspective, the Community has institutionalized the kind of "concurrent majority" arrangement that John C. Calhoun wished for a generation before the American Civil War. Calhoun had feared that a "numerical majority" might gain control of the federal government and would then employ this power to dominate minority sections. He therefore sought to prevent this by having government regard interests as well as numbers, allowing each interest a "concurrent" voice in the making of laws or a veto in their execution. In the European case, although the French government in 1974 announced that it would henceforth define fewer matters as being in its vital national interest, thus increasing the scope for majority voting, the use of national veto power exercised through the Council of Ministers remains a profoundly important and limiting reality for the Community.

To a degree, this Council power is constrained because its decisions are based on proposals made by the Commission, and these may only be amended by unanimous vote. There is, however, a continual process of mutual compromise in an effort at consensus between the Council and Commission and among the members of the Council. On the most crucial long-term decisions, this may mean marathon bargaining sessions running for days and nights, involving package deals, trade-offs among various national interests, and a severe physical and emotional strain on the participants leading to a certain comraderie—and occasionally to heart attacks. The results of this process are mixed: sometimes they produce an upgrading of the common European interest; on other occasions they are no more than an agreement on the lowest common denominator. One consequence of the difficulty in reaching major decisions is that they are often delayed; in addition, little attention is paid to the effects of decisions on

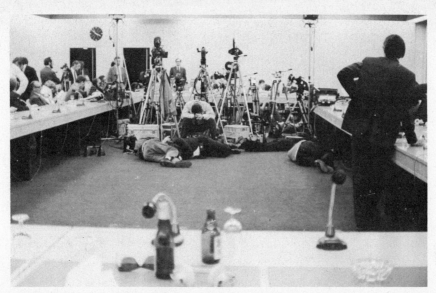

Photographers sleep during a marathon negotiating session.
Courtesy E.C. Photo Library

non-EC members, and decisions once made are difficult to change. The result can be to make Europe a troublesome partner with which to negotiate; and the United States as well as countries of the Mediterranean and Africa have sometimes expressed irritation at this.

Although the Council only meets periodically, it is not wholly dependent on the Commission since its work is prepared by a secretariat and by a *Committee of Permanent Representatives* (known as *Coreper*). The committee is composed of the nine ambassadors to the Community from the member states and supported by committees of national civil servants that deal with each main subject of EC activity. Over the years, Coreper has come to play a greater role in strengthening the hand of the Council vis-à-vis the Commission.

In making its decisions, the Council approves three different kinds of measures: *regulations,* which are supposed to be binding upon member-states and are thus self-executing; *directives,* which are also binding but give individual governments the choice of how to implement them; and *decisions,* which can be self-executory but may require national legislation. To complicate matters, the Commission has the authority to issue all three kinds of measures in those fields where policy has already been established by the Council of Ministers. Finally, the Commission as well as the Council can issue non-binding recommendations and opinions.

This detail should not be allowed to obscure the broader point that the Commission is influential because of its ability to propose, to compromise, and to implement, but that the fundamental political choices which give the Community its direction are made by the Council of Ministers and periodically by summit meetings of heads of state or of governments from the nine countries. These meetings determine the constitutional direction of the Community—for example, on such matters as Britain's entry (the Hague summit, 1969), and the objective of "European Union" by 1980 (Paris, 1972). They reflect a basic fact that no amount of functional integration can overcome: there exists a crucial realm of major integrative decisions that can only be taken on an overriding political basis and are not susceptible to indirect economic and functional processes.

APPLICATION

Once policy is established, the Commission again becomes predominant. The Council may make the major decisions and the summit meetings establish the crucial political choices, but only the Commission has the power to implement these policies. In doing so, it presides over a large European civil service whose employees are divided into some twenty departments, the Directorates General; each member of the Commission supervises at least one of the Directorates, dealing with subjects such as external relations, economic affairs, agriculture, energy policy, and information.

Although small in contrast to bureaucracies of the member states, the Commission's operation does develop a momentum and identity which partially insulates it from political control. Moreover, in implementing broad policies, it gains real leeway in determining the specific means and procedures. Typically, the 1972 Paris summit meeting mandated the Commission to produce a series of specific proposals for implementing its recommendations on transforming the EC into a "European Union," on establishing Economic and Monetary Union, on creating regional development and social funds, and on formulating a policy that guaranteed satisfactory energy supplies. Because of this role and its predominance in daily operations and execution of policy, the Commission very nearly *is* the European Community as far as routine operations are concerned. Thus the Commission and its staff carry out the Community's policies in agriculture, trade, and harmonization of regional, social, and economic policies, and the Commissioners themselves engage in important international negotiations with countries seeking association with the EC (for example, Spain, Finland, Tunisia, Turkey, Israel), with those requesting major trading agreements (Eastern Europe and the more developed countries of Africa and Asia), and with former colonial states seeking foreign aid. Indeed the president of the Commission has met with the U.S. president and other foreign leaders to exchange views on trading, monetary, and political relationships.

The Commission's domination is not unchallenged, and during the 1960's and early 1970's Coreper has come to play a greater role in acting as a watchdog between the periodic meetings of the Council of Ministers. Moreover, by drawing upon skilled specialist committees of national civil servants, Coreper not only scrutinizes the Commission's performance in implementing the Council's decisions, but also possesses the technical expertise to produce proposals of its own on the major subjects of policy. This epitomizes a persistent tension between the Community's supranational elements, embodied in the Commission, and its growing intergovernmental procedures, institutionalized not only in the Council of Ministers but in Coreper and the Davignon Committee.

Advocates of further European unity measures thus face a dilemma; for many of them, unity must be supranational if it is to endure and to erode the forces of nationalism which have bedeviled Europe's political, economic, and social life. Yet some member governments, particularly those of France and Britain, tenaciously guard their sovereignty and prefer to acquiesce in further European measures only on the condition that they can maintain effective control through measures of governmental coordination. European integrationists thus face a difficult choice between very limited supranational progress versus a more extensive European development which is relatively intergovernmental in character. In recent years some Europeanists—for example, Ralf Dahrendorf (a former EC Commissioner)—have asserted that the best way to extend measures of unity is to downplay the insistence on supranational integration as well as the desire for harmonization in all fields (for instance, mayonnaise labeling, highway speed limits), and instead seek to achieve faster progress by whatever means are available—for example, through the intergovernmental Davignon Committee in the foreign policy field. The dilemma, however, remains unresolved and sometimes bitterly contested; at times the result is to frustrate progress as the supranational advocates reject measures which do not come in a sufficiently supranational form, while those such as the French refuse to relinquish further national powers to a European sovereignty.

ADJUDICATION AND ENFORCEMENT

Although the Commission executes policies decided upon by the Council of Ministers, the policies are not universally obeyed. At times, individual companies or, indeed, national governments may not be complying with Community regulations or with provisions of the Rome Treaty. It is the responsibility of the Commission as "watchdog" of the Treaty to take before the European Court the cases of any who violate these provisions. There have been numerous cases, including ones against most participant states; some have been won and some lost.

The Court, located in Luxembourg, originated with the Coal and Steel Community and after 1958 became the judicial body for EURATOM and the EEC. Its nine justices, one from each member state, sit for staggered six year terms. In many respects, the Court is comparable to the U.S. Supreme Court, since it is the final authority on disputes that arise under the Treaties and EC law. Indeed, there is no appeal from its judgments. The other Community organs (Commission, Council of Ministers, European Parliament), the member governments, corporations, and even individuals may bring cases before the Court or be the object of them. The Court decides these cases with the aid of four advocates-general, who present to it impartial conclusions about the case. Like the U.S. Supreme Court, the European Court decides by majority vote, but unlike the Supreme Court it does not report minority opinions or how its justices vote; this lessens the likelihood of governmental pressures on individual members of the Court.

Over the years, the Court has handed down more than 100 judgments, some of which have been landmark decisions in establishing the supreme authority of the Court and of European Community law over national law. The impact of the 1964 *Costa* case (involving an Italian citizen's suit against the nationalized electricity industry) is comparable to Chief Justice John Marshall's 1819 statement of the supremacy of U.S. federal law in *McCulloch* v. *Maryland*. In the *Costa* case the European Court asserted the "preeminence of Community law" and found that the EEC Treaty was incorporated into the legal systems of the member states, with their courts being bound to follow it.[52] In the recent celebrated *Continental Can Co.* case, in which the Commission brought antitrust charges against an American based multinational firm, the Court, on a technicality, overturned the Commission's position but, with a very broad interpretation of the Rome Treaty (Article 86), expanded the Commission's practical authority by upholding its right to exercise sweeping powers to control mergers and monopolies.[53] In related cases, other firms have been fined hundreds of thousands of dollars by the Commission, and the penalties

---

[52] Excerpts from *Costa* v. *ENEL* (*Ente nazionale Energia elettrica impresa gia della Edison Volta*). (European Court of Justice, No. 6/64) July 15, 1964, in Howard Bliss, ed., *The Political Development of the European Community: A Documentary Collection* (Waltham, Mass.: Blaisdell, 1970), pp. 71–73; also see Bliss' comment, p. 41.
[53] A. H. Hermann, "Competition Policy after the Continental Can Case," *European Community* (British edition), April 1973, pp. 11–12.

have been upheld by the Court. In yet another case, the French government was forced to stop the Bank of France from providing preferential interest rates to exporters, in violation of the Rome Treaty. Finally, the Court has decided sex discrimination cases brought by individuals under Article 119 which stipulates that men and women are to receive equal pay for equal work. Some of these cases have been won by women plaintiffs, others lost. (For example, a Belgian stewardess for Sabena airlines contested her forced retirement at age 40. The Court found against her on grounds that the discrimination did not involve the concept of equal pay.)[54]

What these cases show is a remarkable assertion of supranational legal authority overriding national law, at times as decisively as the U.S. Supreme Court is able to overrule a state law or state court. To be sure, this authority is still cautiously exercised so that the European Court has avoided the kind of active intervention in politically sensitive cases which might provoke an extreme national political reaction; in particular, it has stopped short of claiming a power comparable to the Supreme Court's judicial review (the power to declare national laws unconstitutional). Nonetheless, it has implanted itself so that its decisions on European Community matters are regarded as binding upon national governments. An important point here is that unlike the U.S. Supreme Court, the European Court does not have authority on all legal matters, but only on those which relate to the Treaties. Within the Treaties' frameworks, it does function as constitutional interpreter and final legal authority.

For political reasons, some disputes that require adjudication fall outside the Court's jurisdiction. For example, Italy has occasionally failed to comply with Community deadlines and regulations because of bureaucratic failures and domestic political and economic crises. In these cases, the Commission has sometimes sought not to bring Italy before the Court, but instead to negotiate temporary face-saving compromises or resort to loopholes in the Treaty. In another celebrated confrontation involving President de Gaulle's 1965 fight with the Commission and France's six-month boycott of Community institutions, the ultimate resolution in the Luxembourg Compromise was a matter of high politics, essentially transcending the Court's purview.

In the final analysis, however, *enforcement* of European Court decisions, as well as of Community authority more broadly, lies in the hands of national governments of the nine member states. These states comply with Community decisions not because they are compelled to do so but because

[54] Jean Lecerf, "European Law: A Growing Force," *European Community* (U.S. edition), June 1973, pp. 12–14.

they find the continued existence of the EC and their participation in it to be of major benefit economically and politically. Failure to cooperate could thus bring harmful economic consequences, as well as symbolic sanctions (based on their partners' disapproval), and domestic political difficulties because of the generalized public support for European unity. However, on the occasions when a national government is fiercely determined to follow a course of action in violation of Community regulations, —for example, President de Gaulle in 1965–1966—there is little the EC can do to prevent this.

AUDITING AND MONITORING OF POLICY

What are the checks and balances of the European Community system? Democratic control and accountability have not developed at the same pace as have many other aspects of the Community. Policy procedures are heavily bureaucratized and inflexible, and accountability is often indirect. Nonetheless, several factors make the abuse of power by Community officials relatively unlikely. First, the Parliament does maintain an active questioning of the Commission to which Commissioners are required to respond. Because the Parliament lacks significant budgetary authority, its weight is considerably less than that of the U.S. Congress in its exercise of congressional oversight. Yet, its official power to dismiss the Commission does lend credibility to its questions. It also assures that such questions cannot be brushed aside, and that the Commission could not act in a flagrantly abusive fashion.

A second major means of monitoring the Community's performance is informal, through the press and interest groups. Brussels and the Community headquarters are a giant goldfish bowl, in which most significant Community activity attracts some kind of attention. The European press seizes upon major stories, such as the Commission's 1973 approval for the sale of 200,000 tons of EEC surplus butter to the Soviet Union at prices far below what European consumers paid at their local shops. This was as embarrassing to Community officials as the 1972 Russian wheat deal was for the Nixon Administration; a year later a comparable proposal to sell surplus EEC beef to the Russians was temporarily sidetracked.[55] In a less general sense, the hundreds of European and national interest groups jealously scrutinize their own sectors and can resort to vociferous public outcry and pressure upon national and European government institutions when they perceive their interests as being harmed. The Brussels agricultural riot described at the start of this chapter is a visible manifestation

[55] See, for example, *The Economist* (London), July 13, 1974.

of the way an aggrieved pressure group may act in response to the effects of European policies.

Finally, the Council of Ministers and Coreper exercise penetrating national auditing of Commission policies, both to determine whether Community policies are being implemented and to protect—often jealously—their individual national interests. Given this multiple scrutiny, there is ample monitoring of the Commission's activity.

TERMINATION AND AMENDMENT

As a result of this monitoring of the Commission's activity, on-going policies are subject to change as problems develop. The Commission is sensitive to criticism and it may initiate proposed policy changes in response, consulting in the process with Parliament, the Economic and Social Committee and interest groups, and, in effect, beginning another decision-making cycle. The problem of amendment or termination of policy proves more intractable when the Council of Ministers is involved —as it usually is on matters of major policy importance.

Unlike the Commission, the Council is less subject to scrutiny and accountability: its ministers are accountable only to their national heads of government and through them to national political processes. When major policy outlines are the result of package deals, log rolling, or the need to satisfy an intransigent member (typically, but not exclusively, France), the shape of EC policy may prove very difficult to amend. For example, the Common Agricultural Policy is seriously deficient in serving the overall European interest. In particular, its procedures for subsidizing farmers by keeping retail food prices artificially high penalize less well-to-do consumers and result in wasteful surpluses. Yet because achievement of the CAP was the price paid by the Community to satisfy France, there is little prospect of amending it in the foreseeable future. Long-term changes in overall European policies thus must come as a result of national elections which bring to power new governments and—sometimes— new policy programs. In the French case, the demise of first de Gaulle and then President Pompidou and their replacement by the non-Gaullist, moderate conservative Giscard d'Estaing, had the indirect effect of bringing France somewhat more closely into line with its eight EC partners and thus made long-term compromises and progress more feasible. On the other hand, the 1974 oscillation in British government from Conservatives (strongly pro-European) to Labourites (deeply divided, but pledged to renegotiate Britain's membership terms) had a major impact upon the Community's policies and its freedom of maneuver.

In essence, truly major shifts of European policy do not tend to flow from the Community's institutions, as they would if there were a genuine European federal government, but depend upon political and leadership changes within the member states which are then expressed within the Council of Ministers or at major European summit meetings. The effect is as though America's most important domestic and foreign policies were set not by the Congress or the president but by meetings of state governors, and major changes occurred not as a result of national shifts in opinion or needs, but in response to the outcome of gubernatorial elections in California, New York, Pennsylvania, or Texas.

conclusion: performance and prospects

The European Community is not entirely unprecedented; historical counterparts can be found, as, for example, in the treaties that established trading territories which were signed between the ancient rivals, Rome and Carthage, in 508–507 B.C. and again in 348 B.C.[56] But the European Community is unique enough and so surprisingly successful that we may well wonder to what extent national cleavages persist among its component states, which for so long had been rivals and periodic wartime enemies.

HOW UNIFIED IS EUROPE?

Before we can address this question, it is essential to distinguish between two different kinds of measurement. One means of judging how integrated or divided a region may be is to examine opinions held by the general publics involved, to assess the linking of *peoples,* or what has been termed "international community formation." Another approach is to treat the linking of *governments* in their policy cooperation and participation in supranational institutions—that is, in their "international political amalgamation." [57] This distinction is important because the two types of integration (or cleavage) are not always directly related and may even move in opposite directions. Thus it would be a mistake to believe that one kind of measurement alone provides a comprehensive answer about the multidimensional integration process.

As far as the linking of peoples is concerned, the evidence indicates that public opinion, particularly in the original six EEC member states, strongly

[56] William J. Swift, ed., *Great Britain and the Common Market, 1957–69* (New York: Facts on File, 1970), p. 5.
[57] This useful distinction has been drawn by Donald Puchala, "Integration and Disintegration in Franco-German Relations, 1954–1965," in *International Organization* 34 (Spring 1970): 184–85. Another useful classification of integration in economic, social, and political categories can be found in Joseph S. Nye, "Comparative Regional Integration: Concept and Measurement," *International Organization* 21 (1968): 856–74.

supports far reaching political unity.[58] Apart from Great Britain, in many ways a special case because of the recentness of its EC membership and the traumatic nature of the process, European public opinion actually runs far ahead of government policy on European matters. Reliable opinion studies indicate that citizens of the Six share overwhelmingly favorable attitudes (81 percent versus 7 percent) toward European unification.[59] Moreover, they support specific measures of unification, including creation of a European currency to replace national ones (51 percent versus 23 percent), election of the European Parliament by direct universal suffrage (64 percent versus 12 percent), and the formation of a European Government (58 percent versus 23 percent). As a measure of the strength of this pro-European sentiment, most citizens would even vote for a person of another nationality for President of the United States of Europe if his program corresponded better to their own ideas (66 percent versus 19 percent). Nor is it the case that the French public views these questions in an entirely different light; in fact, opinions held by the French people are largely consistent with those of their EEC neighbors, typically coming within a few percentage points of the average of views expressed by other Europeans.[60] Indeed, French opinion even goes so far as to favor by a margin of nearly three to one (65 percent versus 22 percent) creation of a European Army.[61]

If public opinion could thus be taken at face value, and if it were all that mattered, the European Community might seem on the verge of being transformed into a United States of Europe. But in fact there are limits to both the nature and the impact of this opinion. First, an important core of national sovereignty and symbolism remains deeply entrenched. Only a minority of the citizens of France, Germany, Italy, and the Benelux would approve the formation of a European Olympic team that incorporated their national ones (27 percent versus 43 percent), and a majority of nearly two to one oppose the idea of a European flag replacing national flags (27 percent versus 52 percent). Of course, we could interpret these emotional loyalties as meaning that unity can progress quite far provided nothing is done to disturb national symbols—after all, it might

[58] This discussion of European public opinion is elaborated upon in Lieber, "Expanded Europe and the Atlantic Relationship," pp. 40–41.
[59] Jacques-René Rabier, "Europeans and the Unification of Europe." Unless otherwise noted, the following opinion figures are on pp. 160–164. More detailed treatments of major EEC opinion studies are available from the EC information service, for example, Commission des Communautés Européennes, Direction generale de la Presse et de l'Information, *Les Européens et l'unification de l'Europe* (Brussels: June 1972), and *Euro-barometre, Public Opinion in the European Community* (Brussels: Commission of the European Communities, June–July, 1975), no. 3.
[60] See also *Sondages: Revue Française de l'Opinion Publique,* No. 1–2 (1972), "L'Opinion française et l'Union de l'Europe, 1947–1972," p. 106.
[61] *Le Point* (Paris), January 29, 1973.

be argued that retention by the American states of distinct flags and college or professional football teams does not conflict with national loyalty. More ominously, however, the people of Europe do not fully trust each other. Opinion figures have consistently shown that citizens of the original EEC states feel a greater degree of confidence and trust toward the Swiss, Americans and British (none of whom were members of the Common Market) than toward each other. (See Table 6–3 above.) This finding is important because it indicates that one of the essential requirements for integration—mutual trust—is only partially developed. Added to this, European unity is not an issue of pressing political significance. For example, while the French electorate favors the principle of European union, only 11 percent regard it as the most important problem.[62] Finally, opinion polls indicate that if European unity were to require personal sacrifices, there would be a significant decline in support for further measures of integration.

Overall, there exists a kind of passive consensus among the publics of the original Six. Support does exist for dramatic integration efforts if political leaders choose to pursue them, but the support is not intense enough to compel action. Yet (except in Britain) there may be electoral penalties for those who oppose European union. At the height of his power, General de Gaulle was forced into a surprisingly close December 1965 runoff election against François Mitterrand for the French presidency. The narrowness of de Gaulle's victory (55 percent versus 45 percent) partly resulted from a bitter confrontation then in progress between de Gaulle and the EEC Commission.

In short, the constraints of public opinion are exceptionally loose. This point is even evident in the British case, where opinion was initially hostile to membership in the European Community, but not in such a way to prevent Britain's entry. Historically, foreign policy does not play a central role in British general elections, although the Common Market may have been marginally relevant because of the defection of the right-wing Tory, Enoch Powell, and his implied support of Labour's less European policy. The subsequent February 1974 defeat of the Conservative government by Labour owed more to Heath's unpopularity, a damaging confrontation with the miners' union, wide power blackouts, inflation and general economic problems than it did to European issues. In any event, British public opinion shifted in response to both the actual experience of belonging to the Common Market and the advocacy of continued membership by the heads of the Labour, Conservative, and

---

[62] *Sondages*, p. 15. A majority would be indifferent if they learned the Common Market had been abandoned, p. 19.

Liberal parties during the 1975 referendum campaign. As a result, the number of those favorable to political unification grew to include 50 percent of the population, with only 22 percent opposed.[63]

British public opinion remained comparable to French opinion regarding the desired structure of Europe. Thus 39 percent of the French and 46 percent of the British favored a limited European Government that dealt only with the most important issues and that left each country to look after its own problems, while almost identical numbers (32 percent in France, 31 percent in Britain) favored a more limited intergovernmental arrangement (which had been proposed by the Pompidou government) with no European government but regular meetings of the governments of each of the Community countries to agree upon common policies. At the same time, only 5 percent of the French and 11 percent of the British favored a strong European government replacing existing governments.[64] Despite this correspondence, Britons were from 10 to 19 percent less favorable than Frenchmen to a European flag, a common currency, and a European army.

Apart from opinion polls, which measure attitudes, other indicators of the integration of peoples include the growth of mutual transactions involving such communications as mail, phone calls, tourism, student exchanges, and trade. Measured by an index of relative acceptance (the index of relative acceptance calculates how much more or less interchange two or more countries have than might be expected merely on the basis of random probability and their share of, for example, world trade[65]) the Six appear to have experienced moderate but steady growth of mutual preference. An analysis by Karl Deutsch estimated that in 1965, Western Europe seemed to be "less than two-thirds of the way to the level of economic integration normally associated with national states or federations. . . ."[66] More recently, Deutsch and Chadwick have suggested that the trend, if it continues, "should carry the EEC countries within thirty or forty years far toward a community so highly economically integrated that far-reaching political amalgamation will be practicable."[67]

In view of the permissive consensus provided by public opinion and

[63] Twenty-eight percent were indifferent or had no opinion. By contrast in September 1973, only 37 percent had been favorable and 30 percent opposed to political unification. *Euro-barometre* (June–July 1975), no. 3, p. 19.
[64] *The Times* (London), November 16, 1973. Poll by Opinion Research Centre and Sofres.
[65] See Karl Deutsch, Lewis J. Edinger et al., *France, Germany and the Western Alliance: A Study of Elite Attitudes on European Integration and World Politics* (New York: Scribners, 1967), p. 220.
[66] Ibid., p. 237.
[67] Richard W. Chadwick and Karl W. Deutsch, "International Trade and Economic Integration: Further Development in Trade Matrix Analysis," *Comparative Political Studies* 6, no. 1 (April 1973): 92.

the degree of progress achieved in transactions, it is clear that the integration of the peoples of Western Europe is already significant and that national cleavages have diminished. But it is also crucial to examine the actual policies adopted by the participant governments to appreciate fully the national cleavages that do exist within the European Community.

The longest and most prominent national cleavage has been the opposition between France and its partners in the original Common Market. Unlike Germany, Italy, and the Benelux countries ("the Five"), France has continually opposed the autonomy and initiatives of the EEC, EURATOM, and ECSC executives, as well as most efforts to accord greater power or scope to these bodies. Of course, each country has paid attention to its own national interest, but France has done so to a markedly greater degree than any of its partners. Whenever proposals for upgrading the common European interest have been put forward, they have rarely succeeded unless the French government exacted major economic and political advantage from the new initiatives. The French position is in part explained by Gaullist opposition to supranationalism, in part by tenacious pursuit of French national interests, and in part by the advantage France derived by playing upon the other members' strong desires for maintaining European unity.

Britain too has been separated in several key ways from the other European states, initially by its flat opposition to supranational measures and by its non-membership in ECSC, EEC, and EURATOM, and later by its actions to renegotiate the terms of its belated membership. There have been exceptions to this cleavage: during the decade of Britain's attempt to join the Community, it often found itself supported by the Five against the intransigence of France; and more recently, when the issue involved further integration, Britain and France have found themselves together in opposition to the extension of supranationalism. But, more often than not, the pattern of Britain's experience and policy, as well as its chronic economic difficulties, have divided it from most of the Community members.

Though less salient or conspicuous, other national cleavages sometimes become visible within the EC. Italy's perennial political problems have occasionally caused it to fail to comply with Community agreements or regulations, and its inflation and balance of payments problems have added to this failure. More recently, Germany's immense economic strength has become so disproportionate as to threaten the Community's equilibrium. At a time when all the other members have suffered from profound economic problems, Germany has experienced a markedly less severe rate of inflation and an enormous balance of payments surplus (in

1974, Germany held hard currency reserves of nearly $40 billion—a figure substantially greater than that of any other country in the world). Moreover, West Germany's total Gross National Product, which in 1963 was of comparable magnitude to that of France or Britain, has become nearly as large as the GNP of the two other countries combined. In 1973, Germany's GNP of $343 billion, compared to France's $242 billion and Britain's $146 billion, placed it far ahead of its partners in economic strength.[68] As a result, the political balance here shifted toward Germany. Further expansion of Community activities, whether of agricultural policy (the key issue for France), aid to depressed regions (Britain's and Italy's concern), or common foreign aid will require disproportionate contributions from the Federal Republic. The Germans, however, are unlikely to pay the bill for these measures unless their partners accept more extensive measures of unification and carry out changes in their own domestic economic policies which Germany advocates. The resultant cleavage between Germany and its partners is thus no surprise.

Perhaps remarkably, none of these cleavages has so far proved unbridgeable; for all its members, the common economic and political benefits of membership in the Community outweigh other factors. In the last analysis, preserving and enhancing the EC has prevailed over the various national divisions, and with the exception of de Gaulle's 1965 clash, the existence of the Community itself has not been challenged.

When all is said and done, how unified are the nine member states of the European Community? On the negative side, it is clear that there exists no United States of Europe, no European superpower able to deal with the United States or the Soviet Union as an equal. Internally, each of the Nine still retains a national veto power over major EC initiatives. This has been reflected at such crucial moments as the French rejection of the European Defense Community (1954), de Gaulle's vetoes of British entry (1963, 1967), the Luxembourg crisis (1965–1966), disarray during the Middle East War and energy crisis (1973–1974), and renegotiation of Britain's EC membership (1974–1975). Defense policy remains wholly outside the Community and is dealt with on a national basis or sometimes as a NATO matter involving the United States. Foreign policy cooperation is only rudimentary and in crisis situations—as during the October 1973 Arab-Israeli war and energy crisis—it may break down altogether. National struggles continue within the EC, as many members seek maximum gain at minimal cost. When a particular interest within a country is threatened, its government may be tempted to react by trans-

[68] *The Economist* (London), April 20, 1974.

gressing Community rules, as in the case of the 1975 French restriction on imports of cheap Italian table wines which threatened the livelihood of small French wine growers.

Even in the economic sphere, the countries of Europe are not fully integrated. Proposals for Economic and Monetary Union (EMU) were endorsed at the Hague (1969) and Paris (1972) summit meetings of heads of state and government. The achievement of EMU, aimed for 1980, would have in effect created a common European currency and the unification of the economies of member countries. However, under the strains of world monetary fluctuations, recession, inflation, unemployment, and the energy crisis, the plans for EMU were set aside in the mid-1970s. In the absence of coherent democratic governing institutions to make the necessary decisions at a Community level, and without a means to provide for massive resource transfers from wealthier to poorer areas of the EC, the problems of operating an Economic and Monetary Union among the Nine would have created economic and political strains likely to tear the Community apart. In a fully federal system such as that of the United States, backward and depressed regions can appeal to Washington and often obtain substantial measures of economic aid. But in the absence of a full-fledged Community government in Brussels, EMU might have created unmanageable problems for those sectors of Europe unable to compete within a fully open and unified European economy.

At a more mundane level, the organs of the EC appear to spend a disproportionate amount of their time coping with uninspiring bureaucratic tasks and the problems of agriculture. While these efforts may in fact be unavoidable, their nature and slowness (for example, it took over a decade to negotiate a trade agreement with Israel) are hardly likely to capture the imagination and political enthusiasm of the European public.

The balance sheet of European unity does, however, display important successes. The creation of the European Coal and Steel Community and of the EEC; the admission of Britain, Denmark, and Ireland; successful summit meetings and the rudiments of a common approach to foreign policy are by themselves extraordinary achievements if we consider the background of political, religious, and ethnic conflict and warfare which had characterized so much of Europe prior to 1945.

The most tangible successes have come in the fields of trade and agriculture. The achievement of a free trade area, customs union, and Common External Tariff (CET) has eliminated many of the principal obstacles to trade among the Nine and made less likely the kind of protectionist, beggar-my-neighbor reaction to economic crisis which so badly hurt the Europeans during the 1930's. As a result there have been enormous increases in trade among the EC countries as well as between the Nine and the rest of the world. The existence of the CET provides Europe with a uniform tariff toward imports from the outside world and thus facilitates direct trade and commercial negotiations between the EC and foreign countries. Indeed, since January 1973 it has been against EC rules for a member state to negotiate a direct trade agreement with a non-EC country; instead, the EC Commission itself is responsible for such negotiations. As a result, the Community has established numerous trading and commercial agreements with foreign countries; it has also successfully operated on behalf of the Nine in other multilateral trade negotiations such as those in GATT (the General Agreement on Tariffs and Trade).

The Community's Common Agricultural Policy (CAP) has proved to be perhaps the single most important area of Common Market operation. Despite its shortcomings of high consumer prices and occasionally embarrassing surpluses (butter and beef "mountains," wine "lakes"), it has fostered a prosperous European agriculture and the management of labor movement from farms to cities. The reality of Community control of agricultural policy is reflected not only in the Brussels riot, which we noted at the start of this chapter, but in successive coordinated actions by agricultural pressure groups aimed at influencing decisions there. The importance of the CAP is also reflected in the fact that agriculture consumes the lion's share (roughly 75 to 80 percent) of the Commission's time and the Community's budget.

Nonetheless, the EC's operations are not confined to narrow agricultural and commercial matters. From the outside world, the Nine are increasingly seen as a single entity and the reality of this is reflected, for example, in the Community's agreement to provide $4 billion in foreign aid to 46 less developed countries (mostly former European colonies known as the ACP—Africa, Caribbean, and Pacific—regions) over a five year period, 1975–1980. More broadly, the Nine have achieved small but real steps toward a common foreign policy, including cooperation among ambassadors of each of the Nine in foreign countries, a coordinated position and common spokesman in negotiations at the Conference on Security and Cooperation in Europe, which were successfully concluded at Helsinki in 1975, and an EC Commission initiative in dealing with the Communist East European common market (the Comecon, or CMEA).

These examples by no means exhaust the fields in which European unification and common policies have met with success. Among other noteworthy areas, we can cite the achievement of a $1.3 billion Regional Fund, to aid poorer areas within the Community over the 1975–1977 period; operations of the Court of Justice (reflected, for example, in a fine of $115,000 levied in December 1974 against General Motors' Belgian branch for violating EC rules of competition); steps to harmonize the credentials necessary for professionals such as lawyers, doctors, and architects to practice anywhere within the Community; the multiplication of hundreds of pressure groups organized across national lines on the basis of common interests and aimed at exerting influence at Brussels; growing habits of cooperation among bureaucrats and government officials, who increasingly know their counterparts in other countries of the Nine and have learned to consult and act in concert with them; and, finally, the existence of a highly favorable (even if passive) public opinion that supports European unity and further measures toward integration.

In short, the question, "How unified is Europe?", can be answered by pointing both to a long list of areas in which unity does not exist and to a separate—shorter—list of areas where it does.

THE COMMUNITY'S PERFORMANCE

If unity is a story of both successes and failures, what can we say—in bread and butter terms—about the Community's performance in areas in which it has operated with visible importance? What impact has it had on the actual lives of Europeans, and how does its performance compare with that of the Soviet-dominated CMEA?

The most tangible and successful performance of the EC has been in the economic area. The establishment of the Common Market was paralleled by a sharp increase in trade and prosperity. Between 1958 and 1972 trade among the original Six increased by an incredible 724 percent. This increase did not mean that Europe turned its back on the rest of the world. In the same period, the Community's imports from other countries rose by 225 percent and its exports by 256 percent.[69]

Indeed, as Figure 6-1 makes clear, EEC trade rose remarkably faster than that of the United States, USSR, or Japan. One result of these increases was to foster economic growth and increases in real wages, ranging from 75 percent in Italy to 109 percent in France (see Table 6–5).

To be sure, it may be agreed that the development of Western European prosperity was not wholly caused by the existence of the EC, but that it reflected a general growth trend among advanced industrial countries during that period. Nevertheless, the measures undertaken by the Community, the far higher than average increase in trade, and the stimulus to investment caused by the creation of a huge internal market of nearly 200 million people (in the original Six) support the conclusion

[69] Commission of the European Communities, *The European Community: Facts and Figures* (London: November 1974), p. 14.

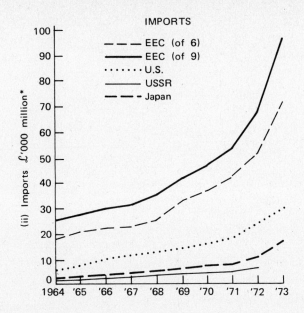

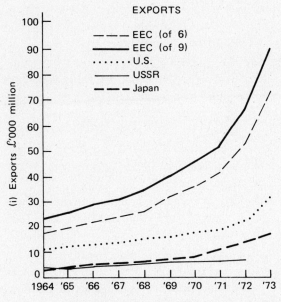

FIGURE 6–1 The Community in World Trade

Source: London, Commission of the European Communities, *Facts and Figures* (November 1974), p. 26.

TABLE 6–5 Economic Growth in the European Community of the Six, 1958–1972

| | GNP per Head [1] | | Real Wages [2] |
	1958	1972	% increase 1958–72
Belgium	1,154	3,351	93%
France	1,196	3,489	109
Germany	1,096	3,840	79
Italy	612	2,008	121
Luxembourg	1,402	(3,255)	75
Netherlands	845	3,193	106

Source: Commission of the European Communities. *The European Community: Facts and Figures.* (London: November 1979), p. 23. [1] $ per year at market prices. [2] Increase of gross hourly earnings of workers in industry October/October, in real terms. [3] Manufacturing industries: September.

that the Community fostered improved economic efficiency, increased total wealth, and higher living standards. Although prosperity did not increase uniformly among the Six, gaps among the members appear to have narrowed somewhat. Thus in 1958, Italy was the poorest member of the EEC, with only 59 percent of average Community per capita GNP. By 1970, however, the gap had narrowed to 67 percent, even though parts of Southern Italy remained desperately poor.[70] There have also been comparable gains in social welfare (health, education, unemployment insurance, leisure, pensions), both in absolute terms and in terms of a narrowing of differences within the Community.

The economic success of the EEC is even more striking when compared with that of the Eastern European Comecon. As Table 6–6 illustrates, gross national product (GNP) per person in the EEC ranged from a high of $6000 in Denmark to a low of $2500 in Italy (or $2100 if we include Ireland, which joined in 1973). But in Comecon, the wealthiest member, Czechoslovakia, enjoyed a GNP per head of only $2300, and the poorest, Rumania, a mere $900 per person (or $500 if we count Mongolia, the sole Asian member).

Superficially, Comecon has been as concerned with promoting unity and prosperity in Eastern Europe as has the EC in the West. The 1960 Comecon Charter declared that "economic cooperation . . . is conducive to . . . raising the standard of living . . . and solidarity of the [CMEA] countries," and it pledged to develop economic cooperation on the basis of an international socialist division of labor in the interests of building communism in their countries. In fact, Comecon provided a vehicle

[70] Roger Broad and R. J. Jarrett, *Community Europe Today* (London: Oswald Wolff, 1972), p. 44.

TABLE 6-6 European Community, Comecon and U.S. Compared

EC	GNP (a) per capita	Steel production tons per capita	Autos per 1000 pop.	TV sets per 1000 pop.	Telephones per 1000 pop.	Passenger kilometers per capita	Messages per capita	Armed forces as % pop.	Milit. expend. as % GNP
Belgium	$4700	1.81	215	207	200	7493	418	1.0	2.3
France	5100	0.45	245	201	161	8639	312	1.0	4.0
W. Germany	5600	0.75	234	262	212	7602	376	0.8	3.3
Italy	2500	0.37	187	170	160	6511	324	0.8	2.7
Luxembourg	5100	(b)	267	183	311	8970	494	0.3	0.8
Netherlands	4500	0.36	200	223	242	6819	483	0.9	3.7
Great Britain	3200	0.55	218	284	253	7263	416	0.7	4.8
Ireland	2100	0.021	125	180	190	4816	279	0.3	0.9
Denmark	6000	0.12	200	320	310	7595	580	0.9	2.4
EC Average	4187	0.44	210	226	227	7301	409	0.7	2.8
Comecon									
USSR	1700	0.48	7	117	41	1621	69	1.4	8–10.0
E. Germany	2200	0.31	85	265	110	3294	198	1.2	6.8
Czechoslovakia	2300	0.80	50	230	124	2970	254	1.4	5.4
Hungary	1600	0.32	16	140	66	1948	172	1.3	3.9
Poland	1600	0.38	64	110	51	1503	83	0.9	5.7
Rumania	900	0.27	2	46	30	1089	48	1.1	2.7
Bulgaria	1500	0.19	NA	42	NA	1410	NA	2.0	3.7
Mongolia	500	NA	NA	5	NA	NA	NA		
CMEA Average	1639	0.31		119	70	1976	137	1.3	5.2–5.5
U.S.	6700	0.62	500	549	617	14,125	1,255	1.5	8.0

NOTE: a=GNP figures for 1973. Note that because of inflation and exchange rate fluctuations, these comparisons are not precise. b=included in Belgium.

SOURCES: GNP figures for EC and Comecon are based on World Bank and Economic Commission for Europe data, cited in *The Economist* (London: August 30, 1973). Other figures c. 1971.

SOURCES: A. J. Groth and W. C. Potter, "Personal Mobility and Communication in the Warsaw Pact States," paper presented at the annual meeting of the American Association for the Advancement of Slavic Studies, Banff, Canada, September 4–6, 1974; C. E. Welch and A. K. Smith, *Military Role and Rule* (N. Scituate, Mass.: Duxbury, 1974), p. 278; R. Broad and R. J. Jarrett, *Community Europe Today* (London: Oswald Wolff, 1972).

for legitimizing Soviet predominance over the East European economies, and progress toward real integration among the East European economies has been slow. The performance of Comecon in raising the living standards of its members has also been meager. Although their industrial production has risen substantially, the East European countries have actually fallen farther behind Western Europe in living standards. Thus East Germany and Czechoslovakia, which had levels of personal consumption only slightly lower than those of West Germany prior to World War II, have dropped to less than 60 percent of current West German levels.[71] In addition, the Soviet Union has maintained a position of trade predominance within CMEA which is without parallel in the EC—for example, it accounts for 54 percent of Bulgaria's foreign trade, 34 percent of Czechoslovakia's and 24.5 percent of Rumania's.[72]

A further illustration of the lag in East European performance may be seen in Table 6–6. Not only do the East Europeans trail badly in GNP per head, but in consumer durables such as automobiles and telephones as well. One reason may be in the relatively higher levels of defense spending as a percentage of GNP (ranging from 2.7 percent to 10 percent) found in Eastern Europe compared to the lower levels characteristic of Western Europe (disregarding Luxembourg, 2.7 percent to 4.8 percent). Similarly, there are more men under arms in the East (0.9 to 2.0 percent of total population) than in the West (0.7 to 1.0 percent). Inasmuch as investment in armaments produces nothing—except rust—the economic performance of the Nine is aided by the lighter military burden. In the early 1970's, the USSR took advantage of a rise in world prices for raw materials to tie the Eastern European economies more closely to its own. Short of foreign currency to buy Western industrial goods and technology, the East Europeans were forced to lean more heavily on the USSR, which provided more than 90 percent of Comecon's petroleum and iron ore, about 70 percent of its steel, grain, and cement, and half its coal.

Unlike the EC, Comecon is a strictly intergovernmental organization. It lacks community-wide organs, such as a parliament or court of justice, and it is without a major supranational bureaucracy to implement its decisions. Apart from the overriding fact of Soviet predominance, the most important differences between the EC and Comecon stem from the democratic pluralistic character of the EC and the closed character

[71] Michael Kaser, *COMECON: Integration Problems of the Planned Economies,* 2nd ed. (London: Oxford University Press, 1967), pp. 204–205.
[72] William C. Potter, "Political Change in Eastern Europe: The International Dimension," paper presented at the Annual Meeting of the American Political Science Association, San Francisco, September 2–5, 1975, pp. 21a, 21b.

of Comecon. The activities of the Community and decisions about its policy and application are carried on amid a lively group struggle. Large nongovernmental organizations and pressure groups seeking to shape the EC's conduct and future have developed throughout the Community. When we speak of the Common Market we are not merely referring to policies of the governments of France, West Germany, Britain, and others, but to a regional supranational organization with an active politics and interest group activity of its own. By contrast, the Comecon lacks such features altogether.

In practice, Comecon has failed to provide the stimulus to economic growth and prosperity characteristic of the EC and it lacks the autonomous nature of its West European competitor. In addition, its citizens do not share the sense of common identity increasingly found among the West Europeans. One reason for this may be the limitation of free movement of persons across each other's frontiers. In the Community, people have been more or less free to come and go as they please; this has promoted a heightened sense of mutual security and acceptance as well as an increased Europeanization of EC public opinion. By contrast, movement among the Communist states has been much more limited and controlled, even when we ignore the stringent limits on travel by East Europeans outside the Communist countries. There also exists very little interchange of labor forces. Illustratively, mobility and communications (as measured by passenger kilometers) and messages (telephone, telegram, letters, and packages) per capita were more sparse in the Comecon than in the EC countries. West Germans, for example, did more than twice the amount of travelling (7602 kilometers) of their East German neighbors (3294) and sent nearly twice the number of messages (376 versus 198).

Obviously, the performance of the EC has been hugely successful in contrast to Comecon and even by its own standards. Nonetheless, there remain significant and politically relevant shortcomings. In essence, those who have taken greatest advantage of the European Community's existence have been the larger businesses and especially the multinational corporations—particularly American-owned ones. From outside, the American firms have been quickest to appreciate and take advantage of the lowering of barriers within the Common Market. Where national firms of France, Germany, or Italy were sometimes slow to operate on a fully international basis, too traditional in their management, or too small in size to make full use of these new opportunities, American firms rushed to invest in Europe. Between 1958 and 1972 American direct investment in the Six jumped from $1.93 billion to $15.7 billion; if Britain is included, the figure rises to $25.9 billion. (By contrast, investment by the Six in the United States rose from $1.4 billion to only

$3.9 billion, and even with Britain the figure is no more than $8.3 billion.) [73] Equally important, American firms gained predominance in many of the most technologically advanced fields—for example, controlling 95 percent of the production of integrated circuits and 80 percent of computers.

By contrast, other groups in society were slower to take advantage of the Common Market. For example, trade unionists, despite formation of the 35 million member European Confederation of Trade Unions (ECTU), failed to acquire the genuine transnational coordination of the multinational corporations and the ability to think and operate on a truly European scale. Benefits to consumers and the general public were largely indirect, in terms of greater prosperity and the like, and food prices tended to be kept artificially high as a result of the Community's Common Agricultural Policy. As a result of these factors, the EC remained at least partly vulnerable to charges that it was a community for the benefit of large corporations, big farmers, and the rich. During the 1975 referendum campaign in Britain, as earlier during the 1972 referenda in Denmark and Norway, these changes became part of the debate over membership.

PROSPECTS: THE FUTURE OF THE EUROPEAN COMMUNITY

Despite periodic crises and premature obituaries (1963, 1965–1966, 1973–1974), the European Community is here to stay. It does, however, remain vulnerable to Willy Brandt's charge of being an "economic giant but a political dwarf." The establishment of the Common Market represented a kind of bargain to seek European political unity via economic means, but while the Community's economic performance has proved generally successful, it has not lived up to the idealistic hopes for political unity. Thus the chief question about its future must be whether Europe can make progress politically.

To be sure, the Community has not been devoid of some limited political accomplishments. The most notable of these has been the achievement of what political scientist Karl Deutsch has termed a security community or a situation in which countries no longer contemplate the possibility of war against one another. In the perspective of two recent World Wars and centuries of previous conflict, this is an achievement of historic magnitude. In addition, citizens of the original six Common Market countries increasingly are able to view themselves and their environment from a European perspective even while their national orientation persists. For example, opinion polls indicate that overwhelm-

[73] *The European Community at a Glance* (Washington, D.C.: European Community Information Service, January 1974).

"What have I done?"
Courtesy E.C. Photo Library

ing majorities of people in all nine EC countries favor the notion of European solidarity in confronting economic problems within the Community, to the extent of their country coming to the aid of another member in economic difficulty.[74] More specifically, European political élites increasingly see political as well as economic problems from a European perspective and remain strongly favorable to far reaching measures of political unification.[75] Finally, the existing institutional structure of the EC, with its at least rudimentary supranational policies and organs (Commission, bureaucracy, court, parliament, and so on) makes the Community politically more than the sum of its nine member states.

In the future, however, the Nine will need to make further progress so that the Community does not stagnate. Direct popular election of

[74] "The 1973 European Community Public Opinion Surveys. Preliminary Findings, November 1973–April 1974." Ronald Inglehart, University of Michigan, Mimeographed, p. 15.
[75] See, for example, Robert J. Lieber, "European Elite Attitudes Revisited." Also note that 75 percent of recent graduates of the prestigious French Ecole Nationale d'Administration (ENA) favor the gradual creation of a supranational European state. *Les Informations* poll, cited in *European Community*, No. 157 (August–September 1972).

the European Parliament may be one such achievement whose time is likely to come. Article 138 of the Rome Treaty commits the members of the Community to this goal, and public opinion in all but Britain supports this. In recent years, increasingly specific proposals have been presented—for example, one which the European Parliament endorsed in 1975. This provided for direct election of the parliament on the first Sunday in May 1978 and would take effect if adopted by the Council of Ministers and notified by the legislatures of each of the nine member states. The proposal included a parliament of 355 members elected for five year terms. Representation, calculated on the basis of population, would give Germany 71 seats, Britain 66, France 65, the Netherlands 27, Belgium 23, Denmark 17, Ireland 13, and Luxembourg 6.

Apart from the question of direct election of the European Parliament, political progress seems possible in the more frequent and regular coordination among European heads of state or government. Since 1975 they have begun to meet not at grand and unusual diplomatic summits, which had all the trappings of international ceremony and formal negotiation between sovereign heads of state, but instead three times per year at more routine, businesslike and informal gatherings known as the "European Council." And, as an indication of at least slight progress, France has agreed to abide by weighted majority rule on issues not of vital national interest. While this is only a minor advance, in that countries still reserve the right to decide for themselves the vital issues on which they will exercise a national veto, the policy does mark a shift away from the almost mystical opposition by de Gaulle (particularly after 1965) to the very concept of majority voting.

A problem, of course, is that these are only small steps on a very long road. The principal political—and often economic—decisions still require unanimity among the Nine, and it is difficult to foresee states which have been sovereign for centuries agreeing to merge themselves into any United States of Europe. It is more realistic to envisage the development of a loose confederation in which elements of national and European sovereignty coexist, but even this type of political unity will not be easy to achieve.

In the short term, the Nine find themselves in a situation in which, because of international interdependence, they have lost many of the traditional powers of decision or control that they often formerly exercised at the national level. For the most part they are no longer masters of their own fate in determining the crucial economic, social, and political decisions that affect them. Instead, and at best, they only partially influence the factors determining inflation, recession, unemployment, investment, capital movements, the activities of multinational corporations, the availability of energy and raw materials, technology, pollution, and even entertainment and culture. Yet this loss of control has not been accompanied by a corresponding increase in supranational European authority nor even in looser European cooperation. There has, however, been a greater willingness to address these and other problems at a European level and to seek cooperative solutions. Thus in 1974, Italy received strong economic and monetary support for its staggering economy from Germany and its EC partners, who feared the effects of the possible collapse of an important trading partner. But the absence of a full-fledged European structure, of democratic means of accountability and control, and of the ability to stimulate the public imagination beyond passive support set limits to the cooperation.

Equally important, the EC remains without the means of its independent defense. The Rome Treaty ignores the subject, and at a national level the Nine individually and as a group lack the means to counterbalance the Soviet Union because they do not have the deterrent capability of the United States. This places major limitations upon their independence, preventing them from dealing with the United States on a basis of real equality or partnership. The resultant European vulnerability also acts to divide the Nine at times of crisis. Thus during the winter of 1973–1974, they split over three distinct responses to the energy crisis. Some members of the EC favored a coherent and unified Community policy in dealing with the Middle East, the Arabs, and the Americans on the problem of energy supply. Others, particularly France, preferred to go their own way, especially in seeking agreement with the Arab oil producers. Finally, most of the Western Europeans began to follow American leadership and to participate in the U.S.-sponsored International Energy Agency.

Interestingly enough, public opinion in Europe favored a more unified response than that adopted by European governments. During the Arab oil boycott, the Nine were divided into three categories by the Arabs: one group (Britain and France) was treated in a favored way and was not to suffer supply cuts; a second group (Germany, Italy, Belgium, Ireland, Denmark, Luxembourg) was to suffer progressive reductions of 5 percent per month; and a third category (the Netherlands—along with the United States, Israel, and others) was to face a total embargo. In response, the European governments failed to hang together; instead they scrambled to save themselves on an individual basis and refused to support the Dutch. Yet even in France, the most independent-minded of the Nine, at least 70 percent of the public favored the sharing of oil with the Netherlands.[76]

---

[76] Based on a SOFRES poll; see *L'Express* (Paris), November 12–18, 1973.

The issue of Europe's place in the world remains unresolved. The Community has been alternately praised and dammed. American governments, which encouraged its birth and development, have often praised and supported the EC—and at times opposed it when the Community appeared to act in a manner too independent for American tastes. The Russians have typically opposed it as a capitalist device and an American tool, but have reluctantly begun to come to terms with it as a reality. The Chinese have warmly applauded the Community—as a means of counterbalancing Russian influence—and have urged its political and military development. And one political scientist has even viewed it as a potentially emergent imperialist superpower, dividing the world and harmful to the interests of the poorer nations.[77]

In fact, the Community possesses only a limited presence on the world stage, but to the extent that questions of international economics become central, it is likely to play an increased role. The EC is already responsible for negotiating trade agreements with outside countries (though there are loopholes in this power), and in the foreign aid field it already contributes more than the United States. For the foreseeable future, the European Community will constitute no more than a civilian power (rather than a military one), and will provide a basis for cooperation both within Europe and between the Nine and the rest of the world. In this sense the world is almost certainly better off than if no such body existed.

It is a paradox that to the extent that the EC performs successfully it reinforces the viability of the states which belong to it. Thus it would be simplistic to assume that, in Europe at least, political life is inexorably shifting from a national to a federal or supranational scale. Of course, the forces of interdependence and transnationalism may make it mutually advantageous for the countries of Western Europe to participate in the Community. Yet it may well be that only states which are viable economically and politically make good partners within the Community. Indeed the problems of Italy and of Britain, which have sometimes hindered the EC's performance, illustrate this point.

Do the forces of history, or of international politics and economics, or of institutional momentum, or even of domestic necessity push the Nine toward closer political unity? In a recent document, the Tindemans Report, even the Commission observes that European union will be spread over a very long period of time on which it prefers not to put a predetermined date. If we consider the specific objectives of this report—a European government with an executive of independent people, responsible to a two house legislature, one house of which has been directly elected—

[77] Johan Galtung, *The European Community: A Superpower in the Making.*

there is nothing automatic or inevitable about such progress. Europe of the Nine is and will be less than a United States of Europe or a European superpower of equivalent rank and stature to the United States and the Soviet Union. How much less is a matter which the Europeans themselves will consciously determine.

At a minimum, the European Community has achieved an impressive amount of harmonization of laws, programs, policies, and institutions across traditional boundaries.[78] It is not yet a federal Europe or a European nation, but if we contrast it with where Europe stood, in the rubble of warfare and economic catastrophe, as recently as 1945, then the degree of progress is remarkable. Perhaps the final word should be that of one of the founders of the Common Market, who observed that the Community was like a gothic cathedral. We should thus keep in mind both that its final completion may take generations and that the outlines of something extraordinary can be seen under construction.

[78] See, for example, Donald Puchala, "The Domestic Politics of Supranational Harmonization in the European Community," paper presented at the Annual Meeting of the American Political Science Association, Chicago, Illinois, August 29–September 2, 1974.

7

alternative european politics

Baltic Sea

North Sea

ATLANTIC
OCEAN

MEDITERRANEAN SEA

Adriatic Sea

Aegean Sea

YUGOSLAVIA

Belgrade

GREECE

Thessaloniki

Trikkala

Ioannina

Athens

Patrai

SPAIN

PORTUGAL

Barcelona

Saragosa

Madrid

Valencia

Malaga

Seville

Oporto

Lisbon

7 ALTERNATIVE EUROPEAN POLITICS

Until this point we have concentrated upon the major European democracies and their chief postwar antagonist, the Soviet Union. We have thus dealt with variants of pluralist democracy (Britain, France, the Federal Republic of Germany, the European Community) and Communist dictatorship (the USSR, the German Democratic Republic, Comecon).

Other significant political patterns exist in Europe that fit neither mold. One of these is right-wing authoritarianism as embodied in the pattern of Mediterranean dictatorships. Another is liberalized communism, of which Yugoslavia is the principal embodiment. It is these two patterns that we treat in the present chapter.

Rightist Authoritarianism: The Mediterranean Dictatorships

background and policy agenda

In the post–World War II period, Spain and Portugal (the latter not a Mediterranean country, to be sure, but one which shares the Iberian penninsula and certain political characteristics with Spain), and also Greece, have all experienced dictatorial forms of rule. The circumstances which have given rise to dictatorships in these three countries seem to have been replicated elsewhere throughout the world; they also appear to recur cyclically. For these reasons, not out of sheer historical antiquarianism, we discuss them here.

These dictatorships represent models of political organization and development that may be usefully compared with those of the major powers discussed earlier: on the one hand, the pluralistic polyarchies or democracies, such as Britain, France, and West Germany; on the other, the more monolithic dictatorships of the far left—the USSR and East Germany or even Yugoslavia.

SOCIAL CLEAVAGES

If we look at the backgrounds of the political systems of modern Spain, Portugal, and Greece, we find in them certain common denominators of deeply pervasive and acute social conflict. In each case, the national history features a legacy of bitter struggles among antagonistic interests. Sometimes these are waged in the form of civil wars, sometimes in widespread riots, civil strife, and armed confrontations, sometimes through revolutionary coups.

In all of these countries there have been intermittent experiments with democracy, usually culminating in violence and disorder, followed by periods of dictatorship, and sometimes the collapse of these regimes, succeeded by shaky experiments in democratic government. In all these countries there have been exceptionally sharp class conflicts, between a large number of very poor people, landless or small landholding peasants and urban workers on the one hand, and small but highly affluent classes of landlords and entrepreneurs on the other. The contrast between the rich and the poor has been sharp, and the feelings attaching to the great chasm between them have been correspondingly strong. Hatred, resentment, and suspicion have long characterized the relations among the classes, with substantial numbers of rich and poor tending to see their relationship as one of all-out struggle: "either them or us."

Another aspect of the polarization of the societies has been a sharp cleavage between the traditional and modern sectors of society. On the one hand, we can find in each of these states the persistence of a rural and handicraft economy, with many social, religious, and cultural values based upon age-old customs and traditions, with strong attachments to the institutions of church, family, village, and region; on the other, we can find, side by side, or in near proximity, the evidence of new social formations, based on the economic, technological, and cultural foundations of the age of industrial and, as some say, postindustrial revolution.

The people who identify with ancient traditions and the status quo of their particular culture face those of their countrymen who have adopted a universalistic, Western, scientific, rational, bureaucratic, and industrial outlook; people who demand change and progress; people who are restive under the rule of the old establishment of landed nobility and its upper bourgeois allies in the cities and towns; above all, perhaps, people who scorn and abhor the old ways and the docility toward one's masters that generally accompanies the acceptance of traditional institutions.

The conflict between old and new is apt to be most severe in societies that have industrialized relatively late in history, and only to a slight or moderate degree. It is precisely in such societies that the differences between life on the farm or in the mountains and life in the city are apt to be at their widest, more so than they might be in Britain, Sweden, or the United States. The cultural distances between the old and the new social formations are likely to be enormous.[1] The urban working class may be taking its cues from the writings of Marxists and anarchists; the new managerial middle class may display all the irreverence of agnosticism, tending to worship science and money; the peasants in the backwoods may well continue to follow the counsels of the parish priest, the local midwife, and the landlord.

Generally, the cleavage of modern society versus traditionalist overlaps the cleavage of poor versus rich in such a way as to augment the effective power of the rich. If the conflicts of these societies ran across strictly class—or income—lines, then the overwhelming number of very poor people might readily overwhelm the relatively few rich people. The strength of the conservative-traditionalist, rightist, elements derives in large measure from the support given them by the masses of relatively poor people who identify with them on the basis of certain important shared values. In all classes, but particularly among rural and lower middle class urban elements, there are many people who are skeptical or hostile toward change; who are deeply attached to religion and often to the whole complex of institutions with which they have grown up; who value order and predictability much more than they value change; who are eager to preserve their particularistic identity against all attempts at innovation; above all, these are people who fear the loss of status and traditional individuality, which they have developed over the ages. They may even prefer a measure of inequality and want to the homogenization of political, social, and economic experiments often advocated by radical or liberal reformers.

In addition to the economic class cleavage, and to the sociocultural cleavage of old versus new, there are often other, more particularistic, cleavages. In Spain, regionalism, for example, embodied by the aspirations of the Basque people in the northeast and the Catalans in the southeastern area around Barcelona, is such a conflict.

All of these underlying social confrontations—atheism and agnosticism

[1] See Stanley G. Payne, *A History of Spain and Portugal* (Madison: University of Wisconsin Press, 1973), p. 600.

against faith and religion; the spirit of science, progress, and pragmatism against the reverence for tradition and the established order; universalism against particularism; the spirit of egalitarianism and internationalism against the values of nationalism, regionalism, and attachment to traditional hierarchy; freedom and change against the worship of order and tranquility—find their expression in political conflict through organized groups and political parties.

POLITICAL CHOICES

Societies like the Spanish, Greek, and Portuguese which suffer from chronic and severe fragmentation are likely to support a great variety of political movements. Under some circumstances (as in Scandinavia), many parties can actually compete within a mutually acceptable framework of rules and policies just as readily as two parties could in Britain or the United States. In bitterly divided societies, however, the multiparty systems tend to aggregate mutually hostile clienteles, and to do so in such large numbers that cooperation within an acceptable framework of rules and policies by a majority is very difficult and sometimes impossible. The parties, the trade unions, and many of the pressure groups are likely to be exclusive organizations, not umbrella organizations. They tend to represent particular, often extreme points of view, seeking combat rather than compromise with most other political forces. They are likely to exhibit ideological rigidity and extremism. The progressives will disdain the slightest stigma of "clericalism." The traditionalists will not sully themselves by any doubtful associations with "godless" socialism and "crass materialism" of secular liberals.

In terms of the impacts of this background of antagonistic fragmentation on the policy agenda, we will usually find policy alternatives as stark either-or choices. Generally speaking, the deeper the gulf between the protagonists the more extreme their policy positions. Among the poor there is likely to be a major tendency toward expropriation of the upper class' land, as well as extermination of the privileged, wealthy strata. The wealthy classes are likely to adhere in very large numbers to policies of repression, rather than of accommodation or gradualist reform. The believers are likely to treat atheists and agnostics as the incarnation of the devil; the progressives are not likely to show tolerance toward the allegedly ignorant and hypocritical believers. Essentially, each side considers the other too evil, dangerous, and untrustworthy to be indulged. Compromises are seen as futile, and attempts at compromise simply as proofs of the naiveté of those involved.

Hence, issues involving distribution or redistribution of resources, regulation by government, autonomy for various societal interests, the terms of participation and equity in the political system, all tend to acquire a kind of all-or-nothing crisis character. The societies are likely to hover precariously between cataclysmic expropriation of proprietors and the certainty of mandated penury for millions of landless and small landholding peasants; between shocking exploitation of the workers and the violent destruction of their factory masters; between compulsory religious instruction and the equally compulsory absence of it; between complete regional independence and the total subjection to a central government. Understandably, where so many of the players are extremist in their thinking and intentions, the stakes of the political game acquire civil war dimensions, whether or not people are actually fighting in the streets.

As Woodrow Wilson once observed, democracy is not so much a form of government as it is a kind of human character. It requires civic virtue, as the ancients called it. Without a high degree of mutual esteem, cooperation, and trust in a society, it is difficult to operate democratic institutions. Thus, in the history of these states, periods of outwardly democratic governments have often coincided with high levels of social tension, unrest, incipient insurrection, military conspiracies, and revolutionary outbreaks.

Portugal's erstwhile strongman, Dr. Salazar, once told an interviewer:

> Speaking generally, I have no horror of party. What I have is a horror of party spirit in Portugal. One can say that for centuries England has existed with two great parties taking turns in power, and so far she has managed quite well on her system. A political education has taught the people to sway between the two parties, influenced by the force of great aspirations or by national needs. But in Portugal our parties have been formed round individuals with mean, greedy little interests. . . . The treatment of a sick nation demands from us that we should stop either for good or at least for a long time all this political action in bits-and-pieces! [2]

On another occasion, the dictator said, not without some post facto justification:

> If the dictatorship were to go, and to give place to the rule of faction, the old causes of chaos and ruin would return, their destructive force accentuated by increased indiscipline, by exacerbated passions, by the collapse of all material and moral defenses against disorder—even to the

[2] See Antonio Ferro, *Salazar: Portugal and Her Leader* (London: Faber and Faber, Ltd., 1939), pp. 242–243.

extent of undermining the conditions necessary to the very existence of society.

Between the forces of an innovative, radical left and those of a conservative, traditionalist right there usually seems little room for compromise or accommodation; all the political arrangements combining them in one community seem more in the nature of an armed truce than peaceful reconciliation. There appears to be a predisposition—activated by the least provocation on either side or perhaps some sudden economic or international crisis—for one side or the other to establish dictatorial dominion, and plunge into civil war in pursuit of it.

Let us now examine the backgrounds of Greece, Spain, and Portugal in further detail.

GREECE

In the history of modern Greece there have been six military coups since 1922. The last occurred in November 1973, when a group of army officers overthrew Colonel George Papadopoulos who had himself seized power from a democratic parliamentary regime in 1967. The military ruled Greece until 1974, when the threat of war with Turkey led to their downfall and the restoration of parliamentary democracy. Greece had been a monarchy virtually from its foundation as a modern nation-state in 1830. However, kings were deposed in 1862, 1917, and 1922; they were exiled in 1941 during the World War, and again after the Papadopoulos coup in 1967. In 1975, the monarchy was abolished by a popular referendum.

The first Greek republic had been established in 1923. Military coups occurred in 1925, 1926, 1933, and 1935. The monarchy was re-established under one of the military governments in 1935, but real power was held by General John Metaxas, who had consolidated a right-wing dictatorship. He was ousted from power following the Nazi invasion of Greece in the spring of 1941. A powerful resistance movement against the Nazis, spearheaded by the Communist Party, the EAM/ELLAS, developed in the early forties. Following the collapse of the German occupation, a civil war broke out between Communist and pro-Communist forces and the moderate and conservative elements. It lasted, with brief pauses, from 1944 until 1949. Enormous material and human losses were incurred on the heels of the great destruction wrought by four years of Nazi occupation.

As in Spain and Portugal, the background of the Greek dictatorship was characterized by deep popular divisions, bitter social, economic, cultural, and political antagonisms, and considerable instability. In the twenty month period preceding the Papadopoulos coup, from August

Greece: George Papadopoulos and military colleagues, Phaedon Gizikis
and Demetrios Ioannidis, dancing, 1973.
Greek Photo Agency—Keystone

1965 to April 1967, Greece had been ruled by four different caretaker
governments.[3]

SPAIN

In Spain there has been only one effective parliamentary government
since 1909—in 1931. Between 1875 and 1902 Spanish cabinets lasted on
the average twenty-two months; between 1902 and 1917 they averaged
ten months; between 1917 and 1923 only six months. More importantly,
however, historian Stanley Payne has pointed out that "the crises of
Spanish parliamentary government occurred not because the system

[3] See Peter Schwab, ed., *Greece Under the Junta* (New York: Facts on File, 1970),
pp. 5–10.

was growing more corrupt and unrepresentative, but on the contrary, as it became less corrupt and more representative." [4] In essence, irreconcilable differences and antagonisms were beginning to be felt more and more acutely with the increasing liberalization or opening up of the political system.

In 1923, a frail and developing Spanish parliamentary regime was overthrown by army general Miguel Primo de Rivera, amidst public disorder and great political agitation. More than half the people could already be described as politically alienated—workers, peasants, the middle classes, and the intellectuals. All of these groups had been thwarted in their particular aspirations, to a large extent by mutual opposition. Only 42 percent of the Spanish electorate voted in the last election before the coup. As Payne notes:

> Under terms of martial law, peace and security were soon restored to the cities and industrial areas. Once the hand of authority was imposed and the opportunity for political maneuver and legal manipulation was at an end, disorder vanished. The dictatorship had, however, few ideas about the long-desired constitutional reform.[5]

Primo de Rivera's "quietist" dictatorship could not long contain explosive social changes in the Spanish body politic. "Law and order" without substantive reform proved a relatively short-term palliative.

In January 1930, Primo de Rivera was forced into exile. Democracy was given another chance. Because of the emergence of strong republican movement in the larger cities of Spain, King Alfonso XII abdicated and the nation became a Republic. A parliamentary democratic political system was formally adopted in the Constitution of 1931 with an extensive bill of rights.

Nevertheless, within a year of the establishment of the Republic (whose thorough anticlericalism profoundly alienated Spain's sizable Catholic opinion) violence, labor unrest, and revolutionary turmoil all began to gather momentum. Anarchists, radicals, Socialists, separatists, moderates, Communists, Falangists, Trotskyists, and numerous other groups involved themselves in a process of growing conflict. When in 1933 the moderate Catholics (CEDA) won a plurality in the parliamentary elections, the Socialists, among others, threatened revolutionary insurrection against what they considered a threat of Fascist rule. Revolutionary risings in Catalonia and Asturias followed the inclusion of the moderate Catholics in the cabinet of October 1934. Republicans, radicals, and

[4] Payne, *A History of Spain and Portugal*, pp. 628–629.
[5] Ibid., p. 617.

Socialists all professed to believe that the moderate Catholic Party was about to stage a coup against the Republic. The CEDA, of course, had reason to suspect its opponents of the same plan.

In the last election before the Civil War, in 1936, the alliance of the parties of the Left (Popular Front) faced an alliance of the parties of the Right. The outcome was a classic split, 34.3 percent for the Left, 33.2 percent for the Right, and 5.4 percent for the Center. Because of the existing Spanish system of electoral districts, the slender Left plurality translated into a sizable majority of seats in the parliament. No sooner was the victory of the Popular Front made known, however, when the poor peasants and city workers proceeded with direct takeover of lands and factories. Strikes and land seizures mounted in the summer of 1936. Churches and convents were looted and burned. Catholic education was virtually proscribed. Conservative and traditionalist Spain felt itself mortally threatened. Such was the backdrop of General Francisco Franco's military coup against the Republic. The Fascist Falanga joined Catholic, middle class, and landed elements in support of the nationalist rising of the army.

The Spanish Republic resisted Franco's right-wing coup, and a bloody and tragic Civil War ensued. On the side of the Republic, there fought a diverse coalition of Liberals, Republicans, Democratic Socialists, Anarchists, Trotskyists, Communists, and even Basque separatists. On the right, Franco's heterogeneous forces were aided by the fascist dictators of Italy and Germany. Mussolini supplied tens of thousands of combat troops. Hitler also provided troops (his Condor legion), as well as air force support and large quantities of weapons.

The Republic found itself almost isolated. A policy of appeasement made the Western democracies loath to antagonize Hitler and Mussolini. They and the United States agreed on a nonintervention policy, in which no weapons would be supplied to either side in the Civil War. In practice this harmed only the Republican (or "Loyalist") side since Germany and Italy were unimpeded in supplying troops and weapons to Franco's forces (the "Rebels").

Spain proved to be an emotional issue in the West, however, and tens of thousands of volunteers from France, Britain, the United States, other European countries, and antifascist refugees from Italy and Germany entered Spain to fight on the side of the Republic. For its own reasons, the Soviet Union sold weapons to the Republicans and provided military advisors, but Stalin's support was not on the scale of Nazi and Fascist aid to Franco. Although prior to the 1936 coup the Spanish Communists had constituted a small minority of the Republican forces, their influence and that of the Soviets grew considerably during the Civil War. In fact, the Loyalists remained a diverse group of Communists and non-Communists and on occasion there were bitter conflicts among them, particularly because of the efforts of Stalinist Communists to purge or eliminate Anarchists and Trotskyists.[6]

After three years of brutal war, in which atrocities were committed on both sides and perhaps a million Spaniards perished, Franco's forces finally defeated the Republicans. In the aftermath of the war, many thousands were executed by the victors. Hundreds of thousands of others became refugees in France, Mexico, and elsewhere; an enduring legacy of fear, bitterness, and division remained within Spain.

PORTUGAL

About Portugal's twentieth century experiment with democracy (prior to 1974), one historian says: "The sixteen-year parliamentary regime of the Portuguese Republic (1910–1926) was the most turbulent and unstable in modern European history."[7]

Terrorism, strikes, bombings, and assassinations (including the murder of an incumbent prime minister and several leading politicians in October 1921) were virtually routine occurrences. The military had attempted to overthrow the Republic with what could only be described as monotonous regularity. When finally, in 1926, General Gomes de Costa succeeded in replacing the Republic with a military dictatorship, it was the eighteenth time that such an attempt had been made (this time successfully) in the sixteen year history of the democratic regime. To be sure, the Republic rested on very precarious social foundations. As late as 1911 nearly 70 percent of the Portuguese population was illiterate. The literate males over the age of 21 who comprised the electorate in 1913 constituted only 6.7 percent of Portugal's population. At about the same time, 57 percent of Portuguese employment was in agriculture, 22 in services and 21 in industry. Nevertheless, Portugal's twentieth century experiment with democracy, like the Spanish, had had important redistributive consequences and implications. All these served to frighten and alienate the middle and upper classes, making them more receptive, not to say eager, to support military dictatorship so as to "keep the lid on."

In both Spain and Portugal, the status of labor and women was improved by democracy. There was tax reform and expansion of education. But the very advances made by workers, peasants, and other heretofore "have-not" groups in these societies provoked a severe counterreaction from the traditionally privileged strata. Illustratively, the right to strike was legally acknowledged and sanctioned by the Portuguese Republic

[6] Ibid., p. 662.
[7] Ibid., p. 572.

for the first time in 1910. This right coincided with the largest outburst of strike activity in the history of the country. Moreover, a count of strike settlements during the parliamentary regime from 1910 to 1925 shows that only 63 out of 518 strikes were ended in defeat for the workers; 182 were won outright, and 196 ended in compromises. The middle and upper classes of Portugal after more than a decade of turmoil, labor unrest, inflation, and redistributive taxation were prepared to return to the more customary bureaucratic rule from the top.

policy process

The victory of the traditionalist, right-wing elements, such as those of Generalissimo Francisco Franco in Spain from 1939 until 1975, Dr. Antonio Salazar in Portugal from 1931 to 1968 and the Greek colonels from 1967 to 1974, involves certain alterations in the problem-solving mechanisms of the political system. These alterations are a departure from pluralistic democracy. Yet, they are also different in certain respects from the models of the various Communist regimes.

Such regimes differ from the pluralistic democracy in the surgical elimination of large strata of the population from political participation. The dictatorship, above all, excludes and represses its principal enemies. For the rightist authoritarians the main enemy is the "mob on the left"— the political parties that organize and represent workers and radical agrarian interests, the free-thinking liberals and the trade unionists. Direct popular participation in government, with its likelihood of reflecting the power of the masses of the poor, is carefully circumscribed.

Neither the Portuguese nor the Greek dictatorships created any mass movements to bolster their power positions in the surrounding societies. They preferred to rely on the bureaucracy, the military, and a variety of traditional interests. Franco, however, recognized the Falanga Espanola as the sole political party in Spain in 1936. This was a radically right-wing group, which sought to make Spain a "totalitarian" society on the models of Hitler and Mussolini, and eager to control both business and the church in the "interest of the state" far more than most Spanish conservatives or traditionalists would have preferred. Nominally, the Falanga has continued as the only legal political party in Spain into the 1970's but its importance and position has seriously declined since the forties. The defeat of Franco's Axis allies in World War II and his subsequent reorientation toward the Western powers brought about its fall.

The means of communication and the rights of association are carefully limited and narrowed to those groups and interests considered loyal and safe: landlords, churchmen, merchants, or military may all be allowed to continue their activities with little harassment by government while others may not be so fortunate. The government itself becomes heavily bureaucratic in its operation with little grassroots popular input and responsiveness to the wishes of ordinary citizens. At its highest levels, the government becomes essentially private and prerogative. One of several incumbents—the dictator or perhaps a junta—arrogates the power to make final decisions on all questions, and does so in a secret and unstructured fashion: that is, without any particular due process or reference to the wishes and judgments of other institutional actors, be they legislators, judges, or some other citizens and officials. What is achieved is a government by decree—without any constitutional centers of interposition.

In terms of our policy-making outline, it implies that the ruler may refuse to share the power of initiative and deliberation of policy with others; that no one can legitimately (that is, openly and with safety of life and limb) interpose in the application or adjudication of the ruler's decisions; that no one may spontaneously or freely monitor the decisional process in public; and that no one can repeal, halt, or change it contrary to the ruler's will, or conduct any "unauthorized" inquiry into the record of the ruler's decisions.

To be sure, the dictator relies on his supporters and delegates power. Thus, observers of the Spanish political scene under the dictatorship have recognized that the regime was far from monolithic. A diverse coalition of economic, cultural, and political interests was held together and managed by the Caudillo (the Leader). The forces around Franco have ranged from right-center to far right, including monarchists, Catholic moderates and conservatives, the out-and-out fascist Falanga, the military, and the politically more "colorless" interests of landed wealth and business. There have been some changes in the coalition around Franco over the years, but the process of government was essentially so private that the political background of these changes could only be inferred from biographical information about the people involved, and speculation about the meaning of related world and domestic events. Between 1939 and 1973, Franco had reshuffled his cabinet on nine different occasions.[8]

Private consultations between the Caudillo and individual ministers have often been more significant than the discussions of larger cabinet meetings. Policy has tended to be poorly coordinated to the extent that the dictator might entrust individual ministers with discretionary authority in their special "fiefdoms," or establish special one-to-one relationships with them. The Caudillo is believed to have defied, on a

[8] See Kenneth N. Medhurst, *Government in Spain: The Executive at Work* (Oxford: Pergamon Press, 1973), p. 73.

number of occasions, some of the major interests supporting his regime, particularly in opting for a pull-out of Spanish forces from Africa in the 1950's and 1960's against the wishes of his military and in his overtures to the United States and the NATO countries during the 1950's.[9]

Given the essentially "quietist" social orientation of the right-wing regime, its methods differ considerably from those of the far left. It is usually nonmobilizational or even antimobilizational. To the extent that it tries to bolster and maintain the mosaic of inherited wealth and privilege, it does not try to organize the masses of people into new movements and synthetic belief systems. Its major effort is devoted to repression and extirpation of hostile and "alien" influences. Beyond this preventive orientation, however, the regime may very well accept a limited amount of social pluralism. This has been illustrated in Franco Spain by the activities of the Church's secular branch, the *Opus Dei*, engaging in cultural, social, and at least implicitly even political activities without major interference from the regime. What will be allowed to churches, of course, may not be allowed to trade unions or peasant cooperatives viewed as threatening to the regime.

The Mediterranean dictatorships pursue a number of characteristic policies, which sharply differentiate them from the liberal democratic political systems. The following are some typical features:

1. The abolition or severe restriction of elective legislative bodies. This usually takes place through curtailment of direct popular elections of representatives (in favor of indirect, or functional, "corporate" representation) and limiting the powers of the elected bodies. This had been accomplished in different ways by both Franco and Salazar. Papadopoulos never convoked a national legislature, though he proposed one in his abortive 1968 Constitution.

2. Abolition of the right to strike.

3. Prohibition of any independent political activity by trade unions or organizations replacing them, such as syndicates, guilds, or mixed employer-employee corporations.

4. Censorship of the press, either prior, post facto, or both. Newspaper articles may require prior clearance for publication and editors are liable to fines, imprisonment, and closure of the presses for "harmful" or "treasonable" articles.

[9] See Medhurst, pp. 76–95. On the coalitional aspects of the regime, see Juan J. Linz, "An Authoritarian Regime: The Case of Spain" in E. Allardt and Y. Littunen, eds., *Cleavages, Ideologies and Party Systems* (Helsinki: Transactions of The Westmarck Society, 1964).

5. Dissolution of political parties and organizations, particularly those with leftist or Marxist leanings.

6. Limitations on the rights of assembly, petition, and association with the application of martial law, curfews, and military or special courts to try offenders against the public order.

7. Removal of ordinary judicial safeguards and recourse for political enemies. Use of "direct action," that is, unrestrained violence against opponents; invocation of secret police, and special courts and detention camps.

8. Heavy investment in military and police sectors of government.

9. Extension of the powers of traditional institutions supportive of the regime. For example, the assignment of oversight of education to the Church; the de facto management of industrial relations to employer groups; the maintenance of public order and security to the military; the representation of interests to the bureaucracy.

10. Emphasis on indigenousness, or sense of national identification, as opposed to cosmopolitanism and universalism, in the fields of culture, education, politics, and the arts.

11. Blurring the distinction between crimes and mere deviance from political–ideological norms of the regime, with heavy police and legal–administrative sanctions attaching to such deviance.

Many of these policies can be vividly illustrated in the case of the Greek colonels' regime. These policies were formalized in a Constitution that Papadapoulos submitted (under appropriate "safeguards" of the police terror) to the Greek electorate and for which he received overwhelming approval in September 1968. One provision called for the establishment of a court which would be able to strip any person guilty of "struggling against the regime" of all his constitutional rights. Another provision defined the role of the armed forces as a defender of "the prevailing regime and social order." The press was forbidden to criticize either the king [10] or the Church or the armed forces or "to propagate illegal views [and] promote outlawed organizations."

[10] The anomalous relationship between a right-wing dictatorship and the monarchy (whose particular incumbents may be "uncooperative" or "inconvenient") is illustrated by one chronicler of the Salazar regime in these terms: "The new Portugal does not tolerate political faction of any kind; it does not tolerate a Royalist faction. That is why, in November 1937, Paiva Conceiro, leader of Royalist disturbances in 1911, 1912, and 1919, was expelled from the country.
"But in 1932, Salazar paid a handsome tribute to the *memory* of King Manoel and gave the impression that, when Portugal is *ready*, she will call back her Kings." See Michael Derrick, *The Portugal of Salazar* (New York: Campion Books, 1939), pp. 119–120. In December 1967, King Constantine II had tried to oust Papadapoulos with a counter coup that failed. The king fled to exile in Rome.

Martial law was to continue until lifted by a parliamentary assembly to be elected in the future. The promise of parliamentary elections was never kept. It merely served to make martial law more palatable for the Greeks. Meantime, thousands of people who had not committed any specific crimes were herded into prisons and detention camps and subjected to torture, solitary confinement, and brutal mistreatments.

performance

In terms of policy consequences, the exclusion from participation and influence of groups eager to redress the balance of rewards in the society, and to promote the economic, social, and cultural opportunities of the masses, frequently leads to unbalanced "outcomes" of the system. While large sums and resources may be lavished on the private comforts and pleasures of the favored élite, the allocations for public education, cultural amenities, health, social welfare and sundry subsidies, aids, and incentives to the poor are likely to suffer. From time to time, the population may benefit by the more or less capricious dispensations of the élite or the principal leader. More often, however, deprived of the leverage of the vote, the right to strike, or even of peaceable assembly and public media of communication, the disinherited are likely to be treated as wards of the mighty.

The economic and social policies of those dictatorships have been geared, above all, to the securing of the perquisites, incomes, and consumption patterns of their most quintessential supporters—generally upper and middle class elements. These middle classes include independent peasant proprietors and exclude radicalized, urban middle class intellectuals. The dictatorships have been generally parsimonious in allocating resources to the public sector of the economy for the benefit of the masses of the poor. Judging by the standards of their own more open types of regime (such as the earlier Spanish Republic from 1931 until 1936 or even 1939, Portugal in the years 1910–1925, or Greece between 1947 and 1967) and still other political models discussed here, the allocations for public education, welfare, health, culture, and recreation have been more severely restricted under the Mediterranean dictatorships.

The contrast between these states and the democracies may be described as one in which there is a "greater tilt" toward private consumption skewed in the direction of the rich and the well-to-do in dictatorships, and a somewhat greater balance between private and public consumption among democracies. The contrast between the Mediterranean and the Marxist-Leninist regimes is even stronger, with still greater concentration of resources on public allocations and relatively skimpy endowments to the private sector among the latter type of regime.

To some extent, of course, the social functionality of the Mediterranean dictatorship (that is, how well it serves particular social interests) is described not by what it *does* but rather by what it succeeds in *preventing* or *suppressing*.

An important indication of the conservative-quiescent character—and from the standpoint of his supporters, *achievement*—of the Franco dictatorship is illustrated by the distribution of land ownership. As of 1969, a mere 0.86 percent of all landowners (51,283 individuals) held 53.5 percent of all the agricultural lands in Spain! On the other end of this lop-sided scale, 52.3 percent of all owners (3,128,953 peasant proprietors) held a mere 4.23 percent of all the land in tiny, dwarf-sized farms.[11]

Similar results in terms of "keeping the lid on" in the countryside had been achieved under Salazar in Portugal. In 1960, farms of under ten hectares constituted 94.9 percent of all farms, but contained only 32.2 percent of the agricultural lands. At the same time, farms of over 200 hectares, which constituted only 0.3 percent of all farms, contained 39.0 percent of the agricultural lands.[12] There were no parallels among any of the well established European democracies, nor among the Communist states.

Dramatic contrasts may be shown between the dictatorships of the revolutionary left (Communist or Marxist-Leninist) and the status quo–right (our Mediterranean type). Shortly before the death of dictator Salazar, Portugal's percentage of population attending school at all levels of education amounted to a mere 13.0 percent, a figure lower than that of *any* contemporaneous Communist state, including even the People's Republic of China, whose GNP/capita was only about one-fifth of Portugal's. The lowest figure among Communist states in Europe was 16.7 percent in the East German Democratic Republic (GDR), a country with an old-population structure. In the USSR the figure was 22.1 percent; in Yugoslavia it was 18.6.

It took the Franco regime six years, from 1940 until 1945, to build some 4,000 new schools in Spain; under the Republic, 6,600 schools had been built between 1931 and 1933. In 1945, only 1.5 percent of the graduates of primary schools in Spain ever went on to a higher education; in 1960 it was still only 2 percent. In Portugal, over the same period, the proportion of primary school graduates going on to a higher education grew from an anemic 2 percent to an equally unimpressive 2.3 percent.

[11] Payne, *A History of Spain and Portugal*, p. 691.
[12] Ibid., p. 674.

In the United States and the Soviet Union the proportion in 1960 was more than 15 times higher than in Portugal. In both Iberian countries the management of the educational enterprise reflected the judgment of a Spanish official who declared that "all the misfortunes of Spain came from the stupid desire to teach Spaniards how to read. To teach a man how to read merely obliges him to assume a position that will cause ill fortune to himself and his fatherland." [13]

In the 1950's, Spain and Portugal were among Europe's most parsimonious spenders on social welfare and cultural programs, both in terms of governmental expenditures and in the percentage of GNP devoted to such purposes.[14] Thus during this period, Spain, with a population close to that of Poland, a roughly comparable national income, and a larger territory, possessed only about one-seventh as many public libraries (683 to 4,585). The annual circulation of these Spanish libraries was only one-ninth as great as the Polish (5,530,000 volumes to 50,198,000 volumes). In 1965, the volumes held in Polish public libraries exceeded the Spanish by a ratio of more than ten to one. In 1965, only half as many people (tourists included) visited museums in Spain as had done so in Poland.

When we look at private consumption items that particularly affect the upper and middle classes, the picture changes considerably. There were almost three times as many telephones per capita in Spain as there were in Poland in 1974 (6.2 per 100 persons, as against 16.5 per 100 in Spain). There were more than five times as many passenger automobiles per capita in Spain as in Poland. Only the diffusion of television sets was approximately equal in the two countries.

Portugal, whose GNP/capita has been closer to Yugoslavia than to Poland, considerably exceeds *both* in the diffusion of telephones and passenger automobiles; so does Greece. Only with respect to television sets, which are used by all the European Communist regimes for political mobilizational purposes, do we find an advantage for Yugoslavia and some of the other Communist states.

Generally, the Mediterranean dictatorships have allowed much greater

[13] Cited by Laurence Fernsworth, *Spain's Struggle for Freedom* (Boston: Beacon Press, 1957), p. 262. Cf. Richard Pattee, *This is Spain* (Milwaukee: Bruce Publishing Company, 1951), p. 419. In 1946, Franco Spain spent almost 60 percent of the state budget on the military and the police, and 7 percent on education. See Richard Clogg and George Yannopoulos, eds., *Greece Under Military Rule* (London: Seeker and Warburg, 1972), pp. 111–112 on analogous patterns in Greece—for example, how the military regime's anti-union policy slowed down the growth of wages in relation to profits and dividends. See also pp. 136–147 on the curtailment of public allocations to education and the authoritarian regimentation of cultural activities in Greece, pp. 148–161.

[14] See J. F. Dewhurst et al., *Europe's Needs and Resources* (New York: Twentieth Century Fund, 1961), pp. 383–399.

freedom of movement and communication to private persons in their societies than have the Marxist-Leninist regimes. If we consider the relative luxury of long-distance travel abroad, we find that Greece with a population of 8.7 million people had 16,557 of its citizens travel abroad in the first year of the Papadopoulos regime. In the same year, Spain, with about 32 million people, sent out 45,800 such travellers; Portugal with about 9.5 million sent 39,200. As noted earlier, however, the Soviet Union sent only 17,600 citizens (officials and tourists, if any) out of its then population of about 240 million people. Among all the Communist states, the highest figure with regard to both population and GNP/capita was Yugoslavia's with 10,100 such travellers out of 20.2 million people. Czechoslovakia, with 10,500 intercontinental travellers out of a population of 14.3 million was more than twice as affluent in per capita terms as either Spain or Greece, about three times as affluent as Portugal, and almost four times as affluent as Yugoslavia.

As of 1970, Spain, Portugal, and Greece all ranked far ahead of comparably developed Communist states, in both the volume of mileage and of messages exchanged. Yugoslavia was the *only* Communist state which, even though it was poorer than Greece in GNP/capita terms, recorded more passenger miles per capita by all conveyances combined. In messages exchanged, the three Mediterranean dictatorships were all ahead of comparably developed Communist states although Yugoslavia came closer to matching the performance of Portugal than the much richer Poland, USSR, and Romania. (See Table 7–1.) [15]

prospects

Inasmuch as prolonged mistreatment, sanctioned by force, is likely to aggravate the sense of injustice and resentment among the victims, the dictatorial regime does not eliminate tensions in the society. It merely represses and manages them to the advantage of the incumbents and their allies. Such management and repression naturally require certain resources and skills. Obviously, there can be no terrorism without terrorists and no censorship without censors. The resources can take the form of substantial amounts of money, managerial skills, foreign assistance, confidence in a particular leader, propitious circumstances in terms of the attitudes of one's opponents as well as those of one's supporters. As circumstances change, sometimes at home and sometimes abroad, so do the resources of the supporters and proponents of the regime. More or

[15] See A. Groth, W. Potter, *op. cit.*, pp. 7–12 and 27–30; all data in this table are for the years 1970–1971.

TABLE 7–1

Country	GNP/Capita	Passenger Kilometers* per Capita	Personal Messages per Capita
Spain	$ 956	2679	244
Portugal	633	2433	121
Greece	1,035	1177	264
USSR	2,018	1621	69
East Germany	2,101	3294	198
Czechoslovakia	2,094	2970	254
Hungary	1,397	1948	172
Poland	1,233	1503	83
Bulgaria	1,102	1410	n.a.
Romania	1,057	1089	48
Yugoslavia	579	1637	115

* Water transport not included.

less "natural" economic and social changes, with new needs and claims arising in the society, can be politically unsettling.[16] The death of a leader, as in the case of Salazar in Portugal in 1968 or Franco in Spain in 1975 can bring about a profound crisis of confidence in the regime. Its supporters can become disheartened and confused; its opponents emboldened. The destruction of a major external supporter of a regime—in Franco's case that of Hitler in 1945—may force a change or relaxation of course, with, conceivably, further destabilizing consequences. Similarly, international pressure, an economic collapse, a defeat and prolonged suffering through war (as in Russia in 1904 and in Portugal in 1974) may bring about the overthrow of even the most repressive regime.

Historically, such an event is often followed by a resumption of the cycle. The most likely immediate alternative to the fallen dictatorship is a regime which either establishes or at the very least firmly commits itself to establishing full-fledged democratic, participatory institutions. The appeal is to the people, to freedom, to equality, and to popular rule. No sooner are the appeals made or the institutions established, however, then the next round of turmoil and conspiracy begins.[17] Sharp differences of outlook among the revolutionaries begin to surface. Soon some accuse

[16] See Max Gallo, *Spain Under Franco* (New York: E. P. Dutton, 1974), pp. 283–299, on the stresses and strains of modernizing change in Spain in the 1960's. The cumulative effect of rapid economic and social development and cultural ferment, induced by increased Spanish contacts with the external world, was to produce new conflicts and pressures upon the Franco regime to "open up," or liberalize its rule.
[17] See Derrick, *The Portugal of Salazar*, pp. 128–129.

others of lacking true fidelity to the "Revolution" and to the "People," who are all pictured somewhat differently by different protagonists. Soon some erstwhile heroes may be seen as the agents of the KGB; others are perceived as in the pay of the CIA. With respect to some cases, at least, both sides may even be right. In any event, the outcome of unresolved cleavage and suspicion soon translates itself into a new round of popular disturbances and a new series of attempts to, on the one hand, "reestablish order," and on the other, to carry out a "true revolution," that is, a change thoroughly transforming the status quo. The sequence is likely to lead from massive unrest and turmoil either directly to a new dictatorship brought about by a military coup, or proceed to the same destination indirectly through the agency of a civil war, winding up either with a revolutionary–leftist or basically status quo–rightist regime.

CASES OF AUTHORITARIAN COLLAPSE

In February 1974, General Antonio de Spinola, deputy chief of staff and ex-governor of Portuguese Guinea, published a book (*Portugal and the Future*) that attacked the regime's policy in Africa. Years of futile war against the guerrilla movement in Mozambique and Angola had drained Portugal of manpower and resources, and had finally undermined the morale and loyalty of the army. Premier Caetano, successor to Salazar, moved to dismiss General de Spinola, as well as the chief of staff, General Francisco da Costa Gomes. Within a few months the attempt to purge the army precipitated a coup. Caetano was exiled to Madeira and subsequently to Brazil. A seven-member military junta took over the reins of power in Portugal, promising to end the colonial wars and to bring a democratic government to Portugal. Momentary euphoria at the overthrow of the dictatorship soon turned to strife and disappointment. The Communist Party attempted to exploit the revolution in order to seize power for itself, even though it had gained only 12.5 percent of the vote in the national elections held in the spring of 1975. Inflation, flight of foreign capital, decline in the tourist trade, an adverse balance of payments, and mounting bankruptcies and unemployment darkened the economic scene. Clashes between the supporters of Left and Right became common. In the first fifteen months after the April revolution, six different governments had succeeded one another. As this book went to press, the fate of Portugal was very much in the balance.

In Greece, mounting popular unrest embracing the military, students, and workers, as well as a largely hostile international public opinion, seemed to cause Colonel Papadopoulos to change course in mid-1973. He announced the abolition of the monarchy in June, thus repudiating his own Constitution of 1968. The king had been fomenting trouble in Greece,

Papadopoulos belatedly discovered. A referendum was to be held, presumably to allow the people to ratify the decision. The referendum of July 29 did not deal actually with the issue of monarchy. It served to confirm Papadopoulos as president for an eight-year term by a very suspect 77.2 percent of the vote. Simultaneously, Papadopoulos promised to hold parliamentary elections sometime in 1974 and to restore civil liberties.

In November, however, large-scale riots in Athens resulted in the deaths of at least 13 civilians and the deployment of tanks in the streets. On November 25, Papadopoulos was overthrown by generals Phaidon Gizikis and Dimitrios Ioannidis, who claimed that their erstwhile leader was about to embark on dangerous electoral adventures.

The dictator had run into a series of difficulties which led to his downfall. The regime's action deposing the primate of the Orthodox Church had alienated some conservative supporters. A high rate of inflation and economic difficulties also contributed to the general dissatisfaction with Papadopoulos. Students and intellectuals were restive under the censorship and the restrictions that Papadopoulos had imposed.

The causes of the downfall of Gizikis and Ioannidis, some six months later, were more clearly international. The Greek rulers embarked on a risky policy of annexation of Cyprus. The objective of achieving a union between Greece and Cyprus was apparently to be secured by means of a coup against the Cypriot government headed by Archbishop Makarios. In mid-July 1974, Turkey, sensitive to the rights and claims of some 20 percent of Cyprus' inhabitants who are of Turkish origin, intervened to forestall a Greek seizure of Cyprus. Turkey's strong military forces swiftly succeeded in occupying much of the island, and humiliated the Greek junta, which was hardly in a position to wage war against the powerful Turks. Constantine Caramanlis, premier from 1955 to 1963, returned from ten years of exile in France to take power. The democratic Constitution of 1952, trampled by the junta in 1967, was restored. Parliamentary elections held in November 1974 gave Caramanlis' moderate New Democratic Party a comfortable 54.3 percent of the vote. In another referendum on the issue of monarchy—this time without terror and intimidation—the Greek people voted by a margin of 69.2 to 30.8 percent to repudiate the crown and institute a republic. Was Greece about to embark on another cycle of democratic rule?

The overthrow of the dictatorship in Portugal produced reverberations and unease in Spain. The economy, buoyant in 1973, sagged in 1974 partly under the impact of increased oil prices and mounting worldwide inflation. Spain's fuel bill rose from $1.1 billion to $3.5 billion in one year. Inflation and recession cut down the volume and profits of tourism in

The military revolutionists in Lisbon, 1974.
UPI Photo

Spain, and the funds sent home by Spaniards working abroad declined. Spanish workers demanded steep wage increases as inflation continued unabated. In July 1974 Franco, approaching the age of 82, suffered from blood clots and did not resume his duties as chief of state until September. The Church increasingly sided with ethnic and worker dissidents. The regime imprisoned 48 priests in 1974 for expressing critical views and supporting the opposition. While arresting some dissidents, the regime was promising to allow all non-Communist groups the right of association —in the near future. Meanwhile, the confluence of inflation and recession,

Portugal: Crowd assaulting Communist Party headquarters, 1974.
AEI—Keystone

the demise of Franco, the example of Portugal, and decline in Church support for the regime, all raised the prospects of further instability in Spain.

Given the conservative, right-wing authoritarian, and even fascist influences and traditions confronting substantial forces of social radicalism in such countries as France and Italy—and the relatively recent memory of the dictatorships of Marshal Pétain at Vichy (1940–1944) and Benito Mussolini as the Fascist Duce (1922–1945)—the problems and dynamics of the Mediterranean dictatorships are not confined to Greece, Portugal, and Spain. The experience of these dictatorships may be relevant in the life of many countries where political disputes become unmanageable through open or pluralist means.

Yugoslavia: Liberalized Communism

background and policy agenda

The Yugoslav model of communism reflects a much more even balance between coercion and participation, between one-party rule and pluralism, than any of the hitherto existent Marxist-Leninist regimes. Yugoslavia is not and may never become a Western-style parliamentary democracy. The League of Communists of Yugoslavia (LCY) is not and may never become a Social Democratic Party on the style of Helmut Schmidt's SPD, François Mitterrand's Socialists, or Harold Wilson's Labour Party. But Yugoslavia is a professedly Marxist-Leninist state, which has broken with the mold established by Moscow and replicated throughout most of Eastern Europe. Since the 1950's it has moved much more closely toward a Western-style, pluralistic, and democratic society than such "hardline" deviants from the Soviet model as China, Albania, or North Korea.

THE LEGACY

Unlike most Communist regimes of Eastern Europe, Yugoslavia's was established largely by the indigenous efforts of the Yugoslav Communist Party. Led by Marshal Tito, the Party's resistance movement during the Second World War won a sizable popular following and succeeded in consolidating power without any substantial assistance from the Soviet Red Army.

Josip Broz Tito had been a loyal Stalinist activist in the days before the outbreak of World War II in the still small and illegal Communist movement in pre–1941 Yugoslavia. If anything, the Yugoslav Communists, under Tito's war-time leadership, gave evidence of being even more militant, orthodox, and pro-Soviet in their attitudes than any other Communists of Eastern Europe. But having won power on his own in 1945, Tito was unwilling to subordinate himself to Soviet control, a condition Stalin regarded as the ultimate proof of Marxist-Leninist and revolutionary loyalty. When the Yugoslav Communists opposed Soviet attempts to dictate their policy and infiltrate their administration with Soviet officials, the Cominform (Communist Information Bureau, a successor to the defunct Comintern or Communist International established in 1918 and dissolved in 1943) expelled them in 1948 as "nationalist deviationists" and "traitors to the cause of proletarian internationalism" (both Soviet euphemisms for those Communists unwilling to accept Russian primacy).

Marshal Tito and the Yugoslav Communist Party were on their own. On one side they faced hostile Communist states loyal to Moscow: Bulgaria, Romania, Hungary, and Albania. Large contingents of Russian troops were stationed within a few miles of Yugoslavia's frontiers. On the other side lay war-torn Greece, pro-Western, Christian-Democrat ruled Italy, and parts of allied-occupied Austria. Between the camps of orthodox Communism and Western democratic capitalism, Yugoslavia's regime seemed an anomalous entity; it was expelled from one camp and completely alienated by ideology, training, experience, and institutions from the other. In this context, the Party regime faced a very difficult task in attempting to reconstruct the country from the ravages of a recently ended war and Nazi occupation, along with a thorough transformation of the social order. All this was to take place without external support and under potential pressure from both East and West.

To be sure, the formal expulsion of the Yugoslavs from the Cominform in June 1948 gradually brought them substantial amounts of Western financial and military aid. Most observers believe, however, that Tito managed to meet the challenge that expulsion from the Soviet bloc posed for him, above all, by mobilizing the latent forces of Yugoslav nationalism: the fierce determination of the people to maintain their independence from foreign rule. Possessed of considerable mountainous, and strategically defensible territory, as well as thousands of experienced guerrilla fighters, Tito discouraged any armed action against Yugoslavia by the Soviets. In due course, Stalin's boast (as reported by Khrushchev at the CPSU 20th Congress) that he would merely shake his little finger and Tito would fall was proved false.

ADAPTATION

In the long run the Yugoslav Communists adjusted their ideology, programs, and institutions in such a way as to maintain and extend a significant, solid base of popular support in the country. The adaptations were gradual, and dealt with ethnic, regional, economic, political, and international areas of concern.

To begin with, Tito's Communists inherited a mosaic of ethnic group identifications. There was actually *no* majority nationality in the country. The Serbs were the largest ethnic component of the population with about 40 percent of the total; next largest were the Croatians with about 20 percent. Several remaining nationalities added up to more than 30 percent of the population. The ethnic heterogeneity of Yugoslavia has always been combined with a very uneven distribution of wealth and resources. Historically, it has been connected with strife, violence, and mutually conflicting claims for autonomy and equity of treatment at the hands of the state. The ethnic cleavage has been compounded by a variety of religious affiliations. Between 40 and 50 percent of the population of modern post–1919 Yugoslavia has been orthodox Christian. This includes substantial numbers of Serbs, Montenegrins, and Macedonians, as well as Russians, Bulgarians, and Romanians. Between 35 and 40 percent of Yugoslavs are Catholic, particularly the Croatians and Slovenes; the remainder, largely Moslem, include some Slavs, Turks, and above all, Albanians. In addition to religious divisions, regional economic differences between the more prosperous northern and western areas of the country, between Croatian, Catholic rich, and southern Moslem poor, have been very substantial.

Yugoslavia also exhibited tremendous differences in literacy and cultural levels between north and south, and east and west. Since the creation of the state at the Peace Conference of Versailles in 1919, Yugoslavia has been characterized by a mosaic of different cultures, histories, and traditions imposed upon the different backgrounds of language, region, religion, and economic development. Some citizens of modern Yugoslavia had been brought up in the context of an independent Serbia before World War I. Some had lived in subjection to the Austro-Hungarian empire, and others under the backward and repressive Turkish empire.

The comingling of all these disparate elements in the state of Yugoslavia, under Serbian monarchy during the 1919–1941 period, brought about a great deal of internal strife and instability. Yugoslavia maintained a precariously democratic constitutional monarchy until 1929, when King Alexander began a period of virtual royal dictatorship until his assassination in 1934. After his death, an authoritarian government of the Regency ruled the country.

During the World War, in the years 1941–1945, Tito's Communist followers succeeded to power by waging not only resistance against the Nazis but a resolute civil war against all the social and political elements connected with the old regime in Yugoslavia: its nobility, landlords, the middle classes, and the élites of the pre–1941 bureaucracy, army, and political parties. Still, the basic ethnic, religious, regional, and even economic divisions of the country were not really affected by the destruction of these old élites.[18]

To win popular support and stabilize his rule after the war, Tito was faced with the need of integrating and reconciling the diverse elements making up modern Yugoslavia. This involved the fundamental issues of

[18] See Wayne S. Vucinich, ed., *Contemporary Yugoslavia: Twenty Years of Socialist Experiment* (Berkeley: University of California Press, 1969), pp. 3–58 and Jozo Tomasevich, pp. 59–118.

extending adequate economic, social, and political opportunities to the several nationalities, allowing them adequate outlets for self-expression and management of local affairs and overcoming the legacy of mutual suspicions and animosities, while maintaining the unity of both country and Party.[19] (See Tables 7-2 and 7-3.)

The general political problem of the Yugoslav Communists consisted in reconciling the desire for maintaining power with the need to accommodate diverse aspirations, wants, and tendencies manifested in the society—short of a highly unpopular, and, in the long run, probably untenable all-out police state. The Party had already eliminated much of the old, pre-war landed nobility, gentry, and the middle class. The work of expropriation of the large estates, factories, banks, and the like, had been completed long before Tito's breach with Stalin. The struggle against the "opium" of religion had also been launched with appropriate orthodoxy well before the breach. All oppositional parties, right, left, and center,

TABLE 7–2 The Ethnic Mosaic of Yugoslavia (c. 1970)

Nationality	Number of Persons	Percentage of Total
Serbs	8,527,200	41.8
Croatians	4,692,000	23.0
Slovenes	1,876,800	9.2
Macedonians	1,142,400	5.6
Montenegrins	550,800	2.7
Moslems [a]	1,060,800	5.2
Yugoslavs [a]	367,200	1.8
Shiptars [b]	999,600	4.9
Hungarians	550,800	2.7
Turks	204,000	1.0
Slovaks	102,000	0.5
Romanians	61,200	0.3
Bulgars	61,200	0.3
Italians	20,400	0.1
Czechs	20,400	0.1
Others and not identified	163,200	0.8
	20,400,000	100.0

[a] = Members of these groups generally consider themselves distinct ethnic entities.
[b] = Albanians.

Source: Reprinted from *The Communist Regimes in Eastern Europe* by Richard F. Staar with the permission of the publishers, Hoover Institution Press. Copyright © 1973 by the Board of Trustees of the Leland Stanford Junior University.

[19] See M. George Zaninovich, *The Development of Socialist Yugoslavia* (Baltimore: Johns Hopkins Press, 1968), pp. 50–57.

Table 7–3 The Ethnic Balance of the Executive Bureau of the League of Communists of Yugoslavia (LCY) (c. 1971)

Tito, Josip Broz	Croatian
Kardelj, Edvard	Slovene
Bakaric, Vladimir	Croatian
Crvenkovski, Krste	Macedonian
Dizdarevic, Nijas	Moslem
Dolanc, Stane	Slovene
Doronjski, Stevan	Serbian
Gligorov, Kiro	Macedonian
Hodza, Fadilj	Albanian
Mijatovic, Cvijetin	Serbian
Pecujlic, Miroslav	Serbian
Soskic, Budislav	Montenegrin
Todorovic, Mijalko	Serbian
Tripalo, Miko	Croatian
Vlahovic, Veljko	Montenegrin

Source: Staar, *The Communist Regimes in Eastern Europe.* (Thus, out of 15 major ethnic groups in Yugoslavia, seven found representation in the Party's highest executive body.)

had been banned and their leaders executed, exiled, or imprisoned. Censorship and propaganda had been applied with as much heavy-handedness in People's Yugoslavia as in any of the East European regimes.[20]

But *after* the breach with Stalin, it became obvious that the Yugoslav Communists could not afford to simply "fake" rank-and-file support of all constituent elements, a course more readily open to those Communists who could rely on the backing of the Red Army. It was vitally important for the Yugoslavs to maintain substantial, genuine support among workers and peasants if they were to continue in power against Moscow, against domestic dissidents, and against the Western emigrés from the old ruling classes. Finally, it became necessary for the Yugoslavs to redefine their Marxism so as to justify and explain their seemingly anomalous international position, out of step with the rest of the world communism led by Moscow.

policy process

THE "OLD MODEL"

Until the break between Moscow and Belgrade, the Yugoslav "model" of domestic political institutions conformed closely to the policy-making

[20] See George Stambuk, "Yugoslavia" in Benes et al., *Eastern European Government and Politics* (New York: Harper & Row, 1966), p. 198.

pattern described here earlier in the chapters on the Soviet Union and East Germany. Although a federal system was adopted by the Yugoslav Constitution of 1946, with gaudy promises of cultural autonomy to the several constituent regions of Yugoslavia, this was no more, or less, than what the federalist Soviet Constitution of 1936 had promised. In fact, in Yugoslavia as in the Soviet Union, power was heavily centralized in the organs of the Party. Tito and his entourage of Politburo colleagues, like Stalin and his principal collaborators, were the real initiators of policy for the whole country. The Party leaders may be said to have "used" the devices of federalism and autonomy as political weapons for gaining support but without relinquishing control any more than the CPSU. The Party controlled the trade unions and all the economic, social, and political and governmental institutions of any importance. These were openly regarded as the transmission belts and levers of the regime designed to serve the Party, not to quarrel with it.

In fact, the Yugoslav Communists took pride in the fact that it was they who first, even before the Russians, pointed out that a people's democracy was simply another form of the dictatorship of the proletariat.[21] And in this dictatorship, the Party, ruled by the iron discipline of Leninist democratic centralism, was the leader and vanguard. The Yugoslavs maintained a secret police, the OZNA, a rigid system of media control and censorship, and they assiduously combined propaganda with terror and repression to consolidate their power and enforce their policies. The result was that the process of policy deliberation, approval, implementation, adjudication, review, and—if need be—amendment, termination, and audit were all safely "in-house" or "in-Party" matters reserved for the decisions of the top leadership of the Party.

NEW FEATURES

After the breach with Moscow, the system became modified toward loosened discipline or hierarchy in the Party and greater pluralism, responsiveness, and sensitivity to the interests, values, and points of view emanating outside the Party. The Yugoslav Communists began to emphasize popular participation and involvement in the political process. They sought to identify themselves as the "participatory Communists," as distinguished from the Stalinist type of "bureaucratic Communists." Tito and the Party executed gradual realignments, producing a new, hybrid version of national communism, an amalgam of Marxian symbols

[21] See statement by Mosa Pijade, Yugoslav Politburo member in the 1940's and 1950's, cited by George Stambuk, ibid., p. 199; see also "Communist Dogma and Yugoslav Practice," *Foreign Affairs* 30, no. 2 (April 1952): 438–439.

and ideas with the particularistic needs of power and national accommodation.

Increased popular participation in power was extended characteristically first to those elements regarded as most amenable to the leadership of a Marxist revolutionary party: the workers. It was extended last, and more slowly, to the potential enemy of revolutionary Marxism in the countryside: the peasantry. Thus a retreat from attempts at collectivization was not fully evident until at least three or four years after the 1948 Tito–Stalin breach. Only by 1952 was the trend to stable and recognized small proprietorship of land clear and convincing. However, as early as 1950 the Yugoslav Communists had instituted workers' councils in all of the larger industrial enterprises. The system of economic self-management growing out of these workers' councils has set the Yugoslav experience apart from the centrally-planned socialist economies of the USSR and Eastern Europe; it has also continually intrigued the Western European democratic socialists in their search for a decentralized socialist economic alternative.

WORKERS' COUNCILS

Self-managed enterprises are expected to take into consideration the interests of the surrounding community and of consumers in general. They must operate within certain broad guidelines of production targets and goals set for them by the state—that is, by the Party leadership. Within those guidelines, however, the question of how the work should be done, by whom, at what rate, and under what conditions is determined by the employees themselves.

Members of the Party are supposed to involve themselves actively in the work of the councils and show leadership by their good examples, dedication, and hopefully—from the Party's point of view—by their superior political, Marxist-Leninist expertise. But the councils are to be vehicles for decision-making participation for *everyone*. The Party has claimed that the institution of workers' councils would serve as a gigantic and practical school of civic education, and that it would contribute to the disappearance of *alienation*, often experienced by workers and employees in highly impersonal work places where individuals have no involvement in or control over the management of their jobs.

With the gradual decentralization of the whole economy, workers' councils have also become profit sharing associations. Each enterprise is given the opportunity—and responsibility—of working for profit, so that those who produced and sold more at less cost would share bigger bonuses (or dividends) at the end of the year than the less efficient producers. Thus, worker management through the councils has not only enhanced the individual's decision-making role but provided material and psychological incentives, too.

In practice, apart from occasional instances of bureaucratic interference from above and plain corruption, the workers' council idea has worked out better in those branches of industry where the quality of the technology and the skills of the labor employed have been high. There, innovations and profitability have flourished. In more backward or poorly capitalized industries the profits and rewards have often been disappointing.

In terms of increasing employee autonomy, further economic reforms, particularly in 1965 and 1966, have reduced the state's central planning to virtually skeletal proportions and have given even more freedom to local groups. The workers' councils' idea has been extended in the sixties and seventies into virtually all other branches of the Yugoslav economy. Government offices, banks, commercial enterprises, and transportation networks have all been organized in the Basic Organizations of Associated Labor.

The efficiency of the self-management concept has come under criticism, however. A recent study of self-management in a Yugoslav shipyard employing some 5000 workers revealed that employee meetings consumed an average of almost 27 full working days in the year. In a country suffering from the highest unemployment and highest inflation rate (32 percent) in the Communist world, this was not good news.[22] To stimulate greater productivity and cut costs, self-management institutions have recently been given the right to fire ineffective employees and have been subjected to a system of substantial monetary fines levied by government ministries for failure to meet assigned standards. In 1975, for example, members of the Yugoslav national airline were told that each late flight would result in a $600 fine against the responsible department or departments.

REGIONAL DECENTRALIZATION

Communes There has also been considerable regional decentralization of power in Yugoslavia, much greater than in any other Communist state. And it has also involved more participatory electoral systems, and more seriously deliberative public assemblies than in any other Communist system thus far. The focus of Yugoslav decentralization initially was *not* federalism. In the 1940's and 1950's, the six Yugoslav republics and two autonomous regions, as set up in 1946, had had most of their powers

[22] See Oskar Gruenwald, "The Silencing of the Marxist Avant-Garde in Yugoslavia," *The Humanist*, May–June 1975.

preempted by the central government. Moreover, elections to their parliaments and governments had been generally indirect and dominated by the Party. It was rather at the district and local level that decentralization and autonomy first became significant.

Beginning with the local people's committees in the 1940's, and the legal reforms of 1952 and 1955, the Yugoslavs have developed a system of commune governments. Throughout the country the communes could raise funds and invest them. They had been given extensive powers in determining the application of federal and republic level laws and regulations; in spending monies both given to them by higher level authorities and raised by each commune locally; in control of security and welfare functions including the administration of health, sanitation, schools, grants, pensions and services to individuals, cultural activities, transportation, and utilities, among others. The communes were also empowered to draft their own plans for annual or even longer-range local development, based upon the priorities and preferences of their own citizenry.

Interest Representation   The elections to the communal councils, unlike virtually all other elections in Yugoslavia, have been direct. The Communist LCY has exercised dominant influence in these elections, to be sure, in the process of nominating candidates and in conducting vigorous election campaigns. It is, after all, the only legally constituted political party in modern Yugoslavia. There have been no anti-Communist or even non-Communist parties to which people could turn. Nevertheless, the relaxation developed in Party discipline since the fifties and sixties has been such that choice among different Party members has not been just a matter of "tweedledum vs. tweedledee." Ethnic, economic, ideological, administrative, social, and cultural differences among Party members have surfaced publicly. In Yugoslavia, the heterogeneity of many parties has found at least some embodiment in the outwardly unified LCY.

Moreover—and this has been particularly important at the local commune level—the representatives of various non-Party organizations, whether trade unionists, agricultural cooperatives, or professional groups, have not been mere "party stooges." The nonparty, nonorganizational, citizen-at-large candidates, frequently elected to commune councils have given them a substantially independent popular input. In practice, all this has meant that while local representatives could not make the broader national and international decisions, they could significantly affect what went on in their particular communities under a relatively loose system of Party controls.

Admittedly, the number of communes in Yugoslavia has tended to decline over the years, thus attenuating the link between each citizen and his local government—from about 8,000 in the late forties to only about 500 in the early seventies. At the same time, however, Party controls over their own members and the society at large have been more relaxed. The communes have played a key role in the day-to-day governance of Yugoslavia. One important illustration of this is that the revenues and expenditures budgeted by the commune governments have exceeded those of the republics by about 2.5 to 1 and have been about 60 percent as large as those of the central federal government in Belgrade.

IDEOLOGICAL INNOVATIONS

In terms of ideology, the Yugoslavs worked out an amalgam between Stalin's own doctrine of socialism in one country and the notion (occasionally given lip service even in Moscow) that revolutions should be neither exported nor imported. The Yugoslavs took the position that they could further the development of their country toward socialism and communism by their own unaided efforts, as much as the Soviets did in the 1920's and 1930's. Moreover, they emphasized worker participation and self-determination which the bureaucratic Stalinists, the Yugoslavs charged, had neglected and stifled. In the Yugoslav view, Stalinists did not lead the working class, they dominated and oppressed it. Symbolically, in 1952, the Party changed its name from the Communist Party of Yugoslavia to the more distinctive, and seemingly also less centralistic, League of Communists in Yugoslavia.

NONALIGNMENT

The Yugoslavs scrapped both the idea that it was their duty to strive for a revolution throughout the world, and the related idea of support (preferably all-out) for the strongest power capable of furthering and subsidizing such revolution—namely, the USSR. They developed the position that there were many different ways of progressing from feudalism or capitalism to socialism, that they could morally support or sympathize with all of them, and that revolution was essentially the domestic concern of each society and each working class. The Yugoslavs viewed Stalinist communism as a dangerous bureaucratic and nationalistic distortion of Communist ideals. In the interest of self-preservation and world peace, it was best for Yugoslavia to adopt a nonaligned position between the hostile and historically doomed capitalist West and the corrupted, despotic communism of the East.

In fact, during the fifties and sixties, Tito successfully attempted to lift the prestige of Yugoslavia and appeal to the pride of his countrymen by seeking to establish a degree of moral-political leadership among the so-called Third World states of Asia, Africa, and the Middle East on a platform of nonalignment between the world's two great power blocs. These efforts were symbolized by Yugoslav sponsorship and participation in the world conferences of nonaligned nations in Bandung, Indonesia, in 1955 and in Belgrade in 1961.

During the late 1940's and early 1950's Soviet and Chinese Communist propaganda ceaselessly attacked Tito for his neutrality in the world struggle between the forces of "socialism" and the forces of "capitalism." The Moscow and Peking hard-liners claimed that such neutrality, in effect, played into the hands of Western imperialism, that it weakened and confused the international revolutionary workers movement. Even after the Moscow-Peking breach, the Chinese continued to accuse Tito of revisionist collusion with the capitalists. Not until after their own particular détente with the United States in 1971, did the Chinese cease to scorn Tito's "bourgeois nationalist" deviation.

After Stalin's death in 1953, the venom of Soviet attacks on Tito and his Party greatly subsided, but more or less veiled criticisms and reproaches of the Yugoslav's "un-Marxist" and "anti-Marxist" positions have appeared intermittently in Soviet and other Warsaw Pact states' media. Soviet overtures, particularly in 1955 when Khrushchev and Bulganin travelled to Belgrade to woo Tito back into the fold, never overcame Yugoslav skepticism of Russia.

INTERNAL ASPECTS, PARTY ROLE

Interestingly, Yugoslav criticisms of the corruption of Soviet communism were easily adapted by domestic critics against the Tito regime. The most famous of these was the attack by an ex-Party leader, Milovan Djilas, in his book *The New Class* in 1957. Djilas charged that the leaders of the Communist Party in Yugoslavia—as elsewhere—had created a system of vested economic, social, and political privileges rooted in the *use* rather than *ownership* of "things" (that is, material possessions and perquisites) and of people, who were made to serve the élites. The difference between *use* and *ownership* was all but semantic, Djilas argued. What was involved was a new form of class dominion by some, a few, over others, the many. Djilas was sentenced to a long term imprisonment for his "slander of Socialist Yugoslavia." The charges which Tito and his colleagues were willing to level at the Soviets were still too dangerous apparently to tolerate in Yugoslavia.

Gradually, however, the LCY began to liberalize. It grew increasingly sensitive to domestic opinion. In 1958 the League took the position that "Marxism is not a doctrine established forever or a system of dogmas. Marxism is a theory of the social process which develops through successive historic phases. [It] implies a creative application of the theory and

Yugoslavia's Marshal Tito at the hunt, 1974.
UPI Photo

its further development, primarily by drawing general conclusions from the practice of socialist development and through attainments of the scientific thinking of mankind." [23]

Following the Soviet invasion of Czechoslovakia in 1968, the Yugoslav Party liberalized its internal structure further. While it had affirmed its role as an ideological teacher and leader for the whole Yugoslav society, the Party explicitly rejected the Soviet model of overlapping control by

[23] Ibid.

leaders of the Party apparatus of the machinery of the state. Full-time LCY functionaries were disqualified from simultaneously holding office in government administration. (The idea was, however, reinstated by the Tenth LCY Congress in 1974.)

The LCY has all but repudiated the Leninist organizational principle that the Party minority must unconditionally obey the decision of the majority. The Eighth Party Congress in 1964 affirmed the members' right to criticize high LCY officials; the 1969 Ninth Congress went even further and secured the so-called right of conscience. Party members may now retain a different opinion from that of the Party leadership on any issue without facing disciplinary proceedings or losing their LCY membership, although officially they may not actually "work" against a decision that a relevant majority—for example, in the 15 member Executive Bureau of the Party—has adopted.

The severity of police sanctions applied by the Party against dissenters and critics in Yugoslavia has tended to decline over the last decade. From the executions, mass and individual, of the 1940's the Party has made a transition to increasingly more selective and shorter jail sentences in the sixties and seventies. After the dismissal of security police chief Alexander Rankovic in 1966, it has gradually become clear, in the words of one scholar, "that only the grossest of deviations would face formal consequences from the state organs." [24]

The Yugoslav Party regime, confronted by the external threat of Soviet intervention and by great internal conflicts at home, has attempted to keep itself afloat by an uneasy balance between the policies of gradual liberalization, on the one hand, and "homogenization" through one-party control and political education or propaganda on the other.

performance and prospects

The Yugoslav policy has produced results that stand in sharp conflict with prevailing Soviet, East German, or other Communist states' practice. In fact, it has produced a decline in the importance of central planning and a gradual deemphasis of a dictatorial role for the Party. It has produced the lifting of prior censorship in Yugoslav mass media (although not yet the fear of more or less veiled post facto reprisals for particularly acute journalistic "misbehavior"). It has also produced a standard of living for many Yugoslavs, and generally for the richer northern and north-western parts of the country, that is quite comparable to Western

[24] George Klein, "Yugoslavia: The Process of Democratization," in Peter A. Toma, ed., *The Changing Face of Communism in Eastern Europe* (Tucson: University of Arizona Press, 1970), p. 222.

Europe. At the same time, however, it has brought on some serious economic problems: large scale unemployment; migration abroad of low-skilled or unskilled Yugoslav workers and peasants unable to find well-paying jobs at home; a high rate of inflation and balance of payment deficits in the relatively freer and more consumer-oriented economy of Yugoslavia; and politically, the reemergence of sharp ethnic, economic, and other societal conflicts now breaking into the open under a more liberal regime and, as in the past, threatening to bring on fratricidal warfare, destroy the fabric of a common Yugoslav statehood, and quite possibly bring on direct Soviet intervention.

FREEDOMS

Among the more interesting and unique consequences of the Yugoslav system have been strikes by workers, public debates of controversial issues in the media, including angry confrontations among Party activists, massive demonstrations by students, and other manifestations of conflict.

According to official information, almost 1,400 strikes had taken place in Yugoslavia between 1958 and 1966. Indeed, in August 1967, ten major strikes occurred simultaneously. Labor outbreaks and stoppages were not suppressed by the regime, although the official union structure professed its "neutrality" in the matter of strikes. Student protests in Belgrade in June of 1968, directed against the privileges of the various political bureaucratic élites, were among the most serious challenges faced by the LCY since its assumption of power after World War II. In the last few years the quarrels of the several nationalities have repeatedly surfaced in the official media, with the Party organ *Borba* publishing letters of mutual recrimination and reproaches by the Serb and Croatian wings of the LCY on such issues as proper usage by officials of the Serbo-Croatian language, the nature of an equitable curriculum in public education for one group or another, or the claims by the Albanian minority that it ought to be given a separate republic of its own within the Yugoslav federation. An illustration of a parliamentary process unthinkable in other Communist countries was the resignation of the government of the republic of Slovenia in 1966 because one of its major legislative proposals had been voted down by the parliamentary assembly. It took three weeks to resolve the impasse between cabinet and legislature.

INCREASING DECENTRALIZATION

With the passage of time, decentralization became extremely important not only at the local but at the federal, republic level. The Constitution of 1963 and the Party Congress of 1969 upgraded the role of Yugoslavia's regional republics: Serbia, Croatia, Slovenia, Montenegro, Macedonia,

Bosnia-Herzgovina. In 1970–1971 the emergent differences between the central regime and the constituent republics seriously threatened the cohesion of the system. In a speech to a Party gathering in April 1971, Tito expressed his concern about the course of Yugoslavian development:

> Comrades, we are a socialist society in which the League of Communists is the ideopolitical protagonist of our entire development. However, the behavior in the League . . . is not good, and I am not pleased. I must say that I am tremendously hurt by this. You know that I have long been at the head of the Communist Party, or rather the LCY, but I believe that up to now we never had a situation such as we have now in the League of Communists. As long as I am in this position and as long as the membership wants to support me, I shall strive to create order in the League of Communists. We must have unity. However, we have some people now who violate this unity, although they too speak about it.[25]

In the early seventies, the autonomy and veto power conferred by the 1969 Constitution on the republics with respect to economics and administration were coupled with continuing fragmentation of the ruling Party and increased assertion of local and regional interests. As a result, there was lively and increasing disarray in Yugoslav political life.[26]

The Tito regime responded to the threat of domestic chaos with a new Constitution, adopted on February 21, 1974, and new Party statutes at the Tenth LCY Congress in May 1974. The effect of both was to increase LCY control over the country, reintroduce indirect elections to communal, provincial, and republican assemblies, and bring back the emphasis on Party identification of government office-holders. Marshal Tito was declared president for life.

SOVIET MOVES AND YUGOSLAV RESPONSES

In the past, each attempt by the Soviets to pressure the Yugoslav regime had produced new efforts to broaden the base of the Yugoslav Party's popular support at home: new emphasis on its differences from Soviet totalitarianism and bureaucratic oppressiveness; new insistence on the Yugoslav Party's greater responsiveness and openness to the people. This was the pattern of 1948 and also of 1958, when, after a brief "flirtation" between Khrushchev and Tito, highlighted by a Khrushchev-Bulganin visit to Belgrade in 1955, the rapprochement was soured by armed Soviet intervention in Hungary in 1956, and the insistence that Yugoslavia

[25] See Paul Shoup, "The National Question in Yugoslavia," *Problems of Communism* 21, no. 1 (January–February 1972): 28.
[26] In the words of one writer, "Yugoslavia harbours a family of nations united by the fear that their hatred of each other may be exploited by the outsiders." George Baily, "Where Titoism was Tried," *Reporter,* July 1, 1965.

"modify" its nonaligned posture between the Soviets and the West. It was also the pattern after 1968, when the Soviets invaded Czechoslovakia and CPSU General Secretary Leonid Brezhnev unveiled his famous Brezhnev Doctrine, asserting a Soviet "right" to use force to protect the regimes of the several "socialist" states, without specifically exempting Yugoslavia from the orbit of its application.

Such Soviet moves have also generally produced renewed Yugoslav orientation to the West, with pleas for economic and military assistance to ensure survival. Nevertheless, Marshal Tito has always been as careful as possible not to provoke Soviet ire by any heavy-handed moves against the other East European states, or attempts to win them away from the existing pattern of Soviet influence. Since the mid-1950's the Yugoslavs have maintained diplomatic, economic, and cultural links with the Soviets and the other Warsaw Pact states. (These had been severed during the Stalin era, 1948–1953.) There has also been continued insistence that the Yugoslavs, however "difficult" and sometimes "unwanted," are part of the family of Communist and Workers' Parties of the world. In the 1960's, this Yugoslav sensitivity to Soviet displeasure led to the imprisonment of a university teacher, Mihailo Milhailov, who had written an article in the Yugoslav periodical *Delo* charging that genocide and concentration camps had been invented not by the Nazis but by the Soviets. Tito's "forebearance" toward his own dissidents was strained beyond the breaking point.

ACHIEVEMENTS

Among the substantial achievements of the 30-odd years of a Communist regime in Yugoslavia have been many typical of other Marxist-Leninist states. There has been massive industrialization and urbanization, with a shifting of the balance from a principally agrarian-rural economy and society before World War II to an industrial and urban society in recent times. Great advances have taken place in the fields of education, social welfare, and popular culture. More people have received higher and technical education than ever before, and great strides have been made in the conquest of illiteracy and improvement of public health. There have been great changes in terms of technological progress and modernization. Yet, Yugoslavia has thus far retained a relative independence and differentness from the surrounding brands of communism in many of its domestic as well as foreign policies.

Yugoslavia has had the lowest volume of trade with the USSR of all the Communist regimes of Eastern Europe; for example, only 12.9 percent of Yugoslavia's total trade in 1971 was with the Soviets. Other East European regimes ranged from 28.7 percent (Romania) to 54.7 percent (Bulgaria). Yugoslavia's trade with *all* the Communist states was only 30.4 percent, while other East European states ranged from 55.2 percent (Romania) to 77.6 percent (Bulgaria). Conversely, Yugoslav trade with non-Communist regimes was higher than elsewhere in Eastern Europe.

Yugoslavia was still substantially less industrialized than the USSR, Romania, Poland, Bulgaria, Czechoslovakia, Hungary, or East Germany. Only 34 percent of its national income derived from industry, where the comparable high figure was 61 percent for Czechoslovakia and the low figure 40.6 percent for Hungary. Yugoslavia has had only 15 percent of its cultivated land under cooperative farm ownership, compared with 14.4 percent for Poland but about 90 percent or more for each of the other Communist states. The Party itself—the League of Communists of Yugoslavia—was less a worker or proletarian dominated organization than was any of the other East European parties. Including agricultural laborers, only 31.2 percent of the LCY was made up of workers as compared with an average of about 40 percent or more elsewhere in Eastern Europe.

Yugoslavia has cast its UN votes with far more independence of the USSR than other East European regimes. Thus, for example, where the Romanians directly defied the Soviets (voted against them) on only six occasions in the several specialized committees of the UN between the 1940's and the mid-1970's, Yugoslavia had done so 188 times. With this independence of Moscow we may also identify some of Yugoslavia's most serious challenges.

Can the liberalized Communist regime long survive its aged and legendary founder, Tito? Can peaceful succession and institutional continuity be accomplished, given the nature of Yugoslavia's long-standing conflicts at home and the aspirations of Soviet as well as some Yugoslav hard-liners to restore the country to a more orthodox and Soviet-aligned model of communism? The arrests and trials of so-called "Cominformist plotters" in 1974 and 1975 cast an ominous shadow.

summing up the alternative European systems

Yugoslavia, and in the recent past Spain, Portugal, and Greece, have all had *authoritarian* political systems, different from the more open, democratic regimes of Britain, West Germany, France, and the United States, but also different from those of the Soviet Union and East Germany.

The political history of our *alternative* systems has been characterized by sharp underlying conflicts of different regions, classes, ethnic elements, and more or less modernized (or secularized) strata of each society.

In terms of the decision-making model of chapter 1, all of these alternative systems have in somewhat different ways narrowed down the scope of popular participation in such functions as the initiation, deliberation, and approval as well as the application of policies. They have significantly resorted to arbitrary and closed adjudication and enforcement methods. They have restricted the capacity of their citizens to exercise interposition through a critical monitoring system, through public power of policy amendment or repeal, and lastly in the refusal to sanction any independent auditing mechanisms, judicial and/or political, to expose and rectify past wrongs.

But the ideological-political *directions* of our alternative systems have been different. The thrust of repression and exclusion in Spain, Greece, and Portugal was directed against the political left and toward the preservation of the possessions and the perquisites of most of the traditional well-to-do socioeconomic strata. In Yugoslavia, the Party directed its effort, above all, against the established elements of the political right and center, the large landlords, and the bourgeoisie. The Party's *avowed* goals included enhancing the well-being of the workers and the poor. In practice, both in Yugoslavia and in the right-wing dictatorships, the rulers became self-appointed trustees of the interests that they set out to protect, enhance, and liberate. Leftist parties (other than the LCY) were as effectively forbidden in Yugoslavia in the fifties and sixties as were rightist or centrist parties. Analogous prohibitions existed, with the exception of the Falanga, in Spain and also in Portugal during Salazar's regime.

Nevertheless, the different ideological objectives, programs, and sociocultural roots of the different regimes have had important practical effects. Landlords and entrepreneurs have been favored by rightist authoritarian regimes in Spain, Portugal, and Greece; in Yugoslavia their fate has been the reverse. In the Mediterranean dictatorships the distribution of land has changed less. Industrial development and urbanization have not been quite so intensive. Educational and cultural mobilization of the people, the advances in school enrollments, literacy, mass access to higher education have not been nearly as substantial. In both the Mediterranean dictatorships *and* Yugoslavia, the regimes have tried to achieve particular and characteristic policy results by destroying, suppressing, or simply impeding various oppositional elements in their respective societies, while enhancing the influence and access of other elements.

The particular way in which they have done this enriches the mosaic of European political models. These models may indicate to us more generally something about the nature of politics in societies where, historically, conflicts and cleavages have been pervasive and severe.

8

postscript: the future of european politics

8 POSTSCRIPT: THE FUTURE OF EUROPEAN POLITICS

The twentieth century has been a time of great crises in the politics of Europe. These crises have taken different forms at different periods. There have been wars, revolutions, depressions, civil strife, economic and diplomatic struggles, persecutions, repressions, and reforms.

There is no indication on the European horizon today (the Helsinki 1975 East-West Summit notwithstanding) that "the corner has been turned," and that a period of quiescence and stability has at last been reached. On the contrary, the dynamics of modernization and change, creating news forms of economic, social, and cultural life in each of the European states as well as among them, the progress of what Karl Deutsch has called *social mobilization*—the forming of new identities and new linkages and the breaking of some old ones—is likely to keep the process of politics as lively as ever. Political institutions throughout Europe are certain to experience considerable stress and strain. Bitter conflicts over the allocation of resources and the shape of the political institutions of the future are all but unavoidable.

Without attempting to anticipate how these conflicts and struggles may work themselves out, it may be useful to point out how the policy-making framework discussed in each of our previous chapters relates to these future conflicts.

We have sought to emphasize in our discussion of policy-making not only its universal characteristics—even if under different names and through different institutions in different systems—but the great *complexity* of the policy process. The enactment of virtually every policy and every rule into practice requires the synchronization of different actors and components of the political system. Approval must be followed by implementation, and implementation by adjudication, if the letter of the law is to be translated into a living reality. Each stage of the policy process, from initiation to post facto audit, usually involves great complexity of procedures and diversity of participants.

In terms of the pluralistic, democratic systems described here, this could mean that crisis level popular conflicts and cleavages may occasionally impede the policy process, exposing its vulnerability and fragility. The power of particular interest groups, parties, regions, and bureaucracies may well cause the policy chain to snag, at times, resulting in a series of frustrating failures with the likelihood of attendant turmoil and strife. Such failures are likely to evoke reactions from the societies in which they occur. Those disappointed in the workings of the policy process will usually seek reforms. Some may seek to change the policy-making rules in the direction of greater participation—or different modes of participation —for interests with which they identify, such as those of labor, farmers, women, youths, or civil servants. Some people are likely to clamor for a streamlining of the decision-making process in the opposite way: by closing it to particular interests: those perceived as hostile, irresponsible, subversive, or radical, and in some cases, those seen as hostile, irresponsible and subversive, but *reactionary* rather than *radical*. Thus, severe conflicts may lead to a polarization of public attitudes toward the political system itself, cause an erosion of popular support for the policy-making process "as-is" and intensify the pressures for some form of authoritarian, or even dictatorial, rule to cope with policy crises (as in France in 1958 over the Algerian issue and in Germany in 1930–1933 over the issue of the economic crisis).

The highly authoritarian political systems that we have discussed exhibit great vulnerabilities in the opposite direction. After all, social, economic, and cultural changes associated with modernization constantly change the constituencies of *all* political systems, and they clearly call for rapid adaptations by the policy-makers to new kinds of problems. Rigidly authoritarian systems may not be able to cope with the strains of change and flux. Closed and arbitrary policy structures may promote conflict and popular resistance instead of peaceful solutions and accommodations. The ideological value system, whether Marxian or traditionalist, upon which the dictatorship may have been initially built is likely to suffer erosion from the cultural changes produced by new patterns of urbanization, by shifts of the working force from land and industry to services, by the diffusion of new types of education, and historically developed new patterns of social values. Dependence on particular incumbents as rulers may prove a handicap.

Faced with such changes, the dictatorship may be unable to keep full control over all the segments of the policy-making process, particularly over its large implementing bureaucracies. Its credibility with the people, in terms of the ability to control and coerce, may decline. Even among the dictatorship's supporters there are likely to be pressures for an opening up of the system, so as to minimize violent conflicts and co-opt the opposition. Among the latter, any signs of weakness and vacillation by the dictatorial regime are likely to evoke demands for still further changes and fresh concessions.

In substance, then, an understanding of the extended policy process not only enables us to appreciate the differences between more and less pluralistic regimes; it also alerts us to the difficulties and perils that both types face in policy-making.

the european prospect

What then is the European prospect? In essence it hinges on two major but interrelated sets of problems. One of these is *performance,* and incorporates the principal social welfare and economic aspects of politics; the other is the problem of *governance* itself, encompassing the nature of the policy process as well as political liberties and legitimacy.

PERFORMANCE

How effective is a political system in meeting the needs of its people? For many, this is the supreme question of politics. Thus a leading official of West Germany's Social Democratic Party (SPD), Herbert Wehner, has observed, "the ability of democracy to develop stands and falls on the security of purchasing power, full employment and freedom from the fear of an insecure old age." [1] From a very different perspective, a comparable question has been posed by the French Communist Party leader, Georges Marchais, who has predicted that Western European regimes will collapse because they are incapable of making people happy.[2]

Together, these tests of economic security and of personal happiness are not unreasonable criteria to use—provided that we apply them across the board and not merely to one type of political regime.

In the case of the democratic political systems we have considered, even in the most avowedly capitalist countries, governments have increasingly intervened in seeking to meet social needs. They have done so by creating welfare states, to provide basic elements of personal security (which the private sector was incapable of meeting) in such areas as health, educa-

[1] Quoted in *The Economist* (London), May 10, 1975.
[2] *Le Défi démocratique* (Paris: Grasset, 1973).

tion, child care, pensions, unemployment insurance, and aid to the disabled. They have also increasingly intervened in the economic sphere by adopting managed economies in order to promote economic growth, full employment, balanced regional development, and technological innovation. Inevitably—indeed, as part of the process of modernization—the percentage of national economic activity falling within the public sector has increased.

The increasing extension of governmental activity into the social and economic realms has taken place throughout the past 75 to 100 years, but it has been particularly accentuated since World War II. The cumulative result of this process has been to place increased demands and burdens upon government and the political process. Such demands and burdens come from citizens and groups who look to the political process as a means of satisfying or protecting their basic interests. As a result, new problems may arise. Among the most pressing of these are the possibility of pluralistic stagnation (discussed in chapter 2), the trade-off between full employment and inflation, and the questions of resource and income distribution.

The record of various societies in resolving these problems has been mixed. In some—for example, the countries of Scandinavia—they are dealt with in part by periodic bargaining between huge umbrella organizations representing business on the one hand and workers on the other, with the result being an agreed figure for yearly wage increases and in effect a series of decisions about resource allocation. In general, however, the resolution of these issues remains a matter of political division between parties of the left (who stress full employment, greater equality of income distribution, and public expenditure) and the right (who give priority to lessening inflation, accept—or even increase—existing inequalities of income, and tend to favor private consumption).

GOVERNANCE

Contemporary performance demands, particularly in meeting the needs of social welfare and economic management, place heavy burdens on governments and political systems. Yet circumstances exist which limit or even reduce governmental abilities to solve or merely to cope with these problems on a national basis. Internally, the power of pressure groups, including huge corporations, trade unions, and smaller special interest groups frequently constrain a government's freedom of maneuver, either because voluntary compliance by such groups is essential if policies are to succeed, or because a government is concerned to retain the allegiance of diverse blocs of voters in anticipation of forthcoming elections.

External constraints are even greater, since governments often have less and less control over many of the most crucial economic and financial factors that influence their domestic life. In a word, this is the problem of growing *interdependence*. The realities of international trade, the world monetary system, investment, technology, communications, transportation, raw material needs, military alliances, multinational corporations, environmental problems, and even cultural interchange all combine to thwart governmental efforts and plans which would operate on an exclusively national basis. Thus, a government that seeks to control inflation or to increase taxes steeply on a multinational corporation may find that a significant portion of domestic price levels is determined by the costs of imported food, raw materials, and even manufactured goods over which it has virtually no control. For example, the energy crisis of 1973–1974 contributed to economic problems which individual governments had difficulty in coping with because they were heavily dependent on imports of foreign oil, whose supply and price were largely outside their control.

To cope with many of the problems of performance and of governance in pluralistic societies, contemporary governments must cooperate among themselves in order to seek multilateral solutions. Much of the continued impetus for the European Community derives from this fact more than from a sense of international idealism. Yet the principal economic and political problems often require action on a scale greater than that of Europe alone, one encompassing the entire developed non-Communist industrial world (Western Europe, North America, Japan)—and on occasion including the countries of Eastern Europe and the less developed world. Nor does it suffice to abdicate responsibility for international interdependence to the multinational corporations (MNCs). It remains true that the MNCs have proved themselves adept at diversifying across national boundaries and even at briefly operating a successful world oil sharing scheme during the Arab oil boycott in the winter of 1973–1974 (albeit at considerable profit to themselves). Yet, whether one consults the historical record (the Hudson Bay Co. in North America, or the East India Company) or more contemporary examples (United Fruit Company and the Central American "banana republics," ITT in Chile), the MNCs are among the world's worst institutions for governing.[3]

Governments thus face difficult and complex tasks of international cooperation to meet their mutual and national needs. Yet their internal problems often make it harder for them to cooperate internationally. Indeed, there is always the danger that frustration at the restricted ability

[3] See, for example, Karl Deutsch, "Between Sovereignty and Integration," *Government and Opposition*, Vol. 9, No. 1 (Winter 1974).

of governments to cope with their tasks on an efficient and individual basis may lead to nationalistic reactions and pressures for drastic and simplistic internal measures.

Two alternatives often posed include right-wing dictatorship or a Communist takeover. A dictatorship would claim to cut through domestic stagnation and political restraints by suppressing trade unions, political liberties, and representative institutions. A Communist regime would seek to overcome economic and political obstacles by destroying autonomous economic powers—not to mention eliminating democratic institutions. But these by no means exhaust the possibilities for change. Other solutions—for example, those posed by European democratic socialists—would seek to overcome domestic economic problems and inequalities of distribution by extending democratic notions of ownership and control to the economic realm while preserving liberty in the political arena.

We are thus concerned with a key question about values, particularly the means by which people can exert control over their own lives. The problems of democratic and representative government bring to mind Winston Churchill's famous aphorism that democracy is the worst form of government—except for any other form of government. If we compare the performance as well as the method of governance of the democratic countries of Western Europe, on the one hand, and the authoritarian regimes of Eastern and Southern Europe, on the other hand, several significant conclusions emerge.

First, the policy process in democratic societies is more likely to keep open the possibilities of flexibility, openness, responsiveness and change. The process of feedback operates more successfully in this type of system than in a right or left-wing dictatorship in which not only are views contrary to those of the ruling élites unwelcome, but actual information at variance with the expectations of these rulers may often be suppressed or held back before it reaches them. To be sure, as revelations about falsified U.S. intelligence estimates of Viet Cong strength have demonstrated,[4] systems of representative government may also suffer this problem, but on balance they are less likely to do so. In addition, the flexibility and adaptability of democratic systems is enhanced by the commonly accepted use of persuasion rather than force as a means of seeking agreement. Minority opinions and ideas may thus, in time, become accepted by majorities, and innovation can occur without the need for disruption or overthrow of an entire system.

Second, from a normative standpoint, systems of representative government may provide the most desirable means of dealing with pluralistic

[4] Sam Adams, "Vietnam Cover-Up: Playing War With Numbers," *Harper's*, June 1975, pp. 41ff.

societies and diverse groups. The chief alternative is the repression by a Stalin or a Pinochet. Yet the boast of Spain's late Generalissimo Franco that his regime was built "not with meaningless ballot-papers but with bayonets," [5] exposes a fatal flaw. In a modern industrial society, authoritarian governments which are unable to win the voluntary cooperation or acquiescence of their people can only achieve their aims by repression. Inevitably, this repression will destroy or corrupt the ideals on which the regime claims to be based, whether those of a classless society or of Christianity, law and order, national unity, and the family. Instead, the prevailing realities will often be ones of institutionalized brutality, torture, propaganda, corruption, racism, and widespread popular cynicism. Not only are these things morally unacceptable, but they lead in turn to another problem.

Ironically, repressive or law-and-order regimes are ways of managing unstable societies (to the special advantage of certain groups within them) not cures for social instability. Most of the political systems of Southern and Eastern Europe (Spain, Portugal, Greece, Yugoslavia, Hungary, East Germany, Poland, Czechoslovakia, and so on) either have been or will be the scene of serious political turmoil. Right-wing and Communist dictatorships may find themselves in unstable equilibrium, both because they lack the consent of the people they govern and because they have not successfully institutionalized the means for transferring power from one leader or group to another. Upheavals (and Russian intervention) in Hungary (1956) and Czechoslovakia (1968), and instability in Poland (1970) are testimony to this fact, as are the events of the early and mid 1970's in Greece, Portugal, and Spain.

Next, the actual performance of authoritarian governments in the economic and social spheres frequently lags behind that of comparable democratic countries. To be sure, left-wing authoritarian governments can be fairly successful in meeting needs for public facilities while right-wing regimes may achieve substantial economic growth, but these are often purchased at a serious price. In the former case, that price may often be of a relatively low standard of living and of personal choice; in the latter, it may be amid real personal hardship and inequality for huge sectors of the population who are not middle or upper class. Indeed, the right-wing regimes, despite their suppression of trade unions have not necessarily been successful in coping with inflation.

A final conclusion, therefore, is that in coming to understand contemporary politics in Europe—and indeed in other developed modern societies—we must be wary of simplistic solutions. The frustrations and

[5] Quoted in *The Economist* (London), November 1, 1975.

complexities of contemporary politics reflect the intricate nature of expanded governmental activity in society and the economy, as well as the profound interdependence of modern Western countries. This by no means rules out the possibility of significant political and economic change—there is, after all, no "final stage" of development—but it does imply that such changes are likely to be successful only to the degree that they take into account these factors of domestic complexity and international interdependence.

INDEX

491

United States (*cont.*)

   compared with Soviet Union, 298, 319, 330–31, 344

   European unity, 369, 373, 385–86

   investment in Europe, 429–30

Universities

   in France, 164

   in Soviet Union, 295

Value Added Tax (VAT), 397, 405

Verba, Sidney, 36, 39

Versailles Treaty, 208

Vichy regime, 129–30

Violence in Britain, 39–40

Volkskammer, 245, 247–48, 250–51

von Hindenburg, 210

Wales, 79

Warsaw Pact, 309

Watergate, 319, 330

Waterloo, 121

Welfare state, 58

West Germany

   Basic Law, 217

   and big business, 246–47

   chancellors, 217–18, 256

   creation in 1949, 215

   compared with Weimar regime, 258

   Common Market, 227–28

   Courts, 253–54

   economic power of, 420–21

   education, 228–29

   elections, 249

   far Left, 234

   far Right, 233–34

   federalism, 215

   foreign policy, 223–27

   future prospects, 269

   housing, 263

   immigrant workers, 231

   income distribution, 228–30

   judicial review, 215–216

   Land governments, 250

   management of the economy, 230–31

   militarism, 269

   monopolistic economy, 229

   and NATO, 226–27

   Nazi influence, 254

   newspaper, 220, 243–44

   1948 blockade, 224

West Germany (*cont.*)

   oil reserves, 231

   Parliament, 248–49. (*See also* Bundesrat; Bundestag)

   policy approval, 248–50

   political attitudes, 270–72

   political parties, 219–22, 249

   president, 217–18

   pro-American stance, 226

   proportional representation, 216

   relations with East Germany, 224–26

   Threshold law, 216–17

   unemployment, 230

   university students, 235

Western European Union, 374

Weimar Republic, 208–209

   decline and fall, 210–11

Wilson, Harold, 44–46, 86, 90–91

Wiretapping in France, 185

Workers. (*See* Trade unions)

Workers' councils, 468–69

Workers' self-management, 169

World War I

   and Germany, 207–209

   and Russia, 286

World War II

   and Germany, 214

   and Soviet Union, 288–89

   and Yugoslavia, 464

Women, role of

   in France, 191–92

   in Soviet Union, 349–50

Yellow journalism, 108

Yugoslavia

   and China, 472

   communes, 469–70

   Communist Party, 463–67, 470–71

   creation of Communist regime, 462–63

   economy, 469

   ethnic groups, 463–66

   industrialization, 478

   nonalignment, 471–72

   regional republics, 475–76

   Serbian monarchy, 464

   and Soviet Union, 463, 465–67, 476–77

   standard of living, 474–75

   trade, 477–78

   worker's councils, 468–69